Best wishes

Colin

GW00384497

The
Complete
Farmhouse
Cookbook

Mary Norwak & Babs Honey

The Complete Farmhouse Cookbook

Compton Russell Ltd

First published in Great Britain 1973
by Compton Russell Ltd, Compton Chamberlayne,
Salisbury, Wiltshire

Published as *Farmhouse Cooking, Book One*
and *Farmhouse Cooking, Book Two*
by Sphere Books Ltd 1973

Printed in Great Britain by
Redwood Press Limited
Trowbridge, Wiltshire
ISBN 0 85955 005 2

Contents

NOTE: All recipes serve 4 to 6 people (according to appetite), unless otherwise stated.

Introduction

Most of us have a child's eye view of farming. We imagine all farms are nice neat buildings, surrounded by orderly fields, grazing cows and scratching chickens. The farmer wears breeches and boots and a soft hat, and strides around with a dog at heel, and sometimes a horse in hand. His wife looks like Mrs Noah, permanently wrapped in a huge white apron, her hair in a bun, living her life in a vast well-scrubbed kitchen surrounded by home-baked bread, honeycombs and cabbages fresh from her well-ordered kitchen garden.

How different is the reality! There are tiny hill farms and vast estates; decrepit cottages and sparkling new bungalows; gloomy Victorian piles and tidy Georgian doll-houses; farmhouses in the centre of village streets and farmhouses miles from anywhere up rough tracks. Farmers and their wives come in different patterns too, but all the men have one thing in common—they like their womenfolk at home, working for and with them. They are traditionalists, bless their hearts, even when they drive sparkling new cars and go abroad for their holidays. Family life is still ruled by the farm. Holidays are taken at odd times of the year, regardless of school terms, because haymaking and harvest are paramount. No farmer's wife will commit herself to village activities between June and September, when her men work all hours of daylight, and food and home comforts are the only things that matter.

All through the year, farmers insist on their hearty breakfasts, potatoes with every meal, pies and puddings, lashings of cut-and-come-again cakes and mouth-watering helpings of their leisure-time game and fish which they dump on the kitchen table.

This collection of recipes reflects this interest in good hearty food during the past two hundred years. We have been sent still-used eighteenth-century recipes; notes of old favourites on the backs of envelopes; Victorian recipes written on black-edged mourning paper; and a number of fascinating scrap-books full of delicious goodies. We received a number of recipes that originated during the 1939–45 war, when many of today's farmers were newly married and struggling to keep up their high standard of food. We have included recipes from an evacuee who grew to love farm life, and from an Italian farmer's wife whose husband was a prisoner-of-war in this country. Some of the recipes reflect the poverty of the country between the two wars of this century; others of the richness of some Victorian farmers, and the 'carefulness' of the Edwardians building up

9

their holdings. Some mirror the interest of today's young wives in foreign dishes, and in labour-saving devices, together with a returning interest in natural foods which discards the synthetic and the standardised convenience product.

Sadly, many of our contributors are unknown to us, for they have left only their names in their friends' cookery notebooks. Three of them however left exceptionally interesting collections of recipes. Thomas Train of Gateshead left a bound copy of *The Female Instructor; or, Young Woman's Companion* whose contents ranged through 'Education, Religion, Conversation, Sensibility and the Government of the Passions, Courtship and Marriage, The Management of Children, FamilyReceipts' but his family had used the book hard, and had written their own recipes on the blank backs of the illustrative plates. They are nice homely recipes which contrast with the rather formal instructions in the book in which they are written.

A little later in time, during the first quarter of the nineteenth century, came Joseph Webb of Kent, who left a neat pocketbook full of recipes 'for horse or man'. There are cures for the mange, nourishing drinks for cows, remedies for milk fever or scab or inflammation of the lungs (often the same remedy seemed to be applied to Mr Webb's animals and children). There are household hints, and recipes for sauces, wines and soft drinks, methods for pickling fruit and vegetables, ways of improving cider and colouring cheese, and even the costs of preparing some recipes. A basic family cake cost $4/5\frac{1}{2}$d in 1823 (one shilling for 1 lb butter, 10 pence for 1 lb sugar, and eggs 1 penny each).

Mrs Garden, perhaps our most prolific source of Victorian recipes, left a notebook which shows clearly the importance of good country food even in a rich and smart household in the second half of the nineteenth century. Her book started life as an Eton College exercise book, full of Greek and Latin exercises. Later it was used to note down jokes about the clergy, household hints, knitting patterns, instructions for dancing the Lancers, lists of useful shops in London and Paris, and above all, recipes. A few of the recipes are rather grand and expensive, with French names, but the majority are friends' recipes, mainly from East Anglia, for harvest cakes, stewed fowl, surplus game, hashed mutton, gingerbread, apple pudding, and the like. The Gardens, like so many Victorian families, were in the transitional stage from their country origins to life in a town. Their staff would still have been mainly recruited from the country, probably from their own ancestral neighbourhood, and both above and below stairs, country food was normally eaten. This tradition of simple country food maintained by the staff was certainly still evident in well-to-do nurseries until the 1939–45 war, and middle-aged men tend to consider 'nursery food' the only sort worth eating. After a century of country people drifting towards the towns, there is an increasing tendency for middle-class families to seek country homes again, with a consequent revival of interest in wholesome farm-based food. Mrs Garden's notebook is as usable today as the most up-to-date cookery manual.

As far as possible we have avoided the professional technicalities of such subjects as salting and cheesemaking, which can be found in official bulletins, but have included the many homely ways in which farmers' wives preserve their surplus produce. We have let our ancestors and our friends speak for themselves and as far as possible kept their original writing which adds such flavour to each dish. Many of them kept commonplace books in which they recorded their recipes, the names of the houses or friends from which they originated, their reliable household hints and medical remedies and their favourite bits of poetry. We hope that you will enjoy today's version of a commonplace book.

I **Breakfast**

A good honest, wholesome, hungry breakfast
Izaak Walton

Farmhouse breakfasts are still pretty solid affairs. They need to be as the farmer often goes out very early after his first breakfast, which is just a snack to 'break his fast'. When the early morning chores have been completed, serious eating begins with the second breakfast. Brawn, faggots and sausages are traditional breakfast foods on the farm, as well as the obvious eggs and bacon; most men like all the fried trimmings as well – potatoes, potato cakes, apples, tomatoes and mushrooms.

FARMHOUSE FAGGOTS

1 *lb pig's fry (lights, liver,*
heart and melt)
1 *pig's caul*
3 *small onions*
3 *oz breadcrumbs*

$\frac{1}{4}$ *oz salt*
$\frac{1}{4}$ *oz white pepper*
$\frac{1}{4}$ *oz ginger*
$\frac{1}{4}$ *oz sage*

Soak caul in tepid water. Cover the pig's fry and onions with water. Simmer for 1 hour. Drain off liquid. Pour a little of the liquor on the crumbs;

keep remainder for gravy. Mince the pig's fry, onion and breadcrumbs. Add seasoning to taste. Beat to a paste with fork, cut caul into 4-inch squares, form mixture into balls, cover with caul, place on greased tin and cook until brown in hot oven.

Mary Horrell, Exeter, Devon

GRANDMA BOY'S SOMERSET FAGGOTS

½ *lb lights*
½ *lb melt*
¼ *lb onions*
½ *lb caul*

½ *lb liver*
6 oz breadcrumbs
Salt and pepper

Put meat and onions through a mincer, mix with breadcrumbs and season with salt and pepper. Shape the mixture into lumps the size of a tea cup. Wrap each in caul, tucking the ends underneath. Place in a tin or pie dish. Half fill with water and bake for 1 hour.

HOG'S PUDDING

**2 *lb liver, heart, lungs and*
trimming of meat
1½ *lb groats or unpolished*
*barley***

**2 *tablespoons salt*
½ *teaspoon pepper*
½ *teaspoon ground nutmeg***

Simmer the liver, etc., for approximately 1 hour. Soak groats in the liquor from the pluck for 12 hours. Cook preferably in a double cooker until quite tender. Mince the meat and mix it with the groats and seasoning. There should be sufficient moisture to make the mixture soft. If the groats soak up all the liquor add water to correct consistency. Fill mixture into large intestines, 12 inch lengths, tying ends together to form a ring. Put the hog's pudding into hot water and cook gently for 25 minutes. It is important to cook slowly, otherwise the skins will burst. Hang up the puddings to keep. They will keep up to ten days, and may be eaten cold or fried.

Currants used to be added and they were mixed in, then the boiled hog's pudding hung up an open chimney to smoke. They were eaten all through the winter.

PORK SAUSAGES

Put ½ lb fat and ½ lb lean pork through mincer with ¼ slice of stale bread, 1 teaspoon anchovy essence, pinch powdered thyme or sage, salt and pepper to taste. Mix *very* thoroughly. Shape into sausages – roll in flour and fry. They smell so good you will find the family will eat them straight out of the frying pan, but if they can bear to wait you can add all sorts of exciting things to them, such as fried onions, fried apple rings, tomato sauce, bacon or scrambled eggs. Make them into sausage rolls as they will *not* be too dry – like commercial sausages which are full of that mysterious thing called rusk – or use for Toad in the Hole.

Mrs Chaplin, Finsthwaite, Lancs

PORK SAUSAGES

9 lb lean pork	**Seasoning**
3 lb firm fat from fat bacon	*3 oz salt*
3 lb bread (before soaking)	*1 oz white pepper*
	½ oz ginger
	¾ oz mace (if you like it)

Soak the bread and wring out. Put lean and fat through coarse plate of the mincer. Mix in seasonings then add the bread and run the whole lot through the fine plate. Attach skins to the filler and fill.

OXFORD SAUSAGES (1)

1 lb lean veal	*6 sage leaves*
1 lb young pork	*1 teaspoon pepper*
1 lb beef suet	*2 teaspoons salt*
½ lb grated bread	*Spring of thyme, marjoram*
Peel of ½ lemon	*and savory*
1 nutmeg grated	

1. Mince all the meats together.
2. Add flavouring, herbs etc.
3. Mix thoroughly together and press into prepared skin.

1869

OXFORD SAUSAGES (2)

Take equal quantities of veal and pork minced, and add half the weight of beef suet. Season with salt and pepper. Add a small quantity of bread soaked in water and 1 chopped anchovy. For seasoning, add lemon peel, nutmeg, lemon thyme, basil or marjoram.

Eighteenth-Century Notebook

EPPING SAUSAGES

Take equal quantities of pork and of beef suet very finely minced. Add salt, pepper, nutmeg, sage, and some bacon. Mix with egg and fry.

Eighteenth-Century Notebook

SMOKED SAUSAGES FROM SCOTLAND

Salt some beef for two days. Mince with suet and season highly with pepper, onion or shallot. Fill large gut, plait in links. Smoke in chimney. Boil to eat.

Eighteenth-Century Notebook

GLAMORGAN SAUSAGES

1 egg	*Pinch mixed herbs*
5 oz breadcrumbs	*A little chopped onion*
3 oz grated cheese	*Salt and dry mustard*

Combine the dry ingredients, season, bind with egg yolk and form into sausage shapes. Roll in flour, dip in egg white and crumbs, fry in lard and serve alone or with garnishings of chip potatoes, fried apple rings, or tomato.

MRS GILBEY'S SAUSAGES

12 lb sausage meat	*1 nutmeg*
4 oz salt	*10 oz breadcrumbs*
$\frac{1}{4}$ oz mace	*$\frac{1}{2}$ pint of hot water, or*
$\frac{1}{4}$ oz cloves	*sufficient to make it of a*
$\frac{1}{2}$ oz pepper	*proper consistency*

Boil sausages before frying them.

Mrs Garden, 1847

OXFORD BRAWN

1 pig's head (pickled if	*4 sausages*
possible)	*Dried sage*
2 feet	*Salt and pepper*
2 tongues	*More salt for covering the*
2 ears (or 4 if possible)	*head*
Some slices of cooked	
ox-tongue	

Cut the head in half and soak for one night. Cover it with salt for another night then boil for 6 hours, very gently. Let it get really cold. Take out the bones and put back in the liquor; now boil in this liquor the feet, tongues and ears for 2 hours. Remove all the bones and gristle then chop all the meat into small pieces, including the 4 sausages which have been boiled for $\frac{1}{2}$ hour with the tongues, etc. Season all the meat with sage, pepper and salt and mix up well. Place the ox-tongue, which should be a nice red colour, in a pattern around the mould or bowl, then put in the meat and press down firmly with a weight on top. Let it stand overnight. The tongues may be put in whole, if liked, in the middle of the mould.

Miss Pocock, Headington, Oxon

Miss Pocock was a farmer's daughter with several brothers. Her mother died when they were all quite young and the only girl had to become the housekeeper – and a wonderful job she made of it. Nor did she stagnate or become a martyred drudge – she would ride to town and study in the evenings to further her education and she became very knowledgeable about local history, among other things.

GRANNY HONEY'S BRAWN

This is very simple and quick to make.

Boil a pig's head very slowly for some hours until the meat is dropping off the bones. In the water in which it is boiling put some chopped onion, with salt and pepper to taste, and a good sprig of parsley if available.

When the meat is cooked leave it in the liquor for an hour or so to cool, but before it is at all cold, remove the meat on to a large dish or tin, and start to cut up. Use every scrap of meat and, chopping it as you go, put it into a big bowl. While you are busy doing this have the liquor on the stove and keep it boiling gently, meanwhile throwing in every bone as it comes clean from the meat.

Finally when all the meat is finely chopped add salt and pepper to taste and a good grating from a whole nutmeg, according to taste. If overmuch liquor has come away with the meat, strain it through a colander before putting in a suitable bowl, tin or mould in which the meat reaches right up to the very top. Place a plate with a weight on top and stand on a tray or large dish overnight.

SAGE BRAWN

| ½ *pig's head* | **10** *sage leaves* |
| 2 *trotters* | *Salt and pepper* |

Clean the head and trotters carefully. Cover with water and add chopped sage leaves and seasoning. Boil gently for 4 hours, until the meat leaves the bones. When cool enough to handle, take out all the bones, and chop up the meat. Mix the meat and the cooking liquid and pour into pudding basins to set. Seasoning should be adjusted before the mixture is poured into basins, and a pinch of nutmeg is delicious.

CHICKEN BRAWN

1 boiling chicken and giblets
½ salt pig's head
12 peppercorns
1 teaspoon salt
Parsley

Strip of lemon peel
1 onion
2 bayleaves
Pinch of nutmeg

Put the chicken and giblets into a pan with water, peppercorns, salt, parsley, lemon peel, and *unpeeled* onion (this colours the liquid). Simmer for 2 hours. Put the pig's head into another pan and cover with water. Bring to the boil, and drain. Cover with fresh water and add bayleaves and nutmeg. Simmer for 2 hours. Slice the chicken meat in neat pieces and put round the bowl or moulds. Put in some chopped pork from the head, and then alternate layers of chicken and pork. Season with pepper as you pack in the layers. Mix the two cooking liquids, strain and pour over the meat.

LANCASHIRE BRAWN

½ salt pig's head
1 pig's tongue
1 pig's heart
6 cloves

Strip of lemon peel
12 peppercorns
Blade of mace
¼ pint vinegar

Simmer the pig's head with tongue and heart and all seasonings, except vinegar, for 4 hours in water to cover. Remove meat, and cut half in chunks. Mince the rest of the meat. Strain the stock and return the meat to the saucepan. Pour over the stock and vinegar, bring to the boil, and pour into basins.

RABBIT BRAWN

1 large rabbit
2 pig's trotters
12 peppercorns

Blade of mace
2 cloves
2 hard-boiled eggs

Cut up the rabbit and leave it to soak in cold salted water. Simmer the trotters in water for 2½ hours. Add the rabbit and spices and continue simmering for about 2 hours until the meat leaves the bones. Cut the meat in pieces. Put slices of hard-boiled eggs in the bottom of a bowl, put in the meat, and pour over the strained stock.

NORFOLK PORK CHEESE

1 salt pork hock with trotter   **Powdered sage**
Pepper

Simmer in water to cover until the meat falls off the bones. Cut the meat into pieces and toss them in pepper and sage. Put the bones back in the liquid and boil them until the stock is reduced to half a pint. Strain over the meat, mix well, and pour into bowls.

SCRAMBLED EGGS WITH KIPPERS

2 kippers   **1 tablespoon butter**
6 eggs   **4 slices buttered toast**
Pepper

Grill the kippers and discard the bones and skin. Flake the flesh and keep warm. Beat the eggs lightly with a fork and season with a little pepper but no salt. Melt the butter in a pan and add the beaten eggs. Add the kipper flesh and cook over a low heat, moving the mixture constantly from the bottom of the pan but not stirring. While the eggs are still creamy, put on to the toast and serve at once.

To keep cracked eggs whole
For boiling, simply wrap them in a plastic bag, *tightly*.

BIRDS' NESTS

Stuffing   **Hard-boiled eggs**

Good rich stuffing made with thyme, parsley, egg and lemon rind. Roll the eggs in the stuffing, wrapping it around neatly. Dip hands in flour to complete the task. Fry the covered eggs in hot dripping. Serve with fried tomatoes but cut the eggs in halves to show their colour.

YORKSHIRE DIP

The word 'dip' has several meanings – the one I have in mind is the kind we have with our breakfast bacon and eggs. Those who can face fried bacon in the morning may not 'curl up at the edges' at the thought of gravy as well! I pour a little tea from the teapot into the hot fat and while sizzling pour it over eggs and bacon. Is this an old Yorkshire custom that is dying out?

Mrs Alden, Yorks

CADGERY

Boil 3 tablespoonsful of rice till very soft. Strain through a sieve – add a piece of butter and the yolk of an egg, 1 tablespoonful of anchovy sauce, white pepper, cayenne ditto and a little salt. Put it on the fire and mix it well together. Add the fish to it in small pieces, let it heat gradually and serve up quite hot. Fish that has been dressed answers the best.

Mrs Garden, 1847

MORNING SCRAMBLE

2 rashers of back bacon
1 slice bread ¼ inch thick
1 oz butter

2 eggs, beaten
Pepper

Remove rind from bacon and cut into half-inch strips. Cut bread into half-inch pieces. Heat butter in a frying pan and fry bacon and bread until crisp and golden brown, take care not to burn butter. Turn heat to low, pour in beaten eggs and pepper and stir continuously until eggs are scrambled.

INSTANT BREAKFAST ROLLS

Self-raising flour – one handful for each roll required. Salt. Milk and water, or just water if pushed for milk. Empty the flour into a bowl, add salt generously and then mix to a fairly stiff dough with liquid. Pinch off pieces and fork or roll into rolls and place on a floured baking tray at intervals making a cross on each one before putting into the *hot* oven. Cook for 12–15 minutes or until done to your satisfaction. Eat hot and well-buttered with boiled eggs.

2 Soups

Good broth and good keeping do much, now and than,
Good diet with wisdom, best comforteth man.

Thomas Tusser

Making soup is one of the greatest kitchen pleasures, and there is no doubt everyone really appreciates the time and trouble taken. While a light soup can be a pleasant beginning to a meal, the heavier winter soups are really best for 'meals-in-one'. Serve from an old-fashioned tureen, and ladle into some really large soup plates or bowls so that everyone can have a generous helping of vegetables and all the trimmings.

Trimmings really make a good home-made soup even better. *Croûtons* are just half-inch dice of bread quickly fried golden in butter and well drained; they give a nice crisp texture to contrast with smooth cream soups. *Crusty bread* heated in the oven and pulled apart, with a lot of un-salted butter, makes another good accompaniment – the butter is blended with a crushed clove of garlic before spreading. *Cheese toasts* are good, par-ticularly in onion soups, and are best made with slices of crusty bread, toasted one side, then spread thickly with grated cheese, salt and pepper and grilled until golden and bubbling before putting into the soup bowls with the soup poured over. *Sausage balls* are marble-sized balls of sausage meat flavoured with a little finely-grated onion and herbs, tossed in seas-oned flour, then cooked in the soup for the final half-hour before serving. *Egg dumplings* are particularly good in meat soups, made by melting 3 oz butter and stirring in 2 oz plain flour and 4 fluid oz boiling water, cooking

21

over low heat until smooth. Leave this mixture to chill, then stir in 2 egg yolks, $\frac{1}{2}$ teaspoon salt and $\frac{1}{4}$ teaspoon sugar, and fold in 2 stiffly whisked egg whites. Drop by teaspoonfuls into the soup, and simmer until dumplings rise to surface.

To start a stock-pot for the winter

Boil some water, then put in all bones, gristle, etc. at hand, with a little salt and a few vegetables, and cover all with cold water. Let the contents come slowly almost to the boil. Just before boiling point is reached, skim the stock. A little salt and a spoonful of cold water will bring the scum up quickly. A day is not too long to let the stock boil, filling up with water as it boils away. In this manner a good stock is obtained at very little cost and with very little trouble.

Rice, potatoes, bread, cabbage (or similar green vegetables) slightly tainted meat, pork, or veal, should *not* be put in the stock-pot, as they cause the stock to turn sour very quickly.

Mrs Ada Wallace, 1911

Browning for Soup

2 oz of powdered sugar and half a pint of water. Place the sugar in a stewpan over a slow fire until it begins to melt, keeping it stirred with a spoon until it becomes black. Then add the water and let it dissolve. Cork closely, and use a few drops when required. Burnt onions may also be used to give colour to soup, or a piece of bread toasted a dark colour, but not burnt, can be put into the cold stock, heated in it, and taken out when sufficient colour is imparted. It must not be put into boiling stock, as in that case it would crumble.

Mrs Ada Wallace, 1911

ARTICHOKE SOUP

1½ *lb Jerusalem artichokes*	1 *pint milk*
1 *large onion*	1 *oz plain flour*
2 *oz butter*	1 *egg*
1 *pint water*	4 *tablespoons cream*

Peel the artichokes and slice them. Slice the onion and soften without colouring in half the butter. Add the artichokes and toss over gentle heat for 8 minutes. Put in the water, bring to the boil, and simmer for 15 minutes, then put through a sieve. Return to the pan. Blend the flour with a little water and put into the pan, and stir while cooking gently. Beat the egg and cream together and gradually pour on the hot liquid. Do not boil. Serve with small squares of fried or toasted bread.

CELERY SOUP

1 *quart stock*	2 *oz flour*
2 *heads celery*	*Salt and pepper*
$\frac{1}{4}$ *pint milk*	

Wash celery and cut into pieces. Simmer gently for 1 hour. Rub through sieve; return to pan. Mix flour with a little milk, throw into soup. Add milk and bring to boil. Season before serving.

TOMATO SOUP

1 *lb ripe tomatoes*	1 $\frac{1}{2}$ *oz flour*
1 *oz butter*	1 *lump sugar*
1 *quart stock or water*	1 *small carrot*
4 *cloves*	$\frac{1}{2}$ *pint milk*
2 *onions (sliced)*	

Put onions, tomatoes, carrot, cloves and stock in saucepan; simmer until tender. Rub through the back of wire sieve with wooden spoon. Melt butter in pan, stir in flour; add salt and pepper; gradually pour in liquid. Add milk and sugar. Bring to boil and serve. Taste all soups with extra spoon to see if seasoned enough.

VEGETABLE SOUP (1)

1 *carrot*	*Bits of celery*
2 *onions*	1 *pint milk*
4 *potatoes*	*Small bunch of thyme and*
2 *pints water or stock*	*parsley*
1 *tablespoonful tapioca*	*Salt and pepper*
$\frac{1}{2}$ *turnip*	

Wash, prepare and cut vegetables into dice; put on to boil with water and two teaspoonfuls salt; also herbs. When tender add tapioca and milk, and simmer until tapioca is clear. Add quarter teaspoonful pepper, sprinkled through fingers. Taste and serve.

VEGETABLE SOUP (2)

Pare and cut into small pieces 1 small turnip, 1 large carrot, and 1 potato; then chop 1 small savoy cabbage and add with the other vegetables to 3 pints of good stock which has been brought to boiling point. Add 1 tablespoonful of sugar, a cupful of rice, 1 oz of butter, and simmer for 2 hours.

23

5 minutes before serving add a gill of milk and a pinch each of salt and pepper.

Mrs Ada Wallace, 1911

POTATO SOUP (1)

1 *lb potatoes*
1 *quart stock or water*
2 *onions*
1 *pint milk*

2 *tablespoonfuls sago*
1 *oz butter or good dripping*
Salt and pepper

Melt fat in large pan; peel and slice potatoes and onions; cook in fat about 10 minutes, shaking occasionally. Add water and cook until tender. Rub through sieve or colander and return to saucepan. Half an hour before serving, add milk and sago.

POTATO SOUP (2)

4 pounds of mealy potatoes, boiled or steamed very dry, pepper and salt, 2 quarts of medium stock. Mash boiled potatoes smoothly with a fork, and gradually put them to the boiling stock; pass it through a sieve, season, and simmer for 5 minutes. Skim well, and serve with fried bread.

Mrs Ada Wallace, 1911

EGG SOUP

1 quart of clear stock, 1 egg, ¼ oz of flour, 1 small tablespoonful of cream, salt and pepper. Put the flour in a basin, break the egg on to it, and mix them smoothly together; then add the milk and a little salt and pepper. Put the clear stock in a pan on the fire; when it boils, hold a pointed gravy strainer over the pan, pour the batter into it, and stir it through with a spoon, moving the strainer about meanwhile over the soup. Let it boil for about 2 minutes, when the cooked batter should resemble fine threads all through the soup. Serve it up in a hot tureen, with croûtons of toasted bread.

Mrs Ada Wallace, 1911

LENTIL SOUP

1 pint of lentils, 1 quart of liquor in which a piece of pork has been boiled, 2 oz of butter, 2 or 3 cloves of garlic, pepper and salt. Put the lentils in a lined saucepan and boil them in water for quarter of an hour; then pour

24

off the water, add a little fresh, with the butter and seasoning, and simmer till the lentils are perfectly soft. Stir in the liquor and the garlic (for which a few dried onions may be substituted if preferred), and serve hot, with or without bread fried in boiling fat.

Mrs Ada Wallace, 1911

PEA SOUP

$\frac{1}{4}$ pound of onions, $\frac{1}{4}$ pound of carrots, 1 head of celery, 1 quart of split peas, a little mint, shredded fine, 1 tablespoon of coarse brown sugar, salt and pepper, 4 quarts of water or stock. Cut the vegetables into small pieces and fry for 10 minutes in a little butter or dripping; pour the water on them, and when boiling add the peas (soaked overnight). Simmer for nearly 3 hours, or until the peas are thoroughly done. Add the sugar, seasoning, and mint; boil for $\frac{1}{4}$ of an hour. There is not another soup that is more widely liked than this.

Mrs Ada Wallace, 1911

GREEN PEA SOUP

Boil till tender some green peas in water, to which a pinch of sugar has been added. Strain off the moisture, then pass the peas through a fine sieve. Return to the saucepan, add a small lump of butter and a little milk thickened with flour, and allow to simmer gently for a few minutes. When the soup is ready for serving, add a piece of beetroot cut into small squares, and 1 or 2 finely chopped spring onions.

Mrs Ada Wallace, 1911

COUNTRY CARROT SOUP

1$\frac{1}{2}$ lb peeled carrots, weighed before peeling	**2 pints light-coloured stock or vegetable stock**
1 large peeled potato	**1 small bayleaf**
1 skinned onion	**$\frac{1}{2}$ pint milk**
2 oz butter	**Salt and pepper**

Chop the vegetables roughly. Melt the butter in a large pan, add the vegetables, and stir them over a gentle heat until the butter is absorbed. Add the stock, bayleaf, salt and pepper, bring the soup to the boil, and simmer it until the vegetables are absolutely tender. Sieve or liquidise the soup, return it to the pan with the milk, reheat and re-season if required.

WATERCRESS SOUP

2 oz butter
1 onion
8 oz potatoes
½ pint chicken stock or water
1½ pints milk
1 bunch watercress

Salt and pepper
Pinch of nutmeg
½ teaspoon cornflour
1 dessertspoon water
2 tablespoons double cream

Melt butter and cooked chopped onion until soft but not browned. Add peeled potatoes and stock or water, bring to boil and cook gently for 15 minutes. Add milk and simmer for 10 minutes. Reserve 4 small sprigs of watercress for garnish, and put remainder into soup. Cook with lid on for 3 minutes, then put soup through a sieve or into a liquidiser. Return soup to pan and season to taste, adding nutmeg and reserved watercress. Blend cornflour with water and stir into soup. Return to boil and cook for a minute. Remove from heat and stir in cream.

TOMATO AND POTATO SOUP

2 leeks
1 oz butter
½ lb tomatoes
¾ lb potatoes
1 teaspoon salt

1 teaspoon sugar
1½ pints water
3 fluid oz single cream
Finely chopped parsley

Remove root and green from the leeks. Split the white part open and wash very thoroughly. Slice finely. Melt the butter and sauté the leeks gently. Chop tomatoes and add these to the leeks, continuing to cook gently for a further 7 minutes. Dice potatoes and add. Season with salt and sugar. Stir well together. Add water, cover and simmer for about 20–25 minutes, or until potatoes are cooked. Sieve and reheat. Adjust seasoning and add the cream and parsley.

BEAN SOUP

2 lb young broad beans
(weighed after podding)
1 small onion (thinly sliced)
6 lettuce leaves (shredded)
Cold water to cover

Salt and pepper
1 pint chicken stock
2 oz melted butter
2–3 tablespoons single cream

Put broad beans, onion and lettuce into a medium-sized saucepan, and add sufficient cold water to cover. Add a little seasoning, cover, bring to the boil, and simmer for about 20 minutes or until beans are tender.

Remove from heat. Strain beans and retain $\frac{1}{2}$ pint of liquid in which they were cooked, add this to the pint of stock. Sieve beans and discard any coarse pieces of skin which will not sieve. (Alternatively, liquidise beans with a little stock.) Add stock to purée, and season to taste. Stir in melted butter. Serve hot or cold; add a little cream just before serving.

CREAM OF ONION SOUP

2 rashers streaky bacon	**1½ pints milk**
8 oz sliced onion	**Seasoning**
1 oz butter	**1½ oz grated cheese**
1 tablespoon flour	**Parsley**

Remove rind from bacon, cut up and fry gently to extract the fat. Add onions and butter and cook slowly until onions are soft, keeping lid on to prevent onions from colouring. Sprinkle in flour, mix well and gradually add milk and seasoning. Bring to boil, stirring, cook for about 10 minutes, then sieve and reheat. Put the cheese in a tureen, pour on the soup, and garnish with parsley.

VICTORIAN PEA SOUP

1 lb dried green peas, soaked overnight	**2 carrots, scraped and sliced**
2 medium onions, skinned and chopped	**4 oz swede, peeled and diced**
	1 ham bone
1 small turnip, peeled and sliced	**4 pints water**
	Seasoning

Put soaked peas and prepared vegetables into a large saucepan, add the ham bone, seasoning and water (you can use 2 pints water and 2 pints of liquid in which a bacon joint has been cooked). Bring to boil, cover pan and simmer until the peas are soft.

Sieve the vegetables. Don't worry if you miss a few, as this adds interest to the texture. Return pulp to liquid, stir, re-heat and the soup is ready.

British Farm Produce Council

MIXED VEGETABLE SOUP

2 oz butter	**2 medium potatoes**
1 onion	**2 leaves cabbage**
¾ lb carrots	**1½ pints hot water**
2 small tomatoes	**Salt and pepper**
2 leeks	**1 oz quick-cooking macaroni**

Melt butter and add chopped onion, cooking until soft but not brown. Add coarsely grated carrots, the choppd flesh of tomatoes, sliced leeks, diced potatoes and water. Bring to boil, season, and simmer with lid on for 15 minutes. Add macaroni and continue simmering for 15 minutes. Just before serving, cut cabbage leaves in thin strips and cook in boiling water for 3 minutes. Drain and add to soup. Serve soup very hot, with grated cheese sprinkled on top.

KING'S SOUP (1753)

4 large onions
4 pints milk
Blade of mace
4 oz butter

2 egg yolks
Parsley
Diced toast

Cut the onions in very thin slices and simmer in just enough water to cover until soft. Add the milk, mace and butter and simmer for 30 minutes. Put the egg yolks into a bowl and break with a fork. Add a little of the hot milk and stir until smooth. Add to the hot soup but do not reheat. Serve with plenty of chopped parsley, salt to taste and diced toast.

PEAPOD SOUP

Peapods from 1 lb peas
1½ pints water
1 tablespoon oatmeal or tapioca

1 onion
Salt and pepper
½ pint milk

Boil the peapods in water for 45 minutes until tender. Sieve and return the purée to the saucepan. Grate the onion and add to the purée. Bring to the boil and add oatmeal or tapioca and seasoning to taste. Simmer for 5 minutes, then stir in milk. Reheat without boiling. This is nice with a garnish of crumbled crisp bacon or with small squares of fried bread.

CROÛTE AU POT

Cut off the bottom crust of a loaf leaving the same thickness of crumbs as crust. Cut it out in rounds. Soak in consommé or broth. Put them in a tin with some butter into the oven and let them be quite dried up. Then lay in the soup tureen with rounds of carrots, turnips, leeks or cabbage boiled in stock and pour good broth over.

Mrs Garden, 1847

GIBLET SOUP MOST EXCELLENT

One pair of Giblets cut in pieces about an inch long. Put them in a saucepan with as much gravy or broth as will cover them or rather more 3 onions sliced and a bunch of sweet herbs. Let them stew well together till almost done, then strain the liquor from them and mash the Giblets. Add to them a full Gill of white wine and the gravy they were stewed in. Put a piece of butter in a stewpan over the fire and add as much flour as will make it a good thickness. Keep it stirring till it is a fine brown and add it to your soup. Season with pepper, salt and mace. Squeeze in the juice of a Lemon. Let them stew slowly till quite tender, be careful to keep them scumming quite clean. 2 eggs boiled hard the yolks broke and thrown into the Tureen. From Mr Gann, Piazza Coffee House.

Mrs Garden, 1847

OATMEAL SOUP

1 *leek*	$\frac{1}{2}$ *pint milk*
1 *oz butter*	2 *fluid oz cream*
2 *oz fine oatmeal*	*Salt*
1 *pint beef stock*	

Slice the leek finely and cook gently in butter until the leek is soft but not coloured. Add oatmeal and stock and stir until it comes to the boil. Simmer for 1 minute. Add milk and cream, and salt to taste and reheat without boiling.

COCK-A-LEEKIE

1 *boiling fowl*	2 *oz rice*
6–8 *leeks*	*Pepper and salt*
3 *quarts stock or water*	2 *tablespoons parsley*

Clean and truss fowl and wash giblets. Place both in a pan with stock or water and seasoning. Bring slowly to the boil, skim well and simmer gently for a good 2 hours. Wash leeks, discarding outer leaves and chop fincly. Add to the pot with rice and cook on for another hour or until the fowl is tender. Cut up meat off bird into neat pieces and place in a hot tureen with the chopped parsley. Remove giblets and skim off any grease from the top of the soup. Pour the soup over the meat and garnish in the tureen. Serve at once. This was traditionally made from an elderly hen which had seen better days.

COTTAGE SOUP

One pound of meat, two onions, two carrots, two ounces of rice, a pint of whole peas, pepper and salt, a gallon of water. Slice the meat and lay one or two slices at the bottom of an earthenware jar or pan, lay on it the onions sliced, then meat again, then the carrots sliced, and the peas, previously soaked all night, and the gallon of water. Tie down the jar and put it into a hot oven for 3 or 4 hours, allowing it to simmer very gently all the time.

Mrs Ada Wallace, 1911

KIDNEY SOUP

Carefully remove the fat from 1 ox kidney, cut into slices, and roll in flour. Place in a saucepan with 1 oz of dripping and fry a deep brown. Peel and slice 2 small onions and add to the kidneys with a generous pinch of salt and pepper. Pour in 6 pints of boiling water and simmer gently for 3 hours, skimming off the fat from time to time. Pare and grate 2 carrots and add to the soup with 2 tablespoons of meat extract. Simmer a few minutes longer and serve.

MARLBOROUGH SHEEP-FAIR DAY 'SOUP'

½ lb lean mutton or lamb (from neck, shoulder or leg)	*2 cups of peas (about 1 lb)*
	1 cupful shredded lettuce
1 or 2 onions, or handful of spring onions using green and all	*1 cupful water*
	Salt and pepper

Cut the meat into very small pieces. Put it into the pan with the peas, sliced onion and shredded lettuce; add the water, and a good sprinkling of salt and pepper. Bring to the boil then cover and cook very gently until the meat is tender (not less than an hour). Add extra, rich stock at this stage but do not make too soupy. Turn into a hot dish or soup tureen and serve with buttered new potatoes, home-made bread, or dry boiled rice. This 'soup' is best eaten in soup plates with spoon and fork.

This was a useful, easily eaten dish for those bygone days when a thriving sheepkeeping community existed on the Marlborough Downs. These days ended in the early thirties, when farming in Britain drifted into the doldrums. The event was held annually in August and the soup made use of the row of late peas.

MUTTON BROTH

5 quarts of water, $\frac{1}{2}$ pound of barley, 1 small turnip, 2 carrots, a little parsley, 1 onion, 4 pounds of scrag of mutton, $\frac{1}{2}$ peck of green peas when in season, 1 teaspoon of salt, 1 teaspoon of pepper. Put the meat into the pot and take off the scum as it rises; then add the vegetables, cut into small pieces, and simmer altogether for 3 hours. Serve very hot.

BEEF BROTH AND PARSLEY DUMPLINGS

8 oz shin beef
2 pints vegetable stock
Salt and pepper
1 carrot
1 onion
1 small turnip
1 stick celery
1 oz dripping
Chopped parsley

Parsley Dumplings
4 oz self-raising flour
2 oz shredded suet
Salt
1 dessertspoon parsley

Cube the meat and cook with stock, pepper and salt for 1 hour. Dice the vegetables and fry in dripping for a few minutes. Add to the meat and simmer for 1 hour. To make the dumplings, mix the dry ingredients and form into soft dough with water. Add the dumplings to the broth 20 minutes before the soup is done. Sprinkle with chopped parsley before serving.

Joyce Kerr

PIGS' PETTITOES SOUP

8 pig's feet and 4 ears
(cleaned)
10 pints water

2 onions
Bunch of herbs

Simmer 4 hours and take out ears. Simmer 1 hour longer and leave to settle overnight. Take off fat. Cut up feet and ears into dice. Season with salt, cayenne, herbs and white pepper. Thicken with flour and butter. Add Madeira and forcemeat balls if liked.

1847 notebook

RABBIT SOUP

1 rabbit, 1 onion, a stick of celery, a turnip, some stock, a bunch of herbs, thickening of flour, a little cream (if at hand), pepper, salt. Skin and wash the rabbit and set aside the head, liver, and kidneys for gravy. Boil the

rabbit in water, then strain it off and add the vegetables and herbs, etc. Cook in the stock till the meat drops off the bones. Take it out, cut the meat into small, neat pieces, putting back the bones and odds and ends into the soup. Boil for another hour, then strain and thicken to a cream-like consistency with the flour. 1 rabbit should make nearly 2 quarts of soup, and milk will answer in it as well as stock; more of whichever is used can be added to make up the required quantity after the soup is strained. When thickened add the pieces of rabbit to the soup to heat through before sending to table.

Mrs Ada Wallace, 1911

MISS BUCHANAN'S IPSWICH PARTRIDGE SOUP

Take a brace or a leash of partridges and nearly roast them, or the remains of partridges dressed the day before. Beat them in a marble mortar bones and all and be careful that all the bones are broken, then take a quart or 3 pints (according to the quantity of soup you wish to make) of good beef broth and put it in a saucepan with the pounded partridges and 6 onions with 2 cloves stuck in each and a carrot. Stew them all together very slowly for 3 or 4 hours, or till the juices are all extracted, and if you have any cold ham in the house add a slice or 2 of the lean. When stewed, strain it through a sieve and press as much of the liquor out as you can do with the back of a spoon. Then take a piece of butter about 2 or 3 ozs and work as much flour into it as you can (at least a tea-cup full) with your hands a little at a time. Then break it in smallish pieces and put it in a basin and take 2 or 3 spoonfuls of the soup when quite hot and put to it. Stir it about till it is mixed and like a thick cream, then put it to the soup and boil it all together, stirring it frequently. Before you send it to table add $\frac{1}{4}$ pint of cream and a little cayenne pepper, but do not let it boil after the cream is in, as it will curdle. It should be about the thickness of pease soup. Hare soup may be made exactly the same with the remains of a hare that has been dressed.

Mrs Garden, 1847

POACHER'S SOUP

2-4 *lb venison*	1 *blackcock or woodcock*
Shin beef	1 *pheasant*
Mutton with bones	$\frac{1}{2}$ *hare or 1 rabbit*
1 *head celery*	2 *partridge or grouse*
2 *carrots and turnips*	6 *small onions*
4 *onions*	6 *peeled potatoes*
Bunch of parsley	1 *small white cabbage*
$\frac{1}{4}$ *oz peppercorns*	5 *pints water*

Cut up venison, beef, mutton, celery, carrots, turnips, onions, and put into the water with parsley and peppercorns. Simmer for 3 hours and strain the stock. Cut up the game, dust with flour and brown. Add to the stock with small onions, some more sliced celery, potatoes, and the cabbage cut in quarters. Season with some black pepper, allspice and salt, and simmer 2 hours. Add some red wine, mushroom catsup and forcemeat balls if liked.

1847 notebook

3 Fish

Oh, the gallant fisher's life!
It is the best of any;
'Tis full of pleasure, void of strife,
And 'tis beloved by many.

Izaak Walton

Most of these recipes are for river fish, since angling has always been a popular country pastime. Until a hundred years ago, fresh fish was rarely seen inland, so many popular farmhouse recipes involve smoked or salted fish which kept well. Today our choice is wider, and these basic cooking methods can be employed.

Shallow Frying is useful for cutlets, fillets or flat fish. Dip the fish in seasoned flour, breadcrumbs, batter or beaten egg, and cook in 2 or 3 oz of smoking hot fat, shaking the pan to prevent sticking. Cook on both sides, allowing 12 to 15 minutes according to thickness, and drain on absorbent paper before serving.

Deep Frying can be used for small whole fish, fillets or fishcakes. Rub fish in seasoned flour, shake off surplus and immerse in smoking hot fat in a wire basket (or use batter, having first dipped the fish in flour). Drain well before serving.

Butter Frying is easy and delicious. Use it for fillets of flat fish or small whole fish not more than half an inch thick. Dip in seasoned flour, shake off surplus, and cook on both sides in hot butter. Allow 2 oz of butter for 4 fillets, and 5 to 8 minutes each side.

Oven Frying is marvellous if you cannot bear a smell in the kitchen. Put 2 oz fat in a baking dish and make it very hot in the oven (400°F or Gas Mark 6). Dip fish in seasoned flour, and in batter if liked. Cook in the oven until golden brown. Thin pieces of fish take about 10, cutlets 15–18 minutes.

Grilling is pleasant and simple. Dip fish in seasoned flour and brush with melted fat. Grease and heat the grill tray and put the fish on it. Put a little more fat over fish while cooking. Whole fish take 3–5 minutes each side (cutlets 5–6 minutes, and fillets 5–10 minutes on one side only). Cook the fish about 2 inches from the grill.

Baking is best for large cutlets or whole fish. Dab the fish with knobs of butter, season well and cover with greaseproof paper, baking in a moderate oven on a greased and heated tray. Allow 10–16 minutes per lb for whole fish, 10–30 minutes for cutlets, and 10–20 minutes for fillets, basting well during cooking.

Braising can be used for large cutlets or whole fish and extra items such as tomatoes, mushrooms can be added. Rub in seasoned flour, brush with melted butter, and put in a covered oven dish with a small glass of wine and water (or use vinegar or lemon juice and water), a small chopped onion, a sprig of thyme and a bay leaf. Baste occasionally, and cook as for the baking method.

Poaching of fillets or flat fish makes a light invalid dish. Put the fish in a buttered baking tin with mushrooms or tomatoes, a little fish stock or wine and water and bring gently to the boil on top of the stove. Cover with a lid or greaseproof paper, and cook in a moderate oven, basting occasionally, and allowing 10–12 minutes for fillets and 15 minutes per lb for whole fish.

Foil Cooking is very clean and allows the fish to cook in its own juices giving plenty of flavour. Coat the fish in melted fat, season, wrap in foil, then proceed as for baking.

Boiling for large fish such as cod and halibut is greatly improved if a good fish stock with plenty of herbs and seasoning is used. Allow $1\frac{1}{2}$ pints of liquid to each 1 lb of fish. Bring to the boil, and simmer slowly, allowing 10–12 minutes for a 6 oz fillet of fish. Skin and fillet the fish after cooking, and drain thoroughly.

SALMON

It is the easiest thing in the world to overcook a salmon and that is the surest way to keep your friends up all night looking for the bicarbonate or whatever. Only 5 minutes too much and it will be spoiled. If you have no fish kettle, find the largest possible self-basting roasting tin and half fill it with water. Put in a bay leaf, a handful of salt and 12 peppercorns. Bring it to the boil. Wring out a cloth in hot water, lay the salmon on it and lift it carefully into the water. Leaving the ends of the cloth out, put the lid on and place it either on a simmering mat over the lowest possible heat or into the bottom of the Aga. Leave it simmering 5 minutes per lb for an 8 lb fish up to a 12 lb fish. Over that weight a little longer as the fish will be thicker, but not more than 10 minutes, under that weight 3 minutes. You can take the fish out immediately and lay on its cloth – on the draining board for a moment before putting it on a dish if you want to eat it hot or cold, but if you want to eat it cold it will be more moist if you leave it to cool in its own juice and drain it off next day. If you have had to cut it in half in the cooking, try to mend it on the plate or have it on a baking tin covered in foil if needs be. Cover the join with slices of lemon and cucumber cut very thin and a little hedge of parsley in the cut. Brown bread and butter and salad – not potato.

Mrs Chaplin, Finsthwaite, Lancs

SALMON CHARLOTTE

1 small tin salmon
½ pint white sauce
2 tablespoons parsley
(chopped)

4 tomatoes, chopped and
peeled
Salt and pepper
4 oz white breadcrumbs

Put salmon in basin and mash, add white parsley sauce and salt and pepper to taste. Grease dish and layer with salmon, tomatoes and breadcrumbs. Layer of breadcrumbs on top, cover and put it in a moderately hot oven.

Nel Fielding, Cirencester

SALMON STEAKS FROM WALES

¾ inch thick steak per person
Salt and freshly ground
pepper

Single cream
Bayleaf

This is a very simple recipe which counteracts its dryness. Season fish well with salt and fresh pepper. Choose a dish just the right size, put in fish and just cover with cream. Tuck in bayleaf and cook at 375°F (Gas Mark 5) for 25 minutes.

LITTLE WYLLIE'S SALMON MOULD

1 lb salmon (cold or tinned)
1 cup breadcrumbs
1 or 2 eggs
1 tablespoon butter

2 teaspoons chopped parsley
Salt and pepper to taste
1 teacup milk

Break salmon up finely. Add breadcrumbs, seasoning and milk warmed (not boiled). Then add eggs. Pour into a pie dish and beat quite smooth. Put butter cut in pieces on the top. Bake in moderate oven for 1 hour.

COLD SALMON CUTLETS

Cutlets are, I think, the best way to prepare salmon. Cut the portion of salmon into slices 1 inch to $1\frac{1}{2}$ inches thick and wash thoroughly. Drain, dry and salt lightly. Melt equal amounts of butter and cooking oil (not olive oil) in the frying pan, grind in a good seasoning of black pepper and add 2 teaspoons of lemon juice. Remove pan from heat and allow to cool. The cutlets should now be dipped on both sides in the pan then wrapped separately in pieces of greaseproof paper with 1 bayleaf in each. Be careful to keep their shape. Cook in a saucepan, with cold salted water to cover, by bringing them to the boil quickly with the lid on and keeping boiling gently for five minutes. No more. When cool, unwrap the cutlets. Serve with cucumber thinly sliced into diluted white wine vinegar, to which a little sugar has been added.

Lynne Wilson

WEST WALES COCKLE DISH

$\frac{1}{2}$ pint cockles
2 onions (minced finely)

1 pint milk (thickened with
arrowroot or flour)

Simmer milk and onion and thicken to taste. Stir in cockles, and just before serving put in chives, then season with pepper, salt and a little vinegar.

Mrs L. George

To keep cod-fish
Take out the eyes, fill the holes with salt, and hang the fish up by the head, in a well-aired place.

Mrs Garden, 1847

LEMON BUTTERED PLAICE

8 plaice fillets　　　　　　　*I teaspoon grated lemon rind*
I egg　　　　　　　　　　　　*Salt and pepper*
5 oz fresh breadcrumbs　　　　*3 oz butter*

Wipe fillets and dip in egg. Mix breadcrumbs, lemon rind, salt and pepper.
Coat fillets in breadcrumbs and press on well. Melt 2 oz butter and fry fish
gently for a few minutes on each side until light golden. Add remaining
butter to fry all the fish. Drain and garnish with parsley. Serve with new
or French-fried potatoes.

STUFFED PLAICE

4 large fillets skinned plaice　　*I tablespoon chopped parsley*
Salt and pepper　　　　　　　　*2 tablespoons melted butter*
4 rounded tablespoons parsley　　*Grated rind and juice ½ lemon*
and thyme stuffing　　　　　　　*4 thin rashers streaky bacon*

Season plaice with salt and pepper. Put stuffing, parsley, salt and pepper,
butter, lemon rind and juice into a basin and add enough boiling water to
give a fairly stiff mixture. Spread stuffing over the skinned side of each
fillet and roll up carefully. Remove rind from bacon and roll each fillet in
bacon. Put a sheet of foil on a baking tin and grease the centre with a little
melted butter. Put the fillets in the middle of the foil, making sure the ends
of the bacon are underneath. Fold over foil to make a loose parcel, and
bake in the centre of the oven, 400°F (Gas Mark 6), for 40 minutes. Serve
very hot with mashed potatoes and a cream sauce.

To bake mackerel

Open them and take out the roes. Wash them and cut off the heads and
tails. Wipe them dry and take out the bones, and season them with pepper,
salt, mace and nutmeg mixed. Lay them as close as you can in a long pan
and cover them with red wine and good vinegar of each an equal quantity.
Cover the pan with paste and bake in a *slow* oven.

Mrs Garden, 1847

WHITING

'The price of whiting fresh from the sea, to be used as dinner fish, fluctu-
ates extremely. Sometimes they fetch 4d and 6d apiece even by the seaside,
whilst at other times they are as cheap as 3d a score, but the low price
holds good only during the great "glut" caught in the herring season.'

A peculiar way of preparing Whiting for breakfast called 'plumping'

A number of moderate-sized whitings are cleaned and washed, laid in salt
for a few hours (more or less according to taste) and afterwards hung up in
the sun for about 2 days, *not longer*. When wanted for use, boil them

lightly on a very clear fire, and serve very hot. The middle-sized are the best for table; the smaller ones bony and the very large of too great a size to fry.

Mrs Garden, 1874

WELSH SOUSED HERRINGS

4 *herrings, deheaded and*　　*Juice of* ½ *orange*
tailed, boned and rolled　　1 *bayleaf*
1 *onion*　　*Peppercorns*
1 *teaspoon browning*　　¼ *pint water*
1 *teaspoon mixed spice*　　¼ *pint vinegar*
Orange rind

Roll herrings up very gently. Cover with other ingredients and cook slowly for 3 hours at 300°F (Gas Mark 2).

CIDERED BLOATERS

4 *whole bloaters*　　2 *red-skinned apples, cored*
½ *pint cider*　　4 *tablespoons oil*
1 *teaspoon salt*　　1 *tablespoon lemon juice*
1 *teaspoon dill seeds*　　*Salt and pepper*
(optional but good)　　½ *bunch watercress*
½ *lb new potatoes, cooked*

Cut heads off bloaters, place bloaters in ovenproof dish. Pour over cider, 1 teaspoon salt and dill seeds. Cover with lid or foil. Bake in moderate oven, 375°F (Gas Mark 5), for 15–20 minutes.

Remove bloaters and cool slightly. Cut each one down the back, exposing 2 fillets. Remove bones and skin. Arrange fish down the centre of large oval serving dish.

Cut apples and potatoes into ½ inch dice and mix together. Beat oil with 4 tablespoons of strained cider and lemon juice. Season. Toss potato salad in half of sauce and pour remainder over fish.

Arrange potato salad around outside of dish. Garnish with line of watercress between potato salad and bloaters.

SWEET-SHARP SOUSED HERRINGS

4 *fresh whole herrings*　　3 *bayleaves*
¼ *pint malt vinegar*　　6 *peppercorns*
¼ *pint water*　　2 *oz demerara sugar*
1 *tablespoon tomato ketchup*　　1 *teaspoon turmeric or*
1 *teaspoon chervil (or*　　*mustard*
parsley)

Remove heads and wash herrings. Bone. Place in an ovenproof casserole dish about 9 inches square. Mix vinegar, water, tomato ketchup, chervil, bayleaves and peppercorns in a jug. Pour over herrings and cover with lid or foil. Bake in moderate oven, 350°F (Gas Mark 4), for 1 hour. Remove herrings from oven and uncover. Mix together sugar and turmeric and sprinkle on top of each herring. Return to oven and continue baking for 15 minutes. Remove and leave herrings to cool in the liquor. When cold, drain fish carefully and serve on a prepared salad.

SOUSED MACKEREL

4 large mackerel　　　　*Bayleaf*
Wine vinegar　　　　　*Salt and pepper*
Pickling spice

Split, bone and roll up mackerel. Pack into an ovenproof dish and cover with equal parts vinegar and water. Add a dessertspoon of pickling spice, bayleaf, salt and pepper. Cover and bake in a slow oven, 300°F (Gas Mark 2), for about 30 minutes, or until tender. Drain off liquid, add fresh vinegar, and leave in a cool place for 24 hours. Serve with salad, brown bread and butter.

BAKED STUFFED HADDOCK

1 medium haddock　　　　*2 teaspoons chopped onion*
(about 2 lb)　　　　　　*2 tablespoons melted dripping*
2 tablespoons oatmeal　　*Salt and pepper*
2 teaspoons chopped parsley　*1 oz melted butter*
2 teaspoons chopped thyme

Clean fish and mix the remaining ingredients except the butter. Stuff fish with this mixture and sew up with needle and cotton. Truss by placing tail through eyeholes. Melt 1 oz butter in a baking dish, put fish in dish and baste. Cook at 375°F (Gas Mark 5) for 40 minutes, basting frequently. When half-cooked, sprinkle with breadcrumbs and parsley and dot with butter. Cover with greaseproof paper and bake at 400°F (Gas Mark 6) for 20 minutes.

HERRINGS WITH MUSTARD BUTTER

4 herrings　　　　　*Salt and pepper*
3 oz butter　　　　　*4 tomatoes*
1 teaspoon dry mustard

Split and bone the herrings and open out flat. Cream butter, mustard, salt and pepper and spread on each fish. Fold fish in half and wrap in foil. Put on a baking sheet with tomatoes cut in half and dotted with butter, and bake in a moderately hot oven, 375°F (Gas Mark 5), for 25 minutes. Serve with brown bread and butter.

KIPPER CREAMS

1 large egg
1 kipper
1 tablespoon cream

Breadcrumbs
A little butter

Scrape the kipper and rub through a wire sieve. Stir in breadcrumbs, butter and cream, make into a soft mixture with the egg, three parts fill small buttered moulds. Steam until firm.

Mrs Page, 1899

BLOATERS À LA SEFTON

2 bloaters
1 oz grated cheese
3 oz breadcrumbs

1 egg
Lard

Put the lard in a saucepan, fillet the fish and cut in nice pieces, dip in flour, then in egg, and then roll in the breadcrumbs and cheese mixed together; when the lard smokes put them in and fry a nice brown, then take up, drain on paper, serve in a circle with parsley in the centre.

Mrs Page, 1899

MRS DOWSON'S STEWED EELS

1 teaspoon black pepper
2 teaspoons salt

½ an onion
Chopped parsley

Simmer eels in 1 pint of milk for ¼ of an hour. Braid a piece of butter in some flour and add to it about 5 minutes before it is served up. A little lemon juice to be added. The eels are not to be put into water and not skinned – to be wiped with a cloth.

Mrs Garden, 1847

EEL PIE

Clean, skin and cut $1\frac{3}{4}$ lb eels into pieces 2 inches long. Dry each piece separately, placing a piece of butter inside, with a little pepper, salt and chopped parsley. Lie them in a pie dish with a cupful of vinegar and water mixed. Thicken with a teaspoon plain flour (or cornflour). Cover with a good puff pastry, and bake in a hot oven. Serve cold for Sunday tea.

PIKE

Boil the pike and let it get cold. In the same water boil macaroni. Take the pike carefully from the bones. Mix the macaroni and fish together with a sauce made of flour, butter and milk, pepper, salt and a little Cayenne. Arrange it in a flat dish *au gratin* and set in a quick oven to be creamy underneath, brown on the top.

Mrs Garden, 1847

CURRIED PIKE

Pike are coarse, ugly fish and not particularly good to eat; try one this way. Cook 1 lb of pike, break into flakes and place in a casserole. Fry 1 finely chopped onion in butter and when brown add a teaspoon of flour and a level tablespoon of curry powder. When mixed cook a further 2 minutes, then add ½ pint milk. Boil slowly for 5 minutes, season the sauce and add lemon juice. Pour over cooked fish in casserole, heat through in the oven or under the grill and serve.

Lynne Wilson

TROUT IN JELLY

After the fish have been cleaned and emptied, form them into circles by skewering their tails into their mouths. Put them into warm water, with salt, vinegar to taste, 2 shallots, a clove of garlic, cook them gently until tender – the time depends on the age of the fish, but a fine knitting needle or a clean matchstick may be stuck into the flesh, but make as small an incision as possible on account of wanting to keep the juices in the fish. Remove from the liquor and place carefully on a suitable dish to get cool. Meanwhile reduce the liquor by half, and following makers' instructions, take some well-known gelatine and make a thick jelly. Baste the fish with this, coat after coat, until they are nicely covered. When set garnish with rings of cucumber and radish, or according to taste.

TROUT CASSEROLE

When the fish are biting and he returns with at least six, this dish is the answer. Medium fry 2 chopped onions, add salt. Line a baking dish with olive oil then brush with a garlic clove. Place the 6 filleted trout in the dish and season. Make a layer with the onions then another of buttered crumbs.

Bake at 350°F (Gas Mark 4) for 15 minutes. Test with a fork and when done sprinkle with chopped parsley and chopped bacon and serve.

Lynne Wilson

TROUT IN BEER

If his luck has only run to a solitary, but good-sized trout, try cooking it in beer. Put ½ pint beer, 1 cup of white wine and 3 tablespoons of vinegar into a saucepan.Bring slowly to the boil. Add the cleaned and gutted fish with a teaspoon of horseradish, a flavour of leaf thyme, ground ginger, and a slice of lemon peel. Simmer until tender and serve fish separately. Strain the sauce and add to taste.

Lynne Wilson

TROUT IN TOMATO

Put 3 filleted trout in an ovenproof dish. Melt 2 oz butter and pour over fish, then add seasoning and some parsley with finely chopped onion. Cook in oven for 20 minutes then drain off butter and cover all with ½ pint of heated tomato sauce. Grill for a few minutes and serve.

Lynne Wilson

CRABTREE FARM FISH PUDDING

1 lb haddock or bream	*3 oz breadcrumbs*
1 chopped onion	*Juice of ½ lemon*
2 eggs	*Salt and pepper*
½ pint milk	*Grated cheese*
3 oz butter	

Poach the fish and cool. Flake the flesh and mix with the finely chopped onion, beaten eggs, milk, softened butter, breadcrumbs and lemon juice. Season well and put into a greased pie dish. Sprinkle with grated cheese. Bake at 375°F (Gas Mark 5) for 40 minutes. Nice with mushroom or tomato sauce. This recipe was invented by a member of the Young Farmers' Club (for the 'TV snack' class) at the Cheshire County Rally. It could be baked in individual dishes.

Margaret Bennion, Malpas, Cheshire

STABLE HOUSE FISH PIE

1 lb halibut	*8 oysters*
8 oz lobster	*4 eggs*
4 oz button mushrooms	*½ pint good white sauce*
2 peeled and seeded tomatoes	*Salt and pepper*
4 oz peeled shrimps	*1 lb potatoes*

Steam the halibut and flake the flesh in large pieces. Mix with lobster meat, mushrooms and tomatoes tossed in a little butter, shrimps and oysters. Whisk the eggs into the white sauce and season well. Bind the fish mixture with the sauce and put into a pie dish. Boil the potatoes and mash them with butter and a little milk, salt and pepper. Pipe them on to the pie, or mark them with a fork. Bake at 350°F (Gas Mark 4) for 30 minutes. This is delicious and rich; some of the shellfish may be omitted if necessary, and it can be fresh, canned or frozen. If time is short, the fish can be heated on top of the stove in the sauce and put into the pie dish, and the potato topping can be browned quickly under the grill.

INVALID'S FISH PUDDING

1 small whiting	1½ oz breadcrumbs
1 egg	1 tablespoon cream
¼ pint milk	

Scrape fish and mix with the crumbs boiled in milk. Add the egg yolk and cream, and light seasoning. Whip the white to a stiff froth and fold into mixture. Put mixture into a buttered basin, cover with a buttered paper, steam until firm.

Mrs Page, 1899

COLD FISH SALAD

The ingredients vary according to taste. You can make it from left-over fish, but Signora Beglia prefers shrimps and, as they are easy to get in her part of the world, she uses mussels as well.

For 4 people you need shelled shrimps, cooked mussels (optional), any amount of cooked fish, olive oil (or other vegetable oil), a clove of garlic, parsley and lemon.

Mix the fish well together in a large bowl. Chop the parsley very finely, then crush the garlic and mix with the parsley. Signora Beglia used a mortar to do this, but an electric mixer is also first class. Next mix in the oil, the chopped parsley and crushed garlic into the fish, add the juice of 2 lemons and season to taste.

This makes an excellent main dish or a first course if it is spread on toast. This recipe comes from Signora Beglia, wife of an Italian farmer who was a prisoner-of-war in England.

STUFFED SPRATS OR HERRING

Large sprats or small herrings, bread soaked in milk (the quantity depends on the number of herrings and as this is eaten cold any amount can be made), mashed potatoes, garlic, grated cheese and breadcrumbs.

Open the fish and clean it. Mix together soaked and squeezed bread and the mashed potatoes in equal quantity. Now mix in finely cut parsley, 2 cloves of crushed garlic (not essential but very good) and the grated cheese. Place this mixture on the fish which are left open. Sprinkle with breadcrumbs and moisten with oil or butter. Bake in a medium oven until the breadcrumbs are brown. Allow to cool and serve with tomato salad.

FISH BAKED IN MILK

$1\frac{1}{2}$ lb of halibut or any kind of fresh fish, 1 pint of milk, $\frac{1}{4}$ of a teaspoon of dried herbs, 1 oz of butter, and salt and pepper to suit taste. Place the fish in a well-greased tin or dish, and cover it with the milk. Add the herbs tied in a small piece of muslin, and the seasoning of salt and pepper. Place a dish over the top, and then bake the fish slowly in a fairly hot oven for $\frac{3}{4}$ hour or until it is tender. The milk, thickened with a little flour, should be used for the sauce, the herbs being taken from the muslin and added too.

Miss Butcher, Newport, 1913

GRILLED GRAYLING

This popular river fish possibly ranks second to trout. Thoroughly clean, split fully and open out. Brush with salad oil, season well with salt and pepper and cook under a hot grill until golden brown. Serve with sliced lemon.

Lynne Wilson

4 Meat

There's no want of meat, sir,
Portly and curious viands are prepared,
to please all kinds of appetites.

Massinger

A friendly swarry consisting of a boiled leg of mutton and the usual trimmings.
'Pickwick Papers'
Charles Dickens

The Vicarage Mutton
  Hot on Sunday,
  Cold on Monday,
  Hashed on Tuesday,
  Minced on Wednesday,
  Curried Thursday,
  Broth on Friday,
  Cottage pie Saturday

Old Jingle

GETTING THE MOST FROM A ROAST

Before a joint can be successfully roasted, there are a number of factors to consider. First, the type of meat – such as beef, lamb, mutton, pork or veal. Second the cut, and every family has its favourite. Third, the amount of fat. Finally, the age and probable ancestry of the meat, and the length of time it has been hung.

46

Personal preference plays a large part in preparing a roast joint. Beef takes the least time, according to the 'doneness' liked. Lamb should not be overcooked, and should have a faint pinkness. Veal and pork must be thoroughly cooked. If you do not use a meat thermometer, a 'touch test' will help to assess the doneness of the meat. If the meat feels firm, it is well done. If it responds like a cake, soft but resilient, the meat is medium rare. Pricking meat loses valuable juices, but if this is done, the meat is rare when the juice is red, medium rare when pink, and well done when colourless. Pork and fowl with light meat must be cooked until the juice is colourless, but most other meats are overdone at this point.

In roasting, everything is done to preserve the dry quality of the heat, and meat should be cooked on a rack which allows air to circulate. Potatoes are best cooked separately in a few spoonfuls of pan drippings. In top quality meat which has a good fat content, there is sufficient moisture in the meat, and no basting is necessary. To start the joint, just rub a little fat over the pan. Very lean meat may be larded with lengths of fat, or brushed with melted fat or oil and then basted, but stock or water used in a pan creates excess steam and spoils the flavour. The best and safest method of basting is with a bulb type baster rather than a spoon.

There are many theories about times and temperatures in roasting, but the latest is that the flavour is best retained by quick browning, followed by cooking at medium heat. The juices are sealed in by the initial hot searing of the meat at 500°F. After 3 minutes, reduce the heat to 350°F and cook for the required time. By this method, no basting is really needed, and there is little pan juice. It is particularly suitable for really choice meat.

With a solid fuel cooker, it is sometimes difficult to reduce oven-heat quickly. Get the oven heat up to the required temperature, put in the meat, then open up the oven door for a minute or two, close up the damper and spin wheel and make up the fire and the temperature quickly reduces, and heat can also be reduced by using the top-plates for cooking.

A really labour-saving and trouble-free method of roasting is to use a meat thermometer. This is marked with the various temperatures and degrees of doneness for various joints. The thermometer is inserted right into the meat on the rack, put into the preheated oven, and checked from time to time until the correct temperature is recorded.

Timing in meat cookery must be a matter of choice depending on the doneness required. At the moderate temperature, beef needs 25 minutes per lb, but for a rare joint take off 5 minutes per lb. Lamb needs 30 minutes per lb as this meat is usually preferred a little more cooked than beef; while pork and veal must always be very well-cooked, so they need 35 minutes per lb. Nowadays, many of us take meat from the freezer, and human nature being what it is we usually forget to allow plenty of time for thawing. If you want to cook meat straight from the freezer, allow double cooking time, and wrap the meat in foil, or cover it with another baking tin. A well-thawed joint has a much better flavour, and it's a good idea to leave the meat to thaw in a well-greased oven tin so that the juices are not lost.

If the joint has been carefully prepared to eat hot, it will also be very good cold. A joint brushed with salad oil, then liberally rubbed with dry mustard and sprinkled with pepper, salt and flour, will have a delicious brown and tender crust. While meat roasted on the bone has the reputation of being sweetest, a boned joint can be stuffed to extend the meat and make more servings.

A roast joint can be made more attractive by basting with a mixture which will give a rich glaze. A $\frac{1}{4}$ pint of fruit juice blended with a tablespoon each of brown sugar and made mustard, and a spoonful or two of the pan drippings, should be spooned over the roast twice during the last 30 minutes of cooking.

Well-chosen accompaniments add to the pleasure of a good joint. Yorkshire pudding, horseradish sauce and mustard, of course, with beef; mint sauce with lamb; redcurrant jelly with mutton; orange or apple with pork and veal. A quick piquant sauce for any hot roast can be made by whipping 1 tablespoon made mustard with 3 tablespoons reducrrant jelly. A creamy gravy is very good with veal or lamb, made by adding milk instead of water to the flour stirred into the pan drippings. Hot fruits are a very good extra, such as hot peach slices with baked ham, hot pineapple slices with lamb, and hot orange slices with veal. Everyone knows how good small baked apples are with pork, but they are equally good with beef.

After taking the roast from the oven, stand it for 15 to 20 minutes before carving; it will cut better and hold the juices.

When a joint has been carefully prepared and served on the first day, the succulent remains will be welcomed on reappearance.

How to make tough meat tender

Soak it in vinegar and water; if a very large piece, for about 12 hours. For 10 lb of beef use $\frac{3}{4}$ pint of vinegar, and soak it for 6 to 7 hours.

Edwardian notebook

VICTORIAN SIRLOIN OF BEEF

Allow $\frac{1}{4}$ hour to each pound of beef.

Make up a good fire; spit or hang the joint evenly, at about 18 inches from it. Put a little clarified dripping in the dripping pan and baste the joint well as soon as it is put down to dress; baste again every $\frac{1}{4}$ hour till about 20 minutes before it is done; then stir the fire and make it clear; sprinkle a little salt, and dredge a little flour over the meat, turn it again until it is brown and frothed. Take it from the spit, put it on a hot dish, and pour over it some good gravy (made) or mix the gravy left at the bottom of the dripping pan with a little hot water and pour it over.

Garnish with fine scraping of horse-radish in little heaps. Serve Yorkshire pudding with it on a separate dish. Sauce: horse radish.

VICTORIAN RIBS OF BEEF, ROLLED AND ROAST

Allow 20 minutes to the pound, or 15 minutes and 30 minutes over.

Order the butcher to take out the bones of the joint; roll it into a round, and fasten it with skewers and a broad piece of tape in the shape of the round. Place it at the distance of 18 inches before a large fire until it is partly dressed; then move it gradually forward towards the fire. Put some clarified dripping in the pan; baste it the moment the dripping melts and do the same every $\frac{1}{4}$ hour. Just before it is done, i.e. about 20 minutes before you remove it from the spit, dredge it with flour, and baste it with a little butter. Remove the tape and skewer, and fasten it with a silver skewer instead. Serve it with good gravy over. Horse radish sauce.

To boil beef

Reckon the time from the water coming to a boil.

Keep the pot boiling, but let it boil very slowly. If you let the pot cease boiling you will be deceived in your time; therefore watch that it does not stop, and keep up a sufficiently good fire. Just before the pot boils the scum rises. Be sure to skim it off carefully, or it will fall back and adhere to the meat, and disfigure it sadly. When you have well skimmed the pot, put in a little cold water, which will cause the scum to rise again. The more carefully you skim, the cleaner and nicer the meat boiled will look.

Put your meat into cold water. Liebig, the great German chemist, advises us to plunge the joint into boiling water, but the great cook Francatelli, and others of the same high standing, recommend cold; and our own experience and practice are in accordance with the cook rather than the chemist. Put a quart of cold water to every pound of meat. Allow 20 minutes to the pound from the time the pot boils and the scum rises.

It is more profitable to boil than roast meat.

Twentieth-century beef

British beef is the best in the world, but, because of its size, the variation in the texture of the muscles and the cooking requirements of the different cuts, it is more difficult for the housewife to understand than other types of meat.

The demand today is for much leaner beef, but it must also be tender and have a good flavour. With modern methods of breeding, feeding and livestock management, it is possible to achieve this, and more and more beef of this standard is being produced annually.

Beef when first cut is dark red, but on exposure to the air the colour brightens. When choosing it, look for a bloom, small flecks of fat in the lean (this is called 'marbling'). It indicates that the animal has been fully prepared for marketing and acts as an internal baster bringing flavour and tenderness to the meat. The fat should be creamy in colour and cuts should be clean and pink in the bone.

A side of beef is divided into two quarters between the tenth and eleventh rib. Most of the roasting joints and steaks come from the hind-quarter.

Hind-quarter cuts

Sirloin: Roast on the bone or, to get the most out of the joint, remove the fillet and use separately cut in steaks for grilling. The loin can also be boned and rolled for roasting. Steaks can be cut from the upper part of the sirloin, e.g. entrecote steaks.

T-bone steak: A trimmed slice of sirloin with the fillet and bone left in, weighing about $\frac{3}{4}$–$1\frac{1}{2}$ lb.

Fillet: Weighs 3–5 lb and is the undercut of the loin. It is very tender and delicately flavoured. Usually cut into steaks and grilled. The whole or half the fillet can be trimmed, neatly surrounded and tied, with beef or pork fat for roasting. This is a luxury dish as it is very expensive.

Porterhouse steak: Defined in the USA as the first cut from the hip end of the loin. Sometimes cut from eye or fore-rib; sometimes from eye of loin. Grill.

Rump steak: Grill or fry.

Silverside: The best joint for salting and boiling and for making pressed beef. Needs long, slow cooking.

Topside: Being lean and containing no bone this is an economical joint. Excellent for slow roasting, pot roasting, braising or boiling. Ask the butcher to tie some fat all round the roasting joint to keep moist.

Thick flank (or top rump): Very lean, and comes from the lower and inner portion of the hind leg. Best for braising, stewing or pot-roasting.

Fore-quarter cuts

Fore rib (chine), middle rib and thick rib: Fore and middle rib are adjoining cuts and both are best roasted on the bone or boned and rolled. The fore rib bone is the longer but the end of it can be cut off to make a separate joint (thick rib). An alternative use for middle rib, when boned, is as a first-class stewing or braising steak.

Porterhouse steak: See description in hind-quarter cuts.

Chuck steak and neck: These cuts are also very good for pies and puddings.

Rolled brisket: Pot roast or braise; otherwise it can be salted and boiled like silverside. It requires long, slow cooking. The fat from the braised joint is excellent for making pastry. The fore leg is called 'shin' and the hind leg is referred to as 'leg of beef'; both are gristly and full of tissue but the meat on both is lean, has a good flavour and is excellent for stewing or for making brawn. Both give a thick jellied stock. It is worth noting that, when roasting meat, the bone helps to conduct heat to the middle of the joint and adds greatly to the flavour and makes the gravy more nutritious. If joints are boned and rolled for easier carving, sit the bones on top of the joint during cooking.

BRISKET CASSEROLE

$2\frac{1}{2}$–3 *lb boned rolled brisket*	1 *bayleaf*
1 *oz plain flour*	*Sprig of thyme*
1 *oz butter*	1 *lb new carrots*
1 *glass red wine*	1 *lb small onions*
$\frac{3}{4}$ *pint stock*	*Salt and pepper*

Brown the brisket on all sides in melted butter in a saucepan. Remove meat and stir in the flour. Add the wine and gradually pour in the beef extract stock. Bring to the boil and stir until thickened. Return the brisket to the saucepan, add salt and pepper, bay leaf and thyme and cover tightly. Simmer over a low heat for $1\frac{3}{4}$ hours. In the meantime scrape the carrots and peel the onions, leaving both vegetables whole. Add these to the meat and gravy and continue cooking gently for a further 45 minutes, or until tender. Serve the joint on a hot plate surrounded by the vegetables and hand the gravy separately.

BERKSHIRE BAKED BEEF

Take a lean piece of beef – chuck steak or whatever can be afforded. Mix well together 1 teaspoon flour, 1 teaspoon sugar, pepper and salt to taste, and rub it on the meat. Lay it in a pie-dish and pour 1 teaspoon vinegar, 1 dessertspoon sauce (Worcester sauce or mushroom ketchup) and $\frac{1}{2}$ cupful water over it. Cover closely with another pie-dish and bake for 2 hours, basting frequently. Serve with jacket potatoes.

DORSET 'DAB-OF-BEEF' STEW

1½ lb stewing beef
Marinade of teacup of cider
vinegar seasoned with a good
pinch of pepper
1 oz lard (melted in frying
pan)

1 good onion
2 cloves
1 bayleaf
Parsley

Cut the beef in good dabs i.e. thickish slices and soak in marinade for about ½ hour. Melt the lard and make it hot. Cook the drained beef on both sides for a minute or two, then put a plate over the top of pan and keep just ticking over for 10 minutes on a low heat. Pour the marinade into a casserole (or thick saucepan) and add the onion, a bayleaf, 1 or 2 sprigs of parsley, the cloves and lastly the meat. Cover to top of meat with water. Cook slowly in oven, or on top of stove, for 3 hours.

CHUCK STEAK – ROLLED AND STUFFED

Take a good slice of chuck steak, about 1 inch thick, lay it flat on the board and put in the centre a mound of sage and onion stuffing such as would be used for duck or goose; roll the steak lightly around, skewer it securely and bind with fine string or yarn, so that the forcemeat cannot escape, fasten a paper greased with dripping over it, lay in a baking tin placed in a moderate oven, and let it cook gently for about a couple of hours. Baste it well from time to time. A ¼ hour before it is to be dished, remove the paper and allow the meat to brown. Serve well seasoned brown gravy with it.

OVEN BEEF AND DUMPLINGS

3 lb salt brisket
½ lb carrots
½ lb onions
4 celery sticks
2 bayleaves
6 peppercorns

Dumplings
6 oz plain flour
1½ teaspoons baking powder
1 level teaspoon salt
1 level teaspoon mixed herbs
3 oz shredded suet

Soak the meat in cold water overnight, and drain. Line the inside of a roasting tin with foil and put the joint in the centre. Cut onions, carrots and celery in large pieces, put round the joint, add bayleaves and peppercorns, and put ¼ pint water over the meat. Cover the tin with a second piece of foil, tucking the edges well under the tin. Cook in the centre of the oven 400°F (Gas Mark 6) for 1 hour 50 minutes. Make the dumplings by sifting flour, baking powder and salt into a bowl with herbs and suet, mixing to a fairly stiff dough with cold water and dividing into 8 pieces. Form each piece into a ball. At the end of cooking time, take foil off meat, put dumplings on vegetables round joint and re-cover with foil. Continue baking for 40 minutes until dumplings are well risen and cooked. This is an old favourite, but it is particularly useful to cook such a meal in the oven when a solid fuel cooker is in use, and there need be no anxiety about the saucepan boiling dry when the cook is coping with something else.

JUGGED BEEF

1½ lb shin beef	*Grated rind ½ lemon*
2 oz plain flour	*Bayleaf, thyme and parsley*
Salt and pepper	*6 small mushrooms*
4 oz chopped streaky bacon	*3 beef cubes in ¾ pint hot water*
2 onions stuck with 4 cloves	

Cut meat into 2-inch pieces and roll them in flour seasoned with salt and pepper. Fry bacon lightly, and add the meat, browning lightly. Add onions, lemon rind, herbs, mushrooms and stock. Cover and cook slowly on top of the stove or in a slow oven at 300°F (Gas Mark 2) for 3 hours. Remove onion and herbs before serving. Serves 4 people.

PRESSED BEEF

2 lb boned and rolled salt	*1 onion*
brisket of beef	*Pepper*
1 pint stock	

Soak the brisket in cold water for 2 hours. Drain and put in a saucepan. Pour in the stock and add the finely chopped onion and pepper. Cover closely and bring to the boil. Simmer gently for 1½ hours.

When cool enough to handle press the meat into a 1 lb loaf tin and fill up with a little of the cooking liquid. Put a plate with a weight on top over the tin and when cold keep in the refrigerator or a cool larder.

Turn out on to a serving dish the following day and surround with crisp lettuce leaves.

POTTED BEEF

1 lb stewing steak	*Salt, pepper and nutmeg*
5 oz bacon	*1 bunch mixed herbs*

Slice stewing steak very thinly, and also the bacon. Arrange alternate layers in an oven dish, seasoning with salt, pepper and nutmeg. Add herbs and just enough water to cover. Put the bacon rinds on top. Cover tightly and cook in a very slow oven for 3 hours. Remove herbs and bacon rinds. This dish will set into a clear pink jelly with very soft meat. If the weather turns cold, it is also delicious served hot.

BEEF IN BEER

4 lb brisket of beef   ½ pint beef stock
6 rashers lean bacon   ¼ pint wine vinegar
1 lb onions   Salt and pepper
½ pint brown ale   Bayleaf

Have the beef rolled and tied. Cut bacon into thin strips and put into casserole. Put in the meat. Slice the onions thinly and put round the beef. Add salt and pepper, depending on possible saltiness of bacon, and bay-leaf. Heat together ale, stock and vinegar and pour over the meat. Cover tightly and cook at 300°F (Gas Mark 2) for 3½ hours. The gravy is rich and delicious, and the meat has a good flavour when eaten cold or in sandwiches.

HUNTER'S BEEF

3 lb rolled ribs of beef   ¼ pint dry red wine
3 rashers streaky bacon   1 beef cube dissolved in ½ pint
2 carrots   water
2 onions   Thyme, bayleaf and parsley
1 stalk celery

Cut bacon in dice, put in a heavy saucepan or casserole, and cover with chopped vegetables. Season with salt and pepper, put on lid and put on gentle heat to soften vegetables in bacon fat. When they are just soft, add wine and stock made with beef cube. Put meat on top of vegetables, add herbs, cover and cook for 2½ hours at 325°F (Gas Mark 3). Slice the meat and serve on vegetables, and reduce gravy by fast boiling before handling separately. This makes a good Sunday meal if there isn't much time to attend to a joint with all the trimmings.

STEAK AND MUSHROOM CASSEROLE

1½ lb chuck steak   Bay leaf
2 oz dripping   Parsley and thyme
4 small onions   ½ pint stock
4 oz button mushrooms   1 dessertspoon cornflour

Cut the steak in cubes and lightly brown in melted dripping. Put into the casserole with onions cut in quarters, mushrooms, herbs and stock. Cover tightly and cook at 350°F (Gas Mark 4) for 2 hours. Before serving, remove herbs and thicken with cornflour. Garnish with a little freshly chopped parsley.

BOILED SPICED BEEF

Choose a piece of beef with as little bone as possible, sprinkle it well with salt, and let it drain for 24 hours. Then prepare the following mixture: 1 lb of common salt, 1 ounce of saltpetre, $\frac{1}{2}$ lb of sugar, and a mixture of pounded mace, cloves and nutmeg. Rub this well into the beef, and let it lie in a crock for a week, turning and basting it daily. Leave it in the pickle for 3 days longer, turning it each day, but not rubbing it. Then drain it well and cook. When cold, this makes very excellent sandwiches.

SPICED BEEF

10–12 lb pickled beef
1 dessertspoon black pepper
$\frac{1}{2}$ teaspoon ground ginger
1 saltspoon powdered cloves

1 saltspoon grated nutmeg
$\frac{1}{2}$ saltspoon ground mace
1 glass claret or port

Drain the beef from the pickle. Mix together the other ingredients (except the wine) and sprinkle them over the entire surface of the meat, which must then be rolled, bound and skewered into a good shape. Put the meat into an earthenware stew-pot with a lid, pour the wine over it, cover the top of the vessel with 2 or 3 thicknesses of greased paper and put on the lid.

As no other liquid than the wine is added, it is absolutely necessary that the steam generated should be kept within the vessel, and for this purpose the lid is frequently covered with a paste of flour and water. The meat should be cooked slowly in the oven for about 4 hours, and then pressed between 2 boards until cold.

A SAVOURY POCKET STEAK

1 small onion and 3 mushrooms chopped finely

1 lb or more of rump steak, 1 inch thick
1 oz butter and breadcrumbs

Cook vegetables in the butter a few minutes, add the crumbs and seasoning. With a sharp knife give the steak a slit through, leaving the bottom of each side $\frac{1}{2}$ inch thick, fill the pocket as a pincushion with the mixture, and skewer up, pour over a little oil, and grill or bake 10 to 12 minutes. Serve with potato chips, and glaze poured over.

Mrs Page, 1899

CORNISH UNDERROAST

2 lb shin beef	Salt and pepper
8 oz ox kidney	1 pint stock
1 lb onions	Potatoes
1 oz plain flour	

Cut up beef and kidney into very small pieces. Slice onions. Toss meat in flour and season well. Fry meat and onions in a meat tin with dripping until meat has changed colour. Pour on stock and leave to simmer while the potatoes are prepared. Peel the potatoes and cut them into pieces about the size of an egg. Put them all over the meat, half below and half above the gravy line like icebergs. Cook at 325°F (Gas Mark 3) for 2 hours until the potato tops are brown and the bottoms soaked in gravy. Serve with plenty of vegetables.

SCOTCH COLLOPS

1 lb fresh minced beef	Salt and pepper
1 large onion	1 tablespoon oatmeal
1 oz butter or dripping	1 breakfastcup water

Brown the beef and finely chopped onion in the fat. Season with salt and pepper, add the oatmeal and water. Cover with a lid and simmer for 30 minutes. Put into a serving dish and surround with mashed potato. Poached eggs may be served on top.

SUFFOLK NESTS

1 small onion	Salt and pepper
1 lb minced beef (raw)	4 eggs
Pinch of mixed herbs	4 tablespoons cream or top
3 tomatoes	milk
1 oz butter	

Chop the onion and cook in butter, then add meat, herbs, tomatoes and seasoning. Cook gently for 15 minutes and put into greased oven dish. Make 4 hollows, drop an egg into each, and top with a tablespoon of cream. Bake at 375°F (Gas Mark 5) until eggs are set (about 10 minutes).

VEAL FRICASSEE

2 lb breast of veal	2 potatoes
2-3 oz cooked peas	Parsley
1-2 egg yolks	$\frac{1}{2}$ gill cream
1 stick celery	Cornflour
2 large carrots	Salt and pepper

Trim the meat and cut into small squares; place them in a larg
Sprinkle with salt and cover with cold water, bring gently to th
moving scum as it rises to the surface. When the water boils clea
the celery, carrots and potatoes cut into small squares. Allow to s.
until the vegetables are cooked, then remove them from the pan.
tinue simmering the meat until it is quite tender, then transfer it to the
dish on which you will serve it, and keep it hot while preparing the sauce.
Strain the liquid into a small pan; blend in 1 dessertspoon of cornflour
previously dissolved with cold water. Reheat the sauce, stirring all the
time, then remove from the heat. Blend into the sauce the egg yolks and
½ gill cream. Add the cooked vegetables and the cooked green peas to the
sauce and reheat all together gently, without allowing it to boil. Pour this
all over the cooked meat and dredge generously with chopped parsley
before serving.

VEAL FILLETS WITH SEMOLINA STUFFING

1 lb veal, cut in the thinnest	*Bacon, chopped*
possible slices	*Nutmeg*
Semolina	*Fresh parsley, chopped*

Cook the semolina in the usual way, leave to cool a little, then add the
chopped bacon, a little nutmeg, and chopped parsley. Leave to set. When
cold, cut the stuffing into fingers. Place a finger of stuffing on a slice of
veal, roll round tightly and secure with a cocktail stick or tie with string.
Heat some butter in a pan and fry the rolls until brown all over. Place
meat in a casserole, dot with butter and cook for 35–40 minutes or until
tender, 350°F (Gas Mark 4).

VEAL WITH SHERRY

4 veal cutlets or chops	*1 tablespoon tomato paste*
6 tablespoons olive oil	*¼ pint dry sherry*
1 stalk celery	*Salt and pepper*
1 carrot	*Chopped parsley*
1 onion	

Heat the oil and fry the meat until brown; add the vegetables and mix
well. Cover and simmer for about 10 minutes or until the vegetables are
tender; mix with tomato paste and sherry together and add to the meat,
together with the seasoning. Cover and cook until the meat is tender –
about 20 minutes, add water during cooking time if necessary to prevent
burning. Sprinkle with chopped parsley.

VEAL FILLETS IN YOGHURT

For each person allow one small round or 'steak' of veal (escallop or 'collop'). Fry the veal 'collops' in butter until tender and cooked and browned lightly on both sides. Sprinkle with salt. Remove the meat and keep hot; meanwhile cook some mushrooms, as required, in the butter. Put the meat back into pan with the mushrooms and pour over sufficient natural yoghurt to cover each escallop. Sprinkle liberally, or to taste, with paprika. Heat most carefully for a few minutes and serve right away.

Mrs Hutchins suggests serving this dish with new potatoes, if in season, or mashed or Duchesse potatoes, peas or French beans and carrots. Garnish with parsley.

Mrs Hutchins, Norfolk

COLD STUFFED BREAST OF VEAL

For 4 people you need 2 lb breast of veal cut in 1 piece, and for the stuffing about 1 lb cut into very small cubes the size of a finger nail or smaller, 4 oz chopped ham, 3 eggs, 4 oz cooked green peas, the same amount of cooked carrot, a cup of grated cheese and oil (or a good knob of butter) and hard-boiled eggs.

Mix all the ingredients well together, excepting the large piece of veal, the oil and the hard-boiled eggs but including the raw eggs; season and then place in a pan and lightly fry in the oil, turning over all the time so that the veal cubes are cooked through and the whole well mixed. Cut open the breast of veal and then alternately fill with a layer of the stuffing and a layer of hard-boiled eggs cut into slices (any number of hard-boiled eggs can be used). When full, sew up the breast, wrap in a white cloth and boil for 3 hours.

Allow to get cold and then serve with salad or with the green sauce.

Signora Beglia, Italy

VEAL BIRDS

You need veal escallops, flour, oil, garlic, small black olives and a little white wine. Dip the escallops in flour. Crush the clove of garlic into the oil so that it becomes quite liquid, mix in wine and some small black olives and pour into an oiled pan over a very hot fire. Drop in the lightly floured escallops. Cook for 5 or 6 minutes. Allow 1 escallop per person.

Signora Beglia, Italy

LANCASHIRE HOT POT (1)

Lamb chops, onions, potatoes. The lamb would be from the neck end. To every $\frac{3}{4}$ lb meat allow $\frac{1}{2}$ lb sliced onions and 1 lb sliced potatoes. Into your casserole put potatoes, then onions, then meat, then start again, adding salt and pepper on top of second lot of potatoes (salt sprinkled on meat makes it tough). Finish with a layer of potatoes. Cover with water. Place lid on top of all and cook in hottish oven for a bit, then in cooler oven for 2–3 hours. Take off lid for about $\frac{1}{2}$ hour before serving to brown top layer of potatoes. (Modern ovens – first $\frac{1}{2}$ hour at 400°F, Gas Mark 6, then 2–3 hours at 250°F, Gas Mark 1.) Add more water if and when it is needed.

LANCASHIRE HOT POT (2)

2 lb potatoes, $1\frac{1}{2}$ lb scrag of mutton, 2 sheeps' kidneys (optional), 1 large onion, about $\frac{1}{2}$ pint water, dripping or butter, pepper and salt. You grease an earthenware casserole or hot pot jar and put in a thick layer of sliced potatoes and then the meat cut into suitably sized pieces. Cover with the sliced onion and season with pepper and salt. Pour on about $\frac{1}{2}$ pint water. Finally place on top of the rest of the potatoes cut in halves to cover the meat etc., completely. Dot the dripping or butter over the top. Cook slowly for $2\frac{1}{4}$ hours adding more water between times and keeping lid or butter paper on top to keep from getting too dried-up. Uncover for last 30 minutes to get brown and crispy.

LAMB AND POTATO HOT POT

1 lb boned shoulder lamb	1 beef cube in 1 pint hot water
1 lb breast of lamb (also boned)	2 bayleaves
	Parsley
$\frac{3}{4}$ lb floury potatoes	1 teaspoon rosemary
2 large onions	12 shallots
Salt and pepper	12 small potatoes
1 stick celery	4 oz grilled streaky bacon

Cut the meat into 2 inch chunks. Peel and slice floury potatoes and onions and put in alternate layers with the meat in a casserole. Season well with salt and pepper, and add the celery, stock, bayleaves, parsley and rosemary. Cover and simmer for 1 hour. When cool, remove meat to a clean casserole, discard celery, bayleaves and parsley, and mash onions and potatoes into gravy. Pour this gravy over meat, and add peeled shallots and small potatoes. Snip grilled bacon into small pieces over the top and continue cooking uncovered for 30 minutes.

LAMB AND MUSHROOM HOT POT

1½ lb best-end lamb cutlets
1 oz plain flour
2 oz butter
1 onion
6 oz button mushrooms

¾ pint stock
Salt and pepper
Pinch of rosemary
1 lb potatoes

Trim fat from cutlets and coat them with flour. Melt the butter and fry cutlets and sliced onion until golden. Put into a casserole with mushrooms stock, salt and pepper and rosemary. Peel the potatoes and cut in ¼ inch slices. Arrange potatoes on top of meat, cover and bake at 300°F (Gas Mark 2) for 1½ hours. Take off the lid and continue baking for 30 minutes. Good with peas and young turnips.

LAMB CASSEROLE

1½ lb middle neck lamb chops
2 large onions
2 lb potatoes

Pinch of marjoram
Stock
Salt and pepper

Take off excess fat and arrange the chops in alternate layers in a casserole with sliced onion and potato, seasoning each layer with a sprinkle of marjoram, salt and pepper, and ending with a layer of potatoes. Half fill the casserole with stock and cook at 375°F (Gas Mark 5) for 2 hours. Take off lid and brown potatoes for 30 minutes.

BOILED MUTTON

Half a leg of mutton, a large onion, carrot, turnip, bunch of herbs, parsley, 12 peppercorns, a little mace, salt.

Weigh the meat, wipe it over with a clean cloth and put into a saucepan containing sufficient boiling water to entirely cover, and let it boil for 5 minutes. Then pour in a little cold water to lower the temperature, and add vegetables, herbs, and spice. Lower the burner and let the meat simmer only till done. 20 minutes to each pound should be allowed and 20 minutes over from the start of the simmering. Remove scum from time to time and close saucepan quickly as possible. About ½ hour before serving, add some salt.

It may be served with a nice thick melted butter sauce poured all over, and with the vegetables cut small, arranged in neat piles round. Celery is good with it.

Mary Bull, 1914

BOILED MUTTON AND BROTH

Leg or shoulder of mutton	*1 large onion*
2 teaspoons salt	*$\frac{1}{2}$ lb sliced carrot and turnip*
Boiling water	*1 oz shredded cabbage*
2 oz pearl barley	*1 tablespoon parsley*

Weigh meat, place in pan of salted boiling water. Boil fast for 10 minutes. Skim and allow to simmer; pour boiling water on the barley, rinse and add to the pan. Simmer for 1 hour; then add the sliced onion and vegetables. The cooking time is calculated as 25 minutes per pound of meat plus 25 minutes for the bone. Remove the meat and $\frac{1}{2}$ pint of the liquid. Add the cabbage to the soup pan, boil for 3 minutes. Skim and check the seasoning. Add the chopped parsley. The meat is good with caper or parsley sauce.

MUTTON IN WINE

This is a good way of turning a leg of mutton into a special dish. Put the joint into a saucepan with a wineglass of water, over strong heat, till the water has evaporated and the meat coloured. Add 1 wineglass of red wine and 2 cups of meat stock, with $\frac{1}{2}$ grated onion, a bunch of parsley and thyme, a bayleaf, salt and pepper. Cover tightly, and simmer on a low fire for 3 hours. Just before serving, remove the joint to a serving plate. Strain the gravy, mix in $\frac{1}{4}$ pint of cream and 2 egg yolks, and warm without boiling. Pour over the meat on the serving dish.

STEWED SHOULDER OF MUTTON

Mutton is not sold much today but lamb is usually one of the cheaper meats and could be used for this.

Remove bone from a shoulder of small mutton or lamb. Make seasoning of breadcrumbs, herbs, onions, butter and a little milk (seasoning in this context is simply the old way of saying 'stuffing'). Mix well together and fill up the space from which the bone has been taken. Sew up tightly, put in a boiler pan (or big saucepan with some sort of tray effect on which to stand meat). Cover meat with hot water and add a little salt to the water. Boil for $1\frac{1}{2}$ hours slowly with lid on. Take the meat from water and skim all fat from liquor; put in some peeled onions, also the mutton and simmer slowly for a further $\frac{3}{4}$ hour. Just before dishing blend some flour with a little cold water sufficient to thicken the gravy in which the meat has been stewed. Serve with boiled, minted, new potatoes, if possible, and green peas.

HASHED MUTTON

Make a white sauce not too thick. Cut up rather fine 2 heads of lettuce and 3 green onions – the white part only of the onions. Put these in the sauce to cook about $\frac{1}{2}$ an hour. Add with pepper and salt the juice of half a lemon. Then put in the sliced-up mutton; leave it to simmer a short time. Then put in the yolks of 2 eggs well beaten with a little cold water. Serve as the eggs begin to thicken.

Mrs Garden, 1847

PORK AND APPLES

4 pork chops
1 large onion
2 apples

Pinch of mixed herbs
Salt and pepper

Wipe pork chops and cook gently in thick frying pan until the fat runs. Turn over chops and surround with sliced onions and apples, sprinkle with herbs and seasoning and continue cooking gently until pork is cooked through, onions are soft and apples reduced to a pulp. Serve with mashed potatoes or with well-drained buttered noodles.

STUFFED APPLES AND PORK

Small joint of pork
Lard for 'dotting' and 1 oz for
stuffing
4 Bramley's Seedling apples
(all about the same size)

1 breakfastcup dry sage and
onion stuffing
1 large onion, peeled and
grated
Salt and pepper

Put joint in a roasting tin, with about 2 tablespoons of water. Dot with lard. Allow 30 minutes to the pound and 30 minutes over at 375°F (Gas Mark 5) cooking time, with the joint towards the top of the oven. Baste frequently. Core apples, and gently cut through the skin round the middle of the apple. Mix the onion with the stuffing mixture. Put the apples in a lightly greased pie dish. Fill core cavities with stuffing and spread the rest over the top of the apples. Melt the lard, pour over the stuffing and season. Put the apples in the lower part of the oven $1\frac{1}{2}$ hours before the meat has finished cooking, basting frequently with juices from the meat tin.

TENDERLOIN IN BRANDY AND CREAM

Cut your slices of tenderloin slightly on the bias so that they hold together. If you can't cut them $\frac{1}{8}$ inch thin – bash them with your husband's mallet or the flat of a heavy knife. Melt a piece of butter in a frying pan – fry the pieces gently on both sides. When you have cooked about 2 or 3 lots the butter will begin to darken – quickly pour in a tablespoon of brandy and set it alight. When the flames have died down pour over half a carton of double cream and let it bubble till it turns dark gold, scraping up the juices meanwhile. Now if you can serve at once do so – if you can't, flatten a sheet of buttery greaseproof paper over the fried pieces and put them to cool quickly and pour the sauce into a separate bowl. Wash the pan and do it again as many times as necessary. When I did it one summer for a silver wedding party we gave for some friends, we had 18 people and most of them came from Scotland. The last people arrived 2 hours late having had an accident and we sat down to dinner at 10.30 instead of 8.30. While we ate the first course the dish of meat was in the slow oven of the Aga and the sauce in a pan on the slow ring. When we were ready the sauce was quickly boiled up and poured over and all was well.

Mrs Chaplin, Finsthwaite, Lancs

PORK CHOPS WITH LEMON

Leave chops to marinate in lemon juice with a pinch of thyme and melted butter in a fireproof dish turning them once or twice during the process. Cook them in the same dish as they are, fairly gently so that they absorb the juice as much as possible. I serve them straight from the dish with mashed or boiled potatoes or just home made bread. A green salad goes well.

Mrs Chaplin, Finsthwaite, Lancs

PORK CHOPS IN ORANGE SAUCE

4 pork loin chops 1 inch thick
2 dessertspoons flour
½ teaspoon salt
2 tablespoons lard
1 dessertspoon soft brown sugar

Pinch of ginger
1 tablespoon grated orange peel
⅓ pint orange juice

Wipe chops with damp kitchen paper and coat with a mixture of flour and salt. Heat lard and brown chops on each side, about 10 minutes in all. Mix together sugar, ginger, peel and juice and pour over chops. Cover and simmer for 45 minutes until chops are tender. Serve with peeled orange rings, mashed potatoes and a green salad.

STUFFED BELLY OF PORK

2 *lb belly pork*   **1 *pig's kidney***
Sage and onion stuffing   **Salt**

Stuff the pork with sage and onion, adding the chopped kidney to the mixture. Rub the scored skin with a little melted lard, sprinkle well with salt and roast for 1½ hours at 375°F (Gas Mark 5).

PORK AND APPLE CASSEROLE

4 *spare rib pork chops*   **¼ *pint stock***
1 *medium onion*   **Pinch of sage or basil**
1 *cooking apple*   **Salt and pepper**
4 *oz tomatoes*

Lightly brown the chops on both sides. Surround with sliced onion, cover with stock and season to taste, adding chosen herb. Cover tightly and cook at 325°F (Gas Mark 3) for 1 hour. Put sliced apple and tomatoes on top, and continue cooking for 20 minutes. Remove lid and allow meat to brown for 15 minutes.

KIDNEYS

The most delicious way of cooking kidneys is to cook them in their own fat. Put the kidneys surrounded by their fat into a casserole or baking tin, and bake in a moderate oven (350°F, Gas Mark 4) for 30 minutes. Cut off the fat, season the kidneys with salt and pepper, and plenty of chopped parsley and return them to the oven for 5 minutes surrounded by their own gravy.

HEARTS

Simmer gently in a little seasoned stock in a casserole until tender, then cut into pieces, removing tubes, and return to the stock with plenty of onions and a little sage. Simmer until onions are cooked, then thicken the gravy.

Those who like the traditional ox heart stuffed with sage and onion, sometimes known as 'mock goose', can vary the stuffing by using a mixture of chopped walnuts and breadcrumbs, or by using bacon and plenty of mixed herbs.

BRAINS

Put brains in a basin under a cold tap for an hour, then remove all skin, ligaments and blood vessels. They should then be cooked by simmering in a little water to cover with a spoonful of white vinegar and a pinch of salt for 30 minutes, before draining and drying.

They are delicious cut in large squares, dipped in batter and deep fried until golden, then served very hot with salt and parsley. They can also be served with a squeeze of lemon, or with home-made tomato sauce.

The most elegant accompaniment is *Black Butter* served over brains which have been simmered, then cut up in pieces and kept warm. This is made by browning 2 oz butter, adding 1 dessertspoon chopped parsley and pouring over the brains, then swilling out the pan with 1 dessertspoon vinegar or lemon juice and pouring this over the brains too. A little chopped garlic or a few capers may be added.

SWEETBREADS

Put sweetbreads in a basin under cold running water for an hour, then remove any skin, hard pieces or blood and dry them well. Blanch them in a saucepan of boiling salted water for 10 minutes, then drain and dry them, and leave to cool.

To serve simply, they can be cut into thick slices, seasoned and floured and fried until golden in butter or olive oil, then garnished with parsley or lemon.

The pre-cooked sweetbreads may also be cut in pieces and threaded on skewers with pieces of thick bacon and small mushrooms, then seasoned and rolled in melted butter and breadcrumbs before grilling under low heat for 10 minutes.

LIVER

Liver can be cut in thin slices, lightly floured, then cooked quickly in butter or bacon fat, to serve with crisp bacon. If onions are also served, clear the pan with a little red wine to make a good gravy, and finish the dish with chopped parsley and squares of fried bread.

The liver can be cut in cubes and threaded with squares of bacon on skewers, finished off with small tomatoes, brushed with oil, salt and pepper and chopped thyme and grilled. Alternatively, cut the liver, bacon and onion in very small pieces, cook them separately and quickly in a little butter or oil, then toss them with plenty of hot buttered boiled rice, a few button mushrooms cooked in butter, plenty of salt and pepper, and herbs, preferably thyme and rosemary.

Liver is particularly juicy cut in cubes and cooked quickly in deep hot fat. Some people like to dip the cubed liver in batter first. If you have a large family, try cooking roast liver, cutting a gash in the solid piece and filling it with a stuffing of bacon, onion, breadcrumbs and egg, then roasting the liver in a moderate oven with a covering of streaky bacon rashers.

This is delicious with a good gravy made from the pan juices, and with redcurrant jelly.

OXTAIL STEW

2 oxtails
1 oz dripping
1 lb carrots
8 oz onions
1 oz flour

Salt and pepper
1 teaspoon tomato purée
1 tablespoon lemon juice
Bunch of mixed herbs

Chop the oxtails into joints, wipe and dry them and fry lightly until golden in dripping. Add thick slices of carrot and sliced onions, and when lightly coloured, sprinkle in flour, and mix well. Add water to cover, or a mixture of water and wine, or cheap red or white wine. Add herbs, salt and pepper, bring to the boil. Simmer or cook in oven set at 300°F (Gas Mark 2) for 2 hours.

Strain off liquid and leave until cold, then take off fat – this can be done the evening before the meal is needed. Put meat and vegetables into casserole, pour on liquid and bring to the boil. Adjust seasoning if necessary, and stir in tomato purée and lemon juice. Cover and cook at 300°F (Gas Mark 2) for 3 hours, and serve sprinkled thickly with chopped parsley.

STEWED OXTAIL

1 oxtail
6 cloves
¼ teaspoon whole white pepper
2 oz butter
1 oz flour

1 tablespoon lemon juice
2 carrots, cut finely
1 large onion, sliced
Bunch of herbs
Salt to taste

Fry the onion slices in the butter, remove from pan when brown; fry the joints of tail in same butter. Take out the joints, stir in the flour, and allow it to get light brown. Return the joints and onions, cover with stock or water, add the seasonings and vegetables, simmer slowly for 3 hours, and add the lemon juice just before serving. The meat should leave the bone easily when sufficiently stewed. Skim off as much fat as possible before serving and arrange the joints neatly in the dish before pouring over the gravy.

WELSH STEWED OXTAIL

1 good sized oxtail   *Sufficient Old Ale to cover*

Leave soaking overnight, before cooking the following morning with suitable vegetables to accompany it according to the time of year. Plenty of onions or shallots, sufficient for one whole one per person. It is best to cook the oxtail alone until nearly tender, then add the vegetables at a suitable time – finishing with sliced potatoes which will also help to thicken the rich gravy. If wished, a dumpling-type covering can be added about 20–25 minutes before dishing.

Dumpling Mixture   *As much good dripping as you*
8 oz self raising flour   *can scoop on to your fingers,*
½ eggspoon salt   *twice*
1 level teaspoon baking   *Water*
powder

Rub dripping (2–3 oz lard may be used if preferred but is not as tasty) into the dry ingredients and mix with sufficient water to make a nice soft dough. This dough can either be used to cover the whole stew in one whole piece, or it can be divided into individual dumplings by flouring the hands and dividing into suitable number of portions. Serve as soon as dumplings are fluffy and cooked.

While on holiday may years ago, this delicious recipe was given to the Honey family by 'Billy the Butch' or Thomas-the-Meat in Haverfordwest, Pembrokeshire. He said that as farmers they would fully appreciate this dish, 'Only,' he warned, 'don't let father get at the ale before you can cook the oxtail.'

FFAGOD SIR BENFRO

1½ lb pig's liver   **2 teaspoons salt**
2 large onions   **½ teaspoon pepper**
3 oz suet   **1-2 teaspoons sage**
4 oz breadcrumbs   **½ oz flour**

Mince the raw liver and onions. Mix thoroughly with the suet, breadcrumbs, seasoning and sage. Form into small balls. Bake in a moderate oven for about 30 minutes. Remove from the tin and keep warm. To make gravy, stir the ½ oz flour into the pan juices and add boiling water or vegetable stock, and seasoning.

This is a Pembrokeshire recipe. It was very popular fifty or sixty years ago after pig killing. The English equivalent would be 'Savoury Ducks' but Ffagods are very much nicer.

Many Welshmen were hill-farming people. Because of this their recipes contained a good deal of carbohydrate, which besides being cheap, provided the energy needed for the hard manual labour of farm work.

HAGGIS

The thrifty Scots would not, indeed could not afford to, waste anything so when a sheep was killed every little bit was used.

The paunch and pluck of a
sheep
2 large handsful of oatmeal
1 lb onions
½ lb grated suet

1 tablespoon chopped parsley
1 teaspoon grated nutmeg
½ pint 'pluck' stock
Salt and pepper to taste

Wash the paunch thoroughly in several cold waters, turn inside out and wash and scrape in very hot water. Leave overnight steeping in cold, salted water. Wash the 'pluck' thoroughly and blanch, then boil gently for 2 hours. Remove windpipe and gristle and mince the heart, liver etc. finely. Toast the oatmeal a little in a warm oven or in front of a fire, chop the onions and mix all ingredients together very thoroughly. Fill the paunch almost full (to allow for expansion), tie or sew up, prick well and place in a pan with sufficient boiling water to cover. Boil steadily for 3 hours.

LANCASHIRE KIDNEY CASSEROLE

I usually use pigs' kidneys, 1 for 2 people, plus onion, carrots and potatoes. Slice and roll in seasoned flour. Brown in saucepan, also 1 onion. Put in casserole, plus carrots and top with sliced potatoes. Add some stock and cook for about 2 hours in a medium oven.

BLACK DISH

To every ½ lb liver, allow 1 large onion, 1 cup water, salt and pepper and a teaspoon of chopped sage. Put all this together in a 'reet gud' dish (a casserole) and cook well with the lid on. And don't be mean with the salt and pepper and add more water if necessary. Serve with mashed potatoes and carrots. In Victorian days, offal was seldom served to the gentry, and the poorer people benefited from this silly fad. These 2 recipes were told to her great-granddaughter by a very old Lancashire lady. She says they were traditional in her childhood and she made them all her life, and she insists they are still good enough for anyone.

OX TONGUE

Put tongue into tepid water with salt; boil for 3 hours, or until the skin is easily removed. When skin is peeled off, curve tongue round in a suitable glass or chrome dish and cover with a flat plate. On plate stand a very heavy weight and leave to cool till the following morning. Ease tongue around with a curvey knife and slide out on to an oval meat dish. Garnish with fresh parsley.

The flavour of the tongue is improved if onions or other suitable vegetables are cooked in the water with the tongue. The resulting liquid is excellent for soup.

TONGUE WITH CUMBERLAND SAUCE

1 salted ox tongue (4-6 lbs)
½ lb root vegetables
Bayleaf, thyme and parsley
Peppercorns

Cumberland Sauce
2 large tablespoons
redcurrant jelly
1 glass port
Juice of 1 orange and ½ lemon
1 teaspoon shredded,
blanched orange rind

Wash the tongue and put in a large pan. Cover with cold water, and bring slowly to the boil. Skim well, add chopped vegetables, herbs and peppercorns, and simmer until the bones at the root of the tongue will pull out easily (about 3 hours). Cool in the liquid, then take off skin and trim away root and bones. Curl the tongue round in a cake tin, and cover with a plate and a weight. Leave 24 hours before turning out. To make the sauce, heat the redcurrant jelly until dissolved, then stir in the rest of the ingredients. Serve cold with tongue, or with ham.

DEVILLED KIDNEYS

4 lambs' kidneys
2 onions
2 tomatoes
1 level tablespoon cornflour
1 level teaspoon curry powder

½ pint beef stock
1 tablespoon chutney
Salt and pepper
Squeeze of lemon juice

Slice kidneys, onions and tomatoes and toss in a little hot oil until onions are just golden. Add cornflour and curry powder, cook for 1 minute, stir in stock and bring to the boil. Add chutney, salt and pepper and lemon juice and simmer for 15 minutes. Serve on toast or with rice or mashed potatoes.

BRAISED LIVER

1-1¼ lb ox liver
2 oz dripping
2 oz onions
8 oz carrots
4 oz turnips
Stick of celery

Bacon trimmings
1 teaspoon flour
Cup of water
Salt and pepper
1 heaped teaspoon arrowroot

Cut thick slices of liver and fry in very hot dripping; remove and next fry the onions and rough-cut vegetables and bacon trimmings. Place in a casserole, lay the liver on top and sprinkle on the flour. Add the water and seasoning and cook, covered, for 1¼ hours, in a moderate oven. Mix the arrowroot with a little water and pour into the casserole; colour with browning if necessary. Cook for another 15 minutes.

A SUBSTITUTE FOR LAMB'S FRY

Lamb's fry is a very expensive dish, but here is a substitute which few can tell from lamb's fry. Cut neat small strips of calf's liver and a lamb's sweetbread into slices; well butter a dish, and screen it with breadcrumbs. Then arrange the calf's liver upon the crumbs, then the slices of sweetbread, and scatter bits of butter here and there. Dust over a little pepper, cover it with a piece of buttered paper, put the dish in a moderately heated oven, and serve with a dish of nicely mashed potatoes.

Mrs Herbert Newton, Norfolk 1913

TRIPE AND ONIONS

1 lb dressed tripe
4-8 oz onions
1 pint milk

1 oz flour
Salt and pepper

Put tripe in cold water and bring to the boil. Remove from the water and cut into small strips. Cut up the onions, place them in cold water and bring to the boil; strain off water and put the onions with the tripe and milk, add seasoning. Simmer for 2 hours. Mix the flour with a little water or milk; add to tripe etc. and boil for a few minutes.

TRIPE ROLLS

1 lb cooked tripe
8 oz bacon pieces
3 onions
3 carrots

Bunch of mixed herbs
Nutmeg
1 pint cider

Cut the tripe in neat slices and cover with slices of bacon. Season with salt and pepper, nutmeg and a sprinkling of herbs, and roll up, tying with cotton. Slice the onions and carrots into a casserole, add a bunch of herbs, put on the tripe rolls and pour on the cider, adding a little water to cover if necessary. Cover and cook at 325°F (Gas Mark 3) for 3 hours. Serve very hot with a purée of potatoes.

THE DOCTOR'S TRIPE HOT POT

1 *lb pre-cooked tripe*
1 *oz flour*
1 *lb onions*
2 *lb potatoes*

3 *tomatoes*
Beef stock
Salt and pepper
1 *tablespoon beef dripping*

Wipe the tripe and cut it into squares. Dip in flour lightly seasoned with salt and pepper. Peel the onions and potatoes, and remove skins from tomatoes. Cut them all in slices. Grease a deep casserole and fill with alternate layers of tripe and vegetables, seasoning each layer, and ending with a layer of potatoes. Pour in the stock so that it comes half way up the dish. Dot with dripping and put on a lid. Cook at 375°F (Gas Mark 5) for 1¼ hours. Remove lid and continue cooking for 15 minutes to brown the potatoes.

TRIPE AND BACON

1 *lb pre-cooked tripe*
8 *oz bacon rashers*
½ *oz plain flour*

¼ *pint water*
1 *dessertspoon tomato sauce*
Salt and pepper

Fry the bacon slowly so that the fat runs. Put the bacon on a warm dish. Slice the tripe and fry it until golden in the bacon fat. Put the tripe with the bacon on the dish. Sprinkle the flour into the fat and cook for 1 minute, stirring well. Add the water, sauce and salt and pepper, stirring all the time. When hot and thick, pour over the tripe and bacon. Serve with mashed potatoes and peas. A few sliced onions cooked with this are very good.

IVERSON GRILLED TRIPE

1 *lb pre-cooked tripe*
1 *tablespoon finely chopped parsley*
1 *tablespoon vinegar or lemon juice*

1 *tablespoon chopped onion*
2 *tablespoons melted butter*
Salt and pepper
Browned breadcrumbs

Wipe the tripe and cut it into bite-sized pieces. Mix together the parsley, onion, vinegar or lemon juice, butter and seasonings. Dip the tripe pieces into this and coat them with breadcrumbs. Brown under a hot grill for 5 minutes each side. This is good with crusty bread and butter, and a winter salad of watercress, chicory and celery.

COTTAGE PIE

A $\frac{1}{4}$ lb of cold meat, 1 lb of cold potatoes, a little gravy, $\frac{1}{2}$ oz of dripping, $1\frac{1}{2}$ teaspoons of flour, $\frac{1}{2}$ an onion, $\frac{1}{4}$ pint of water, and a little salt and pepper. Put the meat through a mincing machine, and mash the potatoes. Then grease a pie-dish, and put in alternate layers of potatoes and meat, seasoned with pepper and salt, also a little gravy and onion, until dish is full. The top layer should be of potatoes. Put the pie in the oven, and bake it until it is brown.

Miss P. Smith, 1913

DORMERS

An old, well-tried way of using up cold meat for hungry, growing teen-agers. Chop up 1 lb scraps of cold lamb, 4 oz or less of suet, $\frac{1}{2}$ lb boiled rice, pepper and salt to taste, and mix. Roll up as sausages, cover with egg and breadcrumbs, fry in hot dripping until golden brown. Serve on a dish of mashed potatoes with carrot 'strips' and peas, with some hot gravy.

MEAT CAKES WITH TOMATOES

Take $\frac{1}{2}$ lb cold meat and chop up finely, or mince. In a saucepan melt a tablespoon of good, tasty dripping and in it gently fry a well chopped, or minced, onion. Then stir in, first, about $\frac{1}{2}$ lb of mashed potato, then the minced meat and finally salt and pepper to taste. Using a little flour on your hands, mould the mixture into rounds and place on a baking dish with a tiny nob of dripping on top. Cook in good oven until light brown, then place on top a slice of tomato or half a small tomato and continue baking until this is cooked. Serve on dish with parsley to garnish. If the meat is a bit scarce, serve the dish without tomatoes and send to table with poached eggs on top of the meat cakes.

PORK RISSOLES

Cut the meat off the bone of cold roast pork. Mince the meat or cut into very small neat pieces; mix it with a well-chopped onion, pepper and salt, breadcrumbs and 1 egg, well beaten, to bind the whole together. Form into shapes the size of an egg, and fry in hot dripping until golden brown. Meanwhile stew the pork-bone in a little water with an onion, salt and pepper and add flour and water thickening. Arrange the rissoles on a dish and pour the gravy round them. Serve with peas and mashed potatoes.

1911

MEAT LOAF

*1½ lb raw lean meat (beef,
veal, rabbit, mutton or a
mixture of any of these)
3 oz fat bacon
1 tablespoon chopped onion
6 oz breadcrumbs*

*Salt and pepper
Nutmeg
½ teaspoon mixed spice
2 eggs
Stock
Brown crumbs*

Cut the meat into small pieces and pass it, with the bacon, twice through the mincing machine. Chop the onion and add to the meat with the breadcrumbs and seasonings. Add the beaten eggs and sufficient stock to moisten. Press tightly into a greased bread tin, cover with greased paper, and steam for about 2 hours. Take off the paper, press the meat mixture down with weights, and leave until cold. Turn out, toss in brown crumbs, and serve cut in thin slices.

PORK SAUSAGE GALANTINE

*1 lb pork sausage meat
2 oz lean bacon
1 egg
4 level tablespoons dried
breadcrumbs
2 teaspoons chopped parsley
Pinch mixed herbs*

*1 tablespoon chutney
1 teaspoon Worcester sauce
1 level teaspoon dried
mustard
1 beef extract cube crumbled
and dissolved in ¼ pint hot
water*

Remove rind and chop the bacon finely. Beat the egg. Wash and chop the parsley. Make the stock. Mix all the ingredients together in a basin adding enough stock to make a fairly soft mixture. Grease a 1-pint pudding basin or a 1 lb loaf tin. Pack the mixture into it and cover with aluminium foil.

Steam for 1½ hours or pressure cook 15–20 minutes allowing the pressure to drop before removing the galantine. Leave the galantine to cool. Turn out, slice and serve.

CURRY

1 *lb meat (uncooked)*
2 *oz fat*
1 *oz plain flour*
1 *onion*
1 *apple*
1 *dessertspoon curry powder*
Raisins or sultanas

2 *oz coconut*
2 *teasponns chutney*
Pinch of sugar
1 *teaspoon redcurrant jelly*
Squeeze of lemon juice
Stock

Cut up the meat and slice the onion and apple. Put the coconut to infuse in a little boiling water. Fry the meat, onion and apple in the fat, and remove to another pan. Fry the curry powder, then the flour. Add the stock and the strained coconut infusion. Boil well, and add chutney, sugar, redcurrant jelly and lemon juice. Pour over the meat and simmer for 2 hours.

Jean Clark, Cherington, Glos.

CAWL

Use any meat from the joint. Bring to the boil and simmer 30 minutes. Add carrots, swedes, cabbage etc. and simmer 30 minutes. Add potatoes and simmer until they are nearly cooked, and then add leeks. Simmer until leeks are tender. This is called Cawl Twmo (Welsh); Cawl 'Warmed Up' (English) and is eaten for a midday meal and warmed up for supper. Mr Raggett says the family were given this every Friday night when they reached home from school in Haverfordwest. When his sister Penny made it she thickened the gravy, whereas his mother did not. He preferred Penny's version. *Everyone* has cawl once a week, he reckons, in those parts.

Mark Raggett, Solva, Pembs

BUBBLE AND SQUEAK

Cut from boiled beef, slices the thickness of a penny piece. Trim and cut them as you please, partly underdone are the best. Plain boil 1 large cabbage, 1 onion, 1 carrot. When cooked, drain and mince very fine, removing any hard parts of cabbage. Put into a sauté pan a piece of butter as large as an egg when melted. Put in beef to warm, taking care it does not dry. This done, remove the meat and put in the vegetables. Stir on the fire till very hot, moisten with stock, add salt, pepper. Place them and the meat on the dish the same as cutlets. Pour a little stock over and serve.

Mrs Garden, 1847

DEVILLED MEAT

1 teaspoon mustard powder
1 teaspoon Worcester sauce
1 teaspoon chutney
½ teaspoon curry powder
1 teaspoon tomato sauce

2 teaspoons vinegar
Pinch of Cayenne pepper
Pinch of sugar
1 oz butter
Cooked meat or poultry

In a small, strong pan, mix together mustard, Worcester sauce, chutney, curry powder, tomato sauce, vinegar, Cayenne pepper, sugar and butter. Melt together and bring to the boil. Pour over slices of meat or poultry and put into a moderate oven, 350°F (Gas Mark 4), for 10 minutes, turning once. Remove the meat and grill on each side for 3 minutes. Serve very hot.

BEEF HASH

3 onions
1 tablespoon fat
1 lb cooked beef

½ lb cooked potatoes
¼ pint beef stock
Salt and pepper

Cut onions in cubes and fry in fat until brown. Add diced cooked beef and diced cooked potatoes, together with stock, and season well with salt and pepper. Continue simmering for 15 minutes.

5 *Ham and Bacon*

They sowes great with fare that come best for to rere
Loke dayly thou seest them and count them full dere.
And yet by the yere have I proved ere now
As good to the purse is a sow as a kow.
And he that will rere up a pig in his house
Shall eate sweter bakon and cheaper fed sowse.

Thomas Tusser

If you're lucky enough to have a whole ham you can store it in a cool dry place by the shank; uncooked hams should not be stored in a refrigerator or a damp atmosphere. Once a ham is cooked, it can be stored in a refrigerator, but the temperature shouldn't be below 40°F. When it's time for cooking, an old-fashioned fish kettle will substitute for a ham pan. Soak a ham for at least 24 hours, though 2 days may be necessary if the ham is very dry and well bloomed. Scrub off the bloom, weigh the ham, put in cold water and bring to boiling point. Simmer very gently (the actual temperature should be 185°F) allowing 15 minutes a lb, and leave the ham to cool in the water for an hour after cooking. To give extra flavour, I like to put a couple of bayleaves in the water and a tablespoon of brown sugar.

After cooling the ham for 24 hours to allow it to set, skin it, and trim off any discoloured meat, and dress the ham with rusk or breadcrumbs. One of the most important things about a whole ham is to see it is carved properly so that everyone has a share of lean and fat meat, and there is no waste. Use a thin-bladed sharp ham slicer for really tempting thin slices, and take the first slice from the knuckle end. Turn the ham round and carve the flank until the knife reaches the small covering bone over the leg joint. Take out this small bone, then turn the ham over and start carving the undercut. Go on cutting alternate slices from these 3 faces, until only the prime face is left, and go on carving this until the bone is clean.

Boiling bacon is a fairly everyday affair, but careful choice and cooking of the original joint can make all the difference between a stringy, salty piece of meat, and a succulent tender and sweet joint.

Forehock is one of the cheap boiling cuts, which can be boned and rolled to save time and trouble; one end is fatter than the other, so carving should be from alternate ends.

End of collar is another cheap piece which can be boiled and pressed lightly; two pieces may be pressed together. Another cut which is good for boiling and pressing is *flank*, rather fatter, which is very good served with rabbit or chicken. These three joints are particularly useful if you like to use up the end pieces in pies or puddings. *Prime Collar* is a middle price cut which is very good if long slits are cut in the meat and a stuffing of chopped herbs inserted. *Slipper* is a small lean joint which is good as a hot joint with spinach or broad beans. *The three gammon joints, middle, corner and hock*, are all choice cuts which respond particularly well to the treatment of boiling, then finishing in the oven with a glaze.

The usual complaint about bacon is that it is too salty. Always allow time for the joint to be soaked for at least 12 hours. If you still have doubts, cook a potato in the water, which will take up the salt. Simmer the joint very gently, allowing 20 minutes a lb. If you want to glaze and decorate the bacon, strip off the rind while the meat is still warm, then put the joint on a rack in a roasting tin before the glaze is used.

CIDER GLAZE

Stud the diamonds with 3 cloves each and sprinkle with 2 tablespoons demerara sugar. Pour over $\frac{1}{2}$ pint medium sweet cider and continue to cook, basting regularly. When joint is cooked and fat golden brown, thicken juice with cornflour and serve with the joint.

APPLE AND MARMALADE GLAZE

Spread the scored fat with $\frac{1}{4}$ lb fairly thick marmalade. Peel, core and slice 1 large apple. Immerse in lemon juice for 10 minutes. Drain. Attach slices of apple on cocktail sticks to the fat. Brush with more marmalade and continue to cook, basting several times and covering with foil if the apples gets too brown.

RAISIN GLAZE

4 oz raisins
Grated rind and juice of 1
lemon

$\frac{1}{4}$ pint water
4 tablespoons honey
Black pepper

Place the raisins, lemon rind, juice and water in a pan and simmer covered very gently for 10 minutes. Strain and add the honey to the liquid with a little pepper. Pour over the joint and continue to cook basting regularly until 10 minutes before the end. Return raisins to the liquor round the joint and serve spooned over the joint when completely cooked.

TREACLE GLAZE

Mix 2 tablespoons plain flour and 2 tablespoons demerara sugar with 2 tablespoons golden syrup and 3 tablespoons warm liquid from bacon. Spread over bacon, put in a hot oven, 400°F (Gas Mark 6), for 20 minutes.

HONEY GLAZE

Spread 2 tablespoons clear honey over the bacon and sprinkle with 1 tablespoon fine breadcrumbs. Mix $\frac{1}{4}$ pint pineapple juice and $\frac{1}{4}$ pint vinegar and pour over joint. Bake for 20 minutes at 400°F (Gas Mark 6) basting occasionally.

MUSTARD GLAZE

Mix 2 teaspoons French mustard, 2 tablespoons wine vinegar and 2 tablespoons cooking liquor, and pour over bacon. Mix together 2 tablespoons fine breadcrumbs and 1 tablespoon demerara sugar, and sprinkle over the joint. Bake at 400°F (Gas Mark 6) for 20 minutes.

CLOVE AND SUGAR GLAZE

Score the fat surface of the joint criss-cross and stud with cloves. Mix 1 teaspoon powdered cloves with 2 tablespoons soft brown sugar, and make a smooth paste with ginger ale. Spread on the bacon and bake at 400°F (Gas Mark 6) for 20 minutes.

A whole ham or a bacon joint always looks attractive with a special garnish. Canned or fresh pineapple rings, sprinkled with demerara sugar and quickly grilled until the surface caramelises, can be arranged on or round the bacon, with maraschino cherries in each circle. Sliced canned peaches and cherries make another garnish, or orange slices dipped in French dressing and sprinkled with chopped parsley. Half maraschino cherries can be fixed into the diamonds scored on a glazed bacon joint with whole cloves.

One of the best things about a joint of bacon or a ham is that there is never a scrap of waste. Use the remains to stuff large firm tomatoes, mixed with a few breadcrumbs and herbs, and a little chopped onion. Or bind the same mixture with an egg, fry and put between buttered baps as 'baconburgers'. Scotch eggs can be covered with minced cooked bacon instead of sausage meat, or apples can be stuffed with minced bacon well seasoned with herbs, and baked in the oven. Most of us know how delicious is bacon and egg pie, but bacon also goes well with onions in a creamy sauce for a supper-time flan (sprinkle the top with grated cheese and give it a golden finish in the oven or under the grill). An old-fashioned bacon roly-poly pudding is usually made with chopped uncooked bacon pieces, but minced cooked bacon is equally good with a little sweet pickle, chopped onion and mixed herbs, rolled up in a suet pastry and steamed for 2 hours, then served with hot tomato sauce. If you have a lot of sandwiches to prepare, make your own sandwich spread with minced cold bacon mixed with a little sweet pickle and onion, mayonnaise to bind and a spoonful of fine white breadcrumbs to stiffen the mixture. This is specially good for brown bread sandwiches with a few slices of tomato or cucumber.

BACON RASHERS

Bacon should have an adequate layer of white, firm fat over the rasher so that it will cook in its own delicious flavour. Remove rind from rashers and fry or grill 'shingled' so that the fat overlaps the lean; fat on top for grilling, underneath for frying. If your pan gets overheated, use a little best pork lard to prevent sticking, but don't allow the fat to smoke while cooking or the bacon will taste burnt. Don't add cooking oil or fat to bacon. Flavour will be at its best and shrinkage at a minimum if you allow 6–8 minutes for frying and 4–5 minutes for grilling. The rashers are cooked when crisp – but not brittle.

Drain off excess fat and use to add flavour when cooking other foods. Use up smoked bacon rinds, crisply fried and crushed, for seasoning soups or stews.

Middle Gammon: Perfect for boiling, or baking, and can also be baked in a crust. Cut into thick rashers ($\frac{1}{2}$ inch) it can be served as delicious gammon steaks.

Top back: Should be grilled in thin rashers, boiled or braised in the piece. A perfect lean cut.

Long Back: Good and lean. Slice thinly to fry gently, or grill quickly, for generous servings.

Streaky Back Rashers: Lean and deliciously streaky at end of rasher, best sliced thin. Perfect for grilling crisp.

Prime Collar: Besides making excellent rashers, this can be served as a whole joint – boiled, well seasoned – it makes a good joint, hot or cold.

BACON AND APPLE ROLL

8 oz flaky pastry
12 oz minced cooked bacon
1 large cooking apple

1 small onion
2 tablespoons of water

Roll the pastry into a rectangle. Mix together bacon, peeled and chopped apple, chopped onion and water. Spread bacon mixture on dough and form into a roll, putting on baking sheet so that the join is underneath. Brush roll with beaten egg, cut slits in surface to allow steam to escape, and bake in a hot oven for 20 minutes until the pastry is beginning to colour. Reduce heat and continue cooking until pastry is golden and crisp (about 1 hour in all). Serve hot or cold.

BACON AND LIVER LOAF

1$\frac{1}{2}$ lb minced lean bacon
$\frac{1}{2}$ lb minced liver
1 teacup fine breadcrumbs
1 egg
Salt and pepper

1 dessertspoon brown sugar
1 dessertspoon ground cloves
$\frac{1}{2}$ teacup milk
4 thin streaky rashers bacon

Mix together bacon, liver, breadcrumbs, egg, salt and pepper, sugar and cloves, and stir in milk. Grease 2 lb loaf tin and line with streaky rashers from which rind has been removed. Bake at 325°F (Gas Mark 3) for 1$\frac{1}{2}$ hours. Cool and unmould. For a picnic, wrap loaf in foil, and serve in slices or on buttered baps.

BACON GALANTINE (1)

8 oz cooked bacon
4 oz stewing steak
4 oz fresh white breadcrumbs
1 large egg
½ teaspoon nutmeg

Pinch of mixed spice
1 teaspoon Worcester sauce
Pepper
Stock or water

Mince bacon and stewing steak together and mix with breadcrumbs, spices, sauce and egg, using just enough water or stock to bind. Shape in a rectangle, wrap in greased greaseproof paper, then in a cloth, leaving a little room for expansion. Steam for 1½ hours in a steamer, keeping water beneath boiling steadily. Lift out galantine, take off cloth and paper, and leave to cool. When cold, glaze the galantine with ½ gill stock flavoured with a little meat extract and thickened with 1 level teaspoon gelatine, using the glaze when it is just on the point of setting. For a party dish, decorate the galantine with a piped pattern of softened butter.

BACON GALANTINE (2)

½ lb collar bacon
½ lb beef sausage meat
4 oz white breadcrumbs
1 teaspoon chopped parsley
½ teaspoon mixed herbs

Salt and pepper
2 eggs
¼ pint strong beef stock
¾ oz gelatine

Mince together bacon and sausage meat, and mix with breadcrumbs, chopped herbs, salt and pepper. Mix with eggs, then with the stock. Form into a roll, wrap in a floured cloth and tie with string. Cover with boiling water and cook gently for 2 hours. Remove and cool in cloth, preferably overnight. For the glaze: mix ½ pint strong beef stock with ¾ oz gelatine softened in 2 tablespoons cold water, and use the jelly just as it is setting.

BACON CASSEROLE

1 lb bacon
2 lb potatoes
1 large onion

1 lb tomatoes
1 gill milk
Seasoning

Arrange a layer of thinly sliced potatoes on the bottom of a well-buttered casserole. Cover with a layer of chopped bacon, sliced onion and sliced tomatoes, season well with salt and pepper and add a little sage if liked. Repeat these layers until the casserole is full, ending with a layer of potatoes, pour the milk over the top, add some pieces of butter, cook in a moderate oven for about 2 hours.

BACON AND TOMATO CASSEROLE

2 *lb gammon slipper*
2 *large onions or leeks*
14 *oz tin tomatoes*

1 *teaspoon basil*
Pepper

Soak the piece of bacon for 6 hours (2 hours if unsmoked). Put into casserole and cover with sliced onions or leeks, and tomatoes. Season with basil and freshly ground black pepper, cover tightly and cook, 350°F (Gas Mark 4), for 1 hour.

WELSH BACON

1-2 *lb potatoes*
4 *rashers bacon*
2 *large onions*

Pepper and salt
1 *oz dripping*
1 *lb broad beans*

Peel and wash the potatoes, and cut into equal-size pieces. Cover the bottom of a saucepan with half the bacon, cut into pieces. Add layers of potatoes and onions, finishing with potatoes. Season. Add the dripping and enough water to cover the bottom of the saucepan well. Cook very slowly until the potatoes are cooked. Add the beans, and cook faster for 15–20 minutes, to brown the potatoes.

BACON AND BEER CASSEROLE

2½ *lb bacon collar*
1 *carrot*
1 *onion*
Pepper
1 *tablespoon black treacle*

1 *bayleaf*
1 *pint ale*
1 *oz butter*
1 *oz flour*

Soak bacon for 6 hours (2 hours if unsmoked). Put in casserole, and add sliced carrot and onion, a shake of freshly ground black pepper, treacle, bayleaf and beer. Bring to the boil, skim, and simmer for 1 hour (or cook at 350°F, Gas Mark 4). Remove bacon, take off skin, and keep joint hot. Blend butter with flour and thicken the strained liquid. This is very good with baked parsnips.

SOMERSET GAMMON STEAKS

4 *slices gammon about* ½ *inch thick*
A little made mustard

2 *medium-sized cooking apples*
Fat for browning
¼ *pint cider*

Remove the rind from the gammon and spread each slice with mustard. Brown on both sides in a little hot fat in a frying pan. Lay each slice of gammon on a piece of foil, large enough to wrap it completely, on a baking tin or meat tray. Peel, core and quarter the apples then cut in thin slices. Lay the apples on top of the gammon pieces. Add the cider to the fat in the pan and simmer for a minute then pour over the meat. Wrap in the foil and bake about 30 minutes at 425°F (Gas Mark 7).

BACON ROLL

1 lb minced ham (left over *Salt and pepper to taste*
from a gammon joint)   *Pinch of mixed herbs*
1 lb minced beef   *1 egg*
1 small onion, finely chopped *½ lb streaky bacon rashers*
1 stick celery, finely chopped

Mix together in a large bowl the minced ham, minced beef, onion, celery, seasoning, herbs and beaten egg. Work together well with the hands and shape into a roll 3–4 inches in diameter. Remove the rinds and bone from the bacon rashers, flatten the rashers well with the back of a knife then wrap firmly around the roll of meat. Overlap the ends of the rashers and try to keep the joins on the underside of the roll.

Lay the roll on a piece of foil, large enough to wrap it completely, on a meat tin or baking tray. Wrap and cook at 425°F (Gas Mark 7) for about 45 minutes then open the foil for about 15 minutes to complete the browning.

WEST COUNTRY OATCAKES WITH BACON

½ tablespoon bacon fat   *Pinch of salt*
3 tablespoons water   *4 bacon gammon steaks,*
4 level tablespoons medium *rinded and slashed*
oatmeal   *4 tomatoes, halved*

Melt the bacon fat with the water in a pan and sprinkle in oatmeal and salt. Work well together until smooth. Roll out the oatmeal on a board dusted with oatmeal to several cakes the size of a small saucer and very thin. Cook slowly on a pre-heated griddle or heavy frying pan for about 10 minutes. Remove to a tea towel in a warm place and leave to harden. Serve quickly with grilled gammon steaks and tomatoes.

YORKSHIRE PEASE PUDDING WITH BOILED BACON

8 oz split peas
Salt and pepper
1 oz butter
1 egg, beaten

Pinch of sugar
3 lb joint of bacon forehock
or collar

Wash the peas and soak overnight in cold water. Tie loosely in a cloth and place in a saucepan with a pinch of salt and cover with boiling water. Boil for 2½–3 hours till soft. Sieve the peas or liquidise in a blender and add the butter, egg, pepper, salt and sugar. Beat together till lightly mixed, then tie up tightly in a floured cloth and boil for another 30 minutes. Serve the pease pudding with the hot bacon joint boiled for 25 minutes per lb, and 25 minutes over with bayleaves, cloves and sliced onion added to the cooking liquor.

COLLAR BACON HOT-POT

3-4 lb collar joint bacon,
boned and rolled
1½ oz dripping
12 button onions, peeled
12 small carrots, peeled

4 leeks, chopped
Stock or beer
Bouquet garni
Bayleaves

Soak bacon in cold water overnight. Place in saucepan, cover with cold water. Bring to boil and simmer for half cooking time, allowing 25 minutes per lb and 25 minutes over. Remove joint, skin and score the fat into squares. Melt dripping in a large fireproof casserole and fry vegetables until lightly browned. Add sufficient stock or beer to cover. Place the joint in the casserole. Add bouquet garni and several bayleaves. Cover and bake at 350°F (Gas Mark 4) for remaining cooking time. 10 minutes before ready remove lid to brown, increasing oven temperature to 425°F (Gas Mark 7). Serve, if liked, with parsley sauce made with the stock from the vegetables.

BACON PANCAKES

Pancakes:
¼ pint pancake batter
Lard for frying

Filling:
2 oz lard
8 oz chopped bacon

2 oz chopped onion
Sprinkle of mixed herbs
Lemon juice
Seasoning
2 oz chopped prunes or
cooking apple

Make the pancake batter. Melt lard in a frying pan and make 6 thin pancakes, leaving the pancakes flat. Put lard, chopped onion, bacon and prunes into a frying pan and cook for 4 to 5 minutes. Add seasoning and mixed herbs to the bacon mixture and divide into 6 equal portions. Reheat the pancakes and place a portion of the bacon mixture in each. Roll the pancakes and serve piping hot.

CIDER-BAKED FOREHOCK WITH CIDER SAUCE

3-3½ *lb forehock (boned and*
rolled)
⅓ *pint cider*
1 *tablespoon brown sugar*
Cloves

Cider Sauce
Cider
1 *teaspoon cornflour*

Soak the bacon in warm water for 1 hour. Rinse and put in saucepan with cold water. Boil gently for 30 minutes. Take out, remove rind and put bacon in baking tin. Mix cider with half the sugar and pour over bacon. Leave to stand for about 30 minutes, basting from time to time. Sprinkle remainder of sugar on top and put cloves in lines across top. Bake at 400°F (Gas Mark 6) for 30–40 minutes, basting occasionally, but not for the last 15 minutes. To make the sauce, put the cider in which the bacon was cooked into a saucepan, and make up to ½ pint with more cider. Bring to the boil. Mix cornflour with a little water and add to the cider. Simmer until thick and serve with the bacon. Apple rings can be served with this dish.

Joyce Kerr

6 Poultry

It was a turkey. He never could have stood upon his legs that bird. He would have snapped 'em short off in a minute, like sticks of sealing-wax.

'A Christmas Carol'
Charles Dickens

CHICKEN

Flavour comes from age (hence the distinction between lamb and mutton, veal and beef), so it can hardly be expected that a 10-week bird can have a full flavour. Hanging time before dressing also gives flavour, and to-day's birds do not remain with their innards so long as the old-fashioned roaster. Set against this loss of flavour are the advantages of reasonable size, tenderness and keen price.

The only way to keep a good flavour in today's birds is to cook them very carefully. Overcooking, particularly in roasting, is the worst crime against good flavour, and better results are often obtained by frying, grilling or casseroling chicken.

The best way of roasting the traditional chicken was with a bunch of herbs and plenty of butter, but today's broiler needs a less subtle approach. In winter, stuffings containing sausages and bacon, or the chicken liver, will give a better flavour. In summer, lighter mixtures which include pineapple, walnuts or sweetcorn, are more acceptable.

Before roasting, the bird's weight should be carefully checked, and cooking time calculated to suit the oven-ready weight. Cook at 375°F and allow 20 minutes a pound plus 20 minutes for all birds up to $3\frac{1}{2}$ lb in weight. The bird should be completely thawed, or cooking will take longer. A giblet gravy will also help to give flavour, or a garnish of streaky bacon rolls filled with pieces of chicken liver.

A jointed bird is often more useful in the kitchen but it's often just as simple to do it yourself – you need a strong sharp knife, a chopping board and a weight. For halving, choose a $1\frac{1}{2}$ to 2 lb bird; for quartering choose a 2 to $2\frac{1}{2}$ lb bird. Remove the giblets, then put the bird on a chopping board. With a sharp knife cut through and along the length of breastbone.

Open the bird out, then cut through along length of backbone, removing it entirely if you like by cutting close along to either side. Tap back of knife sharply with a heavy weight to cut through the bony sections. The bird is now in half.

Put the chicken halves skin side up on a board, and divide each half again by cutting diagonally across between wing and thigh, so that the bird is in quarters (2 wing and breast joints, 2 thigh and drumstick joints). The joints are neater if leg shanks and wingtips are removed.

Chicken joints grill or fry in less than $\frac{1}{2}$ hour, and bake or casserole in less than an hour. For grilling, frying and baking, they need to be moistened frequently with butter or a sauce, and are cooked at a moderate temperature.

ROAST ROSEMARY CHICKEN

1 *roast chicken*, 3-3½ *lb*	¼ *pint stock*
trussed weight	*Salt and pepper*
A small sprig of rosemary	*A little butter*

Put the giblets back into the carcass of the chicken with the rosemary – they help to flavour the gravy. Put the chicken into a roasting tin, sprinkle it with salt and pepper, and dot a knob of butter over it, then pour the stock round the chicken. Roast the chicken in a fairly hot oven, 400°F (Gas Mark 6) for 1 to $1\frac{1}{4}$ hours. Remove the giblets and serve the chicken on a hot dish, surrounded with Duchesse potatoes or potato croquettes. Serve the gravy, which should be thin, separately.

LANCASHIRE CHEESY CHICKEN

1 *hot roasted chicken*	3 *oz butter*
1 *pint milk*	3 *oz plain flour*
A sliced carrot	½ *pint stock*
A sliced onion	6 *oz Lancashire cheese*
A sprig of parsley and thyme,	*Pinch of grated nutmeg*
and one bayleaf	*Salt and pepper*

Cut the chicken into joints, removing the legs at the thigh joints and dividing the thighs from the drumsticks. Cut off both wings with a slice of breast. Cut off the wishbone with some meat, then cut the breast off either side of the bone. Arrange the joints on a hot dish and keep them warm.

Put the milk into a saucepan with the carrot, onion, sprig of parsley, thyme and bay leaf and heat this very slowly to extract the flavours of the vegetables into the milk. When it is almost boiling, take it off the heat.

Melt the butter in a large saucepan, take it off the heat and stir in the flour. Add the stock and whisk or stir the sauce briskly over a very gentle heat until it is warm enough to melt the butter and make the sauce smooth. Strain the hot milk into the sauce and stir it briskly over a moderate heat until it comes to the boil. Take the sauce off the heat and crumble the cheese into it, beating it well to make it smooth, then coat the chicken. Put the chicken under a hot grill for a few moments to brown the top. If the chicken is to be served later or next day the dish can be finished completely, but it will have to be heated thoroughly in a fairly hot oven about 400°F (Gas Mark 6) for about 20 minutes before browning it under the grill.

FRICASSEE OF CHICKEN

Cut the remains of a cold chicken and 2 or 3 oz of ham into neat pieces, season them with pepper, salt and a little lemon juice. In a saucepan put a little white sauce, about $\frac{1}{2}$ pint, stir until hot, and then put in the chicken and ham. Stir over a mild heat until the meat is well warmed in the sauce. Serve it on a hot dish with snippets of toast placed round.

DEVILLED CHICKEN

Remove the skin from the wings and legs of a chicken. Cut a deep incision in several places of the flesh, make a fiery mixture of Cayenne pepper, salt, mustard, anchovy (paste) and butter, and rub it all into the cut parts of the flesh. Broil over a clear fire, and serve on a hot serviette.

If required for breakfast, this could be prepared overnight. The modern version of this is to cook on an electric spit. Otherwise it could be carefully grilled or wrapped in foil and cooked in a hot oven.

The Good Wife's Cook Book, 1870

HONEY GLAZED CHICKEN

1 *roasting chicken (3-3½ lb)*   **3-4** *tablespoons clear honey*
1 *cooking apple*   *Salt and pepper*
1 *large onion*   *Watercress to garnish*
4-5 *tablespoons oil*

Remove giblets from chicken and sprinkle inside lightly with salt and pepper. Peel the apple, cut into quarters and remove the core. Place inside the chicken together with peeled and halved onion. Brush with a little oil and place in a roasting tin. Season. Pour the honey over the chicken and put the remainder of the oil in the base of the roasting tin. Cook at 375°F (Gas Mark 5) allowing 20 minutes to the pound and 20 minutes over. Baste the chicken from time to time. When cooked arrange on a serving dish and garnish with watercress.

Miss Margaret McFarlane, Bath

CHICKEN WITH BAKED RICE

1 roasting chicken, 3 lb in	**1 teaspoon salt**
weight	**4 oz streaky bacon**
2 oz lard, cooking fat or oil	**2 teaspoon black pepper**
2 large onions	**4 oz chipolata sausages**
Pinch of herbs	**8 oz rice**

Boil rice in salted water for 15–20 minutes, drain. Melt fat in baking dish add onion, cut in slices, add chicken and place breast downwards in oven 375–400°F (Gas Mark 5 or 6) and cook for 30 minutes. Remove chicken, mix rice with onion, mixed herbs, salt and pepper, replace chicken on rice resting on its backbone, and continue to cook till bird is tender, $1\frac{1}{4}$ to $1\frac{1}{2}$ hours, turning rice over from time to time and brushing breast of bird with oil.

Meanwhile, roll up bacon and secure on a skewer, bake with sausages in shelf below chicken for 20–30 minutes. Serve chicken on bed of rice garnished with sausages and bacon rolls.

CHICKEN IN TARRAGON

This tarragon chicken recipe is very good with bought chicken joints. It is original and easy, and our sons often make it without cream for a quick easy supper. But it's honestly good enough for dinner.

Fry your chicken joints in half butter and half oil with a sprinkling of dried tarragon. The amount of tarragon is a matter for personal taste. The pan used should have a lid for preference. When done, remove the chicken to serving dish and keep warm. Now add enough cream to absorb or fully blend with the fat (you have to stir like hell). Season, add lemon juice to taste and having got it right, pour it over the chicken and return relaxed, if not smug, to your sherry.

Joan Dampney, Christchurch, Hants

VIENNA CHICKEN

Cut up a chicken into pieces; lay them in a pie dish in a mixture of $\frac{1}{2}$ pint olive oil, the juice of 4 lemons, 1 bayleaf, 2 or 3 sprigs of parsley, and pepper and salt. Let them remain soaking for 4 or 5 hours.

Take each piece of chicken, drain it, dip it in egg and breadcrumbs, and fry to a nice golden colour. When all the pieces are fried, put them in a stew-pan with sufficient white stock to barely cover them, then add the yolk of 1 egg, and $\frac{1}{2}$ a breakfastcup of milk, 24 button mushrooms, salt, pepper etc. to taste. Let them gently stew for $\frac{1}{2}$ hour, thicken the sauce, add the juice of 1 lemon and serve.

CHICKEN MARSEILLAIS

Chop finely $\frac{1}{2}$ lb cold chicken; put it in a basin and mix with it a teaspoon of flour and butter, 2 tablespoons of cream, the yolk of an egg, a teaspoon of chopped parsley, salt and pepper to taste. Thoroughly mix this to a paste. Roll out some flaky type pastry as thinly as possible cut into 6 inch squares, fill with the mixture and fold over and pinch the edges. Bake to a light golden brown in not too hot an oven. Serve hot.

CHICKEN POMPADOUR

Boil $\frac{1}{2}$ lb spaghetti in salted boiling water, but do *not* break up. Drain it in a colander, well butter a basin or mould, line it with spaghetti, twisting it around and fill the centre with $1\frac{1}{2}$ cups of cold chopped chicken, salted and peppered to taste. Pour on top of this $\frac{1}{2}$ cup of cream, 1 oz fresh butter, the yolk of one egg, and a teaspoonful of finely chopped parsley, then cover over with some more spaghetti. Steam it for 1 hour, then turn it into a hot dish, and serve with tomato sauce

SURREY CHICKEN CASSEROLE

1 nice plump chicken, onions, potatoes, thyme and parsley (or dried mixed herbs), leftovers of bacon, not too fat; 1 or 2 hardboiled eggs, if liked, $\frac{1}{2}$ lb sausage meat.
Cut chicken in suitably-sized pieces and fry lightly in dripping or if bacon is fairly fat, fry this first then fry chicken joints, dipped in wholemeal flour, in the resulting fat. Drain well, then taking a good thick casserole dish, put first a layer of sliced potatoes, then a layer of onions; sprinkle this with a little salt and pepper, then put a layer of chicken, potato, onion, sausage meat, potato, onion, chicken, sliced hardboiled egg, bacon, onion and lastly sliced potato, in that order. Pour on $\frac{3}{4}$ pint water or thin stock,

sprinkle with salt and pepper, dot with dripping or butter, cover
buttered paper and casserole lid. Cook gently for 1½–2 hours, bet\
removing lid and paper; return to oven to brown the top layer of potatoes.

GLOUCESTERSHIRE CASSEROLED CHICKEN

1 *cooked chicken*	*home-grown cobs or walnuts*
1 *pint white sauce*	*would do*
2 *cups cooked rice*	*Cooked green peas and/ or*
½ *cup chopped nuts, almonds*	*carrots*
for preference but	1 *cup chopped mushrooms*

Remove chicken from bone and dice. Add to the white sauce and season
with pepper and salt. Put layer of cooked rice in casserole dish, scatter
chopped nuts, peas and mushrooms over, add layer of chicken and sauce.
Continue in layers, finishing with last drop of sauce. Bake in a moderate
oven until done through – about ¾ hour; serve with small snippets of dry
toast and garnish with parsley.

CHICKEN MARYLAND

Fry portions of boned chicken (you need not bone the wings) in egg and
breadcrumbs and lay in a flat dish. Fry mushrooms, also drained pineapple pieces and banana, if you like, in halves. Sometimes a few extra
frozen chicken livers make it extra good. This is all done in one fry pan –
then begin the sauce by either flour or cornflour mixed in a bowl with cold
water, make this rather thick as you will be adding more liquid, pour some
into the hot fry pan, and make a roux, and as it will be much too thick add
white wine or cider (I nearly always add cider), and some of the tinned
pineapple juice. This sauce takes more time to make than the rest of the
meal – as soon as it is like a *thin* sauce pour it over the chicken etc. and
cover the dish with foil and put in oven for ½ hour or longer if guests are
late. Peas and mashed potatoes go well with this as it is rather rich. Salt
and pepper must be added to the sauce.

DOYNTON CHICKEN

4 *chicken joints*	2 *cloves garlic, crushed*
3 *tablespoons olive oil*	1 *pint chicken stock*
4 *rashers unsmoked streaky*	10 *oz frozen peas*
bacon, chopped	*Salt and pepper and sugar to*
6 *oz long grain rice*	*taste*
2 *tablespoons tomato purée*	*Rings of carrots and parsley*
3 *oz onion, chopped*	*to garnish*

Heat the oil in a heavy pan and fry the chicken joints until golden all over. Remove chicken and keep it hot. Add onion and garlic to pan and cook gently for several minutes, then add bacon and rice. Stir and fry until rice begins to brown. Add the stock, tomato purée and seasoning and bring to the boil. Turn the mixture into a casserole, place the chicken joints on top and cover tightly. Bake in a moderate oven, 350°F (Gas Mark 4), for about 40 minutes until rice and meat are tender. Meanwhile, cook the peas, drain and stir into rice. Serve very hot garnished with olives or strips of pimento.

GRILLED FOWL

The remains of cold fowl, juice of ½ lemon, breadcrumbs, pepper and salt, grated lemon peel.

Cut the remains of some cold fowl into pieces, season them with pepper and salt, squeeze over them the juice of ½ lemon, and let them stand for ¾ hour. Wipe them dry, dip them into clarified butter, and then into breadcrumbs with a little grated lemon peel. Put them on a gridiron and broil them over a clear fire. When fried instead of broiled, use the yolk of egg, well beaten, instead of the butter.

TO STEW A FOWL WITH RICE

1 fowl; about 1 quart of mutton broth; pepper and salt; mace; a large cupful of rice.

Truss the fowl for boiling, and stew it in about 1 quart of mutton broth, seasoned with pepper, salt, half a blade of mace, for as long as it takes to cook it tender, letting it simmer as *slowly as possible*, which will improve the fowl's appearance more than fast boiling as it renders them plump and white. Skim the liquor as often as need be; then about ½ hour before the fowl will be quite ready, add a large cupful of rice, and when this too is tender, remove the fowl and keep hot. Meanwhile strain the rice from the liquor and place it on a sieve in front of the fire, to dry and swell; then place it in the centre of a hot dish and hollow out a place for the fowl, arranging the rice rather high in a border around the bird. Serve parsley and butter sauce in a tureen.

STOVED CHICKEN

3 lb chicken joints   1 pint giblet stock
2 large onions   Salt and pepper
2½ lb potatoes   Chopped parsley
2 oz butter

Wipe the chicken joints. Cut the onions in slices, and the potatoes in medium-thick slices. Brown the chicken pieces in half the butter. In a casserole, put a thick layer of potatoes, then onions and chicken pieces. Season well with salt and pepper and add knobs of butter. Put on another layer of potatoes, then onions, chicken and finally potatoes. Season again and pour on stock. Put on a piece of buttered paper and a lid. Cook at 300°F (Gas Mark 2) for 2½ hours, adding a little more stock or water if needed. If an iron casserole is used, this dish may be simmered gently on a low heat on top of the stove. Sprinkle with parsley before serving.

COUNTRY-STYLE GRILLED CHICKEN

4 chicken joints
½ large lemon
1½ oz butter

Salt
2 rashers streaky bacon
2 oz mushroom caps

Rub chicken pieces with cut lemon. Melt butter and brush generously over chicken, then sprinkle with salt. Put chicken, skin side down, in a grill pan with the rack removed, and cook under low to medium heat, with pan 6 inches below heat, for 10 minutes. Turn pieces, brush with butter, and continue grilling for 15 minutes, with 1 or 2 more applications of butter. When cooked, the skin should be crisp and golden, and the juices, when the thigh is pierced with a fine skewer, should be colourless. Cut the bacon in fine strips and fry with sliced mushrooms in remaining butter. When cooked, add the squeezed lemon juice. Serve chicken with this dressing, garnished with watercress, and crisps.

CHICKEN IN THE POT

3-3½ lb chicken
Salt and pepper
2 oz butter
1 tablespoon cooking oil
¼ lb diced bacon
12 button onions

1 lb potatoes, cut in small
cubes
4 oz sausage meat
1 tablespoon fresh
breadcrumbs
1 chicken liver
1 tablespoon chopped parsley

Season chicken inside and out with salt and pepper. Mix together sausage meat, breadcrumbs, chopped chicken liver and parsley, and insert into the neck of the bird. Heat butter and oil in a flameproof casserole and lightly brown the chicken all over. Add bacon and onions, cover closely and cook over a gentle heat for 15 minutes. Baste the chicken, add the potatoes, turning them in the fat and replace the lid. Continue cooking in a moderate oven, 350°F (Gas Mark 4), for 1½ hours. Serve in the casserole, sprinkling the potatoes with chopped parsley and chives.

QUICK CHICKEN CASSEROLE

4 chicken quarters
3 tablespoons cooking oil
1 can condensed mushroom soup
¼ pint creamy milk
Chopped parsley

Heat oven to 350°F (Gas Mark 4). Heat the oil in a frying pan and cook the chicken pieces over gentle heat until golden, about 15 minutes. Put into a casserole. Drain surplus oil from the frying pan, then pour in soup and milk. Heat gently, stirring until boiling. Pour over chicken, cover and cook in centre of oven for 30–40 minutes. Sprinkle with parsley before serving.

CRISP BAKED CHICKEN

4 chicken joints
2 rounded tablespoons flour
1 rounded teaspoon salt
½ level teaspoon curry powder
A little evaporated milk
2 oz potato crisps (or coarse breadcrumbs)

Pre-heat oven to 350°F (Gas Mark 4). Wipe chicken joints, and coat with a mixture of flour, salt and curry powder. Dip the joints in evaporated milk, then coat thickly and evenly with crushed potato crisps or breadcrumbs. Arrange skin side up on a baking sheet and bake for 45 minutes. Serve hot or cold, with green salad. These chicken joints can be wrapped in foil and carried on a picnic without damage.

BARBECUED CHICKEN

2 chicken halves (about 1 lb each)
2 oz butter
4 tablespoons malt vinegar
1 tablespoon Worcester sauce
1 tablespoon tomato purée
1 level tablespoon brown sugar
1 teaspoon finely grated onion
1 teaspoon paprika
½ teaspoon salt

Skewer each chicken half as flat as possible. Melt the butter and brush liberally all over chicken. Arrange skin side down in a grill pan with rack removed, place pan 6 inches below the heat, and grill gently for 15 minutes. Meanwhile add the remaining ingredients to the butter in the saucepan and simmer together for 2 minutes. Turn the chicken, brush with this sauce, and continue grilling gently, with frequent applications of sauce, for 15 minutes, or until the joints move freely. Serve the chicken with the remaining sauce, garnished with watercress, and with crusty rolls and butter.

DEVONSHIRE CHICKEN

4 *chicken joints*
2 *oz butter*
2 *oz finely-chopped onion*
1 *stick sliced celery*
2 *rashers streaky bacon*

1 *oz plain flour*
Salt and pepper
¾ *pint chicken stock*
3 *tomatoes*

Melt butter in a frying pan and fry chicken joints slowly until golden (about 10 minutes). Put chicken into casserole. Add onion, celery and bacon cut into small pieces, and cook until onion is soft but not coloured. Sprinkle in flour and seasoning. Stir for a minute, then add stock and continue cooking until boiling. Add tomatoes skinned, cut in quarters and de-pipped. Pour over chicken, cover and cook at 350°F (Gas Mark 4) for 45 minutes. Garnish with chopped parsley.

HOUSEWIFE'S CHICKEN

4 *chicken joints*
2 *oz butter*
2 *oz bacon*
2 *oz mushrooms*
12 *very small onions*
½ *oz plain flour*

½ *pint stock*
½ *pint dry cider*
Salt and pepper
Parsley, thyme and bayleaf
12 *new potatoes (or 1 can of new potatoes)*

Melt butter and brown chicken pieces all over. Remove chicken and put into casserole. Into fat put bacon cut in strips, mushrooms cut in quarters and the whole onions, and cook until bacon and mushrooms are just soft. Dust with flour, and continue cooking, season with salt and pepper, then add stock and cider. Bring just to the boil, then pour all ingredients into casserole. Add herbs, cover and cook for 45 minutes at 350°F (Gas Mark 4). 15 minutes before serving time, add the potatoes (or the drained can of potatoes) and continue cooking. If new potatoes are not available, use large potatoes cut into small olive shapes. This is a very useful meal-in-one which needs no accompaniments at all except some crusty bread to 'mop up'. The recipe can be used for a whole chicken instead of pieces, if preferred.

GINGER CHICKEN

4 *chicken joints*
2 *oz butter*
2 *medium onions*
Salt and pepper

2 *tablespoons made mustard*
1 *teaspoon ground ginger*
2 *tablespoons orange juice*
1 *bottle ginger ale*

Melt butter and brown chicken all over, then fry sliced onions in same fat until just soft. Smear chicken joints with mustard, then sprinkle with salt and pepper, then return to the pan with all other ingredients. Bring to the boil, cover and simmer for 45 minutes. Thicken the sauce with a little flour if liked. An unusual dish, which is excellent with plain boiled rice or mashed potatoes and a green salad.

DUCK

Roast duck is the traditional Easter treat, and these days birds are bred with broader breasts so that a duckling becomes a reasonable proposition for 6 people. If you want a really delicious bird which is not greasy, but has a crisp skin and full-flavoured meat, try roasting it with $\frac{1}{2}$ inch of water, and with salt on the breast, but no extra fat. The bird should be turned halfway through cooking to brown the breast.

For people who might miss the traditional stuffing, try putting 6 cored apples round the bird, stuffing them with sausage meat and cooking for about 30 minutes. Another good garnish is 12 small whole onions tossed in butter with a rasher of diced bacon, then simmered in a little giblet stock with salt, pepper and a pinch of summer savory.

A delicious sauce to go with duck can be made by adding $\frac{1}{2}$ pint each of good stock and white wine to the pan drippings, stirring in $\frac{1}{2}$ teaspoon each of shredded orange and lemon rind, the juice of 1 orange and 1 teaspoon of lemon juice, simmering for 10 minutes.

When the first new potatoes come in, they are very good with a duck casserole. Joint the bird, dip in flour, and fry in butter until golden, then put into a casserole with $\frac{1}{2}$ lb chopped mushrooms, 1 teaspoon each of minced onion and mint, salt and pepper and $\frac{3}{4}$ pint stock. Cook in a slow oven, 300°F (Gas Mark 2), for $1\frac{1}{2}$ hours, then add $\frac{1}{2}$ pint green peas and continue cooking for 45 minutes.

The First Portion: Place the point of the knife into right leg between tail end of breast, bringing knife forward round thigh part of the leg to middle of back. Turn bird on its side and bring the knife down the centre of the back to the parson's nose, and back between the leg and the tail end of the breast. This is the right leg portion.

The Second Portion: Repeat on the opposite side to give the left leg portion.

The Third Portion: Place the knife on the centre of the tapered part of the breast back, bringing the knife right along the breast in a straight line. Turn bird over, continuing the cut along the back to the end of the meat and tear. This is the right wing portion.

The Fourth Portion: Repeat on the opposite side to give the left wing portion.

The Fifth and Sixth Portions: Bring the knife to the centre back breast as near the breast bone as possible, cutting right along the breast bone and into carcass. Repeat on the opposite side.

GOOSE

September 29, Quarter Day and the beginning of a busy farming year. The day when rents are paid, farms change hands, and servants by tradition are hired. Above all, the feast of St Michael, when the goose was celebration food.

Geese are sadly neglected today, when so many country traditions are dying out, but what can be better than a really tasty bird, with its crisp skin, rich fat and dark flesh? This very richness makes a lot of people wary, but cunning cooking turns a goose into a feast, and there are endless ways of using the remains and offal.

On average, a goose loses half its weight in waste and cooking, so a 12 lb bird would come down to about 6 lb at the table. It needs more cooking for its size than turkey or chicken, but care must be taken to crisp the outside fat without drying the meat.

Start the bird at a high temperature, 450°F (Gas Mark 8), for 30 minutes, then reduce the oven to 400°F (Gas Mark 6) for the rest of the cooking time, allowing 20 minutes for each lb plus 20 minutes. One of the nicest things about a goose is the crisp skin, and this is improved if the bird is rubbed all over with flour before cooking begins, and the oven is turned a little higher for 15 minutes before serving time.

There's a lot of fat in a goose, so cook it on a rack in a large tin, and 20 minutes after you begin cooking, prick the skin with a fork to allow the fat to run out. Drain some of the fat off during cooking to avoid accidents, and baste the bird 2 or 3 times during cooking.

Sage and onion stuffing is usual with goose. Try it with a chopped apple included and a spoonful of made mustard. Those who don't like onions will enjoy Scandinavian fruit-stuffed goose, made by simmering 24 stoned prunes in a little water or red wine, and mixing them with 8 peeled and quartered apples to stuff the bird. Another good stuffing is Scottish, consisting of a mixture of 2 tablespoons chopped onion fried in butter, 2 oz chopped suet, 1 dessertspoon chopped sage, a beaten egg and 5 oz fine oatmeal cooked in a little water. To help 'cut' the fatness of the bird, red cabbage makes a good vegetable accompaniment, or a few baked rosy apples.

Goose 'extras' are particularly useful in the kitchen. The liver can be turned into a rich pâté, or can be soaked in milk, then sprinkled with seasoned flour and cooked in butter until lightly brown, before being simmered with sliced apples and onions until tender. A wineglass of Madeira added at the last minute makes this a very special dish.

The giblets can be turned into an old dish called *Gallimaufry*. Simmer all the giblets except the liver with a little water, seasoning, bayleaf, parsley and thyme until tender. Cut the giblets into walnut-sized pieces and mix with 1 lb steak and the liver cut into cubes. Brown all the meat in a little dripping and sprinkle lightly with flour. Simmer in the giblet stock for another hour, adding a wineglass of port half-way through cooking, and serve very hot with forcemeat balls and small triangles of toast.

Poultry left-overs in our house never present any problem, and indeed have usually been nibbled away by the time a second-day dish is called for.

ROAST GOOSE

1 *goose*	2 *slices bread soaked in milk*
4 *oz pork*	1 *egg yolk*
4 *oz veal*	*Parsley, thyme, sage*
1 *large onion*	½ *wineglass Burgundy*
½ *oz butter*	

Chop the pork, veal, onion, and the goose liver very finely and brown them in butter. Squeeze the milk out of the bread and mix together all the ingredients, chopping herbs finely, and using only a little of the wine to moisten. Season with salt and pepper to taste. Stuff the goose and put into a very hot oven for 15 minutes. Reduce heat to 350°F (Gas Mark 4) and cook for 15 minutes per lb basting with the remaining wine.

GLAZED GOOSE

Take a goose, stuff it, roast it, and then glaze with a packet of aspic enlivened with a little sherry. Glazing is a bit fiddly as you have to catch it just as it is sliding off and it does not easily adhere to the fatty skin of a goose. To show off, try to imprison some decorative foliage or flowers in the glaze. For the stuffing, Theo just takes an arbitrary quantity of chopped onion, sage, white breadcrumbs, seasoned and shovels it into the back-end of the bird. Nothing fanciful.

Joan Dampney, Christchurch, Hants

TURKEY

Take the measurements of your oven first. Your turkey may have to go on the bottom of the oven instead of a runner. A 10–13 lb turkey will serve 10–12 people for one hot meal. Larger birds have a higher proportion of flesh to the bone. Hen birds are preferable to cock birds; and a good bird should have a broad breast. Avoid fresh birds which look dark and scrawny; on a frozen bird watch for browning areas of 'freezer burn'which can indicate long and improper storage, or dehydration.

Many people like to cook the turkey in foil, which speeds up cooking time and gives a moist tender bird. This is not true roasting, however, and sometimes results in a stewed taste, particularly with a frozen bird which may contain a lot of excess moisture. The advantages of slow over quick roasting are debatable. Quick cooking seals the birds and gives better flavour, while the slower and more carefree method reduces shrinkage. The best compromise is to put the bird into a hot oven, 425°F (Gas Mark 7), for 20 minutes, then reduce heat to 375°F (Gas Mark 5) for remaining cooking time. The breast should be covered with bacon, and the turkey basted at intervals. For a bird under 14 lb allow 15 minutes a lb and 15 minutes over. For a larger bird allow 10 minutes a lb and 10 minutes over.

Allow frozen turkeys to defrost naturally before cooking (about 36 hours for a 9 lb bird). Cook the turkey on a rack in a shallow tin and brush the bird with melted butter. Cut the string around the drumsticks after 1 hour when they should be set, so that the heat circulates. Test with a skewer in the thickest part of the drumstick to see if cooking is finished; this can be judged when the skewer goes in easily but no liquid runs out. To prevent the breast drying out before the legs are cooked, cover the breast after the first hour of cooking with a cloth dipped in melted butter.

Allow 20–30 minutes for dishing up and making gravy.

Be sure the dish is large and the knife sharp. Put fork firmly into 'knee' joint, and slice thigh flesh away from body until ball-and-socket hip joint is exposed. Cut joint between thigh and drumstick. Repeat with other leg. Take off wings and divide at major joint if bird is large. Slice the breast beginning at the neck area, and slice thinly across the grain the entire length of the breast. If the bird is large, use only one side, so the rest remains moist for cold serving.

Stuffing is important for turkey. Melted fat or cold water used to bind the bread will give a light loose texture. For a crumbly stuffing with a delicious flavour, fry the breadcrumbs in a little butter. For sausage meat stuffing, add a little chopped parsley or onion. For chestnut stuffing, mix cooked chestnuts with a little fried bacon and minced onion, and put through a sieve or vegetable mill for fine texture. For easy cranberry sauce, cook cranberries in a little boiling water until they pop, and add plenty of sugar.

PRESSED TURKEY

This is a useful way of preparing a bird so that it can be easily sliced, and so that everyone gets a fair helping of light and dark meat. Cook the turkey in foil so that the meat is just cooked but not dry. Carve and pack meat into 2 lb loaf tins. Fill tins to the top and press under heavy weights. Break up carcass and cook in very little water to which has been added generous seasoning and herbs. Cook liquid until it is well flavoured and reduced by half, then pour stock on to meat and press again. Turn out when cold and serve in slices.

SPECIAL SAVOURY STUFFING

Partly cook some onion. Add celery leaves, a liberal helping of parsley, egg and seasoning. Put into the liquidiser and blend. Add breadcrumbs and put into a buttered dish. Pour on a little melted butter or dripping. Cook in oven with poultry or joint.

Pat Brown, Keynsham, Somerset

CELERY AND GIBLET STUFFING

1 *medium-sized head celery*
(chopped)
1 *small onion (chopped)*
2 *oz butter*
Turkey giblets (cooked and chopped)

Rind of 1 *orange*
3 *oz breadcrumbs*
$\frac{1}{4}$ *teaspoon mixed herbs*
Salt and pepper

Lightly fry celery and onion in the butter. Remove from heat, and stir in giblets, orange rind, breadcrumbs and mixed herbs. Season well, and use to stuff the neck end of the turkey. (Sufficient for 10–12 lb turkey.)

SAGE AND ONION STUFFING

4 oz bread, brown or white, without crusts if these are too tough, 1 large onion, freshly chopped sage if possible – if not, dried, rubbed sage, salt, pepper, drippings. Soak the bread, crusts and all in hot water. While this is soaking peel and chop the onion; fry it in enough dripping to keep it from catching. When onion is golden brown take it off the heat. Mash the bread with your hands until no lumps are left, pouring off surplus water as necessary. Add the mashed, smooth, bread to the onions in the frying pan. Chop the sage and add to the rest with pepper and salt, not stinted. Mix well and use as required. If cooking separately in a dish, add more dripping, but for fat birds like duck and goose don't overdo the dripping.

Great-Aunt Anne's version from Cork

Great-Aunt Anne was the youngest of five children, living in the farmlands behind Cork. They were the only Protestants in a Roman Catholic area, and left Ireland in the Troubles. The eldest sister had gone to Cornwall to farm, and Aunt Anne followed her. She is now eighty-two and still going strong.

CHESTNUT STUFFING

1 lb chestnuts
½ pint milk
2 oz bacon
3 oz breadcrumbs
1 teaspoon chopped parsley

Little melted butter
Grated lemon rind
Sugar
1 egg

Make 2 slits in each chestnut, boil them in water for 10 minutes, then skin them. Put the nuts into a pan with enough milk to cover, simmer till tender then rub through a sieve. Pound with finely chopped bacon, add the breadcrumbs, parsley, butter and lemon rind. Season, then blend with the beaten egg.

SAUSAGE STUFFING

1 oz dripping
4 oz breadcrumbs
1 teaspoon parsley

1 large onion
1 lb pork sausage meat
½ teaspoon mixed herbs

Melt the dripping, chop the onion and mix with the sausage meat, lightly fry this mixture in the dripping for a few minutes, add the other ingredients and use as required.

PARSLEY, THYME AND LEMON STUFFING

4 oz breadcrumbs
2 tablespoons chopped parsley
1 egg
2 oz suet

¼ teaspoon thyme
Grated rind of half a lemon
Seasoning

Chop the suet and mix with the breadcrumbs, add the herbs and lemon rind, season well, bind with the beaten egg and use as required.

SAGE AND ONION STUFFING

4 onions
4 oz breadcrumbs
1 oz margarine

6 sage leaves
Salt, pepper and boiling water

Peel the onions, put them into a pan of cold water and bring to the boil. Boil for 5 minutes. Strain off this water, cover with fresh boiling water and cook till tender. Drain, chop finely, mix with rest of the ingredients and use as required.

7 Game

Now soften'd suns a mellow lustre shed,
The laden orchards glow with tempting red;
On hazel boughs the clusters hang embrown'd
And with the sportsman's war the new shorn fields resound.

Bacon

Once the first excitement of the shooting season is over, the country wife is faced with a mounting pile of carcasses, and a waning appetite for plain roast game with all the trimmings. While some men will firmly eat nothing else, and object to casseroled birds, some birds are badly shot or too old to be fit for simple cooking, so that ingenuity must be brought to the task of turning them into tempting puddings, casseroles and pâtés.

A lot of families might find it very odd that others can actually get tired of game. But those with menfolk whose lives revolve round magic dates like 'The Twelfth' or October 1 will know the increasing strain as the winter months continue. Men, and small boys, have a passionate interest in the ultimate eating of any fish, flesh, fowl or good red herring which they have actually done to death themselves – a heritage from the cavemen, perhaps. Their womenfolk, sickened by mounting piles of feathers, gory pelts, or undisposable fish-scales, would sometimes more cheerfully settle for an hygienically wrapped and utterly tasteless chicken trapped in the supermarket.

Nothing can truly beat plainly roasted game with all its delicious accompaniments of crumbs and chips, currant jelly, rich gravy, chestnuts, cabbage or celery, but there is often a moment when even perfection palls and some variety is called for. Additionally, birds may be old or badly shot (or may have lurked in the freezer a long time) and they are not fit for the simple treatment. In the case of partridges, now becoming rare, it may also be necessary to eke out helpings in a way which isn't possible with roast birds.

If a simple casserole is liked, it can be improved if the game is left in a marinade for any period up to 14 days, and the meat cooked in the liquid. A good marinade is a mixture of $\frac{1}{2}$ breakfastcup vinegar with 1 breakfastcup red wine, a bayleaf, a pinch each of pepper, salt and nutmeg, a sprig of thyme, and 4 chopped onions. This is good for hare, pigeon and venison as well as old tough birds (the tough tissues are broken down by the liquid and cooking time is shortened).

A good game soup can be very comforting on a winter evening. If you haven't old birds to spare, use the trimmings and carcasses of pheasants or partridges, and include onions, carrots, celery, a little lean bacon, a good bunch of herbs, and plenty of seasoning including a clove. The soup will taste best if the bacon is crisped before adding to the stock and if the sliced vegetables are cooked in a little butter until golden. A real family soup can have the vegetables left in; for a more elegant version the stock should be strained off and reheated with a little diced game taken from the breast of the bird.

If you like game pie, it can be made with a mixture of game, even with the addition of rabbit, and perhaps a little pork or veal. A little savoury forcemeat can be added for extra flavour. Hot water pastry is best used, and will be easy to handle if put into the refrigerator for just 30 minutes after making before moulding into shape. Stock for the jelly should be made from the game trimmings with a pig's trotter or calf's foot added.

One of the nicest things about game is that it is so delicious with the other traditional autumn foods such as apples, chestnuts, red cabbage and mushrooms. Venison and hare are included here. Likewise are those spreading vermin, pigeon and rabbit, which afford both sport and good food.

POACHER'S POT

Allow 1 small bird (any bird) per person
Seasoned flour

1 oz butter
1 teaspoon mixed herbs

Prepare the birds as for roasting. Dip in well-seasoned flour. Have 1 oz butter very hot in a large saucepan, brown the birds in this, add a small

teaspoon mixed herbs, put on a close fitting lid, and cook slowly for about
$1\frac{1}{2}$ hours. Serve with the liquid in the pan, slightly thickened as gravy,
bread sauce and chips.

SALMI OF GAME OR HARE

1 cooked pheasant or *2*
smaller birds or *hare*
1 teaspoon redcurrant jelly
Seasoning
1 pint espagnole sauce

Wineglass of Port Wine
Garnish: glacé cherries,
  button mushrooms,
  fleurons of puff
  pastry

Joint and skin the birds, or hare, and place them in a casserole. Pour over
the sauce and jelly. Heat thoroughly in the slowest possible way. Pour the
wine over the joints at the last minute and garnish with glacé cherries,
button mushrooms which have been cooked in butter, and the fleurons of
puff pastry.

HERTFORDSHIRE SALMI OF GAME

1 lightly roasted pheasant or
equivalent in other game
¾ pint espagnole sauce
Shallots
4 tablespoons port wine
1 level tablespoon redcurrant
jelly

12 button mushrooms
6 glacé cherries
Fleurons of puff pastry, cut
from remains of pastry case
baked blind, large enough to
hold salmi when cooked

Put the bird(s), cut into easy joints for dishing-up, into a heavy casserole,
sprinkle with finely chopped shallots – a few or many according to taste –
cover with espagnole sauce, the wine and reducrrant jelly. Dot the mushroom stalks around, adding a little thin stock if necessary, and cover
down well before cooking at a gentle pace for about $1-1\frac{1}{2}$ hours until the
birds are really tender.

Have ready the pastry case and arrange the joints in it; pour over the
sauce and garnish with the mushroom heads, sweated, and small fleurons
of the pastry, and finally a few glacé cherries. Serve with buttered carrots
and green peas.

The advantage of this dish is that the 2 stages can be achieved earlier
for last-minute dishing while guests drink their sherry.

GROUSE

In Season: August 12 to December 10.

Young birds have pointed wings and rounded spurs. 1 younger bird will feed 2 people, and an older one will do for 3. Grouse is best roast unless very old, or badly shot. Roast for 20–25 minutes at 400°F (Gas Mark 6) with bacon over the breast; serve on pieces of toast spread with the cooked liver mashed in a little stock. Accompany with gravy, bread sauce, buttered crumbs and wafer potatoes, with a garnish of watercress; rowanberry jelly is delicious with grouse.

ROAST GROUSE

Pluck, singe, draw and truss as a chicken, season inside and out with pepper and salt, put a piece of butter about the size of a walnut inside. Place a few rashers of fat bacon on the bird's breast and roast in a quick oven 20–30 minutes. Baste frequently during cooking, when almost done remove bacon and dredge with flour and return to the oven to brown the breast. Serve with undressed salad and straw potatoes. A piece of toasted or fried bread may be placed under the bird after 15 minutes cooking so the liquid from the bird drains into it, this then can be used when serving.

BRAISED GROUSE (for old birds)

Clean, truss and draw the number of birds you wish to use. Joint them and fry in bacon fat until brown. Put the joints into a casserole with enough stock to cover, with pieces of onion, and sticks of celery, cook gently for 2 hours, draw off the liquid, thicken with a little cornflour; gravy browning will need to be added to give a good colour, pour this over the joints of game.

Serve with creamed potatoes and green vegetables.

DUBLIN ROAST GROUSE

Allow 1 grouse for 2 people. Cook the grouse in a hot oven for about 30 minutes, basting frequently with the dripping in which it is cooked, with the addition of a small wineglass Irish whisky. Pour 1 tablespoon whisky over each bird before serving. Garnish with watercress and game chips and serve on crisp fried bread.

GROUSE ROAST WITH CRANBERRIES

2 grouse **Butter**

Leave grouse to hang for at least a fortnight. After plucking, trussing and dressing, stuff with butter and cranberries. The juicy fruit melts almost away during cooking (25 minutes at 450°F, Gas Mark 8) but the melted, spicy, buttery juice is all the gravy requires.

GROUSE IN ASPIC

3 to 4 grouse **Salt and pepper**
Faggot of herbs **Gelatine or aspic gelatine**

Skin and draw the grouse or pluck and draw. Carefully slice off the meat from each side of the breastbone in 2 neat portions, using as much meat from the wing and leg as possible without cutting into the bone. Simmer rest of the carcass with faggot of herbs for an hour. Strain, season with salt and pepper and simmer breast joints gently in this stock until tender. Remove joints and skin. Place in a shallow dish. Strain stock again, and for each pint of liquid add ½ oz gelatine previously softened in a little warm water, or use aspic gelatine using the stock instead of water. The heat of the stock should dissolve gelatine and when clear and cool, pour gently over joints in dish.

Any remaining jellied stock may be chopped and used as a garnish. A little sherry added to the stock is an improvement.

SALMIS OF GROUSE

2 small grouse **12 mushrooms**
1 oz butter **8 small button onions**
½ gill tomato sauce **Seasoning**
18 stoned French olives **1 croûte of fried bread**
½ pint espagnole sauce **1 small bouquet garni**
¼ gill sherry

Pick, draw, singe and truss the grouse. Put them in a baking dish, cover the breast of each with ½ oz butter, and roast them for about 10 minutes in a quick oven. Take up, untie, and cut the birds into small joints. Cut up the carcasses and fry in a baking dish with the butter left over from the birds. Pour off the fat and put the carcasses in a saucepan, add the wine, cover and let it reduce quickly. Add the espagnole and tomato sauces, boil up, season to taste, skim, and cook for 10 minutes. Peel the onions, fry them in butter, and braise in a little of the sauce. Arrange pieces of grouse in a clean saucepan, season with pepper and salt, add the olives and mushrooms (sliced), and pour the sauce over. Simmer gently for 20 minutes. Lay the bread croûte on an entrée dish and on this lay the pieces of grouse. Garnish with olives, onions and mushrooms. Pour over the sauce. Serve hot, piping hot.

PARTRIDGE

In Season: September 1 to February 1.
First year birds have the first flight feather pointed at the tip, not rounded. The grey partridge is most delicious after only 3–4 days hanging, but the red-legged variety needs 6–7 days. One bird will serve 2 people.

Roast at 350°F (Gas Mark 4) for 25 minutes, with bacon on the breast, basting with butter. Serve split in 2 with clear gravy, watercress, wafer potatoes. A crisp apple and celery salad is a good side dish.

ROAST PARTRIDGE

Prepare the bird, season inside and out by dredging with salt and pepper, stuffing may be used if desired, such as breadcrumbs or parsley. Cover the breast with a little fat bacon and roast in a moderate oven for 30 minutes, basting with its own fat. Try to avoid over-cooking. Serve with straw potatoes and garnish with watercress seasoned and sprinkled with a few drops of vinegar and quarters of lemon.

PARTRIDGE CASSEROLE

2 old partridges	*1 savoy cabbage*
2 onions	*½ pint stock*
2 carrots	*Thyme and parsley*
4 oz streaky bacon	*Salt, pepper*
8 oz chipolata sausages	

Cut the vegetables into neat pieces and brown them in a little butter, together with the partridges. Cut the cabbage into quarters and cook in boiling water with the bacon for 5 minutes. Drain well. Cut bacon and cabbage into small pieces. Put half the cabbage into a casserole, season with salt and pepper, and put on the partridges. Cover with bacon and vegetables, chopped herbs, and the rest of the cabbage. Pour in stock, cover with a lid and cook at 300°F (Gas Mark 2) for 3 hours. Grill the sausages lightly and add ½ hour before serving time. The addition of a glass of dry cider, and a little less stock, makes a good dish.

PARTRIDGE WITH GRAPES

Take 2 plump partridges, 1 lb under-ripe grapes, 4 oz finely cut streaky bacon, pepper and salt. Line a casserole with the rashers and put the birds on top. Add the washed grapes, 1 bayleaf, a pinch of thyme, a sprig of rosemary, season highly with pepper and salt. Pour over the juice of an orange. Cook in a low oven until the birds are tender – this will depend entirely on the age of the birds. Serve surrounded with cooked grapes; the liquor in the caserole is all the sauce that is needed.

OCTOBER PARTRIDGE

2 partridges	*1 small red cabbage*
2 rashers bacon	*¼ pint cider*
Juice of ½ lemon	*6 chestnuts*
Salt and pepper	*1 oz butter*
1 small onion	*1 teaspoon vinegar*

Wipe the partridges inside and out, dust with salt and pepper and sprinkle with lemon juice. Melt butter in a pan and brown the birds slowly all over. Cool slightly, then wrap each bird in a slice of bacon. Slice the onion and red cabbage very finely, season with salt and pepper and put into a saucepan with the cider and vinegar. Bring to the boil and simmer for 20 minutes. Put birds on top and put on lid, then simmer for 1½ hours. Peel the chestnuts, toss in butter and add to the dish 10 minutes before cooking is finished.

BROILED PARTRIDGE

When the partridges have been prepared for roasting, cut off the heads and split up the backs, flatten the breastbone, wipe them inside with a damp cloth, season with cayenne and salt, and broil over a clear, gentle fire for 15 minutes. Have ready some good brown gravy, or mushroom sauce, rub the birds over quickly with butter, place on a hot dish, and serve with the sauce in a tureen.

HARE

In Season: Early autumn to end of February.

Young hare can generally be recognised by white pointed teeth and fresh-looking fur; the older animals will have cracked brown teeth and be scruffy-looking. A hare will feed 10 people easily. The saddle can be roasted (best for a young animal) while other parts are good in casserole, as soup or pâté

ROAST HARE

1 *hare*
4 *or* 5 *rashers of streaky*
bacon

Cooking fat
Stuffing: sage and onion
or sausage meat

Skin and draw then wash the hare in cold water to which a little vinegar has been added to whiten the flesh, dry well and stuff. Heat knob of fat in roasting tin and spoon the hot fat over the hare. Cover the top with bacon and then put a lid on the tin or cover with foil. Cook for about 1½ hours in a moderately hot oven.

Serve with roast potatoes, a green vegetable and redcurrant jelly.

CASSEROLE OF HARE

1 *hare*
1 *onion*
3 *cloves*
Bouquet garni
3 *oz butter*

1½ *pint stock – or equivalent*
in stock and stout – or cider
1 *oz flour*
Fat for frying

Prepare hare and cut into pieces suitable for serving. Fry pieces in 2 oz butter until brown, then pack them into a casserole. Slice and fry onions, add to casserole with cloves, bouquet garni and salt and pepper. Cover closely, simmer for about 2½ hours until tender.

Serve with vegetables of choice and redcurrant jelly.

SOMERSET HARE WITH WALNUTS

Drain a jointed hare after it has soaked for 24 hours in a mixture of sweet Somerset cider and water. Brown the pieces in 3 oz butter mixed with 3 tablespoons of olive oil and then add the grated contents of one cored cooking apple (preferably Bramley's Red Seedling) an eggcup of lemon juice and a little brandy. Cover with a weak stock or water, throw in a bay-leaf, seasoning and a little cinnamon, cover and cook very gently until the meat is quite tender (2–4 hours, in 2 intervals if liked). Then add 4 oz double minced shelled walnuts with a good dessertspoon of flour (whole-meal is good). Cook on top, slowly stirring till the flour is cooked and the sauce has thickened, then serve with forcemeat balls. A wineglassful of port added at the last minute before serving makes this a dish fit for a king.

HARE IN WINE

1 *hare*
1 *bottle claret*
Onion
Garlic
Bouquet garni
Pork fat
2 *rashers bacon*
5 *shallots*

1 *onion*
1 *clove garlic*
Flour
Parsley, thyme, bayleaf
2 *lumps sugar*
Salt and pepper
1 *glass Armagnac*
Croûtons

Put a glass of claret in the blood of the hare. Joint the hare and marinade it in claret with onion, garlic and herbs. Brown the pieces of hare in the pork fat. Cook the bacon, shallots, onion, garlic in the pork fat. Brown the liver. Reduce the claret and add to casserole. Add the pieces of hare, herbs, sugar. Pound the liver and stir into the blood. Add to casserole. Simmer. Cool. Re-heat. Season. Add Armagnac. Serve garnished with croûtons.

CAMBRIDGE HARE IN BEER

1 *hare*
2 *large onions*
8 *oz carrots*

$1\frac{1}{2}$ *oz plain flour*
$\frac{1}{2}$ *pint brown ale or stout*
$\frac{1}{2}$ *pint stock*

Joint the hare. Slice the onions thinly and the carrots rather thickly. Fry the onions in a little dripping until soft but not coloured and put them into a casserole. Coat the hare joints in a little of the flour seasoned with salt and pepper, and cook them in the dripping until golden. Put on top of the onions and add the carrots. Work the remaining flour into the fat in the pan and cook for 2 minutes. Gradually add the beer and stock and cook until smooth. Pour over the hare, cover the casserole, and cook at 350°F (Gas Mark 4) for $2\frac{1}{2}$ hours. Very good with jacket potatoes.

ROAST SADDLE OF HARE

For this cut the back of the hare in 1 piece. Dredge the meat well with black pepper, wrap some rashers of bacon round it, then wrap in grease-proof paper and put into a covered pan with plenty of dripping. Roast for 20–30 minutes. Take out the meat, add a little flour to the fat in the pan, add stock or water and let it thicken. Carve the meat from the saddle, put it into an ovenware dish, pour over it the thickened gravy, add a little port wine, cover and put the dish back into a hot oven to cook for a further 15 minutes.

TO JUG HARE

1 *hare*
Bunch of sweet herbs; chervil,
thyme, tarragon
6 allspice
2 onions, each stuck with a
few cloves

$\frac{1}{2}$ *teaspoon black pepper*
Little lemon peel
2 tablespoons ketchup
Wineglass of port wine
1 oz butter, and 1 oz flour, for
thickening

Wash the hare and cut it into small joints, flour each piece with seasoned flour. Put into a pan with the herbs, the onions, cloves, allspice, salt, pepper and lemon peel. Cover with cold water and bring to simmering point. Simmer until tender, this will take about 2 hours.

Take out the joints of hare and lay them neatly in the dish in which you intend to serve them. Heat the butter, add the flour and cook for 2–3 minutes, add the liquid in which you have cooked the hare and allow to thicken. Then add ketchup and wine. Pour the gravy over the joints of meat and let it stand where it may keep hot but not continue cooking, for 10 minutes. Serve with forcemeat balls and redcurrant jelly.

HERTFORDSHIRE JUGGED HARE

Take 1 hare and marinade it in red wine or vinegar and water for 12 hours minimum, or better still 24 hours, having first cut it into neat joints, dipped in olive oil. Take hare out of marinade and when it has drained well fry it in a little bacon fat or olive oil. Into a casserole, or proper clome jug, put 1 onion stuck with 3 or 4 cloves, a sliced large carrot, a few shallots, a bouquet garni, a few black peppercorns, a small bayleaf, a stick or two of sliced-up celery, some powdered allspice, a level teaspoon of salt, and a little orange peel; then the hare joints carefully placed. Cover the whole with stock and finally seal it with a lid of flour and water paste to prevent its drying out. Cook slowly for $3\frac{1}{2}$ hours, starting off at 350°F and after half the cooking reducing the heat to around 300°F. Then remove the paste or lid (the paste is only strictly necessary if the lid is not really heavy and tight-fitting) and take out the hare joints and keep them hot. Meanwhile strain the liquor and make it as thick as you wish (it should be pretty thick) with flour and water mixed to smooth cream. Simmer this gravy-sauce carefully for a few minutes and then take it off the heat. Use a spoonful or two of this to add to the hare's blood, then pour all that back into the sauce. Add a dash of port wine and a tablespoon of redcurrant jelly and put back on to the heat but do not allow it to boil or the blood will coagulate. Arrange the hare in the cleaned and heated casserole and pour the sauce over it. Decorate with twirls of orange peel and garnish with forcemeat balls.

JUGGED HARE

After the hare has been skinned it should be cut up into joints and suitable pieces, then fried in some fresh butter to a golden brown. Put all the portions into a stoneware jar, with a tumbler of port wine or Burgundy, and sufficient water just to cover the meat. Put in also 1 blade of mace, 6 cloves, 3 eschalots (shallots), 1 clove of garlic, 1 small onion, ½ teaspoon each of allspice and peppercorns, the juice of ½ lemon; and salt to taste. Cover the jar securely and place it in a saucepan, with a small plate at the bottom, turned upside down to prevent the jar from touching the bottom of the saucepan. Fill up with water to about 3 inches from the top of the jar and let the water boil for 4 to 5 hours, replenishing the water as it boils away. When done, the gravy will be plentiful and rich, and it may be thickened with a little cornflour if desired. Take out the jar and put all the joints of the hare into an entrée dish. Strain the liquor through a wire sieve over the hare and serve with redcurrant jelly and some forcemeat balls (fried) which may be placed round the dish.

CORNISH JUGGED HARE

Take 1 hare, 1 bunch sweet herbs, 2 onions, each stuck with 3 cloves, 3 whole allspice, ½ teaspoon black pepper, a strip of lemon peel, thickening of butter and flour, 2 tablespoons mushroom ketchup and some small pieces of bacon, 1 tablespoon clotted cream.

Wash the hare and cut it into small useful sized joints, flour and brown them; put them in a stew pan with the herbs, onions, cloves, allspice, pepper and lemon-rind; cover with hot water, and when it boils remove the scum and let it simmer gently till tender (2–3 hours or more). Take out the pieces of hare, thicken the gravy with flour and a little butter; add the ketchup, let it boil for 10 minutes, add the clotted cream, strain the gravy over the hare joints and serve. A few fried forcemeat balls should be added or they may be stewed for last 10 minutes in the gravy. Serve with redcurrant jelly.

ROAST HARE

On the Wiltshire Downs, the Dorset Downs, the Hampshire Downs and the White Horse Hills, hares were very plentiful and did much damage. Yet roast hare was always something to look forward to.

In selecting a hare for roasting, particular care must be taken to get a young one – one that is not more than three-quarters grown. Old and fully grown hares will do very well for stewing or jugging, but on no account may they be roasted, as they would be too tough and dry.

Let the hare hang as long as possible, 10–14 days is average but this can be varied to please individual preference. (This hanging softens and relaxes the 'strings' in this fast running animal.) Skin and paunch and soak in salt water for an hour or so. Truss the hare ready for stuffing (a suitable stuffing recipe follows later). Fill the hare with a good forcemeat, and lay it in a baking tin, making sure that the stuffing is sewn in securely with strong thread or fine string. Pour over 1 pint of milk and cover the hare with butter which should be spread on evenly all over. Water and dripping can be used for this but milk and butter are considered best. Baste the hare at frequent intervals, never letting it get dried up – a well buttered paper helps to keep the mosisture in; and have the oven turned as low as will keep the hare gently cooking but not 'baking-up'. When the hare is cooked through, sprinkle it with salt and flour and brown it all over. A very young hare would be nicely roasted in 1¼ hours but much depends on the size and age. Remove all string and skewers and send to table with a tureen of rich gravy and some redcurrant jelly.

PHEASANT

In Season: October 1 to February 1
A young cock bird has round spurs in the first year, short pointed ones in the second year, sharp long ones when older. A young hen bird has soft feet and light feathers, while the older one has hard feet and dark feathers. Hen birds are smaller, but less dry and more tender with good flavour. One good bird should feed 4 people. The pheasant is best hung for about a week in normal temperatures; if badly shot or mauled it is better to use the bird more quickly.

Roast pheasant is best cooked at 400°F (Gas Mark 6) for about 45 minutes, according to the size of the bird. Bacon should be tied on the breast, and the bird seasoned inside and out with salt and pepper. The bird is better for basting with butter, and better still if a little red wine is added to the roasting pan at half time. Serve with clear gravy, bread sauce, fried crumbs, wafer potatoes. Mushrooms are a delicious accompaniment, also chestnuts and braised celery.

PHEASANT WITH APPLES

1 *pheasant*	4 *tablespoons cream*
4 *oz butter*	*Salt and pepper*
1½ *lb apples*	

Season the bird with salt and pepper and cook in butter until golden. Peel and slice the apples and line a casserole with half of them. Pour in some of the butter, put in the bird and surround with remaining apples. Pour in the rest of the butter and the cream, cover tightly and cook at 350°F (Gas

Mark 4) for 45 minutes, though time may be a little longer if the bird is old. A wineglass of Calvados (apple brandy) is a delicious addition.

ROAST PHEASANT

1 pheasant
2 oz butter
A few mushrooms

A little fat bacon
Salt and Cayenne pepper

Prepare the pheasant, tie the fat bacon on the breast. Wipe and skin mushrooms and stuff the bird with them adding the 1 oz butter, salt and a few grains of cayenne pepper, truss and cover with a piece of thickly buttered greaseproof paper. Roast for 30 minutes, basting frequently, then take off the paper and roast for a further 10 minutes. Serve with gravy and bread sauce or redcurrant jelly.

PHEASANT SOUP

Take the meat from the breast and wings, put these on one side. Break up the remaining carcass and put all pieces into a pan with onions, leeks, carrots, stick of celery and some herbs. Let this simmer 5–6 hours, put the breast meat through a mincer, then pound it and rub through a coarse sieve, mix with a handful of brown breadcrumbs, and the yolk of an egg until it binds well and can be shaped into small balls. Strain the bones and vegetables from the stock, add the meat balls to it and bring to the boil again. Just before serving add a little fresh cream.

DEVILLED PHEASANT

1 roast pheasant
1 pint cream
1 teaspoon mustard
1 teaspoon Harvey's sauce

1 teaspoon Worcester sauce
Salt
Optional: mushrooms

Roast the pheasant. Whip the cream with the other ingredients. Cut up the pheasant and put it into a flat earthenware dish. Pour over the cream sauce. (If you wish, add the cooked mushrooms at this stage.) Brown but do not boil.

PHEASANT IN CIDER

1 old pheasant
1 lb cooking apples
8 oz onions
2 oz butter

½ pint cider
1 clove garlic
Bunch of mixed herbs
Salt and pepper

Wipe pheasant thoroughly inside and out. Cut apples in quarters after peeling and put into casserole. Slice onions and cook in butter until soft and transparent. Put pheasant on top of apples and cover with onions. Pour in cider, and put in herbs and crushed garlic clove. Season with salt and pepper. Cover tightly and cook at 325°F (Gas Mark 3) for 2½ hours. This dish may be served immediately, or the sauce sieved and poured over it.

PHEASANT WITH CHESTNUTS

1 pheasant
1 oz butter
8 oz peeled and skinned
chestnuts
8 oz small onions
1 heaped tablespoon flour
1 pint stock

Grated rind and juice of ½
orange
1 dessertspoon redcurrant
jelly
1 teaspoon red wine vinegar
Parsley, thyme and bayleaf
Salt and pepper

Brown the pheasant all over in hot butter. Remove from fire and put into casserole. Toss the chestnuts and onions quickly in the fat until they turn colour, and remove from fat, putting round the pheasant. Blend the pan juices with flour, then work in the rest of the ingredients. Bring to the boil and pour over pheasant. Cover tightly and cook at 325°F (Gas Mark 3) for 2 hours. Remove the pheasant and cut in pieces. Put on serving dish with chestnuts and onions. Remove parsley, thyme and bayleaf, skim the liquid and reduce if necessary. Pour over pheasant and scatter with finely chopped parsley.

PHEASANT WITH CELERY SAUCE

1 large old pheasant
1 pint stock
1 head celery
2 oz butter
1 onion

Parsley, thyme and bayleaf
1 clove
Salt and pepper
1 oz butter with 1 oz flour
1 gill cream

The stock for cooking the pheasant should include a carrot and onion, a couple of cloves, salt and pepper and a good sprig of parsley. Poach the pheasant in this until tender (this will depend on the age of the bird). Cut the bird into neat pieces for serving with the celery sauce. Make this by cooking the chopped celery in butter with the onion, herbs, clove, salt and pepper until tender, then simmering in ½ pint stock until really soft (use some of the pheasant stock). Put the celery through a sieve and thicken with the butter and flour worked together. Finally, stir in the cream and pour over the pheasant. The sauce should be rather thick. If time is short and the celery young and without strings, the pieces may be left whole without sieving. If money is short, use a little top milk instead of cream for the sauce. The same recipe may be used for partridges, and this quantity of sauce will be enough for 2 birds.

PHEASANT WITH CREAM

Truss the bird, cover the breast with strips of bacon, and brown in a casserole with 3 tablespoons of butter, 8 shallots, salt and pepper. (Here you can pour in a little brandy and light it, but this is not strictly necessary.) Add $1\frac{1}{2}$ cups of veal or chicken broth, and cook for $\frac{1}{2}$ hour, basting frequently with the juice. Then add 1 good cup of cream, a $\frac{1}{4}$ cup of grated horseradish, and cook for another 20 minutes, basting with the sauce. Season to taste, put the bird on a dish, carve, and pour the sauce round.

Miss Barker, Halstead, Essex

LINCOLNSHIRE PHEASANT (for young birds)

1 *pheasant*	2 *tablespoons flour*
1 *onion*	$1\frac{1}{2}$ *pints stock or water*
1 *carrot*	4 *tomatoes*
4 *oz dripping*	$\frac{1}{2}$ *lb mushrooms, peeled*
Salt and pepper	1 *tablespoon parsley*

Cut up a tender pheasant, peel and shred the onion and a carrot. Melt the dripping in a pan, add the carrot and onion and fry for 5 minutes, stirring with a wooden spoon. Place the pieces of pheasant in this, with a little salt and pepper, and fry for another 5 minutes, stirring all the time. Add the 2 tablespoons of flour and cook for 3 minutes more, gradually adding the stock and stir till it boils. Cut the tomatoes and the peeled mushrooms in quarters, add these to the contents of the pan together with the chopped parsley and simmer for $\frac{1}{2}$ hour. Set the pheasant in the centre of a hot dish, pour over the sauce and garnish with mushrooms. This will only be successful with a young bird; it is a well-known fact that the poacher takes only the best young birds.

PHEASANT AND MUSHROOMS

3 *oz butter*	$\frac{3}{4}$ *pint stock*
8 *oz mushrooms*	$\frac{1}{2}$ *wineglass sherry*
1 *pheasant*	*Salt and pepper*
3 *tablespoons flour*	

Melt half the butter and cook the sliced mushrooms gently for 10 minutes. Season lightly and cool. Stuff the pheasant with three-quarters of the mushrooms. Brown the bird in the rest of the butter, and put in a casserole. Blend the flour into the pan juices, and gradually work in the stock and sherry. Season well and pour over pheasant. Cover tightly and cook at 325°F (Gas Mark 3) for $1\frac{1}{2}$ hours but allow an extra 30 minutes for an older bird. Just before serving, add remaining mushrooms, and garnish with watercress. The sauce is rich and delicious.

PHEASANT IN MILK

1 *pheasant*
Seasoning
Flour

$\frac{1}{2}$ *pint milk*
$\frac{1}{2}$ *pint stock*

Prepare the bird for roasting and dust well with seasoned flour; put into a pan and dredge with more flour. Pour the milk into the pan and then add half a pint of good stock – this should be drenched over the body and breast of the bird. Cook for 40–50 minutes in a good oven, 400°F (Gas Mark 6), basting frequently with the milk-stock liquid. Take out and put on to a hot dish. Stir together all the thick liquid on the bottom of the tin, and serve this as gravy; it should need no additions but may be thinned a little if it is too thick.

NORFOLK CASSEROLED PHEASANT

1 *pheasant*
A little cream
Butter

4 *or* 5 *good cooking apples*
Salt and pepper

Take a pheasant and prepare it in the usual way. When it is clean and dry, melt some nice fresh butter in a largish pan and cook and turn the pheasant in this until it is golden brown all over. Meanwhile slice 4 or 5 good cooking apples and slice them nice and thinly, lay them around the sides of a greased, good-sized casserole dish. Placing if liked a slice of bread under the bird, put the pheasant carefully in the casserole and fill up the spaces with the rest of the apples. Pour over any butter left from the browning operation and add more if necessary; sprinkle well with salt and pepper and cover the bird with a greased paper, before covering tightly. Cook in a moderately hot oven, 350°F (Gas Mark 4), for about an hour (longer if bird is tough). If the bird is then tender uncover it and allow a few minutes longer back in the oven. Serve with forcemeat balls or bread sauce and bacon rolls, mashed potatoes and carrots.

LEDBURY ROAST PHEASANT

Have ready a nice plump pheasant for roasting, wiped inside with clean dry cloth. Dust its breast with salt and pepper and a little flour. Fry some croûtons of bread, white or brown, in butter and stand aside. In the butter in the frying pan, cook a few field mushrooms (if possible). Mix the croûtons and the mushrooms together and place inside the pheasant with a little salt and pepper. Sew up the gap and cover the bird with fat bacon slices or rashers of fat bacon, cover with butter paper and cook in a good oven, reducing the heat after about 20 minutes. After cooking for a further 50 minutes to an hour, remove the paper and bacon and return to the oven to completely brown the breast. Serve on a good hot dish garnished with parsley or watercress. After the first initial hot spell of cooking, it is better to have quite a gentle heat as pheasant can become dry in cooking if care is not taken.

SALMIS OF PHEASANT (1)

Cut up the meat from a pheasant that has been cooked, and is not quite cold. Put the bones and trimmings into a saucepan with 2 glasses of sherry and 1 pint of brown sauce. Let it simmer until reduced by one half. Strain the sauce and put it into a saucepan with the meat from the pheasant, and when it is warm serve.

SALMIS OF PHEASANT (2)

Prepare and joint a pheasant. Stew it in brown sherry sauce, together with some minced ham, and a few mushrooms. Garnish with fried bread croûtons and whole button mushrooms.

PHEASANT WITH APPLES

One lunchtime, soon after we were married, my husband telephoned to say he was bringing two delightful strangers to dinner. With no time for shopping I took two pheasants from the deep-freeze, and prayed that they would thaw, picked some apples and made *Faisan Normande* straight from the cookery book. This was such a success that Theo has slightly adapted it so that he can feel civilised and have a drink when the guests come.

Brown a pheasant in a pan or cast iron casserole in half butter and half oil. Peel, core and chop a couple of Cox's apples and add to the casserole. Add a bouquet garni and some stock and simmer gently till done. Remove pheasant, carve on to serving dish, keep warm but don't let it dry. For the sauce, mash the apples into the stock, remove bouquet, season and add a squeeze of lemon juice. At the last moment add as much cream as you can bear, pour over pheasant, sprinkle with chopped parsley and there you are.

Joan Dampney, Christchurch, Hants

BROILED PHEASANT

After the bird has been prepared for cooking in the usual manner, divide it into neat joints. Place them in a frying pan with a little fat, and fry them until they are browned all over. When they are drained well, sprinkle them with salt and cayenne all over, roll them in egg and breadcrumbs and broil over a clear fire for about 10 minutes. Place on a hot dish, and serve with 'sauce piquante', mushroom sauce, or brown sauce. The remains of any cold pheasant may be treated in the same manner.

NORMANDY PHEASANT

Fry the pheasant in a casserole, then place on a layer of freshly chopped apples (about 4). Add three or four tablespoons of cream and cook for about $\frac{3}{4}$ hour in a moderate oven.

PIGEONS

Pigeons are classed as vermin, but they have the advantage of being in season throughout the year and at their best in late summer and early autumn when stuffed with illicit snacks of ripe corn. Country people affect to despise the birds, but they must still have a soft spot for them, referring fondly to a two-child boy-and-girl family as a 'pigeon pair' with the greatest pride.

Great houses used to breed pigeons for useful food, and the many different species of domesticated pigeons used not only for food but for ornament, sport or messengers rejoice in such names as pouters, carriers, homers, fantails, jacobins, nun, turbits, tumblers and trumpeters. The Star Chamber Accounts constantly carry the price of pigeons, making a difference between the tame or 'house' pigeons and the wild ones. From 1519 to 1535, the usual charge was a penny each or 10d per dozen. By 1590, the price had risen to $2\frac{1}{2}$d each for wild birds and 6d for house birds. In 1602 and 1605 they cost 8d each, and by 1635 were 13s and 14s a dozen. Two and a half centuries later, when they were a favourite on Victorian and Edwardian tables, the price remained at about 1s each. Cassell's Dictionary of Cookery, popular at the beginning of the century, lists no less than forty-three recipes for them, including such delicacies as Pigeon

Cutlets and Pigeons Stewed with Asparagus. Today, the birds are still relatively cheap, and two or three will provide a gourmet meal very cheaply.

Pigeons may be rather dry, and plenty of fat bacon will give them flavour and richness. Fat used in cooking pigeons should not be too hot, as their flesh is delicate, and over-heated fat toughens them and destroys flavour. When the birds are plainly roasted, a slice of crustless toast put under them 10 minutes before serving will absorb gravy and fat and is delicious to eat with the dish.

Pigeons need not be hung, but if they are hung head downwards for an hour immediately after killing, they will bleed freely and the flesh will be paler. Young fat pigeons may be roasted; older birds are close and dry, and need longer cooking. Allow 1 pigeon for 2 people, or 1 each if appetites are hearty.

CIDER PIGEONS

2 *pigeons*	1 *oz flour*
Butter	$\frac{3}{4}$ *pint stock*
1 *small apple*	$\frac{1}{4}$ *pint cider*
1 *small onion*	*Parsley, thyme and bayleaf*

Brown the pigeons in butter, then split them in half. Brown sliced apple and onion in same fat, then sprinkle on flour and cook until golden. Add stock and cider and bring to the boil. Season with salt and pepper, add herbs and halved pigeons. Cover tightly and cook on top of the stove or in a low oven for $2\frac{1}{2}$ hours. Serve pigeons in the gravy with a garnish of fried apple rings and bacon rolls.

PIGEONS WITH CABBAGE

1 *large firm cabbage*	2 *pigeons*
8 *rashers fat bacon*	*Parsley, thyme and bayleaf*
Butter	

This is a very good winter dish made with a firm-hearted cabbage and old birds. Blanch a large firm cabbage in boiling water for 10 minutes, drain very well and chop finely. Mix with 4 rashers of chopped bacon and put into a greased fireproof dish. Season with salt and pepper, and put in a sprig each of parsley and thyme, and a bayleaf. Brown pigeons in a little butter and put them into the dish, covering with the remaining rashers of bacon. Add stock just to cover, cover tightly and simmer for 2 hours. Serve the birds (which may be split in half) on a bed of cabbage. A Victorian version of this dish suggests thickening the gravy before serving with a knob of butter and flour and 2 tablespoons of thick cream.

JELLIED PIGEONS

3 or 4 pigeons
Salt and pepper

Mixed herbs
1 oz gelatine

This is a very good way of dealing with old birds. Simmer the birds in just enough water to cover with plenty of seasoning and herbs for about 1½ hours until the meat leaves the bones easily. Remove the meat from the bones, taste the gravy for seasoning, and dissolve the gelatine (which has been softened in a little cold water) in the hot liquid. Pack the meat into a wetted mould and pour over it the stock. Leave to set before turning out to serve with salad.

POT ROAST PIGEONS

1 bird per person
Seasoned flour
Butter

¼ pint stock
1 teaspoon mixed herbs (for 4 birds)

Dip the birds in seasoned flour, then brown them in a little butter. Add herbs and stock, cover tightly and cook very gently on top of the stove or in the oven for 1½ hours. Serve with the pan gravy, bread sauce and game chips. This is a useful recipe if you are not sure of the age of the birds, but don't want to casserole them.

PIGEONS WITH BACON

With a sharp knife make a slit on each side of the breastbone and insert slices of streaky bacon. Pack the birds into a roasting dish, cover with dripping and greaseproof paper and cook slowly in the oven for 2½ to 3 hours. When cooked, the breasts and bacon will lift away from the birds, and the remains are discarded.

SLOW-COOKED PIGEONS

4 pigeons
12 small onions
3 rashers lean bacon
8 oz mushrooms
1 pint stock
1 wineglass wine or cider (optional)

1 oz butter
¾ oz flour
1 teaspoon sugar
Parsley, thyme and bayleaf tied in a bunch

Use an oven-to-table dish which will allow the pigeons to fit side by side. A cast-iron one is perfect as it can be started on top of the stove, then put into the oven. Peel the onions, cut the bacon into thin strips and wipe the mushrooms. Heat the butter and lightly fry the bacon. Put on to a dish, and cook onions until lightly golden, sprinkling with sugar. Remove to dish. Cook the mushrooms in the same fat and remove to dish.

Brown the pigeons in the fat, very slowly and carefully, and lift out. Work the flour into the fat, cooking until brown. Gradually add stock and wine, bring to the boil and strain. Rinse out the pan, put back the sauce and bring to the boil. Add all the ingredients, cover with a greased paper and well-fitting lid. Cook at 300°F (Gas Mark 2) for 2½–3 hours. Remove bunch of herbs before serving.

POT ROAST PIGEONS

Prepare the birds as for roasting, dip in well-seasoned flour. Have 1 oz butter very hot in a large saucepan, brown the birds in this, add a small teaspoon of mixed herbs, put on a close fitting lid, and cook slowly for about 1½ hours. Serve with the liquid in the pan, slightly thickened, as gravy; bread sauce and chips.

To marinade pigeons

To marinade meat or game means to cover it with a mixture of wine, herbs, spices, onions and vinegar for any period of up to 14 days. The effect of putting tough meat into this mixture is to break down the tissues and shorten the cooking time.

Allow 1 bird per person   **Vinegar**
½ bottle cheap red wine   **Little sliced onion**

Cut up the birds and put them in a large earthenware jar. Allow half as much vinegar as you have wine, mix the 2, add the sliced onion, pour this over the cut joints. Leave for 12–14 days.

When wanted, remove the meat from the marinade, fry some sliced onion, then lightly fry the joints of meat, pack into a greased fireproof casserole, add a little flour to the fat in which you have cooked the birds, and then enough of the marinade liquid to make a thick sauce, pour this over the joints, and put the casserole in a fairly hot oven for about 2 hours.

WOOD PIGEONS WITH CABBAGE

1 large green cabbage   **Salt and pepper**
2 pigeons   **Little parsley, thyme and a**
3-4 rashers fat bacon   **bayleaf**

Blanch the cabbage in boiling water for 10 minutes. Drain and plunge into cold water, leave for 10 minutes. Drain well and press out as much water as possible. Chop, and line a greased fireproof dish with the chopped vegetable and the rashers of bacon. Season with salt and pepper and add the herbs, all except the bayleaf. Have some fat very hot in a pan and brown the prepared, trussed pigeons in the fat, turning so that they are browned all over. Put the birds into the casserole, with the bayleaf, cover with a few more rashers of bacon and put on a close fitting lid. Bring to the boil and allow to simmer for at least 2 hours. The birds can be cut in half and served straight from the bed of cabbage.

ROAST STUFFED PIGEON

Allow 1 bird per person   *Fat for roasting*
Sausage meat, 4 oz per person

Prepare the birds and put into a steamer, cook for 2–3 hours and leave to get cold. When cold, make a shallow cut across the breast of each bird and pull the skin gently off, being careful not to pull the flesh as well. Stuff the birds with the well-seasoned sausage meat, brush with dripping and dredge with breadcrumbs. Have some fat very hot in a baking tin, put the birds in this and bake for about an hour, basting frequently. Serve with good gravy made from the water in which the birds were steamed, a green vegetable and mashed potatoes.

SUFFOLK BRAISED PIGEONS

4 pigeons   *¼ pint dry red wine*
2 small oranges   *(optional, but a great*
Streaky bacon   *improvement)*
Butter   *½ pint stock*
A few sliced mushrooms   *Bouquet garni*
1 onion, sliced   *Chopped parsley*
1 dessertspoon flour

When the pigeons are prepared, peel the 2 oranges and put one half in each bird; truss the birds then wrap each one in a piece of bacon and fry in butter until they are going brown. Drain them then put them in a casserole. Meanwhile fry the mushrooms and onion in the same butter, but not too much; stir in the flour to make a roux and cook for about 3–4 minutes. Gradually blend in the wine and stock, bring to the boil very gently, season to taste before pouring over the birds. Put in the bunch of sweet, fresh herbs (bouquet garni) or if out of season, use dried mixed herbs, cook in a pretty moderate oven (say 325°F) until really tender, at least 1½ hours. After testing, when the birds are well done, remove them from the gravy and arrange them on a flat dish. The gravy can be strained or left as it is, only removing the bouquet garni, and poured over the pigeon joints. Use some nice chopped fresh parsley to garnish. Enough for 4.

JUGGED PIGEONS

Time 3 hours. Some pigeons, two hard-boiled eggs; a sprig of parsley; the peel of $\frac{1}{2}$ lemon; the weight of the livers in suet; the same of breadcrumbs; pepper; salt; and nutmeg; 1 egg; 1$\frac{1}{2}$ oz butter; 1 head of celery; a glass of white wine; a bunch of sweet herbs; 3 cloves; blade of mace.

Pick and draw 4 or 6 pigeons, wipe them very dry, boil the livers a minute or two, then mince them fine and bruise them with a spoon, or beat them in a mortar; mix with them the yolks of 2 hard-boiled eggs, a sprig of parsley, and the peel of half a lemon all shred fine; the weight of the livers in suet, chopped as fine as possible, the same weight of breadcrumbs, and a little pepper, salt, and grated nutmeg; mix it all together with a well beaten egg, and a little fresh butter.

Stuff the pigeons and the crops with this forcemeat, sew up the vents, and dip the pigeons into warm water; dredge over them some pepper and salt, and put them into a jar with the celery, sweet herbs, cloves and beaten mace with a glassful of white wine. *Cover the jar closely*, and set it in a stew-pan of boiling water for 3 hours, taking care the water does not go up to the top of the jar. When done, strain the gravy into a stewpan, stir in a little butter rolled in flour, boil it up again till it is thick, and pour it over the pigeons. Garnish with lemon.

TO FRICASSEE PIGEONS BROWN

Time 1 hour. 5 or 6 pigeons; $\frac{1}{2}$ blade of beaten mace; pepper and salt; 1 pint of gravy or broth; a glass of port wine; a bunch of sweet herbs; peel of $\frac{1}{2}$ lemon; 3 onions or shallots; 2 oz of butter; 1 tablespoon of flour; juice of $\frac{1}{2}$ lemon; and a few pickled mushrooms.

Cut the pigeons into quarters, season them with a blade of mace, well beaten, pepper and salt. Fry them a light brown in butter, and lay them on a sieve to drain, then put them into a stewpan with a pint of gravy or broth, a glass of port wine, a bunch of sweet herbs, the peel of $\frac{1}{2}$ lemon, and 3 shallots choped fine. Cover them closely and stew them for $\frac{1}{2}$ hour, then stir in a piece of butter rolled in flour, season with pepper and salt, add a few pickled mushrooms (or fresh if available) squeeze in the juice of lemon, and add a few forcemeat balls. Let all stew together until both the birds and the forcemeat balls are cooked, skim the gravy if necesasry, put the fricassée on a hot dish and garnish with lemon.

RABBIT

A good rabbit should feed 6 people. If you have a very young one, the legs are excellent if boned, beaten flat, and fried in egg and breadcrumbs, served with slices of lemon. Rabbit casseroles are best with plenty of herbs and seasonings, onions and bacon; leftover rabbit may be minced and potted with butter.

HAMPSHIRE RABBIT

1 rabbit
Seasoned flour
Poultry stuffing
8 oz onions
8 oz tomatoes

4 oz streaky bacon rashers
Dripping
Stock
Salt and pepper

Joint the rabbit and soak in salt and water until blanched. Dry joints and toss in seasoned flour. Put joints in a fireproof dish and surround with balls of poultry stuffing. Cover the rabbit with sliced onions and tomatoes and top with bacon rashers. Dot with dripping, and brown in a hot oven for 20 minutes. Add stock to come half way up the dish, season well with salt and pepper, and cover with a lid. Cook at 325°F (Gas Mark 3) for 2 hours.

BAKED RABBIT

1 rabbit
1 lb onions
1 large carrot

Seasoning
2 oz dripping
Sage

Wash the jointed rabbit in salted water and dry thoroughly. Chop the onions and carrot, and put with the rabbit into a saucepan. Cover with water and simmer until almost cooked. Strain, keeping the stock. Put the rabbit and the vegetables into a baking-tin. Season, and add the dripping and a sprinkling of sage. Bake until browned, basting occasionally. Remove the rabbit joints and keep warm. Make gravy, using the pan juices and stock. Serve separately, or poured over the rabbit.

CURRIED RABBIT

2 fresh young rabbits
½ lb bacon
2 teaspoons butter, or good dripping
1 large sour apple

1 dessertspoon good curry powder
1 dessertspoon flour
1½ breakfastcups water
Salt to taste

Cut the rabbits into pieces sufficient for serving, wash well in salted water and dry; put the butter in a stewpan, and allow it to become hot. Have the bacon cut into small pieces and fry it. Remove cooked bacon to a plate, then fry the pieces of rabbit, which also remove when browned. Have the onions and apple finely chopped then fry these next. When soft crush into a pulp with the back of a wooden spoon, and carefully mix into this the curry powder and flour. Return the rabbit and bacon to the stewpan, and over them pour water, simmer gently for 2 hours, add a little lemon juice, and serve with boiled rice.

Rabbits were once upon a time the standby of many a farmhouse in midweek before the butcher's weekly call on a Friday. Some farmers were so up against it in the hard times before World War II that rabbits, which were thick upon the ground, had to be eaten more than once a week. The farmer's wife would be hard put to it to serve the meat in an acceptable fashion, after a while, as her family would be heartily sick of rabbit in any shape or form. Farmers don't take kindly to 'foreign' dishes but if she didn't overdo the curry powder, she might get away with this dish, for a change.

FRICASSEE OF RABBIT (1)

1 *rabbit*	1 *or 2 strips celery*
½ *pint milk*	1½ *oz flour*
6 *white peppercorns*	1 *blade of mace*
1 *carrot*	*Salt and pepper*
2 *onions*	*White stock*
2 *oz butter*	*Bouquet garni*

Cut the rabbit into neat joints, rinse in warm water, place in a saucepan, and add enough white stock to cover. Bring to the boil and add the washed, prepared vegetables, sliced, the peppercorns and a little salt. Simmer for about 1¼ hours, or until the rabbit is tender, adding a little milk from time to time to replace reduced stock. Melt the butter, add the flour, and stir to a smooth paste. Take out the rabbit and keep hot; strain ¾ pint of the stock on to the flour, stir until boiling, and boil 3 or 4 minutes. Rub the vegetables through a fine sieve, and stir the purée into the sauce. Season to taste, replace the rabbit, and heat through thoroughly. Serve at once.

FRICASSEE OF RABBIT (2)

1 *rabbit*
1 *onion*
2 *oz butter*
½ *pint milk*
4 *mushrooms*
2 *oz flour*

½ *pint white stock*
Bouquet garni
Seasoning
1 *teaspoon lemon juice*
Bacon rolls

Cut the rabbit into neat pieces. Put into a pan with the onion, mushrooms, seasoning and stock and the bouquet garni. Bring to boiling point, cover and cook gently on the simmering side for 10 minutes, then continue cooking for a further 2–2½ hours either gently simmering on top of the stove, or transfer to a gentle oven. Put the meat in a hot dish and keep hot; strain the liquor, melt the butter in the pan, add the flour and cook for a few minutes. Add the strained liquor and milk and stir until the sauce is thickened and boiled. Add the lemon juice and pour over the meat. Garnish with the bacon rolls, lemon, parsley and fried croûtons.

TO FRICASSEE RABBITS BROWN

2 *young rabbits*
Pepper and salt
Flour and butter
1 *pint gravy*
Bunch of sweet herbs

½ *pint fresh mushrooms if*
you have them
3 *shallots*
Spoon of ketchup
1 *lemon*

Take 2 young rabbits, cut them in small pieces, slit the heads in two, season them with pepper and salt, dip them in flour, and fry them a nice brown in fresh butter. Pour out the fat from the pan, and put in 1 pint of gravy, a bunch of sweet herbs, ½ pint of fresh mushrooms if you have them, and 3 shallots chopped fine, season with pepper and salt, cover them close, and let them stew for ½ hour. Then skim the gravy clean, add a spoonful of ketchup, and the juice of ½ lemon. Take out the herbs and stir in a piece of butter rolled in flour, boil it up till it thickens and is smooth, skim off the fat, and serve the rabbits garnished with lemon.

RABBIT STEWED IN MILK

Select a nice rabbit, thoroughly wash and dry it, cut it into small joints, place in a stewpan with about 1½ lb of pickled pork, a large onion stuck with cloves, a blade of mace, a bunch of savoury herbs. Cover it with milk, let it boil, then draw the saucepan to the side and let it simmer gently for 1½ hours. When done, place on a hot dish, strain the liquid, thicken it with flour, and add some finely chopped parsley. Pour over the rabbit and send to table.

Mrs Thorne, 1911

IRISH ROAST RABBIT

1 *rabbit*	**½ *pint scalded milk***
4 *rashers bacon*	**Pepper**
2 *medium onions*	**1 *dessertspoon chopped***
1 *tablespoon flour*	***parsley***
2 *oz butter*	

Cut up rabbit and soak in vinegar and water. Dry pieces well and coat in flour seasoned with pepper. Brown in the butter and put into a casserole. Add chopped bacon, onions and parsley and pour over milk. Cover and bake at 375°F (Gas Mark 5) for 1 hour. Serve with plenty of floury potatoes. Parsley sauce is also good with this.

RABBIT BRAWN

1 *rabbit*	***Pinch of ground cloves***
2 *carrots*	***Sprig of thyme***
2 *onions*	**2 *hard-boiled eggs***
Salt and pepper	**2 *oz gelatine***
Pinch of nutmeg	

Cut up rabbit and simmer until tender in 3 pints of water with diced carrots and onions, seasoning, spices and thyme. Rinse a mould with cold water and decorate the bottom with slices of hard-boiled egg. Cool the cooked rabbit and cut meat into small pieces. Dissolve the gelatine in a little water, then add it to the rabbit stock and boil. Strain over the rabbit meat and leave in a cold place to set. This is much improved if a little cooked ham, bacon or stewing beef is added.

RABBIT WITH ONION SAUCE

1 *rabbit*	**3 *oz butter***
3 *lb onions*	***Some thick cream***

Rabbit and onions have an affinity for each other. This dish goes very well with jacket potatoes. Joint and soak rabbit, then cook in boiling water with seasoning, reducing to simmering heat and cooking for about 1½ hours until tender, depending on the age of the rabbit. Cut rabbit in pieces and serve covered with onion sauce. Make this by cutting onions very finely and stewing gently in butter until they are very soft but not brown, keeping lid on the pan and stirring frequently. Add $\frac{3}{4}$ pint rabbit stock, season again to taste, and stir in some thick, hot cream before pouring over rabbit.

HUNTER'S RABBIT

1 rabbit
1 small hard cabbage
1 lb chipolata sausages
4 bacon rashers
Thyme, parsley and bayleaf

Salt and pepper
1 small onion
$\frac{1}{4}$ pint stock (made with a beef cube)
$\frac{1}{2}$ pint dry cider

Cut rabbit in pieces and soak, then dry thoroughly. Cut cabbage lengthways into 6 or 8 pieces, and boil in very little water for 5 minutes, draining well. Fry sausages and sliced onion. Put cabbage in a casserole, then put in rabbit pieces, followed by sausages and onion, and the chopped, uncooked bacon. Add herbs and seasoning, pour in stock and cider, and cover tightly. Cook at 325°F (Gas Mark 3) for $2\frac{1}{2}$ hours.

JUGGED RABBIT

1 rabbit
1 onion
1 bayleaf
Salt and pepper

Pinch of nutmeg
1 teaspoon sugar
$\frac{1}{2}$ pint dry cider

Soak rabbit joints overnight in 1 pint water with 2 tablespoons vinegar, together with chopped onion, bayleaf, salt and pepper and nutmeg. Drain joints, keeping the liquid, and dry joints well. Fry rabbit in dripping or bacon fat until golden, then cover with liquid and simmer gently until tender (about 1 hour). Add sugar and cider to pan and continue cooking for 15 minutes. Thicken gravy with a little flour or cornflour, and serve with forcemeat balls and redcurrant jelly.

MOCK HARE

Soak rabbit joints overnight in equal parts of vinegar and water, with 1 bayleaf, a chopped onion, salt and pepper and a pinch of grated nutmeg. Take out the joints, drain and dry, and fry till golden. Pour on the liquid and stew slowly till tender. 30 minutes before serving time, add $\frac{1}{2}$ pint cider, and just before serving thicken the gravy with flour or cornflour. Serve with redcurrant jelly and forcemeat balls.

RABBIT WITH LENTILS

Soak ¼ lb lentils in water overnight. Put 1 oz finely chopped bacon into a saucepan and fry till the fat runs; add 1 small chopped onion, and soften without browning. Stir in the lentils and any water remaining, and simmer gently till soft, adding a little more water if necessary to prevent burning. Put through a sieve. Pour ¼ pint cider over the rabbit, add a bunch of mixed herbs, salt and pepper, and simmer with the lid on till it is tender. Add the rabbit liquid to the sieved lentils, simmer till thick, then add the pieces of bacon and rabbit. Serve very hot, accompanied by a green vegetable or a salad.

RABBIT IN CIDER

Joint and soak the rabbit with a good squeeze of lemon juice in the water for an hour, then dry well. Fry the rabbit till brown in bacon fat, and add 4 large sliced onions. Cook till the onions are soft, and add 1 bayleaf, a sprig of thyme, 2 oz chopped bacon and ½ lb peeled sliced tomatoes. Simmer for 10 minutes, then pour on ¼ pint of dry cider. Simmer with the lid on till the rabbit is tender, and season with salt and pepper just before serving, removing the bayleaf.

GLOUCESTER RABBIT

Though this is one of the most simple ways of cooking rabbit, it is extremely tasty because of the preliminary frying of the onions. Joint and soak the rabbit, then dry very well and roll in flour. Melt plenty of butter, and brown the rabbit all over. Put rabbit pieces in a casserole and use the butter for frying 2 lb thinly sliced onions. When the onions are golden, pour in a little stock or water, stir well, pour over the rabbit pieces and cover the casserole tightly. Put in a slow oven for 2½ hours.

RABBIT BRAWN

Cover 2 pig's feet with water and gently cook for 1½ hours. Then put in a jointed rabbit, previously soaked for an hour. Boil together for 2 hours till the meat is tender, adding a little more water if required. Remove all bones, cut meat into neat pieces, and season with salt, pepper and nutmeg. Boil together again for 15 minutes, then pour into moulds or basins well rinsed with cold water. Leave overnight before turning out and serve with salad, or in sandwiches.

A NEW CURRIED RABBIT

1 *young rabbit*
1 *onion chopped*
1 *tablespoon each lemon juice and curry powder*
3 *tablespoons chopped coconut*

1 *teaspoon each sugar and salt*
1 *cup white stock or water*
½ *cup milk*
Boiled rice

Joint rabbit, wash thoroughly and dry each piece upon a clean cloth. Fry a light brown in butter if possible, remove from pan, fry onion, add curry powder, coconut, sugar, salt, milk and stock or water, put in the rabbit and simmer 1 hour; add lemon juice and serve surrounded with rice.

Mary Bull, 1914

TO ROAST A SWAN (1)

Take 2 lb rump steak – chop it fine and season it well with spice, and add a slice of butter; then stuff with the above, taking care to sew the bird up carefully, and let it be tied tightly on the spit so that the gravy may not escape. Enclose the breast of the swan in a meal paste. Afterwards cover the whole bird with paper, well greased with butter. A ¼ hour before it is taken up, remove the paper and paste. Baste well with butter and flour till it is brown and frothy. A swan of 15 lb weight will require 2¼ hours roasting, with a fire not too fierce. To be served up with gravy and redcurrant jelly. *The swan is not to be skinned.*

Mrs Garden, 1847

TO ROAST A SWAN (2)

Take three pounds of beef, beat fine in a mortar.
Put it into the swan (that is when you've caught her).
Some pepper, salt, mace, some nutmeg, an onion,
Will heighten the flavour in gourman'd opinion.
Then tie it up tight with a small piece of tape,
That the gravy and other things may not escape.
A meal paste, rather stiff, should be laid on the breast,
And some whited brown paper should cover the rest.
Fifteen minutes, at least, ere the swan you take down,
Put the paste off the bird, that the breast may get brown.

Mrs Garden, 1847

In Norfolk there is a book recording the 'swan marks' of the peerage and gentry and the Public Record Office has records of marks from other countries. These were intricate patterns made on the beaks of the birds to indicate ownership. Swan was certainly eaten from the middle of the fifteenth century, and always formed part of the feasting in great houses, or for special events. As late as 1931, the Master, Great Hospital, Norwich, was offering cygnets (young swans) dressed for dinner and banquets, or alive for ornamental waters, through an advertisement in *The Times*. The great cook Francatelli gave a recipe in the 1850s for a Norwich-fed cygnet, so it would seem these were certainly superior birds. Cygnets were usually used, and in best condition in September. They were often cooked in the same way as geese.

TRUSSED WOODCOCK

In trussing the woodcock great care must be taken not to tear the tender skin. It must be well plucked, and the head and neck also. Do not draw the bird; cut off the ends of the toes after singeing the hairs. Bring the feet upon the thighs by twisting the legs at the joints. Press the wings to the sides, and the head under one wing, with the beak forward. The legs and breast must have a string tied round them, and also round the head and tip of bill. The bird must hang from the spit feet downwards.

ROAST WOODCOCK

These birds require little time for cooking, as all dark fleshed game is digestible when almost raw, therefore they must not be left from the time they are put down till the time they are taken up. The legs require more cooking than the breast, and this latter should be underdone – very underdone. To obviate this inequality in the cooking, the spit should be stopped while the legs are turned to the fire, constant attention being given to the roasting, when the woodcock are plucked, necks and heads also, they must not be opened but trussed securely. Cover the woodcocks with slices of bacon, put them before a clear fire, nicely bright, feet downwards, fastened to the spit; sprinkle them with flour and baste them continually. Prepare some buttered toast without crust, and when the birds have been down about 5 minutes, place this under them to catch the drippings. When basting hold a dish under them, and they will be sufficiently cooked when the steam draws to the fire. Serve with a piece of the toast under each, garnish with watercress and send to the table with some melted butter.

DEVILLED WOODCOCK

Take a brace of woodcocks that are underdone, and divide them up into joints. Make a savoury powder with $1\frac{1}{2}$ teaspoons of curry powder, $1\frac{1}{2}$

teaspoons salt, 1½ teaspoons of cayenne, and 1½ dessertspoons of mushroom powder. Mix all thoroughly together and well cover the joints with this. Take the brains after splitting the heads, and put them in a basin with the grated rind of a lemon, the yolk of a hardboiled egg, the trail, a pinch of pounded mace, and a tablespoon of soy. Rub the mixture with a spoon until it is quite smooth, and add two dessertspoons of ketchup, the juice of 1½ Seville oranges, and a glass of Madeira. Put the sauce with the birds into a fireproof dish over a gentle fire, and let it simmer very closely until the flesh is thoroughly impregnated with the sauce, stir in 2 teaspoons of salad oil, and serve.

ROAST WOODCOCK

1 *woodcock (per person)*   **½ *lb butter***
1 *piece of toast*

Do not clean out the inside of the woodcock. Skewer its beak through its body. Tie over its breast a piece of fat bacon. Fill it with butter. Heat some butter in a baking dish. Put in a piece of toast. On that put the woodcock and cook it for 10 minutes. Cut off the bacon and string. Cook for another 5 minutes. Pour the juices of the pan over the bird.

WILD DUCK

Under the provision of the Protection of Birds Act 1954, some wild duck are protected by special penalties during the close season, i.e. common scoter, gargany teal, golden eye, long tailed duck, scaup-duck and velvet scoter. Wild duck that may be killed or taken outside the season are the common pochard, gadwall, mallard, pintail, shoveller, teal, tufted duck and widgeon.

ROAST WILD DUCK

Wipe and dry bird. If so desired they can be stuffed with skinned quarter oranges. Season with salt and pepper and place a knob of butter inside. Truss and place on a rack in a baking tin. Roast in hot oven for 30 minutes. Don't overcook. Baste frequently. Dredge with flour then baste again. Serve with orange salad.

If fishy taste is disliked, cover a deep roasting tin to a depth of ½ inch with boiling salted water, put the bird in and bake it for 10 minutes, basting frequently with the salt water.

SALMI OF DUCK, TEAL OR MALLARD

1 *mallard*	1 *oz flour*
4 *oz bacon*	½ *pint stock*
1 *onion*	*Glass of red wine*
Bouquet garni and 1 *bayleaf*	*Few black olives*
Walnut of butter	

Wild duck can carry an unmistakable taste of fish if it has been feeding on salt marshes, so cook it slowly with bay leaves and a glass of red wine.

Dice the bacon and fry lightly, add a bayleaf and the herbs, then transfer half the contents of the pan to a fireproof dish and the rest to a baking tin. Put the bird in the baking tin on the chopped bacon and slice into the tin a large onion. Cover the bird with fat or lard, seeing that the breast particularly is protected so that it does not dry out while cooking. Bake for 20 minutes in a medium oven, 350°F (Gas Mark 4) then remove the bird and slice off all the meat. Have ready the fireproof dish with the rest of the bacon, add the fillets. Make a sauce with the fat, flour, stock and claret, pour this over the meat in the casserole, adding the stoned olives at the same time. Put into a slow oven to cook for a further 30 minutes. Serve just as it is from the dish, with plain boiled potatoes and mixed vegetables.

ROAST SNIPE

2 *snipe*	2 *slices toast*
2 *pieces bacon*	1½ *oz butter*

Snipe, plover and woodcock are dressed without being drawn, truss for roasting, but skin head and leave it on. Wipe dry and place in a baking tin. Cover with bacon. Stand them on a rack in the tin with pieces of toast underneath. Roast for 25-30 minutes, in very moderate oven. Serve on the toast garnished with watercress.

POACHED SNIPE

4 *snipe*	4 *thick slices bread*
½ *lb butter*	

Poach the snipe for 12 minutes in water. Drain and put on the toasted bread. Pour over foaming hot butter.

ROAST TEAL

These birds should be plucked, drawn and trussed like wild duck. Dredge them with flour liberally, put them down to a brisk fire, but do not baste them for the first 3 or 4 minutes, as this will help to keep the gravy in;

after this baste continually. When they are nicely browned, which should be in about 15 minutes, and when the steam draws to the fire, place them in a hot dish with some good brown gravy round them, but not over them, and send some gravy to the table in a tureen. Also send a cut lemon to table, and at the moment of serving sprinkle a little cayenne on the breast, and a squeeze of lemon juice.

ROAST QUAILS

When the birds are firmly trussed a slice of fat bacon should be tied over each, and a vine leaf underneath, if procurable, to correct its deficiency of flavour. If the birds are not drawn they should be served on pieces of toast, which have been placed in the pan 5 minutes after the cooking has commenced. Roast before a clear fire for about 15 minutes, basting continually. Place the quails on the toasts in the centre of a hot dish, pour some good brown gravy round, not over, the quails, and garnish with watercress.

GUINEA FOWL

The guinea fowl forms a convenient substitute for game (says an early Victorian cookbook) as it is in season from February to June. It is rather like pheasant when well-kept, in appearance and taste, and the flesh digestible and savoury.

ROAST GUINEA FOWL

The guinea fowl may be trussed like a young turkey, with the head left on, or like a pheasant, then larded and filled with a good forcemeat. Put it before a clear fire, and to prevent it becoming dry it must be continually basted. Let it cook for about 1 hour, dredge a little flour over it a few minutes before it is taken up, let it froth nicely, and send it to table with bread sauce and gravy.

GUINEA FOWL BOILED WITH OYSTERS

Empty the fowl in the usual way, and dredge 2 dozen oysters with flour; add 2 oz butter, some salt and pepper, and place inside the fowl. Put it into a close fitting jar, and cover with a strong stock or gravy. Place the jar in a saucepan of boiling water, and let it boil very fast for about 2 hours. When the fowl is tender remove it from the jar, drain the liquor and cover it with white sauce or parsley and butter sauce.

VENISON

In Season: Late June to January

The meat should be hung 8–10 days, and is best larded or put into a marinade of wine and herbs before roasting, as there is little fat (a larding needle costs about 5p and is used to thread the meat with strips of fat bacon or pork). Large joints are best roasted; smaller and unidentifiable pieces are best stewed. Chops and fillet may be grilled, and cutlets can be jugged. Cold venison makes excellent cottage pie, or a good galantine if pressed in a mould with plenty of seasoning. Traditional accompaniments are redcurrant, rowan or cranberry jelly.

ROAST VENISON

1 joint venison
½ pint red wine
½ pint vinegar

1 sliced onion
Parsley, thyme and bayleaf

Mix together the wine, vinegar, onion and herbs, and put the venison in it to soak for 2 days, turning the meat from time to time. When ready to cook the meat, put the joint on a rack in a baking tin, with the marinade in the tin. Cook at 375°F (Gas Mark 5) until meat is tender, basting frequently. Strain the pan juices through a sieve, thicken with a little flour, and, if liked, a gill of sour cream or yoghurt.

ROAST VENISON (ROE DEER)

Depending on the weather and whether the beast has been shot that day or bought from a butcher, hang it for 4 days at least in an airy place. We used to have a 'Game Larder' made of perforated zinc, like a bird cage, hanging on the wall outside with a solid roof to keep out the rain and lots of hooks on a beam across the ceiling. If the weather is sultry don't hang it longer than 4 days, but if frosty it is perfectly all right to leave it for 3 weeks – but do watch it and unless you like it strong, 2 weeks is enough, even when the temperature is low. Don't worry about grey mould; it doesn't harm the meat.

When you decide it is time to cook it, take a leg or a saddle for roasting. Wipe it all over with a cloth wrung out in a mixture of permanganate of potash and water, ½ teaspoon to a pint, or salt and water with 1 dessertspoon to a pint. Either spread the joint with butter or wrap it in bacon, wrap it in greaseproof/foil or put it in a self-basting roasting tin – a lid with dimples in. Venison is a very dry meat and care must be taken or it will be uneatable. Roast at a temperature of between 350° and 450°F. If young and well hung at 450°F at 20 minutes per lb., if old and not hung for long at 350°F for 30 minutes per lb. ½ hour before the end of roasting time take the wrappings off the meat to let it get brown on the outside.

Take it out of the tin and lay on a hot dish and to the juices in the pan add 1 glass port, a pinch of mace, 6 peppercorns, a bayleaf and a teaspoon of redcurrant jelly or rowan jelly which has a more bitter flavour. Leave to simmer – add a little stock if necessary. Venison gravy should not be thick.

Mrs Chaplin, Finsthwaite, Lancs

NEW FOREST VENISON ROLL

2 lb venison
½ lb fat bacon
Salt and pepper
Stock or water (to mix)

6 oz breadcrumbs
1 tablespoon chopped parsley
2 eggs

Mince the venison and bacon, add the onion finely chopped, seasonings, breadcrumbs and chopped parsley. Beat the eggs and add to the former ingredients. Add sufficient stock to bind. Flour a pudding cloth and place the mixture on it in a long roll, wrap up, tie the ends with string and boil for 2½ hours. Serve with brown gravy and cranberry or redcurrant jelly. Rowanberry jelly is also good with this dish.

NORMANDY VENISON

Venison is always better if it is marinaded before cooking. This dish should be made with the haunch.

Make a marinade with 1 pint cider, 1 gill wine vinegar, a sprig of parsley and thyme, 1 bayleaf, 2 crushed cloves of garlic, 2 carrots and 2 onions cut in rounds and fried in olive oil until golden, salt and pepper. Mix the marinade and leave the venison in it for at least 4 days.

Drain the joint, cover it with a few rashers of fat bacon and roast it in a hot oven, allowing 10–15 minutes per lb. Halfway through cooking-time, baste with a wine glass of Calvados or brandy, mixed with the juice of ½ lemon and 6 tablespoons of the marinade. While the meat is cooking make a purée of cooking apples with a little of the marinade (add no sugar). Make a gravy with the juices from the meat, a little of the marinade and ½ gill fresh cream. Serve surrounded with apple purée.

VENISON ROAST IN FOIL

Joint of venison
Dripping

A little flour

Rub the meat all over with clarified fat or dripping and wrap in grease-proof paper. Then wrap in foil. Roast by the slow roast method in a moderate oven, 350°F (Gas Mark 4) for 3–4 hours according to the size of joint (40 minutes to the pound) basting often. ½ hour before serving, take off all coverings, dredge with flour, raise the heat of the oven and baste.

VENISON STEWED IN ALE

Venison—stewing cuts   *2 tablespoons black treacle*
½ lb demerara sugar   *1 pint beer*

Dissolve the sugar and treacle in the beer. Put the well-hung meat into a stewpan or casserole, cover with the liquid, put on the lid and bring to the boil. Simmer gently until tender, the time of the cooking being approximately 30 minutes to the pound and 30 minutes over.

ROAST HAUNCH OF VENISON (1)

The joint is best if kept as long as possible before cooking, and to ensure it being in a good condition it must be examined every day. The kernel of the fat should be removed and the parts from which it is taken then wiped dry, and this as well as the whole haunch should be dusted with pepper and powdered ginger. The fatter the meat the better, and to preserve the fat the haunch should be covered with white cartridge paper, well-greased and then with a stiff paste of flour and water rolled out to the thickness of ¾ inch. Tie securely over this with a string or tape 2 additional sheets of greased paper. Put the haunch down to a clear fire, near at first to harden the paste, draw it back after a minute or two, and gradually bring it nearer again. Baste it continually to prevent the outer paper from burning, until the meat is done sufficiently. Remove the paper and paste, sprinkle a little salt on the meat, dredge it with a little flour, and then baste with a tablespoon of dissolved butter. Make a little brown gravy with the fat etc. from the dripping tin, season with salt and pepper and a squeeze of lemon, and strain it over the venison on the dish. Send redcurrant jelly to table with it. The dish and all the plates must be very hot, as the fat of venison hardens very quickly. The time required to roast is from 10 to 15 minutes for each pound in weight.

ROAST HAUNCH OF VENISON (2)

Time – 3 to 4 hours. Haunch from 20 to 25 lb.
This joint is trimmed by cutting off part of the knuckle and sawing off the chine bone, then the flap is folded over, and it is covered in a paste made of flour and water. This paste should be about an inch thick. Stand the

haunch in a suitable roasting dish and cover the paste with dripping. Place in a hot oven to cook the paste but reduce the heat immediately the paste hardens. Baste frequently as venison has very little fat of its own. After 3 to 4 hours, according to the size, test the venison with a thin skewer, running it well in to see if it is done enough, if not, return it to the oven for further cooking. When it is 'dressed' glaze the top and salamander it. Put a frill round the knuckle and serve very hot with strong gravy. Redcurrant jelly in a glass dish or a tureen. Vegetables: French beans.

NECK OF VENISON

Time – ¼ hour per lb.
Cover it with paste and paper as for the haunch, fix it on a spit and roast.
To hash venison: some cold roast venison; wineglass port wine, a little mutton broth; half a shallot; a pinch of cayenne pepper; 1½ oz of butter; a spoonful flour; and salt to taste.
Cut some slices of cold roast venison, nicely, and season them lightly with salt; put the bones, trimmings, any cold gravy from the venison, the shallot etc. and as much broth as you may require into a stewpan, and let it simmer for quite an hour, but slowly, then strain it off. Stir the butter and flour over the fire until sufficiently brown to colour the gravy, taking care it does not burn. Pour the gravy from the bones and the port wine onto it, and let it simmer until it boils. Then draw the stewpan to the side of the fire and put in the slices of venison, and when thoroughly *hot* serve it up, with redcurrant jelly in a glass dish. Garnish with forcemeat balls about the size of a marble.

BRAISED SHOULDER OF VENISON

Remove the bone from a well-hung shoulder of venison, and marinade the meat in equal parts of vinegar and water, with a bunch of savoury herbs. Let it remain in this 3 or 4 days, then chop up 1 large onion, 1 shallot, ½ lb fat bacon, 3 cloves and 3 oz of butter. Let this fry in an earthenware brazing pan; lay the venison on top, squeeze over it the juice of ½ lemon, cover closely, place it in a moderate oven for 3 hours. Just before serving, add a glass of sherry and a teacup of cream. Let it cook a further 10 minutes, and place on a very hot dish, strain the gravy over it, and serve.

STEWED VENISON

Take the remains of a roast haunch of venison, cut it up into small pieces, place it in an earthenware pan with 2 glasses of port wine, a small bayleaf, and the gravy that was left over. Let it stew gently for 15 minutes, and serve it with croûtons of toast and with redcurrant jelly.

VENISON RISSOLES (from the Scottish Highlands)

Roll out some puff paste or shortcrust paste, stamp out in circular pieces, put a teaspoon of minced venison in the centre, brush the edges with beaten egg, fold over to form a half-circle, and press the edges firmly together. Brush over with egg, dip in breadcrumbs and fry in smoking fat to a light golden brown. Drain and garnish with parsley, fried for 1 minute in the fat and then well-drained.

CHESTNUT PURÉE

2 lb chestnuts	**Butter**
½ onion	**Cream**

Slit the chestnuts on the flat side and boil them for 15–20 minutes. Chop the onion finely and cook it in butter. Add the peeled chestnuts and mash them with a fork. Put through a sieve or mill. Melt some butter in a saucepan and add the purée. Season. Add some cream.

BREADCRUMBS

6 slices stale white bread with the crust on.
Leave the slices of bread in a slow oven or the plate drawer to make them hard. Crush them with a rolling pin. Brown in butter. Dry on blotting paper. Keep warm in oven.

FRIED CRUMBS

Some people like to serve fried crumbs with game. Simply melt a lump of butter, about the size of a pigeon's egg, in the heavy frying pan then stir in a cupful of breadcrumbs until evenly blended and cook gently until golden brown all over.

BREAD SAUCE

Take 3 or 4 nice firm onions and cut them with the sign of the cross without scoring right through to their base. In 1 onion, stick 6, 8 or more cloves and remember to account for each one later! In a suitable saucepan pour a little hot water and add 1 oz butter, 1 level teaspoon salt and a good shake of pepper. Place the onions in this and then pour in sufficient milk to nearly cover the onions – the saucepan should be as small as possible in order that too much liquid is not necessary. Cook the onions slowly and carefully – this takes some time according to the texture of the onions. Meanwhile, remove all crust from 4–6 oz of white bread and soak it in a little hot water; when this is all absorbed add a little milk and leave to continue soaking until the onions are really soft and well-cooked, then pour off the onion milk on to the soaking bread. Remove the exact number of cloves and mash the onion with a fork. Add the bread and milk and if liked another knob of butter. Beat well with the electric beater until smooth and creamy and season to taste. Serve in a hot sauce boat.

Mrs Rene Woodhouse

BREAD SAUCE (2)

1 onion
Salt, pepper and nutmeg
1 pint milk

1 cup dried breadcrumbs
Cream

Chop the onion and cook it in milk till it is soft, adding salt, pepper and nutmeg. Add the breadcrumbs and more milk. Just before serving, add some cream.

TO MAKE GAME GRAVY

Take the giblets, bones and any trimmings and just cover with cold water. Add salt and pepper, onions, a bayleaf, any available fresh herbs such as thyme, parsley etc. a clove or two, and a pinch of allspice. Bring carefully to the boil and then simmer well until quantity is reduced. Pour off the fat from the roasting tin, then rinse the tin with a little of the game stock and add to the gravy. Boil again and skim if necessary.

FORCEMEAT STUFFING

For hares and rabbits. Soak some bread, from which all crust has been cut, in a little milk or milk and water. Chop up 1 small onion quite finely and fry in hot pan in which has been cooked small, cut-up pieces of left-over rashers of bacon. Pour off fat if too plentiful, retaining about 2 table-spoons in pan with bacon, now nicely browned, and onion softened but not browned. Beat up an egg, if liked, and add to the mashed-up, lump-free bread, which has been squeezed free of surplus liquid, of milk, or milk and water. To the egg and bread add the onions and bacon with the dripping in which they were fried, season well with salt and pepper and add fresh chopped thyme and parsley, or mixed dried herbs, as required for personal preference, and as available; add a little grated lemon rind or pure lemon juice. Mix all together very thoroughly. If mixture is too soft, a little flour or a few more breadcrumbs may be added to make a better texture for stuffing. Season according to taste. Leave to soak in together, for a while before using, but cover with plate to keep 'bouquet' from evaporating into thin air.

8 Pies

Simple Simon met a pieman going to the Fair
Nursery Rhyme

Little Jack Horner
Sat in a corner
Eating his Christmas pie

Nursery Rhyme

Sing a song of sixpence,
A pocketful of rye,
Four-and-twenty blackbirds
Baked in a pie.
When the pie was opened,
The birds began to sing.
Wasn't that a dainty dish
To set before a King?

Nursery Rhyme

Who can doubt the popularity of the British pie, when we have been singing about it for hundreds of years? All farming families love pastry, and every farm wife knows that a lid or case of melting pastry can transform the dullest meat or the plainest fruit into a luxury dish which is also filling.

For *Shortcrust Pastry*, half as much fat as flour is needed, and the flour rubbed in with the fingertips. For the richer types, *Rough Puff* and *Flaky*, the fat is rolled in, and lemon juice is added (for rough puff, use 4–6 oz fat to 8 oz flour and 2 teaspoons lemon juice; for flaky pastry, use 6 oz fat to the same amount of flour and lemon juice). *Hot Water Pastry* uses one-third as much fat as flour, and the fat is melted before adding, while an egg yolk is an optional extra.

Basically, a good quality plain flour should be used, and everything kept as cool as possible. Rich pastry needs 'resting' in a cold place between rollings, or before use. Dry ingredients should be sieved to incorporate air and lighten the mixture. Water should be added all at once to make the mixture bind without being sticky. Pastry should be rolled lightly, but firmly, rolling on one side only. A hot oven is necessary, the richer the pastry the hotter the oven being a good general rule; the temperature can be decreased as soon as the pastry is firm and brown. A professional finish makes all the difference to savoury pies. For meat pies and patties and sausage rolls, brush over before baking with beaten egg, or egg yolk mixed with a little water.

Fillings can be varied endlessly to suit the family taste and purse. Small pies for the lunch-box can be filled with leftover meat, egg, cheese or fish mixtures; a thick white sauce or good gravy should be used for binding the mixtures.

For supper-time, the favourite bacon and egg pie can be improved with the addition of a few mushrooms or with slices of pork sausage. Again, cooked bacon and hard-boiled egg may be combined in a creamy sauce to give variety.

For more formal occasions, the traditional steak pie can appear in many disguises. Pieces of pigeon or game can be included, hard-boiled eggs, diced vegetables, mushrooms, forcemeat balls, kidneys, or even a few canned oysters. This type of pie is delicious if the meat is rolled round a forcemeat filling and packed firmly into the pie-dish with some onions and a quantity of strong beef stock.

Chicken pies are a useful way of using the odd old boiler, or of eking out the remains of a roast bird. One mixture can be a combination of chopped, cooked chicken and ham, onion and hard-boiled eggs and small forcemeat balls, with plenty of herbs and good chicken stock, and a topping of flaky pastry. This use of good stock and plenty of herbs is always important in a chicken pie.

INSTRUCTIONS FOR PASTRY MAKERS, 1870

We believe it is utterly impossible to teach verbally how to make good paste or pie-crust; a lesson from a good cook would be worth whole volumes on this subject. Some general directions, however, may be given on this important art. First, the cook should have smooth *cold* hands – very clean – for making paste or crust. She should wash them well, and plunge them in cold water for a minute or two in hot weather, drying them well afterwards before beginning her paste.

The pastry slab, if possible, should be made of marble; if it is a wooden paste-board, it should be kept scrupulously clean.

The crust used for homely pies need not be as delicate as that used for company; it may be made of clarified beef dripping or lard instead of butter.

Be very careful about the proper heat of the oven for baking pies, as if it be too cold the paste will be heavy, and have a dull look; if too hot, the crust will burn before the pie is done.

Try if the oven is hot enough by holding your hand inside it for a few seconds; if you can do so without snatching it out again quickly, it is too cold; it is best, however, to try it by baking a little piece of the crust in it first.

Always make a small hole with a knife at the top of the pie to allow the gases generated in it by the cooking to escape. This aperture is also useful for pouring gravy into the pie when it is done, if more is required. The hand of a pastrycook should be light, and the paste should not be worked more than is absolutely required for mixing it.

We give first three plain receipts for pie crust, such as people of small means can use, and will find good, and also instructions for clarifying dripping, so as to render it fit for making pie-crusts.

To Clarify Beef Dripping

Put the dripping into a basin, pour over it some boiling water, and stir it round with a silver spoon; set it cool, and then remove the dripping from the sediment, and put it into basins or jars for use in a cool place. Clarified dripping may be used for frying and basting, everything except game or poultry, as well as for pies etc.

To Make a Short Crust with Dripping

1 lb flour
¾ lb clarified beef dripping

1 wineglass of very cold water
Pinch of salt

Take care that the water you use is cold, especially in summer. Cut the flour, well dried, into a large basin (which should be kept for the purpose) with a pinch of salt; break up the clarified beef dripping into pieces, and mix them *well* with the flour, rubbing both together till you have a fine powder. Then make a hole in the middle of the flour, and pour in water enough to make a smooth and flexible paste. Sprinkle the pasteboard with flour, and your hands also, take out the lump of paste, roll it out, fold it together again, and roll it out – i.e. roll it 3 times; the last time it should be the thickness required for your crust, that is, about ¼ inch or even thinner. It is then ready for use.

Or, a still Plainer Crust for Children

1 lb flour   **Cup of water**
5-6 oz clarified beef dripping

Put the flour into a bowl, and work it into a smooth paste with about a cupful of water. Divide the clarified dripping into 3 parts, roll out the paste, and put over it, in rows, one portion of the dripping broken into pieces the size of a bean; flour it, fold over the edges, and again roll it; repeat this folding, spreading and rolling 3 times, dredging a very little flour over the paste and rolling-pin each time. It will be fit for any common purpose, or for children.

Common Puff Paste

1 lb sifted flour   **½ teaspoon salt**
¼ lb lard   **½ lb butter**

Put 1 lb of sifted flour on the slab, or in an earthen basin, make a hollow in the centre, work into it a ¼ lb of lard and ½ a teaspoon of salt. When it is mixed through the flour, add as much cold water as will bind it together, then strew a little flour over the pasteboard or table; flour the rolling-pin, and roll out the paste to ½ inch in thickness; divide ½ lb of butter in 3 parts; spread evenly over the paste, fold it up, dredge a little flour over it and the paste-slab or table; roll it out again, spread another portion of the butter over, and fold and roll again; so continue until all the butter is used; roll it out to ¼ inch in thickness for use.

Mrs Giles, Shaftesbury, Dorset

BEEF AND BACON PIE

This is good hot or cold. Make it with cheap bacon pieces.

1 onion   **¼ pint water**
8 oz bacon pieces   **Pinch of fresh mixed herbs**
8 oz minced raw beef   **Salt and pepper**
1 tablespoon plain flour   **8 oz short pastry**

Chop the onion and bacon in small pieces, put in a heavy pan, and cook gently until the fat runs from the bacon, and the onion and bacon are soft and golden. Add the mince and cook until mince browns. Stir in flour mixed with a little water, and the rest of the water, herbs and seasonings and cook until mixture is thick and well blended. Roll pastry into 2 rounds and line an 8 inch pie plate. Put in filling, and cover with second round of pastry. Bake at 400°F (Gas Mark 6) for 30 minutes.

CHESHIRE PORK PIE (1)

Take the skin off the loin of pork, and cut it into steaks. Season them with pepper, salt and nutmeg, and make a good crust. Put into your dish a layer of pork, then a layer of pippins, pared and cored, and sugar sufficient to sweeten it. Then place another layer of pork, and put in a ½ pint of white wine. Lay some butter on the top, close your pie, and send it to the oven. If your pie is large, you must put in a pint of red wine.

Thomas Train, Gateshead, 1812

CHESHIRE PORK PIE [1870] (2)

Time to bake – 1½ hours

2 lb pork	**Pepper, salt and nutmeg**
3 oz butter	**½ pint white wine**
6-8 pippins (sweet apples)	**Enough puff paste**
2 oz sugar	

Take the skin and fat from a loin of pork, and cut it into thin steaks; season them with pepper, salt and nutmeg; line a pie-dish with puff paste, put in a layer of pork, then of pippins pared and cored, and about 2 oz sugar; then place in another layer of pork and a ½ pint of white wine, and lay some butter on top; cover it with puff paste, pass a knife through the top to leave an opening, cut the paste even with the dish, egg it once and bake it.

Mrs Giles, Shaftesbury, Dorset

ROMAN PIE

¾ lb pastry	**1 egg**
2 oz fine spaghetti or	**¼ teaspoon grated lemon rind**
vermicelli	**¼ pint white sauce**
1 lb cooking veal	**Salt, pepper and nutmeg**
¼ lb ham	**(grated)**

Well butter a dish and line it with the pastry right through. Throw the vermicelli into a pan of fast boiling salted water, and let it boil for 5 to 10 minutes, until it is tender; then drain well. Put a layer of vermicelli in the dish, pressing well round on the sides, so that it lines the pastry. Next put

147

in the meat cut into neat cubes, add the grated lemon rind, add a seasoning of pepper, salt and nutmeg. When the dish is full, pour in the sauce, cover the top with pastry as you would any pie, bake it for ¾ hour, loosen the edges, turn out the pie, brush over with beaten egg and return to the oven for a few minutes to set. Mutton or beef can be used instead of veal. It is delicious eaten hot or cold.

POTATO PIE

Allow as much meat per person as possible (4 oz per person is ample). Cook together stewing steak, onions (as required), potatoes, in water to cover, adding salt and pepper to taste. When meat is tender (1½–2 hours according to cut of meat used) take the dish out of oven (or turn into dish if stewed on top). Cover with a thickish crust of pastry and cook again until golden brown and cooked through. This is best cooked in oven from the start.

DORSET LAMBS' TAIL PIE

For those fortunate enough to find a good supply, put tails in bucket and sprinkle over a handful of salt. Cover completely with boiling water and leave to steep for 20 minutes or so. Then using very sharp pointed knife, cut sharply down length of tail to peel off outer skin and wool. Drop into cold salted water each tail as it is cleaned and finally drain all tails and cook immediately.

Take 2 lb (say) lambs' tails, 3 or 4 hard boiled eggs, 5 slices streaky bacon, salt and pepper and sweet herbs – thyme, parsley and marjoram. Place lambs' tails in sufficient water to cover and cook till tender, on a slow simmering heat. Onions may be added at this stage if liked.

Meanwhile make pastry using ½ lb lard to 1 lb self-raising flour with ¼ teaspoon salt dissolved in sufficient ice-cold water to make a firm paste. The secret is to rub fat into flour as little as possible leaving lumps of lard the size of marbles to be rolled into the paste to make air-flakes. This quantity is for a deeper dish, for a shallow flatter one use ¾ lb lard to 1½ lb flour. Put pastry aside to 'rest' in a cool place.

Remove cooked tails from liquor and arrange one layer in dish then cover with sliced hard-boiled eggs and bacon. Continue in this fashion until dish is full, then pour over liquor to which has been added salt and pepper to taste and chopped mixed sweet herbs. Cover whole with pastry rolled to required thickness and brush with egg yolk or milk. Cook in hot oven until pastry is beginning to turn colour, then reduce heat until pastry is golden brown. Cool slowly and preferably leave overnight. Serve cold with new potatoes and salad.

STEAK AND KIDNEY PIE (1)

1½ lb skirt of beef
6 oz ox kidney
1 oz seasoned flour
1 oz dripping
2 large onions or 8 pickling onions

¼ pint dry red wine
¼ pint stock
½ teaspoon dried thyme
1 bayleaf, crumbled
½ lb flaky pastry

Trim the meat and cut into approximately 1 inch pieces. Cut the kidney into pieces of about the same size. Discard the core. Dust the meat and kidney with well-seasoned flour. Heat the fat and brown the meat very slowly. Remove from the heat, pour over the red wine and the stock (or omit the wine and make up the total amount of liquid in stock). Add the thyme and the crushed bayleaf and additional salt and pepper if necessary. Allow to cool, and if possible stand for 2 to 3 hours (covered). Transfer to a pie dish. Cover with the pastry supported in the centre and sealed around the edges of the dish. Cut slits in the pastry cover. Decorate if wished and brush with a little milk or beaten egg to glaze. Place on a low shelf in the oven at 400°F (Gas Mark 6) and cook for about 20 minutes or until the pastry is golden brown. Cover the pie completely with grease-proof paper then reduce the oven heat to 300°F (Gas Mark 2) and continue cooking for a further 3 hours or until the meat is tender. If necessary additional stock may be added through the slits in the pastry during cooking.

STEAK AND KIDNEY PIE (2)

1½ lb steak and kidney (for 4)
1 small onion

Stock
Seasoned flour

Dice meat and roll in seasoned flour. Brown in hot dripping, add onion and cook all slowly until tender – approximately 1½ hours.

Pastry

8 oz flour (mix plain and wholemeal)
1 teaspoon baking powder

6 oz margarine and lard mixed
Salt

Rub in fats. Little water needed as fat proportion is high. Put meat in pie-dish and cover with pastry. Decorate top with leaves and 'flowers'; brush with egg or milk. Cook in hot oven for 1 hour or until pastry is well browned.

STEAK AND KIDNEY PLATE PIE

1 *lb stewing steak*	1 *oz fat*
$\frac{1}{4}$ *lb kidney*	1 *smallish onion*
1 *rounded tablespoon*	$\frac{1}{2}$ *pint water*
well-seasoned flour	1 *teaspoon made mustard*

Cut meat into small pieces and toss in seasoned flour. Fry the sliced onion slowly until brown. Move to one side and brown the meat lightly in the fat. Add the water; cover and simmer very gently for $1\frac{1}{2}$ to 2 hours. Stir in mustard and correct seasoning to taste.

Take 6 oz plain flour, $\frac{1}{4}$ teaspoon salt, 2 oz butter or margarine, 2 oz lard or vegetable fat, squeeze of lemon juice and water to mix.

Sift flour and salt. Cut the fat into almond-size pieces and drop into the flour. Add the lemon juice to about 5 tablespoons water and mix the flour and fat to a stiff dry dough, handling quickly and lightly. Turn on to a floured board, roll to an oblong. Fold in 3 and give a half turn so folds are on the side. Stand in cool place for a few minutes. Repeat the rolling and folding 3 or 4 times to flake the fat into the flour.

Roll to a thin sheet, about $\frac{1}{2}$ inch thick. Cut a strip and line moistened edge of 9 inch pie plate, and moisten top of strip.

Turn hot filling into the plate. Cover with pastry, trim and cut up edges, using flat of finger along edge of pastry while slitting into pastry with the flat knife blade. Decorate with pastry leaves and slit centre. Brush top with beaten egg or milk. Bake in a hot oven at 450°F (Gas Mark 8) for 10 to 15 minutes. Reduce heat to moderate and bake a further 10 minutes until the pie is golden and flaky. Serve hot, with hot greens, jacket potatoes and mustard.

EGG AND PARSLEY PIE

8 *oz short pastry*	1 *tablespoon dripping*
4 *eggs*	*Salt and pepper*
1 *teacup chopped parsley*	*Pinch of Cayenne pepper*

Roll out the pastry and cut into 2 rounds the size of a pie plate. Wash and dry the parsley thoroughly, and remove sprigs from stalks. Chop the parsley finely. Line the pie plate with one round of pastry. Put a thick 'cross' of pastry on the bottom. In each space, put an egg. Season with salt, pepper and cayenne pepper, and pour over melted dripping. Sprinkle remaining parsley over the eggs. Cover with pastry, and mark lid lightly with a knife between the eggs. Bake at 400°F (Gas Mark 4) for 40 minutes. Cut the pie along the marked lines so each portion contains an egg. Serve with sauce, gravy or chutney.

SAUSAGE AND ONION PIE

8 oz short pastry
8 oz sausage meat
1 onion

1 egg
Mixed herbs

Roll out the pastry and cut into 2 circles to fit a pie plate. Line the plate with 1 round of pastry. Mix the sausage meat, chopped onion, beaten egg and plenty of chopped fresh herbs. Cover with a pastry lid. Bake at 425°F (Gas Mark 7) for 30 minutes.

Gillian Tetlow, Debden, Essex

PORK AND KIDNEY PIE

1 lb pork shoulder or hand
of pork
3 pigs' kidneys
2 teaspoons basil
$\frac{1}{2}$ pint stock

Pinch of nutmeg
1 medium onion
2 medium carrots
6 oz short pastry

Cut pork and kidneys in pieces and put into a pie dish with basil, stock, nutmeg, chopped onion and carrots. Cover with a lid or piece of foil and cook at 325°F (Gas Mark 3) for 1 hour. Cover with pastry lid and bake at 400°F (Gas Mark 6) for 30 minutes.

LAMB AND MUSHROOM PIE

1 lb shoulder lamb
2 lambs' kidneys
Seasoned flour
1 onion

$\frac{1}{2}$ pint stock
4 oz mushrooms
Salt and pepper
8 oz short pastry

Cut the meat into cubes and cut the kidneys into small pieces. Toss in a little seasoned flour and brown in a little fat with the sliced onion. Add stock and mushrooms. Bring to the boil and simmer until tender. Season with salt and pepper to taste and put into a pie dish to cool. Cover with pastry, glaze with a little beaten egg and bake at 400°F (Gas Mark 6) for 40 minutes.

BEEF AND COW HEEL PIE

13 oz shin beef
$\frac{1}{2}$ cow heel
1 onion stuck with cloves

Salt and pepper
6 oz self-raising flour
3 oz shredded suet

Cut up the beef and cow heel, cover with water and add the onion, salt and pepper. Simmer for 3 hours. Strain, and keep the liquid. Remove bones and onion and cut the meat into neat pieces. Put into a greased pie dish, moisten with cooking liquid, and taste for seasoning. Mix the flour and suet with a pinch of salt, and mix to a soft dough with cold water. Roll out and put on top of the meat. Bake at 400°F (Gas Mark 6) for 1 hour. Make gravy with the remaining cooking liquid, and serve the pie with gravy, mashed potatoes and a green vegetable.

CHICHESTER CHICKEN PIE

1 chicken or boiling hen (cooked until entirely tender – preferably in a clay casserole) using water or stock with salt, pepper, one bayleaf, an onion stuck with cloves (4–6). Allow this to cool sufficiently for any fat to form on top. Remove all fat carefully.

½ lb sausage meat made into   *1 large onion*
small balls   *4-6 oz bacon 'bits'*

Take all (cooked) meat off chicken bones and cut up into neat smallish pieces. Fry bacon and if available field mushrooms; dip sausage balls in flour and fry them in bacon fat with the onion sliced and chopped. Mix all ingredients together with a few peas if liked. Make a white sauce well seasoned and add to other ingredients. Cover with pastry made in the following way: ½ fat to flour rubbed in very roughly; pinch salt; sufficient iced water to mix to neat dough which should then be left in very cool place to 'rest' for as long as possible. Cover ingredients with the pastry and cook until golden brown in a pretty brisk oven.

CHICKEN PIE (1)

Remains of cold fowl cut into neat joints; remove skin, pack it in a pie dish alternately with forcemeat balls, slices of hard-boiled eggs, and thin slices of bacon or ham. Sprinkle well with pepper and salt, half-fill the pie dish with chicken stock (made from boiling skin, bones, giblets etc. with an onion, salt and pepper). Allow to cool, wet the edges of pie dish with water and cover with pastry. Brush round the edge with water, make hole in middle and brush all over with egg yolk. Cook quickly 20 minutes and slowly for another ½ hour.

1870 CHICKEN PIE (2)

Time to bake – $1\frac{1}{4}$ hours.

2 small chickens	*Cup of good gravy*
Some forcemeat	*A little flour and butter*
A sweetbread	*4 eggs*
Few fresh mushrooms	*Some puff paste*

Cover the bottom of a pie-dish with some puff paste, upon that round the side lay a thin layer of forcemeat; cut 2 small chickens into pieces, season them highly with pepper and salt; put some of the pieces into the dish, then some sweetbread cut into pieces well seasoned, a few fresh mushrooms, and the yolks of 4 or 5 hard-boiled eggs cut into pieces of 4, and strewed over the top. Put in a little water and cover the pie with a piece of puff paste; glaze it, ornament the edges and bake it. When done, pour in through the top a cupful of good gravy, thickened with a little flour and butter.

Mrs Giles, Shaftesbury, Dorset

INDIVIDUAL CHICKEN PIES

8 oz rough puff pastry	*1 teaspoon parsley*
1 small chicken	*$\frac{1}{2}$ teaspoon salt*
4 oz mushrooms	*$\frac{1}{2}$ teaspoon Worcester sauce*
4 hard-boiled egg yolks	*Stock made from chicken*
1 medium onion	*carcass*
1 tablespoon vinegar	*4 rashers streaky bacon*

Make rough puff pastry. Remove flesh in neat pieces from an uncooked chicken, and simmer carcass in water for an hour to make stock. In a bowl mix pieces of light and dark flesh, sliced mushrooms, mashed egg yolks, finely chopped onion, vinegar, parsley, salt, sauce and chopped bacon, and divide mixture between four individual pie dishes. Half-fill each dish with stock, and cover with pastry. Brush tops with beaten egg, make an air vent in each, and cook at $375°F$ (Gas Mark 4) for 1 hour.

CHICKEN PIE

1 lb cooked chicken	*Salt and pepper*
1 lb potatoes	*Chopped parsley*
$\frac{1}{2}$ pint chicken stock	*12 oz puff pastry*
$\frac{1}{2}$ pint evaporated milk	

Cut the chicken and the peeled potatoes into small cubes. The chicken stock should be made from the broken carcass and should be rich and strongly flavoured with plenty of herbs. Mix the stock and milk and pour over the chicken and potato in a pie dish. Season well with salt and pepper, and add plenty of freshly chopped parsley. Cover with a pastry lid and bake at 425°F (Gas Mark 7) for 40 minutes.

Harold C. Palmer, Great Bardfield, Essex

NEW YEAR CHICKEN PIE

Line a pie dish with bacon rashers, top with cooked chicken, and then with sausage meat. Just cover with some chicken stock. Bake at 325°F (Gas Mark 3) for 30 minutes. Top with breadcrumb stuffing well flavoured with herbs. Bake for 30 minutes more. Turn out when cold. Quantities can be as variable as you like, and as suits your numbers. This is a useful dish to make in the post-Christmas season when there is cold poultry around (turkey can be used instead of chicken); it is a sort of elementary terrine, and very delicious.

AUTUMN CHICKEN PIE

8 oz *plain flour*	1 *teaspoon tarragon or*
1 *teaspoon salt*	*parsley*
2 oz *lard*	*Grated rind* ½ *lemon*
2 oz *margarine*	*Salt and pepper*
2 *eggs*	1 lb *cold cooked chicken*
½ *pint milk*	

Sift together flour and salt, rub in lard and margarine, and add about 6 teaspoons cold water to make stiff dough. Leave to rest for 10 minutes, then line a 7 inch flan ring or sponge tin with ⅔ of the pastry. Blend eggs and milk, add tarragon or chopped parsley, lemon rind, salt and pepper, and chicken cut in ½ inch strips. Put mixture into pastry case, cover with remaining pastry, seal and flute edges. Cut slits in the top, and bake at 425°F (Gas Mark 7) for 20 minutes. Remove flan ring and continue baking at 350°F (Gas Mark 4) for 40 minutes. Serve cold with salad. This is a good evening meal to follow soup, but is excellent for a packed lunch with whole tomatoes.

GIBLET PIE (1)

Scald the giblets, clean them, place in a saucepan, cover with cold water, and let it come to the boil; skim well, add pepper and salt, simmer gently about 2 hours. When soft, cut the giblets into small pieces, place in a pie dish, and dredge with flour. Cut up ½ lb of beef steak and mix with it, also a large onion cut in thin rings, 2 or 3 cloves, and 2 hard-boiled eggs cut in quarters. Fill up the dish with stock from the giblets, cover with a good short crust (give 2 little cuts on the top to let out the steam), decorate according to taste. Bake in a moderate oven for ¾ hour. Serve hot.

Mrs Thorne, 1911

GIBLET PIE (2)

This is real old-fashioned pie and if no blood is available with the giblets, add 8 oz chopped black pudding to the ingredients. Clean the giblets, cut the neck into neat pieces, cut the liver in pieces, and slice the flesh from the gizzard. Put into a pan with 1 lb chuck steak cut into cubes, a small onion stuck with three cloves, salt and pepper. Cover with water and simmer 1½ hours until tender but not broken up. Put meat into a pie-dish, with any blood from the bird, and remove the onion. Cover with short pastry and bake at 375°F (Gas Mark 5) for 1 hour, covering the top if it browns too quickly. Serve with jacket or mashed potatoes, and swedes, carrots or parsnips.

EXMOOR MUTTON PATTIES

½ *lb cold mutton*	*dried mixed herbs*
2 *oz cold boiled bacon or ham*	*Salt and black pepper to taste*
1 *rounded teaspoon plain flour*	½ *lb flaky pastry*
1 *level teaspoon chopped parsley*	1 *teacup thickened mutton gravy*
½ *teaspoon crushed herbs or*	*Cold water*

Chop mutton and bacon or ham. Mix with the flour, parsley, herbs and seasoning to taste. If liked, stir in 1 rounded teaspoon of finely chopped onion. Roll out pastry fairly thinly. Cut 6 rounds for lids. Pile trimmings together, roll out a little thinner and cut out rounds for lining patty tins. Then line them smoothly. Fill with mixture. Srpinkle a tablespoon of gravy over each filling. Brush edge of lining with cold water. Cover with pastry lids. Press edges lightly together and notch. Make a slit in the centre. Decorate centre of each patty with leaves made from trimmings of pastry. Bake in moderately hot oven, 400°F (Gas Mark 5), for about 20 minutes. Heat remainder of gravy. When patties are ready, lift up leaves and add a little gravy.

1870 MUTTON PIE

Time to bake – $1\frac{1}{2}$–2 hours.

2 lb loin of mutton	*3 mutton kidneys*
Pepper and salt	*Gravy made from the bones*
A little forcemeat	*Pastry*

Strip off the meat from the bones of a loin of mutton without dividing it, and cut it into nice thin slices, and season them with pepper and salt; put a pie-crust round the edge of a piedish, place in it a layer of mutton, then one of forcemeat, and again the slices of mutton with 3 or 4 halves of kidneys at equal distances; then pour in a gravy made from the bones seasoned and well cleared from fat. Moisten the edge with water. Cover with a paste $\frac{1}{2}$ inch thick, press round with your thumbs, make a hole in the centre, and cut the edges close to the dish, ornament the top and border according to your taste, and bake it.

Mrs Giles, Shaftesbury, Dorset

HOT MUTTON PIES

Pie made on a 2 lb jamjar:

$4\frac{1}{2}$ *oz plain flour*	*3 tablespoons water*
$1\frac{1}{2}$ *oz lard*	$\frac{1}{8}$ *teaspoon salt*

Pie made on a 1 lb jamjar:

3 oz plain flour	*2 tablespoons water*
1 oz lard	$\frac{1}{8}$ *teaspoon salt*

Filling (sufficient for larger pie):

$\frac{3}{4}$ *lb lean mutton*	*Salt, pepper and nutmeg*

If smaller pies are required, a larger quantity of pastry can be made and then moulded on tumblers.

Sieve the flour and salt into a bowl. Put the water and lard into a pan and bring to the boil. Pour into the flour and mix well with a knife. Grease and flour an upturned 2 lb jam jar. Mould $\frac{2}{3}$ of the pastry over the jar and leave to go cold. Carefully take away the jar and fill the pastry case with the meat cut into small pieces and seasoned with salt, pepper and nutmeg. Roll out the remaining pastry for the lid. Seal the edges well, decorate with leaves. Make a hole in the centre to allow the steam to escape.

Tie a piece of greaseproof round the pie so that it will keep a good shape. Bake approximately 30 minutes at 375°F (Gas Mark 5). Remove the paper, brush over the whole pie with egg wash and return to the oven for a further 30 minutes. Serve very hot with gravy poured into the hole.

MUTTON PIES

Have a pan containing $\frac{1}{2}$ pint of boiling water. Add 4 oz beef dripping and 1 teaspoon salt. Pour it on to 1 lb of flour. Mix. When cool, form it into a lump. Knead this on a floured board. Divide $\frac{2}{3}$ of the dough into 6 to 9 small straight-sided tins. Fill these with $\frac{3}{4}$ lb lean lamb or mutton, chopped small. Add salt, pepper, and nutmeg and then moisten with gravy. Make the rest of the pastry into lids. Damp the edges, put them on, make a little hole in each, brush with milk. Bake in a moderate oven, 350°F (Gas Mark 4), for 40 minutes. Fill up each pie with gravy before serving.

BACON PASTIES

12 oz short pastry	*1 large onion*
8 oz minced raw steak	*Salt and pepper*
6 oz streaky bacon	*$\frac{1}{2}$ teaspoon Worcester sauce*
4 oz lambs' kidneys	*Egg for glazing*

Roll out pastry and cut out 6 7-inch rounds. Chop the bacon, kidney and onion, and mix with the steak, seasoning and sauce. Put mixture on half of each round and fold over pastry. Pinch edges together. Put on to a wet baking sheet. Bake at 425°F (Gas Mark 7) for 15 minutes; then at 350°F (Gas Mark 4) for 45 minutes. Serve hot or cold.

SAUSAGE AND EGG ROLL

Cheese Pastry:	*1 egg yolk*
3 oz butter	*Water to mix*
6 oz plain flour	**Filling:**
Pinch of salt	*1 lb pork sausage meat*
Pinch of ucayenne pepper	*4 hard-boiled eggs*
3 oz cheese (grated)	*Milk or beaten egg to glaze*

To make pastry, rub butter into sieved flour, and seasoning. Add cheese, and mix to a stiff dough with egg yolk and water. Roll to a rectangle approx. 11×8 inches. Flatten sausage meat on a floured board to approx. 11×5 inches. Place sausage meat on pastry and arrange eggs in a line along centre. Fold sausage meat over eggs. Wet edges of pastry and fold over to enclose sausage meat. Seal edges. Use pastry scraps for decoration. Glaze with milk or beaten egg. Bake in a fairly hot oven, 400°F (Gas Mark 6), for 30 minutes, then reduce heat to 375°F (Gas Mark 5) for a further 30 minutes. Leave until cold. Wrap in foil or greaseproof paper.

BEEF PATTIES

1 lb self-raising flour	*1 minced onion*
6 oz lard or dripping	*2 tablespoons thick brown*
¼ pint water	*gravy*
6 oz beef	*Seasoning*

Make the pastry, cut into rounds, and line some patty tins with it. Cut the meat into small pieces, or mince finely with the onion, mix with the gravy, onion and seasoning. Place a spoonful in each pastry case, put on pastry lids and press the edges together. Bake in a good oven till brown. Reduce heat and leave in oven for a few more minutes to finish. Serve on a hot dish, garnished with parsley.

MUTTON PASTIES

Cut ½ lb cooked lamb or mutton into small pieces, add ½ lb peeled and sliced potatoes, 1 chopped onion, 1 teaspoon chopped parsley, ½ teaspoon salt, ¼ teaspoon pepper, 2 tablespoons water. Roll 1 lb plain pastry into ¼ inch thickness, stamp into rounds, using small teaplate as guide, and place a heap of mixture in centre of each round. Wet the edges of pastry, fold over meat and press edges together. Brush with beaten egg and bake in hot oven for 15 minutes, or until pastry is lightly browned, then reduce heat and continue cooking for a further 15 minutes. Cover with a greased paper and leave 10 minutes before serving.

CORNISH PASTIES (1)

Allow 3–4 oz pastry per pasty according to age and capacity of appetite. Have ready sufficient peeled and 'shripped' potatoes (i.e. potato which has been cut up in fine small wafers by constantly turning the potato in order that the corners can be 'shripped' off – a worndown potato peeler sometimes makes a good 'shripper') allowing one potato per person.
1½ lb of test raw chuck steak – the better the meat the better the pasty is. Onions as desired, and/or swede.
Make pastry well in advance using the usual shortcrust recipe and having consistency pliable but not too wet. Have clean dishcloth or rag handy. Keep shripped potatoes in bowl of water to cover, to prevent their going brown. Take 3–4 oz pastry (about a good handful) and roll out until pastry is smooth and firm trying to keep it as near circular as possible. Use 6 inch plate to cut round if possible. On this circle of pastry place about 2 tablespoons of shripped potato and sprinkle with salt. If onion is desired, arrange on top of this.

Now take 3–4 oz meat and place carefully on top of onion – the meat can be rolled on a floured paper if liked in order to keep pieces of meat separate from one another. Wet around edge of pastry then sprinkle top of meat with pepper. Now dry fingers in clean cloth and then start to 'crimp' edges of pasty by first bringing front half-moon up to meet back half-moon in centre. Press wetted edges together then move fingers down to righthand corner and pinch, roll and crimp altogether in one movement. This takes practice! But don't despair – 'patches' of pastry can always be added both before and during cooking to repair those splits in the pastry cover. Make sure there are no gaps anywhere in the pasty and then brush with milk and stand on piece of butter or lard paper, place on baking sheet and just before popping in good oven, 425°F (Gas Mark 7), make cut up near crimped edge for steam to escape. Settle the pasty slightly back on itself and bake for about 15 minutes or until pastry is golden brown, then reduce heat to finish cooking until meat, tested through steam-hole, is tender. Keep hot by covering with thickish clean cloth in very low oven.

When Cornish men worked down in the lead mines, the usual Cornish 'docky' of bread and fish or meat was not practicable because of the danger of lead poisoning. Eventually the traditional 'docky' became the hot Cornish pasty which could be eaten by holding the pointed end in paper and eating through from the other pointed end. To this day it is customary for a man working away from home to take his pasty with him and many a farmer's wife is asked if 'the missus will warm me pasty for I? If you be so kaind'.

CORNISH PASTIES (2)

Shortcrust Pastry	**Filling**
4 oz plain flour	*Potato, finely sliced (not diced)*
2 oz fat	
Pinch salt	*Onion and/or turnip, finely cut*
Water to mix to a firm dough	
	4 oz steak (Chuck or Skirt)
	Seasoning

Roll pastry into round or rounds. Pile up sliced potato on about half the pastry. Put onion and/or turnip on potato. Cut meat in small pieces and spread over. Season with salt and pepper. Put a few thin pieces of potato on top to save the meat drying. Damp edges of pastry. Fold over to semi-circle and crimp edges. (Crimp by pinching the pastry with the left hand and fold over with right hand, forming a rope-like effect on the side of the pastry.) Place on unfloured baking sheet and bake at 425°F (Gas Mark 7) for 10–15 minutes, reducing to 350°F (Gas Mark 4) for a further 30 minutes.

Mrs Thomas, Truro, Cornwall

SAVOURY BEEF ROLL

1 lb minced beef	**Pastry**
1 teacup breadcrumbs	6 oz flour
½ egg	2 oz butter or margarine
1 onion	½ teaspoon baking powder
¼ teaspoon spice or ground ginger	1 teaspoon salt
	A little milk
½ teaspoon mixed herbs	
Seasoning	

Put mince (uncooked meat is best for making the roll) into a basin, add breadcrumbs, onion very finely chopped, the herbs and the spice. Mix thoroughly with hand, then form into roll. Place in a well-greased tin, cover well with greased paper, bake 20 minutes in a good oven. Meanwhile prepare pastry. Sieve dry ingredients into a basin, rub in butter till free from lumps, then add enough milk to make a stiffish paste. Turn this on to floured board and roll into an oblong. Remove the roll from the oven and taking off paper, wrap it quickly in the pastry. Put a few pastry leaves on top, brush over with milk or beaten egg, and return to oven. Cook about ½ hour longer, until the pastry is brown and thoroughly cooked. Serve with brown or tomato sauce.

CURRIED EGG PIE

8 oz short pastry (8 oz plain flour, 4 oz mixed butter and lard)	1 tablespoon curry powder
	Juice of 1 lemon
	1 medium apple
6 hard-boiled eggs	1 tablespoon tomato purée
1 oz butter	or 2 ripe tomatoes
1 small onion	Salt and pepper
2 tablespoons plain flour	

Make pastry and roll out 2 10-inch circles to fit pie plate. Melt fat, add chopped onion and fry until pale gold. Stir in flour and curry powder and cook until mixture bubbles. Add ¼ pint plus 3 tablespoons water, and stir until smooth. Add lemon juice, peeled and chopped apple and either tomato purée or peeled and quartered tomatoes. Season to taste and simmer with lid on for 30 minutes. Cool. Line pie plate with one round of pastry. Cut eggs in half and put cut side down on pastry. Spread curry sauce over eggs. Cover with second piece of pastry, seal, and glaze with beaten egg or milk. Bake at 425°F (Gas Mark 7) for 30 minutes. Serve with crisp lettuce and tomatoes.

COTTAGE CHEESE PIE

8 oz plain flour	2 tablespoons cooked peas
6 oz lard	2 tablespoons chopped
3 eggs	parsley
8 oz cottage cheese	$\frac{1}{2}$ teaspoon mixed herbs

Sieve flour with a pinch of salt and add cut-up lard. Mix with a squeeze of lemon juice and enough iced water to make a stiff dough, using a knife to avoid breaking up fat. Form into an oblong and roll lightly into a long strip. Fold into 3, enclosing as much air as possible, close and seal ends. Give pastry a half turn and repeat rolling and folding twice more. Leave pastry for 20 minutes, then roll out 2 6-inch rounds to fit deep pie plate or flan ring. This rough puff pastry is good for savoury pies. Whisk eggs and mix with sieved cottage cheese. Add peas, parsley, herbs and plenty of salt and pepper. Pour into lined pie plate or flan ring. Cover with remaining pastry and seal edges. Make a cut to allow steam to escape and glaze with beaten egg. Bake at 425°F (Gas Mark 7) for 10 minutes, then reduce heat to 350°F (Gas Mark 4) for 35 minutes.

FISH ENVELOPE

8 oz cooked cod or haddock	$\frac{1}{4}$ pint white sauce
fillet	Salt and pepper
1 hard-boiled egg	8 oz short pastry
1 tablespoon capers	

Flake fish and chop egg, and add fish, egg and capers to sauce, seasoning with salt and pepper. Roll out pastry thinly to form a square, put fish filling in the centre, brush edges of pastry with beaten egg or milk and draw sides up over the centre to form an envelope. Seal edges well, decorate with trimmings and brush with beaten egg or milk. Bake at 400°F (Gas Mark 6) for 30 minutes, and serve hot or cold. This filling can be varied by using canned salmon instead of the fish, or by adding a few mushrooms or shrimps to the mixture.

CURRIED LAMB PIES

½ lb flaky pastry
1 dessertspoon lard
1 teaspoon minced onion
1 dessertspoon plain flour
½ pint stock
1 teaspoon curry powder

Salt and pepper
½ lb cubed cooked lamb
½ diced apple
2 talespoons coconut
2 tablespoons sultanas

Line individual patty cases with pastry. Melt lard and brown onion lightly. Stir in flour, then stock, curry powder, salt and pepper to taste, and stir until the mixture thickens and boils. Add meat, apple, coconut and sultanas, heat through and leave to cool. Put a spoonful of the mixture into each patty case, top with rounds of pastry and seal edges; make a small hole with a skewer in the top of each, and bake at 450°F (Gas Mark 8) for 20 minutes. Serve hot or cold. These pies are excellent for the lunch-box.

FRIED MEAT PIES

½ lb short pastry
1 medium onion
1 tablespoon lard
1 lb minced raw beef
½ pint stock

2 teaspoons chopped parsley
Salt and pepper
2 tablespoons flour
2 chopped hard-boiled eggs

Chop onion finely and soften in melted lard. Add minced beef, stock, parsley, salt and pepper to taste, and simmer with a lid on for 30 miuntes. Stir in flour, heat and stir until thick, then add egg and leave to cool. Roll out pastry thinly and cut in circles the size of a saucer; this quantity should make 6 circles. Put 3 tablespoons of meat mixture on one side of each circle, fold over the other side, damp and pinch edges to seal them. Fry in hot deep fat for about 3 minutes until golden. If there is any meat mixture over, add a little water and simmer until the mixture is like a sauce, then use to pour over the pies at serving time. These pies are a variation of a favourite South American recipe, and make a very pleasant change when served really hot with a crisp salad. The filling may be varied by using corned beef flavoured with a little tomato purée or table sauce; a little chopped green pepper is also good cooked with the onion.

HAND-RAISED PORK PIES (1)

This is for 2 pies over large and small moulds (large: $5\frac{1}{4}$ inches diam. × $3\frac{3}{4}$ inches depth; small: $3\frac{1}{2}$ inch diam. × 3 inches depth).

2 lb plain flour	*$2\frac{1}{2}$ lb seasoned pork*
$12\frac{1}{2}$ oz lard	*1 egg*
2 teaspoons salt	*Stock*
$\frac{1}{2}$ pint water	*Gelatine if necessary*

Bring fat and water to the boil and simmer for 5 minutes. Make well in sifted flour, pour in quickly and work up with wooden spoon. Put in refrigerator for 30 minutes. Knead with hands and turn on to floured board. Cut off enough paste for the tops. When you are not using paste, cover with cloth to keep it warm, for it is more pliable when hot. Flour the moulds well, and also the paste on the side going over the moulds. Roll out and mould paste over moulds upside down. Tie a double band of greaseproof paper round paste ($2\frac{1}{2}$-inch for large mould; 2-inch for small mould). Turn right way up and cut round edge level with moulds. Make tops as large as pie. Fill with pork 1 inch from top, moisten the inside rims of pies with beaten egg, press lids in position and nip round with fingers. Cut 3 air holes in lid with scissors. Bake in middle of the oven at 375°F (Gas Mark 5). The top may be glazed with beaten egg. If you want to glaze the sides, take pies out of oven and remove paper and brush over with egg 30 minutes before cooking time is finished. Allow $1\frac{1}{2}$ hours for large pie; 1 hour for small pie. Simmer bones and trimmings for 3 to 4 hours. Let pies cool 1 hour, then pour just warm stock through small funnel at intervals so stock has time to soak through.

HAND-RAISED PORK PIE (2)

Pastry	*$\frac{1}{2}$ teaspoon powdered sage*
12 oz self-raising flour	*Salt and pepper*
$\frac{1}{2}$ teaspoon salt	
4 oz lard	**Jelly**
$\frac{1}{4}$ pint water	*Pork bones or a trotter*
1 egg	*2 pints water*
	1 onion
Filling	*Seasoning*
$1\frac{1}{4}$ lb shoulder pork	*1 teaspoon gelatine*

Sieve the flour and salt into a bowl. Boil the lard and the water in a pan. When dissolved, pour into the centre of the flour. Work all together until a smooth dough is obtained. Cut $\frac{1}{3}$ off dough and reserve for lid. Work the remainder on a floured board, gradually moulding to form bowl shape. (A cake tin can be used as a guide.) Put on to a greased baking sheet and fill the centre with the diced pork, sage and seasoning. Roll out the reserved $\frac{1}{3}$ for lid, brush edges of the pie with beaten egg and seal on the lid. Use trimmings to form leaves for decoration. Make a hole in the top and brush all over pie with the egg. Bake in oven 400°F (Gas Mark 6) for 30 minutes, then reduce heat to 350°F (Gas Mark 4) for further $1\frac{1}{2}$ hours. Make a jelly from the bones, water, onion, and seasoning by boiling for about 2 hours. Strain and add the dissolved gelatine. Allow to cool. Pour some of this into the hole in the lid when the pie is cool and leave to set before cutting.

RAISED PORK PIE (3)

1 *lb flour*	$\frac{1}{2}$ *pint water*
$\frac{1}{4}$ *lb butter*	Pinch salt
1 *egg*	

Rub butter into flour, beat egg and water together, and mix all into a dry dough. Grease cake-tin well and line with pastry. Cut stewing pork into dice removing any fat, and cook partly; drain quite free from liquor, put layer of pork into pie, sprinkle well with salt and pepper, layer of finely minced onion and sage leaves; continue until tin is full; brush round edge with egg, and lay pastry cover on, rolled out not too thinly. Brush top over with yolk of egg, and ornament with leaves. Make a slit in centre. Before the pie is covered put in 2 or 3 tablespoons of stock. Stand on another tin and bake in steady oven for 2 hours. Turn carefully out of tin and brush around sides with egg yolk, and put back in oven to glaze.

ECONOMY PORK PIE

Pastry	$\frac{1}{3}$ *pint milk*
5 *oz lard*	1 *lb flour*
1 *teaspoon salt*	
Filling	1 *tablespoon breadcrumbs*
1 *lb pork pieces or meat from*	*Salt and pepper*
the blade	4-5 *hard-boiled eggs*
$\frac{1}{2}$ *lb pork sausage meat*	*A little beaten egg*
$\frac{1}{4}$ *teaspoon mixed herbs*	$\frac{1}{4}$ *oz gelatine*
Pinch of mace	$\frac{1}{4}$ *pint stock or water*
1 *bayleaf*	

Heat the lard with salt and milk and when boiling beat into the flour which has been sieved into a warm bowl. When smooth, cover with a cloth and prepare the filling.

Chop or mince the meat and sausage meat, add herbs and spices and breadcrumbs. Season well with salt and freshly ground pepper. Use the warm pastry to line a cake tin or pie mould, taking care to seal all the joins by wetting the edges. Place a little of the mixture in the pie case, add the hard-boiled eggs and pack the remaining mixture into the pie together with a spoonful of water. Cover the pie and decorate the edge. Brush with beaten egg. Make a few leaves and a rose or tassel from the scraps of pastry.

Bake at 425°F (Gas Mark 7) for $\frac{1}{2}$ hour. Cover with greaseproof paper and reduce to 325°F (Gas Mark 3) for a further $1\frac{1}{2}$ hours. Cool and remove from the tin. Dissolve the gelatine in the stock and pour into the pie (under the rose) and serve cold with a crisp green salad. Endive can be used with tomato, vegetable and potato salads.

VENISON PASTY

8 oz shortcrust pastry	*6 peppercorns*
12 oz cold cooked venison	*$\frac{1}{4}$ teaspoon mace*
$\frac{1}{2}$ pint stock	*1 dessertspoon redcurrant*
1 bayleaf	*or 1 teaspoon rowan jelly*

Line a pasty dish with half the pastry. Mince the meat – not too fine. Simmer the stock with the rest of the ingredients for 20 minutes and strain enough over the minced meat to make it moist but not sloppy. Mix it well and leave for a minute or two for the meat to absorb the stock. Put it into the prepared pastry case. Roll out the rest of the pastry and make a lid, moistening the edges. Make a few slits in the pastry to let out the steam and cut out leaves and put them on, moistening the underside first to make them stick. Paint the whole thing over with egg yolk and water and put fairly near the bottom of a brisk oven for 15–20 minutes. If it is overcooked it becomes dry and crumbly and impossible to eat tidily. Like Haggis it is best with vegetables with a high percentage of water in them – turnips, swedes, marrows, carrots. Mashed potatoes with a *lot* of butter.

Mrs Chaplin, Finsthwaite, Lancs

GAME PIE

Pastry	*6 tablespoons milk*
12 oz plain flour	*4 oz lard*
2 level teaspoons salt	*2 egg yolks*
Filling	*1 pheasant, drawn*
12 oz sausage meat	*Salt and pepper*
4 oz raw lean ham	*$\frac{1}{4}$-$\frac{1}{2}$ pint jellied stock*
6 oz lean chuck steak	*Gelatine*

Assemble a $7\frac{1}{2}$-inch raised game pie mould with a hinged side. Grease. Place on a baking sheet. Sieve the flour and salt together. Make a well in the centre. Warm together the milk and lard, and when lard has melted, pour into the flour with beaten egg yolks. Gradually work in the flour with a wooden spoon to give a smooth pliable dough. Knead lightly on a floured board until smooth. Leave to cool slightly. Line the mould with $\frac{3}{4}$ of the prepared pastry, rolled out to $\frac{1}{8}-\frac{1}{4}$ inch thickness. Press the pastry to the sides of the tin, so that there are no cracks or wrinkles. Line the pastry with sausage meat, reserving a little to make small balls. Cut the ham and steak into small cubes. Cut the flesh away from the carcass of the pheasant. Cut in small pieces. Mix the prepared meats with the seasoning and fill up the pie mould. Add a little stock. Cover with remaining pastry. Decorate as desired. Make a hole in the centre for the steam to escape.

Bake at 425°F (Gas Mark 7) for $\frac{1}{2}$ hour. Reduce the heat 375°F (Gas Mark 5) for a further $\frac{1}{2}$ hour. Finally reduce to 350°F (Gas Mark 4) for a further 30–35 minutes. If pastry shows signs of over-browning, cover with greaseproof paper. Remove the pie from the oven, fill up with hot stock, leave to cool. Remove tin mould when the pie is cold. Fill with more jellied stock. Serve when set, garnished with watercress and sausage balls.

Cook some tiny sausage meat balls in the oven until golden brown. Cool and glaze in jellied stock.

REV. R. W. PEDDER'S GAME PIE

Small pie dish holding about 2 pints. Cut lean raw game into large dice and fill pie dish almost full. Have ready some *jellied* stock in saucepan with $\frac{1}{2}$ saltspoon mixed herbs, $\frac{1}{2}$ inch cinnamon stick, $\frac{1}{2}$ inch square of bayleaf, 2 cloves, 2 saltspoons salt, sprinkling of pepper or 3 peppercorns. Let it infuse and then strain it over the meat in the dish. Cook in slow oven for 3 hours (or 2 if the game is young). Eat cold – tomorrow – not before. Keep lid on pie dish in oven.

He always made this with roe deer venison but any game will do – varying in richness. I made one with only pheasants and mallard in equal numbers and added a glass of port for richness.

Mrs Chaplin's father was a sporting, farming parson, once a traditional character in English life, but now alas rare. She is always the person to turn to when a delicious recipe for game or salmon is needed. Like many old game 'pie' recipes, this contains no pastry. Occasionally one finds beautiful unglazed oven dishes, decorated with elaborate modelling of game, and used for this kind of pie.

Mrs Chaplin, Finsthwaite, Lancs

GAME PIE

If venison is used for this, the delicacy of its flavour will entirely depend on its having been hung long enough. Trim the best end of the neck, and rub it with cayenne pepper, nutmeg, mace and salt. Boil down the trimmings of the venison, and the inferior joints of hare or any other game used, and make a rich gravy. Make a forcemeat of the raw liver of the hare and shallots all finely minced together. Remove the bones from the principal parts and fill with forcemeat. Line a dish with shortcrust, place the venison and hare in it and fill in the spaces with forcemeat; add a little of the gravy, cover the top of the pie with pastry, ornament the top with leaves or whatever, and bake in a hot oven for 10 minutes. Then reduce the heat and let it cook in a slower oven for $1\frac{1}{2}$ hours, and when the oven is quite cooled down, it can remain in it to finish cooking. If venison is not obtainable or is not liked, another hare, a rabbit or whatever is available may be used instead.

Farmers on the edge of Savernake Forest had the right to kill deer if they became a menace to their crops – and one or two deer grazing on a field of growing wheat or oats can do irreparable damage to that year's crop – consequently venison was on the menu in this part of Wiltshire. Also in the New Forest regular shoots were arranged to thin out the deer population for the sake of its own survival. These were properly undertaken with a minimum of chosen game at a certain time of year, by the verderers and those in charge.

This is a very old recipe from the Wiltshire/Hampshire border.

GROUSE PIE

Make a farce of $1\frac{1}{2}$ lb calf's liver and $\frac{1}{2}$ lb fat bacon. Cut it up and put in stewpan with a shallot and a little chopped parsley. Let it heat gently on the fire, skimming occasionally. When the meat is tolerably done, turn all into a mortar and pound thoroughly. Have ready the meat cut from bones of 3 grouse and $\frac{1}{2}$ lb veal cut in thin slices. Put layer of thin fat bacon at bottom of the pie, then a layer of the farce, then one of the grouse, then the veal and so on till the dish is full and a slice fat bacon over the top and 2 bayleaves. When nearly cold, fill in with the gravy drawn from the bones and set with a little gelatine. Run it through a sieve, let it get cold and skim off all fat. Heat it again and then put over the pie. Cover with paste of flour and water and bake 4 hours.

Mrs Garden, 1847

GROUSE PIE

2 grouse	**Salt, pepper and herbs**
$\frac{1}{2}$ lb pie-crust pastry	**Few yolks hard-boiled eggs**
Game forcemeat	**Few slices raw ham**

Cut up a brace of grouse, each of them in 5 parts, and season with pepper and salt. Mask the bottom of a pie dish with a layer of game forcemeat, in which place the pieces of grouse; sprinkle over a little cooked fine herbs; fill the cavities between the pieces with a few yolks of hard-boiled eggs, and place on top of the grouse a few slices of raw ham; pour in good gravy, to half the height, cover the pie with paste, egg it, and put it in a moderate oven, 350°F (Gas Mark 4) for 1½ hours.

GROUSE AND STEAK PIE

2 casserole grouse   *Parsley*
1 lb steak   *Pastry*
2 onions

Cut the flesh of two 'casserole' grouse. Make a stock with the carcasses. Fry some finely chopped onion golden in butter. Add the steak cut in cubes and brown. Cut an onion and parsley into a pie dish, add some stock and cover with pastry. Cook for about 2 hours.

1870 PLAIN PIGEON PIE

Time to bake – 1¼ hours.

2-3 pigeons   *A little gravy*
1 rump steak   *2 oz butter*
Pepper and salt   *Puff paste*

Lay a rim of paste round the edge and sides of a pie-dish, sprinkle a little pepper and salt over the bottom, and put in a thin beefsteak; pick and draw the pigeons, wash them clean and cut off the feet, press the legs into the sides; put a bit of butter, and a seasoning of pepper and salt into the inside of each one, and lay them in the dish with their breasts upwards, and their necks and gizzards between them; sprinkle some pepper and salt over them, and put in a wineglass of water; lay a thin sheet of paste over the top, and with a brush wet it all over; then put a puff paste ½ inch thick over that, cut it close to the dish, brush it over with egg, ornament the top, and stick 4 of the feet out of it, and bake it. When done, pour in a little good gravy. You may put in the yolks of 6 hard boiled eggs, or leave out the beefsteak, if you think proper.

Mrs Giles, Shaftesbury, Dorset

PIGEON PIE (1)

Take 2 or more dressed pigeons and stew them until tender – this should be done the night before. If you have a pressure cooker, a great deal of cooking-time is saved by cooking the pigeons in this, following makers' instructions. When the birds are properly cooked, and cooled, pull them apart using fingers and a sharp pointed knife, and place the joints or pieces in a dish. Meanwhile boil up the liquor in which they were cooked until it is reduced by half. Over the meat sprinkle some fresh sweet herbs chopped (parsley and thyme or marjoram) or 2 teaspoons of dried mixed herbs, some finely chopped onion or shallot, some grated lemon peel ($\frac{1}{2}$ lemon to 2 birds) salt and pepper to taste; then place 1 layer of cut up rashers of bacon, and 1 layer of sliced hard-boiled eggs. Pour over the liquor now cooled, and cover the whole with a good pastry. Bake in a good oven until the pastry is nicely browned and cooked right through. Reduce heat, cover pastry with a butter-paper and leave in oven for a further 10 minutes. Remove from oven and stand to cool leaving butter-paper undisturbed for about 15 minutes.

Pigeons are more numerous than they have ever been in living memory and do tremendous harm to standing crops such as brussel sprouts, cabbages etc. which of course makes the loss of income reflect in the market prices, because of depleting the supply. Pigeons are on sale in many well-known chain suppliers these days and are an economical and welcome addition to the menu. Pigeon pie eaten cold, with dressed lettuce, spring onions and cold new potatoes, cooked with a nice sprig or two of mint, is a banquet fit for even your richest relations. This is a version which came from a Dorset grandmother.

PIGEON PIE (2)

Prepare $\frac{3}{4}$ lb shin of beef and $\frac{1}{4}$ lb ox kidney, by cutting them up into small pieces and stewing them with $\frac{1}{2}$ pint of stock or water until quite tender, in a pie-dish. Take 2 pigeons, each cut into 4 pieces. Cut up 2 onions, 4 shallots, very finely, and 3 teaspoons chopped parsley, and cut up into slices 2 hard-boiled eggs.
Put a layer of meat in the bottom of the pie-dish, sprinkle a layer of onion, shallot, parsley, salt and pepper and hard-boiled egg, and then a layer of pigeon, and so on until the pie-dish is filled. Melt a little gelatine into $\frac{1}{2}$ pint of stock, put this to the gravy in the pie, and cover with a good puff pastry. Ornament top and edges, brush over with the yolk of an egg. Bake in a moderate oven for $\frac{3}{4}$–1 hour or until pigeon is cooked. If the birds are tough, cover the pastry with greased paper and reduce heat, so that the prolonged cooking will not dry up the pastry.

PIGEON PIE (3)

4 pigeons, take the livers, gizzards, and chop them up fine, add to them pepper, salt and Cayenne to taste, fry them lightly in butter, then add 2 tablespoons of breadcrumbs, then divide the whole into 4 portions. To

each portion put a small knob of butter about as big as a blackbird's egg, and place in the body of each pigeon for seasoning. Truss the birds neatly, and place them breast down in a deep dish; fill the dish half full with water, lay on top a piece of steak peppered, cover with good pie crust and bake for ¾ hour.

PIGEON PIE (4)

6 pigeons
8 oz chuck steak

Salt, pepper and mace
8 oz pastry

The nicest pie is made with breasts only, in which case the remains of the birds should be simmered in a little water to produce a rich gravy. Small mushrooms and/or hard-boiled eggs are a good addition to the pie. Remove the breasts from the pigeons with a sharp knife, and put into a pie-dish with the steak cut into small pieces. Just cover with water, season well with salt, pepper and a pinch of mace, cover with a lid, and simmer in a medium oven for an hour. Cover with pastry, brush with beaten egg and bake in a hot oven, 425°F (Gas Mark 7) until golden.

PIGEON PIE (5)

5-6 pigeons
8 oz medium quality steak
8 oz pastry crust

Seasoning
Little good gravy

Joint the birds so that each one yields 4 joints, 2 breast joints and 2 leg joints, put the rest of the carcasses to stew in a little water, for the gravy. Cut the steak into small thin pieces each about the size of a tablespoon, line a pie dish with these slices, then lay the pigeons on top, cover with water, add plenty of seasoning, cover with greased paper and put into a medium oven, allow to simmer for 1 hour. Take out the dish, have ready a good pie crust pastry, cover the pie with this. Brush the top with beaten egg, and put back into the oven, bake until the pastry is a golden brown. Mix a dessertspoon of cornflour with a little cold milk, add a cupful of the hot bone stock, and allow to thicken, season to taste, and when the pie is done, lift up the crust and add the thickened gravy.

COMPANY PIGEON PIE (6)

Use only the pigeons' breasts. To save plucking and drawing, slit the skin over the breast, fold back skin and feathers, and cut out the breasts. Put into a dish with an equal quantity of steak (veal or pork will do). Season well and fill dish with stock. Cover with a lid and cook at 350°F (Gas Mark

4) for 1 hour. Take off the lid and add a little more stock and a layer of hard-boiled egg slices. Cover with short or flaky pastry and bake at 400°F (Gas Mark 6) for 30 minutes.

PARTRIDGE PIE (1)

2 partridges
½ lb veal
½ lb fat bacon
6 mushrooms
Salt and pepper

2 oz butter
2 hard-boiled eggs
Parsley
¼ pint of stock
Shortcrust pastry

Cut each partridge into 4 pieces. Melt the butter in a pan, put in the joints and fry lightly. Cut the veal and bacon into thin slices, line the pie dish with the sliced meat, cover with the joints of partridge and season well, adding the parsley and mushrooms, finishing with a layer of bacon and veal. Cover the pie with short pastry and bake for 1 hour in a hot oven. When cooked fill with a good stock and serve hot or cold.

Game is excellent in pies, and an economical way of serving. You can vary the above recipe by using the game you have available.

PARTRIDGE PIE (2)

2 partridges
8 oz lean veal
8 oz boiled bacon or ham
¼ pint onion sauce
1 oz butter
2 hard-boiled eggs

1 tablespoon chopped parsley
4 oz mushrooms
Salt and pepper
Pinch of nutmeg
Puff pastry
Rich stock or gravy

Cut the birds in halves and cook them lightly with butter until just coloured. In a pie-dish put a layer of mixed chopped veal and bacon. Put in partridges. Add parsley, mushrooms and seasoning, and put on a second layer of veal and bacon. Pour on the onion sauce and cover with slices of egg. Cover with pastry, glaze with beaten egg and bake at 400°F (Gas Mark 6) for 1 hour. When the pie is removed from the oven, pour in a little rich hot stock or gravy. Serve hot or cold.

HARE PIE (1)

Cut hare meat into small pieces and roll them in a little flour seasoned with salt and pepper and a pinch of mixed spice. Put into an oven dish with half the meat weight in butter. Cover tightly and stand the dish in a tin of hot water. Cook at 350°F (Gas Mark 4) for 1½ hours. In a large pie dish, put a layer of sausage meat. Cover with the hare and its gravy, and add a wineglass of red wine or port and some fried forcemeat balls. Cover with a good short crust and brush with egg or milk. Bake at 400°F (Gas Mark 6) for 30 minutes. As the pie cools, pour some melted stock or consommé (jellying consistency) through a hole in the pastry. Leave until completely cold.

HARE PIE (2)

3 joints hare	**8 oz plain flour**
1 teaspoon fresh herbs	**Pinch of salt**
Salt and pepper	**2 oz lard**
3 tablespoons cider or red	**½ gill milk and water**
wine	**Stock**

Chop or mince the hare finely, season with herbs, salt and pepper, and leave to stand overnight in cider or wine. Sieve flour and salt in a warm bowl. Bring lard, milk and water to boil together and pour into the middle of the flour, stirring until cool enough to handle. Knead until smooth, adding more hot milk and water if necessary. Cover with a tea towel damped in hot water and wrung out, and stand bowl in warm water for 15 minutes, keeping dough only just warm. Roll out ¾ of pastry and line a pie mould or cake tin with removable bottom. Mix hare meat well and stir in a spoonful of stock, and put filling into pastry case to within 1 inch of the top. Brush top edge with egg, cover with pastry lid, and glaze with beaten egg. Make a hole in the centre of the lid. Bake at 400°F (Gas Mark 6) for 20 minutes, then reduce heat to 350°F (Gas Mark 4) for another hour, covering the pastry with thick paper to prevent its burning. When pie is cool, pour in a little cold jellied stock almost at setting point, using a funnel in the hole. Leave in tin until completely cold. This is a very useful way of using hare, and is particularly good for a harvest supper table.

1870 PLAIN RABBIT PIE

Time to bake – 1¼ hours.

1 large rabbit	**Pepper and salt**
12 oz rather fat bacon	**1 shallot**
Sprig of parsley	**Puff paste**

Skin and wash a fine large rabbit; cut it into joints, and divide the head. Then place it into warm water to soak until thoroughly clean; drain it on a sieve, or wipe it with a clean cloth. Season it with salt and pepper, a sprig of parsley chopped fine, and 1 shallot if the flavour is liked (but it is equally good without it). Cut the bacon into small pieces, dredge with flour the

172

rabbit, and place it in the pie-dish with the bacon, commencing with the inferior parts of the rabbit. Pour in a small cupful of water, or stock if you have it; put a paste border round the edges of the dish, and cover it with puff paste about $\frac{1}{2}$ inch thick. Ornament the top and glaze it, make a hole in the centre, and bake it.

Mrs Giles, Shaftesbury, Dorset

SUSSEX RABBIT PIE

Cut up a young wild rabbit into 12 or 14 pieces. Do not use the head. Wash the pieces and place them in a pie-dish with 1 lb pickled pork or suitable pieces of rashers of cold boiled bacon, cut up into suitably-sized pieces; sprinkle over pepper and a little salt to taste, add a blade of mace, 2 cloves, and 1 shallot or small onion minced. Barely cover the meat with some good veal or other white stock. Cover the pie with a tin or plate and cover with a good paste. Brush over with egg to which has been added salt, and bake in a brisk oven until the pastry is done. This pie may be served hot or cold. If you are short on bacon or pickled pork, 1 or 2 hard-boiled eggs are a great addition to the protein content and the flavour.

RABBIT PIES

1 rabbit
$\frac{1}{2}$ pint thick white sauce
$\frac{1}{2}$ lb cooked ham or corned beef
4 tablespoons breadcrumbs
$\frac{1}{2}$ teaspoon grated lemon rind
1 teaspoon chopped parsley
Pepper and salt
Short or puff pastry

Simmer the rabbit pieces gently until tender, cool, and mince the flesh with the ham or corned beef. Add breadcrumbs, lemon rind, parsley and seasoning and bind with white sauce. Roll out pastry thinly and cut into 4 inch rounds. Cover half the rounds with rabbit mixture and top with the other half, pressing edges together. Brush tops with milk and bake at 450°F (Gas Mark 8) for 20 minutes. These little pies are delicious for a packed meal.

RABBIT PIE

Joint a rabbit and soak in cold salted water for 2 hours, then dry thoroughly. Cut $\frac{1}{2}$ lb steak into cubes, and form $\frac{1}{4}$ lb pork sausage meat into small round balls. Arrange layers of rabbit, steak and sausage meat balls in a pie-dish, sprinkling thickly with salt, pepper, grated nutmeg and chopped parsley. Cover with stock or water, put on a pastry lid, and bake at 450°F (Gas Mark 6) for 20 minutes, then reduce to 350°F (Gas Mark 4) for another $1\frac{1}{4}$ hours.

ROYAL RABBIT PIE FROM HUNTINGDON

1 *nice rabbit*	**¾ *pint water***
About ½ lb stewing steak	**1 *level tablespoon cornflour***
(or shin, well cooked)	***Onion or mushroom if liked***
Chicken stock (if possible)	**1 *lb pastry (puff for***
½ *lb bacon*	***preference)***
Salt and pepper	***Egg for glazing***

Make the pastry and put to 'rest' in a cool place. Meanwhile skin, wipe and dry the rabbit. Cut up the beef and bacon and arrange in pie-dish. Add onion or mushroom if desired. Blend the cornflour with a little cold water and add to the chicken stock; bring carefully to the boil, stirring all the time, and cook for a further minute or so. Place the joints of rabbit in the pie-dish on top of the other ingredients and pour the 'gravy' over all adding more stock or water if necessary. Bring to the boil, gently, then cover the pie-dish and place in a medium oven, 350°F (Gas Mark 3) until all the meat is cooked but not falling apart – about 1 hour. Take out of oven and cool the pie-dish and its contents, then cover with the prepared pastry. Decorate the pie as required and brush with beaten egg before returning to a good oven for the best part of ½ hour. Garnish with parsley, and serve with brussels sprouts or kidney beans, if in season, and mashed potatoes. This pie is also delicious eaten cold with beetroot and green salad, says Mrs R., who sent the recipe.

ESSEX RABBIT PIE

In one Essex family about fifty years ago, rabbit pie was served regularly for Monday morning breakfast. During the month of May (and May only) the pies contained a mixture of rook and rabbit. At other times, the mixture could be moorhen and rabbit.

ROOK PIE (1)

6 *rooks*	***Powdered mace***
4 *oz stewing beef or mutton*	**2 *cloves***
Salt and pepper	***Short pastry***

Skin and clean the rooks and cut away the backs and ribs, leaving the breasts with the two upper wing bones attached, also the two legs without the fat. Wash and dry. Dip in flour and arrange in a pie-dish with meat cut in cubes. Season with salt and pepper, a pinch of mace, and cloves. Cover with water and put on a lid, and simmer very slowly until the meat leaves the bones. Cool and add some hard-boiled eggs if liked. Cover with short pastry, brush with egg, and bake at 400°F (Gas Mark 6) for 45 minutes.

1870 ROOK PIE (2)

Rooks must be skinned and stewed in milk and water before being put into the pie-dish; they may then be treated as pigeons. Epicures assert that only the breast must be used, but if when the rook is drawn and skinned it is laid on its breast and an incision made on each side of the spine of about a finger width, and that piece removed, the whole of the bird is wholesome food, that being the really bitter part.

4 rooks	*3 hard-boiled eggs*
½ lb puff paste	*About 2 oz butter*
Pepper and salt	*Small piece of rump steak*

Lay the rump steak in the pie-dish, cut the rooks as directed, and lay them in the dish well seasoned, add the butter in knobs and some hard-boiled eggs. Bake as you would a pigeon pie.

Mrs Giles, Shaftesbury, Dorset

YORKSHIRE ROOK PIE

After skinning and cleaning the rooks, cut away the backs and ribs, leaving the breasts with the two upper wing bones attached, also the two legs without the feet. Wash, dry, dip in flour and arrange in pie dish. If the dish is small, cut the breast in two down the breastbone. Season with salt and pepper, a large pinch of mace and 2 cloves for every 6 rooks. Cover with water and a lid, and stew very slowly until the meat leaves the bones, filling up with cold water if necessary. When cold, cover with pastry and bake in usual way until pastry is golden brown. If a little stewing beef or lamb is available, cut it up and add to the pie allowing ¼ lb to 6 rooks. Hard-boiled eggs are also an improvement.

1870 VEAL AND HAM PATTIES

6 oz ready dressed lean veal	*lemon peel*
3 oz ham	*Some Cayenne pepper and salt*
1 oz butter rolled in flour	*1 spoon essence of ham*
1 tablespoon cream	*1 spoon lemon juice*
1 tablespoon veal stock	*Puff paste*
A little grated nutmeg and	

Chop about 6 ozs ready-dressed lean veal, and 3 ozs of ham, very small and put into a stewpan with 1 oz of butter rolled in flour, a tablespoon of cream, the same of veal stock, a little nutmeg and lemon peel, some cayenne pepper and salt, a spoonful of essence of ham and lemon juice. Mix well together and stir it over the fire until quite hot, taking care it does not burn. Prepare the patty-pans as for oyster patties, and bake them in a hot oven for ¼ hour; fill the mixture and serve.

Mrs Giles, Shaftesbury, Dorset

1870 OYSTER PATTIES

Light puff paste　　　　　　　　*A little grated lemon peel*
2 dozen large oysters　　　　　　*A little Cayenne pepper*
1 oz butter rolled in flour　　　　*Salt*
½ gill good cream　　　　　　　*1 teaspoon lemon juice*

Roll out puff paste less than ¼ inch thick, cut it into squares with a knife, cover with it 8 or 10 patty pans, and put upon each a bit of bread the size of a walnut; roll out another layer of paste of same thickness, cut it as above, wet the edge of the bottom paste and put on the top, pare them round and notch them about a dozen times with the back of the knife, rub them lightly with yolk of egg, and bake them in hot oven about ¼ hour. When done, take a thin slice off the top, and with a small knife or spoon take out the bread and the inside paste, leaving the outside quite entire. Parboil 2 dozen large oysters, strain them from their liquor, wash, beard, and cut them into four, put them into a saucepan with 1 oz of butter rolled in flour, ½ gill of good cream, a little grated lemon peel, the oyster liquor strained and reduced by boiling to one half, a little Cayenne pepper and salt, and a teaspoon of lemon juice; stir it over the fire for 5 minutes, fill the patties, put the cover on the top, and serve.

Mrs Giles, Shaftesbury, Dorset

1870 VEAL AND OYSTER PIE

Time to bake – 1½ hours.

1½ lb veal cutlets　　　　　　　*Peel of ½ lemon*
¾ lb ham　　　　　　　　　　*Pepper and salt*
50 oysters　　　　　　　　　　*Puff paste*
A cup of weak gravy or broth

Cut 1½ lb of veal into small neat cutlets, and spread over each a thin layer of minced or pounded ham, season them with pepper, salt and grated lemon peel, and roll each cutlet round. Line the pie-dish edge with a good paste, put a layer of rolled veal at the bottom over the veal a layer of oysters then of veal, and the oysters on top; make a gravy with a cupful of weak gravy or broth, the peel of $\frac{1}{2}$ a lemon, the oyster liquor strained and a seasoning of salt and pepper; cover a crust over the top. Ornament it in any way approved, egg it over, and bake it in a moderate oven. When done, more gravy may be added by pouring in through a funnel into the hole in the top, and replacing the ornament on it after the gravy has been added.

Mrs Giles, Shaftesbury, Dorset

1870 LOBSTER PATTIES

Time – 20 minutes

Some puff paste
A hen lobster
1 oz butter
$\frac{1}{2}$ tablespoon veal gravy
1 teaspoon essence of anchovy

1 teaspoon lemon juice
1 tablespoon flour and water
A little Cayenne pepper and salt

Roll out the puff paste about $\frac{1}{4}$ inch thick, and prepare the patty pans as for oyster patties; take a hen lobster already boiled, pick the meat from the tail and claws, and chop it fine, put it into a stewpan with a little of the inside spawn pounded in a mortar until quite smooth, with 1 oz of butter, the $\frac{1}{2}$ teaspoon of cream, the same of veal gravy, essence of anchovy, lemon juice, Cayenne pepper, and salt, and a tablespoon of flour and water. Let it stew 5 minutes, fill the patties, and serve.

Mrs Giles, Shaftesbury, Dorset

1870 CONGER-EEL PIE

Time to bake—rather more than 1 hour

A piece of conger-eel
A quart of water
$\frac{1}{4}$ onion
A bunch of sweet herbs
Pepper, salt and spice

A sprig of parsley
4 sage leaves
15 oysters
$\frac{1}{2}$ lb puff paste

Cut a piece of a moderate-sized conger into pieces of convenient size; take out the bone, and put it on the fire with any odd bit of the fish there may be to spare, with a quart of water, a quarter of an onion, a bunch of sweet herbs, pepper, salt, and a little spice, and let it simmer to make the gravy. Season the pieces of conger with pepper and salt, and boil them with parsley and sage minced finely. Arrange them in a pie-dish, pour in the gravy (which should be strong enough to jelly when cold), put the oysters on the top, and pour in their liquor, cover the pie with a good puff paste, and bake it in a moderate oven.

Mrs Giles, Shaftesbury, Dorset

BACON AND EGG FLAN

8 oz short pastry
3 oz streaky bacon
1 small onion
2 eggs

¼ pint creamy milk
1 oz butter
Pepper and salt
1 oz grated cheese

Line sponge tin or flan ring with pastry. Chop bacon and onion in small pieces and soften in butter. Put into flan case. Beat eggs and milk lightly together, season with salt and pepper, and pour on top of bacon and onion. Sprinkle on grated cheese. Bake at 375°F (Gas Mark 5) for 30 minutes. Serve hot or cold.

BACON AND MUSHROOM FLAN

6 oz short pastry
4 oz back bacon
4 oz mushrooms
1 oz butter

2 large eggs
½ pint milk
Salt and pepper

Line a pie plate or flan ring with the pastry. Chop the bacon and mushrooms and cook in the butter until the mushrooms are just soft. Put into the pastry case. Whisk the eggs with the milk and seasoning (the bacon may be a bit salt already). Pour into the pastry case and bake at 425°F (Gas Mark 7) for 35 minutes. Scatter a few chopped chives or a little parsley on the top and serve hot or cold.

CHEESE AND MUSHROOM FLAN

6 oz short pastry
8 oz mushrooms
1 oz butter
¼ pint cream

2 eggs and 1 egg yolk
2 oz grated Cheddar cheese
Salt and pepper

Line an 8-inch flan ring with pastry. Fry sliced or chopped mushrooms in butter. Beat up cream, eggs and egg yolk, and add drained mushrooms and cheese. Season with salt and pepper, and pour into pastry case. Sprinkle with a little cheese, and bake at 375°F (Gas Mark 5) for 40 minutes.

MUSHROOM FLAN

4 oz short pastry
1 small onion
2 oz bacon
1½ oz butter
8 oz mushrooms

2 eggs
¼ pint milk
2 oz grated cheese
Salt and pepper

Line 7-inch flan ring with pastry. Chop onion finely and dice bacon and cook in butter until soft. Add sliced mushrooms and cook until just tender. Season well with salt and pepper and put into flan case. Beat together eggs and milk and add most of the cheese, and pour over mushroom mixture. Sprinkle with cheese and bake at 350°F (Gas Mark 4) for 40 minutes.

MRS HIBBERD'S PASTRY

Take 1½ lb self-raising flour, ½ teaspoon salt and ¾ lb lard, or lard and butter or margarine. Rub the fat into the flour but *not* too finely, leave lumps of fat but not too big. Add sufficient, very cold water (iced if possible) to bind together into a pastry nice to handle and *leave* for an hour or 2 in the cool before rolling out.

This method is so quick to do that the pastry can be made in an odd moment and put aside.

INSTANT PASTRY MIX

3 *lb self-raising flour*   1½ *lb lard and/or margarine*

Rub fat into flour, but stop before the mixture reaches the breadcrumb stage. It should be lumpy. Store in a very cool place up to 2 to 3 weeks. Just add ice-cold water to make flaky-type pastry. You can make instant crumbles, rockbuns, puddings, etc. by adding sugar and more elbow grease. This is a useful standby in the Honey household.

9 *Savoury Puddings*

'Goose and dumplings,' observed Trumper; 'goose and dumplings: suppose you can dine off them?'
'Nothing better,' said Scott; 'nothing better.'
'Lots of onions!' added Trumper; 'lots of onions!'
'That's your ticket,' replied Scott; 'that's your ticket.'

'Hawbuck Grange'
R. S. Surtees

Suet-based pastry has always been a favourite in country kitchens. Steak, pork, minced meat, offal, poultry, game and bacon have formed the fillings of delicious gravy-soaked puddings and roly-polys for centuries. The thick suet crust has helped to make scarce meat go a long way. In many cases, there has been no meat at all, and some of these puddings have been simply flavoured with herbs and oatmeal, to serve with a gravy and take the place of meat. Similar puddings, sometimes made with a batter, were often devised to eke out expensive roasts (Yorkshire pudding is the classic example), and were usually cooked under the meat, but served first with gravy to curb the appetite. Dumplings have also been traditionally used to extend stewed meats for large families, or to make the best of small pieces of bacon or offal.

In some of the recipes there are individual measurements for the suet pastry.

If you want to make up your own recipe to suit the amount of filling you have available, allow 1 oz flour to ½ oz shredded suet for 1 helping of pudding. For a 4- or 5-person family, a suet crust of 8 oz flour and 4 oz suet will give enough for a good-sized pudding which will allow for some second helpings.

Flour can be self-raising, or plain with the addition of baking powder (a teaspoon to 8 oz flour). Black treacle (about 1 teaspoon to 8 oz flour) gives a rich-tasting and well-coloured crust. 6 tablespoons of cold water will be enough to mix this proportion of suet pastry.

Some people prefer to line the basin before putting in the filling, but others say this takes up too much of the meat juices and prefer all the crust on top. Some 'dry' puddings are better cooked as savoury rolypolys, to be served with gravy or a knob of butter, and this is a good method for the various types of bacon and onion pudding.

To cover a pudding, use kitchen foil or double greaseproof paper, brushed with melted fat, or use a pudding cloth. Make sure the water is at boiling point when the basin is put into the steamer or saucepan. A ½ pint of water will evaporate in 30 minutes when boiled, so puddings which are to be left to steam on their own for 2 or 3 hours should be put in a pan containing not less than 3 pints of boiling water. 'Topping up' should always be with boiling water.

STEAK AND KIDNEY PUDDING

8 oz self-raising flour
4 oz shredded suet
Salt and pepper
6 tablespoons water

1 lb stewing steak
3 lambs' kidneys or 4 oz ox kidney

Cut steak into thin pieces and chop kidney in small pieces. If liked, wrap a piece of meat round each piece of kidney, but otherwise just mix the 2 meats. Mix flour, suet, salt and pepper to a firm paste with water. Line a greased basin with ⅔ of the pastry. Put in the meat, and season well with salt and pepper and add a sprinkling of flour. Add water or stock almost to the top of the basin. Cover with remaining pastry and seal edges. Cover and steam for 4 hours.

Variations: Either add 1 small chopped onion or substitute 3 sliced onions for kidney. 2 oz chopped mushrooms may be added and/or 8 oysters for a special occasion (tinned ones can be used). 1 lb minced steak mixed with 4 oz mushrooms and a small chopped onion also make a good pudding, with a pinch of thyme mixed with the seasoning.

RABBIT OR HARE PUDDING

8 oz self-raising flour
4 oz shredded suet
Salt and pepper
6 tablespoons water
1 small rabbit

½ teaspoon sage
2 sliced onions
2 sliced tomatoes
2 oz chopped mushrooms

Make in the same way as for steak-and-kidney, using rabbit joints and stock or water.

HARE PUDDING

1½ lb meat cut from hare
2 sliced onions
1 sliced apple

1 tablespoon red wine or
redcurrant jelly

Make as for steak-and-kidney, adding red wine or redcurrant jelly to stock or water, and using plenty of seasoning. As hare joints are so large it is better to strip the meat from them before using.

KENTISH PORK AND APPLE PUDDING

8 oz self-raising flour
4 oz shredded suet
8 oz fresh lean pork
Medium-sized cooking apple

Salt and pepper
Sage
Stock or water

Prepare pastry with flour and suet and enough water to make a firm paste. Line basin with pastry, and put in pork cut in squares, chopped apple, salt and pepper, a good pinch of chopped sage and stock to cover. Put on pastry lid, cover and boil for 4 hours.

NORTHAMPTONSHIRE BACON ROLL

8 oz self-raising flour
3 oz suet
Salt and pepper

6 oz chopped mixed bacon
and onion

Make suet pastry, using just enough water to make a firm dough. Roll into a rectangle and put on bacon and onion, and plenty of seasoning. A little chopped sage may be added. Roll in a floured cloth and boil for 1½ hours. Serve with gravy.

ESSEX PORK PLUGGA

This is made in the same way as Northamptonshire Bacon Roll but using diced streaky pork instead of bacon.

SUSSEX BACON PUDDING

The bacon, onion and some chopped herbs are added to the suet mixture, together with a beaten egg and a little milk (instead of the usual water to make the pastry). The mixture is steamed in a basin for 1½ hours and served with gravy.

SUFFOLK LAYER PUDDING

6 oz self-raising flour
6 oz plain flour
¼ teaspoon salt
4 oz suet

1 lb cooked minced meat
1 medium onion
Salt and pepper

Mix suet pastry with the two kinds of flour, salt, suet and milk to moisten. Line a pudding basin with half the mixture. Use meat left from the joint, or fresh mince which has been cooked, and use a little stock or gravy to moisten. Mix meat with chopped onion and seasoning. Put a layer of meat mixture into basin, then a thin layer of suet pastry, then more meat and pastry until basin is full, ending with pastry layer. Cover and steam for 2 hours. Serve with gravy or parsley sauce.

SUFFOLK ONION PUDDING

4 oz plain flour
2 oz suet

8 oz onions
Salt and pepper

Mix flour and suet with water to a stiff dough – and roll out. Cut up onions, salt and pepper them, and put on to dough. Roll up into a cloth. Boil for 1¼ hours. Serve with a slice of butter. This is very good with boiled bacon or a piece of beef.

CHICKEN PUDDING

12 oz self-raising flour
6 oz suet
1 old chicken
1 chopped onion
1 chopped garlic clove
(optional)

Bayleaf
Salt and pepper
1 dessertspoon chopped
parsley

Make up suet pastry with enough water to give a firm paste. Cut flesh from legs, wings and breast of bird. Line a basin with suet pastry. Fill with alternate layers of meat and onion, with garlic, seasoning and parsley. Put bayleaf in the centre. Just cover meat with stock or water, and top with pastry. Steam for 4 hours. Serve with gravy made from chicken stock, using carcass of bird, or with parsley sauce.

STAFFORDSHIRE LIVER PUDDING

8 oz self-raising flour
4 oz suet
2 lb ox liver

2 large onions
Salt and pepper

Make suet pastry with enough water to give a firm paste. Put diced liver and onions in a basin, mixing well, and season with salt and pepper. Cover with stock and put on pastry lid. Steam for 3 hours.

PIGEON PUDDING (1)

8 oz self-raising flour
4 oz suet
2 pigeons

8 oz shin beef
1 kidney

Make up suet pastry and line a pudding basin. Cut pigeons in quarters and put in basin with diced beef and kidney. Season well and cover with stock. Put on pastry lid and steam for $2\frac{1}{2}$ hours.

PIGEON PUDDING (2)

8 oz self-raising flour
$\frac{1}{2}$ teaspoon salt
4 oz shredded suet
3 pigeons

8 oz chuck steak
3 hard-boiled eggs
Salt, pepper and mace

Make a suet pastry by mixing flour, salt, suet and $\frac{1}{4}$ pint cold water. Line a pudding basin with pastry, leaving enough for a lid. In the basin put the breasts of the pigeons, the steak cut in small pieces, the egg yolks, salt, pepper, and a pinch of mace. Pour in stock from the bones and trimmings, to just cover the meat. Cover with suet crust, tie on a pudding cloth, and cook in a saucepan of boiling water for 3 hours.

GAME PUDDING (1)

1 old grouse or partridge　　**Salt and pepper**
1 oz butter　　　　　　　　　**Mace**
1 onion　　　　　　　　　　　**Suet pastry**
1 lb stewing steak

Line a basin with half the suet pastry, made with 8 oz flour. Cut the bird into quarters and brown them in the butter. Cut steak in cubes and roll it in flour. Put game and steak into basin, add chopped onion, salt and pepper and a pinch of mace. Fill up with stock. Cover with remaining suet pastry and steam for 3 hours. Chopped parsley or other herbs may be added, and so can mushrooms and/or ham or bacon. Stock can be made from game livers and carcasses and used as extra gravy.

GAME PUDDING (2)

8 oz suet pastry　　　　　　　**Salt, pepper and nutmeg**
4 pigeons or 2 partridges　　　**Stock made from game**
8 oz stewing steak　　　　　　**trimmings**
Yolks of 3 hard-boiled eggs

If pigeons are used, the breasts only can go into the pudding, and the rest be simmered for stock. If partridges are used, they can be split in half. I like the addition of a little bacon and a chopped onion, and sometimes a few mushrooms to this pudding, but they are optional. If appetites are very hearty, the quantity of suet pastry may be increased so that the bowl can be lined as well.

Line the bowl with $\frac{1}{2}$ inch thick pastry if liked. Put in pigeon breasts or halved partridges, chopped steak, egg yolks, seasoning, and gravy to come half way up the bowl. Put on pastry lid and cover with cloth. Cook for 3 hours.

BACON LAYER PUDDING

8 oz suet pastry　　　　　　　**2 onions**
8 oz chopped bacon　　　　　　**2 carrots**

Roll out the pastry thinly and cut out a round to fit the bottom of a greased 2-pint basin. Put in a layer of bacon pieces. Grate the onions and carrots, and put a little of the mixture on top of the bacon. Put on another layer of pastry, then bacon and vegetables. Continue until basin is full, topping with pastry. Cover and steam for 2 hours. Serve with gravy.

NORFOLK BEEF PUDDING

8 oz self-raising flour
3 oz shredded suet
Pinch of salt

12 oz stewing steak
1 shallot
Salt and pepper

Make up a suet crust with flour, suet, salt and water. Roll it out and put on to a piece of greased greaseproof paper. Cut up the meat and shallot finely and put on to the suet pastry. Sprinkle with water and season with salt and pepper. Tie up in a cloth and steam for 3½ hours.

NORFOLK MUSSEL PUDDING

8 oz self-raising flour
3 oz shredded suet
Pinch of salt

2 pints mussels
Salt and pepper

Make the suet crust with flour, suet, salt and water, and roll out. Put on to a piece of greased greaseproof paper. Wash the mussels well and remove their beards. Put them in a pan on a very low heat and they will open quickly. Put them on to the dough, season with salt and pepper. Tie up in a cloth and steam for 1½ hours.

PARTRIDGE PUDDING

1½ lb flour
½ lb suet
¼ lb rump steak
Brace of old partridges
½ teaspoon pepper
1 teaspoon salt

¼ lb mushrooms
1 teaspoon each freshly
chopped parsley, thyme and
tarragon
¾ pint brown stock
¼ pint sweet stout

Line a 2-pint pudding basin with a suet crust made with the flour, suet and enough cold water to make a stiff dough, leaving enough crust for a cover. Cut the rump steak in thin slices and put on the bottom, cut the partridges into neat joints and season with pepper and salt, and put into the basin mixed with sliced mushrooms and herbs. Pour in stock mixed with stout, cover with suet crust and pinch the edges together. Tie a pudding cloth or foil over the basin, place in boiling water, and keep boiling for 3 hours.

GROUSE PUDDING

8 oz *plain flour*
1 *teaspoon baking powder*
½ *teaspoon salt*
4 oz *suet*
1 *old grouse*

1 lb *stewing steak*
1 *onion*
1 oz *butter*
Salt, pepper and nutmeg

Sift together flour, baking powder and salt, and add the grated or chopped suet. Stir in enough cold water to make a pliable dough, and line a pudding basin with two-thirds of the pastry. Cut the flesh of the grouse into neat chunks, stewing the bones and trimmings in water to make a good stock. Brown the grouse and cubes of steak in the butter and put into the basin with salt, pepper and a pinch of nutmeg, chopped onion, and enough stock or water to half fill the basin. Cover with the top crust, put on paper and a cloth, and steam for 3 hours, adding boiling water to the saucepan to keep it almost to the top of the basin. Make a hole in the top crust before serving and pour in hot stock or gravy.

1870 PORK PUDDING
Time to boil – 2½ hours.

1½ lb *pork*
¾ lb *sausage meat*
A few leaves of sage

1 *onion*
Pepper and salt
Suet crust

Line the pudding basin and lay in the slices of pork, add the sausage meat, season highly, cover with the crust, and boil in a floured cloth.

Puddings may also be made in a similar way from ox-kidney slices, and mutton kidneys.

Mrs Giles, Shaftesbury, Dorset

KIDNEY PUDDING

3 *sheeps' kidneys*
2 *teacups breadcrumbs*
1 *teacup milk*
1 *egg*

1 *teaspoon suet*
Nutmeg, parsley and mixed herbs
Salt and pepper

Skin the kidneys, mince them and mix with the suet. Put into a basin with the breadcrumbs. Add a little chopped parsley, some mixed herbs, grated nutmeg, salt and pepper. Beat the egg, mix with the milk, then stir both into the pudding mixture. Pour into a buttered basin and steam for 1½ hours. Turn out and serve with green vegetables and thick gravy.

VENISON PUDDING

1 lb thin fillet of venison   8 oz suet crust pastry
2 oz diced bacon   ½ pint stock
4 oz mushrooms   A little red wine if available

Thoroughly grease a pie dish. Flour a thin fillet of venison and lay it at the bottom. Season, and add diced bacon and small mushrooms. Set it in the oven, dry, to cook for about 20 minutes, while you make a light suet crust. Season the crust lightly and roll it out to fit the pie dish. By now the floured meat in the dish should have browned slightly and the bacon be crisp. Fill up the dish with stock and a little red wine if available. Put on the paste and cook until the crust is well risen, about $1\frac{1}{4}$ hours at 350°F (Gas Mark 4)

After putting on the crust, but before baking, score the top fairly deeply into squares, this gives the dough a better appearance. Suet is advised for the crust as the pie needs long baking. If the steak is cut in small pieces and well fried in the dish first, it should be tender by the time the crust is done.

RABBIT PUDDING

Cut a young rabbit into joints, soak and dry well. Line a pudding basin with suet pastry, and put in alternate layers of rabbit, chopped onion, sage and chopped mushrooms. The layers should be well-floured, and strips of fat bacon inserted at intervals, with a good sprinkling of salt and pepper. Fill the basin with water, cover with a suet crust, and tie on greaseproof paper. Steam for 3 hours. The pudding will make its own rich thick gravy.

MRS CHAPMAN'S BACON ROLL

Mix well together 12 oz flour, 4 oz suet (or dripping), 1 teaspoon of baking powder, $\frac{1}{4}$ teaspoon salt. Add enough water to make a stiff paste, then roll out $\frac{1}{4}$ inch thick. Cut $\frac{1}{2}$ lb thin, streaky rashers into pieces, peel and chop 3 large onions. Put the bacon and onions in alternate layers on the pastry. Sprinkle with pepper and a cautious quantity of salt, then roll up. Tie securely in a pudding cloth, and boil for 3 hours. Serve with a good brown gravy, carrots and cabbage cooked in very little water for a minimum of time.

This comes from a very happy Oxfordshire family of 10 children – 5 boys, 5 girls. Their mother was a past master (or should it be mistress?) at making her slender housekeeping allowance stretch to its limit; this recipe was one of her standbys and one will never forget the atmosphere as they all sat round the big kitchen table after just such a delicious dish, which, with home-grown vegetables, cost so little yet fed so many so well.

BUCKS DUMPLING

8 oz liver
8 oz streaky bacon
1 lb flour
6 oz shredded suet

2 large onions
1 dessertspoon chopped sage
Salt and pepper

Cut liver and bacon very small. Mix flour and suet to a stiff dough with a little water and a pinch of salt. Roll out to a rectangle. Cover dough with liver and bacon. Grate onions over the top, together with chopped sage and plenty of pepper and salt. Roll up tightly in a floured cloth and boil 2½ hours. Serve with a good gravy.

KIDNEY DUMPLINGS

Put a well-seasoned lamb's kidney into the scooped-out centre of a large onion, and wrapping the onion in suet pastry, bake at 350°F (Gas Mark 4) for 1¼ hours, and serve with good rich gravy.

SUFFOLK DUMPLINGS

¾ lb flour
6 oz suet
1½ gills water
2 lb lean pork

1½ lb onions
½ teaspoon salt
Seasoning to taste

Grease a pudding basin and find a pudding cloth big enough to tie over the basin and a disc of greased paper which will cover the top. Make a crust from flour, suet and a little water mixed to a thick pastry consistency. Line the basin with the crust, keeping back enough to cover the top. Cut the pork into pieces and mix with the chopped onions. Put into basin in layers with seasoning between. Add remaining water until basin is full. Cover with top crust, which should not be too thin. Cover with paper, wrap in the cloth, and steam for 4 hours.

A TASTY BATTER PUDDING

1 oz shredded suet
4 oz flour
2 eggs

1 pint milk
Pinch of salt

Mix suet and flour with salt. Beat eggs, and add to the mixture, and make into a batter with the milk. Put into a greased pie dish and bake for 1½ hours in a moderate oven. Serve with meat, or by adding 2 tablespoons of sugar and a few currants, make it into a sweet pudding.

SAVOURY PUDDING

2 oz shredded suet
6 oz stale bread
½ pint milk
2 oz fine oatmeal

3 eggs
Salt and pepper
Cayenne pepper
Thyme, sage and marjoram

Soak bread in hot milk and leave it to get cold. Mix dry ingredients with bread. Beat eggs and mix well in. Melt some dripping in a tin to boiling point. Spread in mixture with a fork. Bake for 30 to 40 minutes in oven with joint. Serve like Yorkshire pudding.

YORKSHIRE SAVOURY PUDDING

4 large onions
2 teaspoons chopped sage
8 oz bread without crust

1 oz oatmeal
3 oz shredded suet
Salt and pepper

Pour some boiling water over the bread and leave to stand for 30 minutes. Drain well but do not squeeze out moisture. Chop the onions finely and mix with bread and other ingredients. Put into greased oven tin and bake at 375°F (Gas Mark 5) for 1 hour until well browned. Cut into slices to serve with thick gravy and vegetables.

DUCK PUDDING

3 oz bread without crust
1½ gills milk
1 egg
2 oz shredded suet

1 teaspoon flour
1 onion
½ teaspoon chopped sage
Salt and pepper

Pour the milk over the bread and leave for 10 minutes, then beat well with a spoon. Stir in the egg, suet, flour, finely-chopped onion, sage and seasoning. Grease and warm some small patty tins, and put in the mixture. Bake for 15 minutes at 450°F (Gas Mark 7). Take out and put under roasting duck or pork for the last 15 minutes' cooking time. The mixture can also be baked in an oven tin in a hot oven for 25 minutes until risen, and then be put underneath the duck or pork. Cut into slices to serve.

OATMEAL PUDDING

Mix 2 oz fine Scotch oatmeal in ¼ pint of milk. Add to it a pint of boiling milk and stir over the fire for 10 minutes. Then put in 2 oz sifted bread-crumbs, or as much as will make the mixture rather stiff. Take it off the fire and mix with it 2 oz suet, two eggs and a teaspoonful chopped marjoram and sage. Butter a Yorkshire pudding pan, put in the pudding and bake for an hour in a moderate oven. Turn out on a hot dish and have a little good gravy in a boat.

Mrs Garden, 1847

LINCOLNSHIRE PUDDING

A Yorkshire pudding with sultanas in.
Served before meal with a good gravy.

NORFOLK DUMPLINGS

A yeast dumpling.
Served before meal with gravy.
Make a dough as for bread, but mix with milk, plunge into boiling water and boil for 20 minutes. Serve at once with gravy or sugar and butter. Do not touch with a knife, but tear apart with 2 forks.

SUFFOLK OR LARD DUMPLINGS

1 lb flour   **½ pint water**
½ saltspoon salt

Mix and form into round dumplings, put into boiling water and boil ½ to ¾ of an hour. Serve with roast or boiled meat, sometimes boiled with the meat.

Empire Marketing Board, 1929

MRS CROWFOOT'S DUMPLINGS

2 eggs   **8 tablespoons milk**
8 tablespoons flour

Made into two dumplings and boiled ¾ of an hour. The thick gravy is made by dredging the meat well with flour and adding a little water.

Mrs Garden, 1863

SUSSEX DRIP PUDDING

Serve this instead of Yorkshire pudding. Make a suet pudding and cook it the same time as you roast a joint of beef. (By tradition all Sussex puddings are cooked in a cloth but if you steam it in a basin, the effect is the same.) When the roast is ready, remove it from the pan, cut the pudding into slices and soak well in the hot dripping. Place the slices on a hot dish and brown in the oven while making the gravy.

MEALY PUDDINGS

Long pudding skins
1 lb oatmeal
½ lb suet

2 large onions (parboiled)
¼ teaspoon salt
¼ teaspoon pepper

Wash pudding skins in warm water and leave to soak in cold water and salt. Chop onions, mix with oatmeal, suet and seasonings. Tie end of pudding skin with thread, put in enough mixture to make length of a sausage. Tie skin again, leaving enough room for pudding to swell. Continue until mixture is finished. Put into pan with boiling water and salt, pricking puddings first to prevent their bursting, and simmer for 20–30 minutes.

Mrs Biggan, Kirkcudbrightshire

LEEK (OR ONION) PUDDING

4 oz self-raising flour
2 oz suet
2 leeks or onions

Water to mix
Seasoning

Sieve flour, add suet and seasoning. Mix to a stiff dough with water. Roll out ⅔ thinly to line greased pudding basin. Chop leeks and fill up centre; cover with ⅓ suet pastry rolled out to form lid. Alternatively, the chopped leeks may be mixed in with the suet pastry, and all turned into the basin. Cover with foil and boil in pan of water for 2 hours. Serve in slices with meat dishes instead of dumplings.

Mrs Biggan, Kircudbrightshire

PEASE PUDDING

½ pint split peas
½ oz butter

1 mashed potato
Salt, pepper and sugar

Tie peas in a pudding cloth (loosely to allow for swelling) and boil for 3 to 4 hours until soft. Drain well, pass through a wire sieve, beat in butter, potato and seasonings. Turn out into a dish and serve with boiled salt pork and baked or boiled ham.

Mrs Biggan, Kircudbrightshire

SAVOURY PUDDING

6 oz stale bread
½ pint milk
6 oz oatmeal
½ lb boiled onions (optional)

4 oz suet or dripping
1 or 2 eggs
Salt and pepper
1 teaspoonful baking powder

Break bread into small pieces, soak in milk and mash well with fork. Add the oatmeal, salt, sage, onion and suet or dripping and stir well. Stir in the beaten eggs, dust well with pepper and add the baking powder. Place in a greased baking tin and bake in a moderate oven, 375°F, for ½ hour.

This dish can be eaten with sizzling sausages for supper or with pork, as a change from sage and onion stuffing. It is delicious eaten with fried or grilled trout which has been dipped in wholemeal flour, served with horseradish sauce.

SAVOURY BAKE

Peel 3 large onions and cook them until tender, then drain well and chop finely. Chop 4 oz suet, crumble 4 oz bread, rub ½ oz thyme and ½ oz sage to a fine powder, or if fresh herbs used, chop them finely; and beat up with 1 egg. Put all these ingredients into a basin, season with pepper and salt, and mix well together, adding a little milk if necessary to moisten. Melt a little dripping (1 oz) in a tin, pour in the pudding and cook for an hour in a moderately hot oven. Serve with good brown gravy. Sausages or odd scraps of bacon chopped and fried could be served with this, with vegetables added to make a main meal.

CHEESE AND ONION ROLY-POLY

8 oz plain flour
½ level teaspoon salt
½ level teaspoon baking
powder
4 oz suet
Cold water to bind

4 oz thinly sliced onions
8 oz thinly sliced Cheddar
cheese
Pinch each pepper, salt and
nutmeg
A little milk

Sieve the flour, salt and baking powder, mix in the suet and sufficient cold water to make a soft dough. Knead lightly and roll out to an oblong strip. Scatter the onions and cheese over the surface with pepper, salt and nutmeg, damp the edges and roll up like a Swiss roll. Brush with milk, bake in fairly hot oven at 400°F (Gas Mark 6) for 40–45 minutes until browned, or roll in greased greaseproof paper and steam for 1½ hours. Serve hot with tomato sauce.

CHEESE AND LEEK PUDDING

$8\frac{1}{2}$ oz plain flour
$\frac{1}{2}$ level teaspoon salt
2 level teaspoons baking powder
3 oz suet
10 oz grated Cheddar cheese

Cold water to bind
1 lb leeks
$\frac{1}{2}$ oz butter
$\frac{1}{2}$ pint milk (or milk and water)

Sieve 8 oz flour, salt and baking powder, mix in the suet and 2 oz cheese, and bind with cold water. Use $\frac{2}{3}$ of this dough to line a greased pint-size pudding basin and reserve $\frac{1}{3}$ for the 'lid'. Wash the leeks thoroughly and cut into rounds. Make cheese sauce with the remaining $\frac{1}{2}$ oz flour, cheese, butter and milk, or milk and water. Fill the pudding with alternate layers of leeks and cheese sauce, ending with leeks. Put on the 'lid' and seal the edges. Cover with greased greaseproof paper or foil and steam for $1\frac{1}{2}$ hours. Turn out and serve hot.

10 *Egg and Cheese Dishes*

When fish is scant, and fruit of trees,
supply that want, with butter and cheese.

Thomas Tusser

An egg boiled soft is not unwholesome
'Emma', Jane Austen

Farm wives like to use a lot of eggs and cheese in their cooking. Traditionally, they have been easily available and quick to use on busy days, and a lot of favourite farm dishes combine the two ingredients into tasty snacks.

Most of us know the pleasure of a good hunk of Cheshire or Cheddar with a corner of new bread, creamy butter, and perhaps a crisp radish or onion. Not so many have enjoyed experimenting with Wensleydale, Stilton, Double Gloucester, Derby, Lancashire, Leicester and Caerphilly, with the rare Dorset Blue Vinney, and the more difficult to find Dunlop and Orkney. All of them repay searching out, as do the increasing variety of interesting cream cheeses which appear regionally.

Price for price, these cheeses represent excellent nutritional value compared with meat, but what most of us care about is the taste. To get the best cheeses, in perfect condition, with full flavour, seek out a grocer who really knows his business, and there are still quite a lot of them about. When you can see large pieces of cheese side by side, it's so much easier to compare texture and flavour (no good cheese merchant will begrudge you a small 'taster' when you are comparing and buying). Today the trend is towards neat even slices tightly wrapped in plastic; excellent for the bedsitter or the occasional picnic when you can't be bothered with leftovers, but useless for the normal family.

Buy only enough cheese for a week's supply at a time, because cheese will deteriorate after cutting. Keep cheese away from draughts or too much air circulation which will dry it out. Keep the cheese in a polythene bag, foil, or greaseproof paper and store it in a cool place. It can be kept in the refrigerator away from the ice-making compartment, and should be taken out at least an hour before eating to regain temperature and full flavour.

If you find a really good big piece of cheese, it can be frozen, wrapped in polythene (if it has a strong flavour, wrap it in freezer paper or foil, then in polythene, to prevent cross-flavouring in the freezer). Don't try to store the cheese longer than 2 months, and don't expect perfect texture (many cheeses crumble when cut after freezing), but the flavour will still be good.

If you get a lot of cheese ends, grate them finely (easier if the cheese is dried out naturally in a cool airy place), and store the grated cheese in a loosely covered jar in a cool place. This makes an excellent standby for quick and easy cooking, and for adding extra flavour to soups, salads and pasta.

Perhaps most of us tend to forget, or never know, how good these British cheeses can be for cooking. Most of us basically use Cheddar, but Double Gloucester, Wensleydale and Cheshire also give excellent results, and best of all is Lancashire, known to so many as the only cheese for toasting. Orkney, recently introduced, is rather like a mild Cheddar, and though it is too soft for grating well, it is creamy and delicious for Welsh Rarebit. Here are their characteristics:

Cheshire: A mellow, open-textured cheese with the salty tang of the Cheshire pastures. There are red, white and blue varieties, 'Old Blue' being the richest – and rarest. It has been produced in the county since the twelfth century.

Cheddar: The 'prodigious cheese . . . of delicate taste' of which William Camden wrote in the days of the first Elizabeth. Made under the shadow of the Mendip Hills, close by Cheddar Gorge, genuine Cheddar is coveted for its unique 'nutty' flavour.

Wensleydale: 'An apple pie wi owt tha Cheese is like a kiss wi owt a squeeze.' That is what they say in Yorkshire, where this subtle flavoured and flaky textured cheese comes from. The recipe has come down from the abbots of Jervaulx Abbey. Its special peculiarity is the delicious honeyed after-taste, redolent of the lush dale pastureland.

Stilton: A connoisseur's cheese. Rich, mellow Blue Stilton comes from

Melton Mowbray, from Hartingdon in the Dove Valley and from the Vale of Belvoir. A creamy young White Stilton is popular in the North Country.

Double Gloucester: A pungent, smooth-textured, cheese somewhat similar to Cheddar, but fuller in flavour. It was once carried round in the old Gloucestershire May Day processions, garlanded with flowers. Charles Lamb's favourite supper cheese.

Derby: A mild, close-textured, creamy cheese with a pale honey colour that develops a fuller flavour in four to six months. Sage Derby, flavoured with sage leaves, is a traditional Christmas delicacy.

Lancashire: 'Many's the night I've dreamed of cheese – toasted mostly', said Ben Gunn in Stevenson's *Treasure Island.* He probably meant the famous old toaster from north of the Ribble, the original 'Leigh Toaster'. Although possessing a mild flavour when young, this cheese develops a full and rather pungent flavour as it matures. Its loose texture makes it ideal for crumbling over soups and hot-pots. Also obtainable as 'Sage Lancashire' – this contains chopped sage leaves mixed in with the curd during cheesemaking.

Leicester: A fine dessert cheese of mild flavour, becoming more piquant with maturity. Millstone in shape, and with a rich russet colour that looks particularly well on the board.

Caerphilly: The small creamy white cheese that nowadays comes from the West of England as well as from the small Glamorgan village that gave it birth. Gentle and milky in flavour – a cheese for those who like buttermilk and yoghurt. A delicacy in Wales, where it is served for tea, together with celery and thin slices of bread and butter. A great favourite with children.

Hints on separating eggs

There are many ways of separating eggs without the use of a separator:

1. Break an egg on a saucer, invert an eggcup over the yolk and drain off the white.

2. Break the egg in 2, and hold the half-shells like 2 cups. Gently tip the yolk from one half-shell to the other, and the white will gradually drop into a bowl placed beneath.

3. Set a small, wide-stemmed funnel in a glass. Break the egg in the funnel and the white will slip through to the glass.

4. With a needle, prick a smallish hole in the round end of an egg. Gradually enlarge it until the white runs out. Take care not to prick the yolk with the needle.

Never attempt to whip egg whites that contain even the tiniest speck of yolk. The yolk contains fat and this will prevent the whites beating stiffly. So will any smear of grease on whisk, basin or other utensil used.

Egg yolks

They are better if used immediately, but they can be kept for 2 or 3 days if placed, whole, in a screw-topped jar, covered with cold water and put in the refrigerator.

Add an egg yolk to the mixing of pastry, scones and batters, to cream sauces and soups (but do not let the liquid boil after adding the yolk). Add an extra yolk or 2 to scrambled eggs. Or make this dish with yolks alone, adding 2 tablespoons of milk for each yolk when mixing; cook in a greased basin set in a pan of water. Poach them hard (this can be done in an eggcup standing for 15 minutes in simmering water), rub through a sieve and use the resulting Mimosa balls to garnish soups, salads and rice dishes.

Egg whites

They will keep for several days in a covered bowl in the refrigerator (away from the freezer).

Add an extra white or 2 to soufflés, or to any sweets or savouries of the mousse type. Or whisk a white into a just-setting jelly. Give a meringue top to plain milk puddings – jut a few minutes in a hot oven is sufficient cooking. Egg whites can be used in place of egg and breadcrumbs in coating meat cakes and vegetables. Whisked stiffly, they can be added to fruit purée and cream to make a delicious dessert.

WENDOVER EGGS

A plate of cold boiled ham. Chop up 1 or 2 soft-boiled eggs (7 minutes) on top. Whites will be set, yolks creamy. Add butter, pepper, salt.

EGG AND TOMATO SCRAMBLE

Heat some butter in a small saucepan. In this soften a tomato cut into 8. Pour in 1 or 2 well-beaten eggs, stir over gentle heat, until the eggs are set.

EGG AND VEGETABLE SCRAMBLE

Heat any leftover vegetables, bacon pieces, and/or sliced sausage pieces, in fry-pan. Stir in egg and water and scramble.

EGGS IN A NEST

There are many ways of making these. Make the nest from a baked potato with some of the inside scooped out, break in the egg and pop back in the oven. Or choose large firm tomatoes, cut off the tops, and scoop out the insides. Into the hollows flake morsels of butter. Now pop a raw egg in each, season well, and cook on greased baking sheet for about 15 minutes at 400°F (Gas Mark 6).

EGG ROLLS

This is just right for the family. Mix 1½ lb mashed potatoes with 6 chopped hard-boiled eggs and 3 oz grated cheese. Season and add flavouring – 6–8 chopped spring onions do very nicely. Mould into 8 rolls, dip in beaten egg, coat with breadcrumbs and then fry in deep fat until golden brown.

EGG HUBBLE-BUBBLE

Fry diced cooked potatoes, and any vegetable you may have handy (mushroom, tomato or peas do very well), in butter. When cooked, pour in 3 or 4 lightly beaten seasoned eggs. Sprinkle with grated cheese. Cook very slowly, with a plate over the top, until the eggs are set.

EGG-ON-POTATO CAKES

Add an egg to about 1 lb cold mashed potatoes, season well, add (according to preference) cooked peas, cooked chopped beans or carrots, or grated cheese, mould into patties, dip in beaten egg and then breadcrumbs. Fry in shallow fat, and serve with fried, poached or scrambled egg.

ADD-AN-EGG PIE

The beauty of this dish is that it can be reheated without spoiling. If you are going out, just bake it in the morning – leave it for the family to heat up, and you will not have to feel guilty at all. Using 8 oz short-crust pastry, line the bottom of an 8 inch shallow tin, leaving some pastry for the lid. Layer with 4 sliced hard-boiled eggs, 2 peeled and sliced tomatoes, and 4 thin rashers of bacon. Season well. Cover with pastry lid and bake about 30 minutes at 425°F (Gas Mark 7). You can also use 8 oz cooked fish with this recipe, substituting for the bacon. Smoked haddock, for instance.

FLUFFY EGGS

Beat egg white stiffly and fold in some finely grated cheese. Fill individual dish, or pile up on toast. Make a hollow in the centre and drop in egg yolk. Bake at 350°F (Gas Mark 4) about 10 minutes.

SCOTCH EGGS

4 hard-boiled eggs　　　　**1 beaten egg**
1 lb sausage meat　　　　**Brown breadcrumbs**

Divide the sausage meat into 4 pieces. Roll out thinly, put an egg in the centre of each piece, then roll up neatly; moulding with your fingers. A little beaten egg brushed onto the join wil keep the eggs from bursting out. Dip each ball into beaten egg, roll in breadcrumbs and fry in hot fat. Allow to get quite cold, then slice and serve with salad.

FRICASSEE OF EGGS

6 hard-boiled eggs　　　　**1 heaped teaspoon minced**
3 teacups chicken or veal　　**onion**
stock　　　　**1½ oz butter**
1 heaped teaspoon minced　**3 level tablespoons flour**
parsley　　　　**4 tablespoons milk**
　　　　　　　　　　　　Salt and pepper to taste

Shell and slice eggs. Melt butter. Stir in onion. Fry 2 minutes, then stir in flour. Gradually add stock. Stir till smooth and boiling. Season with salt and pepper to taste. Add eggs, milk, salt and pepper to taste. Mix lightly, then serve in a baked pastry case, or hollow out a mound of fluffy mashed potatoes, and pour in fricassée. Sprinkle with the parsley.

EGGS IN POTATO CASES

Take some potatoes which have been baked in their skins, cut them in halves, and scoop out all the potato pulp. Then mix it with a little butter, pepper and salt. Return the pulp to the skins, leaving a hollow in the centre. Boil some eggs soft. Shell them, and place them in the potatoes. Make a rich cheese sauce, and pour a little over each one. Place them in the oven till they are hot and a pale brown. Then sprinkle a little parsley over them, and serve them very hot.

Mrs Everard, 1911

EGG-IN-A-BED

2 oz butter　　　　**4 oz Cheddar cheese, grated**
4 oz mushrooms, sliced　　**4 eggs**
2 tomatoes, skinned and　　**4 tablespoons single cream**
chopped　　　　**Chopped parsley (optional)**
Salt and black pepper

Melt butter, fry mushrooms and chopped tomatoes, until tender, season to taste. Put the mixture plus half the cheese in the bottoms of 4 individual greased fireproof dishes. Break an egg into each dish. Pour 1 tablespoon cream gently over each, then top with the remaining cheese. Bake at 350°F (Gas Mark 4) for 8–10 minutes until eggs are set and cheese has melted. Serve immediately garnished with parsley.

LANCASHIRE EGGS

1 oz butter
1 teaspoon olive oil
½ lb Lancashire cheese

4 eggs
Salt and pepper

Put butter into a shallow fireproof dish with olive oil. Cover with slices of cheese, and melt over heat. Break the eggs on top and put into a moderate oven until the whites are set. Sprinkle with salt, pepper and grated cheese and brown under the grill.

EGG NESTS

1½ lb potatoes
2 tablespoons thin cream or
top milk

1 oz butter
4 eggs
1 oz grated cheese

Cook potatoes, drain well, mash with milk and butter. Divide into 4 portions and shape into round cakes. Hollow out the centre of each one, break in an egg and bake in a moderate oven for 10 minutes. Top with cheese and brown under the grill. For greater speed, poach eggs while you mash the potatoes, slip eggs into hollows, cover with cheese and brown the tops.

DEVILLED EGGS

2 tablespoons grated cheese
¼ teaspoon mustard
1 teaspoon tarragon vinegar
4 hard-boiled eggs

1 tablespoon melted butter
Salt and Cayenne pepper to
taste

Cut eggs in halves lengthwise. Remove egg yolks. Mash with cheese, mustard, vinegar, butter and enough milk to moisten. If liked, add a teaspoon grated onion or minced chives. Fill egg whites. Serve on tiny rounds of fried bread, or with sardines and potato salad as an hors-d'oeuvre course. Allow 2 halves per person.

EGGS IN PARSLEY SAUCE

6 hard-boiled eggs
2 teacups medium-thick parsley sauce

Grated cheese to taste
Salt and black pepper to taste

Shell and slice eggs. Place in a greased pie-dish. Season with salt and black pepper to taste. Add pinch of ground mace to taste to sauce and pour over. Sprinkle thickly with grated cheese. Cover with stale breadcrumbs Dab here and there with butter. Bake in a moderate oven until brown.

CHICKEN OMELETTE

1 teacup finely chopped chicken
1 oz butter
2 tablespoons flour

1 teacup milk
4 eggs
4 tablespoons hot water
Salt and pepper to taste

Melt butter in a small saucepan. Add flour. Stir till frothy, then add milk. Stir till smooth and boiling. Season with salt and pepper to taste. Add a rounded teaspoon of minced chives or parsley if liked, a pinch of ground mace, or grated cheese to taste. Keep hot. Beat egg whites till stiff. Beat yolks till thick and lemon-coloured. Beat in hot water and salt and pepper to taste. Fold in stiffly beaten egg whites. Melt about 1 teaspoon of butter, just enough to cover bottom of small omelette pan. When hot, add egg mixture. Cook over a slow fire till puffy and light brown below, then slip under grill or in oven till top is dry. Don't overcook or it will be tough. Loosen edges, make a dent in centre, slip on to a flat hot dish, fill with creamed chicken, and fold in 2. Serve with spinach or green peas.

MUSHROOM OMELETTE

6 eggs
Salt and pepper
4 oz mushrooms

2 oz butter
Pinch of nutmeg
3 tablespoons cream

Beat eggs lightly with a fork and season with salt and pepper. Wipe the mushrooms and chop them finely, and cook until soft in half the butter. Season with salt and pepper and a pinch of nutmeg, remove from heat and add the cream. Keep hot. Heat the remaining butter, pour in the eggs, and cook until the top is just beginning to set. Pour mushrooms on top, fold over and sprinkle with a little chopped parsley.

TOMATO OMELETTE

Peel 6 tomatoes, and cut them into small pieces. Beat up a tablespoon of flour with a little milk into a smooth paste. Add 4 well-beaten eggs, pepper, salt and the tomatoes. Put $\frac{1}{2}$ oz butter into a white enamelled frying pan, pour into the pan just sufficient of the mixture to just cover the pan, let it cook quickly, fold it over, and slide it on to a hot dish, and continue cooking the rest in the same manner.

DICK'S HOLIDAY COOK-UP

When our children were small we all 11 used to cram into one moderate-sized car to go on holiday. Later when the boys grew too big to be accommodated we used to select the half-fare-sized ones to travel by British Rail while we took the dog with us. Father was always cook for this one day each year and true to fashion he cooked what his mother had done for the 8 of them (we come from long lines of big families). Her object in those hard times in the early thirties, was to make a little go a very long way, but Dick adapted it for speed before the journey. It's really quick and easy to eat.

A panful of cold potatoes squashed up and put into hot frying pan with a little, not too much hot dripping. As many eggs as can be spared. Bacon previously cooked – if there are many more mouths than slices of bacon, just snip whatever you have into small pieces and cook these first, putting the potatoes on top and mashing bacon and potato together. When potato is cooking nicely, sprinkle with salt and pepper to taste (but don't be too mean with the pepper). Now pull the potato on one side in order to fry as many eggs as you have and put them, *unbroken*, on top of the potato – you may need to use 2 pans at this stage. Place the eggs carefully on top of the nicely browned potato, and in front of the assembled company break the yolks so that they run all over the spuds. Dish up really smartly on to nice hot plates.

Babs Honey

EGG RAREBIT

6 oz *Cheddar cheese*	2 *tablespoons brown ale or*
1 *level teaspoon dry mustard*	*milk*
Pepper	4 *slices bread*
	4 *eggs*

Grate cheese; place in a medium-sized saucepan, with mustard, a shake of pepper and ale or milk. Heat gently until cheese has melted, about 10 minutes, stirring occasionally. Poach eggs and put on to buttered toast. Pour on cheese mixture and brown under grill.

1866 EGGS AND CHEESE

1 oz butter
1 teaspoon olive oil
8 oz Lancashire cheese

4 eggs
Pepper

Melt the butter and oil in a shallow dish on top of the stove. Cut the cheese into slices, reserving about 1 oz for grating. Put cheese into the dish and melt cheese gently. Break the eggs on top. Cook at 350°F (GasMark 4) for 8 minutes. Sprinkle with pepper and grated cheese, and brown under the grill.

BOILED CHEESE

4 oz of good mild rich English cheese cut in thin slices, a piece of butter the size of 2 walnuts, 2 tablespoons of good cream. Put all into a stewpan and keep stirring till it boils and is quite smooth. Then add the white and yolk of an egg. Stir it quickly, put it into a dish and brown it before the fire. No cheese must be used that is old or with the blue mould. Dry toast is to be sent up into it.

Mrs Garden, 1847

CHEESE AND POTATO DISH

2 lb potatoes
A little finely chopped onion (optional)
8 oz grated Cheddar cheese
1 level teaspoon salt

½ level teaspoon pepper
½ level teaspoon nutmeg
4 tablespoons hot stock or water

Scrub and peel the potatoes; put into cold salted water, bring to the boil and parboil for about 15 minutes. Drain and, when cool enough, cut into ½ inch dice and toss with the finely chopped onion, if used. Put alternate layers of diced potato and grated cheese into a greased fireproof dish, seasoning each layer; finish with a layer of grated Cheddar cheese. Add the stock or water, cover and place in a fairly hot oven, 400°F (Gas Mark 6). After 20 minutes uncover and brown in the oven or under the grill.

CHEESE CUSTARD PIES

If you have a little pastry left over, line as many small patty tins as your pastry will run to and fill with cheese custard. Make the cheese custard by beating together 2 eggs, a ½ pint of milk, about 2 oz grated cheese, a mustardspoon of made mustard, some pepper and salt. Bake in a moderate oven until the custard has set. Serve with a green salad.

CHEESE BALLS

Beat egg white stiff. Fold in tablespoon grated cheese. Drop spoonfuls into deep smoking fat. Drain on paper. Keep yolks for soups.

SUSSEX RAREBIT

Allow 3 oz Cheddar cheese for each person. Grate the cheese and put in a pan with some butter and a little old ale. Add some freshly ground black pepper, a teaspoon of mustard and a dessertspoon of cream for each person. Melt slowly, stirring until all the ingredients are well blended. As soon as it bubbles, serve on rounds of hot toast in deep plates into which you have poured a little spiced beer.

BOMBAY TOAST (1)

From slices of bread half an inch thick, cut out rounds small or large, as preferred, fry them a nice brown. Spread a layer of any kind of minced or potted meat on them, and place a little chutney on top of meat. Place a little grated or thinly sliced cheese on top of all and grill quickly until cheese is toasted. If liked, the cheese may be toasted separately and added last before serving.

BOMBAY TOAST (2)

2 eggs
1 oz butter
Some chopped chutney

Some rounds of buttered toast
1 teaspoon anchovy essence
Salt and Cayenne pepper

Melt the butter in a saucepan and then add beaten eggs. Stir well and just before eggs are set add other ingredients; continue stirring until mixture thickens properly but be careful not to overcook. Spread this mixture on the rounds of buttered toast and serve very hot, immediately.

CHEESE PATTIES

Put 1 oz of butter in a saucepan over the fire with $\frac{3}{4}$ oz of flour. When mixed stir in $1\frac{1}{2}$ gills of milk, let it cook well; then set aside to cool. Beat up 3 yolks and 2 whites of eggs, stir into the saucepan with salt, Cayenne, and 2 ozs of grated cheese, and mix well together. Line some patty pans with pastry, fill with the cheese mixture, and bake till the pastry is done. Serve hot.

Mrs Holt, Oldham

CHEESE FRITTERS

1¼ *lb raw potatoes*
2 tablespoons self-raising flour
8 oz grated Cheddar cheese

Pinch of salt
Fat for frying
1 oz castor sugar and pinch of ground mace

Peel the washed raw potatoes, mince or grate them finely. Stir in the flour and cheese. Drop tablespoons of the mixture into a pan containing ½ inch of fat at frying temperature. Fry gently, turning to brown on both sides. Lift from the fat carefully and drain. Sprinkle with sugar and ground mace, and serve hot.

CHEESE SCOTCH EGGS

6 oz grated Cheddar cheese
1½ *oz flour*
1 level teaspoon salt
Pinch Cayenne pepper
½ *teaspoon Worcester sauce*
1 egg

1-2 *tablespoons milk or cream*
4 hard-boiled eggs
Dried breadcrumbs
Deep fat for frying

Mix the grated cheese, flour and seasonings, add the Worcester sauce, beaten egg and milk or cream and beat well. Using wet hands coat the hard-boiled eggs completely with the cheese mixture. Roll them in dried breadcrumbs. Fry in hot deep fat to a golden brown, taking about 2 minutes to allow the cheese mixture to cook through. Drain, cool slightly and cut across in half. Garnish and serve hot with tomato sauce or cold with salad.

CHEESE ONION BAKE

4 large onions
4 slices buttered toast
4 oz grated Cheddar cheese
1 egg

¼ *pint milk*
1 level teaspoon salt
Pinch of paprika pepper
½ *oz butter*

Peel the onions and cook until almost tender in boiling salted water. Drain and cut into rings. Prepare the toast and arrange neatly in a fireproof dish. Pile on the onion rings and sprinkle liberally with the grated cheese. Beat the egg, add the milk and seasonings, and pour over the onions. Dot with butter and bake in a moderate oven at 350°F (Gas Mark 4) for approximately 30 minutes.

HOT CHEESE SAVOURY

2 eggs
¼ pint double cream
4 oz grated cheese -
Lancashire for choice

Salt and pepper
Cayenne pepper
Grated nutmeg

Beat eggs. Stir in cream and cheese. Season with salt and pepper, a little cayenne and a little nutmeg. Divide mixture between 4 individual heat-proof dishes or one small casserole. Sprinkle with remaining cheese. Bake in a hot oven at 400°F (Gas Mark 6) until just beginning to brown on top for 20–25 minutes. Serve really hot with toast.

CAULIFLOWER CHEESE

1 medium-sized cauliflower
1 oz butter
1 oz plain flour
½ pint milk or milk and
cauliflower-water
4 oz grated Cheddar cheese

½ level teaspoon salt
1 level teaspoon made
mustard
Pinch nutmeg
1 tablespoon browned crumbs

Soak the cauliflower in cold water for about 15 minutes, then break into flowerets. Cook in a little boiling salted water in a covered pan until tender and arrange neatly in a fireproof dish. Melt the butter, add the flour and cook for 1 minute. Remove from heat, add milk or milk and cauliflower water gradually. Bring to the boil, stirring well. Cook for a minute, re-move from the heat, add the seasonings and 3 oz cheese, and stir until the cheese has melted. Coat the cauliflower with the cheese sauce. Mix and sprinkle over the remaining cheese and browned crumbs. Brown under a hot grill or in a fairly hot oven at 400°F (Gas Mark 6). Serve hot.

CHEESE AND ONIONS

4 medium onions
¼ pint milk

Salt and pepper
4 oz grated cheese

Peel and slice the onions. Cook until tender in very little water. Add milk and seasoning. Bring to the boil and turn into an ovenproof dish. Cover with cheese and brown under the grill. Serve with bread and butter. A nice supper dish.

EIGHTEENTH-CENTURY CHESHIRE RAMEKIN

'Take some old Cheshire Cheese, a lump of fresh butter and the Yolk of a hard boiled new-laid Egg, and beat them very well together in a Marble Mortar. Spread it on some slices of Bread toasted and buttered, hold a Salamander over them and send them up.'

CHEESE PUDDING

1 pint milk
¼ lb breadcrumbs
1 tablespoon butter
2 eggs

¼ lb grated Double
Gloucester
Pepper and salt

Pour hot milk on to breadcrumbs, adding a tablespoon of butter, leave to cool then add 2 beaten eggs, grated cheese, salt and pepper to taste. Turn into a greased pie dish and bake in a moderate oven until the mixture has set and the top is nicely browned. Time about 40 minutes.

GLOUCESTERSHIRE POTATO CAKES

½ lb cooked potatoes
2 oz flour
2 oz grated Double
Gloucester

1 egg
A little butter

Mash the potatoes thoroughly with a little butter. Work in the flour and cheese. Beat the egg and add it to the mixture. Roll out and cut into small round cakes which can either be baked in the oven, 325°F (Gas Mark 2), or cooked on a girdle or heavy frying pan.

DALE APPLE SAVOURY

Breadcrumbs
2 large apples

4 oz grated Wensleydale
cheese
¼ pint milk

Grease a baking dish and line it with breadcrumbs. Peel, core and slice the apples in rings, and layer the bottom of the dish with half the amount. Cover with half the grated Wensleydale and repeat the layers. Cover with the milk and finally sprinkle some buttered breadcrumbs on top. Bake in a moderate oven, 375°F (Gas Mark 4), for about a ½ hour until the apples are done.

WENSLEYDALE PUDDING

2 oz breadcrumbs
2 oz grated Wensleydale
cheese

1 egg
¼ pint milk
tomato

Grease pie dish. Beat egg yolk and milk. Mix breadcrumbs and cheese, and pour milk and egg yolk over this, whip egg white until stiff and fold into the mixture. Sprinkle with a little more grated cheese and a few slices of tomatoes. Bake at 400° F (Gas Mark 6) for 15–20 minutes.

CHEESE PUFFS

4 rounds of toast
2 egg whites

4 oz Wensleydale cheese
¼ teaspoon baking powder

Whip egg whites until stiff, add cheese and baking powder. Pile on to the toast and grill.

11 Vegetables and Salads

*'Tis not her coldness, father,
That chills my labouring breast;
It's that confounded cucumber
I've ate, and can't digest.*

'Legends of Mirth and Marvel', Thomas Ingoldsby

First Early Vegetables

Beetroot: Try baking these for the fullest flavour. Wrap them in foil, stand on a rack, and cook in a moderate oven for about 1 hour (young roots). If the flesh yields when pressed, the beetroot is done.

Broad Beans: When young, cook in boiling salted water for 15 minutes. When old, allow 30 minutes, and slip the beans out of the skins to serve.

Carrots: Wash and scrub carrots, and cook whole in as little water as possible for 15 minutes, rubbing off the skin after cooking.

French Beans: Use very young and fresh, and if small, cook them whole or in chunks (the same applies to runner beans, as shredding dissipates flavour into the cooking water). Just cover in salted water with a lump of sugar, and cook for 15 minutes.

Globe Artichokes: Cut off stems, and invert artichokes in a deep bowl of cold water for 1 hour. Plunge into boiling salted water and cook until the leaves pull away easily. Drain very thoroughly before serving.

Peas: Cook in just enough quickly boiling, salted water to cover, with a lump of sugar and a sprig of mint, for about 15 minutes with the lid off.

Potatoes: Wash them, leaving the skins on and plunge into boiling salted water. Cook for 15–20 minutes, remove skins, and toss in melted butter.

Turnips: Peel thickly, and cook in boiling salted water for 20 minutes.

Choosing potatoes

Certain varieties of potato are more suitable for different ways of cooking than others, choose the right varieties for your dish, and see that you cook them in the best possible way.

Boiling (red or white varieties): Just cover with cold salted water, bring to the boil and when tender drain off all the water and stand the pan over a low heat allowing the steam to escape, for 2–3 minutes. If they have to be kept hot longer than this, do not put back the lid of the pan, instead cover with a crumpled tea cloth pressed well down on top of the potatoes. This will absorb any steam still left and keep in the heat.

To boil new potatoes, have ready some boiling salted water, put in the potatoes and boil till just soft.

Steaming (red or white varieties): See that the water is fully boiling before putting the potatoes in the steamer. Cook $1\frac{1}{2}$–2 hours.

Mashing and Creaming (red varieties): Cook as for boiling, add hot milk and butter till you have the required consistency. Stir with a lifting movement to keep the potatoes light.

Deep Frying (white varieties for chips or crisps): Cut the potatoes into fingers or wafers, rinse well in cold water then dry in a clean cloth. Do not attempt to cook too many at one time, as the fat must be able to circulate round the potatoes.

Sauté-ing (red or white varieties): Partly boil unpeeled potatoes, peel and dice them, then fry in hot melted butter until a golden brown. Drain and serve very hot.

Roasting (red or white varieties): Put the raw peeled potatoes into really hot dripping around the joint, cook in a hot oven and baste or turn the potatoes once or twice during cooking to ensure a glistening brown crust.

Baking in skins (red or white varieties): Scrub the skins, prick with a fork or skewer and rub lightly all over with butter or cooking fat. Bake in a hot oven, 1 hour. Before serving, cut a cross in the top squeeze gently to let out the steam and press a knob of butter into the cut.

Salads (white varieties): Cook the potatoes until just done so that they do not break up. If you want the flavour of the dressing to be absorbed by the potatoes then add it while still hot. To keep the potato flavour distinct add dressing when the potatoes are cold.

1915 VICTORIA POTATOES

Peel and boil the usual amount of potatoes, but take them off the fire when they are almost, but not quite cooked. Strain them, and cut each one into thin slices. Butter a pie-dish, and put in the potato.

Make a white sauce with a $\frac{1}{2}$ oz of butter, a $\frac{1}{2}$ oz of flour, and a $\frac{1}{4}$ pint of milk, boil it up well, and pour over the potatoes. Sprinkle a $\frac{1}{2}$ oz of grated cheese over the top, and bake in a moderate oven until the top is nicely browned.

If you prefer quite plain potatoes, steam them instead of boiling. You haven't a steamer? Well, use a colander, stand it in a pan of boiling water and it will answer the same purpose.

When the potatoes are cooked, turn them into a hot dish and sprinkle them lightly with salt.

If I have any good dripping in the larder, I steam the potatoes, season and mash them up with about a $\frac{1}{2}$ oz of it.

About vegetables

If boiled potatoes have to stand awhile before being served, cover them over with a thick cloth, and stand the pan where they will keep warm, but will not scorch. The cloth absorbs the moisture, and helps to make the potatoes floury.

To remove the smell of cooked onions from a pot, fill it with boiling water and drop in a red-hot cinder.

If you wish to prevent green vegetables from boiling over, drop a piece of dripping the size of a walnut into the centre of them, just as they commence to boil.

When peeling onions, hold them under a tap of running water, or stand at an open window. No matter how weak one's eyes may be, they will not smart if onions are peeled in either of these ways.

If a cauliflower is tied up in a piece of muslin it can, when cooked, easily be lifted from the pan to the colander. There is no risk of its being broken. This will also keep it free from scum.

Miss T. Hempsall, Moorthorpe, 1913

BOILED NEW POTATOES

A root of potatoes freshly dug rarely has equal-sized potatoes on it, yet it seems wicked to cut the beautiful big young ones. So when peeled, have ready your pan of boiling salted water and put the large ones in for about 7 minutes before adding the smaller ones. About 5 minutes before they are all cooked, add 2 or 3 sprigs of freshly picked mint. Before straining off the potato water remove the mint from the pan. Dish the potatoes into a hot dish and serve with dabs of butter.

BAKED POTATOES

Potatoes for baking should have the skins brushed with melted butter or cooking fat, and pricked to allow the steam to escape. Bake 1–1¼ hours at 400°F (Gas Mark 6). To serve, mark a cross on top of the potato, squeeze gently, held in a cloth, sprinkle with salt and place a knob of butter in the cross.

The potatoes may be cut in half, the cut side wiped dry, and placed cut side down on a greased tin. This will reduce the cooking time to 30–40 minutes.

Variations for baked potato fillings

When the potato has been baked, scoop out the flesh, mash, and add any of the variations listed below:

1. Chopped cooked meat, beef, ham, bacon and garnish with parsley.
2. Flaked fish and butter.
3. Chopped grilled kidney, garnished with fried onion rings.
4. Chopped boiled egg and mayonnaise, garnished with sieved egg yolk.
5. Chopped fried mushrooms.
6. Sultanas and cubes of cheese.
7. Minced ham and savoury sauce.
8. Grated cheese and egg yolk.
9. Flaked salmon and squeeze lemon juice.
10. Chopped chives and tomato purée.
11. Flaked cooked kipper fillets and lemon juice.
12. Cottage cheese and chopped chives.
13. Scrambled egg and chopped fried bacon.
14. Minced chicken and sauté-ed chopped mushrooms.

BAKED CHEESEY POTATOES

4 large potatoes   *1 egg*
1 oz butter   *Salt and pepper*
2-3 oz grated cheese

Scrub the potatoes, dry them and brush with melted fat. Bake in a hot oven for about 1 hour. Cut a slice from the top of each potato, scoop out the inside and mash well with the butter, cheese, egg yolk and seasoning. Whisk the egg white and fold into the mashed potato. Place the potatoes in the skins again, and heat in the oven for 5–10 minutes.

POTATO SAUSAGE ROLLS

Scrub average size potatoes, remove the centres from each with an apple corer. Fill cavities with sausage meat mixed with a little finely chopped onion if liked. Wrap each potato in a rasher of bacon, cover with foil, and bake at 400°F (Gas Mark 6) for 1 hour.

FOIL POTATOES

4 large potatoes   *2 medium onions*
2 oz butter   *Salt and pepper*

Peel potatoes and cut crosswise in 4 slices. Spread butter thickly between each slice and on top. Reassemble potatoes with onion slices between. Season with salt and pepper and wrap each potato tightly in double foil. Bake at 325°F (Gas Mark 3) for 1½ hours. Open foil and sprinkle with parsley, or brown in the oven. These potato parcels may be prepared in advance, then cooked at the right time.

SCOTS POTATO FRITTERS

6 large potatoes   *1 tablespoon lean ham*
2 eggs   *Dripping*
1 tablespoon breadcrumbs

Parboil the potatoes and cut them in thick slices (about ¼ inch). Beat up the eggs with the finely grated breadcrumbs and grated ham. Dip each slice of potato in this mixture and fry in plenty of good hot dripping. These are grand by themselves or for serving with any kind of fried meat.

SCALLOPED NEW POTATOES

3 oz butter   *2 oz fresh breadcrumbs*
1½ lb new potatoes (all   *Salt and pepper*
similar in size, scraped)

Melt 2 oz butter in a medium to large saucepan. Add the whole potatoes. Spread them out so they cover the base of the pan in one layer, and cover. Cook very slowly to prevent butter from burning. Turn the potatoes over, several times during cooking, so that they turn golden all over. Cook for ½–1 hour (depending on size of potatoes). When tender, add remaining 1 oz butter. Turn the heat up and add the breadcrumbs and seasoning. Cook 3–4 minutes, stirring continuously until the breadcrumbs have absorbed the butter, and have turned crisp and golden.

NORTHUMBERLAND PAN HAGGERTY

2 *lb potatoes cut in slices*   3 *oz grated cheese*
1 *lb onions sliced*   *Salt and pepper*
1 *tablespoon dripping*

Place layers of potatoes, onion and grated cheese in a heavy frying pan.
Season each layer, fry gently till brown. Keep a lid on the pan and cook
until the vegetables are brown.

DELICIOUS POTATOES

3½ *lb potatoes*   3 *oz grated cheese*
3 *oz butter*   *Salt and pepper*
1 *carton double cream (5 oz)*

Peel potatoes thinly and cut into slices ⅛ inch thick. Place on a large piece
of foil, season well, add cream, sprinkle with cheese and dot with butter.
Make a secure parcel of the foil, put into a baking tin and bake in a hot
oven for 45 minutes to 1½ hours, or until potatoes are soft. Serve as an
accompaniment to meat or savoury dishes. Oven temperature 400°F (Gas
Mark 6).

Michael Jeffs

POTATO PAN HASH

1 *lb mashed potatoes*   *Salt and pepper*
Bacon fat or butter

Heat fat or butter in a frying pan. Add potato, smooth over, and cook
gently until crisp and brown underneath. Fold over with a fish slice and
slide on to a warm plate. Serve with mushrooms, bacon, tomatoes, eggs or
a little grated cheese.

STELK

2 *lb potatoes*   *A little milk*
2 *oz butter*   *Salt and pepper*
Bunch of spring onions

Boil potatoes in salted water, drain and mash, add the butter and keep hot.
Chop onions and cook until tender in a little milk, then beat into potatoes
until light and fluffy. Pile on serving plates, and put a good lump of butter
in a 'well' in each serving. The idea is to eat from the outside, dipping each
mouthful into the pool of butter. A comforting dish for tired children.

It's also excellent with a bit of boiled bacon, or with a few crisp rashers or sausages.

WELSH POTATO CAKES

1 lb boiled potatoes
4 oz plain flour
1 teaspoon baking powder
1 egg

1 oz butter
1 tablespoon sugar
Pinch of salt

Mix all the ingredients except the butter. Melt the butter and mix thoroughly with the rest. Roll out 1 inch thick. Bake on a girdle, or at 425°F (Gas Mark 7) for 20 minutes. Serve hot with a lot of butter. Cold potato cakes can be fried with the breakfast bacon.

WELSH ONION CAKE

1 lb potatoes
½ lb onions

4 oz butter
Salt and pepper

Use a well-buttered cake tin. Peel the potatoes, slice them fairly thinly and arrange in a layer on the bottom of the tin. Sprinkle a layer of finely chopped onion on the potatoes, add flakes of butter, salt and pepper. Continue in layers until the tin is full, finishing with a layer of potatoes and a few flakes of butter. Cover with a lid and bake at 350°F (Gas Mark 4) for 1 hour. Eat with hot or cold meat.

POTEN BEN FEDI

2 lb potatoes
½ lb minced cooked meat
1 rasher bacon

1 medium onion
1 oz butter
1 tablespoon wholemeal flour

This is a sort of Welsh washday dish, excellent for dealing with oddments from the weekend joint. Boil the potatoes and mash them with the butter and flour, then mix in the meat. Chop bacon and onion and cook in the fat which runs from the bacon until golden. Mix well into the potatoes, season to taste, and turn into a greased pie dish. Bake at 350°F (Gas Mark 4) for 30 minutes until the top is golden.

WELSH HOT POT

1 lb potatoes
8 oz onions

8 oz bacon
Salt and pepper

This can be cheaply made with bacon pieces. Slice potatoes fairly thickly, slice onions and cut bacon in neat pieces. Arrange in alternate layers in a casserole, season with salt and pepper. Cover with a lid and cook at 325°F (Gas Mark 3) for 2 hours. Remove lid and continue cooking for 20 minutes. Another version of this made in a saucepan and with the addition of water used to be called 'The Miser's Feast', with the miser eating the mashed up potatoes one day, and saving the slices of bacon to eat a second day.

CHAMP

8 *large potatoes*   **Salt and pepper**
6 *spring onions*   **Butter**
⅓ *pint milk*

Let the peeled potatoes stand in cold water for 1 hour. Drain and cover with cold salted water, and boil until tender. Drain well and dry off by putting a folded cloth on top and returning the pot to a gentle heat for a few minutes. Chop the spring onions very finely, using the green tops as well as the bulbs, put them into a bowl and pour on boiling water to cover them. Drain the onions and add to the milk. Bring to the boil and pour on to the mashed potatoes, with pepper and salt to taste. When very light and fluffy, pile up on individual plates, making a well in the middle, and put a piece of butter in the 'well'. The potato is scooped up into the melted butter as it is eaten. Sometimes this is known as *thump* in Ireland. Another version, called *colcannon* includes chopped boiled curly kale or cabbage. The Welsh mixture of vegetables is a *stwns*, being a mixture of potatoes and swedes; potatoes and peas; or potatoes and broad beans, sometimes with buttermilk poured over.

BOXTY

2 *large raw potatoes*   **1 *teaspoon bicarbonate of***
¾ *lb mashed potatoes*   **soda**
2 *tablespoons plain flour*   **1 *teaspoon salt***

Grate the raw potatoes and squeeze out the liquid. Add to the mashed potatoes and salt. Mix the soda with the flour and add to the potatoes. Roll out ½ inch thick in a circle. Cut in 4 quarters and put on an ungreased girdle. Cook on gentle heat for 30 to 40 minutes, turning bread once. The farls or quarters should be well browned on both sides. A teaspoon of caraway seeds can be added to the dough.

STRAW POTATOES

Cut up some potatoes about the thickness of wooden matches. Well wash and dry them on a clean cloth. Place them in a wire basket, not more than a cupful at a time, and plunge them into a bath of boiling fat. Shake the potatoes until they are quite crisp and of a golden-yellow colour. Lift them out, put them on a clean cloth to drain, sprinkle with salt, and serve on a hot dish.

PEASE PUDDING (1)

1½ pints split peas *2 oz dripping*
2 eggs *Salt and pepper*
½ teaspoon bicarbonate of soda

Soak peas overnight in hot water, to which is added the soda. Mash them and tie loosely in a muslin bag. Boil for 2 hours. Press through a sieve, reheat and add fat, beaten eggs, pepper and salt. Tie in a floured cloth and boil for 1 hour. Serve hot.

PEASE PUDDING (2)

Put 1½ pints of split peas into a clean cloth; tie loosely in order to allow them room to swell. Place in cold water, and let them boil until tender. They should be cooked enough in 2½ hours if the peas are new. Take them from the pot, remove them from the cloth, rub them through a sieve, add pepper, salt and a knob of butter about ½ oz, beat all together thoroughly for 5 or 6 minutes, put into a floured cloth, tie it tightly, and let it boil again for ¾ hour. This dish may be served with boiled or roast pork, or boiled beef.

JEANNIE'S PEASE PUDDING

Take a small handful of peas per person and soak for a while in cold water. Bring to the boil very carefully and cook slowly until tender 2½–3 hours. Then mash well, add pepper and salt to taste, a little finely chopped onion and a good sized knob of dripping. Place in a tin and bake in good oven for 25–30 minutes until nice and brown on top. Serve with cold boiled beetroot and cold meat.

Jeannie was a Scottish orphan brought up in a home and evacuated in 1940. She said they had pease pudding served every Monday without fail with cold meat. Just the same she had quite a liking for the dish.

Pease pudding hot; pease pudding cold,
Pease pudding in the pot 3 days old (or 3 weeks old if she was remembering unhappiness).

(The traditional time was 9 days.)

GARDENER'S CASSEROLE

1 lb lean salt pork
1 lb small carrots
6 small onions
1 dessertspoon flour

2 lb green peas (weighed before shelling)
1 lb new potatoes
Parsley, thyme, bayleaf
Salt and pepper

Dice the salt pork and brown in a saucepan. Add the whole carrots and onions and cook together for 5 minutes. Stir in the flour, mix well, and add hot water to cover. Cover tightly and simmer for 30 minutes. Add peas and potatoes, with a good sprinkling of chopped parsley and thyme, and a bayleaf. Season to taste and simmer for 1 hour.

VEGETABLES IN THE MILKY WAY

¾ lb young carrots (prepared and sliced)
1 medium-sized swede – approx. 12 oz (prepared and diced)

Sauce
1 oz butter

4 tablespoons double cream
4 tablespoons milk
1½ level tablespoons cornflour
5 tablespoons cider
1 level teaspoon castor sugar
Salt and pepper

Cook carrots and swedes together in boiling salted water for about 15 minutes, or until cooked. To make sauce, melt butter in a saucepan, add cream and milk. Blend cornflour with 2 tablespoons of the cider, and add to the cream mixture, with the remainder of the cider. Bring to the boil, stirring continuously. Add sugar and seasonings, and simmer for 2–3 minutes. Drain vegetables and mix with sauce. Serve hot.

BUTTERED PEAS AND CARROTS

2 lb peas (in pods)
1 lb new carrots
1 small lettuce heart

1 small onion
2 oz butter
Salt and sugar

Cut the carrots in small strips and cook in boiling water for 5 minutes. Drain well. Put shelled peas, shredded lettuce, chopped onion, and a pinch each of sugar and salt in a pan with the carrots and just cover with boiling water. Cook very gently until the water is nearly absorbed, then add the butter and serve at once.

STAFFORDSHIRE SAVOURY VEGETABLE MARROW

1 *large marrow*	3 *tablespoons breadcrumbs*
1 *lb cold meat*	1 *oz dripping*
1 *oz flour*	2 *oz ham or bacon*
1 *teaspoon salt*	1 *teaspoon chopped parsley*
½ *teaspoon pepper*	1 *or 2 tomatoes*

Cut marrow through about 2 inches from the end. Remove all seed and pulp. Peel the larger part and boil for 5 minutes. Mince the meat and all the ingredients except the dripping. Moisten with stock or water, mix well. Dry marrow well on outside, stuff it with the mixture, replace the cut off end, tie on firmly, put in a baking dish, bake in a moderate oven for 1 hour basting with the dripping. Serve hot together with tomato sauce or gravy.

STUFFED CABBAGE

1 *cabbage*	*onion and parsley*
2 *tablespoons rice*	½ *lb sausage meat, seasoned to*
1 *tablespoon each chopped*	*taste*

Take a firm head of cabbage, pour boiling water over it, let stand for 15 minutes, drain cover again with boiling water, let stand for 30 minutes, drain and shake dry. Make a stuffing of the meat, onion, parsley, rice and seasoning, cut stalk out, put in some mixture, fold over 2 or 3 leaves, cover with another layer of mixture, and continue until each layer is stuffed; press all firmly together and tie in a cloth; put in a pan of salted water, and boil for 1½ hours. When cooked, remove cloth, put cabbage in a deep dish and serve with melted butter or white sauce.

CREAMED CABBAGE

Take 2 white cabbages (sometimes called cow cabbages) and shred them. Throw them into fast boiling water. Let them boil for about ½ hour until tender, drain through a colander, press them between 2 plates to drain away all moisture. Put 2 oz butter into a stewpan, pepper and salt, and work in a tablespoon of flour, adding gradually $\frac{1}{2}$ pint of milk or a little cream. Stir in the cabbbage and let it cook about 10 minutes, and serve.

RED CABBAGE CASSEROLE

1 *small red cabbage*	*Salt and pepper*
1 *oz dripping*	*Flour*
1 *onion*	$\frac{3}{4}$ *pint stock*
1 *apple*	3 *tablespoons vinegar*

Shred cabbage finely. Melt dripping, add chopped onion and apple, season with salt and pepper, sprinkle with flour, stir well and add cabbage. Pour in stock and vinegar. Cook with lid on for $2\frac{1}{2}$ hours at 325°F (Gas Mark 3).

BRAISED CARROTS

Cut the carrots into rounds about 1 inch thick. Put them into boiling salted water and when nearly done, remove them into a stewpan with a little cayenne and $1\frac{1}{2}$ oz butter. Let them simmer gently in this for about $\frac{3}{4}$ hour or less, shaking them continually to prevent their burning. Remove the carrots to a hot vegetable dish, pour the liquor over them, sprinkle with chopped parsley and serve.

MASHED CARROTS

Take 6 or more large carrots, wash and scrape them, place them in boiling water salted, and when soft remove and mash them. Replace in the saucepan with only a little of the water they were boiled in, add 1 oz butter, pepper, and a little gravy or milk. Stir them over the fire until they are nearly dry, and serve in a hot vegetable dish.

GLAZED CARROTS

Scrape and cut into even slices 6 or 7 large carrots. Throw them into boiling salted water and let them partly boil. Remove them, and place them in a saucepan with a lump of sugar, 2 oz butter, and sufficient stock to cover them. Let it boil very quickly until the stock is reduced to a glaze, shake over the fire until the carrots are covered with the gravy and serve.

MRS C's FANCY WAY WITH CARROTS

2 lb carrots　　　　　　　　　　**Salt and pepper**
4 oz butter

Use a large flat saucepan. Melt the butter, add pepper to taste, and toss the prepared carrots in the melted fat. Add hot water to cover and salt to taste, and bring to boil. Simmer to taste. This is delicious. Mrs C. comes of farming stock but was left a widow with two very young children. She became a 'dinner lady' and eventually came to work for the Honey family. She was a pillar of strength, helping once or twice a week when there were 10 or more to feed every day. She managed to do a great deal of voluntary work for Boys' Clubs, Army Cadets, etc. and now runs a canteen for Old Age Pensioners in Bath.

BOILED CELERY

Cut off the outer leaves of the celery, wash it carefully, make the stalks even, put into boiling salted water, but do not cover it with the lid. Let it boil gently for $\frac{3}{4}$ hour if the celery is young or longer if older. Have ready some pieces of toast, and when the celery is cooked, dip the toast into the liquor the celery was boiled in. Place it on the toast, pour over some melted butter and serve.

BRAISED CELERY

Take the required heads of celery, cut off the roots, outer leaves, and green tops, cut into halves, and then into even lengths. Place in a saucepan 2 oz butter, and when it is melted put 2 oz each of onion, carrot and turnip in the same saucepan. Wash well and blanch the celery in boiling salted water for 15 minutes. Remove it, and place it on top of the other vegetables. Cover with a buttered paper, put on the lid of the saucepan, and fry all together for 12 minutes. Add $1\frac{1}{2}$ pints of stock, braise it gently for 2 hours, or until the celery is tender. Divide the pieces again, and place them on long snippets of bread, and serve.

TO COOK FRENCH BEANS

12 oz French beans　　　　　　　**Pinch of salt**
3 tablespoons butter　　　　　　**Few grains of ucayenne pepper**
1 tablespoon lemon juice　　　　**4 tablespoons water**

Cut large beans in chunks, but leave small ones whole. Cover them with cold water, and bring to the boil only. Drain the beans. Melt the butter in a heavy saucepan and add the lemon juice, salt and pepper and water. Add the beans and cook slowly for 10 minutes. This method can be used for frozen beans now, but the preliminary cooking will not then be necessary.

HARICOT BEANS

Chop 1 onion very finely, and put it into a stewpan with a little butter and flour. Let it cook until the butter is browned. Pour in a little water or stock, and stir until it thickens. Add to this the haricot beans, which have been soaking all night in water, and boil until tender. Simmer for about 25 minutes and serve hot.

HARICOT BEANS IN TOMATO SAUCE

Soak the beans overnight, put them into a saucepan and cover with cold water. Add 1 carrot, 1 onion, 1 turnip, $\frac{1}{2}$ a head of celery, pepper and salt to taste. Let them boil slowly until sufficiently cooked. Remove the vegetables, drain the beans, place them in a hot dish and cover them with tomato sauce, and serve with croûtons round the dish.

LEEKS

Leeks are delicious if fried in dripping (or butter) or roast round beef, lamb or pork (for about 25 minutes), drained and served in hot dish. The resulting fat from the draining makes a tasty foundation for the accompanying gravy, or for soup.

SAVOURY LENTILS

Wash 1 lb dried lentils overnight, and leave soaking in clean cold water. Next day drain them. Meanwhile place in a suitable saucepan the lentils, 3 or 4 rashers of streaky bacon, 1 chopped clove of garlic (if liked), 1 diced carrot, 1 chopped onion, 1 bay leaf and a sprig of thyme. Barely cover with cold water and bring slowly to the boil. When boiling, transfer the pan to the oven and allow to go on cooking gently until the lentils are quite soft. Add more liquid during this cooking if necessary. Serve the lentils with boiled ham, pork or bacon.

BOILED LENTILS

There are two kinds of lentils, the red and the green. The red are perhaps preferable. Soak the required quantity in water overnight. In the morning drain them and throw them into boiling salted water, and let them cook without breaking for about a $\frac{1}{2}$ hour, or longer if not soft enough. Drain them, return them to the saucepan, add 1 oz of butter, pepper, and a dessertspoon of vinegar, shake over the fire till hot, and serve.

LENTIL PUDDING

This is very nice with boiled pork.

Mix with a teacupful of milk 2 oz cornflour and 3 oz of lentil flour. Boil a pint of milk with pepper, salt and powdered herbs to taste. Add this to the mixed lentil flour and cornflour. When this is cool, whisk in 3 eggs, boil for 2 hours, and serve with a white sauce.

CREAMED LENTILS

Soak a pint of lentils overnight in cold water. Next day throw them into salted, boiling water, and allow them to boil for 3 hours. Strain them, and add half a teacup of thick cream, pepper, salt (if required) and simmer gently for 5 minutes. Serve very hot.

FRIED LETTUCE

Carefully wash and dry lettuce leaves. Fry them in butter until brown on both sides. Season with salt and pepper and serve as a garnish for boiled chicken or ham.

DRESSED LETTUCE

Wash and dry some crisp lettuce leaves. Shred lengthways in 1 inch wide strips. Chop a few leaves of fresh mint and sprinkle on the lettuce. Chop very finely some young onions and sprinkle on lettuce. Sprinkle with a little salt and pepper and a little sugar. Cover the whole, but do not make awash, with equal quantities of vinegar and milk to which has been added a little made mustard.

BRAISED LETTUCE

4 small well-hearted lettuce
1 small onion
1 rasher lean bacon
1 tablespoon olive oil
1 tablespoon butter
4 tomatoes

1 dessertspoon chopped parsley
Salt and pepper
1 lump of sugar
Pinch of nutmeg

Wash the lettuce but keep them whole, plunge into boiling salted water and bring water to boil again. Take out lettuce and drain them thoroughly. Heat oil and butter and add chopped bacon and onion, stir until lightly coloured, and add skinned and chopped tomatoes. Stir until the mixture begins to form a sauce, then put in lettuce, parsley and seasonings. Cover pan tightly and simmer very gently for 30 minutes. If liked add a dozen stoned olives before serving. This is very good with lamb. Most people are surprised at cooking lettuce, but it's a useful answer to the glut, and delicious.

CREAMED FIELD MUSHROOMS

Field mushrooms   *Creamy milk*
Butter   *Salt and pepper*

This simple dish is best made with field mushrooms and is very good for breakfast or supper. The mushrooms may be served with crisp bacon, or on toast. Wipe and slice the mushrooms and cook gently in a little butter until it is almost absorbed. Add a teacup of creamy milk and continue cooking for about 10 minutes. Add a little more milk and cook 2 or 3 minutes longer, so the mushrooms are in a light creamy sauce. Season to taste.

MUSHROOM SALAD

8 oz mushrooms   *1 clove garlic*
8 tablespoons olive oil   *Salt and black peppercorns*
2 tablespoons lemon juice   *Chopped parsley*

Many people have not tried raw mushrooms, but they are delicious served as a salad, in particular with shellfish.

Wipe mushrooms and slice thinly, including the stalks. Mix oil and lemon juice, crushed garlic and freshly ground black pepper. Pour over mushrooms. Leave for a couple of hours until they have absorbed most of the dressing. Just before serving, season with salt and sprinkle with chopped parsley.

MUSHRUMPS IN CREAM

1 lb mushrooms   *Salt and pepper*
3 tablespoons butter   *8 fluid oz cream*
2 tablespoons plain flour   *Parsley*
Pinch of thyme

225

Wipe the mushrooms and leave whole or cut in thick slices according to size. Toss in the butter until just soft. Sprinkle with flour and add thyme, salt and pepper. Add the cream and cook over very low heat for 5 minutes, stirring gently. Serve with plenty of chopped parsley. (Mushrooms were commonly referred to as mushrumps in eighteenth-century recipes.)

Eighteenth-century Recipe

BUTTERED MUSHROOMS

Take ½ lb button mushrooms; put them in a saucepan with 3 oz butter and let them get slightly browned. Sprinkle salt and pepper over them and let them cook without burning until they are quite tender. They should be served as they are, on toast, and will be found to make a nice breakfast dish.

STEWED MUSHROOMS

Trim and clean a pound of mushrooms, and put them into a saucepan with ¼ lb fresh butter, ½ pint veal stock, and salt and pepper to taste. Let this stew very gently for 1½ hours. If required, thicken with a little corn-flour. Serve in an entrée dish with snippets of dry toast around.

GRILLED MUSHROOMS

Take some large field mushrooms, peel the outside top skin, and trim the stalks. Season with pepper and salt and steep them in a marinade of oil, or fresh butter melted. Grill over a clear fire, but not too fierce, on both sides. Serve with melted butter on a hot dish, and a squeeze of lemon on each mushroom.

BAKED ONIONS

Take the required number of medium-sized Spanish onions. Remove the outer skins and boil them in salted water for 15 minutes, then throw them into cold water. Drain well, cut them in halves, and arrange on a well-buttered baking tin. Bake in a quick oven, basting them with butter until they are tender and brown, and serve.

BRAISED ONIONS

Peel 6 or more large onions, or, if preferred, choose medium ones; place them in a pan with 4 oz beef dripping, cover the pan with a closely fitting lid, and let them cook until quite soft and brown. Then take out the onions, thicken the liquor with a little cornflour, salt and pepper to taste, and the juice of $\frac{1}{2}$ a lemon. Serve with steak or roast beef.

BOILED ONIONS

Peel the required number of onions and throw them into boiling salted water for 10 minutes; take them out and put them in cold water for 1 hour. Drain the onions and place them in a saucepan with sufficient water to cover them, and a little salt. Let them boil gently until quite tender, take them up, drain them and place on a hot dish with some melted butter poured over them.

ONIONS BAKED IN THEIR JACKETS

Choose decent-sized onions, 1 per person, or more for gluttons. Remove only very loose outer dried up leaves, retaining as much outer cover as possible. Place on a baking tin in the bottom of an oven and cook until tender in the middle, testing with a skewer or knitting needle. Take from the oven, cool only enough to be able to remove the onions on to a suitable dish. Eat on side plates, with a spoon, accompanied by butter, salt and pepper. Very good for children's or older people's supper dish, served with grated cheese and wholemeal bread.

IRISH BAKED ONIONS

Parboil as many onions as are needed, then drain them. Mix together some cold minced meat, chopped parsley, a little brown stock or gravy, and seasoning. Scoop out a teaspoonful from the centre of each onion, blend this with the meat mixture, and fill up the centres.

Bake the onions in a moderate oven until they are tender. Then stand each one upon a round of fried bread, and pour some thick brown, or tomato sauce round the dish, and garnish with sprigs of fried parsley.

1915

STUFFED ONIONS

4 *medium-sized onions* 2 *oz butter*
2 *oz fresh breadcrumbs* *Salt and pepper*
6 *oz grated Cheddar cheese*

Peel and parboil the onions for 20 minutes. Remove from the pan and cool slightly. Take the centres out very carefully and chop them. Mix with the breadcrumbs and 4 oz cheese. Season and stuff the onion cases. Put into an ovenproof dish and dot with butter. Bake in a moderately hot oven 375°F (Gas Mark 5) for 45–55 minutes. Sprinkle the remaining cheese on top of the onions 15 minutes before end of cooking time. Serve with toast and quartered tomatoes.

ONION SAVOURY

1 lb onions	**2 eggs**
1 pint milk	**Parsley**

Cook the sliced onions in the milk, then beat in the egg yolks. Whisk the egg whites until stiff, fold them into the onion mixture, add a little chopped parsley, salt and pepper to taste. Bake in a greased dish in a moderate oven until firm.

VICTORIAN SEAKALE

An excellent vegetable and most easy of digestion. When in full season it may be bought quite cheaply. It must be well washed to free it from grit and sand, all the dark parts are to be cut away near the roots and tied into small bundles and thrown into plenty of boiling salted water; when quite soft take them up, drain thoroughly, untie the bundles and arrange on a folded napkin on a dish. Serve with melted butter.

This is a most delicious and different addition to the menu – the poor man's asparagus, in fact and as easy to grow as brussels sprouts. The leaves are a beautiful silvery blue useful in floral decorations.

VICTORIAN SALSIFY

Put into a stewpan ¼ lb beef suet, cut into small squares, add one bayleaf, 3 or 4 cloves, 1 onion, a little piece of thyme, and a teaspoon of salt. Stir it all together on the fire for about 5 minutes, then add 2 tablespoons of flour, stir well and gently add 3 pints of water. Prepare about a dozen salsify by scraping until they are white; rub them with lemon, and put them in cold water for about ½ hour before they are required. When the ingredients in the saucepan are nearly boiling put in the salsify and let them simmer till tender, which will be in about 1 hour.

SORREL PURÉE

Fry in butter 2 large onions until they are a golden yellow colour. Dredge a little flour over them, add a pinch of grated nutmeg, a small piece of sugar, salt, pepper and a ½ pint of gravy or stock. Take a peck (2 gallons) of fresh sorrel, pick away the stalks, wash it in 3 or 4 waters, and boil it for $\frac{1}{4}$ hour, or until tender in a very little water, say, $\frac{1}{2}$ pint. Drain the sorrel thoroughly, and add it to the other ingredients, stir it over a gentle fire for 15–20 minutes, rub it through a hair sieve, and place it in the centre of a hot dish, with cutlets of veal, lamb or mutton around it.

STEWED SORREL

Pick $\frac{1}{2}$ a peck (1 gallon) of sorrel leaves, wash thoroughly in several waters, drain them, and place in a fireproof dish or earthen jar, and let them stew gently in the open oven until tender. Mix 1 oz of butter with them, add pepper, salt and Cayenne to taste, beat all together until the leaves are smooth, and serve. Serve with roast meat.

BAKED TOMATOES

Well butter a flat baking-dish, and put in tomatoes cut into halves. Sprinkle over them some breadcrumbs, grated cheese, chopped onion, shallot and parsley. Place them in a hot oven, and when ready to serve, squeeze a lemon over the whole, with salt and pepper.

TURNIP TOP GREENS

When young and freshly cut they are very excellent as a vegetable. Owing to their slightly bitter taste they are considered a very healthy article of diet to eat in the spring. Cut away the stems and dead leaves, wash them in several waters, and finally let them remain in fresh water for 1 hour. After draining them, put them into a saucepan of slightly salted water, fast boiling. If young, they should be cooked and quite tender in 15 minutes or so. Strain through a colander, squeeze out as much of the water as possible, put them into a hot vegetable dish, and cut them across each way. Place a little butter, salt and pepper on top.

BOILED TURNIPS

Turnips that are to be served plainly boiled must be small and very young; the larger ones should be mashed. Put the necessary quantity of turnips into slightly salted boiling water and let them boil for 25 minutes. Drain through a colander, and serve with a white sauce poured over them.

TURNIP PURÉE

Pare and wash 6 turnips. Cut them into quarters and boil them in salted water until tender. Mash, and pass them through a hair sieve. Put them in a stewpan with 1 oz of butter and $\frac{1}{4}$ pint of cream. Dredge in a little flour, and stir it over the fire until the mass becomes stiff. Serve this purée in the centre of the dish and arrange the meat around it.

APPLE AND WALNUT SALAD

8 fresh walnuts
4 crisp eating apples

1 gill mayonnaise, sharpened with vinegar
A little salt

Shell and skin walnuts; peel, core and cut apples into dice. Put a thin layer of nuts into a glass dish, sprinkle very lightly with salt, and next a layer of chopped apples with a little mayonnaise over. Continue until all is used, reserving a few walnuts as garnish. Top with mayonnaise, sprinkle over remaining nuts and serve at once. This must be prepared just before serving or the apples will brown and lose their crispness. To save time, however, the apples may be peeled shortly beforehand, and if kept covered in cold water with a little salt added, they will keep white. Wash well before chopping up.

Mrs Butcher, Ely, Cambs.

APPLE AND CABBAGE SALAD

1 small head of cabbage
2 small apples
$\frac{1}{4}$ cup cream

1 tablespoon vinegar
1 tablespoon sugar

Grate cabbage and apple. Add cream, vinegar, and sugar. Mix well.

ORANGE SALAD

2 oranges
2 lettuces

Squeeze of lemon juice
Salt and pepper
3 tablespoons olive oil

Peel the oranges rather extravagantly with a knife and cut out the segments of orange, leaving no pith or skin. Mix with the hearts of the lettuce. Dress with lemon juice, salt, pepper and oil. Good with cold chicken or pork.

BEETROOT AND HORSERADISH SALAD

3 or 4 beetroot, cooked and
diced
Salt and pepper
Horseradish sauce

Horseradish sauce
Juice of a lemon
1 dessertspoon vinegar
1 teaspoon mustard
Salt and pepper
Good pinch of brown sugar
2 or 3 tablespoons fresh
horseradish, grated
$\frac{1}{4}$ pint double cream, whipped

To make the sauce, mix all the ingredients together and season well, cover with the whipped cream and stir thoroughly. Cover the beetroot with the horseradish sauce and stir until the sauce is consistently pink.

CELERY SALAD

1 head celery
1 large onion
A few lettuce leaves
Some chopped parsley or

chives or a little fresh
watercress
French dressing
Salt

Prepare the celery and dice it. Chop the onion very finely and mix it with the diced celery in a bowl. Put the mixture into a wooden salad bowl which has been lined with a few crisp lettuce leaves, and sprinkle with a little salt. Pour 3 or 4 dessertspoons of French dressing over the celery, onion and stir gently, taking care not to bruise the lettuce. Garnish with chopped parsley, chives or a few sprigs of fresh watercress.

12 Sauces

> *Ne wette hir fyngres in hir sauce depe.*
> *Wel koude she carie a morsel, and wel kepe,*
> *That no drope ne fille upon hire breste.*
>
> *The Prioress in 'The Canterbury Tales', Geoffrey Chaucer*

Two large potatoes, passed through kitchen sieve,
Unwonted softness to the salad give.
Of mordant mustard add a single spoon
Distrust the condiment that bites so soon,
But deem it not, thou Man of Herbs, a fault
To add a double quantity of salt;
Three times the spoon with oil of Lucca crown,
And once with vinegar procured from town.
True flavour needs it, and your poet begs
The pounded yellow of two well-boiled eggs.
Let onion atoms lurk within the bowl,
And scarce suspected animate the whole:
And lastly on the flavoured compound toss
A magic teaspoon of Anchovy sauce.
Then though green turtle fail, though venison's tough,
And ham and turkey be not boiled enough,
Serenely full the epicure may say,
'Fate cannot harm me – I have dined today.'

Sidney Smith

GUBBINS SAUCE

Melt $\frac{1}{2}$ oz butter in a bowl over a pan of simmering water, stir in 2 teaspoons made mustard, 2 teaspoons wine vinegar, 1 teaspoon tarragon vinegar, $\frac{1}{2}$ teaspoon sugar and 3 tablespoons single cream. Season to taste with salt, pepper and cayenne pepper. For chicken, turkey, pheasant and partridge.

CUMBERLAND SAUCE

Peel the zest of 1 orange and $\frac{1}{2}$ lemon and shred finely, plunge in boiling water for 2 minutes and drain. Melt 4 tablespoons redcurrant jelly over a low heat and add 1 teaspoon finely chopped shallot, cook gently for a few minutes. Add $\frac{1}{4}$ pint port, lemon and orange zest. Blend together 1 teaspoon made mustard, $\frac{1}{8}$ teaspoon cayenne pepper, $\frac{1}{8}$ teaspoon ground ginger with the juice of the orange and lemon. Add to the port and simmer gently for 10 minutes. Adjust seasoning. For cold venison and ham.

ROBERT SAUCE

Melt 1 oz butter in a pan and gently fry a finely chopped small onion until transparent. Add $\frac{1}{4}$ pint white wine and reduce by half. Stir in $\frac{1}{2}$ pint of good brown sauce, coating consistency, and bring to the boil, stir in 1 teaspoon made mustard, 1 teaspoon vinegar and $\frac{1}{2}$ teaspoon sugar. For grilled meats, especially pork.

MUSTARD SAUCE

Melt 1 oz butter in a pan, add 1 oz flour and cook for a minute without browning. Draw the pan aside and gradually add $\frac{1}{2}$ pint milk. Return to the heat, bring to boil, stirring, boil 2–3 minutes. Blend together 2 teaspoons dry mustard and 2 teaspoons vinegar and add to sauce. Season to taste adding a little sugar if liked. For herrings, cauliflower and boiled meats.

PIQUANT SAUCE FOR LEFTOVERS

$\frac{1}{4}$ pint vinegar
2 chopped shallots
A sprig of thyme
A crushed clove of garlic

$\frac{3}{4}$ pint of gravy or thickened brown stock
2 tablespoons chopped gherkins
Seasoning

Cook the vinegar and flavourings gently in an uncovered pan, remove the thyme and garlic and, when the vinegar is reduced to $\frac{1}{8}$ pint, add the gravy and gherkins and season well. In this sauce, minced cooked meat or sliced leftover meat may be reheated. As an alternative the gherkins may be sliced and arranged as a garnish on the dish.

WILDFOWL SAUCE

2 glasses port
1 tablespoon Harvey's sauce
1 tablespoon mushroom
ketchup
1 tablespoon lemon juice
1 slice lemon peel, chopped
fine

1 large chopped shallot
Cayenne pepper
1 blade mace
2 cloves
1 tablespoon white roux
$\frac{1}{2}$ pint game stock
1 tablespoon redcurrant jelly

Simmer the chopped shallot, Cayenne, mace and cloves in the stock. Strain on to the roux in the top of a double boiler. Add the port and other ingredients. Heat and strain into a sauceboat.

BREAD SAUCE

1 medium-sized onion
1 clove
$\frac{1}{2}$ pint milk
2 oz fresh white breadcrumbs

Seasoning
1 tablespoon cream and $\frac{1}{2}$ oz
butter or 1 oz butter

Put the onion and clove in a saucepan with the milk and bring to the boil. Add the breadcrumbs and seasoning. Simmer for about 15 minutes, stirring occasionally. Remove the onion and clove and stir in the cream and butter.

1742 CUCUMBER SAUCE

2 oz butter
1 large cucumber
Salt and pepper

1 teaspoon grated onion
$\frac{1}{2}$ pint gravy made from pan
juices
1 teaspoon lemon juice

Melt the butter. Add the cucumber which has been peeled, sliced and drained. Toss in fat until golden. Add salt and pepper, onion and gravy and simmer until the onion is cooked. Add the lemon juice and serve with mutton.

1742 HORSERADISH SAUCE

2 oz grated horseradish
1 tablespoon ground mustard
1 tablespoon sugar

4 tablespoons vinegar or *oil*
1 teaspoon turmeric
Salt and pepper

Mix all ingredients together and serve with beef.

1831 COMMON SAUCE

Unsalted butter   *Walnut pickle or catsup*

Melt the butter gently and when just soft add a spoonful of walnut pickle or catsup. Stir well and serve with fish.

1831 CELERY SAUCE

1 head celery
½ pint cream
Powdered mace

Powdered nutmeg
½ oz butter rolled in flour

Cut celery in small pieces and simmer in just enough water to cover until tender. Add cream, mace and nutmeg to taste, and the butter rolled in flour. Stir over very gentle heat until thick and well-blended, but do not boil. Serve with fowl, turkey, partridge and other game.

1831 EGG SAUCE

4 hard-boiled eggs   *4 oz butter*

Chop the eggs not too finely and add to just-melted butter. Very good with poached or baked cod or fresh haddock.

READING SAUCE

Take Wallnuts and beat them until thay becum a pulp. Squeeze the pulp from them and let it stand and settle the day then pour of the clear and to every pint of juice put ½ pound of anchovys 1 oz of Shallotts. Let it stand on the Fire untill the Anchovies is quite Disolved then add ¼ oz Mace ¼ oz Cloves ¼ oz Jamaica Pepper ¼ pint White Vinagar. Let all boil together Quarter of Hour. Strain it off it should Drip through the Bag jently.

Joseph Webb's Book, 1823

TARTARE SAUCE

Take yolks of 2 eggs in a basin with pepper and salt. Drop salad oil into these keeping it stirred well till quite thick and firm – then add in drops a dessertspoon of tarragon vinegar and teaspoon of chili vinegar still keeping briskly stirring. This will make it about the thickness of cream. Serve cold with salmon, soles or turbot.

Mrs Garden, 1847

HOT SAUCE

2 *teaspoons French mustard*
1 *teaspoon common mustard*
1 *teaspoon anchovy sauce*
1 *teaspoon Harvey sauce*

Half a teaspoon chili vinegar
1 *teaspoon salt mixed in a*
teacup full of good gravy

Boil together.

Mrs Garden, 1847

SAUCE FOR CHICKENS

Take the heads and necks of the chickens, with a small bit of scrag of veal, or any scraps of mutton you may have by you, and put them into a saucepan, with a blade or 2 of mace, and a few black pepper corns, an anchovy, a head of celery, a slice of the end of a lemon, and a bunch of sweet herbs. Put to these a quart of water, cover it close, and let it boil till it is reduced to half a pint. Then strain it, and thicken it with a $\frac{1}{4}$ lb of butter mixed with flour, and boil it 5 or 6 minutes. Then put in 2 spoonfuls of mushrooms, and mix the yolks of 2 eggs with a teacupful of cream, and a little nutmeg grated. Put in your sauce, and keep shaking it over the fire, till it is near boiling; then put it into your boats, and serve it up with your chickens.

Thomas Train, Gateshead, 1812

SAUCE FOR A BOILED DUCK

Take 1 large onion, a handful of parsley clean washed and picked, and a lettuce. Cut the onions small, chop the parsley fine, and put them into a $\frac{1}{4}$ pint of good gravy, with a spoonful of lemon juice and a little pepper and salt. When they have stewed together a $\frac{1}{2}$ hour, add 2 spoonfuls of red wine. Lay the duck in your dish and pour the sauce over it.

Thomas Train, Gateshead, 1812

LEMON SAUCE FOR BOILED FOWLS

Take a lemon, and peel off the rind, then cut it into slices, take the kernels out, and cut it into small square bits. Blanch the liver of the fowl and chop it fine. Mix the lemon and liver together in a boat, pour on some hot melted butter, and stir it up.

Thomas Train, Gateshead, 1812

ORANGE SAUCE

5 tablespoons sugar
2 tablespoons water
1 tablespoon white vinegar
Juice of 2 oranges

Segments of 1 orange
Grated rind of 1 orange
1 teaspoon arrowroot

Mix arrowroot with a little orange juice. Dissolve sugar in water. Bring to boiling point until solution is golden brown. Watch carefully, remove from heat and add vinegar, remains of orange juice. Add rind and segments and blended arrowroot. Bring to boil and boil 2 minutes. Serve with roast duck.

Pat Brown, Keynsham, Somerset

VAL'S BARBECUE SAUCE

2 oz lard
1 clove garlic
3 onions
2 lemons (rind and juice)
4 oz brown sugar

$\frac{1}{4}$ pint vinegar
4 tins tomato purée
4 tablespoons Worcester sauce

Cook all together to make a thick sauce. Serve with sausages or beef fondue.

Pat Brown, Keynsham, Somerset

TONATTO

A creamy sauce to serve with cold veal. This sauce is a mixture of mayonnaise made in the usual way and into which is mixed crushed tuna, anchovies, and capers to taste (but not too much), until quite smooth. It is delicious.

Signora Beglia, Italy

GREEN SAUCE DRESSING

This dressing can be served with any cold dish. Used for spaghetti only, it should be heated up quickly after it has been mixed in with the spaghetti.

You need basil, a couple of cloves of garlic, grated cheese, salt and olive oil. As it is a sauce which can be kept, the quantity may vary but the correct proportions are 1 cup of basil to 2 cloves of garlic and $\frac{1}{2}$ a cup of cheese.

Mix all these ingredients together with the oil. Signora Beglia uses a mortar and works hard at it, but an electric mixer will also do the job. The sauce should be liquid with the basil and solids settled at the bottom, so when serving the spoon should dive deep in order to bring up the solid and the liquid. Well seasoned this is delicious on cold ham, cold meat or fish.

Signora Beglia, Italy

SAUCE FOR COLD CUTS FROM THE SUNDAY JOINT

Add 2 tablespoons chutney, 1 teaspoon made mustard, $\frac{1}{4}$ teaspoon curry powder and blend well.

OXFORD BRAWN SAUCE

Blend 1 teaspoon salad oil with 2 teaspoons caster sugar and 1 teaspoon dry mustard; when smooth beat in 2 tablespoons vinegar and 2 tablespoons salad oil. Season to taste. Add 1 teaspoon chopped parsley and spoon over meat slices. For cold meats and brawn.

MUSTARD CREAM SAUCE

Blend $\frac{1}{4}$ pint lightly whipped double cream with 2 tablespoons made mustard and season to taste. For herrings, mackerel and grills.

MUSTARD BUTTER

Cream 4 oz butter with 1 tablespoon made mustard. Shape into a roll, wrap in greaseproof paper, put in refrigerator, slice and use as required. For meat and fish steaks.

LEMON DRESSING

Juice of 2 lemons
1 tablespoon clear honey

Chopped fresh herbs

Combine all ingredients. Dress salad just before serving, or serve separately.

SALAD CREAM

$1\frac{1}{2}$ *pints milk*
$\frac{3}{4}$ *pint vinegar*
4 oz margarine
4 heaped tablespoons flour

3 heaped tablespoons sugar
1 level tablespoon mustard
2 eggs

Melt margarine in saucepan. Take from heat, add flour, sugar and mustard. Stir in milk and return to heat, stirring all the time to avoid sticking. When mixture begins to thicken, take from heat and beat quickly to avoid lumps. Put to cool. When cool, beat in 2 eggs and add vinegar to required thickness. This will keep 4–6 weeks and Mrs Ball makes it before haymaking to last through the summer. She multiplied the quantity by four to make enough for 130 people at a YFC Harvest Supper.

Mrs Ball, Compton Greenfield, Glos.

SALAD CREAM (to keep)

2 oz plain flour
4 tablespoons sugar
6 oz butter
8 egg yolks

4 teaspoons salt
1 pint cream
$\frac{1}{2}$ *pint vinegar*
1 teaspoon dry mustard

Mix dry ingredients. Add melted butter, eggs and cream. Carefully add vinegar, stirring. Cook slowly in double saucepan, stirring frequently.

Pat Brown, Keynsham, Somerset

SALAD DRESSING

1 hard-boiled egg
1 tablespoon sugar
2 tablespoons mixed mustard

1 tablespoon oil
Little salt
Milk and vinegar

Mix sugar, mustard, salt, oil and egg yolk into smooth paste (mix salt, sugar and egg first) then add by degrees alternately milk and vinegar to taste.

Lewis' Mother's Cookbook, Mary Horrell, Exeter

SALAD DRESSING

1 egg
¼ teaspoon mixed mustard

¼ teaspoon salt
¼ teaspoon pepper

Well mix, then add 3 teaspoons Tarragon vinegar, 2 teaspoons pounded sugar. Well mixed. Add 4 teaspoons vinegar and a little Worcester sauce and ¾ teacupful cream.

Lewis' Mother's Cookbook, Mary Horrell, Exeter

MINT SAUCE TO STORE

Pick fresh young mint leaves. Warm 8 oz golden syrup and put in liquidiser. Add mint leaves and liquidise until fine. Store in jar and add vinegar as required.

Pat Brown, Keynsham, Somerset

SALAD CREAM

1 oz butter
½ oz flour
¼ pt milk

1-2 tablespoons vinegar
Salt, pepper, mustard
1 teaspoon sugar

Melt butter, add flour. Add milk slowly. Bring to the boil. Cool slightly, add remaining ingredients. This is good, but is not for keeping.

13 Packed Meals

Keen appetites and quick digestion wait
On you and yours.

Dryden

He that will have cake out of the wheat must
tarry the grinding.

Shakespeare

In the country there is always a need for packed meals. Whatever the weather, farmers may have to eat miles from home and need nourishing, compact food to last them from early breakfast to a late evening meal. In more relaxed moments, usually in the depth of winter, there is need for the handy sandwich for hunting and shooting families, and the more elaborate picnic for the numerous outdoor events in the winter calendar.

Many of the recipes throughout this book are just as good for outdoor eating, but here are some of the trusted favourites for lunch boxes of all kinds.

SAUSAGE LOAF

1 lb pork sausage meat	**Pinch of sage**
1 tablespoon tomato sauce	**2 slices bread**
1 grated onion	**1 beaten egg**
Salt and pepper	

Mix together sausage meat, sauce, onion, seasoning, crumbled bread and egg. Press into a greased loaf tin and bake at 400°F (Gas Mark 6) for 40 minutes. Leave until cold, then wrap in foil for carrying. Eat with buttered baps.

SAUSAGE SHAPE

1 *lb beef sausage meat*
1 *lb pork sausage meat*
1 *lb cooked ham or tongue*
1 *dessertspoon chopped*
pickles
1 *teaspoon mixed spice*

Pinch of freshly ground black
pepper
1 *tablespoon sweet stout*
1 *tablespoon Worcester sauce*
Pinch of rosemary
Salt

Mix together the sausage meats and finely chopped ham or tongue. Add pickles, spice, pepper, stout, Worcester sauce, rosemary and salt to taste. Tie in a cloth, and cook very slowly in stock for 2 hours. Lift out and press between 2 dishes under heavy weights until cold. This may be used for sandwiches, or may be glazed when cold, to serve with salad.

PORK CHEESE

1 *lb cold roast pork*
Pinch mixed herbs
Grated lemon rind
2 *teaspoons chopped parsley*
2 *blades of mace*

4 *sage leaves*
Pinch grated nutmeg
Good stock made from meat
bones and strengthened
with a little gelatine.

Cut the meat into small pieces. Season well, add the herbs. Mix well and put into a greased mould, fill with the gravy, and bake in a moderate oven about an hour. Turn out when cold.

BEEF LOAF

1 *lb beef steak*
4 *oz bacon*
4 *oz white breadcrumbs*

1 *teaspoon chopped parsley*
$\frac{1}{2}$ *teaspoon thyme*
2 *eggs*

Mince the meat and bacon finely, and mix with the rest of the ingredients. Add the well-beaten eggs, and a little stock to moisten if necessary. Put into a greased oblong tin and steam for 3 hours. When cold, turn out and sprinkle with brown breadcrumbs. Leave to chill before cutting, as it will crumble if cut warm.

CHICKEN ROLL

Put some cold (roast) fowl through a mincer with a little ham, season with pepper, sauce, nutmeg, a little minced shallot or onion, a dessertspoon chopped parsley; moisten withh a cupful of white sauce which has been nicely flavoured and the yolk of 1 egg. Spread the mince out on a flat dish, make into rolls on a floured board, dip into a beaten egg, cover well with breadcrumbs, allowing the crumbs to harden, and fry in boiling fat. Cool and eat with crusty bread.

VEAL CAKE

Slices of cold roast veal	*Some gravy*
Slices of ham	*2 sprigs of parsley*
3 eggs	*Pepper and salt*

Cut a few slices of ham and veal *very* thin, taking off the skin from the veal, chop 2 sprigs of parsley fine, and cut the eggs hard-boiled into slices. Take any nice shaped mould, butter it, and put the veal, ham, eggs and parsley in layers until the mould is full, seasoning each layer with a little pepper and salt. Placing a few slices of egg at the bottom of the mould at equal distances, fill up with good stock and bake for 30 minutes. When cold, turn it out.

STEAMED MEAT MINCE PUDDING

$\frac{1}{2}$ lb minced cold meat	*1 egg*
4 oz breadcrumbs	*$\frac{1}{2}$ teaspoon curry powder*
2 oz suet (dripping or lard	*Stock*
would do)	

Mix all together, adding a little flour if necessary; steam in greased bowl for 2 hours. Cool, and turn out.

CAMP PIE

$\frac{1}{2}$ lb lean ham	*$\frac{1}{4}$ teaspoon Jamaica pepper*
$\frac{1}{2}$ lb mutton	*1 teaspoon salt*
$\frac{1}{2}$ lb steak	*1 egg*
$\frac{1}{2}$ teacup breadcrumbs	*1 teacup milk*
$\frac{1}{4}$ teaspoon black pepper	

Mince together the ham, steak, and mutton. Mix well all the other ingredients, put in a buttered mould, and boil for 3 hours. Serve cold.

Mrs Higgins, Falkirk, 1911

BACON AND MUSHROOM PICNIC LOAF

1 *small loaf white bread*
4 *oz butter*
4 *rashers lean bacon*
8 *oz chicken livers*

4 *oz mushrooms*
1 *onion*
Salt and pepper

Cut a 'lid' from the top of the loaf and scoop out the soft bread (this can be saved to use for breadcrumbs). Leave about 1 inch wall all round inside the bread. Melt 3 oz butter and fry the outside of the loaf and lid until golden brown and crisp and leave to cool. Chop the bacon, chicken livers, mushrooms and onion finely. In the remaining butter, cook the bacon for 1 minute, and add the onion. Cook until the onion is transparent, and add chicken livers and mushrooms. Season with salt and pepper and cook for 2 minutes. Pack the mixture into the loaf and cover with the lid. Wrap in foil and chill for 2 hours. Serve cut into slices with salad.

SHOOTER'S SANDWICH

1 *large thick rump steak*
1 *sandwich loaf*

$\frac{1}{4}$ *lb mushrooms*
Salt and pepper

Grill the steak medium rare, and fry the chopped mushrooms in butter. Cut off the end of the sandwich loaf, remove some of the crumbs, and put in the well-seasoned steak and mushrooms. Put back the crust, wrap the loaf in blotting paper, then greaseproof paper, and tie into a neat parcel with string. Put under heavy weights for 6 hours, and do not slice until needed.

SANDWICH FILLINGS

The most conventional sandwich fillings such as egg, meat, cheese and fish can be improved with imaginative additions. If you intend to freeze sandwiches, avoid hard-boiled egg, mayonnaise or salad cream, and lettuce, tomato and cucumber which do not react well to low temperatures. These can be packed into the lunch box separately. Here are the main ingredients with their flavouring combinations:

Beef: Chopped ham, lettuce, horseradish sauce. Lettuce, fried onion, cucumber. Tomato, lettuce, salad cream.

Lamb: Apple sauce, chopped mint. Mint jelly.

Pork: Apple sauce. Sliced pineapple, mustard, salad dressing. Salad dressing spiced with curry powder.

Ham: Dates and salad dressing. Hard-boiled egg, capers.

Tongue: Redcurrant jelly, lettuce. Hard-boiled egg, onion, salad cream.

Chicken or turkey: Chopped crisp bacon, lettuce, salad cream. Ham, chopped parsley, green pepper.

Crisp bacon: Chopped cooked chicken liver, tomato, mayonnaise. Mashed liver sausage, cucumber.

Egg: Sardines, lemon juice. Anchovy paste or anchovy fillets.

Cheese: Radishes, corned beef, salad dressing. Shredded raw cabbage, sliced apple, mayonnaise.

Cream cheese: Chutney, walnuts. Liver sausage, egg, chives, salad dressing.

EGG SANDWICHES

Mash hard-boiled egg with butter and curry powder, or with gherkins or anchovies. Even easier, try scrambled egg sandwiches.

BACON AND EGG SANDWICHES

Cook egg on both sides to seal yolk, and with the bacon put between bread and butter.

SAVOURY BUTTERS

These are delicious used alone for tea-party sandwiches, or as a lift to heartier sandwiches or rolls filled with salad or hard-boiled eggs.

SALMON BUTTER

Remove skin and bones from contents of 1 small tin salmon. Mash fish with a squeeze of lemon juice, plenty of pepper and salt, and work in 2 oz butter. Good with cucumber sandwiches.

SARDINE BUTTER

Mash 2 oz sardines and blend with 2 oz softened butter and a squeeze of lemon juice, pepper and salt to taste.

KIPPER BUTTER

Grill or poach 4 kipper fillets, cool and remove bones. Mash flesh with 2 oz butter, pepper and salt and a dash of Worcester sauce. Eat with plenty of crisp lettuce.

CURRY POWDER

Cream 3 oz butter and work in 1 oz chopped mango chutney, 1 teaspoon made mustard, ½ teaspoon curry powder, a squeeze of lemon juice, pepper and salt. Useful with cold meat or poultry sandwiches.

14 Wines, Beers, Punches, Possets and Soft Drinks

From wine what sudden friendship springs!

Gay

Though gay companions o'er the bowl
Dispel awhile the sense of ill;
Though pleasure stirs the maddening soul
The heart – the heart – is lonely still.

Byron

A GALLON OF FLOWERS

Wines made from spring flowers are popular, but often a recipe calls for a 'gallon of flowers' and the weight is difficult to determine. This is best interpreted as a gallon container full of flowers under their own weight, not compressed. If a pocket spring balance is used while picking, measuring is easier. For instance, 3 lb dandelion petals only equals 1 gallon; 2 lb dandelion whole heads equals 1 gallon; 2 lb elderflower flowers stripped from bunches equals 1 gallon.

ELDERFLOWER DRINK

1 cluster of elderflowers with the pollen on it, 4 quarts cold water, 1½ lb lump sugar, 1 lemon and finely grated rind, 1 teaspoon tartaric acid. Put ingredients into a pan, stir often. After 24 hours strain and bottle. Stand bottles upright for a fortnight, then lie on side. Use screwtop bottles, or wired corks. The former are far better.

Lewis' Mother's Cookbook, Mary Horrell, Exeter

NETTLE WINE

1 gallon young nettles	**3 lemons**
3 lb white sugar	**2 oz root ginger**
1 gallon water	**½ oz yeast**

Boil the nettles, ginger, rinds and juice of the lemons together until a dark green, then strain and add the sugar. Put the yeast on toast, and put it on the wine when it is blood heat. E. Shepphard is my friend who makes it, and when she bottles it, she adds a few raisins.

Miss Mabel Nokes, Priston Mill Farm, Bath

PARKSIDE ORANGE WINE

12 large juicy oranges	**3 lb sugar**
1 gallon boiling water	

Wash the oranges and slice them thinly, including the peel. Put into a china basin and pour over the water. Cover with a cloth and leave for a week, stirring 2 or 3 times a day. Strain the liquid. Heat up a pint and stir in the sugar until dissolved. Add to the remainder. Pour into bottles and cork lightly until fermentation has ceased, and then seal. Ready in 4 months.

APPLE WINE

Cut ripe apples and to each gallon of fruit allow 4 pints of water. Put on a low heat, bring to boil and simmer for 20 minutes. Cool and strain, and add 8 oz of brown sugar or honey to each quart of liquid.

Put in cask with whites of two eggs and 2 oz bruised cinnamon stick to each gallon. Let it work and bung tightly.

Ros Hill, 1864

POPLAR COTTAGE APPLE WINE

6 lb apples   **1 gallon water**
2 lb sugar

Cut up the apples, including skins and cores. Cover with the water, and mash and stir for 2 days. Strain the liquid and heat up 1 pint. Pour this over the sugar. Stir well to dissolve, and then add the rest of the liquid. Leave to stand for 3 days. Skim, strain and bottle, corking lightly at first. Push corks in firmly later.

BRAMBLE AND ELDERBERRY WINE

Use half and half ration, i.e. 2 lb Brambles and 2 lb Elderberries – 7 pints of water – $3\frac{1}{2}$ to 4 lb sugar – $\frac{1}{2}$ oz yeast or all-purpose wine yeast. These proportions can be varied – 1 lb Elderberries to 3 lb Brambles – there is no hard and fast rule.

Crush the fruits, and leave to soak in warm atmosphere for 24 hours. Then strain the juice, place in pan and bring to the boil for no longer than 2 minutes. Remove the rising scum, add the sugar, and when the liquid has cooled to blood heat, add the yeast. Keep the must in a warm, even temperature closely covered until fermentation has ceased. I find that the large glass sweet jars make handy fermentation vessels and can be obtained from your local shop.

A few reminders: Never put wine into screw top bottles for fear of explosion. Incidentally, if such a disaster should occur, and I sincerely hope it never does, it is in no way an indication that the wine is extra strong and potent . . . merely that the wine has been bottled before the fermentation has ceased.

Always keep the wine closely covered – 3 thicknesses of polythene is a happy medium. Secure the neck of the jar with string.

Add one Campden tablet finely crushed to each gallon of wine; these or sulphur tablets, which kill bacteria, are obtainable from any chemist.

On one farm in Cheshire they used to bury their rhubarb wine for 40 years. Seasoned topers 'blacked out' after drinking 1 gill of its potency!

Mrs Ward, York

PARSNIP WINE

4 lb parsnips   **3 lb white sugar**
1 teaspoon ground ginger   **$\frac{3}{4}$ oz baker's yeast or 1**
Rinds and juice of 2 lemons   **teaspoon dried yeast**
and 1 orange

Scrub parsnips, but do not peel them. Cut into $\frac{1}{4}$ inch to $\frac{1}{2}$ inch slices. Boil in a gallon of water with ground ginger and citrus rinds until tender. Place sugar in bucket and strain over parsnip liquid. Stir and leave to cool. When the liquid, or must, as it is called, has cooled to lukewarm, add the citrus juices and prepared yeast. Cover closely and leave for 24 hours. Pour the must into a jar. Insert an airlock and leave to ferment. When all fermentation has ceased, rack off into bottles, and store.

RICE WINE

3 *lb rice*
1 *lb raisins*
3 *lb white sugar*

Juice of 2 lemons and 1 orange
$\frac{3}{4}$ *oz baker's yeast or 1 teaspoon dried yeast*

Soak rice overnight in 3 pints water. Chop or mince raisins. Mix raisins, rice, rice water and sugar in bucket; pour on 5 pints of boiling water. Stir well, cover and leave to cool. When at room temperature, add fruit juices and prepared yeast. Cover well; stand in warm place to ferment, stirring daily.

When fermentation slows, strain into fermentation bottle and fit airlock. Allow to clear, then rack off into a clean jar. Allow any further fermentation to cease before bottling.

CARROT WINE

6 *lb carrots*
4 *lb white sugar*
1 *lb wheat (available from a health store)*
Rind and juice of 1 lemon and 1 orange

$\frac{3}{4}$ *oz baker's yeast or 1 teaspoon dried yeast*
4 *oz raisins*

Scrub and peel carrots; boil until tender in 1 gallon of water. Strain liquid into bucket over sugar, wheat and rinds; stir well. When lukewarm, add fruit juices and prepared yeast. Stir well and leave for 7 days, stirring daily.

Remove rinds, but not raisins, and pour into fermentation jar with lock. Bottle when all fermentation has ceased.

ORANGE WINE

12 *medium-sized oranges*
2 *lemons*
1 *lb minced or chopped raisins*

$3\frac{1}{2}$ *lb white sugar*
$\frac{3}{4}$ *oz baker's yeast or 1 teaspoon dried yeast or 1 champagne yeast tablet*

Wash oranges and lemons. Peel half the oranges and place rinds in oven to dry crisp and brown. Squeeze all oranges and lemons and mix in bucket with raisins and sugar. Add 6 pints cold water and stir well. Cover.

Place rind from oven in a jug or bowl and pour over 2 pints of boiling water. Leave for an hour. Prepare yeast.

Strain liquid from peel into bucket and mix well. Add the yeast liquid. Cover and leave to ferment for 3 days, stirring daily. Do not strain. Pour into jar; fit airlock.

When all fermentation has ceased, rack off into a clean jar. Wait 2 weeks, to make sure all fermentation has ended, then bottle.

POTATO WINE

5 lb old potatoes	*3½ lb demerara sugar*
Juice and rind of 2 lemons	*¾ oz baker's yeast or 1*
and 1 orange	*teaspoon dried yeast*
1 teaspoon ground ginger	*4 oz seedless raisins*

Scrub potatoes and cut into large pieces. Boil in 1 gallon of water for about 15 minutes; strain off liquid while potatoes are still quite firm. Boil liquid again with rinds and ginger for 10 minutes, adding more water if level has dropped below 1 gallon mark.

Place sugar in bucket and pour over boiling liquid. Stir well, and when lukewarm, add fruit juices and yeast liquid. Cover and leave to ferment, stirring daily.

When fermentation slows, pour into fermentation jar, add raisins and insert airlock. Leave for at least 9 months, then rack off into bottles.

APPLE WINE

6 lb chopped apples	*¾ oz baker's yeast or 1*
(including crab apples)	*teaspoon dried yeast*
Rind and juice of 1 lemon	*½ lb seedless raisins, minced*
3 lb white sugar	*or chopped*

Boil apples and lemon rind in a gallon of water until soft, about 10 minutes. Strain into a bucket over the sugar. When lukewarm, add lemon juice and prepared yeast. Cover well and leave for 24 hours.

Pour into a fermenting jar; leave for 4 weeks, then rack off into a clean jar. Add raisins. Insert airlock and leave until you are sure fermentation has ceased. Cork, and leave for 6 months, then rack into bottles.

RAISIN WINE

3 *lb seedless raisins* $\frac{3}{4}$ *oz baker's yeast or* 1
3 *lb demerara sugar*   *teaspoon dried yeast*
Juice and rind of 1 *lemon*

Chop or mince the raisins. Mix with half the sugar and lemon juice and rind. Pour over 7 pints lukewarm water (half boiling, half cold will get the right temperature). Add prepared yeast. Stir vigorously, then cover and stand in a warm place for 10 days.

During the first 2 days, stir frequently to prevent raisins and sugar settling. Then stir once daily.

After tenth day, boil up remaining sugar in a pint of water, allow to cool and add to mixture when lukewarm. Stir well; do not strain. Pour into fermenting jar and fit airlock. Keep in a warm place until fermentation ceases, then rack off into bottles.

CIDER

This is a simple recipe. It is ready to drink just as soon as all the fermentation has ceased. Windfall and weathered apples are best, so don't be in a hurry to bring them indoors. Try to mix varieties as much as possible.

For large quantities, cut and mash the apples so that they are thoroughly squashed; for small quantities, use a mincer. Use every part of the fruit – skin, pips, and cores.

Put the pulp in a nylon straining bag or something similar and press out the juice. Some people use a wooden mangle or a clothes wringer. A rolling pin is useful, or it is possible to buy a fruit press. Keep pressing until the pulp is 'dry', i.e. when you have extracted the maximum amount of juice from it.

Pour juice into a fermenting jar and plug neck with cotton wool. (Fermentation is usually fierce at first, and if you insert an airlock, the froth may find its way up the inside.) Stand the jar on a tray in a warm place to continue fermenting.

Renew the cotton wool if necessary. When fermentation dies down, clean the jar and insert an airlock. Let it finish fermenting.

It is best served from the jar, otherwise use strong cider bottles.

Near almost every Somerset farm, and some other houses too, you will notice a small orchard. There may be an eating apple or two; a cooking apple or two; but the rest will be old, unpruned, straggling cider apple trees. In spring they are a mass of bees and blossom, and in the autumn they bear a crop of small bright red apples. They are not, of course, picked in the normal way; small apples and unpruned trees would make it very difficult. You will often see a long pole attached to a high branch and this is used to shake the apples down.

The farmer's family or workers pick up the apples into buckets and empty them into sacks. In bigger orchards this is a useful source of seasonal income for the local women. The sacks are eventually collected up and taken to the cider press in the farm buildings.

Although many of these old trees are being cut down to make way for barns and silage pits, and the farmer buys his cider, odd trees can still be seen. They are decorative in their own right; white with blossom in the spring; a welcome patch of shade in the heat of summer; red and yellow with apples and autumn leaves in the fall; and a lacy silhouette against a frosty blue sky in the winter.

They seem to be part of the old farmsteads near which they grow, and which were old when they were planted many years ago.

Mrs Berkeley, Somerset Farm Wives' Club

BEER (1)

Most beers are rather complicated to make, but this is a simple recipe for bitter beer of average strength.

To make 4 gallons of beer you will require:

¼ *lb dried hops*	2 *lb preserving sugar*
1 *dessertspoon caramel*	½ *teaspoon citric acid*
colouring	2 *teaspoons dried yeast*
2 *lb malt extract*	

For such a large quantity, you will need an extra-large fermenting vessel such as a small plastic dustbin.

Boil as much water as your largest pan will conveniently take. While this is heating, tie the hops in a muslin bag and add them, with the caramel colouring, when the water boils. Simmer for 45 minutes.

Warm the tin of malt extract in water to soften it a little. Remove hops.

Place extract and sugar in the dustbin and pour over the boiling liquid. Add tepid water to make up to 4 gallons, then add citric acid. Stir all the ingredients together vigorously.

Allow to cool to room temperature, then add prepared yeast. This will make a lot of froth, hence the need for a large container. Cover with dustbin lid or a sheet of polythene tightly tied, and allow to ferment for at least 3 days, but no more than 7, keeping temperature as constant as possible.

After the first day or two, remove some of the froth (this is bitter to the taste). The beer is ready for bottling when the froth has died down to a ring in the centre.

The beer will be still or only sparkling. If you want to give it more bite, add 1 level teaspoon of sugar to each quart bottle – no more or the bottles may burst.

Screw-top cider or beer bottles are best. Screw very lightly for the first day or two, then tighten up. Keep in a cool place until the beer clears. There will be a slight deposit in the bottom of the bottles, so pour the beer very carefully.

BEER (2)

2×1 gallon fermentation jars, 2 bored corks, 2 fermentation locks, a plastic funnel, a length of plastic tubing for syphoning. Strong bottles e.g. cider bottles (and plenty of patience).

1 oz hops	**1 lb jar plain malt extract**
½ lb demerara sugar	**½ teaspoon gravy browning**
2 oz flaked rice	**1 teaspoon granulated yeast**

All the above can be bought at Boots the Chemists.

Put the demerara sugar, malt and flaked rice into large container e.g. a 2 gallon plastic bucket, and pour on 3 pints warm water, stir till it has dissolved, meanwhile put the hops into a saucepan with 1 pint of cold water. Bring to the boil and simmer for about 10 minutes, then strain the liquid into the bucket. Put another pint of water on to the hops again bring to the boil and again strain off the liquid into the bucket. Repeat once more with another pint of water. Add the ½ teaspoon of gravy browning and stir well, put a little of the warm liquid into a cup and sprinkle on the granulated yeast. Leave for about 10 minutes until it is frothy. Make up the liquid in the bucket to 1 gallon with cold water, and when lukewarm, stir in the frothy yeast. Now pour it all into the fermentation jar and put a plug of cotton wool in the top. Stand in a deep dish in a warm place. When the first violent ferment has ceased, take out the cotton wool, wipe the neck of the jar clean, and insert a bored cork and an air lock, making sure that there is water halfway up the airlock. Leave in warm room till it has ceased working (4 to 7 days) then syphon off into a clean jar making sure you do not disturb the sediment on the bottom. Put on the airlock again and leave till liquid has cleared. Syphon off carefully into strong bottles, add 2 lumps of sugar to each bottle and screw down tight. Put in a cold place for about a week, when the beer should be ready for drinking. When syphoning the liquid from the yeasty deposits, it is better to filter it through a cloth placed in the plastic funnel. This is very, very good.

Harper Adams Agricultural College, Salop.

CORNISH MEAD

The honey used in this should be light and well ripened, and throughout the whole process the utmost cleanliness must be secured. Use 4 lb honey to each gallon of water, and allow the honey to dissolve, then put into a large boiler or copper, add 1 oz hops and $\frac{1}{2}$ oz ginger per gallon, and boil for one hour, skimming off the scum as it rises. When sufficiently boiled pour it into a wooden vessel and when its temperature is reduced to 120°F add 1 oz brewers yeast per gallon, mix well with the liquor which must then be covered and allowed to stand for about 8 hours in the same vessel. Next, pour it into a perfectly clean barrel, and as the contents ferment, the barrel must be filled with more of the liquor, an extra half-gallon having been prepared for this purpose beyond what the barrel holds. When fermentation has ceased, dissolve $\frac{1}{4}$ oz isinglass in a cupful of water, pour it into the barrel and stir well; this is to clear the liquid. After about 6 days draw off the liquor into a second perfectly clean barrel, filling the barrel completely, and drive in the bung as tightly as possible. Leave for at least 6 months, after which it may be bottled. The bottles must of course be perfectly clean, the corks new, and they should be fastened with wire and covered with tinfoil, a neat label being pasted on each bottle.

'*The Practical Bee Guide*', *The Rev J. G. Digges*, 1904

MEAD (1)

This may be made with honey straight from the bees, but can also be made with shop honey. Blend together 1 gallon of water, 1 pint of honey, and 4 oz sugar and bring to the boil. Skim and pour into an earthenware crock to cool. When lukewarm, add the peel of an orange cut in slices, the juice of an orange, and 2 oz yeast creamed with a little warm water. Put a lid on the crock, and leave to 'work' for a fortnight, stirring 3 times a day for the first 3 days. Strain, bottle and keep for 3 months before using.

MEAD (2)

1 oz dried hops	2 gallons water
2 lb honey	1 oz yeast

Put hops and honey into water and boil slowly for 1 hour. Cool and when lukewarm add the yeast spread on a piece of toast. Cover and leave for 4 days. Strain, bottle and cork loosely until fermentation has ceased, then cork tightly. Keep 1 year before using.

MR NIGHTINGALE'S WHISKEY

3 *lb raisins*
3 *lb sugar*
½ *pint wheat*

2 *potatoes*
1 *gallon water*
Yeast

Steep raisins, sugar, wheat and potatoes in water for one month, stirring each day. Strain, add yeast and allow to work. Restrain and bottle.

BRITISH SACK

To every quart of water put a sprig of rue; and to every gallon put a handful of fennel roots. Boil these ½ an hour, then strain it; and to every gallon of liquor put 3 lbs of honey. Boil it 2 hours, and skim it well. When it is cold, pour it off, and turn it into a cask or vessel that will just hold it.

Thomas Train, Gateshead, 1812

BRITISH CLARET

Take 8 pounds of Malaga raisins, well bruised, and put these into 6 gallons of water, and 2 gallons of cyder; place them in a warm situation, and let them stand close covered for 14 days, not forgetting to stir them well every other day. At the expiration of that time, strain off the liquor into a clean and well-seasoned cask, and add to it a pint of the juice of raspberries, a pint of the juice of black cherries, and a quart of ripe barberries. To work it up, throw in a little mustard seed, then cover it with a piece of dough, and let it stand 3 or 4 days by the side of the fire. After that, let it stand a week, and bottle it off. When it is worked fine, and is sufficiently ripe, it will have the taste and colour of common claret.

Thomas Train, Gateshead, 1812

ELDERFLOWER DRINK

Well-established idea that elderflowers are health-giving. Dry blooms and use as 'tea'.

1 *cluster of elderflowers with*
the flower on it
4 *quarts cold water*

1½ *lb lump sugar*
1 *lemon and finely grated rind*
1 *teaspoon tartaric acid*

Put ingredients into pan, stir often. After 24 hours, strain and bottle. Stand bottles upright for a fortnight, then lie on side. Use screw top bottles.

BARLEY WATER

3 oz pearl barley
1 lemon

2 pints boiling water
Sugar to taste

Wash the barley in a little boiling water. Drain off the water, and put the barley into a jug with the grated rind and juice of the lemon, and a little sugar. Pour over it the boiling water. Stir occasionally while cooling and strain before using.

LEMONADE (1)

1½ lb lump sugar

1 pint boiling water

Put ½ oz tartaric acid in a jug and pour on the hot syrup; when nearly cold add about 16 drops of essence of lemon.

LEMONADE (2)

1 orange
1 lemon
1¾ lb sugar

½ oz tartaric acid
3½ pints boiling water

Mince orange and lemon, rind, pips and juice. Put in bowl with sugar, tartaric acid and water. Leave 24 hours. Strain through colander and sieve and bottle.

Mrs E. Jones

OLD-FASHIONED LEMONADE

3 lemons
3 tablespoons sugar

1 quart boiling water
Sprig of mint

Dice lemons and put into a jug with the sugar. Pour on boiling water, leave for 30 minutes, then strain. Put the mint into serving jug, pour on lemonade and add a few slices of fresh lemon. Serve with ice-cubes.

LEMON SYRUP

2 lemons
1¾ lb lump sugar

1 oz tartaric acid
1 pint boiling water

Peel lemons very thin. Add the peel to the lump sugar and pour on it the boiling water. Squeeze the juice of the lemons into a basin. Mix the tartaric acid with it, then stir all together. Put through a strainer and bottle off.

A drop or two of brandy or whiskey will keep it for many weeks. About 2 tablespoons to a tumbler of water.

Mrs Garden, 1847

GINGER BEER

Place 2 oz baker's yeast, or $\frac{1}{2}$ oz dried yeast, in a large glass jar and add $\frac{1}{2}$ pint tepid water, 2 level teaspoons each of sugar and ground ginger. When stirred it will soon begin to froth and seethe. Daily, for a week, feed the plant with 1 teaspoon each of sugar and ground ginger.

At the end of a week, strain the liquid carefully through butter muslin, retaining the residue, and add the juice of 2 lemons, 1 lb sugar and 2 pints of lukewarm water. Stir mixture well to dissolve sugar. Bottle when cool.

Carefully scrape the reserved residue into two jars, and carry out the whole process again, omitting the yeast this time. Remember, the plant won't live for more than a week or 10 days unless it is rejuvenated and started again.

The ginger beer is ready to drink in about a week. Cork lightly at first. Serve chilled.

MR JONES' PERSIAN SHERBERT

1$\frac{1}{2}$ *lb sugar bruised fine*	*4 oz tartarick acid*
$\frac{1}{4}$ *lb carbonate soda*	$\frac{1}{4}$ *oz essence lemon*

Be sure and pound it fine and sift it through fine muslin. 2 teaspoons to $\frac{1}{2}$ pint Water.

Joseph Webb's Book, 1823

RHUBARB SHERBET

Cut some rhubarb into short lengths and to every pint of fruit put a quart of water and let it boil for 20 minutes; strain into a jug and sweeten with 8 lumps of sugar which have been rubbed into the rind of a lemon. When cool drink as a cooling beverage.

Lewis' Mother's Cookbook, Mary Horrell, Exeter

LAURA'S LEMONADE

4 large lemons	*1 teaspoon oil of lemon*
2 lb sugar	*1 dessertspoon tartaric acid*
2 pints water	

258

Squeeze the lemon juice over the sugar in a basin. Add the oil of lemon and the acid. Stir well and pour on boiling water. Stir until dissolved, and cool. Bottle when cold. Dilute to taste.

DAMSON GIN

This is a variation of the traditional sloe gin. Choose perfect fruit and wash them well, then prick them with a thick needle. Use half fruit and half gin, and to each estimated bottle add 8 oz sugar candy (or granulated sugar if the candy sugar is not available). Put fruit into a jar with the sugar and a teaspoon of almond essence and top up with gin. Stand jar in a warm place and shake or stir at least 3 times a day for a week. Store, and decant after 3 months.

CHERRY BRANDY

1 lb Morello cherries
4 oz sugar candy
¼ oz shredded bitter almonds

½ inch cinnamon stick
Brandy

Remove stalks from cherries, wipe fruit and prick with a thick needle. Half-fill wide-necked jars with the fruit. Add sugar, almonds and cinnamon in the correct proportions, and fill jars to the top with brandy. Cover tightly and leave for at least 6 months. The brandy can be strained from the cherries, and the cherries are good to eat.

PUNCHES AND MULLS

Winter punches and mulls are cockle-warmers and tongue-looseners, and they can be very inexpensive, but they must be carefully prepared. Punch needs a strong spirit or wine base, and should be served very hot, preferably in handled mugs or glasses (pour it in over a metal spoon to avoid cracking). It's a good idea to heat the punch in a preserving pan which can easily be carried to a serving table and holds the heat better than a china bowl. Use inexpensive wine for punches, but use good whole spices to avoid cloudiness. As a variation on mixed drinks, try mulled wine, ale or cider, but suit the strength to the time of day.

Serve these hot drinks hot, but don't keep them on the boil, for a boiling drink soon loses its kick. Mulled wine can be poured back into the bottles after making and kept standing in hot water. For a really Olde Worlde touch, warm the mixture with a redhot poker to make the mull smoother.

MULLED WINE

Use cheap red wine for this. It's the traditional remedy for preventing or curing a cold. In Shakespeare's day, they used to add a well-beaten egg to the mull when it was taken from the fire. Heat 2 tablespoons sugar in 4 tablespoons water until the sugar has dissolved. Add 1 bottle red wine and heat to boiling point. Pour into glasses containing a slice of orange or lemon, and grate on a little fresh nutmeg.

MULLED ALE (1)

3 eggs
2 pints milk
1 pint ale

4 oz castor sugar
Little grated nutmeg

Bring the ale to the boil in a saucepan, then set aside. Beat the eggs, and stir in the milk, pour this mixture into the ale. Add the sugar and nutmeg, and heat slowly, but do not boil. Let it thicken, stirring meanwhile. Serve very hot.

MULLED ALE (2)

In a saucepan, mix together 1 quart brown ale, $\frac{1}{4}$ pint brandy, 1 tablespoon caster sugar, 4 cloves and a pinch each of nutmeg and ginger. Bring almost to the boil, add a piece of fresh butter the size of a walnut, and serve very hot.

MULLED CIDER

Boil 1 quart cider with 2 whole allspice, 2 whole cloves and 3 inch cinnamon stick for 5 minutes. Remove spices and add 3 oz brown sugar. Reheat and serve hot with a few lemon slices.

BUTTERED RUM (1)

6 lumps sugar
$\frac{1}{2}$ teaspoon ground allspice
$\frac{1}{2}$ teaspoon ground cloves

8 fluid oz rum
6 teaspoons fresh butter
6 tablespoons hot water

Dissolve the sugar in half the water. Add the other ingredients except the butter. Add remaining boiling water and pour into hot mugs. Add a knob of butter to each, and serve hot.

BUTTERED RUM (2)

For each person, warm a tumbler or mug and put 1 teaspoon caster sugar. Add $\frac{1}{2}$ teacup boiling water, $\frac{1}{2}$ teacup rum, and a lump of butter. Sprinkle with grated nutmeg.

RUM PUNCH

Boil 6 cloves and 1 inch cinnamon stick in $1\frac{1}{4}$ pints water for 5 minutes. Rub 12 lumps of sugar over the rind of an orange until they are yellow and full of zest. Add to the spiced water and boil for 5 minutes. Strain liquid on to 1 pint dark old rum, and serve very hot.

NEGUS

Put 1 pint of port into a jug. Rub a lemon with 12 lumps of sugar, and then squeeze the lemon juice and strain it. Mix sugar and lemon juice with the port, pour on 1 quart of boiling water. Cover the jug until the liquid has cooled slightly, then serve in glasses with grated nutmeg.

BISHOP

Stick a lemon with 12 cloves and roast it. Rub another lemon with 2 oz lump sugar and put into a bowl with juice of $\frac{1}{2}$ lemon. In the bowl put the roasted lemon, 1 pint boiling water, a pinch of mixed spice and 1 quart of port which has been brought nearly to boiling point. Serve very hot.

LAMBSWOOL

Slit the skin of 4 large apples round the centre and bake them until the flesh will mash easily. Heat together 1 quart brown ale, 1 pint sweet white wine and 3 inch cinnamon stick, with $\frac{1}{2}$ teaspoon each nutmeg and ginger. Mash the apples and stir them into the liquid. Take out cinnamon stick, and sieve the mixture, pressing down well. Reheat, adding sugar to taste.

WASSAIL

Slit the skin of 3 small red apples and bake them in the oven with 3 tablespoons soft brown sugar and $\frac{1}{2}$ teacup brown ale, basting well until the apples are soft. Heat 1 quart brown ale with $\frac{1}{2}$ pint sherry, $\frac{1}{4}$ teaspoon each of cinnamon, nutmeg and ginger, and a thin strip of lemon peel, and simmer for 5 minutes. Add the apples to the ale, with more brown sugar to taste, and serve very hot.

DR JOHNSON'S CHOICE

Heat 1 bottle red wine with 12 lumps of sugar and 6 cloves. Just before boiling point, add 1 pint boiling water, 1 wineglass orange Curaçao and 1 wineglass brandy. Serve with grated nutmeg.

CAMBRIDGE MILK PUNCH

This is a delicious, and apparently innocuous, drink, which is just the thing for maiden aunts. Put the thin rind of $\frac{1}{2}$ small lemon into 1 pint new milk with 12 lumps sugar. Simmer very slowly to extract the flavour of the lemon, take off the fire and remove the lemon rind. Stir in the yolk of an egg mixed with 1 tablespoon cold milk, 2 tablespoons brandy and 4 tablespoons rum. Whisk very thoroughly, and serve when frothy.

CARDINAL'S MULL

Make this like Bishop, but using claret or burgundy instead of port, flavouring with cinnamon and nutmeg and substituting an orange for the roasted lemon.

SIR ROGER DE COVERLEY

Heat together 1 bottle light red wine, 1 glass port and 2 tablespoons orange Curaçao, with 1 small teaspoon cinnamon, 1 small teaspoon mixed spice, a dash of nutmeg, 6 cloves and sugar to taste. Bring slowly to boiling point, simmer 2 minutes while stirring, strain and serve in warm glasses (10 glasses).

MADISON MULL

Stud an apple with cloves and bake in a moderate oven for 30 minutes. Heat to boiling point 1 pint of dry vintage cider with the apple, and 1 bottle claret. Heat without boiling, strain into a bowl and add 2 tablespoons Calvados (16 glasses).

MALMSEY MULL

Stud 1 large sweet orange with cloves and bake in a moderate oven for 1 hour. Heat 1 bottle Malmsey Madeira and 4 tablespoons apricot brandy and a pinch of ground ginger, with the orange floating on top, to boiling point. Just before serving, add $\frac{1}{2}$ pint boiling water (15 glasses).

APPLE POSSET

In each glass, put 2 tablespoons Calvados and fill up with hot apple juice, stirring with a cinnamon stick.

FLAMING PUNCH

Stick an orange with cloves and bake in a moderate oven for 1 hour. In a saucepan, combine 2 bottles claret, 1 sliced lemon, 1½ inch cinnamon stick, 2 oz blanched whole almonds, 2 oz raisins and 2 oz sugar. Add the orange and simmer uncovered for 15 minutes. Remove cinnamon stick and pour punch into serving bowl. In a saucepan, put 2 oz sugar and ¼ pint brandy. Heat very gently, ignite with a match, and while flaming pour into punch bowl (12 glasses).

OATMEAL CAUDEL

1 pint hot water *Pinch of cinnamon*
2 tablespoons oatmeal *Blade of mace*
Lemon rind *1 pint ale*

Boil the oatmeal in the water with the lemon rind, and spice and enough brown sugar to taste. When thick, pour into the heated ale, stirring meanwhile.

MILK POSSET

1 pint milk *Pinch of ground ginger*
A little sugar *Pinch of nutmeg*
Squeeze of lemon *1 glass white wine or sherry*

Heat the milk, when it froths add the wine or sherry. Strain and add lemon juice, sugar to taste, and stir in ginger and nutmeg. Serve hot.

SPICED CIDER

2 pints cider *1 teaspoon ground nutmeg*
2 tablespoons honey *1 teaspoon ground cinnamon*
2 tablespoons lemon juice

Place all ingredients into saucepan and bring gently to the boil. Simmer 10 minutes. Strain through muslin before pouring into glasses. Garnish with apple slices and lemon slices.

SPICED RED WINE TODDY

1 *bottle good cheap red wine*
2 *oz soft brown sugar*
4 *cloves stuck into ½ large*

orange or 1 small orange
1 *teaspoon whole allspice*

Place all ingredients, except those for decoration, into saucepan and heat gently until sugar dissolves. Bring nearly to boil and simmer gently for 10 minutes. Strain before pouring into glasses. Decorate each glass with halved sliced orange and maraschino cherries.

OLD TIME MULLED CLARET

Pour into a large saucepan 3 bottles claret, ½ bottle port and ¼ bottle cognac. Add 4 spirals of lemon peel, 3 sticks of cinnamon, 1½ teaspoons of grated nutmeg, 1 dozen cloves spiked into the lemon peel. Add sugar to taste according to the dryness of the claret. Cover the saucepan with a lid and heat slowly to very hot, but not to *boil*.

MULLED BURGUNDY

2 *bottles red burgundy*
2 *limes or 1 lemon, cut into*

thin slices and seeded
½ *banana cut into slices*

Tie the fruit together with 2 sticks of cinnamon, 1 dozen whole cloves and a variety of mixed spices into a piece of cheesecloth. Put along with wine into a covered pot, simmer for not over 10 minutes. Discard cheesecloth and contents, then add 1 cup dark rum, ½ cup of brown sugar to taste and 1 cup of soda water. Stir and serve foaming, garnish with curl of lemon peel.

RED WINE CUP

3 *bottles red wine*
½ *bottle port*
¼ *bottle brandy*

Sugar, cloves and lemon rind to taste

Heat red wine, sugar, cloves and lemon rind together. Add brandy just before serving.

HOT CHRISTMAS PUNCH

1 *bottle cider*
12 *lumps sugar*
2 *oranges*
8 *cloves*
1 *level teaspoon ground*
nutmeg

1 *stick cinnamon*
4 *tablespoons water*
2 *lemons*
1 *sherry glass rum*
1 *sherry glass brandy*

Rub the sugar over the rind of 1 of the oranges to remove the zest. Cut this orange in halves, squeeze out the juice and put into a pan with the sugar. Cut the other orange into 8 sections, stick a clove into the skin of each section and then sprinkle with the nutmeg. Add to the pan with the cinnamon, water and rind of the lemons, cut into strips. Heat gently until the sugar dissolves and then simmer for 5 minutes. Leave to cool until needed.

Remove the cinnamon, pour in the cider and heat until really hot, but not boiling. Add the rum and then the brandy and heat again for a minute. Divide the orange section and lemon rind between 8 glasses, add the hot cider and serve at once.

CIDER PUNCH

$\frac{1}{2}$ *gallon cider*
$\frac{1}{2}$ *bottle brandy*
1 *bottle red wine*
1 *lb sugar*
2 *oranges*

2 *lemons*
1 *stick of cinnamon*
Root of ginger
Cloves and nutmeg to taste

Squeeze the juice from 2 oranges and 1 lemon, put in a saucepan and add the sugar. Put remains of fruit, cinnamon, ginger, cloves and nutmeg in a cloth and boil with juice and sugar. Add cider and bring to boil. Just before serving remove cloth, add brandy and red wine and bring to boil. Serve piping hot with slices of lemon.

OXFORD PUNCH (HOT)

3 *parts rum*
2 *parts brandy*

1 *part fresh lemon juice*
6 *parts boiling water*

Add sugar to taste. Stir well.

HOT TEA PUNCH

1 *bottle rum*
1 *bottle brandy*
2 *sliced oranges*

1 *sliced lemon*
3 *pints freshly brewed tea*

Add sugar to taste. Mix well in a bowl. Mull with a red-hot poker.

WHITE WINE CUP

1 *liqueur glass orange*
Curacao
2 *liqueur glasses brandy*

1 *bottle hock*
1 *syphon soda water*

Put Curaçao and brandy in a jug with a large lump of ice. Pour on a bottle of iced hock and add soda water. Stir well and serve very cold.

SILVER WEDDING PUNCH

1 *medium tin apricots*
1 *medium tin pineapple*
6 *oranges*
1 *bottle cheap white wine*

1 *wineglass brandy*
1 *wineglass orange Curaçao*
Soda water

Mix together sliced apricots, pineapple and oranges. Add wine, brandy and Curaçao. Chill and dilute with soda water to taste.

Rene Woodhouse's recipe, as used at Oaksey Park, Cirencester

COLD PUNCH

2 *gallons best Fine Old Rum*
2 *dozen Oranges*
2 *dozen lemons*

16 *quarts spring water*
16 *lb lump sugar*
1 *pint new milk*

Pare your oranges and lemons quite thin pour the Rum on the Parings and let it stand 30 Hours then pour the boiling water on the Sugar and let that stand untill it is quite Cold. Strain the Rum from the parings to which add the Juice of the Lemons and Oranges after which add to your Ingredients the Milk put it into a cask let it stand 3 Weekes then bottle it.
NB it is proper it should be made in March then it will keep any length of time and do not foment.

Joseph Webb's Book, 1823

SNAPDRAGON

1 *lb seedless raisins*   **1 *wineglass whisky or brandy***

It is an old Christmas custom to snatch hot raisins from flaming spirit. Prepare them by putting the raisins in a large shallow fireproof dish and heating them for 10 minutes in a low oven. Remove from the oven, pour over spirits, stir well and set light to the mixture. It burns steadily with a blue flame. Put the dish in the centre of the table, and let everyone snatch and eat the raisins while still flaming.

RUM AND EGG FLIP

4 *fresh eggs*   ***Juice of* 3 *lemons***
½ *pint double cream*   **½ *lb castor sugar***
½ *pint Jamaica rum*

Place the perfectly clean whole eggs (in shells) in china bowl. Extract the juice from the lemons, and pour this over the eggs. Leave for four days, turning the eggs over daily, using wooden spoon. On fourth day, beat the eggs and juice well together, and pass through nylon, or hair sieve. Whip the cream and sugar till thick, then gradually mix in the egg and lemon juice. Beat well, and finally add rum. Stir well. Bottle and label. Store in cool place.

Miriam Ward, York

SHOOTING DRINKS

1) Strong green tea, with a little brandy in it is a capital drink for shooting.
2) Milk and whisky; quantity according to taste, the less spirit the better.
3) Melt or dissolve by a gentle heat 1 oz of black currant jelly in ½ pint of syrup (sugar and water); when cold, add the same quantity of rum (or gin if you prefer it), shake well and bottle.

The Country House Collection of Useful Information and Recipes 1867

TREACLE POSSET

½ *pint milk*   ***dark treacle***
1 *tablespoon golden syrup, or*

Bring the milk to the boil and pour it over the syrup or treacle in a jug, stir well and serve very hot.

APPLE CIDER

4 lb apples (grated)   **2 gallons cold water**

4 lbs apples (grated), 2 gallons cold water. Stir every day for fortnight. Strain off. 3 lb sugar, 4 oz lump ginger (well bruised), 1 teaspoon cloves, 1 teaspoon cinnamon. Stir till sugar is dissolved. Leave a fortnight. Strain. It is then ready for use.

Mrs Kittie Lister, Chatham

DAMSON WINE

4 gallons of damsons, 4 gallons of boiling water. To every gallon of liquid allow $3\frac{1}{2}$ lb lump sugar. Pour water over damsons and let stand for 4 or 5 days, stirring each day, then strain and add sugar. When this has dissolved pour into cask. It may be bottled for 12 months.

ROUGH CIDER

Leave apples to mellow and soften. Press hard between earthenware dishes, or through an old heavy mangle to extract juice. Leave tub of juice in a temperature of 60°F until frothing ceases and sediment has gone to the bottom. Remove clear liquid to a wooden cask and store in a cool place. To prevent the cider turning vinegary, put into strong clean stoppered bottles after 2 weeks and store in a cool place.

SIMPLE APPLE WINE

6 lb apples   **2 lb sugar**
1 gallon water

Cut up apples, including skins and cores. Cover with water, mash and stir every day for 2 days. Strain and heat up 1 pint of the liquid, then pour over the sugar. Stir well to dissolve sugar, and add rest of liquid. Leave to stand for 3 days, then skim, strain and bottle, corking lightly at first, then pushing corks in firmly after 3 days. This is a very light and delicious wine which stores well.

COTTAGE PERRY

10 lb windfall dessert pears   **1 lb white sugar**
1 lb raisins   **1 gallon water**
5 Campden tablets   **Yeast**

Wash fruit and slice into a china bowl with the chopped raisins and crushed Campden tablets. Dissolve the sugar in the water and pour over the fruit. Leave 3 days covered with a cloth, stirring twice daily. Cream 1 oz yeast with a little of the liquid and return to bowl, and leave in a warm room until gas bubbles no longer form. Pour off the liquid, strain the pulp through a thick cloth and add to the liquid. Put liquid into large jars, filling them and corking well. Leave in a cold room for several weeks until the perry becomes clear. Syphon off the liquid, leaving deposit behind. Dissolve $\frac{1}{4}$ lb sugar in every gallon of liquid and put into bottles (champagne bottles are best for this). Cork and tie down and store bottles on their sides in a cool place for at least 3 months.

DAMSON WINE

Bruise 8 lb damsons and pour on 1 gallon boiling water. Leave 48 hours. Strain; add $2\frac{1}{2}$ lb sugar to each gallon juice.

Cover it and let it ferment. When this ceases, fill cask or bottles. Do not cork tightly till wine settles. Ready in 9 months, after straining again.

ELDERBERRY WINE (1)

Pick elderberries when quite ripe, strip from stalks, crush. Pour 1 gallon boiling water on to 8 pints berries. Stir occasionally, leave 2 weeks. Strain. To each quart of juice add $\frac{3}{4}$ lb sugar, $\frac{1}{2}$ oz crushed whole ginger, 2 cloves. Boil together 25 minutes. When cool pour into tub or cask or large basin, add 1 oz yeast spread on slice of toast and allow to ferment. This takes a week or two. Strain and bottle. Do not cork too tightly. Keep 4 months before using.

ELDERBERRY WINE (2)

Put 4 lb ripe elderberries in vessel with 1 gallon cold water, let it stand until berries burst. Strain through close muslin, add 4 lb sugar to 1 gallon juice. Stir until all sugar is melted, then pour into gallon jars and let it remain until finished working. Bottle and cork tightly.

AUTUMN FRUIT WINE

Plums, damsons or blackberries make an excellent wine, particularly damsons which provide a rich, dark wine. 1 lb fruit, 1 quart boiling water. Place ripe fruit in earthenware bowl. Pour 1 quart boiling water over each pound of fruit. Let it stand for 5 days, stirring well each morning. Strain liquor, squeeze fruit well through muslin. To every quart of juice add 1 lb sugar. Put into bottles, putting over bottlenecks paper pricked with a pin. Let it stand 4 weeks. Strain again, bottle and cork well. In a week the wine is ready for use.

RHUBARB WINE

To every 5 lb rhubarb allow 1 gallon of water. Cut fruit up in small pieces. Let stand in water for 10 days, stirring every day. Strain. To each gallon of liquid allow $3\frac{1}{2}$ lb sugar, juice of 2 and rind of 1 lemon, $\frac{1}{2}$ oz isinglass dissolved in a pint of the liquor, warmed. Pour this into the wine when cool. Stir all together and let stand for 7 or 9 days. Leave to settle. Skim often during fermentation. Strain into stone jars. At end of 6 months, strain into bottles. Cork well. 2 sultanas put into each bottle will improve the wine.

BEETROOT BEER

1 lb beetroot *1 breakfastcup white sugar*
1 pint stout

Wash beetroot and slice into bowl. Sprinkle on sugar and leave 24 hours. Strain, add stout, bottle and cork. Ready 7–14 days.

HOP BEER

1 lb malt extract *1 gallon water*
1 oz hops *Yeast*

Boil malt, hops and water for $1\frac{1}{2}$ hours, adding water to make up original quantity. Strain through muslin. When liquid is cool, add yeast and leave covered for 3 days. Syphon off and bottle. Put 1 lump of sugar in each, bottle and cork. Ready in 7 days.

15 Salting and Smoking

The important art of pickling or salting meat was, until refrigeration was thought up, the job which called for 'the housekeeper's best attention' to quote an early Edwardian cookery book. Nowadays, buying bacon requires very little skill, but in those days every farmer's wife was responsible for catering for enormous appetites, usually for enormous families, without the sophistication of refrigerators or deep freezers. She was compensated for this lack by having, invariably, more space, more help and in many farmhouses ample provision made for storing in cool conditions, meat and other perishable goods. This was, of course, essential since the farmer, it seemed, produced the food for his own larder before thinking of markets and other outlets for his surplus stock. Now we have, on the whole, smaller families, smaller houses and smaller profits so there are hundreds of farmers' wives who are in the (super) market for cheap food, the same as any other housewife.

GUIDE TO BACON CURING

1. If you live in Hampshire, Wiltshire or Dorset you must singe the pig – after killing it. If you live in Yorkshire, Lincolnshire or any of those northern counties you must scald the pig – this is traditional.

2. Great care must be taken in the preparation of the meat for salting. It must be carefully examined to see that it is *fresh* and *good* (i.e. sweet and wholesome smelling).

3. Having ascertained this, it must be wiped, sprinkled with salt, and afterwards left to drain a few hours before it is rubbed with the salt. *This will ensure that the meat is thoroughly cleansed from the blood.* If this is not done the meat will 'turn' and taste 'strong'.

4. It should then be placed in the pickling pan and turned every morning, it should also be rubbed with the pickle.

5. The cover of the pickling pan should fit very closely and have a weight on it to keep it down.

6. If a large quantity of salt meat is frequently required, the pickle may be boiled up, skimmed well, and when *cold* poured over any meat which has been sprinkled and well drained (as 3. above).

SWEET CURE

This is a sweet pickle for ham or bacon, using a carcass of about 8 score. Split the carcass, and from each side cut a rounded ham and a round shoulder (fore-ham). Debone the middle except for the chump end of the loin, which can be used fresh or lightly salted. To make packing easier, the middle may be subdivided into back and belly. Rub the knuckles with salt, and sprinkle salt on the joints, then pack into a crock. Pour over a pickle (for 15 lb ham or fore-ham) consisting of $\frac{1}{2}$ lb block salt, 1 lb black treacle, $\frac{1}{2}$ lb brown sugar, 1 pint malt vinegar and 2 pints old ale, with 1 tablespoon saltpetre. Turn the joints twice daily for the first week, then once daily for four weeks. Hang meat to drain for 24 hours, then encase in clean cotton bags and suspend from hooks. The hams are ready for use in 6 months and do not need soaking before cooking.

For 15 lb bacon, use a pickle of $\frac{1}{2}$ lb salt, $\frac{1}{2}$ lb brown sugar, 2 oz black treacle, $\frac{1}{4}$ pint vinegar and no saltpetre. Pack in crocks and pour over pickle, and turn joints twice daily for 3 weeks. The bacon can be used immediately after curing, or it can be soaked for 1 week with several changes of water before cooking as required.

DRY CURE

This is a dry cure method for a carcass of 16 to 20 score, using 28 lb salt and 8 oz saltpetre. Singe the flesh to remove hair and cut the carcass, removing the head, the spine with some of the back meat, and the ribs with a coating of lean meat.

Clean by sprinkling the flesh side with salt, and rubbing salt into the skin. Leave the sides, flesh side down, to drain for 24 hours, then wipe with a clean cloth. Sprinkle saltpetre on the flesh side of the shoulders and hams. Sprinkle half the salt over the sides which are placed one on top of the other. After 7 days, sprinkle half the remaining salt on, and put the top side at the bottom. After 7 more days, add remaining salt, and reverse positions of sides. The sides are in cure for about 4 weeks. Wipe off sides after curing, and hang up to dry for 7 days. Store sides whole, or for convenience cut into hams, middles and shoulders before hanging them up in clean cotton bags.

HEAVY CARCASS CURE

This is most suitable for a heavy carcass, which may be cut in three different ways. One method involves removing a chine of 6–8 inches wide and salting the 'long side'; the carcass can be simply split; or it may be cut into hams, fore-hams and middles. The ingredients for curing are 28 lb salt, ½ lb saltpetre and 1 lb demerara sugar. Rub saltpetre in first, spreading most thickly on blood patches. Sprinkle meat with salt and pack on a layer of salt in a trough. Place hams on top and every day for a fortnight, sprinkle on salt. When meat is cured, wipe salt off and sprinkle with flour. After being dry for 3 months, pack in a bin containing slaked lime.

TO CURE BACON

Time – 3 weeks

1 *lb saltpetre*   **1 *lb salprunella***
1 *lb bay salt*   **1 *lb moist (brown) sugar***

Pound the salprunella and bay salt very fine, mix the coarse salt and the sugar well together, and rub it into your bacon, hams and cheeks, putting all in the same brine. Turn and rub the bacon for a week every day; afterwards every other day. Let it remain in the brine for 3 weeks, and then send it to be smoked or dried. Large sides of bacon take a month to dry, small ones 3 weeks.

TO CURE HAMS

For 2 large hams:

1 *lb common salt*
3 *oz bay salt*
2 *oz saltpetre*

1 *lb coarse brown sugar*
1 *quart stale strong beer or*
ale

Boil all the above ingredients in the quart of beer or ale, and when cold pour it onto the hams and turn them every day for a fortnight; then smoke them well.

MRS JEWRY'S WAY TO PICKLE PORK

One third saltpetre   *Two thirds white salt*

Mrs Jewry says some people prefer pork pickled with salt alone (the legs especially); others in the following manner: Put a layer of salt at the bottom of the tub; then mix the saltpetre and salt well. Cut the pork in pieces, rub it well with the salt and lay it close in the tub, with a layer of salt in between every layer of pork till the tub is full. Have a cover, just large enough to fit the inside of the tub, put it on, and lay a great weight at the top, then as the salt melts, it will keep it close. When you want to use it, take a piece out, cover up the tub again and it will keep for a good long time.

MRS JACKSON'S YORKSHIRE WAY WITH HAMS, TONGUES AND BEEF

1½ *lb brown sugar*
2 *oz saltpetre*

1½ *lb common salt*
2 *oz pepper*

On the night you get the meat, rub it all over with common salt; next morning rub it well with a mixture of the above ingredients.

With hams – take them into the kitchen and rub them *before the fire* every day and turn them, every day for 10 days, then every other day for 10 days. If it is a very big thick ham, it may need a few days longer.

Mrs Jackson lives on a remote farm in the East Riding and has successfully brought up 4 sons and 2 daughters. They all had hearty appetites, so she was used to providing tables full of food. She played the village church organ for many years and filled her spare time in joining in all village activities with gusto. She is a great cook to this day and long may she continue to encourage folk to 'wrap theesen around this and ye'll not feel the wind!' as she plies one with good food.

MRS BRIDGES' GLOUCESTERSHIRE CURE

This is a very old receipt which has been handed down from generation to generation. The whole simple process is spread over 4 weeks and the result is a delicious ham of a delicate flavour.

Take one good ham. Note: the best ham is obtained from a once-farrowed 'hilt' (gilt)

First week: Put ham into trough or 'lead'. Take a bar of salt and rub salt all over ham working well into every crevice and crease. Continue the treatment every other day for 1 week.

Second week: Prepare mixture for second week's treatment. Chop 1 lb salt into a dish; add $\frac{1}{2}$ lb *only* of saltpetre, 1 lb dark brown sugar and mix well together. Rub some of this mixture into the front and the back. Turn every other day for a week, gradually using more of the mixture but keeping back sufficient for the final week. When brine forms, baste this over as well.

Third week: With rind side down in brine, cover with remainder of brine mixture rubbing and pressing into the surfaces. Cover with golden syrup and leave untouched for 3 days.

Fourth week: Dust with rice flour, then hang up to dry.

Take care that no flies can get in by using plenty of butter muslin. After this, leave for 2 *years* – if you can.

Jim Woodhouse, Oaksey Park, Glos.

W. ARNOLD'S PICKLING RECIPE

For Beef and Pork

1 *gallon water*	$\frac{1}{2}$ *oz saltpetre*
6 *oz coarsest raw sugar*	$\frac{3}{4}$ *lb bay salt*

Hams and Tongues

2 *quarts water*	1 *oz saltpetre*
3 *oz coarsest sugar*	14 *oz bay salt*

Boil till no more scum rises, then set by till quite cold. Let the meat be entirely covered and if you have reason to keep it long it will be necessary to boil the pickle every 6 weeks and to move the scumming as before and adding to the above quantities $\frac{1}{2}$ oz coarset moist sugar and 2 oz of common salt. If these instructions are carefully attended to the Pickle will keep for 12 months. In extreme hot weather it is necessary to rub the meat with a little salt and let it remain a few hours that all the blood may be drawn from it before it is put into the pickle. Meat thus cured never becomes hard and dry as when salted in the usual way.

Mrs Garden, Slough, 25 September, 1861

FOR PICKLING A HAM WITH BOILING PICKLE

For a ham 26 lb.

5 quarts water
3 lb common salt
1 oz saltpetre

1 oz salt prunella
1 lb moist sugar

Put all in the water to boil, and throw it while boiling on the ham. Keep a month in pickle and smoke – if preferred.

Lewis' Mother's Cookbook, Mary Horrell, Exeter

EVERYTHING BUT THE SQUEAK

How to deal with the rest of the pig

Liver: The liver of the pig is particularly good for highly seasoned patés. If cooked as a main meal, it is excellent seasoned with sage, onion and apple.

Pork Fillet: This is the lean strip of meat lying beneath the loin, weighing 8–12 oz. It is a delicious piece of meat. The fillet may be slit, stuffed and roasted in a hot oven for 45 minutes, before serving with a good gravy. The meat is best wrapped in bacon, and well basted with a little dripping, and should be cut diagonally to serve. It is also delicious if cut in small pieces and tossed in oil or butter with chopped mushrooms, onions and green peppers until golden and cooked through, then served in its own juices with rice or mashed potatoes.

Ears: Leave them for 24 hours in coarse salt, then wash well and scald. Make a stuffing with 4 oz sausage meat, 4 oz bread soaked in stock, 4 oz chopped mushrooms, 1 small onion, 1 egg. Fill the ears with this stuffing putting one ear on top of the other to contain the stuffing, and tie up. Brown in a little fat, then simmer in good stock for two hours. Serve in the reduced liquor with pease pudding, lentils or butter beans.

Trotters: Wash, scrape and singe the trotters thoroughly. Cut them in half, and leave them covered in salt for 24 hours. Wash very thoroughly, match up the halves again, and tie each tightly in a clean cloth. Put in a pan of cold water with a good bunch of mixed herbs, a carrot, an onion stuck with cloves, salt and pepper, bring to the boil, then simmer for five hours. Leave to cool in the stock remove when just tepid, and leave until completely cold before taking out of cloth. Roll each trotter in melted butter or in oil, and then in breadcrumbs. Grill slowly for 20 minutes.

Head: The head makes superb stock, and if this is left to chill, lard may be removed from the top of the stock. The meat from the head can be eaten in many ways, but its best known use is in brawn.

Chitterlings: Cut 'tubes' in lengths of about 4 inches and clean thoroughly under running water. Scald in boiling water for 30 minutes. Thoroughly rinse again by running cold water through. Soak in salt and water for 5 days, then rinse thoroughly again. Some people like to eat these cold with salt, pepper and vinegar; others fry them and season with salt and pepper. *Brains:* Leave brains in cold running water for an hour. Put in a pan of cold salted water and bring to the boil. Boil for 5 minutes, remove from heat, and leave to cool in the liquid. A good way of serving these is to dip walnut-size pieces in batter and deep-fry them, serving with a sharp sauce. *Heart:* Thoroughly wash the heart, removing core and piece at top. Make 4 deep cuts into the flesh, wash again in cold water and stuff the cuts with sage and onion stuffing. Skewer together, sprinkle with salt and pepper, and wrap in foil. Put in a dish and bake at 350°F (Gas Mark 4) for 2 hours. Serve with rich gravy.

HOME SMOKING

Smoked food has been a tradition in Britain for centuries. From the humble haddock, bloater and kipper to the grand salmon and trout, and from the everyday rasher to the succulent ham, there is a delicious smoked food for any meal of the day.

Those with good supplies of fresh meat and fish, wonder whether they might not try their hand at home-smoking. It is possible to tackle the job on a do-it-yourself basis, but good results are only obtained by careful attention to detail.

The point of smoking is to remove moisture from the food very slowly, like drying, and to give additional flavour and to preserve. Smoking which is meant to preserve food for a length of time needs space, skill and scrupulous hygiene.

It is necessary to build a smoke-house, though this can be of a simple type, or to adapt a farmhouse chimney with a smoke box. Foods which can be smoked include eel, herring, salmon, trout, sprats, cod's roe, ham and bacon, tongue, turkey, goose, duck and chicken, and a variety of home-made sausages. Some of these items need brining before smoking; ham, bacon and salmon need elaborate preparation and are not really practical to smoke on a small scale.

If an individual flavour is required for home-produced or home-caught products, it may be preferable to prepare the meat or fish with an individual cure but get it smoked by a local bacon factory.

In addition to the basic smoke-house, there must be a good supply of wood. The best smoke is produced by slow combustion hardwood shavings; oak, beech, birch and hornbeam are excellent, with additional flavour provided by juniper and bay. The addition of thyme, sage or heather makes a good variation.

Resinous woods should be avoided because they can give an unpleasant flavour. The object of creating the smoke is to make fumes which solidify the albumen in the meat. This halts decomposition; the flavour is a bonus.

The simplest form of smoke-house can be constructed in a 10-gallon drum with the bottom cut out and a replaceable top which has a few holes punched in. This is particularly good for smoking trout or haddock, suspended over a concentrated source of heat and smoke. Haddock should be split, cleaned and beheaded, rubbed inside and out with salt, and left overnight, then dried in the open air for 3 days. Trout need not be split or beheaded, but the gut should be removed.

The fish should be suspended by the tail on a rod across the top of the drum, and tied with a piece of wire at least 1 foot from the fire. The drum should then be upended over the fire – best made between bricks on which the drum stands. The heat must be evenly maintained during smoking – which will take from 9 to 12 hours.

A slightly more elaborate smoke-house can be constructed for permanent use. This can be a drum or a packing case which has been made smoke-proof at the joints, standing across a trench. The trench should be about 10 ft long, 1 ft deep and 1 ft wide, dug in the direction of the prevailing wind, with old paving stones or sheet iron to roof it over. If the lid of the house is hinged, it will be esaier to use, and it should have small holes or a tube inserted as a vent.

To use this type of smoke-house, light a fire at the end furthest from the box, cover with stones or iron sheets, and open the lid of the box. When the fire is red-hot, draw it to the end of the trench and put a load of hardwood sawdust between the fire and the box. Leave a little flue space, cover the trench and seal all spaces with earth. The food can be hung across the box and the lid closed and not opened for 48 hours.

The idea is to build up a progressively dense smoke which dries and flavours the fish gradually; if the first smoke is too dense it will form a dry coating on the food which will not be penetrated by the later smoking.

For this type of smoking, the food should be brined first in a strong brine (with enough salt to float a potato). A small fish need only be brined for 20 minutes, but a salmon needs several days, and elaborate preparation.

The smoking method which is most likely to appeal is the one using the old-fashioned farmhouse chimney, which can be used for hams and sausages. These must be prepared first, and are then best left to hang and dry for two or three days before smoking.

The food to be smoked can be hung above the opening of a bread oven so that the smoke gently enfolds them; the temperature should never rise above 90°F at which point the fat melts and meat is spoiled. The fire should be smouldering, not flaming. On the first day, the meat should be smoked for 30 minutes, then rubbed down with pepper, thyme and chopped bay leaves, which will cling to the fat.

After cooling and drying for 48 hours, the meat should be smoked again for 1 hour. After further drying for 48 hours and 1 hour's smoking, a light flavour will be obtained.

The meat should be hung in the chimney for 2 or 3 weeks before being stored in a cool dry place. The meat will lose about $\frac{1}{4}$ of its weight in smoking.

The wide chimney can be used for complete smoking, with the meat suspended high up on a bar, or on hooks on wire, but the fire will need careful attention.

Smoke the meat for about an hour a day, allowing a total of at least 3 weeks for complete smoking.

The best method of regulating the smoke-flow is to construct a smoking box for the fireplace, to fit on a wall above the fire. A sheet of metal has to be fitted across the whole chimney with a piece of piping going through it and the wall into the smoking-box. A second piece of piping should then go out of the top of the box and back into the chimney. Meat in the box needs about 2 hours a day for 8 consecutive days.

16 Freezing

St James's Park

'As Lately Improved by His Majesty'

(on the royal ice well)

> *Yonder, the harvest of the months laid up*
> *Gives a fresh coolness to the Royal Cup;*
> *There ice, like crystal firm, and never lost,*
> *Tempers hot July with December's frost;*
> *Winter's dark prison, whence he cannot fly,*
> *Though the warm spring, his enemy, draws nigh.*
> *Strange! that extremes should thus preserve the snow.*
> *High on the Alps, or in deep caves below.*

Edmund Waller, 1606–87

GARDEN PRODUCE

APPLES

Firm apples for freezing in slices; fluffy apples for purée or sauce. For slices, peel and core fruit and put into basin of cold water, then slice medium apples into twelfths, large ones into sixteenths. Use dry sugar pack for preference (8 oz sugar to 2 lb fruit). Freeze baked apples in individual waxed tubs or foil dishes. Make apple sauce in the oven with a minimum of water, adding a squeeze of lemon juice. Storage time for baked apples: 1 month. Storage time for slices, pulp or sauce: 1 year.

ARTICHOKES (GLOBE)

Remove outer leaves, trim stalks, remove 'chokes' and wash artichokes very thoroughly. Blanch in sizes in 4 quarts boiling water with 1 tablespoon lemon juice for 7 minutes. Cool in ice water, and drain upside down. Pack in boxes (polythene will tear). If preferred, blanch only bottoms for 5 minutes. To cook whole artichokes, plunge into boiling water and boil 5 minutes. Storage time: 1 year.

ASPARAGUS

Remove woody portions and small scales and wash well. Sort into sizes, and blanch each size separately (small spears: 2 minutes; medium: 3 minutes; large: 4 minutes). Cool and drain and pack in boxes lined with moisture-vapour-proof paper, or wrap in freezer paper. To cook: allow 5 minutes in boiling water. Storage time: 9 months.

BLACKBERRIES

Fully ripe, dark glossy berries. Wash in chilled water and drain on absorbent paper. Pack dry and unsweetened, or in dry sugar pack (8 oz sugar to 2 lb fruit) or in 50 per cent syrup. Storage time: 1 year.

BEANS (BROAD)

Small young beans with tender outer skins. Blanch 1½ minutes, cool and pack in cartons or polythene. To cook, allow 8 minutes in boiling salted water. Storage time: 1 year.

BEANS (FRENCH)

Tender young beans left whole or cut in 1 inch pieces. Blanch whole beans 3 minutes, cut beans 2 minutes, and pack in polythene. Cook whole beans for 7 minutes in boiling salted water, cut beans for 5 minutes. Storage time: 1 year.

BEANS (RUNNER)

Tender young beans cut in pieces (not shredded, as they become pulpy and tasteless). Blanch 2 minutes and pack in polythene. Cook 7 minutes in boiling salted water. Storage time: 1 year.

BROCCOLI

Compact heads with tender stalks not more than 1 inch thick, of uniform green colour. Discard woody stems and trim outer leaves. Wash very well and soak in salt solution (2 teaspoons salt to 8 pints water) for 30 minutes, then wash in clean water. Cut in sprigs and blanch 3 minutes for thin stems, 4 minutes for medium and 5 minutes for thick stems. Pack into bags or boxes (alternate heads in boxes). Cook 8 minutes in boiling water. Storage time: 1 year.

BRUSSELS SPROUTS

Small, compact heads, graded for size before blanching. Blanch 3 minutes for small sprouts, 4 minutes for medium ones, and pack in cartons or bags. Cook for 8 minutes in boiling water. Storage time: 1 year.

CHERRIES

Red varieties freeze better than black. Firm cherries in chilled water for 1 hour, then dry, and remove stones which may flavour fruit. Pack in glass or plastic containers, as the acid in cherry juice tends to remain liquid in freezing and may leak through cardboard. For pies, pack cherries in dry sugar (8 oz sugar to 2 lb pitted cherries or in syrup depending on tartness). Storage time: 1 year.

CAULIFLOWER

Firm compact heads with close white flowers, broken into sprigs not more than 1 inch across. Add juice of 1 lemon to blanching water and blanch for 3 minutes. Pack in lined boxes. Cook for 10 minutes in boiling water. Storage time: 6 months.

CORN ON THE COB

Fresh tender corn, frozen as cobs or kernels. Remove leaves and 'silk' and grade cobs for size, cutting stems short. Blanch small cobs for 4 minutes, medium 6 minutes and large 8 minutes. Cool and dry in paper. Pack individual ears in freezer paper and freeze immediately in coldest part of freezer. Store quantities in bags for easy handling. Kernels can be scraped from cobs and packed in containers. Storage time: 1 year.

Correct cooking after freezing is very important for corn. Either put frozen cobs in cold water to cover, bring to fast boil, and simmer for 15 minutes, or thaw in packaging in refrigerator, plunge in boiling water and cook for 10 minutes.

CURRANTS

Black, red and white currants should be stripped from stems, washed in chilled water, and dried. For jam making, pack dry in bags. For later cooking, use dry sugar pack (8 oz sugar to 1 lb berries, mixing sugar until dissolved). *Boskoop Giant* and *Wellington* are good for freezing. Storage time: 1 year.

GOOSEBERRIES

Wash in chilled water, dry, and freeze without sweetening. For future jam-making, freeze fruit slightly under-ripe. Purée can be made with little water, sieved and sweetened. *Careless* is a good variety for freezing. Storage time: 1 year.

HERBS

Wash parsley, mint or chives, chop finely, pack into ice-cube trays and fill with water. Freeze, wrap cubes in foil, and package in bags. Flavour is not strong, though colour is good. Do not freeze herbs in sprigs for garnishing, as they go limp on thawing.

PLUMS

Plums, greengages and damsons can be treated in similar ways. Chill fruit in chilled water, dry well, cut in halves, removing stones, and pack in 40 per cent syrup. Damson skins can be very tough, and they are best frozen in pulp form. Very good plums can also be frozen in a dry sugar pack. Storage time: 1 year.

PEAS

Young sweet peas, not old starchy ones. Shell and blanch for 1 minute, lifting basket in and out of water to distribute heat evenly between layers of peas. Chill and pack in polythene bags or cartons. Cook in boiling water for 7 minutes. Storage time: 1 year.

POTATOES

Young new potatoes can be scraped and washed, blanched for 4 minutes, cooled and packed in polythene bags. Cook in boiling water for 15 minutes. Storage time 1 year. Or slightly undercook, drain, toss in butter, cool, pack and freeze. Cook by plunging frozen bag in boiling water, removing pan from heat and leaving 10 minutes. Older potatoes can be frozen as mashed potatoes, chips, or baked potatoes, for no longer than 3 months.

RASPBERRIES

Discard hard, seedy fruit, and wash in chilled water. Freeze in dry pack, or in sugar, allowing 4 oz to each lb raspberries. *Norfolk Giant* and *Lloyd George* are best for freezing. Storage time: 1 year.

RHUBARB

Young pink sticks can be frozen unsweetened for pies. Pack in cartons or polythene or foil. If lightly blanched for 1 minute, stems will pack more easily. Also can be packed in 40 per cent syrup, or in purée form. Storage time: 1 year.

STRAWBERRIES

Strawberries are best frozen dry, when they will be less pulpy when thawed. If packed in dry sugar or syrup, slice or lightly crush fruit (dry sugar pack: 4 oz sugar to 1 lb fruit or 40 per cent syrup). *Cambridge Vigour*, *Cambridge Favourite* and *Royal Sovereign* are best for freezing. Storage time: 1 year.
Apricots, blueberries, cranberries, fresh figs, grapes, melons, peaches and quinces may also be frozen.

SPINACH

Young tender spinach without heavy leaf ribs. Remove stems and wash very well. Blanch for 2 minutes, moving container to separate leaves. Cool, press out excess moisture, and pack in rigid containers or polythene bags. To serve, cook 7 minutes in a little melted butter. Storage time: 1 year.

TOMATOES

Tomatoes cannot be frozen for salad use. For cooking, they can be frozen whole, after wiping clean, in polythene bags. Thaw for 2 hours at room temperature before using. Storage time: 10 months. Tomatoes can be frozen as pulp, by removing skins, pips and cores, then simmering tomatoes in their own juice for 5 minutes before sieving and packing in cartons. Storage time: 1 year. Tomato juice is made by simmering ripe tomatoes in a covered container for 15 minutes, then putting juice through muslin and packing in containers. Juice should be thawed in containers in refrigerator. Storage time: 1 year.

FARMYARD AND FIELD

POULTRY

Birds to be frozen should be in perfect condition, and should be starved for 24 hours before killing, then hung and bled well. When the bird is plucked, it is important to avoid skin damage; if scalding, beware of over-scalding which may increase the chance of freezer-burn (grey spots occurring during storage). The bird should be cooled in a refrigerator or cold larder for 12 hours, drawn and completely cleaned. With geese and ducks, it is particularly important to see the oil glands are removed, as these will cause tainting.

A whole bird should be carefully trussed to make a neat shape for packing. Birds may be frozen in halves or joints. When packing pieces, it is not always ideal to pack a complete drum in each package; it may be more useful ultimately if all drumsticks are packaged together, all breasts or all wings according to the way in which the flesh will be cooked. *Giblets* have a storage life of 2 months, so unless a whole bird is to be used within that time, it is not advisable to pack them inside the bird. Giblets should be cleaned, washed, dried and chilled, then wrapped in moisture-vapour proof paper or bag, excluding air; frozen in batches, they may be used for soup, stews or pies. *Livers* should be treated in the same way and packaged in batches for use in omelettes, risotto or pâté.

Bones of poultry joints should be padded with a small piece of paper or foil to avoid tearing freezer wrappings. Joints should be divided by two layers of Cellophane. Bones of young birds may turn brown in storage, but this does not affect flavour or quality.

Geese and ducks have a storage life of 6–7 months; turkey and chicken frozen whole 8–12 months, and in pieces 6–10 months. Giblets and livers should not be kept longer than 2 months.

Stuffing can be put into a bird before freezing, but it is not advisable as the storage life of stuffing is only about 1 month. Pork sausage stuffing should not be used, and if a bird must be stuffed, a breadcrumb stuffing is best. It is better to package stuffing separately, but this is unnecessary as a stuffing may be prepared during the thawing time of the bird.

GAME BIRDS

All game birds should be kept cool between shooting and freezing; care should be taken to remove as much shot as possible, and to make sure shot wounds are thoroughly clean. Birds should be bled as soon as shot, kept cool and hung to individual taste. After plucking and drawing, the cavity should be thoroughly washed and drained and the body wiped with a damp cloth. The birds should then be packed, cooled and frozen, as for poultry. Game will keep in the freezer 6–8 months.

HARES AND RABBITS

Hares and rabbits should be beheaded and bled as soon as possible and hung for 24 hours in a cool place. Skin and clean, washing cavity well, and wipe with a damp cloth. Cut into joints and wrap each piece in Cellophane, excluding air, then pack joints together in moisture-vapour-proof bag or paper, seal, label and freeze. Hares and rabbits will keep in the freezer 6–8 months.

VENISON

Venison needs careful butchering, but if help is not immediately available, the carcass should be kept in good condition, the shot wounds carefully cleaned, and the animal kept as cold as possible. The venison should be beheaded and bled, skinned and cleaned, and the interior washed and wiped. Hanging should take place in a very cool place (preferably just above freezing point) with the belly propped open so air can circulate. 5 to 6 days' hanging will make the meat tender. The meat should be cut in joints, packed like meat, sealed, labelled and frozen. Since this is a large animal, it is best to keep only the good joints whole. The rest of the meat can be minced to freeze raw for later use as hamburgers and mince, or can be casseroled or made into pies and frozen in this form. Since the meat is inclined to dryness, it is often marinaded before cooking. The marinade should be poured over the meat while it is thawing. Venison will keep in the freezer 8–10 months.

HAM AND BACON

Cured and smoked meats are best stored in a cool atmosphere, protected from flies and dust, and there is no advantage in freezing them. They may, of course, be frozen, and are then better in the piece rather than slices, but storage time is limited to 3–4 months. Meat stored in this way should be overwrapped. Sliced bacon may for convenience be stored in the freezer, wrapped in moisture-vapour-proof wrapping, but storage time is limited to 3 weeks.

MEAT

Good quality meat should be chosen, and hung for the required time. Meat should be packed in quantities suitable for use on one occasion. If possible, meat should be boned and surplus fat removed so as not to take up unnecessary freezer space; if bones are not removed, ends should be wrapped in several layers of greaseproof paper to avoid piercing freezer wrappings. Meat should be packed in polythene for easy identification, and labelling is very important as with all freezer items. It is most important to exclude air from packages so that the freezer wrap stays close to surface of meat. If a whole animal or a variety of different meats are being prepared for freezing at one time, begin with the offal, then pork, then veal and lamb, and finally beef as this will keep best under refrigeration if delays occur. Normally, no more than 4 pounds of meat per cubic foot of freezer space should be frozen at one time for best results.

It is important that wrapping for meat should be strong, since oxygen from the air which may penetrate wrappings affects fat and causes rancidity (pork is, of course, most subject to this problem). In addition to moisture-vapour-proof wrapping, an overwrap of brown paper, grease-proof paper or stockinette will protect packages and will guard against punctures from projecting bones or other packets. It is worth taking this precaution, since meat is likely to be the most costly item stored in the freezer.

BAKING DAY

COOKED YEAST MIXTURES

Bread, buns and rolls freeze particularly well when 1 day old. Freeze in polythene bags. Thaw in wrapping at room temperature; $1\frac{1}{2}$ lb loaf takes about 3 hours. In emergency, bread can be thawed very quickly in a moderate oven, but will become stale very quickly.

SCONES

These may be frozen cooked or uncooked; unbaked ones will only store for 2 weeks, otherwise 2 months. If scones are unbaked, they can be baked in a hot oven without thawing, or partly thawed and then cooked.

CRUMPETS AND MUFFINS

These bought seasonal delicacies can be frozen in polythene bags for future use. Thaw at room temperature and toast.

PANCAKES AND GRIDDLE CAKES

Thin pancakes, griddle cakes and drop scones should be cooled before packing. Stack large pancakes with layers of Cellophane or greaseproof paper between, then wrap in freezer paper or polythene. Separate while frozen, or thaw in one piece at room temperature. Wrap around filling and heat in a low oven, or on a plate over steam covered with a cloth. Thaw griddle cakes or drop scones before buttering.

SPONGE CAKES

Fatless sponges can be stored for 10 months; those made with fat can be stored for four months. Delicate sponges can be frozen in freezer paper or polythene, then packed in boxes to avoid crushing. Thaw baked cakes in wrappings at room temperature unless they are iced (see Icings and Fillings).

FRUIT CAKES

Rich fruit cakes store well in tins, so there is little point in taking up freezer room. Dundee cakes, sultana cakes and other light fruit mixtures freeze very well. Thaw in wrappings at room temperature.

SMALL CAKES

Small fruit cakes and sponge drops may be frozen in polythene bags. Small butter-iced cakes are best made in paper or foil cases, iced and frozen in single layers, then packed in boxes with greaseproof paper between layers. Choux pastry and meringues can be frozen well, if unfilled, and should be frozen in single layers, then packed in boxes.

BISCUITS

Baked biscuits store well in tins. Unbaked biscuits freeze very well. Make up batches of biscuit mixture, form into cylinder shapes and freeze in freezer paper, polythene or foil. To use, thaw in wrapping in refrigerator for 45 minutes, cut in slices and bake. These unbaked biscuits will store for 2 months.

ICINGS AND FILLINGS

Do not fill cakes with cream, jam or fruit. Be sure a butter-iced cake is absolutely firm before wrapping and freezing. The easiest packing method is to put the cake on a board or cardboard plate, and slip it into a polythene bag. Foil wrappings can also be used. Remove wrappings before thawing to avoid smudging icing. If sponge or flavoured cakes are to be packed ready for future icing, put layers together with Cellophane, foil or grease-proof paper between.

FLAVOURINGS AND DECORATIONS

Use only pure flavourings, vanilla in particular. Highly spiced foods develop off-flavours, so avoid spice cakes, though gingerbread will be satisfactory if stored for no longer than a month. Chocolate, coffee and fruit-flavoured cakes freeze very well. Do not decorate with nuts, coloured balls, sweets or grated chocolate before freezing, or moisture may be absorbed and the cake icing show colour changes.

SLICED CAKES

It is usually most convenient to pack cakes whole. It can happen that a cake may be started, but the remainder might be left for some time, when it can then be frozen in slices for future use. It is also useful to have meal-size wedges or individual pieces for lunch boxes. Pieces can be wrapped and frozen individually. It is easier to slice the whole cake in wedges before freezing, and withdraw slices as they are needed without thawing the whole cake.

PIES AND FLANS

Pies and flans can be stored baked and unbaked. Do not use custard fillings which separate, or meringue toppings which toughen and dry during storage. Baked flan cases, patty cases and vol-au-vent cases are usefully frozen, and can be thawed at room temperature before filling.

UNBAKED PIES

Pies may be prepared with or without a bottom crust. For fruit fillings, brush surface of bottom crust with egg white to prevent sogginess, for meat pies, brush crust with melted lard. Do not cut air vents in pastry before freezing. To prevent sogginess, freeze unbaked pies *before* wrapping them. Make fruit pies with cooked or uncooked fillings; apples tend to brown after 4 weeks, even if treated with lemon juice. Meat pies are best made with cooked filling and uncooked pastry; to bake, cut slits in top crust and bake unthawed as for fresh pies, allowing 10 minutes longer than normal cooking time.

BAKED PIES

Cook pies in normal way, cool quickly and freeze. These are best prepared and frozen in foil containers, packed in freezer paper or polythene. Pies may be eaten thawed but not reheated. A cooked pie should be heated in a moderate oven for 45 minutes (double crust) or 30 minutes (single crust).

FRESH FRUIT PIE FILLINGS

Surplus fruit may be frozen in the form of pie fillings which can be used with fresh pastry when needed. Simply combine fruit with sugar to sweeten, and add 1 tablespoon lemon juice and 2 tablespoons tapioca flakes to each lb of fruit, leave to stand for 15 minutes, then put into a pie plate with foil lining, leaving a rim of foil to fold over. Fold over foil and freeze, then remove filling from pie plate and store in freezer. To use, line pie plate with pastry, put in fruit filling, dot with butter, cover with pastry lid, make slits in top crust, and bake at 425°F (Gas Mark 7) for 45 minutes.

COMPLETE MEALS

FIRST COURSES

Keep a small selection of prepared starters. Vegetable soup, kidney soup and tomato soup are worth keeping in the freezer. Chicken stock or meat stock can be quickly turned into clear soup with a few fresh vegetables. Pâté is another good first course. Keep a roughcut one which will make a complete meal, and a smooth chicken liver or fish pâté for grander occasions.

MAIN COURSES

Main courses can be prepared in batches for freezing, though most people prefer to cook a double quantity, serving half fresh and freezing the rest for future use. Steak and kidney pies and chicken pies are excellent frozen. If they are completely cooked before freezing, they can also be taken out to eat cold for a packed meal. Steak and kidney pudding or game pudding can be either large or individual sizes. Shepherd's pie is most easily prepared with a cooked meat base and cooked mashed potato, frozen before the final browning process. All casseroles are successful, but thicken with cornflour if necessary. Meat balls and meat loaves can be made in large batches to use in a number of ways. Left over meat and poultry are best sliced and covered in sauce or gravy before freezing.

ACCOMPANIMENTS

Even the quickest freezer meal loses its point if potatoes have to be peeled or sauces prepared. Freeze rice, spaghetti and macaroni when slightly undercooked and well-drained, packed in bags. They may be reheated in the oven or in boiling water. Potatoes are good if mashed and formed into croquettes, or piped into pyramids which can be quickly browned in the oven or deep-fried; plain mashed potatoes should be reheated in a double saucepan with a little hot milk.

Later in the year, freeze large baked jacket potatoes wrapped individually in foil. Bread from the freezer is always useful, after heating in the oven, to go with soups or salads. Sauces can be prepared well in advance when there is more time for simmering and stirring.

PUDDINGS

Pastry flan cases and sponge flan cases can be made ready for filling with fruit or ice cream. Ready-cooked fruit pies and mincemeat can be used for packed meals. Fruit with sponge toppings and fruit crumbles freeze well. These are best with the fruit partly cooked and the topping raw to cook during the reheating.

All kinds of steamed puddings, sponge and suet varieties can be frozen with jam or syrup toppings, dried fruit, or chocolate flavouring. I like to cook these for slightly less than the full time before freezing, then complete cooking during the reheating. Light mousses and fruit whips are excellent for hot evenings. Milk puddings and custards do not freeze well.

17 Buttermaking and Cheesemaking

But huswives, that learne not to make their owne cheese;
with trusting of others, have this for their feese.
Their milke slapt in corners their creame al to soat;
their milk pannes so slotte that their cheeses be lost.

Thomas Tusser

Butter and hard cheeses are not easy to make at home these days, for large quantities of fresh untreated milk are needed, and the sort of equipment not often found in today's kitchens. Small quantities of butter, yoghurt, clotted cream, and soft cheeses, can, however be made with little equipment. Some of the very old traditional recipes for these foods can still be easily used.

DIRECTIONS TO THE DAIRY-MAID

The business of the dairy-maid is of the most beneficial nature, as by her knowledge and industry we are furnished with several of the most essential articles necessary for the preservation of our existence. We shall therefore give such directions as may enable the inexperienced to become proper proficients in so valuable an employment.

Directions for making butter

When you have got a sufficient quantity of cream, strain it through a clean linen cloth into the churn, which must be put to stand in the coolest place of the dairy, in summer; but in winter it must stand in the warmest. When you churn, let it be with solid heavy strokes, for they will make the butter much better than slight quick ones. When you find the butter begins to break, cleanse the inside of the lid, and then strike the church-staff more softly, to prevent the butter from heating. If the summer is hot, it would be proper to set the churn in a leaden cistern filled with cold water, and in winter before a slow fire. When the butter-milk is drained off, let the butter be taken out and washed in clean cold water, and it will be ready to be made up in rolls for present use.

To make Common Cheese

Take as much milk as you have ready, and when it has been made milk-warm, take a calf's bag that has been washed clean, and put in it some salt with curd. Keep it fastened with a skewer, and when you use it, put it in a pan of water mixed with salt, then boil it, and make small holes in it to let out the liquor, which must be poured into the milk. Take great care the milk be not too warm, otherwise you will spoil your cheese; for it should not be warmer than when it comes from the cows. When it has curdled, pour the whey from it, and let the rest be pressed out; then let it stand a day to dry, when it must be carefully crumbled as small as possible; then put to it a little salt properly mixed, and then put into the mould. If the cheese is pressed hard it will keep much longer than what is pressed soft; but the latter, when new, will have a better taste.

To make Cream Cheese

Put 2 spoonfuls of rennet into 12 gallons of milk, just as hot as when it comes from the cow, and in a $\frac{1}{2}$ hour it will be curdled. Break the curd with a delf plate, and take care to keep it from getting to the bottom; then let it stand a $\frac{1}{2}$ hour, when you must draw a plug fixed to the middle of the vessel to let the whey run out. When it is properly drained, put the curd into a clean canvas bag, and roll it up and down till the rest of the whey is drained off, then hang it up till it be dry, when it must be put in a thick mould, and a flat stone laid over it. When you take it out of the mould, cut it in slices of an inch thick, by drawing a silken thread gently and regularly through it. Put the slices thus cut up on a clean board, and sprinkle a little salt over them, taking care to turn them twice each of the first 4 days. Then lay them on strewed nettles 8 days more, when they must be set up to dry. They will be ready to eat in a few days.

To make Sage Cheese

Prepare the curd in the same manner as before, and squeeze as much of the juice out of sage and spinnage as will give it a fine greenish colour; put it to the curd, with which it must be properly mixed, then put it into the mould, and press it in a moderate manner; then put it by about 6 months, and it will eat fine.

To make Cheese as in Cheshire

Instead of breaking the curd, you must draw it gently to one side with your hands, and press it as softly as possible, that the whey may run out without hurting the milk. When you have got out the curd, put it in a vat, and keep turning it, and mixing with it a great deal of salt; then mix the curd as small as possible, and put it in a mould 8 inches deep. It must be pressed very hard, and when taken out, let it be put upon a shelf and turned once every day for a month; then cut a hole in the middle and pour in a $\frac{1}{2}$ pint of sack, which will immediately dissolve through the cheese, when you must put in the piece that was taken out, so close that it may not be damaged; then set it in the cellar, and in a year it will be ready for use.

To make Cheese as in Gloucestershire

When you have prepared the curd, let it be taken off gently, and put it into a vat covered with a clean linen cloth till it is dry. Then cut it into small pieces, and put it into boiling water mixed with salt; then take it out, and, having wrung it from the water, let it stand a day longer in another vat, only that you must turn it several times. Put it into the press, and when it has laid 24 hours, take it out and set it up. Turn it several times for a month and in 8 months it will be ready for use.

1812

INSTRUCTIONS TO A DAIRY-MAID

To Make Cheese

Put the milk into a large tub, warming a part till it is of a degree of heat quite equal to new; if too hot, the cheese will be tough. Put in as much rennet as will turn it, and cover it over. Let it stand still completely turned; then strike the curd down several times with the skimming-dish, and let it separate, still covering it. There are 2 modes of breaking the curd; and there will be a difference in the taste of the cheese, according as either is observed; one is, to gather it with the hands through the fingers till it is cleared, and lading it off as it collects. The other is, to get the whey from it by early breaking the curd; the last method deprives it of many of its oily particles, and is therefore not advised.

Put the vat on a ladder over the tub, and fill it with curd by the skimmer; press the curd close with your hand, and add more as it sinks; press the curd close with your hand, and add more as it sinks; and it must be finally left 2 inches above the edge. Before the vat is filled, the cheese-cloth must be laid at the bottom: and when full, drawn smooth over on all sides.

There are 2 modes of salting cheese; one by mixing it in the curd while in the tub after the whey is out; and the other by putting it into the vat and crumbling the curd all to pieces with it, after the first squeezing has dried it. The first method appears best on some accounts, but not on all; and therefore the custom of the county must direct. Put a board under and over the vat, and place it in the press; in 2 hours turn it out and put a fresh cheese-cloth; press it again for 8 or 9 hours; then salt it all over, and turn it again in the vat, and let it stand in the press 14 or 16 hours, observing to put the cheeses last made undermost. Before putting them the last time into the vat, pare the edges if they do not look smooth. The vat should have holes at the sides and bottom, to let all the whey pass through. Put on clean boards, and change and scald them.

To preserve Cheese sound

Wash in warm whey, when you have any, and wipe it once a month, and keep it on a rack. If you want to ripen it, a damp cellar will bring it forward. When a whole cheese is cut, the larger quantity should be spread with butter inside, and outside wiped to preserve it. To keep those in daily use moist, let a clean cloth be wrung out from cold water, and wrapt round them when carried from table. Dry cheese may be used to advantage to grate for serving with macaroni, or eating without. These observations are made with a view to make the above articles less expensive, as in most families where much is used there is waste.

To make Sage Cheese

Bruise the tops of young red sage in a mortar, with some leaves of spinach, and squeeze the juice; mix it with the rennet in the milk, more or less according as you like for colour and taste. When the curd is come, break it gently, and put it in with the skimmer, till it is pressed 2 inches over 1 vat. Press it 8 or 10 hours. Salt it, and turn every day.

Cream Cheese

Put 5 quarts of strippings, that is, the last of the milk, into a pan, with 2 spoonfuls of rennet. When the curd is come, strike it down 2 or 3 times with the skimming-dish, just to break it. Let it stand 2 hours, then spread a cheese-cloth on a sieve, put the curd on it, and let the whey drain; break the curd a little with your hand, and put it into a vat with a 2 lb weight upon it. Let it stand 12 hours, take it out, and bind a fillet round. Turn every day till dry, from 1 board to another; cover them with nettles, or clean dock-leaves and put between 2 pewter-plates to ripen. If the weather be warm, it will be ready in 3 weeks.

Another – Have ready a kettle of boiling water, put 5 quarts of new milk into a pan, and 5 pints of cold water, and 5 of hot; when of a proper heat, put in as much rennet as will bring it in 20 minutes, likewise a bit of sugar. When come, strike the skimmer 3 or 4 times down, and leave it on the curd. In an hour or 2 lade it into the vat without touching it; put a 1 lb weight on it when the whey has run from it, and the vat is full.

Another sort – Put as much salt to 3 pints of raw cream as will season it; stir well and pur it into a sieve in which you have folded a cheese-cloth 3 or 4 times, and laid at the bottom. When it hardens, cover it with nettles on a pewter-plate.

To a quart of fresh cream put a pint of new milk warm enough to make the cream a proper warmth, a piece of sugar, and a little rennet.

Set near the fire till the curd comes; fill a vat made in the form of a brick, of wheat-straw or rushes sewed together. Have ready a square of straw, or rushes sewed flat, to rest the vat on, and another to cover it; the vat being open at top and bottom. Next day take it out, and change it as above to ripen. A ½ lb weight will be sufficient to put on it.

To Make Butter

During summer, skim the milk when the sun has not heated the dairy; at that season it should stand for butter 24 hours without skimming, and 48 in winter. Deposit the cream-pot in a very cold cellar, if your dairy is not cool. If you cannot churn daily, change it into scalded fresh pots; but never omit churning twice a week. If possible, put the churn in a through air; and if not a barrel one, set it in a tub of water 2 feet deep, which will give firmness to the butter. When the butter is come, pour off the butter-milk and put the butter into a fresh-scalded pan, or tubs which have afterwards been in cold water. Pour water on it, and let it lie to acquire some hardness before you work it; then change the water, and beat it with flat boards so perfectly that not the least taste of the butter-milk remain, and that the water, which must be often changed, shall be quite clear in colour. Then work some salt into it, weigh, and make it into forms; throw them into cold water, in an earthen pan and cover. You will then have very nice and cool butter in the hottest weather. It requires more working in hot than in cold weather; but in neither should be left with a particle of buttermilk, or a sour taste, as is sometimes done.

To Preserve Butter

Take 2 parts of the best common salt, 1 part of good loaf sugar, and 1 part of saltpetre; beat them well together. To 16 ozs of butter thoroughly cleansed from the milk, put 1 oz of this composition; work it well, and pot down, when it will become firm and cold.

The butter thus preserved is the better for keeping, and should not be used under a month. This should be kept from the air, and is best in pots of the best glazed earthenware, that will hold from 10 to 14 lbs each.

To Preserve Butter for Winter, the best way

When the butter has been prepared, as above directed, take 2 parts of the best common salt, 1 part of good loaf-sugar, and 1 part of saltpetre, beaten and blended well together. Of this composition put 1 oz to 16 ozs of butter, and work it well together in a mass. Press it into the pans after the butter is become cool; for friction, though it be not touched by the hands, will soften it. The pans should hold 10 or 12 lbs each. On the top put some salt; and when that is turned into brine, if not enough to cover the butter entirely, add some strong salt and water. It requires only then to be covered from the dust.

To manage Cream for Whey Butter

Set the whey 1 day and night, skim it, and so till you have enough; then boil it and pour it into a pan or 2 of cold water. As the cream rises, skim it till no more comes; then churn it. Where new-milk cheese is made daily, whey-butter for common and present use may be made to advantage.

To scald Cream, as in the West of England

In winter let the milk stand 24 hours, in the summer 12 at least; then put the milk-pan on a hot hearth, if you have one; if not, set it in a wide brass kettle of water, large enough to receive the pan. It must remain on the fire till quite hot, but on no account boil, or there will be a skin instead of a cream upon the milk. You will know when done enough, by the undulations on the surface looking thick, and having a ring round the pan the size of the bottom. The time required to scald cream depends on the size of the pan, and the heat of the fire; the slower the better. Remove the pan into the dairy when done, and skim it next day. In cold weather it may stand 36 hours, and never less than 2 meals. The butter is usually made in Devonshire of cream thus prepared, and if properly, it is very firm.

Butter-milk

If made of sweet cream, is a delicious and most wholesome food. Those who can relish sour butter-milk, find it still more light, and it is reckoned more beneficial in consumptive cases. Butter-milk, if not very sour, is also as good as cream to eat with fruit, if sweetened with white sugar, and mixed with a very little milk. It likewise does equally for cakes and rice-puddings, and of course it is economical to churn before the cream is too stale for anything but to feed pigs.

To keep Milk and Cream

In hot weather, when it is difficult to preserve milk from becoming sour and spoiling the cream, it may be kept perfectly sweet by scalding the new milk very gently, without boiling, and setting it by in the earthen dish, or pan, that it is done in. This method is pursued in Devonshire, and for butter, and eating, would equally answer in small quantities for coffee, tea, etc. Cream already skimmed may be kept 24 hours if scalded without sugar; and, by adding to it as much powdered lump-sugar, as will make it sweet, will be good for 2 days, keeping it in a cool place.

To choose Butter at Market

Put a knife into the butter if salt, and smell it when drawn out; if there is any thing rancid or unpleasant, it is bad. Being made at different times, the layers in casks will vary greatly, and you will not easily come at the goodness but by unhooping the cask, and trying it between the staves. Fresh butter ought to smell like a nosegay, and be of an equal colour all through; if sour in smell, it has not been sufficiently washed; if veiny and open, it is probably mixed with staler or an inferior sort.

To prepare Rennet, to turn the Milk

Take out the stomach of a calf as soon as killed, and scour it inside and out with salt, after it is cleared of the curd always found in it. Let it drain a few hours; then sew it up with two good handfuls of salt in it, or stretch it on a stick, well salted; or keep it in the salt wet, and soak a bit, which will do over and over by fresh water.

From Mrs Bing Smith, Lancaster, 1900

CORNISH CREAM

Put new milk into rather deep straight-sided pans, enamel if possible. Leave it to stand for 24 hours, and set over a slow fire. Heat very slowly to a temperature of 150°F. Remove from heat without shaking the cream, and leave to stand in a cold place for 24 hours. Skim off the cream.

DEVONSHIRE CREAM

Leave the milk to stand for 12 hours after milking, or 24 hours in the winter, for the cream to rise. Put the pan in a second pan of boiling water and let the water simmer gently, until the cream on the surface of the milk is thick and yellow, and small air bubbles come to the surface. When a ring appears on the cream inside the rim of the pan, remove it from the heat. Leave to stand for 12 hours, and skim off the cream. A note on this old recipe says that a pinch of saltpetre, put into each basin with the milk strained over it, will take away the taste of turnips.

BUTTER WITH AN ELECTRIC MIXER

Use 4-day-old double cream. Put into mixing bowl and mix with a heavy beater at low speed. As soon as the butter begins to form, reduce speed and continue until the butter comes into one lump. Drain off buttermilk. Wash the butter in cold water until the water remains clear. Squeeze to extract water. Salt to taste and pat butter into shape. 1 pint cream is the most practical quantity to use.

BUTTER WITH AN ELECTRIC BLENDER

Blend top milk or fresh cream at high speed for 1 minute. Drain off buttermilk. Put clean, cold water into the blender goblet, and blend for a few seconds. Drain off water, and squeeze butter to exclude moisture.

To remove the taste of turnips from butter

Dissolve 1 tablespoon saltpetre in 1 breakfastcup boiling water. Put a tablespoon of this liquid into a 10-pint pail and milk the cow into the pail. At once put the pail into a copper of boiling water and leave for about 3 minutes until the milk reaches 104°F. All taste of turnip will disappear. (This recipe dates from 1909.)

CONSTANT YOGHURT

Bring a pint of milk to the boil, bubble gently 1 minute and allow to stand 15 minutes in a warm kitchen. Meanwhile take 4 empty cartons or small jars, and an ovenproof dish or cake tin to stand them in. Fold a clean tea-towel in 2, lay it in the dish and place a cork mat on top.

Take 1 spoonful of commercial yoghurt and blend with 3 of hot milk. Divide the rest of the milk among the jars and stir in a spoonful of yoghurt and milk mixture. Place the jars on the cork mat, cover with another mat and wrap the ends of the towel over the top. Cover all with a lid or a plate and leave in a warm part of the kitchen 6 to 8 hours, disturbing as little as possible.

YOGHURT

Boil 1 pint milk then cool to blood heat. Add carton of plain yoghurt. Tip into coffee jar and wrap. Leave for 24 hours. Next day take $\frac{1}{2}$ a carton of this mixture and add to 1 pint boiled milk. Continue indefinitely to make supplies.

COTTAGE CHEESE

Put sour milk in a warm place until thick. Add ½ teaspoon salt to each pint of milk. Put into a muslin bag and leave to drain overnight. Press between 2 plates for an hour, and then mix with a little fresh cream to serve.

SOUR MILK CHEESE WITH HERBS

2 pints thick sour milk　　*1 fluid oz cream*
1 oz butter　　*Salt and pepper*
1 tablespoon salt　　*Chopped fresh herbs*

Scale the sour milk until the curd separates from the whey, but do not boil. Add all the other ingredients except the herbs and beat well. Add herbs to taste.

EIGHTEENTH-CENTURY CREAM CHEESE

Put a wet double napkin into a pewter soup plate. Put in a pint of cream, cover it and let it stand for 24 hours, unless the weather is very hot. Turn the cheese, add a little salt and leave 12 hours. Put into a dry napkin, salt the other side and leave another day. Some keep it in nut leaves to ripen.

FRESH CHEESE

Use 2 pints of warm new milk with a pint of sweet cream and 2 spoons of good rennet. Cover and leave to stand until it is a hard jelly. Break this up and put into a hair sieve. Let the whey drain off. Put the cheese in a dish with a beaten egg yolk and sugar to taste. Serve with sweet thick fresh cream and more sugar.

TWENTY-FOUR HOURS CREAM CHEESE

Leave 3 pints of cream to stand for 24 hours until thick. Put into a thick cloth and press with 4 oz weight, turning every hour until it is thick, and putting in a clean cloth each time. Chill in dairy or on ice.

HERB CHEESE

Heat some creamy milk to blood heat. Add just enough rennet to curdle, and let it coagulate. Hang in a muslin bag to drip. When the curd is firm, add plenty of chopped chives or parsley to make a green cheese.

DRY CREAM CHEESE

Take 1½ pints of very thick fresh cream, and put it into a cloth. Put this on a board and put another board on top, weighted with 4 lb. Leave for an hour and remove the cream to a bowl. Add a little salt and put into a clean cloth. Repeat pressing, and changing the cloth 3 times more until the cheese is firm.

FRESH CREAM CHEESE

Put 2 pints very thick sweet cream into a muslin cloth and hang it up all night. Next mornng, line a small hair sieve with fresh nettles and put a square of fine-mesh netting on the nettles. Pour in the cream, fold a cloth on top, and cover with nettles. Put in cold dairy, or on ice. When well chilled, put a piece of fresh wet muslin into the sieve, cover with nettles and put cream upside down on them. Cover with more nettles and 8 oz weight. Put back in dairy or on ice until the evening.

TO MAKE STILTON CHEESE

Take 60 quarts of new milk, and 6 quarts of cream. When lukewarm, put rennet, as for other cheeses. Press the curd in the usual manner, and when put into the cheese-vat, turn it over 4 or 5 times a-day into clean cloths. The cheese-vat should be 10¼ inches deep, and 8¼ inches over. Stilton cheeses are seldom used till 2 years old. See that the rennet is perfectly sweet, for on that the flavour of the cheese greatly depends.

1872

18 Potted Meat and Fish and Pâtés

What a breakfast ! Pot of hare; ditto of trout;
pot of prepared shrimps; dish of plain shrimps;
tin of sardines; beautiful beef-steak; eggs, muffins,
large loaf, and butter, not forgetting capital tea.

'Wild Wales', George Borrow

Potted meat and fish have been popular in Britain for many hundreds of years. They were traditionally eaten for breakfast, but are now more acceptable as a first course for luncheon or dinner, or for high tea or supper. Many delightful litttle china pots were produced to hold these delicacies, but today the same mixtures can be pressed into small soufflé dishes or ramekins. Originally 'potting' was a useful method of preserving meat, game and fish, and the dishes were covered with clarified melted butter to keep out air. This same method can be employed today, but once a 'pot' has been started, it should be eaten quickly.

More hearty pâtés are also included in this chapter, since they contain so many similar ingredients. They can be covered with butter also, or with aspic. Pâtés and 'pots' freeze well, but the butter or aspic coating should not then be used. These finishes may be added after thawing for serving. Both types of recipe are useful for using up meat, game and fish from other dishes, or for preserving a surplus quantity. They are nicest eaten with thin bread and butter, or with fresh toast, while some of the firmer mixtures may be sliced and eaten with salad.

POTTED BEEF

1 lb shoulder steak (beef)
1 teaspoon salt

⅛ teaspoon pepper
4 oz butter or margarine

Wash and dry the meat and cut into very small pieces. Season and place in a stone jam jar or in a basin; cover with aluminium foil or greased grease-proof paper and stand in a pan of water. Cover the pan and simmer for 2½ hours. Strain the liquid into a bowl and add 3 oz of the margarine. Mince the meat several times till very fine. Mix with the liquid. Put into a clean jar or bowl and pour on the remaining melted margarine. Keep in a cool place and use within 2 days.

MRS JEWRY'S POTTED BEEF

Allow yourself about 3½–4 hours to complete this task, she says, but 'be assured it is well worth the time spent'. (Actually, most of this time involves the meat being cooked.)

2½ lb lean beef
5 oz butter

Pepper, salt and mace

Take a piece of lean beef and remove carefully the skin and gristle; put it into a covered stone jar with 3 dessertspoons of hot water, and stand it in a deep stewpan of boiling water to boil slowly for *nearly 4 hours*, taking care that the water does not reach the top of the jar. When done, take it out and mince it fine, then pound it in a mortar with a seasoning of pepper, salt and mace (also pounded). When smooth like a thick paste, mix in some clarified butter and a very little of the gravy from the jar. Press it into pots, pour over butter on to the tops and tie down for use.

POTTED LIVER

8 oz calves' liver
1 medium onion
2 oz butter

1 hard-boiled egg
1 tablespoon double cream
Salt and pepper

Cut the liver in small pieces and chop the onion. Cook them slowly in the butter until the onion is soft but not brown. Mince liver, onion and egg, with the pan juices. Add the cream and season to taste and put into small pots. Serve on toast or in sandwiches.

POTTED PORK

1 lb hand, shoulder or blade of pork
1 lb pork sausage meat
¼ teaspoon garlic salt
¼ teaspoon basil
¼ teaspoon black pepper
¼ teaspoon salt
¼ teaspoon marjoram
Pinch of nutmeg
1 pint water
1 oz gelatine

Cut the pork into very small pieces and put into pan with the sausage meat, seasonings and water. Bring to boil. Put lid on, reduce heat and simmer for about 1 hour. Strain off the liquid. Dissolve gelatine in a little cold water and stand over hot water until gelatine is syrupy. Add gelatine to liquid and leave until cold. Skim off fat and add meat mixture to liquid. Put into 2 lb loaf tin or dish and leave until set. Cut in slices to serve with salad or in sandwiches.

TO POT OX CHEEK

When you stew an ox cheek, take some of the fleshy part, and season it well with salt and pepper, and beat it very fine in a mortar, with a little clear fat skimmed off the gravy; then put it close into your potting-pots, and pour over it clarified butter, and keep it for use.

Thomas Train, Gateshead, 1812

MRS HILLIER'S POTTED OX-TONGUE

1½ lb cooked tongue
6 oz butter
Nutmeg and cloves
1 small spoon mace
A little Cayenne pepper

Take about 1½ lb from a boiled tongue and remove the rind. Pound it as fine as you can with the butter and the spices. When the meat is nice and smooth and free from bits and the spices are properly worked into the meat, press the mixture into little suitable pots and pour melted butter over them. You can add a little cold roast meat with the tongue such as lamb or veal. It all helps the flavour.

Mrs Hillier is now very old indeed, over 90, but she still works hard and it is always a pleasure to hear her talking of the good old days when her husband was a vet. in some pretty hard hunting country. She had long, lonely days when her husband was out hunting, but she found plenty to occupy her time; there were many parties around the various farmhouses where the large kitchens would be cleared and dancing would begin after supper and carry on to the early hours, when the horses would take them safely home.

POTTED MEAT (1)

Procure 1 lb of lean hock and a nap or kneebone. The hock costs little and the knee even less. Wash the hock and nap carefully, and place in a large pot, covering the whole with cold water. Bring to the boil, and skim well; then boil slowly for 4 hours. Take out the meat and bone. Mince the meat very finely, also any small pieces of soft gristle adhering to the bone, but these can be left out if liked. Put back the minced meat into the liquid again, and boil for another ½ hour, adding salt to taste and also 2 teaspoons Jamaican pepper (red pepper). Dish into bowls of fancy shapes, and leave until cold.

POTTED MEAT (2)

1 pig's cheek
1 cow heel
1½ lb shin of beef
Seasoning

If the pig's cheek is too salt, boil it by itself; when cooked cut into small pieces and add it to the cow heel and beef, which should be boiled until the meat comes freely from the bones. Cover the cow heel and shin with water, boil a bag of pickling spices with these for about an hour of the cooking time – cook the meats until very tender. The bag of spice consists of 1 tablespoon peppercorns, 12 cloves, 3 blades of mace, or a little nutmeg, ½ teaspoon Cayenne pepper, and 3 bayleaves; tie in a muslin bag and suspend from saucepan handle with string into the liquid.

Remove all meat from bones and chop or mince very finely. Place in basins or moulds and cover with the liquid, which you have previously reduced, by boiling, until only a little remains. Stir these juices into the minced meat and leave to set. It is advisable to rinse moulds or basins with cold water.

POTTED MEAT (3)

1½ lb beef
2 tablespoons anchovy sauce
½ gill water
Pepper and salt to taste
4 oz salt butter

Cut the meat up into cubes and put in an earthenware pot with the water. Let it simmer for 5 hours. Put through a mincer twice and mix well with the sauce, seasoning, and 2 oz butter. Fill small jars with the mixture. Melt remainder of the butter and pour over the top.

WILTSHIRE MEAT PASTE

1 *lb lean beef, the better the*
cut, the better the paste
1 *tablespoon anchovy paste*
or sauce

¼ *teaspoon pepper*
Salt to taste
¼ *grated nutmeg*

Put all in a basin when thoroughly minced and steam for at least 2 hours, or according to the cut of the beef. Suitable for spreading on home-made scones or bridge rolls, or on snippets of dry toast.

LIVER PÂTÉ

Get very fresh calves' liver, parboil it, pass it through a mincing machine, mix the same weight of cold tongue, which must be cut into dice, 2 dozen button mushrooms cut into small pieces, 2 onions minced and fried in butter; salt, pepper and parsley to taste.

Line a dish with well made puff pastry, fill with the mixture and cover with a thin layer of pastry. Bake from ¾ to 1 hour.

SIMPLE PÂTÉ

¾ *lb pig's liver*
2 *lb belly pork*
3 *heaped tablespoons onion*
softened in butter
1 *large egg beaten with*

1 *heaped tablespoon flour*
Salt and pepper
Nutmeg
Bay leaf

Mince or chop liver and pork and mix all ingredients together, seasoning to taste. Put into terrine (or loaf tin). Cover with lid or foil and bake at 350°F (Gas Mark 4) for 1½ hours (the terrine should stand in a baking tin of water). The pâté will be cooked when a metal needle or skewer comes out clean. Cool for an hour, then weight gently until next day. The pâté may be finished with meat jelly; or with a layer of lard for storage in a cool dry place. Before the pâté is cooked, the terrine may be lined with pieces of pork fat, or with thin strips of streaky bacon.

CHICKEN LIVER PÂTÉ

Equal quantities by bulk of cooked livers (I do them inside the birds when roasting or simmer with the stock), butter and stock from chicken carcasses. Press livers through a sieve. Mix thoroughly with melted butter and as much of the stock as you like. The full quantity may make it too wet for some tastes, but I find that an hour in the fridge makes it pretty solid. Season to taste with salt and fresh ground pepper and ring the changes with thyme/parsley/chives.

Useful for supper for 2 when the family have had roast chicken for lunch.

Mrs Chaplin, Finsthwaite, Lancs

PORK AND SAUSAGE PÂTÉ

½ *pig's liver*	4 *oz mushrooms, finely*
½ *lb pork sausage meat*	*chopped*
1 *oz white breadcrumbs*	¼ *teaspoon sage*
Salt and black pepper	1 *dessertspoon tomato*
4 *oz lean bacon*	*chutney*

Remove the gristle from liver and rinds from the bacon. Mince liver and bacon and then mix them together, stirring in all the other ingredients. Mix thoroughly. Press into a 1½-pint sized basin, cover loosely with foil and bake at 325°F (Gas Mark 3) for 1½ hours. Leave loaf in basin until cold.

PRESSED FOWL

Old boiling hens are often obtainable at small country markets and are more tasty, as well as being a better buy, than frozen chicken. Place a dressed fowl (i.e. ready-for-cooking) in a saucepan with cold water, to cover and let it simmer gently over a moderate fire until the meat falls off the bone, about 2–3 hours. When done pick to pieces – this is best done with only the fingers, when the bird is cool enough to handle. Put the bones back in the liquor in saucepan and boil until the content is halved; then strain. Season with salt and pepper, and pour the strained liquor over the "picked" meat and mix well again. Pour the whole into a mould. When quite firm turn out and slice thinly.

BUTTERED GROUSE

The birds (young ones are essential) are rubbed with butter, a lump of butter is put inside them, and they are wrapped in a piece of fat bacon. Roast them in a preheated oven at 425–450°F (Gas Mark 7 or 8). Baste frequently. They will take 30–35 minutes. Remove from the oven, cut each bird in half, and arrange neatly in a pie dish. Pour the hot juices from the roasting pan into a saucepan, add, for 2 birds, ½ lb of butter. Let it melt, season with a very little mace, cayenne pepper and salt. Pour over the birds, and eat cold next day.

POTTED GROUSE

2 old grouse
1 carrot
1 onion
2 oz streaky bacon

Butter
Bunch of mixed herbs
Salt and pepper

Slice the carrots and onions, and cut the bacon in neat pieces and fry in butter until golden. Put into a casserole with the herbs and plenty of salt and pepper, and put the grouse on top. Cover with stock and cook at 300°F (Gas Mark 2) for 2½ hours. Remove the carrot. Take meat from the bones of the grouse, and put the mixture through a mincer, then pound, sieve or put in a liquidiser. Press into a shallow dish and cover with melted butter. A small glass of port improves this dish. Serve with hot fresh toast.

POTTED GROUSE

2 grouse
Salt and pepper
6 oz butter

¾ pint jellied consommé
1 wineglass red wine or sherry

Salt and pepper the birds and put a knob of butter into each. Pack into an earthenware casserole and pour over the consommé (this may be home-made or canned). Add the wine or sherry and remaining butter. Cover tightly and bake at 325°F (Gas Mark 3) for 2 hours. Leave until cold and set when the birds will be in wine-flavoured jelly with a firm butter top. Serve half a bird to each person with toast, and small pickled gherkins or reducrrant jelly.

DEVON TERRINE OF HARE

Line an earthenware terrine with slices of bacon. Remove all bones from the hare and cut up into small pieces. Place it in the terrine with ½ lb pickled pork, cut into small pieces, and flavourings of thyme, marjoram, parsley, one shallot, 1 clove of garlic, salt and pepper to taste, and then pour over the whole a glass of Madeira or sherry. Close the lid tightly with an edging of paste, and put it in the oven – a slow one – to bake gently for 4 hours.

HARE PÂTÉ (1)

1 lb cooked hare, removed
from bones
2 oz mushrooms
1 thick slice bread soaked in
milk
Rich gravy

2 oz butter
2 egg yolks
6 tablespoons brandy or
Madeira
Pepper and salt
1 bayleaf

Strip the hare from the bones and cut up meat in small pieces. Mix with sliced mushrooms cooked in butter and the soaked bread. Mince and pound until smooth. Moisten with a little gravy and mix with butter, egg yolks, brandy or Madeira and seasoning. Put the bayleaf in the bottom of a dish, put in the meat mixture, cover and steam for 2 hours (the dish may be placed in a tin of water and cooked at 325°F, Gas Mark 3, for 2 hours). Leave until very cold under a weight. This pâté will keep for several weeks in a refrigerator.

HARE PÂTÉ (2)

Joints of hare
2 onions
Bayleaf
Mixed herbs

1 lb fat bacon, cut in cubes
3-4 rashers bacon
½ pint red wine
Lemon juice

Put the hare, fat bacon, onions, bayleaf and herbs into a pan and cook very slowly until the meat will just leave the bones. Take out and remove meat from bones, put hare and bacon through the mincer, add more seasoning and lemon juice. Lay some rashers of bacon on the bottom of a fireproof dish, press the minced meat into the dish, add the red wine and some more rashers of bacon on top. Put the dish, standing in a baking tin containing water, into a moderate oven 300°F (Gas Mark 3) for 2–3 hours. Take out and apply light pressure until the pâté is cold.

HARE PÂTÉ (3)

Crisp 1 lb fat diced bacon in a large pan before adding and browning the jointed hindquarters of a hare. Then pour in ¼ pint dry red wine and ½ pint of chicken stock. Add a dozen peppercorns, bayleaf and thyme, simmer, covered for 1 hour adding 6 oz thickly sliced calf's liver to cook for the last 5 minutes. Let cool, strip the hare flesh from the bones and double mince together with the liver, bacon, 1 medium onion and 2 garlic cloves. Thereafter cream the mixture with the fat from the cooking liquor together with some of the liquor itself, 2 tablespoons brandy and seasonings to make a medium-stiff purée. Turn this into a greased casserole, cover with foil and bake for an hour in a moderate oven, first seating the casserole in a shallow pan of water.

HARE PÂTÉ (4)

Joint the hare, and stew until tender with an assortment of herbs and vegetables until the meat is ready to fall off the bone. Then take the meat and mince finely, or put it through a sieve. Add a glass of port or brandy, and 2 tablespoons of redcurrant jelly. Mix well, put into jars, pour melted butter on the top.

POTTED HARE

Remains of jugged hare   **Butter or aspic**

Put the remains of a jugged hare through a sieve or mill with just enough of its sauce to moisten it but not so much as to make it runny. Press down in a dish. Cover with melted butter or liquid aspic. Put in the refrigerator.

HARE TERRINE

Put all the joints but the saddle into a casserole with 2 or 3 sliced onions, a bayleaf, a teaspoon of marjoram and 2 lb of fat bacon, cut into cubes. Add enough stock to cover all ingredients, or, if you have it, use stock and half a bottle of cheap red wine. Cover closely and cook in a slow oven, 45 minutes. Let it cool, then put all the meat, including the bacon, through the fine plate of the mincer.

Season well with ground black pepper, salt if needed, more herbs and a little grated lemon peel.

Grease a mould. This should be a 2-pint terrine, that is a straight-sided china mould, but if you have not got such a thing use a basin or a straight-sided fireproof dish, do not use a metal mould.

Put the meat into the mould, do not press it down. Put a few rashers of bacon on the top and moisten with some of the stock in which you have cooked the joints. Put greaseproof paper on the top and stand the mould in a pan of hot water. Put this pan into a low oven and cook for $1\frac{1}{2}$–2 hours. When you take the pan out of the oven press evenly down on the greaseproof paper so that all the meat is consolidated, leave the paper on top while the terrine cools, it can then be stored in a cold larder until required.

If wanted to be kept for 2–3 weeks, run melted butter over the top of the meat; when cold cover with tinfoil. It can then be safely kept for 2–3 weeks.

POTTED PARTRIDGE

2 partridges   **½ pint stock**
8 oz butter

Season the birds inside and out and put a lump of butter in each. Put into a casserole with some good stock and the rest of the butter, cover with double cooking foil and a lid and cook at 350°F (Gas Mark 3) for 1½ hours. Leave until cold, when the butter will form a seal on top. Do not uncover until they are to be eaten; they will keep several days. Serve garnished with parsley, and with redcurrant jelly.

PHEASANT TERRINE

1 pheasant   **½ wineglass Madeira**
1 lb fat pork   **½ wineglass brandy**
½ lb thin-cut streaky bacon   **Salt and pepper**
rashers   **Mixed herbs (parsley, chives,**
1 wineglass white wine   **basil, tarragon, garlic)**

This is a rather expensive recipe but makes a large quantity of a very superior pâté and is well worth while for a special occasion. The recipe may be used for other game birds, hare, duck or chicken, and the mincemeat layers can consist of chopped-up poultry or game, pork, liver or tinned liver pâté.

Take the breast and thighs from a plump pheasant, cut the meat in slices and leave for 24 hours in the wine, Madeira, brandy and herbs. Mince the pheasant trimmings and liver with pork and season well with salt and pepper. Line a terrine (if you haven't the correct dish, use a deep pie dish or an earthenware casserole) with rashers of bacon. Put in a layer of the mincemeat, then the pheasant slices, and continue in layers, finishing with a layer of mincemeat. Cover with bacon rashers and put on a lid. Stand the dish in a tin of water and cook at 325°F (Gas Mark 3) for 1½ hours. Leave until cold with a weight on top. This makes an excellent beginning for a shooting picnic.

POTTED PIGEONS

2 pigeons   **8 small onions**
1 oz butter   **½ pint stock**
2 rashers streaky bacon   **Salt and pepper**

Brown the birds all over in the butter, then take out the pigeons, and cook the onions and the bacon cut in strips in the fat. Put onions and bacon in a casserole and add pigeons split in half. Season well with salt and pepper and add stock. Cook at 350°F (Gas Mark 4) for 1½ hours.

PIGEON PÂTÉ (can be made from either young or old birds)

3 pigeons	**Small teaspoon grated thyme**
1 cup red wine	**Grating of nutmeg**
½ cup vinegar	**Salt and pepper**
Bayleaf	**4 finely chopped onions**

Make a marinade of the seasonings, the herbs, the wine and the vinegar, add the chopped onion, and pour all this over the jointed birds. Leave to soak, 3–4 days. Take the meat from the birds, 8 oz sausage meat, 8 oz bacon rashers, seasoning, little milk and 1 slice of bread (crusts removed). Mince the meat twice, mix with the sausage meat, add seasoning. Soak the crumbled bread in enough milk to moisten it, then beat this in to the meat mixture. Have ready an ovenware dish with a close fitting lid. Lay some rashers of bacon at the bottom, press in the meat mixture, put more rashers on top, put on the lid and bake in a moderate oven 2–2½ hours.

RICH PIGEON PÂTÉ

10 pigeon breasts	**½ glass wine, sherry, brandy**
½ small onion	**or whisky**
1 teaspoon mixed herbs	**Salt**
(including basil and	**Ground black pepper**
rosemary if possible)	**Garlic (optional)**
½ oz streaky bacon	**6 crushed juniper berries**
4 oz lard	**(optional)**
4 oz butter	

Cut the pigeon breasts into cubes about 1 inch square. 'Melt' bacon and onion in butter and lard in a thick frying pan so that they are cooked but not browned. Turn up heat and sauté the pigeon breasts. This should take only a few minutes, and they should be faintly pink inside. Remove from the pan and put aside. Add the herbs, seasoning (plenty of black pepper) and wine to the butter and let it bubble for a few seconds. Add to the pigeon and place in a liquidiser until well pounded. (If you do not possess one, simply pass the meat through a fine mincer and then beat in the butter and wine with a fork.) Put into an earthenware dish or terrine and cover with melted butter. Place in a refrigerator. Serve well chilled with piping hot toast.

Mrs. Archie Coat

PIGEON WALNUT PÂTÉ

Separate the flesh from the bones of 2 pigeons that have simmered till quite tender in a little stock and then mince it up. Mix it together with ½ lb double minced dry walnuts, garlic and onion, creaming in at the same time a little of the greatly reduced stock in which the pigeons cooked, together with seasonings and a good dash of Cayenne.

POTTED RABBIT

Joint a rabbit and put into a casserole with tightly-fitting lid. Add 2 oz butter, 1 lump sugar, 1 onion stuck thickly with cloves, 12 allspice, 6 peppercorns, and a good sprinkling of nutmeg. Put on lid and cook in a slow oven till the meat leaves the bones easily. Cool the meat, remove the bones and put through a mincer twice. Beat in ½ lb butter, 1 dessertspoon Worcester sauce and a pinch of sugar. Put into small pots, covering the tops with melted butter. This is delicious on toast, and will keep in the refrigerator for a few days.

POTTED ROOKS

4 rooks   **Gelatine**
Salt and pepper   **1 oz butter**

Skin and clean the rooks and cut away the backs and ribs, leaving the breasts with the 2 upper wing bones attached, also the 2 legs without the feet. Put into a double saucepan with salt and pepper to taste and butter. Cook slowly until the meat comes away from the bones, which may take 8 or 10 hours. Take the meat off the bones and put into a jar. Put the bones back in the liquid and continue simmering for 2 hours. Strain liquid and add very little gelatine. Pour over the meat and leave until cold. Cover with a layer of melted butter.

TO POT WOODCOCKS

Pluck 6 woodcocks, draw out the train, skewer their bills through their thighs, and put the legs through each other, and their feet upon their breasts. Season them with 3 or 4 blades of mace, and a little pepper and salt: then put them into a deep pot with 1 lb of butter over them; tie a strong paper over them, and bake them in a moderate oven; when they are tender enough, lay them on a dish to drain the gravy from them;

then put them into potting-pots, and take all the clear butter from your gravy, and put it upon them. Fill up your pots with clarified butter, and keep them in a dry place.

Thomas Train, Gateshead, 1812

POTTED KIPPERS

Remove all skins and bones from some cooked kippers, mash the flesh until nice and smooth, then add sufficient melted butter to work into a soft paste. Add pepper, and salt if required, and a pinch of nutmeg. Fill some empty paste pots with the mixture and seal with a thin layer of melted butter. This is very acceptable to someone who has been ill and needs a change of diet.

POTTED PERCH

Take the heads off your perch and the tails, and take out the insides unless the fish are less than 2 inch long. Butter a baking dish and lay them in – packing them as tight as possible. Dot with butter, sprinkle with a pinch of salt, black pepper and mace and cook very slowly with the lid on over a piece of foil for 4 hours. All the bones will have melted by this time. You can serve them in the dish in which they were cooked or pound them up and put them into individual ramekins and run clarified butter over them. For tea serve from the dish with large hunks of new bread and butter – for dinner for a first course in ramekins with thin brown bread and butter or with toast.

Mrs Chaplin, Finsthwaite, Lancs

SALMON PÂTÉ

Mince and pound cooked salmon till it will go through a sieve, then put into a dish leaving $\frac{1}{2}$ inch headroom. Pour over half the weight of the fish in butter, melted, with pinch of mace, black pepper and salt to taste, while the fish is still warm. Serve as for Potted Perch.

Mrs Chaplin, Finsthwaite, Lancs

POTTED HERRINGS

6 herrings slit down back. Do not remove tails. Remove bones; wash; dry and season; pepper and salt. Roll up; skin outside and tails uppermost. Place in pie-dish, add 2 tablespoons vinegar and 2 of water. Cover dish. Bake very slowly for 1 hour or more. Serve cold; garnish parsley.

TO POT SALMON

Let your salmon be quite fresh, scale and wash it well; dry it well with a cloth, split it up the back, and take out the bone. Season it well with white pepper and salt, a little nutmeg and mace; let it be 2 or 3 hours, then put it in your pot, with $\frac{1}{2}$ lb of butter; tie it down, put it in the oven, and bake it an hour. When it comes out, lay it on a flat dish, that the oil may run from it; cut it to the size of your pots, lay it in layers till you fill the pots, with the skin upwards; put a board over it, lay on a weight to press it till cold, then pour over it clarified butter; when you cut it, the skin makes it look ribbed. You may send it to the table either cut in slices, or in the pot.

Thomas Train, Gateshead, 1812

19 Steamed Puddings, Dumplings and Sweet Sauces

If you want a good pudding, to teach you I'm willing,
Take twopennyworth of eggs, when twelve for a shilling,
And of the same fruit that Eve had once chosen,
Well pared and well chopped at least half a dozen;
Six ounces of bread (let your maid eat the crust);
The crumbs must be grated as small as the dust;
Six ounces of currants from the stones you must sort,
Lest they break out your teeth and spoil all your sport;
Six ounces of sugar won't make it too sweet,
Some salt and some nutmeg will make it complete.
Three hours let it boil, without hurry or flutter,
And then serve it up – without sugar or butter.

Sydney Smith

The English have long been famous for their sweet puddings served after the meat course. The price of sugar fell with the opening up of trade with the East in the seventeenth century, and the serving of fruit tarts or puddings became increasingly popular with prosperous citizens about the middle of the century. These were commonly made of flour, milk, eggs, butter, suet, marrow and raisins.

SUSSEX WELL PUDDING (sometimes called POND PUDDING in some families)

½ lb self-raising flour
or ½ lb plain flour and 1
teaspoon baking powder
Pinch of salt

2–4 oz suet
1 egg (if liked)
Milk or water to mix
4–6 oz dried fruit
Filling:
Butter and brown sugar

Mix all dry ingredients, then mix to an elastic dough with milk or water. Turn on to a floured board and roll into a neat round about size of breakfast plate. Take generous portions of butter and brown sugar and place in middle of pastry. Gather edges together at the top and make secure. Tie in cloth or place in greased basin and boil for 2 hours. Serve on large dish deep enough to catch the delicious filling which comes out once the 'football' has been cut into.

LIVERPOOL PUDDING WITH LEMON SAUCE

¼ lb breadcrumbs or bread
(soaked)
¼ lb flour
¼ lb suet
2 good tablespoons treacle
1 saltspoon nutmeg (fresh
ground)
2 oz currants

1 teaspoon baking powder
2 oz brown sugar
Juice and rind of 1 lemon
2 eggs (beaten)
A little milk
¼ teaspoon salt
A little mixed peel or 1
tablespoon marmalade

Mix all dry ingredients together. Add rind and juice of lemon, and syrup. Add squeezed out bread (if soaked) and mix into other ingredients with egg and milk. Mix altogether briskly but well then pour into greased mould or bowl. Cover with greased paper and steam for 2 hours. Serve with lemon sauce if preferred or thin custard.

Lemon Sauce – Melt knob of butter or margarine in small warm saucepan. Pour into it ½ pint of lemon squash. To this add 1 good heaped teaspoon cornflour and stir till all is smoothly blended. Add ¼ pint of cold water and

cook very carefully until thick and smooth. Add a little white sugar if
needed.

GOLDEN LAYER PUDDING

½ *lb self-raising flour*	**Filling:**
3–4 oz suet	*Golden syrup*
½ *teaspoon salt*	*Breadcrumbs*
Cold water to mix	*Lemon juice*

Mix all dry ingredients then add sufficient water gradually to mix to an
elastic dough. Roll out this dough thinly and cut into rounds to fit a
1½ pint pudding basin. Spread layer of filling-mixture in bottom of basin,
then cover with layer of pastry, then filling and so on up the sides of basin
finishing with pastry. Boil for 2½ hours and turn out carefully on to hot
deep dish.

MARMALADE PUDDING (very light)

2 oz breadcrumbs	*2 oz margarine*
2 oz self-raising flour	*1 egg*
1 oz castor sugar	*1 tablespoon milk or water*
2 oz chopped mixed peel	*2 tablespoons marmalade*
1 grated lemon rind	

Rub margarine or butter into flour. Add sugar and breadcrumbs. Next
add marmalade and stir in beaten egg and milk adding more milk or
(preferably) a little water if need be to make a nice soft consistency. Boil
in lightly greased basin for 2 hours. Turn out onto hot plate.

HAMPSHIRE SIX-CUP PUDDING

1 cupful each of:	*Milk*
Self-raising flour	*A mixture of raisins,*
Breadcrumbs	*sultanas and currants*
Suet	*1 teaspoon bicarbonate of soda*
Brown sugar	

Mix all dry ingredients together except the bicarbonate of soda. Warm the
milk and dissolve bicarbonate of soda in it; allow to cool a little. Now add
milk to other ingredients. Place in greased bowl and for 4 hours steam in
just boiling water.

BERKSHIRE GINGER PUDDING

6 oz self-raising flour
3 oz golden syrup
3 oz lard

½ teaspoon ground ginger
½ gill milk
Pinch of salt

Mix flour, salt and ginger in bowl. Warm lard, syrup and milk in saucepan, taking care not to heat up too much (lukewarm if possible). Add contents of saucepan to dry ingredients and boil for 2 hours in a greased basin. Turn onto hot dish and serve with extra syrup if desired.

CHOCOLATE CRUMB PUDDING

1½ pints milk
2 level tablespoons cocoa
2 eggs, beaten
5½ oz stale breadcrumbs

2 oz sugar
½ teaspoon salt
1 teaspoon vanilla essence **or**
¼ teaspoon mixed spice

Heat milk to scalding point. Add breadcrumbs and let stand until soft. Combine cocoa, sugar and salt and add to eggs. Add egg mixture to breadcrumb mixture and stir well. Add flavouring Pour into greased pudding dish, place in a pan of hot water and bake in a moderate oven or steam about 1 hour until set. Serve hot or as party sweet, cold and decorated with whipped cream and chocolate peppermint crisps.

FRILSHAM FRUIT BATTER

2 oz margarine
4 oz self-raising flour
2 oz sugar

1 pint rhubarb—sliced,
fresh, bottled or deep frozen
can be used for this adaptable
recipe

Rub margarine into flour. Stir in salt, sugar, rhubarb and just enough milk to make a nice thick batter. Bake in a greased pie-dish for about ½ hour till batter is cooked through at 400°F (Gas Mark 6). Serve with cream or smooth thin custard.

A very simple pudding quickly made but delicious if unexpected visitors arrive.

GINGER SNAP WITH APPLE SAUCE

1½ cups ginger snap crumbs
2 oz sugar, preferably soft
brown

1 level teaspoon mixed spice
1 beaten egg
3 teacups milk

Grease a pie-dish and sprinkle in snap crumbs. Add sugar, spice and egg and milk. Mix till blended. Stand dish in baking tin to contain hot water reaching halfway up tin. Bake in a moderate oven, 350°F (Gas Mark 4) for about ½ hour until set. Serve with thinly sliced, stewed, sweetened apples.

GOOSEBERRY PUDDING

Make a suet crust with 4 oz suet, 1 oz butter and 8 oz self-raising flour, with a pinch of salt. Line a small greased pudding basin with crust, leaving enough for a lid. Top and tail gooseberries and fill basin, adding 2 oz sugar. Cover with crust, and seal edges. Cover with foil, and cook in a pan of boiling water for 2½ hours. Turn out and serve with hot apricot jam and cream.

CHERRY AND CURRANT PUDDING

Prepare a suet crust with ½ lb of flour, 4 oz of suet, 1 teaspoon of baking powder, a little salt, and about 1 gill of water. Mix the dry ingredients together, and mix them to a stiff paste with the cold water. Turn this on to a floured board, and roll it out to the size of the basin you are using, saving enough for the top. Line the basin closely with the suet crust, leaving no spaces or holes, and allow the crust to overlap the edges of the basin a little.

Half fill it with prepared cherries and currants, and then add 1 oz of brown sugar, and fill up with fruit. Turn the overlapping edges in towards the basin and fit on the piece of crust reserved for the top, tie the pudding down with a scalded and well-floured cloth, and boil for about 2 hours.

1911

CURRANT AND APPLE PUDDING

Rub together 4 oz of sugar and 2 oz of cooking butter until it is thick and creamy. Then add 1 unbeaten egg, 4 oz of flour and 1 good teaspoon of baking powder. Mix well together and add sufficient milk to form a rather stiff batter. Beat the ingredients thoroughly well together, adding 3 small chopped up apples (in dice) and ½ a cupful of prepared currants.

Turn the mixture into a well-buttered mould and steam it for not less than 1½ hours – custard sauce is the correct accompaniment.

1911

OXFORD PUDDING

6 oz self-raising flour
2 oz ground rice
4 oz chopped suet
4 oz thick marmalade

4 oz golden syrup
1 egg, beaten
2 tablespoons milk
2 oz soft brown sugar

Grease a 1½ pint basin and press the sugar round sides and on the base.

Sift flour and rice, stir in suet, syrup and marmalade, and mix with egg and milk. Turn into basin, cover down and steam for 3 hours. Serve with warmed syrup.

STEAMED CARAMEL PUDDING

Caramel:
3 oz granulated sugar
3 tablespoons water

Sponge:
3 oz butter
3 oz castor sugar
2 eggs (separated)
6 oz self-raising flour
6 tablespoons milk

Put the sugar and water into a small pan over a very gentle heat, and leave until a light golden brown. Pour into a warmed 2 pint basin and coat the inside. Cream the butter and sugar together until light and fluffy and beat in the egg yolks. Add the flour and milk a little at a time. Whisk the egg whites until stiff and lightly fold into the mixture. Put into the basin. Butter a piece of greaseproof paper and make a pleat in it. Secure it over the basin and tie with string. Steam for 1½ hours. Turn out on to a warm plate and serve at once, with sugar.

BAKED GINGER FRUIT PUDDING WITH SYRUP SAUCE

4 oz butter
4 oz castor sugar
2 eggs
2 tablespoons milk
4 oz self-raising flour
Pinch of salt
½ level teaspoon ground ginger
1 oz stem or crystallised

ginger (chopped)
3 oz sultanas

Sauce:
6 rounded tablespoons golden syrup
1 tablespoon lemon juice

Cream butter, add sugar and beat together until light and fluffy. Beat in eggs, 1 at a time, with a little of the flour. Add milk. Sieve in remaining flour, with the salt and ground ginger. Add chopped ginger and sultanas, and fold into mixture lightly until well mixed. Turn mixture into a well-buttered 2-pint ovenproof dish and bake in a moderate oven, 350°F (Gas Mark 4) for about an hour. To make sauce, heat together the syrup and lemon juice, stirring. Turn out pudding, and serve with sauce.

SPICED ORANGE PUDDING

3 oz butter
2 oz soft brown sugar
Grated zest of 1 orange
3 oz black treacle
1 large egg

6 oz self-raising flour
1 teaspoon ground cinnamon
1½ oz chopped glacé cherries
2 oz seeded raisins or chopped dates

Grease 1½-pint pudding basin and line bottom with a circle of greased paper. Cream butter, sugar and orange zest until light and fluffy. Beat in treacle. Whisk egg and add gradually. Stir in sifted flour and cinnamon and lastly add fruit. Turn into pudding basin, cover with foil and steam 1½ to 1¾ hours. Turn out and serve with orange sauce.

Orange Sauce – Make up the juice of 2 oranges to ½ pint with water. Blend a little of this with 1 level tablespoon of cornflour and stir this into heated juice. Bring to boil, stirring. Sweeten to taste.

OLD-FASHIONED RHUBARB PUDDING

1 oz butter
Brown sugar

Suet Crust:
8 oz self-raising flour
1 teaspoon salt
3 oz suet
¼ pint water

Filling:
1½ lb young rhubarb
1 oz chopped candied peel
2 oz currants
Grated rind and juice of
½ lemon
4 oz sugar
Pinch of cinnamon
½ teacup water

Butter 2-pint pudding basin thickly and sprinkle plentifully with brown sugar. Make suet crust by sieving together flour and salt and working in suet and water. Knead pastry until smooth and cut off one-third pastry for lid. Line the basin with suet crust. Cut rhubarb into 1 inch pieces and put half into the basin. Sprinkle over peel, currants, lemon rind and juice, half the sugar, and the cinnamon. Add the rest of the rhubarb and sugar, and pour in water. Cover with suet crust lid, and a greased paper on top. Bake at 350°F (Gas Mark 4) for 1¼ hours. Turn out to serve, with cream or egg custard.

GREAT GRANDMA'S STIR-IN PUDDING

1 *lb self-raising flour* ⎫ *Rub together to fine crumbs*
7 *oz lard* ⎬ *and add ½ lb sugar*
½ *teaspoon salt* ⎭

Stir in prepared gooseberries, chopped apple, halved plums or chopped rhubarb. Mix with sufficient milk and water to make a soft dough which will drop easily but cleanly into a greased basin. Cover with butter paper and then foil. Steam 2 hours. Serve with fresh cream or smooth, creamy custard.

This is an old Dorset recipe, handed down from generation to generation; very adaptable and useful.

GINGER FRUIT PUDDING

8 *oz self-raising flour*
½ *level teaspoon salt*
2 *rounded teaspoons ginger*
4 *oz butter or margarine*
3 *oz soft brown sugar*

4 *oz mixed dried fruit*
2 *large eggs, beaten*
Approximately 6 tablespoons milk to mix

Sift together dry ingredients, rub in fat, add sugar and fruit, then stirring briskly, mix to a soft dropping consistency with the beaten eggs and milk. Turn into a very well-greased fluted mould. Cover with greaseproof paper or aluminium foil, and steam steadily for 1½ hours. Turn out on to a warm dish and serve with Marmalade Sauce.
Marmalade Sauce – Blend 4 tablespoons marmalade with 2 tablespoons water in a saucepan. Heat gently until boiling.

BLACKCURRANT JAM PUDDING

6 *oz self-raising flour*
3 *oz butter or margarine*
2 *oz soft white breadcrumbs*
2 *oz castor sugar*
1 *level teaspoon salt*

2 *tablespoons blackcurrant jam*
2 *eggs, well beaten*
2 *tablespoons milk*

Rub fat into flour, then add breadcrumbs, sugar and salt. Stir in the jam and eggs, then mix to a slack consistency with the milk. Well-grease a pudding basin or mould, put a little jam in the bottom, then fill with the pudding mixture. Cover with greased paper or aluminium foil, and steam for 1½ hours. Turn out and serve warm with additional jam and sour cream, sweetened to taste with icing sugar and sprinkled with nutmeg.

323

SYRUP SPONGE PUDDING

4 oz butter or margarine	2 standard eggs
4 oz sugar	6 tablespoons milk
4 level tablespoons golden	8 oz self-raising flour
syrup	Pinch of salt

Cream fat, sugar and 2 tablespoons syrup till light and fluffy. Beat in eggs, one at a time, then fold in sifted dry ingredients alternately with the milk, to make a fairly slack mixture. Well-grease a 2 pint fancy mould or pudding basin and pour in remaining syrup. Top with pudding mixture, spread evenly, then hollow out centre slightly. Cover with aluminium foil or with 2 sheets of greased greaseproof paper. Steam for 2 hours. Turn out on to a warm dish.

APPLE SUET ROLL

Sift 8 oz self-raising flour, a pinch of salt and a pinch of mixed spice into a bowl and stir in 4 oz shredded suet. Mix well and add enough cold water gradually to form a pliable dough. Roll out $\frac{1}{8}$ inch thick into an oblong. Peel, core and chop 1 large cooking apple and put on pastry, leaving 1 inch uncovered at each side. Sprinkle with 2 oz cleaned currants, 2 oz soft brown sugar, grated rind of 1 lemon and 2 tablespoons golden syrup. Roll up pastry and tie in a piece of clean cloth, securing firmly. Put into top of steamer or into a large pan of boiling water, and cook for 2 hours.

BAKEWELL PUDDING

Yolks of 5 eggs	4 oz butter
Whites of 3 eggs	Almond essence
6 oz castor sugar	Strawberry jam

Line flan ring or baking tin with puff pastry, spread with jam. Melt together butter and sugar, mix in egg yolks and whites and essence, bake in hot oven, 350°F (Gas Mark 4) for 25 minutes.

The first Bakewell Pudding was the result of a misunderstanding between the mistress of the Rutland Arms Inn, Mrs Greaves, and her cook. Mrs Greaves was the wife of William Greaves, who kept the inn in the coaching days of the last century. On a day when important visitors were expected Mrs Greaves instructed her cook how she wanted the pastry made for the strawberry tart; the egg mixture was to be mixed into the pastry. The cook misunderstood her mistress and poured it on top of the jam and what should have been a tart went to the table as a pudding. When the guests complimented Mrs Greaves on her pudding she was mystified and questioned her cook who confessed what she had done. Mrs Greaves' very words to her cook were 'Continue to make them in that way', and so they have been made for 100 years.

Mrs Burton, Kirk Langley, near Derby

GRANNY'S SIX CUP PUDDING

1 *teacup flour*	1 *teacup currants*
1 *teacup sugar*	1 *teacup raisins*
1 *teacup breadcrumbs*	2 *large eggs*
1 *teacup grated suet (from*	*Allspice to taste*
the butcher if possible)	*Candied peel if liked*

Beat eggs. Sieve flour and spice, add dry ingredients together then eggs and mix well. Almost fill basins with mixture. Steam 3 hours. The longer the steaming the darker the pudding. These puddings can be reheated as desired.

Mrs Naylor's grannie came to Lancashire almost 100 years ago as a nurse maid. This recipe was used at the house where she was employed. She used it herself for Christmas puddings and Mrs Naylor prefers it for Christmas and usually makes about half a dozen.

Mrs Naylor, Cowpe, Rossendale

BROWN BREAD PUDDING

6 *oz brown breadcrumbs*	2 *oz raisins (or chopped*
½ *pint milk*	*candied peel)*
3 *oz butter*	*Grating of nutmeg*
4 *oz sugar*	1 *teaspoon cinnamon*
3 *eggs*	*Pinch of salt*

Put breadcrumbs in a bowl and pour on hot milk. Add the spices, raisins, salt. Cream butter and sugar, and add the eggs one at a time. Gradually work in the breadcrumb mixture. Put into a well-buttered mould, cover with foil or buttered paper and steam for 2 hours. Serve with jam, fruit syrup or custard.

LEMON PUDDING

Take 4 oz each of breadcrumbs, suet, flour and sugar. Mix with this a teaspoon of baking powder, the grated rind and juice of 1 lemon, and

2 well-beaten eggs. Stir all well together, place in a buttered mould, and steam for 3 hours. Serve with any sweet sauce preferred. Tried with great success.

Mrs F. Arden, Swinton, Manchester, 1911

TREACLE PUDDING

2 teacups of flour, 2 teacups of breadcrumbs, 4 oz of beef suet, 1 teaspoon of ground ginger, 4 tablespoons of treacle, and a little milk. Chop the suet fine, then mix with the other dry ingredients. Put the treacle and milk in a basin, and stir until thoroughly mixed. Then pour into the dry ingredients, and mix well. Put into a greased basin, and steam about 3 hours. Serve with sweet sauce.

Miss Kathleen Brooks, Hove, 1911

SYRUP SPONGE

1 heaped breakfastcup flour	**2 eggs**
1 teacup sugar	**3 tablespoons syrup**
¼ lb butter	**A little milk**
2 tablespoons baking powder	

Butter a basin, and pour in the syrup. Mix flour and baking powder together, and rub in butter with hands till it has the appearance of breadcrumbs; add sugar. Well beat eggs and sufficient milk to make a nice consistency. Pour into basin, and steam for 3 hours.

1911

SUSSEX PLUM DUFF

1¼ cups pastry flour	**1 cup raisins**
⅔ cup suet	**1 cup currants**
⅔ cup brown sugar	**Pinch of mixed spice**
Milk to mix	

Chop the suet finely, then rub into the flour. Mix in the sugar, raisins, currants, and spice and mix to a stiff paste with a little milk. Put the paste into a floured cloth, tie up like a ball and drop into a pan of boiling water. Boil for 1½ hours.

CHOCOLATE CHIP SPONGE PUDDING

*4 oz chocolate or chocolate
chips
4 oz margarine
4 oz castor sugar
2 eggs*

*8 oz plain flour
2 level teaspoons baking
powder
Milk to mix*

If you are using block chocolate, use the plain variety, and cut it into neat pieces with a sharp knife before starting to make the pudding. Cream margarine and sugar and beat in each egg separately. Fold in sieved flour and baking powder, and add milk to give a soft dropping consistency (if liked, add a little orange or lemon essence too). Stir in chocolate, and put into a greased pudding basin or a fireproof oven dish. Steam for 1 hour, or bake at 425°F (Gas Mark 7) for 15 minutes, then lower heat to 375°F (Gas Mark 5) for 30 minutes. Serve with jam sauce or chocolate sauce.

SPICED APPLE AND RAISIN PUDDING

*½ lb cooking apples
2 tablespoons water
12 oz self-raising flour
1 level teaspoon cinnamon
½ level teaspoon mixed spice
3 oz butter*

*1 oz walnuts
3 oz stoned raisins
4 oz soft brown sugar
2 eggs
4 tablespoons milk*

Lightly grease a 1½ pint pudding mould or basin. Peel, core and slice apples and stew in water. Cool and sieve. Sieve flour, cinnamon and spice, rub in butter, and add chopped walnuts and raisins and sugar. Lightly beat eggs and fold into dry ingredients, together with apple purée. Blend well, adding enough milk to make a soft dropping consistency. Put into the mould and cover with greased greaseproof paper and foil. Steam for 2½ hours. Serve with a jam or honey sauce.

KISS ME QUICK PUDDING

*2 eggs and their weight in
flour, sugar and butter*

*2 tablespoons raspberry jam
1 small teaspoon soda (bicarb)*

All beaten up. Steam it 1 hour and ½.

Mrs Garden, 1847

MRS TOWNLEY'S FULBOURN APPLE PUDDING

Peel 2 dozen russetts, remove the cores and cut them in slices. Put them into a deep saucepan with 4 oz butter, the rind of 2 lemons, 12 oz pounded sugar and 1 lb apricot jam. Toss the whole over a slow stove fire until the apples begin to dissolve and then set them aside to cool. Next, line a good-sized basin with some light-made suet paste. Fill this with the prepared apples – place a covering of paste on the top and fasten it down securely and steam it for about 2 hours. It may also be served up with some warm apricot jam poured over it. This apple preparation is also best for apple Charlottes or for apples served with rice, or whipped cream.

Mrs Garden, 1847

DRIPPING PUDDINGS

The weight of 3 eggs in their shells in dripping, $\frac{1}{2}$ teacup currants, tablespoon powdered sugar, flour to thicken. Beat up the 3 eggs, add the sugar and currants also the dripping (melted if too hard); beat up all together, thickening it with flour, but do not make it too stiff or they will not be light. Bake in small tins.

Mrs Garden, 1847

MANOR HOUSE MARROW PUDDING

Take 1 pint of breadcrumbs, $\frac{1}{2}$ pint of currants, $\frac{1}{2}$ lb of raisins, lemon and orange peel, $\frac{1}{2}$ lb suet cut very fine – the marrow out of a round of beef bone is the best if you have it. Mix all together then take a small piece of puff paste and line the dish you intend to bake it in with the paste. Fill the dish half full of the mixture. Take 6 eggs beaten well, as much sugar as will sweeten to your taste, 1 quart of new milk and mix with the eggs, nutmeg according to fancy. Put in $\frac{1}{2}$ glass of brandy. Pour this custard in the dish with the other mixtures. It will take $1\frac{1}{4}$ hours to bake. From the Manor House, Brentwood.

Mrs Garden, 1847

BAKED APPLE PUDDING

Take 6 apples cut small and simmer them in a pan with lemon peel, lump sugar and cinnamon and cloves according to your taste. Boil a lemon whole till quite soft, beat it up and mix it with the apples. Take 6 yolks and 4 whites of eggs, beat them up and when the apples are quite cold, stir them together. Then have it baked with a paste round it. Strew almonds on the top. This recipe, and variations on it, appear in a number of old manuscript books, but Mrs Garden's version is the easiest and clearest. Possibly it was copied from a popular book or magazine of the period.

Mrs Garden, 1847

1898 CUP PUDDING

1 *breakfastcup flour*   1 *oz butter*
½ *cup sugar*   1 *egg*
1 *teaspoon baking powder*   *A little milk*
1 *oz lard*

Butter basin and fill half full of jam. Put in mixture and steam for 2 hours.
Miss Jeffrey, Hambledon, Hants.

1898 JAM SPONGE

2 eggs, their weight in flour and butter, the weight of one in sugar; 3 tablespoons strawberry jam. Mix altogether. Butter a basin well and fill it 3 parts full. Steam it for 2 hours.

Miss Jeffrey, Hambledon, Hants

1898 TREACLE SPONGE

½ *lb treacle*   2 *oz suet*
1 *teacup milk*   2 *teaspoons baking powder*
¾ *lb flour*

Warm milk and treacle. Boil 3 hours.   *Miss Jeffrey, Hambledon, Hants*

COTTAGE PUDDING

2½ *oz shredded suet*   4 *tablespoons milk*
8 *oz flour*   ½ *tablespoon cream of tartar*
4 *oz stoned raisins*   ¼ *teaspoon bicarbonate of soda*
4 *oz sugar*   *Pinch of salt*
1 *egg*

Mix the suet, flour, raisins, sugar, cream of tartar and salt together. Dissolve the soda in the milk, add it to the well-beaten egg, mix well, and stir into the dry ingredients. The mixture must be rather stiff, but at the same time, thoroughly moistened. Turn into a greased Yorkshire pudding tin, and bake in a moderate oven from 30 to 40 minutes. Cut the pudding into squares, and serve, after dusting it over with white sugar.

GERMAN PUDDING

1 *lb flour*   ½ *oz spice*
½ *lb golden syrup*   ½ *oz ground ginger*
½ *lb suet*   *Pinch of salt*
1 *oz sugar*

Mix the syrup with a little milk slightly warmed. Mix all together, put into a greased basin, tie down and boil $3\frac{1}{2}$ hours.

Lewis' Mother's Cookbook, Mary Horrell, Exeter

HIGH CHURCH PUDDING

Take $\frac{1}{2}$ lb fine flour and nearly $\frac{1}{2}$ lb chopped suet, 1 teacup of jam, 1 of milk, 1 teaspoon of bicarbonate of soda. Mix together, put in a buttered basin and tie loosely, and boil slowly 2 hours as the pudding will swell Serve with wine sauce.

Lewis' Mother's Cookbook, Mary Horrell, Exeter

PRUSSIAN PUDDING

Stew very slowly until quite dry and tender 3 oz of well-washed rice in rather more than a pint of milk. Let it cool a little, then mix it with 3 oz of finely rolled and rubbed suet. Add a little finely shredded candied peel, 3 oz of raisins or sultanas carefully picked over, and a couple of well-beaten eggs. Boil in a well-greased basin for 2 hours. Serve with custard sauce.

Lewis' Mother's Cookbook, Mary Horrell, Exeter

SPICED HONEY PUDDING

Boil $\frac{3}{4}$ pint milk and stir in 2 oz semolina. Cook for a few minutes, stirring all the time, then pour into a basin. To this add 4 oz honey, 4 oz breadcrumbs, the juice and grated rind of a lemon, 1 teaspoon ground ginger, 4 egg yolks and 2 oz butter. Beat well, then fold in well-beaten whites of 3 eggs. Put in a buttered dish and steam for an hour. Serve with melted redcurrant jelly.

BOILED BATTER PUDDING

Take a quart of milk, beat up the yolks of 6 eggs, and the whites of 3, and mix them with a $\frac{1}{4}$ pint of milk. Then take 6 spoonfuls of flour, a teaspoon of salt, and 1 of ginger. Put to these the remainder of the milk, mix all well together, put into your cloth, and boil it $1\frac{1}{4}$ hours. Pour melted butter over it when you serve it up. A batter pudding may be made without eggs, in which case proceed thus: take a quart of milk, mix 6 spoonfuls of flour with a little of the milk first, a teaspoon of salt, 2 of beaten ginger, and 2 of the tincture of saffron. Then mix all together, and boil it an hour.

Thomas Train, Gateshead, 1812

JEAN'S STEAMED PUDDING

2 oz breadcrumbs
2 oz castor sugar
2 oz suet
2 tablespoons golden syrup

1 egg
Milk mixed with small
½ teaspoon bicarbonate of soda
Add ginger if liked

Pouring mixture. Steam for 1½–2 hours.

Pat Smith, Keynsham, Somerset

DATE PUDDING

¾ cup plain flour
1 teaspoon bicarbonate soda
¾ cup boiling milk
1 tablespoon sugar or golden syrup

¼ lb dates or other dried fruit
1 tablespoon fat (suet, lard, margarine or dripping)
Small teaspoon vanilla essence

Put sugar, fat, soda, dates in greased basin, pour over boiling milk, quickly stir in flour, add essence. Mix well. Steam at once for 1 hour or a little less.

NEWCASTLE PUDDING

2 oz butter
2 oz castor sugar
3 oz flour
¾ teaspoon baking powder

2 eggs
1 teaspoon vanilla essence
4 oz glacé cherries

Beat butter and sugar to a cream. Sift flour with baking powder, and add flour and eggs alternately. Beat well and add essence. Grease a mould and decorate with halved cherries. Pour in mixture and steam 1¼ hours. Pour *Jam Sauce* round dish. Make this by boiling 2 tablespoons raspberry jam and 2 oz sugar with 1 gill water. Add ½ teaspoon arrowroot mixed with a little water. Bring to the boil and serve.

GYPSY PUDDING

12 oz shredded suet
1 lb currants
1 lb raisins
1 lb breadcrumbs
1 lb sugar
8 oz mixed peel
8 oz apples
8 oz flour

8 oz grated carrots
4 oz chopped blanched almonds
6 eggs
½ oz mixed spice
1 teaspoon baking powder
1 teaspoon vanilla essence

Add a silver thimble for the old maid, a button for the old bachelor, a nut for wealth, a ring for marriage, and a sixpence for good luck. Steam for 6 hours when made and 3 hours more when wanted. Will keep for months if well steamed at making.

WELCOME GUEST PUDDING

$1\frac{1}{2}$ oz almonds
2 oz shredded suet
4 oz breadcrumbs
2 oz sugar

$1\frac{1}{2}$ oz candied lemon peel
1 gill milk
2 eggs
1 teaspoon vanilla essence

Blanch the almonds and chop roughly. Mix the suet, breadcrumbs, sugar and peel. Beat together the milk, eggs and essence, and mix into dry ingredients. Pour into greased basin, cover with greased paper and steam for 1 hour 20 minutes.

SOUTHPORT PUDDING

6 oz apples (weighed after peeling)
6 oz breadcrumbs
3 oz suet

6 oz brown sugar
Good pinch of nutmeg
1 oz candied peel
2 eggs

Grate the apples and mix with breadcrumbs, suet, sugar, nutmeg and peel. Mix with beaten eggs and pour into a greased basin. Steam for 2 hours. Serve with a sweetened apple sauce flavoured with cloves.

APPLE DUMPLINGS

8 oz flour
4 oz suet
1 level teaspoon salt
2 level teaspoons baking powder

1 gill water
3 lb Bramley's Seedling apples
3 oz sugar

Sift flour and baking powder, add salt, mix in suet. Mix to a soft dough with water. Divide pastry in 2 pieces of $\frac{1}{3}$ and $\frac{2}{3}$. Grease a 2 pint basin, line it with $\frac{2}{3}$ of the suet crust. Peel, core and slice the apples. Put half the apples into the lined basin, add the sugar then the rest of the apple. Cover the pudding with the remaining $\frac{1}{3}$ of the suet crust and seal edges. Cover basin with greased greaseproof paper or kitchen foil. Steam for 2 to 3 hours until fruit and pastry are cooked. Turn out and serve very hot.

FRUIT DUMPLINGS

Three-quarters fill a small basin or stone jam jar with any fresh fruit. Sprinkle with sugar, cover with saucer. Place in a large saucepan with water coming half-way up basin. Cover, boil till fruit is soft.

Rub $\frac{1}{2}$ teaspoon butter or margarine into 2 tablespoons self-raising flour and a pinch of salt. Mix quickly with water to soft dough, divide into 4, drop on top of fruit. Cover closely. Simmer for 10–15 minutes. Serve straight from basin.

Mrs L. Ward, London

QUICK FRUIT DUMPLINGS

2 cups flour
2 teaspoons baking powder
½ teaspoon salt
1 tablespoon sugar

1 cup milk
2 tablespoons fat
Large bottle cherries or blackberries

Rub fat into flour and other dry ingredients and make into very soft dough with milk. Bring the fruit and juice to boil, using pan that has tight lid. When boiling, drop dumpling mixture by tablespoons on to fruit, cover at once, very tightly, cook without raising lid 15 minutes. Serve hot.

CLOOTIE DUMPLING (1)

3 oz plain flour
3 oz breadcrumbs
3 oz chopped suet
2 oz sugar
1 tablespoon golden syrup
¾ cup milk or sour milk

1 teaspoon ground cinnamon
1 teaspoon ground nutmeg
2 oz currants
2 oz sultanas
1 level teaspoon bicarbonate of soda

When mixed, tie in a cloth. Boil for at least 2 hours. Serve with sauce or custard. This is from a farmer's widow with many grandchildren, who still rears calves for her son.

Mrs Corrie, Burnside of Auchengool, Kirkcudbright

CLOOTIE DUMPLING (2)

4 teacups flour
1½ teaspoons baking powder
2 teaspoons cinnamon
1 teaspoon mixed spice
¼ lb chopped suet

1 cup sugar
½ lb raisins (blue)
½ lb sultanas
¼ teaspoon salt
(Peel if desired)

Mix dry ingredients, add fruit and enough milk to mix to fairly stiff consistency. Have pot boiling with a plate on the bottom. Dip cloth in boiling water. Sprinkle cloth with flour; shape dumpling into round on cloth and tie securely. Put into boiling water and make sure water does *not* cover dumpling. Keep at boiling point for $3\frac{1}{2}$–4 hours.

A very old recipe – can be eaten hot as a pudding or sliced cold and fried with bacon. Mrs Usher says she finds this 'disastrous for one's figure, but very useful for filling the bottomless holes inside our seven grandchildren'.

Mrs Antonia Usher, Argyll

FLUFFY BRANDY SAUCE

1 *egg separated*
4 *oz icing sugar*

$\frac{1}{4}$ *pint whipped double cream*
3 *tablespoons brandy*

Beat the egg white until it is foamy. Add 2 oz of the icing sugar, a little at a time, beating well after each addition until the mixture is stiff enough to stand up in peaks. In a second bowl, beat the egg yolk and remaining 2 oz sugar until the mixture thickens. Fold into the egg white and sugar mixture together with the whipped cream and brandy.

This sauce can be made in advance and kept in the refrigerator until needed. It is good with rich fruit puddings.

SPICED APPLE SAUCE

1 *lb cooking apples*
4 *oz granulated sugar*
2 *tablespoons water*

$\frac{1}{4}$ *teaspoon cinnamon*
$\frac{1}{8}$ *teaspoon grated nutmeg*

Wash, core and peel apples. Cut into quarters, and place in a medium-sized saucepan with granulated sugar, water, cinnamon and nutmeg. Simmer gently for 20 to 25 minutes, stirring occasionally. Serve with light fruit puddings.

20 Pies and Tarts

'Miss Bates, let Emma help you to a little bit of tart – a very little bit. Ours are all apple tarts. You need not be afraid of unwholesome preserves here. I do not advise the custard.'

'Emma', Jane Austen

KENTISH APPLE TART

Grate 2 large cooking apples in basin, add 3 oz sugar, 1 beaten egg, 2 oz butter, rind and juice of lemon. Mix well. Pour into pastry case and bake about ½ hour in quick oven.

Mrs Padgham, Minehead, Somerset

NORFOLK APPLE PIE

Roll out 12 oz short pastry and line a deep pie plate or an 8 inch sandwich tin with half of it.

2 lb cooking apples
Small knob of butter
1 tablespoon granulated sugar

2 tablespoons orange
marmalade
1 tablespoon cleaned currants

Peel, core and slice the apples and cook them without any water, adding the small knob of butter to prevent burning. When they are soft, stir in the sugar and beat them to a pulp. Pour half of this into the pastry case, spread over the marmalade, and sprinkle on the currants. Put the remaining apple pulp on the top. Make a lid from the other piece of pastry and put on top. Trim and decorate the edges. Bake in a hot oven, 400°F (Gas Mark 6) for about 15 minutes, then reduce heat to 350°F (Gas Mark 4) for a further 20–25 minutes. Dredge the top with castor sugar and serve hot with custard or cream.

BLACKBERRY PIE

1½ *lb large ripe blackberries*
2 *tablespoons butter*
1 *lb sugar*
4 *tablespoons cornflour*
8 *oz short pastry*

Butter a deep pie dish and put in 1 lb of blackberries. Dot with butter and stir in 6 oz sugar. Cook remaining blackberries with the rest of the sugar and very little water until soft, and put through a sieve. Thicken with cornflour blended with 6 tablespoons water. Pour over the raw berries and cover with pastry. Bake at 400°F (Gas Mark 6) until lightly brown, then reduce heat to 350°F (Gas Mark 4) and cook for 30 minutes. Serve cool with cream.

FEN COUNTRY APPLE CAKE

1½ *lb cooking apples, peeled, cored and sliced*
Juice of ½ *lemon*
1 *oz butter*
2 *oz castor sugar*
2 *rounded tablespoons semolina*
6-8 *oz short pastry or rough puff pastry*
1 *oz currants, washed and dried*
3 *level tablespoons black treacle*

Put apples, lemon juice and butter into a pan, cover, then simmer slowly till soft and pulpy. Add sugar and semolina, bring very slowly to the boil, then cook gently for 5 to 7 minutes or till mixture has thickened. Remove from heat and leave till completely cold.

Divide pastry in two. Roll out 1 portion and with it line a 7–8 inch heatproof plate. Spread with half apple filling to within ½ inch of edges; sprinkle with currants and add treacle then top with remaining filling. Roll out rest of pastry into an 8–9 inch round, moisten edges with water and cover pie. Press edges well together to seal and knock up with the back of a knife. Brush top with beaten egg or milk then bake towards top of a hot oven, 425°F (Gas Mark 7) for 25–30 minutes or till pale gold.

RAISIN PASTRY

12 oz short pastry
2 level tablespoons oatmeal

2 tablespoons black treacle
3 oz raisins

Roll out the pastry thinly and use half to line 1 inch plate. Cover with the oatmeal and pour on the treacle. Sprinkle the raisins evenly over the tart. Moisten the edges of the tart with water and cover with the rest of the pastry. Press edges together to seal, and trim off surplus pastry. Flute the edges. Bake in a hot oven, 425°F (Gas Mark 7) for 20–30 minutes. Serve hot or cold.

ELDERBERRY PIE

1 lb elderberries (use ripe
elderberries, stripped from
stalks)
1 tablespoon golden syrup

Warm water
2 or 3 cloves
$\frac{1}{2}$ lb pastry

Nearly fill pie-dish with berries, add cloves. Sweeten with syrup. Pour over 2 or more tablespoons water according to size of pie. Cover with pastry. Bake in brisk oven till crust is browned. Then lower heat and allow fruit to simmer for a further 10–15 minutes.

PEACH PIE

Flaky pastry
1 lb fresh peaches or large can
peach halves

4 oz ground almonds
4 oz icing sugar
3 eggs

Line a pie plate with pastry. Arrange peach halves (strain if using canned). Add almonds and icing sugar to the well-beaten eggs and pour over the peaches. Bake in a moderate oven until brown.

FRUIT AND ALMOND TART

8 oz plain flour
1 teaspoon cinnamon
2 oz castor sugar
4 oz lard
1 egg yolk
2 tablespoons cold water

4 egg whites
6 oz castor sugar
4 oz ground almonds
1½ lb cooked fruit (plums,
gooseberries, rhubarb)

Sift flour with a pinch of salt, cinnamon and 2 oz castor sugar, and rub in lard until mixture is like fine breadcrumbs. Beat egg yolk with water and use to make a stiff dough; leave in cold place for 15 minutes. Whisk egg whites until stiff and fold in sugar and ground almonds. Roll out pastry and line 9 inch flan ring. Spread egg mixture in pastry case and arrange well-drained fruit over filling. Bake at 400°F (Gas Mark 6) for 10 minutes, then at 350°F (Gas Mark 4) for 35 minutes. This is a party pie which is particularly good with early rhubarb or cooked dried apricots.

RASPBERRY PIE

Lay into a tart dish a border of puff paste and 1½ pints of fresh raspberries well mixed with 3 oz sugar. Beat thoroughly 3 large eggs with 3 oz more sugar and pour over the fruit. Bake the pudding 25–30 minutes in a moderate oven 350°F (Gas Mark 4).

MRS C'S SPECIAL FLAN

1 × 8 *inch flan case*	4 *oz currants*
2 *oz castor sugar*	1 *oz glacé cherries*
2 *oz butter*	½ *teaspoon mixed spice*
4 *eggs*	2 *drops vanilla essence*
4 *oz sultanas*	1 *wineglass sherry*

The pastry case should be about 2 inches deep. Bake the flan case until it is just set but not coloured. Beat together butter and sugar, the egg yolks, and 2 of the egg whites. Add the sultanas and currants, cherries, spice, essence and sherry. Whip the remaining egg whites until very stiff and fold in carefully. Pour into the pastry case. Bake at 350°F (Gas Mark 4) for about 25 minutes until set and golden brown. Serve with cream. It makes a change from mince pies.

AUNT LUCY'S OPEN APPLE TART

2 *oz butter*	*Almonds and raisins, if liked*
1 *cup sugar*	*Pastry*
1 *good-sized lemon*	1 *egg*
1 *large apple*	

Melt butter, stir in sugar and beaten egg. Add finely chopped apple, the grated rind and juice of the lemon and almonds and raisins if liked (but these are only for festive occasions). Stir all ingredients well together. Line a pie-dish with sweet pastry. Pour in the mixture and bake.

STRAWBERRY FLAN

4 *oz plain flour*	2 *oz castor sugar*
Pinch of salt	1 *lb strawberries*
Yolk of 1 *large egg*	6 *tablespoons raspberry*
2 *oz butter*	*jelly or jam*

Sieve flour and salt on to pastry board, and shape into a circle. In the centre of the circle, put the egg yolk, sugar and butter, and use the tips of the fingers to pinch these ingredients together. Gradually work in the flour, using a palette knife to push in the flour from the outside ring. When the dough is made, knead lightly until free of cracks. The mixture is soft and delicate but should not be made too dry with additional flour. Wrap the dough in greaseproof paper and leave to rest in a cool place for an hour before using. Roll mixture and put into a flan ring (handle it very carefully), and bake blind at 400°F (Gas Mark 6) for 30 minutes. Remove flan ring and allow pastry to finish until it is light golden in colour. Cool completely. Arrange strawberries in neat circles on pastry. Melt jam or jelly with 3 tablespoons water (sieve if jam is used) until a smooth syrup is achieved. Glaze the strawberries by spooning this syrup lightly over them, starting in the centre of the flan and working outwards, and being careful to avoid the pastry edge.

ALMOND FRUIT TART

½ lb plain flour
Good pinch of salt
1 teaspoon cinnamon
2 oz castor sugar
4 oz lard
1 egg yolk
1-2 tablespoons cold water

Filling:
4 egg whites
6 oz castor sugar
4 oz ground almonds
1½ lb cooked fruit (plums,
gooseberries, rhubarb,
apricots)

Sift flour, salt, cinnamon and sugar and rub in lard until the mixture resembles fine breadcrumbs. Beat egg yolk with a little cold water and use to form a firm dough. Allow to relax for 15 minutes.

Whisk egg whites until stiff and fold in sugar and ground almonds. Roll out the pastry to line a 9 inch flan ring and spread the egg mixture in the pastry case. Drain the fruit thoroughly and arrange over the filling. Bake at 400–425°F (Gas Mark 6–7) for about 10 minutes: then reduce temperature to 350°F (Gas Mark 4) and cook for a further 30–35 minutes until the pastry is browned.

RHUBARB AND ORANGE TART

For the flan:
4 oz plain flour
1 tablespoon cornflour
1¼ oz lard
1¼ oz margarine

1 teaspoon castor sugar
Lemon juice
Pinch of salt
Cold water to mix
1 egg yolk

Sieve the flour, cornflour and salt. Rub in the fats. Add the sugar, stir in the beaten egg yolk and a few drops of lemon juice. Mix to a stiff dough with cold water. Roll out thinly and line a large flan case with it.

For the filling:

1½ *lb rhubarb*	1 *heaped teaspoon cornflour*
3 *dessertspoons castor sugar*	*A little boiling water*
	2 *oranges*

Wipe the rhubarb and cut into very small pieces. Keep the skin on unless it really is stringy and tough. Arrange in the pastry case in circles. You may have to pile it up a bit in the middle. Sprinkle with sugar. Now heat up the juice of the oranges with a little boiling water and a little sugar. Mix cornflour to a smooth paste with a little water and pour the boiling fruit juice over it, stirring constantly. Return to pan and stir till boiling. Pour over the rhubarb, covering it all if possible. Bake in a fairly hot oven for about 25 minutes.

ORANGE TART

½ *pint milk*	2 or 3 *oranges*
2 *eggs*	2 *tablespoons marmalade*
1 *tablespoon flour*	*A few drops rum essence or*
1 *dessertspoon cornflour*	1 *dessertspoon rum (optional)*
2 *tablespoons sugar*	*Flaky pastry*

Bring the milk to the boil. Meanwhile separate the egg yolks from the whites. Mix the egg yolks with the flours and sugar, blend thoroughly. Slowly add the boiled milk. Return to the saucepan over a low heat, stirring all the time until the mixture thickens. Remove from heat. Add the grated rind of 1 orange and stir in the marmalade. Leave to cool. Add the rum or essence and fold in the stiffly beaten egg whites.

Have ready the pastry case on a plate, fill with orange cream and cover with thinly sliced orange. (I have seen it with the peel left on – although it looks prettier that way, it is also more indigestible, so I prefer to peel the oranges before slicing.) Bake in a moderate oven, 350°F (Gas Mark 4) for 35–40 minutes.

KATIE'S TART

Puff or flaky pastry	**Topping:**
3 *egg yolks*	10 *oz castor sugar*
2 *oz sugar*	5 *tablespoons water*
1 *tablespoon flour*	6 *oz soaked desiccated*
½ *pint milk, boiled*	*coconut*

Thoroughly blend the egg yolks with the sugar and flour. Slowly add the boiled milk. Return to the saucepan over a low heat, stirring constantly until the mixture thickens. Do not allow to boil. Allow to cool.

Meanwhile, line a pie plate with the pastry. Prepare the topping by melting the sugar with the water in a saucepan over a low flame. Stir until it begins to thicken. Add the strained coconut and boil until transparent. Pour the filling into the pastry case and cover with the coconut topping. Bake in a moderate oven until the pastry is cooked and the top brown.

MINCEMEAT AND APPLE TART

Pastry:
6 oz flour
¼ teaspoon salt
1 level dessertspoon castor sugar
4 oz butter or margarine
1 egg yolk

Filling:
Mincemeat
Apple purée
Juice of 1 orange
2 oz ground almonds

Sieve the flour, salt and sugar together. Rub in the fat very lightly. Mix to a stiff dough with the egg yolk. Leave in a cool place for at least an hour. Knead well, roll out thinly and line a shallow pie-dish. Prick well. Fill this case with alternate layers of mincemeat and apple purée. Pour over the orange juice and cover with ground almonds. Bake in a moderate oven, 350°F (Gas Mark 4) for 35–40 minutes.

NORFOLK TREACLE TART

Line a 9 inch pie plate with short pastry. Take 1 egg, 2 tablespoons of golden syrup, the rind and juice of half a lemon. Beat the egg. Warm the syrup and beat the egg into it. Stir in the lemon-rind and juice. Pour into the pastry case and bake at 375°F (Gas Mark 5) for about 35 minutes. Eat cold, when the mixture will have set like a jelly.

TREACLE CUSTARD PIE

6 oz short pastry
1 level dessertspoon semolina or rolled oats
1 level tablespoon black treacle
½ pint milk
2 eggs
1 oz castor sugar

Roll out pastry and with it line a 7–8 inch heatproof pie plate. Sprinkle base with semolina or oats then pour in treacle. Combine milk and eggs and beat till well blended. Stir in sugar then pour custard into lined pie plate. Bake in the centre of the oven, at 450°F (Gas Mark 8) for 10 minutes, then at 325°F (Gas Mark 3) for 30 minutes or till firm to the touch. Serve warm or cold.

CINNAMON PLUM TART

4 oz butter
6 oz plain flour
10 oz castor sugar
1 egg yolk

1½ dessertspoons lemon juice
1½ lb plums
1 teaspoon cinnamon

Rub 3 oz butter into flour and stir in 3 oz castor sugar. Mix to a dough with egg yolk, 1 teaspoon lemon juice and 3 tablespoons iced water. Chill pastry well, then roll out to fit a 9 inch pie plate or sandwich tin, fluting the edges. Halve and stone plums and arrange in a pattern, cut side up all over the pastry. Mix together remaining sugar and cinnamon and sprinkle half on plums. Pour over remaining lemon juice and dot with remaining butter. Bake at 350°F (Gas Mark 4) for 40 minutes, then sprinkle with remaining cinnamon sugar. Serve warm or cold.

LEMON PIE

Short crust. Take slice of bread 1 inch thick, remove crusts, pour ¾ cup granulated sugar on it, and pour 1 breakfast cup of boiling water over it, the grated rind and juice of 1 lemon, 2 egg yolks, and beat all together, then boil for 2 or 3 minutes. Whip whites of eggs with a little sugar put on top of filling in open tart and brown under grill.

Mrs Beck, Felixstowe

SUFFOLK PIE

2 egg yolks
1 oz sugar
1½ gills milk
1 oz breadcrumbs
2 oz ground almonds

1 oz butter
Almond or vanilla essence
1 egg white
1 tablespoon raspberry jam

Make a custard by blending the egg yolks with the sugar and pouring the warm milk over, mixing well. Return to the pan and cook over gentle heat, stirring all the time, until the custard just coats the back of the spoon. Do not allow it to boil. Stir in the crumbs, almonds, butter and flavouring, then fold in the stiffly whisked egg white. Spread the jam over an 8 inch pastry case, pour in the filling and bake for 35–40 minutes in a fairly hot oven, 350°F (Gas Mark 4).

COUNTRY GOOSEBERRY AMBER PIE

1½ *lb green gooseberries*   1 *oz butter*
4 *oz sugar*   2 *eggs*

Sufficient short crust pastry rolled thinly to line a pie-dish or enamel plate. Have this ready and 'resting' in cool place while preparing and cooking the fruit, etc.

Prepare the fruit by topping and tailing and washing if necessary. Place them in a saucepan with ½ a teacup of water and cook until softened a little, then add sugar and let it dissolve. Continue simmering gently until fruit is pulped. Remove from stove. When fruit has cooled a little, beat in butter and egg *yolks* only. Fetch pastry case from the cool and fill it with the fruit and egg mix. Bake in good oven for 35–40 minutes until filling is 'setting' or firming to the touch. Beat whites of egg until stiff with, if liked, a little extra sugar. Spread over the pie and return to oven to colour and crisp just to brown.

LOUGHBOROUGH LEMON PIE or GRANNY-KNOWS-BEST

1 *egg*   1 *oz sugar*
1 *oz plain flour*   *Short crust pastry*
½ *pint milk*   1 *lemon (or orange or*
¼ *oz butter*   *equivalent pure lemon juice)*

Make a thin sauce by blending the flour with the milk and sugar, then adding butter. If preferred the butter can be melted first, the flour and sugar stirred carefully into this and the milk gradually added to make smooth paste. Cook gently stirring all the time. Separate yolk from the egg white and beat the yolk with the lemon juice (and rind if whole fruit used – the rind improves flavour). Blend egg-lemon mixture with the sauce, being careful to see that the sauce is not too hot at the time. Pour into the pastry case. Beat egg white until very stiff and 'peaky' and cover top of pie with it. Bake in moderate oven until top is golden brown. Serve hot or cold with cream.

For using that odd scrap of left-over pastry to make an easy and yet 'special' pudding suitable for lunch or Sunday tea.

POULTON MORELLO CHERRY PIE

½ lb short pastry
¼ pint water
¾ pint milk
½ lb Morello cherries (other
varieties will do, or black
eating cherries)
½ teaspoon almond essence

2¼ level dessertspoons custard
powder
1-2 tablespoons sugar,
according to variety of cherry
¼ oz gelatine with
2 tablespoons cold water

Roll out the pastry thinly and line a pie plate. Trim the pastry so that it just overlaps the edge, double it under so that it rests on top of the plate's rim, then pinch into flutes. Prick pastry at base and sides with a fork and line it with a round of greased paper, and weigh it down with a few clean stones. Place to chill in a very cool place for ½ hour before cooking it in a hot oven.

When nearly cooked, remove the paper and weighting and return the case to a cooler oven for a while to dry off the pastry base. Then leave to get cold. Wash and stalk the cherries and stew until tender with the water with ¾ of the sugar or to taste. Then drain off juice, and measure it. Thicken the juice with cornflour allowing 1 level dessertspoon to ¼ pint juice. Cook this for 2 or 3 minutes and, when cool, turn it out into the pastry shell and let it set. Make a custard with the milk and custard powder and add the remainder of the sugar and the almond flavouring. Leave this until cold but stirring at frequent intervals. Stone ¼ pint of the cooked cherries and add it to the custard. Soften the gelatine in the cold water then dissolve it gently over a low heat and strain into the custard. Add more sugar or flavouring if required and, when it is beginning to set, turn it out into the pastry shell. When it is quite set, decorate pie with the remainder of the fruit. Serve with cream.

APRICOT PIE

Coddle 6 large apricots very tender. Break them very small, sweeten them to your taste. When they are cold add 6 eggs (only 2 whites) well beaten. Mix them well together with a pint of good cream. Lay a puff paste all over ye dish and pour in your ingredients. Bake it ½ an hour. Don't let the oven be too hot. When it is enough, throw a little fine sugar over it, and send it to the table hot.

Mrs Garden, 1847

BAKED APPLE DUMPLINGS

8 oz short crust pastry ¾ oz brown sugar
4 small cooking apples ¾ oz butter
1 oz seeded raisins ¼ teaspoon cinnamon

Make shortcrust pastry and roll out, cutting 4 circles round a saucer. Peel and core apples and put one in the centre of each piece of pastry. Fill centre of apples with mixture of raisins, sugar, butter and cinnamon. Enclose apples completely in pastry and invert on baking sheet. Brush pastry with egg or milk and bake at 425°F (Gas Mark 7) for 25 minutes. Sprinkle with castor sugar as they come out of the oven and serve hot or cold with cream. They are also very good served with heated sieved apricot jam, and make a pleasant variation of apple pie.

APPLE AND GINGER DUMPLINGS

Make 8 oz of your usual short crust pastry. Divide it into 4 equal pieces and roll out each to a round large enough to enclose a peeled and cored cooking apple (a Bramley Seedling, for preference). Place each apple on a piece of pastry. Drop a piece of crystallised ginger or ginger in syrup into each core cavity and fill up with demerara sugar. Wet a margin half-way round the inner rim of each piece of pastry, fold over and pinch the joins firmly together.

Place, join sides down, on a baking sheet and brush with milk. Form the rolled-out pastry trimmings into 'leaves', place them in position and brush them, too, with milk.

Bake for 10 minutes at 425°F (Gas Mark 7), then lower the heat to 350°F (Gas Mark 4) and bake for a further 30 minutes. Serve warm and pass the cream with the apples.

HEREFORD ORANGE AND APPLE DUMPLINGS

4 good cooking apples, peeled and cored. Take care to keep them whole, cover with water. 1 medium egg
Cold water to mix
A little milk and sugar to glaze
A few dates, raisins or sultanas Grated rind from 1 large orange

For Pastry:
8 oz plain flour or ½ plain and ½ self-raising flour Orange sauce:
Juice of an orange
4 oz fat, either all lard or lard and margarine mixed Water
1 teaspoon sugar 1 heaped tablespoon sugar
1 level tablespoon cornflour

Make pastry by rubbing fat into flour until like breadcrumbs; then stir in the grated rind of the orange. Add sugar. Then beat egg with a little water and mix with rest to make a firm dough. Divide pastry into 4 and roll out each piece on floured board. Drain apples and fill with dried fruit. Mould pastry covers over each apple bringing any surplus up to top. Dampen inside and pinch well together, cutting off overflow to use for leaves for garnishing. Turn dumpling upside down and press gently but firmly on to a greased baking sheet. Arrange pastry leaves around top of dumpling. Brush with milk and press in a little sugar, taking care not to spill around bases. Put well down in oven and cook for 40–50 minutes or until apples are cooked inside, if this takes longer than 50 minutes reduce heat for last few minutes. Meanwhile make sauce. Using juice from the orange and enough water to make this up to ½ pint, mix cornflour in a saucepan with a little of this liquid. Add sugar and rest of liquid and stir well. Cook gently over heat until boiling point is reached but taking care to stir all the time. Continue cooking for 1 minute. Pour into warmed sauceboat and serve with the dumplings.

D'ARCY APPLE CRISPS

6 oz short pastry
1 lb apples
6 tablespoons apricot jam

5 tablespoons soft
breadcrumbs

Roll out the pastry and line a tin about 10 × 8 inches. Sprinkle with half the crumbs. Warm the jam slightly and spread half of it over the crumbs. Peel the apples and cut them in neat slices, and arrange them in lines on the pastry. Brush with remaining jam and scatter on the rest of the crumbs. Bake at 425°F (Gas Mark 7) for 20 minutes, and then at 350°F (Gas Mark 4) for 10 minutes. Serve hot or cold with cream. Rather crisp eating apples are nicest to use for this.

APRICOT TURNOVERS

8 oz plain flour
1 teaspoon salt
5 oz lard
3 dessertspoons cold water

2 oz sugar
2 breakfastcups cooked
apricots

Sieve flour and salt together, cut in lard and add cold water a little at a time until the dough just holds in a ball. Roll out thinly and cut into 5 inch squares. Place a few apricots on each square. Moisten edges with cold water, fold to make a triangle and press edges with a fork. Bake at 375°F (Gas Mark 5) for 40 minutes. This mixture makes about 12 turnovers. These are a good variation on the usual apple pie, and are very easy to carry for a picnic.

APPLE TURNOVERS

12 oz short crust or flaky pastry
1½ lb cooking apples

4 tablespoons brown sugar
1 oz raisins
2 oz butter

Roll out pastry and cut into 4 inch circles (cut round a saucer for the shape). Peel and slice apples and cook gently with sugar, raisins and butter until soft. If you like a pinch of cloves or cinnamon, add during the cooking. Put a spoonful of mixture on to half of each circle, fold over and press edges together, damping them a little first. Bake at 425°F (Gas Mark 7).

APPLE TREACLE SQUARES

Short crust pastry:
8 oz plain flour
4 oz butter or margarine
Pinch of salt
Water to mix

Apple filling:
1½ lb cooking apples
2 tablespoons black treacle
1 oz brown sugar
1 level teaspoon cinnamon

Place long strips of greased greaseproof paper along the length of the bottom of a 7 × 11 inch swiss roll rin. Let the paper come well over the shorter sides of the tin.

Sieve together the salt and the flour. Rub in the butter until the mixture resembles fine breadcrumbs. Sprinkle on the water and lightly mix with a round bladed knife until the pastry holds together. Turn on to a floured board and knead very lightly until smooth. Divide into 2 and roll each piece into an oblong shape to fit the tin. Line the tin with one half of the pastry and lightly prick with a fork.

Peel, core and slice the apples. Mix together the apple slices, black treacle, sugar and cinnamon and spread over the pastry. Moisten the edges of the pastry with water and top with the second piece of pastry. Press down gently along the edges to seal.

Bake in a hot oven at 425°F (Gas Mark 7) for 15 minutes, and then at 350°F (Gas Mark 4) for approximately 30 minutes, until the pie is evenly brown and the apple is tender.

Allow to cool slightly. Carefully lift the pie out of the tin by gently raising the greaseproof paper strips. Sieve the icing sugar over the top. Cut into squares and serve with brown sugar and fresh dairy cream. Makes 12 squares.

ALMOND TARTS

Line tart tins with pastry. Put spot jam in each. Beat 2 egg whites with 5 oz sugar. Add 4 oz ground almonds. Put spoonful in each case and bake in moderate oven.

BALMORAL TARTS

1 oz butter	1 oz glacé cherries, peel, etc.
1 oz castor sugar	½ oz cornflour
1 egg	A little lemon rind
1 oz sponge cake crumbs	A little lemon curd

Make flaky or short pastry. Line patty pans with very thin pastry and place a little lemon curd in each. Cream butter and sugar. Beat in egg yolk and a little lemon rind. Fold in crumbs, cornflour and fruit. Whisk egg white stiffly, fold into mixture. Place a little filling in each tart. Bake in a moderate oven, 375°F (Gas Mark 5) for 25 minutes.

RASPBERRY-CURRANT TARTS

Line some deep patty pans with short pastry, prick well with a fork and bake in a hot oven for 12 minutes or till golden. Leave to cool. In a saucepan, mix together ¼ lb raspberries, ½ lb red currants and 8 oz sugar, and stir over a low heat for 10 minutes. Mix together 2 tablespoons of cornflour and 2 tablespoons of cold water, stir into the fruit, and continue cooking till thick and clear. Chill well, and just before serving fill pastry cases and garnish with sweetened cream.

MRS GORONWY'S MARMALADE TART

2 oz butter	1 egg
2 oz sugar	Flaky or puff pastry
2 tablespoons marmalade	

Line a dish with pastry. Cream together the butter, sugar, well-beaten egg and marmalade, and use as filling. Bake for a ½ hour in a warm oven.

OPEN TART

Make short pastry, roll out fairly thinly and put in round flat tin about 1½ inches deep. Put a layer of purée of prunes (stewed and sieved), a layer of apples cut in thin slices and arranged nicely in rings. Bake for about 30 minutes till apples are golden brown.

21 Hot Sweets

I've done it, said brave Mr Banting,
And so may each overfed Briton,
If he'd only adopt resolution severe
And avoid—if he would not grow fatter and fatter—
All bread, butter, sugar, milk, 'taters and beer.

William Banting published *A Letter on Corpulence addressed to the Public* in 1863, telling his own story. He had adopted a diet consisting mainly of meat, fish and fruit, giving up milk, butter, sugar and potatoes. He lost 2½ stone in nine months and gained better health than before. His name is still used as a slang term for slimming.

FLAMING PEARS

4 large pears	**½ pint water**
4 oz sugar	**8 tablespoons brandy**

Peel the pears, but leave on the stems. Put into a casserole and cover with the sugar and water. Cover and bake at 350°F (Gas Mark 4) for 45 minutes. Arrange pears on a serving dish, and pour a little of the syrup round them. Sprinkle each with a little sugar and the brandy, and set on fire at the table.

BAKED PEARS

2 lb cooking pears (or hard
eating pears)
4 oz castor sugar
½ pint cider

½ pint water
Shredded almonds
A twist of lemon peel

Peel the pears, leaving the stems on, and arrange them upright in a deep casserole. Sprinkle on sugar and pour over cider and water and add lemon peel. Cook at 300°F (Gas Mark 2) until pears are tender and can be pierced with a fork. Leave to cool in the juice, then reduce this juice until thick and syrupy. Spike with almonds and serve with thick cream. The pears may also be cooked in red wine. Quinces are excellent cooked this way in cider, using honey instead of sugar.

MRS BROWN'S PEARS IN WINE

2 lb firm eating pears
½ pint cheap red wine
4 oz brown sugar

1 teaspoon ground ginger
2 pinches saffron
1 tablespoon wine vinegar

Mix together wine, sugar, ginger, saffron and wine vinegar and simmer until the sugar melts. Peel the pears and cut in quarters or eighths. Poach in the sauce until tender. Drain off sauce and put pears in a serving dish. Thicken the sauce with a little cornflour or arrowroot and pour over the pears.

FANCY STEWED APPLES

Peel and core 7 or 8 apples, place them in a syrup and stew until soft, turning occasionally so they are cooked through. The syrup should be made of ½ lb castor sugar, the juice of 2 lemons and enough lemon rind to flavour simmered till thick. Dish the apples carefully so as to keep them whole. Colour the syrup with cochineal and pour around. Have ready some blanched sweet almonds. Stick the apples thickly with these, and on the top of each put a piece of redcurrant jelly.

Lewis' Mother's Cookbook, Mary Horrell, Exeter

APPLE CANDY CRUMBLE

1 lb peeled and sliced apples
½ pint water
4 oz plain flour

4 oz butter
8 oz sugar
1 teaspoon cinnamon

Put apples into a buttered baking dish. Pour over water. Rub together flour, butter, sugar and cinnamon till the mixture is like breadcrumbs. Pat down firmly on top of apples and bake at 350°F (Gas Mark 4) for 30 minutes until crust is brown. Serve warm with cream.

GOOSEBERRY TANSY

Simmer 1 lb gooseberries in 4 oz fresh butter until cooked. Stir in 2 beaten egg yolks and ¼ pint lightly whipped cream. Add 4 oz sugar and boil gently. Turn into dish and sprinkle with the juice of 1 lemon and a little sugar. Serve hot or cold.

APPLE CHARLOTTE (1)

Butter a pie-dish and coat with 1½ tablespoons of brown sugar mixed with a little ground cinnamon, or ground cloves, nutmeg or ginger. Line the dish with slices of bread and butter and fill it with peeled, cored and sliced apples. Sprinkle each layer with the chosen spice and another dessert-spoon of brown sugar. Warm ½ a cup of golden syrup with ½ a cup of water and pour it over the apples. Put another layer of bread and butter on top, sprinkle another tablespoon of sugar over it and dot with butter. Bake at 350°F (Gas Mark 4) for 45 minutes. Turn out and serve with cream.

APPLE CHARLOTTE (2)

2 lb apples (firm or soft as
preferred)
A little grated lemon rind
¼ pint water

Bread and butter
3 tablespoons brown sugar
3 tablespoons syrup

Stew the apples with the lemon rind and water until very soft. Butter a fireproof dish, and line the sides with bread and butter, buttered side inwards. Pour in the apple pulp and cover with buttered bread, buttered side uppermost. Dredge thickly with sugar, pour on the syrup, bake in a good oven, 400°F (Gas Mark 6) for ½ an hour.

GOOSEBERRY MARMALADE CHARLOTTE

3 slices bread, butter
and marmalade
½ lb lightly stewed

gooseberries
½ pint milk
1 egg

Remove crusts from bread, cut into fingers and line the base and sides of a pie-dish. Put the gooseberries (no juice) inside. Mix the milk and egg together and pour over the gooseberries. If time, leave for 30 minutes. Bake near the bottom of a moderately hot oven, 375°F (Gas Mark 5) for 1 hour.

SOMERSET LOGANBERRY AND APPLE CHARLOTTE

Basketful loganberries-	*2 oz butter*
about ½ lb	*Saltspoon cinnamon*
3 large or 4 medium cooking	*4 oz white breadcrumbs*
apples	*4 oz demerara sugar*

Peel core and slice thinly the apples. Wash loganberries if need be. Melt butter in pan; mix breadcrumbs with cinnamon and sugar and throw into hot butter. Sprinkle thin layer of well-stirred crumbs onto bottom of a lightly greased pie-dish (1½ pint size). Cover with a layer of apple, then a layer of crumbs. Do this twice. Cover with loganberries, then crumbs. apple and lastly crumbs, as thick a layer as possible. Bake in a gentle oven for about an hour until top is golden brown. If apple is not quite done, reduce heat and continue gently cooking until it is soft. Serve with cream or creamy custard.

This pudding can be made with blackberries or raspberries, whortle-berries or mulberries substituted for loganberries.

BLACKBERRY SPONGE

Small bowlful blackberries-	*Wineglass milk*
about ½ lb	*3 oz sugar*
3 oz butter	*6 oz self-raising flour*
2 standard eggs	

Douse blackberries with cold water and quickly get out to drain off. Layer them in bottom of a pie-dish. Cover with a little of the sugar—1 heaped tablespoon. Cream the rest of the sugar with the butter, gradually add well-beaten eggs and milk. Fold sifted flour into this creamy mixture using metal spoon and flicking wrist right over quite awkwardly.

Spread soft mixture evenly over fruit and smooth off top with the back of the spoon. Bake in a moderately hot oven, 400°F (Gas Mark 6) for 40–45 minutes using lower shelf. Sponge will be well risen and golden brown. Serve with Cornish cream.

RASPBERRY OMELETTE

Clean and sugar a ½ lb of fresh raspberries. Beat 4 egg yolks till pale lemon-coloured, and slowly add 1½ oz of castor sugar and a ½ teaspoon of grated lemon rind. Beat the egg whites with a pinch of salt till stiff peaks form and gently fold into yolk mixture. Melt butter in an omelette pan, pour in mixture and cook over a low heat with a lid until browned at the edges. Put in a moderate oven (350°F, Gas Mark 4) for 5 minutes till centre is well done. Drain fruit, place on ½ the omelette, fold over and serve dusted with icing sugar.

1915 TREACLE SLIPS

4 oz of flour, a little salt, 1 egg, and ½ a pint of milk. Sieve the flour and salt, break the egg into it, and beat well without letting it get lumpy. Add ½ the milk, stirring it in gradually, and then beating with the back of a wooden spoon to put plenty of air into the mixture. Beat it until bubbles appear.

Add the rest of the milk, and stand the batter aside for ½ hour if possible. Then fry it as for pancakes, only make them a shade thicker. As each one is cooked turn it on to a sugared paper, sprinkle with lemon-juice, and spread with golden syrup.

HONEY, NUT AND DATE PUFF

1 lb puff pastry	**A little egg white**
Castor sugar for dusting	**¼ lb cream cheese**
4 oz chopped dates	**1 heaped tablespoon thick**
1 heaped tablespoon flaked	**honey**
almonds	**2 teaspoons orange juice**
Finely grated rind of 1 orange	

Cut the pastry in half and roll out into 2 squares of equal size, and ¼ inch thick. Mix all the remaining ingredients except egg white and castor sugar, until smooth and thick. Put one square of pastry onto baking sheet and spread with nut and date mixture. Wet the surface of second square and with wet side downwards, press over mixture. Brush all over with egg white, dust with castor sugar. Bake at 375°F (Gas Mark 5) for 25–30 minutes until golden brown. Serve with custard or cream.

MIDFORD APPLE CAKE

4 peeled apples	*2 eggs*
3 oz butter	*2 oz flour*
¼ pint milk	*3 tablespoons sugar*

Slice apples and fry in hot butter. Mix milk, eggs and flour. Stir in apples and butter and bake for 20 minutes at 375°F (Gas Mark 5). Turn out, sprinkle with sugar, and brown in oven or under grill.

AUNT TOMMY'S ORANGE SWEET

5 oranges	*3 eggs*
3 oz castor sugar	*1 tablespoon cornflour*
1 pint milk	*2 tablespoons icing sugar*

Peel the oranges and cut them in thin slices. Put into a fireproof dish and scatter the sugar over the fruit. In a double saucepan, bring the milk to the boil. Pour a little milk on to the egg yolks and mix well. Return to the remaining milk, together with the cornflour mixed with a little water. Stir constantly until it thickens, and then pour over the fruit. Whisk the egg whites to stiff peaks. Fold in the icing sugar, and spread the mixture over the custard. Bake at 325°F (Gas Mark 3) for 15 minutes.

QUAKING PUDDING

Take a quart of cream, boil it and let it stand till almost cold; then beat up 4 eggs very fine, with 1½ spoons of flour: mix them well with your cream; add sugar and nutmeg to your palate. Tie it up close in a cloth well buttered. Let it boil an hour and then carefully turn it out. Pour over it melted butter.

Thomas Train, Gateshead 1812

BOILED RICE PUDDING WITH RAISINS

1 pint milk	*2 oz sultanas or raisins*
2 oz Carolina rice	*Nutmeg*
2 oz sugar	

Add rice to the milk and bring to the boil. Add the sugar and dried fruit. Simmer for ½ hour stirring occasionally. Add grated nutmeg.

Mrs Biggar, Kirkcudbrightshire

CRUSTY PLUMS

Cut thick slices of bread and spread with butter and black treacle on one side. Press into this side stoned, raw half plums. Put a little butter and brown sugar into each half plum and place slices in a buttered fireproof dish. Cover with buttered paper and bake for 30 minutes in a moderate oven, 350°F (Gas Mark 4). Serve with cream.

RHUBARB TANSY

1 lb rhubarb	**2 egg yolks**
4 oz butter	**$\frac{1}{4}$ pint double cream**
2 oz sugar	**2 tablespoons lemon juice**

Prepare and chop the rhubarb into $1\frac{1}{2}$ ins. pieces. Simmer gently in the butter until cooked. Add the beaten egg yolks and the lightly whipped cream, sweeten to taste, then gently boil the mixture until it is just firm. Turn out at once on a serving dish. Sprinkle with lemon juice and a little castor sugar to taste. Serve hot or cold.

LEMON SPONGE

1 oz butter beat well with 3 oz sugar; add juice and rind of 1 lemon and yolk of egg; add 1 large tablespoon of flour and $\frac{1}{4}$ pint milk. Whisk white of egg and add last. Put in well-greased pie-dish; stand in pan of water. Bake at 400°F (Gas Mark 6) for 25 minutes.

Mrs Beck, Felixstowe

HOT STRAWBERRY PUDDING

Hull 2 lb strawberries and put them in a fireproof dish with 1 lb sugar and a pinch of cinnamon. Put in a very low oven until the sugar has melted, then drain off the syrup. Stir in 2 wineglasses of red wine, pour the liquid over the fruit and return to the oven until hot. Just before serving, add a dessertspoon of honey and a dessertspoon of lemon juice, and serve very hot with thick cream.

FRESH PLUM PUDDING

1 egg	**Sugar**
Butter	**$\frac{1}{2}$ lb small ripe plums**
Flour	**Soft brown sugar**

AUDLEY END SAUCE

2 oz cornflour	1 egg
1 pint milk	½ gill top milk or cream
2 oz butter	1 tablespoon moist brown
1½ oz sugar	sugar

Weigh the egg and weigh out the equivalent in butter, flour and sugar. Remove stones from plums and cut them in half. Cream butter and sugar, add beaten egg and flour. Spread a layer of this sponge mixture in a greased oven dish, add the plums face down and sprinkle lightly with sugar, then add the rest of the sponge mixture. Bake at 350°F (Gas Mark 4) for 30 minutes until golden and firm. Make the sauce by mixing cornflour with a little water then cooking gently for 5 minutes with the boiling milk, butter and sugar. Gradually whisk in the egg and top milk or cream. Put sauce into a buttered dish, sprinkle sugar on top and caramelise under a hot grill. Serve sauce either hot or cold.

VICTORIA PLUM SPONGE

1 lb Victoria plums, halved and stoned	4 oz softened butter
2-3 oz sugar	2 eggs
2 tablespoons water, or	
1 lb 3 oz can plums, drained	**Topping:**
1 oz hazelnuts, roasted and husks removed	2 oz plain flour
	1 level teaspoon mixed spice
	1 oz butter
	2 oz demerara sugar
Sponge:	1 oz hazelnuts, roasted, husks removed, roughly chopped
4 oz self-raising flour	
1 level teaspoon baking powder	2 tablespoons plum jam, warmed

Place plums, sugar, water and hazelnuts in a greased 2½ pint ovenproof dish, and add hazelnuts.

Sift flour and baking powder together. Add remaining sponge ingredients and beat for 2 minutes. Spoon mixture over plums and spread evenly. Bake at 375°F (Gas Mark 5) for 30–35 minutes until sponge is risen and golden.

Meanwhile prepare topping, sift flour and mixed spice together. Rub in butter and mix in sugar and nuts. Remove pudding from oven and quickly spread top of sponge with jam. Sprinkle topping evenly over sponge. Return pudding to oven for a further 10–15 minutes until topping is lightly browned. Serve hot with cream, custard or ice cream.

LEMON DREAM

2 oz butter
4 oz castor sugar
2 eggs

1 oz plain flour
1 lemon
¼ pint milk

Cream butter and sugar, and beat in egg yolks. Stir in flour and juice and grated rind of lemon. Add the milk (the mixture will look curdled). Whisk egg whites stiffly and fold in. Pour into well-buttered 1½ pint oven dish, stand in a shallow pan of warm water and bake at 350°F (Gas Mark 4) for 35 minutes. This gives a delectable lemon pudding with its own sauce underneath.

Loraine Honey, Harewood End

ORCHARD PUDDING

1 lb apples
¾ pint milk
½ oz butter
1 teaspoon almond essence
Rind of ½ lemon

4 oz sugar
3 oz fresh white breadcrumbs
2 eggs
1 oz chopped almonds

Bramley's Seedling apples are best for this. Peel and core the apples. Cut four rings and slice the rest. Put the apples into a pan with the milk, butter, essence, lemon rind and 1 oz sugar. Heat very gently just to soften the apples slightly. Remove the apple slices and rings carefully. Pour the milk mixture on to the breadcrumbs and leave to soak for 20 minutes. Separate the eggs and mix the yolks into the breadcrumb mixture. Put into a fireproof dish and put the dish into a tin of warm water. Cover the dish with a piece of wet greaseproof paper. Bake at 325°F (Gas Mark 3) for 30 minutes. Top with the apple slices. Whisk the two egg whites stiffly and fold in the remaining sugar. Stir in the nuts and pile on top of the pudding. Decorate with the four apple rings set into the meringue. Bake at 250°F (Gas Mark ½) for 30 minutes and serve hot.

OATMEAL PUDDING

1 tablespoon fine oatmeal
1 dessertspoon flour
1¼ pints milk
1 egg

Pinch of salt
1 oz sugar
Butter

Mix the oatmeal and flour together into a smooth cream with a little of the milk, then add the rest of the milk to the oatmeal and flour. Stir and simmer for five minutes. Add the salt and sugar and cool slightly. Add the beaten egg and turn into a dish which has been greased well with butter. Bake at 325°F (Gas Mark 3) for 20 minutes. Serve with syrup or brown sugar and cream.

QUEEN ANNE'S SEMOLINA

1 pint milk
Pinch of salt
8 level tablespoons fine semolina

2 eggs
8 oz castor sugar
3 tablespoons redcurrant jelly

Warm milk and sprinkle in salt and semolina, bring just to boil and simmer for 2 minutes. Remove from heat and stir in beaten egg yolks and half the sugar. Turn into $1\frac{1}{2}$ pint heatproof dish, cool slightly and spread thinly with redcurrant jelly. Whisk the egg whites until stiff, add 3 tablespoons of remaining sugar and whisk again to firm peaks. Fold in rest of the sugar and pile lightly on top of pudding. Place in a very hot oven, 450°F (Gas Mark 8) for 3 minutes, until pale golden. Dot with small blobs of redcurrant jelly and serve hot or cold.

CHOCOLATE FUDGE PUDDING

2 oz castor sugar
1 oz cocoa
$\frac{1}{4}$ teaspoon cinnamon
2 oz fine semolina
1 teaspoon baking powder
1 oz butter

$\frac{1}{2}$ teaspoon vanilla essence
2 eggs
1 tablespoon walnuts
$\frac{1}{2}$ pint hot water
3 oz brown sugar
$\frac{1}{2}$ oz extra cocoa

Sift sugar, cocoa, cinnamon, semolina and baking powder. Melt butter and blend with vanilla essence and beaten eggs, and stir into dry mixture. Add chopped walnuts, and put into well-greased $1\frac{1}{2}$ pint pie dish. Blend hot water, brown sugar, and extra cocoa, and pour gently in circular movement over top. Bake at 375°F (Gas Mark 5) for 30 minutes. Serve warm. This recipe makes a spiced chocolate pudding with its own sauce in one dish.

DEBDEN CHOCOLATE PUDDING

6 oz sugar
4 oz flour
2 teaspoons baking powder
Pinch of salt
1 oz plain chocolate
2 tablespoons butter

Scant $\frac{1}{4}$ pint milk
3 oz brown sugar
4 oz castor sugar
3 tablespoons cocoa
$\frac{1}{8}$ pint cold water

Stir together 6 oz sugar, flour, baking powder and salt, and blend with melted chocolate, butter and milk. Pour into a buttered baking dish (about $1\frac{1}{2}$ pint size). Over the top scatter brown and castor sugars and cocoa, without mixing, and pour on cold water. Bake at 325°F (Gas Mark 3) for 1 hour. Leave to stand at room temperature for 1 hour, and serve cool but not chilled. The pudding makes its own fudge sauce beneath a cake-like top, and is for a person who likes a really rich chocolate confection. Whipped cream or ice cream are delicious as a topping, but only possible for the iron digestion of the schoolboy.

BLACKBERRY PUDDING CAKE

This can be eaten as a cake, but it is also excellent when served as a pudding with cream or custard. Cream together 4 oz butter and 4 oz sugar, and beat in 1 egg. Gradually add 8 oz plain flour sifted with 2 teaspoons baking powder and $\frac{1}{4}$ teaspoon salt, and beat to a smooth batter with $\frac{1}{4}$ pint milk. Pour into a buttered square or rectangular tin, and sprinkle thickly with well-washed and drained blackberries. Cream together 2 oz butter with 4 oz sugar, 2 oz plain flour and $\frac{1}{2}$ teaspoon cinnamon until the mixture is of a crumble consistency. Sprinkle on blackberries, and bake at 350°F (Gas Mark 4) for 1 hour.

DEVONSHIRE PUDDING

3 eggs
3 oz soft brown sugar
3 oz flour

1 large tin apricots
Grated rind of $\frac{1}{2}$ lemon

Separate eggs and beat yolks with sugar until pale and creamy. Mix in flour and blend well. Beat egg whites until stiff and fold into the mixture. Drain off juice from apricot halves, mix them with the lemon peel into the sponge base and turn into a buttered baking dish. Bake at 350°F (Gas Mark 4). Serve with cream.

CHERRY PUDDING

Take 1 lb of cherries, 4 oz sugar, 2 oz plain flour, 2 oz castor sugar, 3 eggs, 1 gill of thick cream, 2 or 3 tablespoons of milk, the grated rind of a lemon and a pinch of mace.

Cook the cherries with a little water and 4 oz of sugar until tender. Allow to cool and remove the stones. Mix the flour and milk together, then add the castor sugar, and cream, and mace, and warm slowly before beating in the egg yolks. Add the grated lemon rind and lastly the egg whites beaten stiffly. Well butter a mould or basin and fill with alternate layers of cherries and the mixture until full. Cover with greased paper or foil and bake in a moderate oven for $\frac{3}{4}$ of an hour.

LEMON SAUCE PUDDING

8 oz castor sugar
1½ oz plain flour
½ teaspoon baking powder
Pinch of salt
2 eggs

1½ teaspoons grated lemon rind
1 tablespoon melted butter
⅓ pint milk
4 tablespoons lemon juice

Sift 6 oz of the sugar with flour, baking powder and salt. Beat egg yolks until light and creamy. Fold in melted butter, milk and lemon juice, and stir into flour mixture. Beat egg whites, fold in remaining sugar and beat well, then fold into lemon mixture. Put into buttered pie-dish and bake at 350°F (Gas Mark 4) for 1 hour. Serve warm with cream. The pudding is a light sponge with a lemon sauce underneath.

BREAD AND BUTTER PUDDING

1 oz butter
4 slices white bread
4 oz raisins
2 oz chopped dried apricots
2 oz sugar

2 eggs
1 pint milk
1 tablespoon granulated sugar

Butter a baking dish. Remove crusts from the bread, butter the slices and cut into 1 inch wide fingers. Arrange half the bread, butter side up, in the bottom of the dish and cover with dried fruit and 2 oz sugar. Top with remaining bread. Beat eggs with the milk and pour over the pudding. Leave to stand for 15 minutes, sprinkle the surface with 1 tablespoon granulated sugar and bake in a moderate oven, 300°F (Gas Mark 2) for 1½ hours.

RHUBARB BUTTERSCOTCH CRUMBLE

3 cups rhubarb
Pastry of your choice
3 oz brown sugar
2 tablespoons flour (level)
Pinch of salt
1 egg, beaten
2 tablespoons cream

Chop up rhubarb and put into a pastry-lined pie plate. Now mix together the brown sugar, flour, salt, egg and cream. Spread this mixture over the rhubarb, and bake the pie in a hot oven for 10 minutes. Then reduce the heat to moderate and bake for 20 minutes more. Serve warm or cold.

RHUBARB BROWN BETTY

4 oz fresh white breadcrumbs
2 oz suet
2 oz sugar
1 lb young rhubarb
2 tablespoons golden syrup
½ teacup water

Mix breadcrumbs with suet and sugar and put in a thin layer at the bottom of a greased basin. Cover with a layer of chopped rhubarb. Dissolve syrup in water, and use half of this to pour over the rhubarb. Add another layer of crumb mixture, then rhubarb and syrup, and finally top with crumbs. Cover and steam for 1½ hours, or bake at 325°F (Gas Mark 3) for 1½ hours. Serve with cream or egg custard.

RHUBARB PUDDING

2 lb rhubarb
3 oz sultanas or currants
3 oz butter
1 egg, large
½ teaspoon mixed spice
Lemon peel (about a 4-inch
strip)
3 tablespoons golden syrup
6 tablespoons plain flour
3 teaspoons baking powder
Pinch of salt
1½ breakfastcups milk

Cut the rhubarb into 1 inch pieces and put in a fireproof dish with the sultanas or currants. Add 1 tablespoon syrup dissolved in warm water, the spice and the lemon peel. Cream the butter, add the well-beaten egg, and the rest of the syrup. In another basin sieve the flour, baking powder and salt together. Add to this the milk and the egg mixture alternately till all is mixed. Pour over fruit. Bake in moderate oven for about 50 minutes.

GINGERBREAD PLUM PUDDING

1½ lb yellow plums
6 oz castor sugar
2 oz butter
3 oz black treacle
1 oz golden syrup
5 tablespoons milk

1 egg
4 oz plain flour
1 oz granulated sugar
1 teaspoon mixed spice
1 teaspoon ground ginger
½ teaspoon bicarbonate of soda

Mix plums and castor sugar and put into a buttered oven dish. Warm together butter, treacle and syrup, then add milk and beaten egg and leave to cool. In a bowl, mix sieved flour, granulated sugar, spices and soda, add cooled treacle mixture and blend well together. Pour over fruit, spreading evenly. Bake in the middle of a low oven, 325°F (Gas Mark 3) for 1¼ hours.

TOSSED APPLES

Peel very small eating apples, but leave on stalks. Heat some butter in a thick pan and toss apples in it until brown. Drain and arrange on thick layer of castor sugar. Serve warm or cold.

Mrs Georgina Hill, 1864

APPLE SLICES

Butter thin bread on both sides and put in a baking dish. Halve apples without peeling, but remove cores. Put half an apple on each piece of bread, hollow side up, and put thick cream in each hollow. Scatter soft brown sugar on bread and fruit. Cook at 325°F (Gas Mark 3) for 45 minutes, renewing cream and sugar half way through cooking. Serve warm.

Mrs Georgina Hill, 1864

DEEP-FRIED APPLES

Make a thick batter with 3 eggs, ½ a pint of milk, a pinch of nutmeg, a liqueur glassful of brandy and enough flour to give the consistency of thick cream. Dip in apple slices and deep-fry in hot lard. Drain and sprinkle with sugar.

Mrs Georgina Hill, 1864

APPLE CHARTREUSE

Boil 8 oz of Carolina rice in 2 pints of milk until the rice is tender and has absorbed milk. Peel and core 9 medium pippins; put raspberry jam in holes and fill up with cream.

Line a deep pie-dish with rough puff pastry. Put in apples and fill in spaces with rice. Brush over apples and rice with egg yolk, dust with sugar and decorate with candied peel. Bake at 400°F (Gas Mark 6) for 20 minutes, then at 375°F (Gas Mark 5) for 25 minutes. Serve hot.

Mrs Georgina Hill, 1864

APPLE OMELETTE

Slice eating apples thinly and dip in brandy. Dust with grated lemon peel and fry quickly on both sides in hot lard. Beat up eggs (allow 2 for each person) and pour into a little hot butter in an omelette pan. Spread apple slices over eggs and cook until eggs are just set.

Fold over omelette, dust with icing sugar and glaze under grill or in oven.

Mrs Georgina Hill, 1864

APRICOT DELIGHT

6 oz breadcrumbs	*¾ oz ground almonds*
3 oz sugar	*2 oz bitter almonds*
3 oz suet	*1 or 2 eggs*
Some apricot jam	*Squeeze lemon juice*

Beat the egg, stir in the sugar, the jam and the lemon juice, add the finely chopped almonds. Mix suet with breadcrumbs. Grease a pie-dish and put into it alternate layers of the breadcrumbs and the jam mixture, beginning and ending with crumbs. Bake in a moderate oven for about an hour or until firm. Serve with cream or custard.

BASIC BATTER

4 oz plain flour	*1 egg*
Good pinch salt	*½ pint milk and/or water*

Sieve the flour and salt into a basin. Make a well in the centre and drop in the egg. Add about ½ the liquid, bit by bit, and mix from the middle outwards. Beat well until the mixture is smooth like cream. If possible give it time to 'rest' for ½ an hour by covering and leaving in the cool. Finally add the rest of the liquid and beat again. Some people add 1 tablespoon of boiling water just before they pour into the cooking dish but this takes courage.

PANCAKES

(The basic recipe makes 8 pancakes.)
Heat a little lard in a frying pan. Pour in a little batter, tilt the pan until covered evenly, cook quickly until the pancake is golden brown underneath. Then toss or turn and brown the other side. Turn out on to sugared paper, roll up and sprinkle with lemon juice.

JAM PANCAKES

Spread a little warm jam on the pancakes before you roll them up.

APPLE BATTER

Add 2 tablespoons of sugar to the basic batter. Peel, core and slice 2 or 3 medium-sized apples. Heat a knob of butter in a baking tin. Add the apples and the batter. Sprinkle with cinnamon or nutmeg. Cook like a Yorkshire pudding.

PANCAKES WITH HONEY AND WALNUT SAUCE

8 pancakes
1 rounded tablespoon thick
honey
10 oz chopped walnuts
Juice of 1 lemon
1 oz butter

The pancakes can be made fresh or made before the meal. Place the butter in a shallow pan, and when it has melted add honey, nuts and lemon juice. Stir until blended. Slide one pancake into the mixture fold in halves and into quarters in the pan and then slide in next pancake until all pancakes are in the pan. Remove pancakes and arrange on a heated serving dish, pour remaining mixture over the top.

BLACKBERRY PANCAKES

Blend together 4 oz flour, 2 tablespoons sugar, 1 egg yolk, $\frac{1}{2}$ pint milk, and $\frac{1}{2}$ lb blackberries to a smooth batter. Add 1 tablespoon melted butter and fold in the stiffly beaten white of the egg. Fry small pancakes of this mixture in butter browning on both sides. Serve very hot with plenty of vanilla ice-cream.

SOMERSET FRITTERS

8 oz plain flour
1 egg
Enough milk to make a stiff
batter
2 tablespoons sugar

2 tablespoons currants
4 apples
1 teaspoon mixed spice
½ teaspoon bicarbonate of soda

Make a batter with flour, egg and milk just stiff enough to drop from a spoon. Mix in sugar, currants, grated apples, spice, and the bicarbonate of soda mixed with a little milk. Melt some lard in a frying pan. Put in spoonfuls of batter and brown on both sides. Pile on to dish and sprinkle with sugar.

GERMAN PUFFS

2 tablespoons flour, 2 eggs well beaten, ½ pint new milk, 2 oz butter just melted. Stir all together add a little nutmeg and sugar, put the mixture into teacups, half filling them. Bake in a quick oven ¼ of an hour, turn into a dish, and strew sugar over.

Lewis' Mother's Cookbook, Mary Horrell, Exeter

1911 SUNDERLAND PANCAKES

2 eggs, 2 oz of butter, 2 oz of sifted sugar, 2 oz of flour, and ½ a pint of new milk. Beat the eggs thoroughly, and put them into a basin with the butter, which should be beaten to a cream. Stir in the sugar and flour, and when these ingredients are well mixed, add the milk, which should be slightly warm. Keep stirring and beating the mixture for a few minutes; put it on buttered plates, and bake it in a quick oven for 20 minutes. Serve with a cut lemon and sifted sugar, or pile the pancakes high on a dish, with a layer of preserve or marmalade between each layer.

NORTHALLERTON PUDDING

4 oz plain flour
1 egg
½ pint milk

1 tablespoon castor sugar
2 drops vanilla essence
1 oz lard

Sieve flour into a mixing bowl. Make a well in the centre, add the egg and sugar and gradually beat the egg into the flour, adding a little milk to make a smooth paste. Add vanilla essence and beat in remaining milk until small bubbles rise to the surface. Leave to stand for 30 minutes.

Heat lard in a baking dish until smoking, add batter and bake, 425°F (Gas Mark 7) for 30 minutes. Serve with golden syrup and cream.

APPLE BATTER

4 *small cooking apples*
4 *dessertspoons mincemeat*
3 *eggs*
1 *oz sugar*

2 *oz flour*
¼ *pint milk*
Pinch *of salt*

Peel and core apples and put into a buttered oven dish. Put mincemeat into each one. Beat together egg yolks, sugar, flour and milk with a pinch of salt, then fold in stiffly beaten egg whites. Pour over apples and bake at 350°F (Gas Mark 4) for 1 hour. Sprinkle with sugar and serve at once.

APPLE AND OATMEAL CAKES

3 *oz oatmeal*
6 *apples (large, firm)*
2 *oz sugar*

1 *oz flour*
Butter *for frying*

Cook the oatmeal in water until well swollen, then strain and turn into a basin. Peel and core the apples, chop into small pieces. Mix the apples, the oatmeal and the sugar together, binding with the flour. Form into small balls with the hands, and fry in hot butter until just brown. Sprinkle with sugar and serve very hot with custard.

APPLE FRITTERS

2 *apples (firm)*
2 *tablespoons flour*
½ *teaspoon baking powder*

1 *egg*
A little milk

Peel and core the apples, and cover with a little sugar to prevent them browning. Make a batter of the flour, baking powder and milk, with the yolk of egg. Whisk the white and fold it in to the batter. Dip slices of apple into the batter, then drop in very hot fat, and fry until golden brown. Sprinkle with castor sugar and serve very hot.

APPLE CRISPS

Some large apples (firm)
2 *or 3 thick slices of white bread*

Butter
Sugar

Peel and cut up the apples, cut the crusts off the bread, and cut it into cubes. Fry the apples in butter in a frying pan, and as soon as they are cooked, lift out and put into a dish, and sprinkle them with sugar. Fry the bread cubes in the remaining butter, lift out to drain, then mix with the apples and serve with custard or cream.

22 Cold Sweets and Ices

Things sweet to taste prove indigestion sour.
William Shakespeare

A perpetual feast of nectared sweets
Where no crude surfeit reigns.
Milton

AUTUMN PUDDING

1 lb blackberries
2 large apples

4 oz sugar
White bread

Simmer blackberries with peeled and sliced apples, sugar and ½ pint water until soft. Strain, keeping the juice, and rub the fruit through a sieve. Add half the juice to the fruit pulp and sweeten with more sugar to taste. In the bottom of a soufflé dish or straight-sided casserole, put a layer of thinly-sliced white bread without crusts. Cover with a layer of blackberry purée, then another layer of bread and purée until the dish is filled, making sure each layer of bread is well-soaked with the fruit, and finishing with a layer of bread. Put a plate on top with a heavy weight, and leave overnight. Turn out to serve, with the rest of the blackberry juice thickened with cornflour to make a sauce and with cream if liked.

BLACKBERRY PUDDING

1 lb blackberries   **8 oz castor sugar**
½ pint cider   **5 slices white bread**

Simmer the blackberries with cider and sugar. Take the crusts from the bread, and use some of the bread to line a pudding basin. Pour the hot fruit into the basin and cover with bread. Put a plate and a weight on top and leave in a cold place for 24 hours. Turn out and serve with cream.

BLACKBERRY MOULD

Line a mould with pieces of bread and put a layer of blackberries and apples previously boiled, then a layer of bread and so on until the mould is full. Set to cool overnight, turn out and serve with custard or cream.

Lewis' Mother's Cookbook, Mary Horrell, Exeter

POLKA PUDDING

Mix 2 teaspoons of arrowroot in ½ pint of cold milk. Beat 2 eggs well, add to them 1½ oz of fresh butter cut into small pieces, a dessertspoon of rosewater, a few drops of any essence you like, ½ a teacup of powdered sugar. Boil ½ pint of milk in a stewpan. When boiling stir in these ingredients without taking the pan off the fire. Boil 5 minutes keeping it well stirred, then put into a mould and serve cold.

Lewis' Mother's Cookbook, Mary Horrell, Exeter

FUDGE PUDDING

2 oz butter   **teaspoons coffee essence**
2 oz plain flour   **2 tablespoons golden syrup**
1 pint milk   **2 oz plain chocolate**
½ teaspoon vanilla or 2

Make a plain white sauce with the butter, flour and milk, and add essence. Grease a small thick saucepan, put in the golden syrup and heat it to a rich brown colour. Be careful that it does not burn, or it may curdle the milk. Stir this quickly into the sauce and mix well. When cool, pour into a pretty serving dish. Just before serving, grate chocolate on top.

NO-BAKE RHUBARB CRUMBLE

1 lb young rhubarb   **water and sugar)**
2 tablespoons water   **2 oz butter**
4 oz sugar (or use 4 oz   **6 oz fresh white breadcrumbs**
raspberry jam instead of   **2 oz soft brown sugar**

Cut rhubarb into 1 inch lengths and cook gently with water and sugar (or jam) until tender, then cool. Melt butter, remove from heat and mix in crumbs and sugar. Fill a serving bowl with alternate layers of rhubarb and crumb mixture. Top with whipped cream. Add a grating of lemon or orange, a pinch of ginger, or a few shreds of angelica for extra flavour.

POPLAR COTTAGE RAISIN FLAN

8 oz digestive biscuits
4 oz melted butter
6 oz seedless raisins
8 fluid oz water

1 tablespoon cornflour
½ teaspoon ground cloves
½ teaspoon ground cinnamon
4 oz brown sugar

Crush the biscuits into crumbs and mix with the melted butter. Press into a flan dish and chill. Cook the raisins in the water for 10 minutes until plump and soft. Stir in cornflour mixed with a little water, and simmer until thick. Add spices and sugar and stir until the sugar has dissolved. Cool and fill the flan case. Serve with thick cream.

BETTY'S ORANGE MERINGUE

1 tin mandarin oranges
1 lemon
Sugar to taste

2 tablespoons cornflour
2 eggs

Drain oranges and put in bottom of buttered Pyrex dish, saving some to decorate. Make liquid up to ½ pint with water and lemon juice. Make blancmange with liquid and cornflour and sugar. Grate lemon rind finely and add. Cool and add 2 egg yolks. Whisk whites stiffly and fold on top. Add sugar. Cook 1 hour in slow oven. Decorate with oranges.

STRAWBERRY SHORTCAKE

10 oz plain flour
4 teaspoons baking powder
2 tablespoons castor sugar
½ teaspoon salt
3 oz butter

1 egg
5 tablespoons milk
1½ lb strawberries
Whipped cream

Heat oven to 425°F (Gas Mark 7) and grease and flour an 8 inch cake tin. Mix flour with baking powder, sugar and salt, and cut in butter until mixture looks like breadcrumbs. Make a well in centre, add beaten egg and milk and stir quickly until well mixed. Spread in cake tin and bake for 15 minutes until golden and firm. Leave in the tin until partly cool, then turn out on to rack. While the shortcake is still warm, split and butter the bottom layer. Cover with halved berries, sprinkle with sugar and top with the second half. Spoon on more sliced berries and whipped cream, and garnish with whole berries. Serve at once.

ORANGE CREAM ROLL

$\frac{1}{4}$ *pint double cream*
2 level tablespoons icing sugar
3 level tablespoons orange juice
2 level teaspoons grated orange rind
15 ginger biscuits

Whip cream, fold in sugar, orange juice and rind. Mix gently until mixture is dropping consistency. Sandwich ginger biscuits together with cream and place in a roll on a dish. Cover roll completely with remaining cream. Cover roll with a lid and leave to chill in refrigerator overnight. To serve, cut diagonally into slices.

ANGIE'S GINGER ROLL

Dip ginger nuts in sherry (quite quickly or else they almost disintegrate) sandwich with whipped cream into a long shape. Then cover with cream and chill. Then before serving decorate with chopped stem ginger. The ginger nuts can also be put together with leftover brandy butter, instead of cream.

Mrs Hollest, Saffron Walden, Essex

RICE SOLID

6 oz rice
Quart of milk
Sugar to taste
Lemon rind for flavouring
Filling

Boil the rice until cooked in the milk, which has been sweetened, and flavoured by adding a strip of lemon rind. Turn it into a pretty mould, and leave it until cold and set. Then turn it out gently scoop out 2 tablespoons of rice from the centre, and fill the cavity with baked apple, putting a little strawberry jam on the top. Put the scooped out rice round the base of the mould, and stand it in some whole fruits from the jam for decoration.

Mrs Lowelle, Birmingham, 1915

AN ECONOMICAL JELLY

Take two calves' feet, when thoroughly cleaned cut them into pieces, place in a stewpan, with 2 quarts of cold water; let them boil, skin, then gently simmer for 5 or 6 hours, when the liquor should be strained through a wire sieve, and set aside until the next day. Remove every particle of fat, warm the jelly in an enamel saucepan, with the rind and juice of 2 lemons, loaf sugar to sweeten, 4 cloves, a small stick of cinnamon, the whites and shells of 2 eggs, a pinch of dried saffron. Let it all come to a boil, strain through a jelly-bag into a basin; when cool add 2 wine-glasses of sherry, and pour into damp moulds.

Mrs Thorne, 1911

APPLES IN RED JELLY

Choose rather large apples, peel and take out the cores with a scoop and put into each apple 2 cloves, then fill them up with sifted sugar, place them in a pie-dish and add more sugar, the juice of 1 lemon and 2 teacups of water. Bake ½ hour, do not let the apples break. Lift them out carefully, then strain the liquor in which they have been stewing into a lined saucepan, add the rind of a lemon and 1 tablespoon of gelatine, which has been dissolved in cold water, and if not sweet enough, add more sugar and 6 cloves. Boil till quite clear. Colour with a few drops of cochineal and strain the jelly through a double muslin into a jug and let it cool a little, then pour it into the dish around the apples. When quite cold put on the top of each apple the white of an egg beaten to a stiff froth. A very pretty supper dish.

Lewis' Mother's Cookbook, Mary Horrell, Exeter

APPLE CUSTARD

Boil 1½ lb loaf sugar in a pint of water until it hardens when poured into cold water. Then add 2 lb of apples pared and cored, the peel and a little of the juice of 2 lemons. Boil till quite stiff, put into a mould. When cold, put into a glass dish and pour custard around.

Lewis' Mother's Cookbook, Mary Horrell, Exeter

APPLE FOAM

2 lb apples   **2 egg whites**
Sugar to taste   **2 cartons natural yoghurt**

Peel and core apples and cook gently with sugar to taste but no water. When fruit is tender, sieve and cool. Whip egg whites and fold into pulp with yoghurt. Chill well.

BLACKBERRY AND APPLE COMPÔTE

1 lb blackberries
2 large apples

8 oz sugar
4 tablespoons water

Wash blackberries, and add peeled and sliced apples, sugar and water. Bring to the boil, cover and simmer for 5 minutes until apple is tender. Chill thoroughly, and serve with cream.

SOFT APPLES

Use small eating apples, peel them and prick with a coarse needle. Put into a jar inside a saucepan of boiling water. Put in 2 tablespoons of honey for 8 oz apples. Tie brown paper over jar and shake frequently but gently. When soft, put in dish and pour on liquid from cooking. When cold, top with thick cream.

Mrs Georgina Hill, 1864

RASPBERRIES WITH RED CURRANT SAUCE

Simmer a ½ lb red currants with 6 oz sugar for 15 minutes. Strain the liquid and chill; serve over raspberries.

COLD RASPBERRY SOUFFLÉ

Sieve ½ lb fresh raspberries, measure the purée and make up to a ½ pint with water. Sprinkle 1 tablespoon gelatine in 4 tablespoons of cold water and leave to soften. In a double boiler, cook together 4 egg yolks with 4 oz sugar and cook over hot but not boiling water until thickened (about 10 minutes). Add the softened gelatine and stir till dissolved, then let the mixture cool for 15 minutes. Stir the raspberry purée into the cool gelatine mixture. Beat 4 egg whites till stiff peaks form. Whip a ½ pint cream stiffly, fold into the meringue and gradually add the raspberry mixture. When thoroughly combined, turn into a soufflé dish and chill for at least 2 hours. Decorate with whipped cream and a few raspberries.

MRS D.G.'S APPLE JELLY

To 1 lb apples pared and cored add 1 lb sugar powdered and ¼ pint water. Boil it until it is stiff with some strips of lemon peel. It may then be put into a mould and turned out when cold.

Mrs Garden, 1847

VICTORIAN APPLE MARMALADE JELLY

2½ lb peeled and cored 'good' cooking apples, stewed in only sufficient water to prevent burning. Beat them to a smooth pulp. For each lb of pulp take ¾ lb sugar and boil it to a thick syrup adding as little water as necessary for making the sugar boil. Add this syrup to the apple pulp with about ½ teaspoon of minced or grated lemon peel. Stir over a good heat for about 25 minutes or till the apples cease to stick to the bottom of the pan. The jelly may now be poured into moulds which have been dipped in cold water. This will turn out into a nice stiff jelly, which may be stuck with blanched almonds, and a custard poured round it on the dish. The apples will take about ¾ hour to reduce to pulp, and 25 minutes to boil after the sugar syrup has been added.

VICTORIAN LEMON JELLY

Take a clean saucepan and put into it 1½ pints of water, the juice of 8 lemons and the rind of 2, pared very thinly, ½ lb sugar, 1 inch stick of cinnamon, 3 oz leaf gelatine (see instructions on side of modern packets of powdered gelatine for equivalent quantity) and 4 cloves.

Stir this over the fire with a wooden spoon until the gelatine is entirely dissolved, then add the crushed shells of 2 eggs and the whites well beaten up, but not the yolks. Whisk the contents in the stewpan until it comes to the boil, then stop, let the scum rise and remove it. Turn a chair upside down on another chair, take a cloth and tie a corner of the cloth to each of the 4 legs, place a basin underneath the cloth and first of all pour some boiling water through the cloth to make it hot. Empty the basin and replace it; now pour the contents of the pan through the cloth so that it will run through into the basin. Repeat this operation 3 times, each time rinsing the basin first in hot then in cold water, leaving it cold and wet each time. After the third operation the jelly will become very brilliant, and brilliancy in a jelly is to be aimed at. When the jelly is nearly cold it may be poured into an ornamental mould, which has been previously scaled and rinsed in cold water and left wet.

WINE JELLY

Any kind of wine jelly may be made from the preceding recipe by substituting a pint of wine in lieu of water, and using only 2 lemons.

GLOUCESTER GOOSEBERRY MOULD

1½ lb prepared gooseberries   **Sugar to taste**
½ oz gelatine   **½ pint water**

Soak the gelatine for 1 hour in a gill of water. Cook fruit in rest of water until tender. Add sugar and dissolve. Bring fruit again to the boil, just, stirring all the time. Beat in the softened gelatine and when quite dissolved, turn all into a wetted mould or basin and leave to set. Turn onto fancy plate and serve with cold, creamy custard or real cream.

RHUBARB THING

8 oz digestive biscuits   **1 pint stewed rhubarb**
2 oz butter   **1 orange jelly**
Castor sugar to taste

Crumble the biscuits and mix with melted butter and sugar. Press into a flan dish and chill. Melt the jelly in a little hot water and add to the rhubarb. Whisk well, or whirl in the blender. Just before setting, pour into the biscuit case. Chill before serving.

Jean Clark, Cherington, Glos.

OATMEAL FLUMMERY

Steep 3 large handfuls of very fine oatmeal in cold water for 24 hours, then add the same quantity of water again and leave for a further 24 hours. Strain through a fine sieve and boil until very thick, stirring well, and working in 1 tablespoon castor sugar and 2 tablespoons orange flower water. Pour into shallow dishes and serve with cream and sugar, and fresh fruit in season.

RICE FLUMMERY

Scald 1 pint of milk with a piece of lemon peel and a pinch of cinnamon, and stir in 2 oz castor sugar. Mix 3 oz ground rice with a little cold milk, then stir in the boiling milk with 1 oz fresh butter and 4 drops almond essence. Cook gently, stirring all the time, until the mixture thickens and leaves the sides of the saucepan. Pour into a wetted mould and leave until cold. Turn out and serve with cream, custard, jam, or fresh fruit.

EDWARDIAN FLUMMERY

Soften 2 oz gelatine in 1½ pints warm water, and add a wineglass of sherry and ½ wineglass brandy, with the juice of 3 lemons and sugar to sweeten lightly. Leave until cold, then stir in 1 pint lightly whipped double cream. Put into a wet mould and leave until set. Turn out, and decorate with split blanched almonds and glacé cherries. (The original recipe says this will make 2 moulds for a cost of 3/– (15p). One mould would be enough for a modern family, though the cost is far higher!)

SUMMER FLUMMERY

In a saucepan, put $\frac{1}{2}$ pint water with 5 tablespoons white wine, cider or lemon juice. Heat gently and scatter 6 level tablespoons fine semolina on the warm but not boiling liquid. Bring just to boil and reduce heat. Stir and cook for 3 minutes, then add 4 level tablespoons castor sugar. Continue stirring for 5 minutes, then remove from heat and cool. Beat 2 egg whites very stiffly and fold into lukewarm mixture. Pour into well-oiled 1-pint mould to chill and set firmly. Turn out and decorate with a few strawberries or raspberries, and serve with a sauce made from $\frac{1}{2}$ lb strawberries or raspberries which have been sweetened, crushed and very lightly cooked.

LEMON FLUMMERY

Boil $\frac{1}{2}$ pint water with $\frac{3}{4}$ oz butter and the grated peel of 1 lemon. Mix in a bowl 1 oz plain flour and 4 oz castor sugar. Make a well in the centre and put in the hot liquid, whisking to avoid lumps. Blend 1 egg yolk with a little of the hot mixture, then return all the liquid to the pan. Bring slowly to the boil and cook gently for 10 minutes. Whisk 1 egg white until stiff, add the juice of the lemon to the saucepan, then pour into a bowl and fold in the egg white. Cool, then scatter top with crushed macaroons or digestive biscuits. Serve cold with cream.

GOOSEBERRY FLUMMERY

Stew 1 lb green gooseberries with 8 oz sugar and very little water in a covered saucepan until the skins burst and the fruit is pulpy. Remove from heat and add 1 teaspoon lemon juice. Warm $\frac{1}{2}$ pint milk and sprinkle in 4 level tablespoons fine semolina. Bring just to boil, then simmer 3 minutes to thicken. Remove from heat and stir in cooked gooseberries. Tint a pale green if liked. then pour into a bowl to chill and set. Stewed rhubarb may be used instead of gooseberries, tinted lightly pink.

SIMPLE GOOSEBERRY FOOL

This is one of the few old recipes which recommend sieving the fruit. Top and tail 1 lb green gooseberries, and boil with 12 oz sugar and $\frac{1}{3}$ pint water. Put through a coarse sieve, and mix very gradually with 1 pint milk or 1 pint cream. Serve very cold.

RICH GOOSEBERRY FOOL

Stew 1 lb green gooseberries in $\frac{1}{4}$ pint water with 8 oz sugar, until soft and pulpy. Whisk them well, then blend with 1 dessertspoon orange-flower water and $\frac{3}{4}$ pint cream.

SUFFOLK MIXED FRUIT FOOL

This recipe is about 150 years old, and very rich, but well worth while for a special occasion. Bruise together $\frac{1}{2}$ pint strawberries and $\frac{1}{2}$ pint raspberries, and put them through a fine sieve. Mix pulp with 4 oz castor sugar and 1 dessertspoon orange-flower water. Scald $\frac{3}{4}$ pint cream and stir until cold, then mix the fruit pulp and cream well together. Cool in a bowl, and decorate with whole fresh strawberries or raspberries.

STRAWBERRY OR RASPBERRY FOOL

Put 1 quart strawberries or raspberries in a pan with 4 oz castor sugar and heat them just enough to draw the juice. Sieve and mix with as much creamy milk as will give the consistency of custard. Serve very cold. A richer mixture may be made if the yolks of 2 eggs are mixed with the milk and gently stirred over a low heat (preferably in a double boiler) until the custard has thickened.

APPLE FLUMMERY

Put 4 tablespoons pearl barley in 2 pints water and bring to the boil. When boiling, add $1\frac{1}{2}$ lb peeled and sliced sweet apples and cook until barley and apples are soft. Sieve them and put back into the pan with $1\frac{1}{2}$ oz castor sugar and the juice of 1 lemon. Bring to the boil, cool and stir in 3 tablespoons of cream. Serve very cold.

BLACKBERRY FOOL

Stew 1 lb blackberries in just enough water to cover them, and sweeten with castor sugar to taste. Put through a fine sieve, and mix with 1 pint cream. Serve cold in small glasses with shortbread biscuits.

BLACKBERRY FLUMMERY

Simmer 1 lb well-washed blackberries with 8 oz sugar till soft. Put through a sieve, and thicken with 2 tablespoons cornflour and a pinch of salt. Continue to cook for 5 minutes, stirring well. Add 1 teaspoon lemon juice, and cool. Serve with sugar and cream.

BLACKCURRANT FLUMMERY

1 lb blackcurrants   **4 oz castor sugar**
1 pint water   **2 teaspoons lemon juice**
1 dessertspoon cornflour   **2 eggs**

Remove stalks and wash currants; stew gently in the water until tender, then sieve them. Mix the cornflour to a smooth paste with a tablespoon of the blackcurrant purée. Put rest of purée on to boil with the sugar. When boiling, add the blended cornflour and the lemon juice, and cook for 2 minutes, stirring all the time to prevent sticking. Leave to cool. Separate the eggs, beat the yolks, and add to the cooled blackcurrant-cornflour mixture, mixing well. Whip egg whites to a stiff foam and fold into the mixture when cold. Pour into glass serving bowl; serve with cream or egg custard.

RHUBARB FOOL

2 cups stewed rhubarb   **Sugar to taste**
½ pint whipped evaporated   **Lemon juice to flavour**
milk

Sweeten the stewed fruit to taste and allow to become cold. Scald the tin of evaporated milk in a pan of boiling water for ½ an hour, cool and then chill thoroughly. Beat the milk and then fold in the stewed fruit. Flavour with a little lemon juice.

LEMON FLUMMERY

4 eggs   **½ oz gelatine**
4 oz castor sugar   **½ pint cream**
2 lemons

Separate eggs. Beat egg yolks and sugar until creamy; add rind and lemon juice slowly. Add gelatine previously dissolved in 2 tablespoons hot water. Beat ¼ pint cream until half thick. Stir in, fold in egg white. Decorate with ¼ pint thickly whipped cream, violets and angelica.

Pat Brown, Keynsham, Somerset

RASPBERRY CREAM

Rub a quart of raspberries, or raspberry jam, through a hair sieve to take out the seeds, and then mix in well with cream. Sweeten it with sugar to your taste; then put it into a stone jug, and raise a froth with a chocolate mill. As your froth rises, take it off with a spoon, and lay it upon a hair sieve. When you have got as much froth as you want, put what cream remains into a deep china dish, or punch bowl, pour your frothed cream upon it as high as it will lie on.

Thomas Train, Gateshead 1812

DAMASK CREAM

1 *pint cream*
Blade of mace
1 *cinnamon stick*
Icing sugar

Rosewater
Pinch of salt
Rennet

Heat the cream gently with the mace and cinnamon stick, but do not let it boil. When the cream is well-flavoured, remove the pan from the heat, take out spices, and sweeten to taste with icing sugar. Add rosewater to taste and salt. Cool to bloodheat and set with rennet (using the amount required for 1 pint milk). When it is cold, pour on a layer of fresh cream flavoured with rosewater, about ¼ inch thick. Decorate with rose petals.

Eighteenth-Century Recipe

POLLY'S STRAWBERRY CREAM

1 *lb strawberries*
½ *pint milk*
2 *eggs*
5 *tablespoons castor sugar*

½ *pint cream*
1 *miniature bottle Kirsch*
3 *drops rosewater*

If the strawberries are large, cut them in half. Leave small ones whole. Put strawberries into a bowl with half the Kirsch. Make a custard with the milk, egg yolks and 1 tablespoon sugar. Chill and mix in remaining Kirsch. Whip the cream and the rosewater. Into the cream, fold the custard, stiffly whipped egg whites, strawberries and Kirsch, and the remaining sugar. Serve very cold.

STONE CREAM

Cover the bottom of a glass dish about an inch thick with apricot jam. Plum or Strawberry will do. To a pint of cream put a little white powdered sugar and just enough isinglass to make it a *very* little stiff. *Nearly* boil it and when the isinglass is dissolved strain it. When nearly cold, pour over the preserves in the glass dish. You can put any ornaments you please on the top.

Mrs Garden, 1847

378

GERANIUM CREAM

½ pint double cream
6 oz cream cheese
4 tablespoons castor sugar

2 sweet-scented rose
geranium leaves

Put the cream into a double saucepan with the sugar and geranium leaves and heat over boiling water until the cream is hot but not boiling. Cool, leaving in the geranium leaves. Mix with the cream cheese until smooth and put into a bowl. Chill with a cover on for 12 hours. Remove the leaves just before serving. Serve with fresh sugared raspberries or blackberries.

CARAMEL CUSTARD

For the custard:
½ pint milk
3 eggs
1½ oz castor sugar
Vanilla flavouring

For the caramel:
4 tablespoons sugar and
2 of water

Make caramel by boiling sugar and water in a pan until golden-brown. Pour the caramel into the greased mould, or moulds. Leave until quite cold. Mix the custard, pour on top of the caramel, steam gently until set. Cool slightly before turning out. Serve hot or cold.

FROZEN APPLE CREAM

½ pint apple sauce
Cinnamon and nutmeg
1 teaspoon melted butter

2 teaspoons lemon juice
½ pint whipped cream

Put apple sauce through a sieve and add a pinch each of cinnamon and nutmeg. Stir in butter and lemon juice, and chill in refrigerator for 1 hour. Fold in cream and put into freezing tray. Freeze at lowest refrigerator setting until firm.

SCOTS CREAM-CROWDIE

1 pint double cream
2 oz coarse oatmeal
2 oz castor sugar

1 tablespoon rum
4 oz fresh raspberries or
blackberries

Cast the oatmeal in a thick-bottomed saucepan over the fire until crisp. Beat the cream to a thick froth and stir in the oatmeal, sugar, rum and fresh fruit. Serve at once.

GOOSEBERRY CREAM

Cover 2 lb prepared gooseberries with cold water and boil until tender. Sieve, and reheat the pulp, sweetening to taste. Add 1 oz butter, then 2 beaten eggs, and stir gently, but do not boil. When the mixture is thick, remove from heat, and when nearly cold add 1 teaspoon orange-flower water and a little green colouring. Stir well and put into small serving glasses. Serve with cream and sponge fingers.

GINGER CREAM

½ *pint double cream*
¼ *pint cold custard (the same*
consistency as the cream)
1 oz sugar

½ *oz gelatine*
3 tablespoons water
1 oz chopped crystallised
ginger

Dissolve the gelatine and sugar in the water. Whip cream until thick (don't overwhip) and fold into custard. Add the gelatine and stir until the mixture begins to set. Stir in the ginger. Pour into a mould to set.

ALMOND CREAM

½ *pint double cream*
1 oz sugar
¼ *oz gelatine*

3 tablespoons water
2 oz almonds
Almond essence

Blanch and skin almonds. Chop them coarsely (leaving a few for decoration) and toast till light brown. Cool. Add almond essence to the water and dissolve the sugar and gelatine in it. Whip the cream until thick (don't overwhip). Add gelatine mixture and cold chopped almonds. Mix lightly. Pour into individual moulds. Leave to set. Turn out and decorate with the whole almonds.

STRAWBERRY CREAM

2 lb strawberries
1 tablespoon lemon juice
6 oz castor sugar

2 envelopes gelatine
¼ *pint double cream*

Clean strawberries and press through a sieve, then combine with lemon juice and sugar, and stir until sugar dissolves. Melt gelatine in a little cold water, and stand bowl over hot water until gelatine becomes syrupy. Blend gelatine into strawberry mixture, then refrigerate until mixture is like unbeaten egg white. Whip cream until just stiff, fold in strawberry mixture and pour into mould. Refrigerate 2 hours before unmoulding.

COMMON SYLLABUB

Put a pint of cyder and a bottle of strong beer into a large bowl; grate in a small nutmeg and sweeten it to your taste. Then milk from the cow as much milk as will make a strong froth. Let it stand an hour, and then strew over it a few currants, well washed, picked and plummed before the fire, and it will be fit for use.

Thomas Train, Gateshead, 1812

EVERLASTING SYLLABUB

This is a very old country recipe, with a rather misleading name. The syllabub will certainly not last as long as the recipe has.

Place ½ pint thick cream in a deep bowl. Pour in about ½ pint wine. Traditionally raisin wine was used, but the cream can be flavoured with brandy, sherry, or what you will. Having added the wine, add 4 oz castor sugar and the grated rind of a lemon. Whip up the mixture briskly. As the cream rises, remove the top with a fish slice. Place the cream so sliced off in a wide glass. Continue until you have filled as many glasses as there are diners. Set aside in a cool larder or a refrigerator.

NORFOLK SYLLABUB

4 fluid oz white wine
1 tablespoon sherry
2 tablespoons brandy

1 lemon or 1 bitter (Seville)
orange
2 oz castor sugar
½ pint double cream

Put the wine, sherry and brandy into a basin. Peel the lemon or orange very thinly and squeeze out the juice. Put peel and juice into the wine mixture. Leave overnight, and remove peel. Stir in the sugar until it dissolves. Add the cream and whip until the mixture forms soft peaks. Put into tall wine glasses, jelly glasses or custard cups. This syllabub will hold its shape for 12 hours. Originally a syllabub was made by milking the cow into the wine mixture and skimming off the froth which arose into serving glasses.

HONEYCOMB MOULD (1)

1 pint of milk, 2 eggs, ½ oz of gelatine, and sugar and flavouring to suit taste. Put the milk on to boil, and beat the whites and the yolks of the eggs separately. Stir the yolks into the hot milk with the sugar and the gelatine. Let it cook until it is just thick, and then add the whites of the eggs. Then turn it into a mould to set.

Mrs Lavelle, Birmingham 1913

HONEYCOMB MOULD (2)

Juice and rind of 2 lemons *½ oz gelatine*
3 egg yolks   *¾ pint milk*
3 stiffly-beaten egg whites *3 tablespoons cream*

Beat the egg yolks in a large basin. Add the thinly-pared lemon rind, gelatine, sugar, milk and cream, and stir to a thick custard over a pan of simmering water. Mix in the lemon juice, and fold the custard into the stiffly-beaten whites. Pour into a jelly mould.

MY FRIEND'S LEMON SOLID

Put 1 quart of milk in a saucepan with ¾ lb of loaf sugar and 2 oz of gelatine. Let it get hot enough to dissolve the gelatine, then stand aside to cool, and when cool, stir in the juice of 1 good-sized lemon. Pour into a wetted mould and leave till next day, when it will turn out ½ a solid-looking custard and the other ½ a clear jelly.

Miss R. Harding, 1913

LEMON SOLID

1½ pints milk   *2 lemons*
½ pint single cream *5 oz granulated sugar*
1 oz gelatine

Put gelatine to stand in 1 pint of milk. Put remaining milk and cream mixed in a pan with the sugar. Warm until melted and bring to near boil. Add the rind of the lemons. Pour in the other milk and slowly stir in the juice of the lemons. It should slightly curdle. Pour into mould, set and turn out.

Pat Brown, Keynsham, Somerset

CAFÉ MOUSSE

Make a teacup of strongest and clearest coffee; use ¼ lb to a teacup water. When made put coffee with 2 yolks of eggs and 1 oz sugar in a gallipot into a saucepan boiling water and stir over the fire until the mixture thickens. Then let it get cold. Whip a pint of cream quite stiff and add the mixture by degrees so that it is smooth and thick. Serve in china cups and saucers.

Mrs Garden, 1847

LEMON MOUSSE

3 *eggs*
3 *oz castor sugar*
1 *large lemon*

1 *oz gelatine*
4 *oz tin evaporated milk*
or ½ *pint cream*

Separate the eggs. Whisk the egg whites to a stiff peak in one basin. Whisk the evaporated milk or cream to soft peaks in another basin. Put egg yolks and sugar into a double saucepan and whisk over heat until creamy. Add the lemon juice and grated lemon rind. Pour into the whipped cream and whisk gently, gradually adding the gelatine melted in a little hot water. Fold in the egg whites, mix well and chill. As a change, use 4 oz grated chocolate, a little coffee and rum instead of the lemon juice and rind.

Jean Clark, Cherington, Glos.

ICE CREAM

To 1 lb of preserved fruit, which may be of what kind you choose, add a quart of good cream, the juice of 2 lemons squeezed into it, and some sugar to your palate. Let the whole be rubbed through a fine hair sieve, and if raspberry, strawberry, or any red fruit, you must add a little cochineal to heighten the colour. Have your freezing pot nice and clean, and put your cream into it, cover it and put it into your tub with ice beat small, and some salt, turn the freezing pot quick, and as the cream sticks to the sides scrape it down with your ice-spoon, and so on till it is frozen. The more the cream is worked to the sides with the spoon, the smoother and better flavoured it will be. After it is well frozen, take it out, and put it into ice shapes, with fresh salt and ice; when you serve it, carefully wash the shapes for fear any salt should adhere to them, dip them in water lukewarm, and send them up to table.

Thomas Train, Gateshead, 1812

FRUIT ICES

These may be made either with water or cream. If water, 2 lb of fruit, 1 pint of spring water, 1 lb of clarified sugar, and the juice of 2 lemons.

Thomas Train, Gateshead, 1812

NO-BEATING ICE CREAM

4 *eggs*
4 *oz sifted icing sugar*

½ *pint double cream*
Flavouring to taste

This will fill one 2½ pint or 2 × 1½ pint refrigerator containers with lids if the freezing compartment is big enough. If not, use an ice tray and cover with a lid of foil. Set the refrigerator to coldest setting. Separate the eggs and whisk the egg yolks in a small bowl until well blended. In a larger bowl, whisk egg whites until they form stiff peaks. Beat in the sifted icing sugar a spoonful at a time until it has all been included. Slowly whisk the blended egg yolks with the white meringue mixture. Lightly whip cream until it is frothy and will form stiff peaks. Fold this into the egg mixture and add any flavouring. Mix thoroughly and pour into container. Cover and freeze for at least 2 hours before serving.

Joan Gay, Marlborough, Wilts

IVY COTTAGE ICE CREAM

Make a custard with ½ pint milk, 2 eggs, 3 oz sugar. Cool a little. Add 4 oz plain chocolate or chocolate chips. Now add 1 level teaspoon gelatine dissolved in 1 tablespoon of water. Cool this chocolate-custard-gelatine mixture. Take ½ pint evaporated milk and whisk it till it doubles in volume. Now add the other mixture and chill together in freezer. *Note for evaporated milk*—Boil if for 20 minutes in *unopened* tin. Store in refrigerator until needed.

This recipe is quite successful for coffee flavouring.

For best results turn the refrigerator to COLDEST setting ½ hour before making the ice cream, as the faster it sets the creamier it will be.

ICE CREAM

Whip ¼ pint of cream, stir in 4 level tablespoons icing sugar. Fold into two stiffly beaten egg whites, add flavouring. No need to stir while freezing.

M. Shepherd, Tywardreath

BLACKBERRY ICE

Boil together 4 oz castor sugar and ¼ pint water for 5 minutes to make a syrup. 2 rose geranium leaves steeped in the syrup or a tablespoon of rosewater will greatly improve the flavour of the ice. Sieve 1 lb black-berries very finely, and blend into the syrup. Pour into refrigerator freezing tray, cover with aluminium foil, and freeze at normal ice-making temperature for 2 hours.

STRAWBERRY ICE

8 oz strawberries　　　　　*12 oz sugar*
Juice of 1 orange　　　　　*1 egg white*
¼ pint water

Sieve strawberries with orange juice. Dissolve sugar in water and boil for 10 minutes. Cool and add strawberries and orange juice. Freeze at lowest setting of refrigerator until mushy. Put into chilled bowl, add stiffly-whipped egg white and beat well. Return to freezer for a further hour.

HONEY ICE CREAM

1 lb fresh or frozen
raspberries
¼ pint double cream
1 small carton plain yoghurt

10 level tablespoons honey
2 tablespoons lemon juice
Pinch of salt
4 egg whites

Put raspberries through a sieve and add cream, yoghurt, honey, lemon juice and salt. Mix thoroughly, put into ice trays and freeze. Put into a mixing bowl and stir until smooth, then fold in stiffly whisked egg whites. Return mixture to ice trays and refreeze. Serve in chilled glasses.

This is a delicious, light and refreshing ice with a distinctive flavour of honey and raspberries, which is very good after a heavy meal.

MICHAEL'S BIRTHDAY PUDDING

Years ago there was a BBC competition for summer sweets. Being self-confident in those days, I composed this recipe and sent it up without ever actually making it. When I collected first prize and had it demonstrated on television I could not confess and had to think quickly to avoid awkward questions. Subsequently I have frequently made it, as it is easy and keeps for ages in the deep freeze.

Make your favourite ice cream (I use blackberry with ½ pint of frozen pulp). Put some lightly crushed meringues in the bottom of a ring mould. Fill up with ice cream and cover with more crushed meringue. Press them firmly into the ice cream. Turn out and serve with more meringues and whole blackberries in the centre.

Joan Dampney, Christchurch, Hants

23 *Cheesecakes*

The calves then that come betwene new yere and lent:
save gladly for store lest thou after repent.
For all thing at that time that colde feleth some:
shall better beare colde when the next winter come.
Weane no time thy calfe under xl daies olde:
and lay for to save it as thou savest golde.
Yet calves that doe fal betwene change and the prime:
has seldome to rere them, but kill them in time.

Thomas Tusser

MRS SHUTTLEWORTH'S YORKSHIRE CHEESECAKE

About a quart of beastings
3 oz sugar
1 egg, beaten
Lemon rind
Short crust pastry (10 oz flour
to 4½ oz lard and 1½ oz butter
or margarine)

Pinch of freshly grated
nutmeg
Baking powder
A little melted butter

386

To make the curd: put the beastings into a heavy-based pan and stand over a gentle heat (a double saucepan could be used). You must be careful to avoid letting it burn—it quickly turns solid in the pan as it is *very high in protein*.

When it is solid, turn it out into a large basin, straining it through a sieve. Before the curd is quite cold, break it up with a fork, not too finely. To make the cheesecakes line a deep saucer or tin with a good short crust pastry and fill it with the following mixture: to $\frac{1}{2}$ lb curds add 3 oz sugar, the egg and nutmeg. Stir in the currants and lemon rind. Finally stir in 1 teaspoon of baking powder and a scant oz of melted butter. Bake at about 400°F (Gas Mark 6) for 30 minutes or until golden brown.

From Mrs Shuttleworth comes this recipe which 'could never be found in any modern cookbook'. She says it is a recipe which has been handed down to her through the tattered pages of her husband's grandmother's cookery book. In the West Riding, she says, they usually just call them curd tarts, but in some districts they are known as 'beastings' tarts. You will need to know a diary farmer to procure the 'beastings' or first milk. or colostrum, of a freshly calved cow. Once procured, however, it will keep in a freezer for a while. She says 'I guarantee that this will disappear like magic, before your very eyes, which is just as well because *they should be eaten while fresh* to be at their best.'

HONEY AND WALNUT CHEESECAKE

Short pastry
3 tablespoons sultanas
1 tablespoon chopped
candied peel
8 oz cottage cheese
2 tablespoons double cream
1 tablespoon honey
2 eggs
1 dessertspoon lemon juice
1 level teaspoon cinnamon
3 oz walnut kernels

Line a pie plate with pastry and sprinkle the bottom with sultanas and peel. Blend sieved cottage cheese with cream, honey, egg yolks and lemon juice. Whisk egg whites stiffly and fold in mixture. Put into pastry case and sprinkle with cinnamon. Bake at 425°F (Gas Mark 7) for 10 minutes, then reduce the heat to 375°F (Gas Mark 5) and bake for 30 minutes. Sprinkle thickly with very finely-chopped walnuts before serving.

HONEY CHEESECAKE

4 oz cottage cheese
2 oz honey
2 oz castor sugar
$\frac{1}{2}$ level teaspoon cinnamon
2 beaten eggs
Short pastry
Cinnamon
Castor sugar

Blend together sieved cottage cheese, honey, sugar, cinnamon and eggs. Line a pie plate with short pastry and fill with the cheese mixture. Sprinkle thickly with a mixture of cinnamon and extra castor sugar, and bake at 375°F (Gas Mark 5) for 35 minutes.

SONIA'S CHEESECAKE

2 oz butter
4 oz castor sugar
4 eggs
1 lb cottage cheese
2 tablespoons whipped cream

1 level tablespoon cornflour
2 tablespoons lemon juice
1 teaspoon grated lemon rind
Sweet biscuit crumbs

Cream butter and sugar and beat in egg yolks. Add sieved cottage cheese, whipped cream, cornflour, lemon juice and rind. Blend all ingredients thoroughly and fold in stiffly whisked egg whites. Butter an 8 inch tin, and sprinkle with crushed sweet biscuit crumbs. Pour in cheese mixture and bake near the top of oven at 325°F (Gas Mark 3) for $1\frac{1}{4}$ hours. Leave to cool slightly in the turned-off oven before serving.

ALMOND CHEESECAKE

2 oz butter
2 oz castor sugar
Grated rind of 1 lemon
3 egg yolks
1 lb cottage cheese

2 oz ground almonds
1 oz sultanas
2 oz soft breadcrumbs
Pinch of salt

Cream butter and sugar with lemon rind. Beat in egg yolks. Stir in sieved cottage cheese, ground almonds, sultanas, breadcrumbs and salt. Put into a buttered 8 inch tin, and bake at 400°F (Gas Mark 6) for 40 minutes. Leave to cool with the oven turned off. Sprinkle with sugar before serving.

OLD-FASHIONED CHEESECAKES

8 oz cottage cheese
6 oz castor sugar
6 egg yolks
2 oz butter
Finely grated rind of 2 lemons
Pinch of salt

Pinch of nutmeg
Puff pastry
Chopped mixed peel
Currants
Sultanas

Blend together sieved cottage cheese, sugar, egg yolks, butter, lemon rind salt and nutmeg. Line tartlet tins with puff pastry, and spoon the cheese mixture into the cases. Sprinkle with peel, currants and sultanas. Bake at 375°F (Gas Mark 5) until the pastry is light and golden.

COVENTRY TARTS

8 oz cottage cheese *4 oz butter*
4 oz castor sugar *1 egg*
Pinch of salt *Short pastry*
Pinch of nutmeg *Apple, cranberry, quince or*
1 tablespoon orange juice *currant jelly*

Blend together sieved cottage cheese, sugar, salt, nutmeg, fruit juice, butter and beaten egg. Line tartlet tins with short pastry and fill with mixture. Bake at 375°F (Gas Mark 5) until pastry is light and golden. Top each tart with jelly before serving.

There seem to be several traditional English cheesecakes, some dating from the seventeenth century, usually made from cottage or curd cheese. The name 'cheesecake' was also given to those made with fresh cream and fruit juices, since the mixture formed a curd. The famous Yorkshire curd cakes were made with new cheese curd rubbed into a custard with milk and eggs, and baked in a pastry case, sometimes with currants.

Today, curds are not often obtainable, and pasteurised milk is not suitable for making our own soft cheese, but cottage cheese is widely available. This is best sieved for use and mixed with a little fresh cream. Soured cream is also available in cartons, or fresh cream may be soured with a little lemon juice. Traditionally cheesecakes have a pastry base and are cooked in a slow moderate oven. Some modern versions which masquerade under the same name are unbaked and set in the refrigerator; they make delicious puddings but won't please the husband who wants a cheesecake 'just like Mother made'.

TRADITIONAL YORKSHIRE CHEESECAKE

4 oz plain flour *2 eggs*
Pinch of salt *Grated rind of 1 lemon*
2½ oz butter *2 teaspoons cornflour*
Juice of 1½ lemons *2 tablespoons double cream*
8 oz curd cheese (or cottage *1 tablespoon melted butter*
cheese) *Raisins*
2 tablespoons castor sugar

Sift flour and salt, rub in butter, and add juice of ½ lemon and enough water to bind. Roll out thinly and use to line 10 inch plate. Bake blind at 425°F (Gas Mark 7) for 10 minutes. Sieve cheese and mix with sugar, eggs, lemon rind and remainder of lemon juice. Beat until smooth and add

389

cornflour mixed with cream to a smooth paste. Fold in melted butter and blend well. Pour into pastry case and sprinkle with raisins. Bake at 350°F (Gas Mark 4) for 30 minutes. Serve cold.

Black Bull Hotel, Freath, Yorks

NINETEENTH-CENTURY CHEESECAKES

8 oz puff pastry	*2 oz butter*
8 oz cottage cheese	*Pinch of nutmeg and salt*
6 oz sugar	*Grated rind of 2 lemons*
6 egg yolks	

Line small tart tins with pastry. Sieve cheese and mix with all ingredients, and put into tart cases. Sprinkle top of each with a mixture of chopped candied peel, currants and sultanas. Bake at 375°F (Gas Mark 5) until pastry is golden, about 20 mintues.

RAISIN AND PINEAPPLE CHEESECAKE

8 oz plain flour	*2 oz seeded raisins*
Pinch of salt	*8 oz cottage cheese*
5 oz butter	*10 oz soured cream*
1 oz castor sugar	*2 oz castor sugar*
1 egg yolk	*2 eggs and 1 egg white*
2 pineapple rings	*1 teaspoon grated lemon rind*

A flan ring is best for this cheesecake, but if you are uncertain about using one successfully, a china flan dish will look decorative. Grease the container well. Sieve flour and salt and rub in butter until the mixture is like bread-crumbs. Add sugar and bind together with the egg yolk blended with 1 teaspoon water. Line flan ring and chill, saving trimmings for lattice strips. Chop pineapple and put with raisins on the bottom of the pastry case. Sieve cottage cheese and beat in remaining ingredients. Pour into pastry shell. Bake at 425°F (Gas Mark 7) for 20 minutes. Remove from oven, lattice top with strips, sprinkle with extra castor sugar and bake at 325°F (Gas Mark 3) for 35 minutes.

CHRISTMAS CHEESECAKE

8 oz rich short pastry	*2 oz sultanas*
16 oz cottage cheese	*1 oz chopped candied peel*
1 oz ground almonds	*5 oz soured cream*
2 eggs and 2 egg yolks	*1 oz castor sugar*
4 oz castor sugar	*Candied lemon and orange*
Grated zest of 1 large lemon	*slices*
5 oz soured cream	

Line Swiss roll tin with pastry and bake blind at 425°F (Gas Mark 7) for 7 minutes. Mix together sieved cottage cheese, ground almonds, eggs, yolks, sugar, lemon zest, soured cream, sultanas and chopped candied peel. Fill pastry case and bake at 300°F (Gas Mark 2) for 1 hour 10 minutes. Mix together soured cream and sugar for topping and spread on top of cheesecake 15 minutes before end of baking time. Turn off oven and leave cheesecake in oven for 1 hour. Chill and remove from tin. Decorate with halved slices of candied orange and lemon. This makes a delicious contrast to traditional Christmas foods.

24 Bread and Yeast Cakes and Buns

There is no mystery about breadmaking. The rules are simple, but these are the basic instructions for preparing the best possible bread.

Warm basin and flour to avoid chilling the dough, which slows up the working of the yeast.

Make the dough on the soft side for a light loaf; if it's too stiff it cannot expand under the influence of the yeast.

Work the dough thoroughly to ensure an even distribution of yeast to allow it to work properly in raising the dough.

Keep the dough warm and warm the tins.

Don't make the dough too hot or it will produce a coarse, breakable crumb of irregular texture.

Don't try to shorten the rising or proving time of the dough. Under-proving or under-fermentation will give a heavy, soggy loaf with a crust breaking away from the top.

Don't let the dough rise for too long. Over-proving or over-fermentation results in a loss of strength, colour, scent and flavour.

Don't bake the bread at too low a temperature, or it will be pale, moist and flavourless.

Yeast products freeze particularly well and you can keep a good supply of bread, buns and yeast pastries which will taste just as delicious as they were fresh from the oven. Uncooked yeast mixtures can also be frozen for future baking.

Equipment

Any type of cooker can be used, and the oven must be preheated before baking. You need a large mixing bowl, a wooden spoon, a clean cloth to cover the dough, and loaf tins and/or baking sheets. Once these tins have been greased and used regularly, they should not be washed but wiped clean, greased and floured for each using.

A dough hook for an electric mixer is cheap and will save a lot of hard work.

Ingredients

Large quantities of flour can be stored for about 3 months in a small dustbin. 3 lb bags are convenient for a batch of bread or buns.

Fresh yeast can be kept for about 10 days in a covered bowl in the refrigerator. If supplies are erratic, it is worth buying 8 oz or 1 lb packages which can be stored in the freezer (divide the yeast into 1 oz cubes and wrap each cube in polythene or foil); frozen yeast will be ready for use after 30 minutes at room temperature.

Dried yeast is convenient to store and use, though it sometimes has a stronger flavour. The maker's specific instructions must be carefully followed. 1 oz of dried yeast is equal to 2 oz fresh yeast if you are following a recipe which does not specify dried yeast. 3 lb flour requires 1 oz dried yeast, and the yeast takes longer to start working than fresh yeast (usually about 15 minutes) before being added to the flour.

Fat and sugar added to the basic mixture give a richer, longer-keeping bread. Salt is an essential in bread and should be dissolved first in a little water, as dry salt affects the growth of the yeast cells.

Storage

Home baked bread is best stored in a refrigerator in a polythene bag. The addition of 1 oz fat to 3 lb flour keeps bread fresh longer.

Bread and buns freeze best when 1 day old. They can be packed in foil or polythene, and should be thawed in wrappings at room temperature. A $1\frac{1}{2}$ lb loaf will take 3 hours to thaw.

Bread may be thawed in a moderate oven, but will then stale very quickly. Richer yeast doughs, such as used for tea breads and savarins, will keep for 3 months in the freezer; yeast pastries which include fat, are best kept for only 1 month.

Uncooked yeast mixtures may be frozen for up to 2 weeks, but proving after freezing takes a long time, and the texture may be heavier. Unbaked dough for freezing should be proved only once, and then either shaped for baking, or kept in bulk if storage in this form is easier.

The surface should be brushed with a little olive oil or unsalted melted butter to prevent toughening of the crust. A little extra sugar should be added to sweet mixtures.

Wrap the dough or shaped bread in freezer-paper or polythene. The dough should be thawed in a moist warm place as quickly as possible to give a light-textured loaf, then shaped and proved again before baking. Shaped bread and rolls should be proved at once in a warm place before baking.

Making the dough

Before work begins, the flour should be sieved and warmed. Warm liquid must be added—1 part boiling water to 7 parts cold tap water gives an approximately correct temperature.

When the yeast is added, it is set working by the addition of water and/ or sugar, then well kneaded into the flour mixture.

Kneading is best done on a floured board, folding the dough over on itself and pushing with a firm, rocking motion until the dough becomes smooth and shiny.

The dough must then prove in a warm place, covered with a damp cloth. A rack over a cooker, or in front of a fire, are suitable warm places, but the dough should not be over direct heat or steam, or in a draught. When the dough has doubled in size, it should be lightly re-kneaded and shaped.

Baking and finishing

Bread is baked in a hot oven 450°F (Gas Mark 8), though sweet light mixtures are cooked at a lower temperature. A dish of water in the oven gives a crisp crust. Bread is ready when it sounds hollow if tapped underneath with the knuckles.

A professional finish can be added. Plain loaves painted with rich milk or cream before baking have a gleaming brown crust; beaten eggs give a dark crust; melted butter or margarine a crisp, crunchy crust. Thick milk and sugar syrup painted on after baking, gives a sweet, sticky finish.

WHITE BREAD

2½ lb white bread flour　　　**½ oz salt**
1 oz fresh yeast　　　　　　　**1½ pints warm water**
2 oz fat (butter, margarine
or lard)

Put flour in a large warm bowl, make a well in the centre, and sprinkle salt around the edge. Cream yeast with a little warm water and pour into the well. Add the rest of the water and the warmed fat and mix well to a soft putty-like consistency. Leave to prove until double in size. Put into tins and leave to prove again until bread reaches top of the tins. Bake at 450°F (Gas Mark 8) for 45 minutes, turning bread once in the oven. Cool on a wire rack.

WHOLEMEAL BREAD

3 lb wholemeal flour　　　　　**1½ oz fresh yeast**
1 oz salt　　　　　　　　　　**1½ pints warm water**
1 oz sugar

Take half the flour and make into a batter with all the water. Cream the yeast with 2 tablespoons of warm water and mix well into the batter. Cover the basin with a damp cloth and let the batter stand for 15 minutes. Add the rest of the flour, salt and sugar, and make the dough. Mix well and knead for 10 minutes. Warm and lightly grease 4 × 1 lb loaf tins, and divide dough amongst them. Flatten each piece and roll up to fit lengthwise in the tin, pressing down to avoid cracks and folds. Leave for 1 hour in a warm place until the dough doubles in volume. Bake at 450°F (Gas Mark 8) for 45 minutes, turning the loaves (moving them through a right-angle in the oven) half way through cooking time. Turn the loaves on to a wire tray and cool thoroughly before cutting.

WHOLEWHEAT BREAD

3 lb wholewheat stoneground　　**2 level tablespoons brown**
flour　　　　　　　　　　　　**sugar**
2 level teaspoons salt　　　　　**1 oz dried yeast**
2 level teaspoons vegetable　　**1½ pints warm water**
fat or oil

Dissolve 2 teaspoons of the sugar in ⅔ of the water. Sprinkle yeast into liquid, whisk and disperse with a fork, and leave to stand for 15 minutes in a warm place until frothy. Dissolve rest of sugar and salt in remaining water. Add oil, and add to flour. Pour in yeast mixture and mix thoroughly to a smooth dough. Knead for 5 minutes. Prove in a warm place for about 20 minutes and wait until double in size. Knead again and shape into loaves (this quantity will fill 4 × 1 lb tins). Prove for 20 minutes. Bake at 450°F (Gas Mark 8) for 35 minutes, and brush tops with oil as soon as loaves come out of oven.

BEGINNER'S BREAD

1½ *lb wholemeal flour*
1½ *lb plain flour*
4 *level teaspoons salt*
1 *level tablespoon syrup or*
brown sugar

1¾ *pints lukewarm milk and*
water
1 *teaspoon honey*
2 *oz yeast*

Put the flour, salt and syrup (or sugar) into a warm basin and leave in a warm place. Whisk the milk and water with the honey and yeast in a jug. Add to the flour, mix with your hands to a stiff dough.

Half fill greased bread tins, press down firmly with damp fingers, cover with a damp cloth, and put to rise in a warm place until the dough has filled the tins. One rising only is necessary because you're using wholemeal flour.

Remove the cloth, brush the tops of the loaves with milk or melted butter, and bake in a hot oven, the first 5 minutes at 450°F (Gas Mark 8), then reduce the heat or move to a lower shelf, and cook for a further 25–30 minutes or until done.

Turn the loaves out of the tins and tap the bottoms. If they sound hollow, the bread is done, if not, put back in oven, out of tins and cook for a further 5 minutes. Cool on a wire rack.

QUICK BREAD

3 *lb plain flour*
1 *level teaspoon sugar*
¼ *pint boiling milk, mixed*
with

1¼ *pints cold water*
1 *teaspoon honey or syrup*
2 *oz yeast*
4 *level teaspoons salt*

Put 1 lb of flour into a bowl, add the sugar, and leave in a warm place. Mix the boiling milk, the cold water, the honey or syrup together in a jug. Add the yeast and stir thoroughly. Add all this liquid gradually to the warmed flour, mixing with a wooden spoon to a smooth batter. Beat well, cover with a cloth and stand in a warm place again for 15 minutes. The mixture will rise and bubble. This period counts as the first rising.

Sieve the salt with the remaining flour and add to the batter a little at a time, using a spoon first to stir, then your hand, as the batter becomes a dough knead well until the dough feels elastic. Shape into a ball with well-floured hands, put into a well-greased baking tin, cover with a damp cloth and stand again in a warm place until the dough has doubled its size.

Turn the dough onto a floured board, divide into 4 pieces and shape each piece into a roll. Flour and flatten each piece, and roll up like a Swiss roll. Do this 2 to 3 times to each piece. Put each roll into a greased 1 lb bread tin, press down well. Cover with a damp cloth and put in a warm place until the dough rises to the tops of the tins. Brush tops with milk. Bake in a hot oven, 500°F (Gas Mark 9) for 10 minutes, then 400°F (Gas Mark 6). Small loaves 20 minutes or large loaves 30–35 minutes.

JOYCE GARDENER'S AIRING CUPBOARD BREAD

To a 3 lb bag of stoneground wholemeal (plain) flour, I add 2 heaped teaspoons salt and rub in 2 oz lard. I put the flour and bowl in a warm place some hours before making. When I am going bread making I remove the clothes and use the airing cupboard for rising. I think the bread has a better flavour if it does not rise too quickly. I put $\frac{1}{2}$ oz dried yeast (1 oz if you use fresh, but I found it so unreliable) in a cup with a heaped teaspoon sugar (I use brown) and a little warm water and stir, put this in the airing cupboard (saucer on top) then rub in lard into the flour and put back in the cupboard. When the yeast is working well (about 12 minutes) I make a hole in the flour and pour in the yeast and $1\frac{1}{4}$ pints water, warmer than tepid but not too hot. Mix well and gather together, turn onto a board and knead for 5 minutes. I do not flour the board, as I find this quantity of water is enough to make a soft dough without being sticky, also the final loaves stand up better. Then return to bowl and cover with damp cloth and return to cupboard for 1 hour. Then knead for 5 minutes and return to cupboard covering with cloth again, after $\frac{3}{4}$ hour I look at it. If I consider it has doubled its size I knead for 5 minutes and return to cupboard for $\frac{1}{2}$ hour covering with cloth. Then knead for a few minutes, divide and shape into 4 loaves making cuts across the top with a sharp knife and put in the tins and place in the cupboard for 40–45 minutes, covering with cloth. When I have shaped the loaves I turn the oven as high as it will go and then turn it down to 500°F when I put the bread in, 2 loaves on a shelf; after $\frac{1}{4}$ hour I swap the shelves over and turn down to 450°F (Gas Mark 8), and turn off the oven after $\frac{1}{2}$ hour. I give the loaves a few minutes more (usually 5) then remove from oven and place on racks and cool quickly.

JUNE'S BREAD

2 lb strong flour (10-12 oz
wholemeal flour and white)
2 teaspoons salt
1 oz yeast (fresh)
2 teaspoons castor sugar

1 egg (optional)
1 pint (lukewarm) liquid
including egg ($\frac{1}{2}$ milk, $\frac{1}{2}$ water)
$1\frac{1}{2}$ oz lard

Rub in fat to flour and salt. Put Castor sugar with yeast into liquid. Make a well in flour and add yeast and liquid. Mix in. Stand in warm place about $\frac{1}{2}$ an hour or until it is bubbling. Knead for about 7–8 minutes until dough leaves side of bowl (the longer you do it, the better the bread). Stand again until it doubles in size. Knead again and put in tins. Leave to rise and double. Bake rolls at 425°F (Gas Mark 7) for 30 minutes, and loaves for 45 minutes.

EMERGENCY BREAD

Mix 1 lb flour with 1 teaspoon salt and 1 teaspoon bicarbonate of soda. Add $\frac{1}{2}$ pint sour milk and mix to a dough. Grease a loaf tin and place the dough in this, making a shallow trough down the centre so that the bread rises evenly. Bake in a fairly hot oven, 400°F (Gas Mark 6) for about 45 minutes. Let it get cold before cutting.

IRISH GRIDDLE BREAD

8 oz wholemeal flour
8 oz plain flour
1 level dessertspoon sugar
1 level teaspoon bicarbonate
of soda

1 level teaspoon salt
1 dessertspoon dripping
Milk

Mix together flours, and add sugar, soda and salt. Rub in dripping and mix to a batter with milk, to make a dough which is stiff but will roll easily. Roll out in a round 1 inch thick, and cut into 4 sections. Cook on a hot griddle for 10 minutes each side.

BROWN SODA BREAD

1 lb white flour
3 lb brown wholemeal flour
1 tablespoon baking powder
1 teaspoon bicarbonate of soda

1 tablespoon sugar
$\frac{1}{2}$ teaspoon salt
2 oz butter or lard
$1\frac{1}{2}$ pints warm milk

Sift flour, baking powder, bicarbonate of soda, sugar and salt into a large bowl. Rub fat into flour and mix to a stiff dough with warm milk. Knead until smooth and shape into an oblong loaf. Score a cross on the top and bake at 400°F (Gas Mark 6) for 1 hour.

OATMEAL AND WHOLEMEAL BREAD

8 oz wholemeal flour
6 oz medium or coarse oatmeal
2 teaspoons cream of tartar

(not required if sour milk is used)
1 teaspoon bicarbonate of soda
1 teaspoon salt
Milk and water to mix

Mix dry ingredients. Add enough milk and water to make stiff dough. Work together as quickly as possible with hands and put in floured tin or form into round loaf. Bake in fairly hot oven.

MALT BREAD

1½ lb white flour (or a mixture of plain white and wholewheat flour)
1 oz fresh yeast
¼ teaspoon salt

¼ pint warm water
2 tablespoons black treacle
2 tablespoons extract of malt
2 oz butter
2 oz sultanas

Sieve flour into bowl. Cream yeast with a little water, and dissolve salt in rest of water. Add the yeast and water to the flour, then add treacle, malt, butter and sultanas. Knead to an even texture, prove till double in size, knead again and shape into tins. Prove until the mixture reaches the top of the tins, then bake at 425°F (Gas Mark 7) for 45 minutes, turning the loaves half-way through cooking time. Remove to a wire tray and glaze with milk and sugar syrup.

CURRANT BREAD

1½ lb white flour
4 oz sugar
Pinch of salt
1 oz fresh yeast

4 oz warm butter
½ pint warm milk
8 oz mixed dried fruit
2 oz chopped mixed peel

Mix flour, sugar and salt, and add yeast creamed with a little sugar. Work in warm butter and milk, knead and leave to prove for 1½ hours. Knead in fruit and peel, and shape into loaves or buns to prove for 45 minutes. Bake at 375°F (Gas Mark 5) for 45 minutes, turning after 20 minutes. Small buns will need about 20 minutes cooking time. Remove to a wire tray and glaze with a mixture of milk and sugar.

BAPS

1 lb plain flour
2 oz lard
2 level teaspoons salt
1 level teaspoon sugar

1 oz yeast
½ pint lukewarm milk and water

Sieve the flour, rub in the lard and sugar. Cream the yeast in half the liquid and dissolve the salt in the rest. Mix into the flour, knead and prove until double in size. Divide into pieces and make into small loaves about 4 inches across. Brush with milk, put on to a greased baking sheet, prove again, and bake at 450°F (Gas Mark 8) for 20 minutes.

MUFFINS

1 egg	**1 lb flour**
½ pint milk	**1 teaspoon salt**
1 oz butter or margarine	**½ oz fresh yeast**

Beat together egg, milk and warm butter. Put flour and salt into a bowl, and put in yeast creamed with a little warm water. Add butter, milk and egg mixture, and knead thoroughly to a soft but not sticky dough. Cover and prove for 1½ hours. Roll out dough to ½ inch thickness on a floured board, and cut out muffins with a large tumbler. Bake on a griddle, turning as soon as the bottoms are browned, or on a baking sheet in a hot oven at 450°F (Gas Mark 8) for 15 minutes, turning half way through cooking.

CORNISH SPLITS

1 lb strong plain flour	**1 oz yeast**
2 oz fat	**½ pint warm milk**
1 teaspoon salt	**1 teaspoon sugar**

Warm milk and add sugar and yeast. Sieve flour and salt. Work in fat finely. Add liquid altogether. Mix and knead. Allow to rise till double in size in a warm place. Knead again till fine in texture. Divide into equal sizes, roll into balls and place on floured baking tray. Allow to rise again. Bake at 375°F (Gas Mark 5) for approximately 15 minutes.

FRUIT BANNOCK

Batter ingredients:	**Additional ingredients:**
2 oz plain flour	**6 oz plain flour**
1 oz melted butter or lard	**1 oz castor sugar**
⅛ pint warm milk	**⅛ pint warm milk**
¼ oz fresh yeast	**1 oz sultanas**
	1 oz currants
	½ oz candied peel

Blend batter ingredients together in a mixing bowl and leave for 20–30 minutes until the batter is frothy. Add the additional ingredients and mix well. Knead the dough thoroughly for about 10 minutes on a lightly floured board. Put the dough to rise in a warm place under a damp cloth and leave for 1 hour, until the dough springs back when pressed gently with a floured finger. Knead the dough again and shape into a ball. Flatten with the hands to approximately 8 inches across and ½ inch thick. Put on a greased and floured tray and slash with sharp knife into 8 equal sections. Brush top with milk, cover with a greased paper and leave to rise until the dough feels springy (about 45 minutes). Brush top again with milk, and bake towards the top of a fairly hot oven, 400°F (Gas Mark 6) for 20 minutes. Cool on a wire tray.

BATH BUNS

12 oz plain flour	*3 oz sugar*
4 oz butter	*Grated rind of 1 lemon*
¾ oz yeast	*1 oz chopped mixed peel*
⅛ pint milk	*2 oz sultanas*
2 eggs	*Sugar crystals or crushed*
½ teaspoon salt	*loaf sugar*

Rub the butter into the warm flour. Cream the yeast with a little milk and add with the rest of the milk and the eggs to the flour, stirring in the salt. Knead well and leave to rise until double its size. Knead in sugar, lemon rind, peel and sultanas, and make into 10 rough balls. Leave to prove again for 10 minutes. Brush with egg, sprinkle with crushed loaf sugar or sugar crystals, and bake at 450°F (Gas Mark 8) for 15 minutes.

CHELSEA BUNS

12 oz plain flour	*1½ gills milk*
3 oz melted butter	*2 oz castor sugar*
½ oz yeast	*2 oz currants*

Put the flour in a warm basin, and add 2 oz of the melted butter. Cream the yeast with a pinch of sugar and add to the flour mixture together with the milk. Knead well and leave to rise until double its size. Re-knead to a square shape. Brush with remaining melted butter and sprinkle with the sugar and currants. Roll up like a Swiss roll, and cut into slices 1½ inches thick. Place cut side up on greased baking sheet, leaving room to swell. Leave to prove for 10 minutes. Brush with egg and bake at 450°F (Gas Mark 8) for 15 minutes.

ICED PLAIT

8 oz *plain flour*
Pinch of salt
½ oz *yeast*
¾ *gill milk*
1 oz *butter*
2 oz *sugar*

1 *egg*
3 oz *mixed dried fruit*
Water icing
Chopped nuts and glacé
cherries

Put the flour and salt into a warm bowl. Cream the yeast with a little sugar, and add to the flour, together with the butter, sugar, warm milk, egg and dried fruit. Mix well, knead thoroughly, and leave in a warm place until double its size. Re-knead, form into a long roll, divide into three and plait together, pressing the ends together firmly. Prove for 15 minutes, then brush with egg and bake at 450°F (Gas Mark 8) for 15 minutes. When cold, coat with white water icing and sprinkle thickly with chopped nuts and glacé cherries.

SALLY LUNNS

12 oz *plain flour*
½ *teaspoon salt*
½ oz *yeast*
1 *teaspoon sugar*

1½ *gills milk*
2 oz *melted butter*
1 *egg*

Warm the flour and salt. Cream the yeast with the sugar, add warm milk, and stir into the flour with melted butter and egg. Knead well and divide in half. Shape the pieces to fit 2 greased 6 inch round cake tins or soufflé dishes. Leave in a warm place until risen to the top of the tins. Brush with egg and bake at 450°F (Gas Mark 8) for 30 minutes. If the Sally Lunns are to be eaten hot, they should be split in 4 and spread thickly with butter, then the slices replaced and cut into wedges. They should be covered with a damp cloth and reheated in the oven until the butter has melted.

TEA CAKES

8 oz *plain flour*
Pinch of salt
½ oz *butter*
½ oz *yeast*

1 *teaspoon sugar*
1 *egg*
¼ *pint milk*
2 oz *sultanas*

Warm the flour and salt and rub in the butter. Cream the yeast and sugar and add to the flour, together with the egg, milk and sultanas. Knead well and leave in a warm place until double its size. Knead well again and divide into 3, shaping into rather flat round cakes. Put on greased tins, and prove for 10 minutes. Bake at 450°F (Gas Mark 8) for 12 minutes. Brush over with milk and sugar glaze immediately after removing from oven.

LINCOLNSHIRE PLUM BREAD

12 oz plain flour
1 teaspoon baking powder
¼ level teaspoon nutmeg
Pinch of salt
4 oz butter
6 oz castor sugar
6 oz currants

3 oz sultanas
3 oz raisins
2 oz mixed peel
2 oz chopped glacé cherries
1 oz yeast
½ pint warm milk

Sieve flour, baking powder, nutmeg and salt into a basin. Rub in butter. Add most of the sugar, keeping a little back and add dried fruit. Cream the yeast with remaining sugar, make a well in dry ingredients, and add yeast and warm milk, mixing well together. Turn mixture into a greased 2 lb loaf tin and bake in a very moderate oven, 325°F (Gas Mark 3) for 2½ hours, covering with thick brown paper after 1½ hours. Turn out on wire rack to cool. Slice and spread with butter.

BARA BRITH WITH YEAST

½ pint milk
½ oz yeast
1 egg
1 lb plain flour
2 oz soft brown sugar

½ level teaspoon salt
1 level teaspoon mixed spice
2 oz cooking fat
10 oz mixed dried fruit
2 oz candied peel (chopped)

Heat the milk until lukewarm. Dissolve the yeast in 1 tablespoon of the milk. Beat the egg and add to remainder of milk. Sift the flour, brown sugar, salt and spice into a bowl, and rub in the fat. Stir in the dried fruit and peel. Make a well in centre of dry ingredients and pour in egg, milk and yeast. Beat until smooth and beat or knead for a further 5 minutes. Place in a well greased 2 lb loaf tin. Put to rise in warm place until double its bulk. Bake for 15 minutes at 425°F (Gas Mark 7) and for 1 hour at 375°F (Gas Mark 5).

HARVEST CAKES

Make a piece of dough as if for loaf of bread with warm milk. Let it stand till quite light. Then work in a *small* piece of butter, a *very little* sugar and a very few currants. Then make the cakes about as large as a light dumpling. Let them stand again till light. Bake on flat tin.

Mrs Garden, 1847

BARLEY CAKES

3 oz sugar
2 oz butter
2½ oz barley flour
1½ oz plain flour
½ teaspoon baking powder

1 egg
About 1 teaspoon milk
Vanilla or almond essence
Pinch of salt

Cream fat and sugar, add egg and flavouring. Mix flour, barley, baking powder and salt, add to fat and sugar, mixing lightly with sufficient milk to make fairly stiff mixture. Bake in paper cases or small greased tins 20 minutes in moderate oven, 375°F (Gas Mark 5).

DEVONSHIRE YEAST CAKE

1 lb plain flour
6 oz dried fruit
1 oz yeast

2 oz lard
4 oz sugar
Warm water

Warm flour and put into warm bowl. Rub in fat, add fruit and sugar. Make a well and crumble in yeast, sprinkle with a teaspoon sugar, then pour in about a breakfastcup warm water. Mix with hand to a sticky dough and put aside in a warm place to prove for 1 hour. Turn out, knead lightly and make into small dough cakes about the size of a sticky bun or into 2 large, as required. Prove again for 10 minutes and bake at 450°F (Gas Mark 8) to a light brown, about 25 minutes.

Mrs Bidder

SULTANA DOUGH CAKE

1 lb bread dough
3 oz caster sugar
3 oz butter

7 oz sultanas
1 egg

Line 7 inch tin with greaseproof paper. Put butter, sugar and fruit into warm bowl and stand it in a warm place to bring temperature up to that of bread dough, and warm the egg. This should be done immediately after rolling dough and putting it to rise (about 20 minutes). When dough is ready, add it to the mixture in the bowl and with the hands break it into small pieces. Add the egg, then continue working all the mixture together until thoroughly blended. It should then be of a soft consistency and be almost poured into the tin. Cover, and let rise in a warm place for 30 minutes. Bake in middle of oven at 400–420°F (Gas Mark 6–7) for 1–1¼ hours.

Mrs Wesley

WILTSHIRE LARDY CAKE

8 oz flour
¼ teaspoon salt
¼ teaspoon mixed spices
¼ oz yeast
1 teaspoon sugar

¼ pint warm milk
2 oz lard
2 oz sugar
2 oz dried fruit

Warm flour, salt and spice. Cream yeast and sugar together and add to flour, mix with enough warm milk to make a soft dough. Beat well. Cover and stand aside in a warm place till doubled in size. Roll out on well floured board to ¼ inch thickness. Spread on half lard, sugar and fruit. Fold in 3, turn to left (flaky pastry-wise) and roll again. Repeat with rest of lard, etc. Roll out to oblong 1 inch thick. Place in deep tin and leave till well risen. Score top with knife, brush with sugar and water. Cook in hot oven about 30 minutes.

Mrs A. Padgham, Minehead, Somerset

25 Tea Breads, Scones and Rusks

Now for the banquet we press;
Now for the eggs and the ham!
Now for the mustard and cress!
Now for the strawberry jam!
Now for the tea of our host!
Now for the rollicking bun!
Now for the muffin and toast!
Now for the gay Sally Lunn.
                                    W. S. Gilbert

Mealtimes have varied considerably over the centuries. In the early eighteenth century, the leisured classes took a late breakfast at 10 or 11 o'clock, followed by a cup of coffee or chocolate around noon. Dinner was eaten in the late afternoon, about 5 or 6 o'clock, and supper very late. This followed an earlier custom of dinner at 11 a.m. and supper at 6 p.m. Towards the end of the century, there was a swing back to this more natural division of the day, and dinner went back to 2 or 3 p.m. and supper to 7 or 8 p.m. At this period, afternoon tea was introduced about 5 o'clock, with thin bread and butter, and toast, much in evidence.

DATE LOAF

Soak overnight 1 packet of dates cut small and covered in boiling water with $\frac{1}{2}$ teaspoon bicarbonate of soda. Rub in 2 oz margarine into $\frac{1}{2}$ lb self-raising flour and add 4 oz soft brown sugar, 1 dessertspoon golden syrup and 1 very small egg. Add date mixture and put in *lined* loaf tin. Bake at 300°F (Gas Mark 2) for approximately $1\frac{3}{4}$ hours. Cool, slice and butter.

Pat Brown, Keynsham, Somerset

ORANGE LOAF

2 oz butter	**2 tablespoons milk**
6 oz castor sugar	**7 oz plain flour**
1 egg	**2½ teaspoons baking powder**
Grated rind and juice ½ large orange	**½ teaspoon salt**

Cream butter and sugar until light and fluffy. Add beaten egg gradually with orange rind, juice and milk. Sieve flour, baking powder and salt, and fold into creamed mixture. Put mixture into buttered 2 lb loaf tin, and bake at 375°F (Gas Mark 5) for 1 hour. Cool, slice and spread with butter.

HONEY LOAF

4 oz butter	**10½ oz plain flour**
4 oz castor sugar	**3 teaspoons baking powder**
6 tablespoons honey	**1 teaspoon salt**
1 egg	**¼ pint milk**

Cream butter and sugar until light and fluffy, and mix in honey thoroughly. Beat in egg. Sieve flour, baking powder and salt, and stir into creamed mixture alternately with milk. Put into buttered 2 lb loaf tin and bake at 350°F (Gas Mark 4) for $1\frac{1}{4}$ hours. Cool, slice and spread with butter.

DATE AND WALNUT LOAF

8 oz self-raising flour	**Pinch salt**
1 teaspoon bicarbonate of soda	**½ pint milk**
2 tablespoons golden syrup	**2 oz chopped walnuts**
2 oz dates	

Melt milk and syrup in saucepan with dates, add walnuts and dry ingredients when slightly cool; pour into greased tin and put a few chopped nuts on top. Cook for 25 minutes at 325°F (Gas Mark 3). Keep in a tin for a few days to get moist.

Mrs Saunders, Bedfordshire

MALT BREAD

2 *cups self-raising flour*
2 *tablespoons sugar*
2 *tablespoons fruit*
½ *teaspoon bicarbonate of soda*

2 *tablespoons Ovaltine*
2 *tablespoons golden syrup*
1 *tablespoon chopped nuts*
(optional)

Mix all together with ¼ pint milk into a stiff mixture, and bake in a moderate oven for 1 hour.

Mrs Evelyn Walker, Derby

WALNUT BREAD

This sweet cake-bread is excellent sliced and buttered and is good with honey. Stir together 12 oz self-raising flour, ½ teaspoon salt and 8 oz castor sugar. Add 6 oz chopped walnuts, 2 beaten eggs, 8 fluid oz milk and 2 oz melted butter. Beat well together, leave to stand for 20 minutes, then put into a tin lined with greaseproof paper (about 9 × 5 × 3 inches). Bake at 350°F (Gas Mark 4) for 1 hour 10 minutes.

ETHEL'S HARVO

3 *cups white flour*
1 *cup sugar*
1 *lb golden syrup*
2 *cups (or more) milk*
1 *cup brown flour*

6 *oz lard*
1½ *teaspoons bicarbonate of soda*
Fruit if desired

Melt syrup, rub fat into flours, add other ingredients, mix to soft dough and bake in slow oven. Eat buttered.

Eaten at harvest-time, when families doubled up to help their neighbours with the harvest in return for help with their own. The wives all worked together to produce the grub to fill the many who sat around the large kitchen table.

Mrs Alden, Selby

MALT LOAF

3 *oz malt extract*
2 *oz brown sugar*
1 *oz butter*
8 *oz wholewheat flour*
2 *teaspoons baking powder*

¼ *teaspoon salt*
¼ *pint milk*
2 *oz currants and sultanas*
1 *oz chopped mixed peel*

408

Warm the malt extract, sugar and butter together till dissolved. Cool a little. Sift dry ingredients into a bowl, and pour in the liquid. Mix well, stir in the fruit and put into a greased and floured loaf tin. Bake at 325°F (Gas Mark 3) for 1½ hours.

SPICE BREAD

10 oz self-raising flour
½ teaspoon mixed spice
1 teaspoon ginger
6 oz sultanas
2 oz butter

6 oz syrup
6 tablespoons milk
1 egg
4 oz brown sugar

Mix flour with spices and stir in sugar and fruit. Melt butter and syrup together over gentle heat. Stir into dry ingredients, together with an egg beaten up in milk. Mix well, pour into a well-greased loaf tin, and bake for about 1½ hours at 350°F (Gas Mark 4). Turn out as soon as possible after it is cooked. Slice and butter.

GINGER AND WALNUT TEABREAD

8 oz self-raising flour
¼ level teaspoon salt
2 level teaspoons ground ginger
1 level teaspoon baking powder
2 oz butter
2 oz sugar

3 oz walnuts, chopped
1 oz crystallised ginger, finely chopped
1 egg, beaten
¼ pint milk

For topping:
1 teaspoon demerara sugar

Sift together flour, salt, ginger and baking powder. Rub in butter until mixture resembles fine breadcrumbs. Mix in sugar, walnuts and crystallised ginger. Mix most of the beaten egg with the milk and add to flour and butter. Beat thoroughly. (This makes a very sticky dough.) Turn into a greased 1 lb loaf tin. Brush top with remaining beaten egg and sprinkle with demerara sugar. Bake in a moderate oven, 350°F (Gas Mark 4) for 1 hour 5 minutes, until golden brown and sounds hollow when tapped underneath. Serve sliced and spread with butter.

AUSTRALIAN TEA CAKE

4 oz sultanas
4 oz raisins
4 oz brown sugar
Cold tea

1 tablespoon whisky
1 egg
4 oz flour

Soak the fruit overnight in cold tea, put into a basin and add sugar, flour, beaten egg and whisky. Bake for 1½ hours at 300°F (Gas Mark 2). Don't drown the fruit—just cover with cold tea.

Miss Mabel Nokes, Priston Mill Farm, Bath

FARMHOUSE TREACLE LOAF

8 oz wholemeal flour
8 oz plain flour
4 oz sugar
6 oz black treacle
5 oz raisins

1 oz chopped nuts
1 egg, beaten
½ pint milk
1 level teaspoon bicarbonate of soda

Sift the flours together. Mix in sugar, raisins and nuts. Make a well in the centre. Heat the milk and treacle to lukewarm temperature, add the bicarbonate of soda and pour into flour, add beaten egg. Stir well and put into 2 well-greased 1 lb loaf tins. Bake in a moderate oven, 350°F (Gas Mark 4) for 1½ hours. Slice and spread with butter to serve.

As this loaf contains no fat, it is not a good keeper, but is delicious sliced and buttered while still warm.

BARA BRITH

1 lb self-raising flour
4 oz black treacle
4 oz sugar
4 oz butter, margarine or cooking fat
½ lb sultanas
1 egg

Juice and rind of 1 lemon
¼ level teaspoon salt
1 level teaspoon mixed spice
1 level teaspoon bicarbonate of soda
Milk to make the beaten egg up to ½ pint

Rub fat into flour. Add the salt, spice, sugar, grated lemon rind and sultanas. Mix well together, then add the treacle, egg, milk and lemon juice, mixing the bicarbonate of soda with the last tablespoon of milk mixture. Mix well and put in a well-greased 2 lb loaf tin and bake in a moderate oven 325°F (Gas Mark 3) for 2 hours. Turn out and cool on a rack. Slice and butter to serve.

PHILLIDA'S TEA BREAD

12 oz mixed fruit (including cherries)
1 cup tea
6 oz brown sugar

10 oz self-raising flour
1 egg
A little milk

Soak fruit in tea overnight. Mix all ingredients together. Bake at 325°F (Gas Mark 3) for 2 hours. Good eaten as cake, or sliced to eat with butter.

Miss P. Walpole, Wolterton Hall, Norfolk

CORNISH FRUIT BREAD

8 oz plain flour	*1 egg*
2 teaspoons baking powder	*½ pint milk*
¼ teaspoon salt	*1½ oz butter*
½ teaspoon cinnamon	*4 oz sugar*
½ teaspoon nutmeg	*3 oz mixed dried fruit*
¼ teaspoon ground ginger	*2 oz chopped walnuts*

Sift flour, baking powder, salt and spices together and stir in the sugar. Beat the egg and most of the milk together and stir into the dry ingredients. Add the nuts, fruit and melted butter. If necessary, add a little more milk to make a fairly sticky dough. Put into a greased and floured loaf tin and bake at 350°F (Gas Mark 4) for 1 hour.

GREAT AUNT HARRIET'S TEA BREAD

4 oz butter	*3 tablespoons orange rind*
5 oz sugar	*and 2 tablespoons juice*
10 oz flour	*4 oz chopped walnuts*
½ teaspoon salt	*4 oz chopped raisins*
2 eggs	*A little more than ¼ pint milk*

Cream the butter, add sugar gradually and cream till smooth. Beat in the eggs one at a time then add rind and juice. Sift flour and salt, add to the mixture alternately with the milk ending with flour. Add nuts and raisins. Bake in a 1 lb tin at 350°F (Gas Mark 4) for about 1 hour.

My great aunt Harriet used to serve this in slices, buttered, just like bread, but my family like it as cake too. As far as I can gather, this recipe was used by my great-aunt's grandmother though the original recipe was for three times as much again.

Mrs St Clare, Stroud

STEAMED SULTANA BREAD

1 cup All Bran cereal	*1 teaspoon bicarbonate of*
1 cup wholemeal flour	*soda*
2 cups plain white flour	*1 tablespoon black treacle*
½ teaspoon salt	*1½ cups thick sour milk*
1 tablespoon sugar	*½ cup sultanas*

Use a breakfastcup for measuring the ingredients. The bread is best steamed in straight-sided earthenware marmalade jars, but otherwise can be cooked in small bowls or in cylindrical tins. Mix together bran cereal and the two flours with the salt, sugar and bicarbonate of soda. Beat the treacle into the milk and stir into the dry ingredients. Add the sultanas and mix well. Fill jars or tins about $\frac{2}{3}$ full and tie on greaseproof paper. Put into a pan of boiling water, put on a lid and boil steadily for 3 hours, adding more boiling water as necessary. Turn out on to a wire rack and leave until cold. Cut in slices and serve with cheese.

STOVIES

1 oz bacon fat or dripping
2 lb potatoes
$\frac{1}{2}$ lb onions

$\frac{1}{2}$ pint hot water
Salt and pepper

Melt fat. Slice and fry onions without browning. Add sliced potatoes, hot water and seasonings. Cover and cook very slowly for $1-1\frac{1}{2}$ hours, stirring or shaking occasionally to prevent browning. Serve with mince collops or casseroles.

Mrs Biggar, Kirkcudbrightshire

POTATO SCONES

8 oz cooked potatoes
$\frac{1}{2}$ gill milk

About 2 oz flour
Pinch of salt

Mash or sieve potatoes, add salt; knead enough flour into this as it will take, then add enough milk to make a stiff dough. Roll out very thinly on floured board. Cut into rounds and prick with a fork. Bake on hot girdle for about 5 minutes, turning when half-cooked. Butter, roll up and serve very hot; or fry with bacon.

Mrs Biggar, Kirkcudbrightshire

BROTHER DON'S POTATO CAKE

12 oz self-raising flour
4 oz margarine
4 oz sugar
6 oz hot potato, mashed

1 egg
2 tablespoons milk
4 oz raisins

Rub the fat into the flour. Add the sugar, raisins and potato. Mix well. Add the egg and 2 tablespoons milk to bind. Cook in a coolish oven, about 350°F (Gas Mark 4), in a sandwich tin, well greased, for about 1 hour. Serve hot with lashings of butter.

My brother Don lives in the New Forest, and once when his wife was ill he had to do the cooking. Now he still bashes out the very first recipe he tried all those years ago. He reckons if he can do it, anyone can! It's a great standby in times of emergency.

IRISHMAN'S MUFFINS

Peel and grate potato to fill a breakfast cup and drain off the liquid which forms. Work in half as much flour, plenty of salt and a dash of pepper. Thin with a little milk till it will drop from a spoon. Heat enough dripping to give a $\frac{1}{4}$ inch in the frying pan and drop in dessertspoons of the mixture. Fry well, turning frequently, till brown both sides. Dip in salt or melted butter.

Mrs Toulson says that long before the days of the modern barbecue a group of schoolchildren would gather at the bottom of their orchard, where her father had built them a square of loosely arranged bricks, about 4 or 5 bricks high, to form their own barbecue. Sticks and wood were the fuel and on this they made their feast.

Mrs Toulson

WALNUT AND HONEY SCONES

1 lb self-raising flour	**2 oz finely chopped walnuts**
1 level teaspoon salt	**2 tablespoons clear honey**
4 oz butter	**10 tablespoons cold milk**
2 level tablespoons castor sugar	

Sift flour and salt into a basin and rub in butter. Add sugar and walnuts and mix to a soft but not sticky dough with honey and milk. Turn on to lightly floured board, knead quickly and roll out to $\frac{1}{2}$ inch thickness. Cut into rounds and put on greased baking sheet. Brush tops with beaten egg or milk and bake at 425°F (Gas Mark 7) for 10 minutes.

COTTAGE CHEESE GRIDDLE CAKES

1 tablespoon melted butter	**2 oz self-raising flour**
4 oz cottage cheese	**1 tablespoon milk**
2 eggs	

Add butter to cottage cheese and gradually whisk in eggs. Stir in flour and milk and mix to a smooth thick batter. Drop spoonsful on to a hot greased griddle or frying-pan and turn several times. Serve freshly baked with crisp hot bacon, honey, jam or jelly. These scones are very light and digestible, and particularly good for those who do not want much starch in their diet.

413

GOLDEN DROP SCONES

8 oz self-raising flour
½ level teaspoon salt
½ level teaspoon grated
nutmeg
1 level dessertspoon castor
sugar

1 egg
2 level tablespoons black
treacle
Scant ½ pint cold milk

Sift dry ingredients into bowl. Make well in centre, and drop in egg and treacle, then gradually mix to thick batter with the milk, drawing in flour from sides of bowl. Beat with back of wooden spoon till batter is smooth and creamy. Drop dessertspoons on to well greased griddle, thick frying pan or hot plate of an electric cooker. Cook for about 1 minute each side. Serve hot with butter.

DROP SCONES OFTEN CALLED PANSCONES

8 oz self-raising flour
1 dessertspoon golden syrup

1 egg
½ pint milk

Mix to a batter. Grease a hot girdle or hot plate slightly. Drop the batter in spoonsful on to the hot plate. When the scones bubble, turn over with a knife. They should be golden brown on both sides. Cool in a clean towel. Cover them until cold.

Mrs Corrie, Burnside of Auchegool, Kirkcudbrightshire

PITCARTHLY BANNOCK

6 oz flour
1 oz rice flour
4 oz butter
3 oz castor sugar

1 oz almonds
1 oz candied orange or
citron peel

Blanch and chop almonds finely. Shred and chop peel finely. Sieve flour, rice flour and sugar, rub in butter and work all together with the lard. Form into a cake or press into shortbread mould. Prick well, and bake in steady oven until beginning to colour, moderate the heat and allow to crisp off slowly for about 1 hour.

Mrs Biggar, Kirkcudbrightshire

LARGE ROUND SCONE

6 oz sifted white self-raising
flour
2 oz wholewheat stoneground
flour
2 oz margarine

1 level teaspoon baking
powder
A little salt
Sugar to taste
Mix with a little milk

Rub fat into flour, add salt and sugar, mix with a little milk. Put into enamel plate (cutting round into 12 segments). Bake at 400°F (Gas Mark 6) for about 15–20 minutes.

Miss Grace Butler, Southstoke, Somerset

LANCASHIRE SCONES

½ lb self-raising flour
¾ oz butter
3 oz crumbled Lancashire cheese

A little salt
¼ pint milk

Mix the flour and a pinch of salt. Rub in butter and add cheese. Make into a fairly soft dough by adding about ¼ pint milk. Roll the mixture out ¾ inch thick, and cut in small circles. Bake in a hot oven, 425°F (Gas Mark 7), until brown. Split, spread with butter and eat them hot. Lancashire cheese was often referred to as 'Leigh Toaster' because it is so good when cooked.

WHOLEMEAL SPOON SCONES

10 oz wholemeal flour
6 oz plain flour
1 level teaspoon salt
2 oz granulated sugar
1 level teaspoon bicarbonate of soda

2 level teaspoons cream of tartar
2 oz butter
1 tablespoon black treacle
Scant ½ pint milk

Sieve together dry ingredients and stir in sugar. Rub in butter, then mix with treacle and milk to give a heavy dropping consistency. Drop dessert-spoons of mixture on to a baking sheet, dusted with wholemeal flour. Brush lightly with milk and dredge with flour or rolled oats. Bake at 450°F (Gas Mark 8) for 15 minutes.

SCOTTISH TREACLE SCONES

2 oz butter or margarine
8 oz self-raising flour
1 oz castor sugar

2 oz black treacle
1 egg
1 oz currants

Rub the fat into the sifted flour, add the sugar and dried fruit, and mix in the well-beaten egg and the black treacle, adding a little cold milk if necessary to make a soft, but not sticky dough. Roll out to 1 inch thickness and cut into 2 inch rounds with a plain cutter. Well grease a hot girdle, or thick frying pan or electric hotplate. Cook the scones on a gentle heat for about 5 to 7 minutes on each side. Pile between folds of a napkin and serve, split and buttered, while still warm.

MRS BLENKIN'S SCONES

1 lb self-raising flour
6 oz granulated sugar
4 oz margarine
4 oz lard

Currants or sultanas
1 egg
Milk to mix
Beaten egg

Stir together flour and sugar and rub in fat. Add dried fruit to taste, egg and a little milk to mix. Roll out and cut in circles, and brush with beaten egg. Bake at 425°F (Gas Mark 7) for 10 minutes, and at 350°F (Gas Mark 4) for 5 minutes.

When Babs Honey had to travel to Hull one autumn day, she arrived at the station in the evening, having left early from Somerset. Her instructions were to have tea in the big store opposite the station and then to catch the bus to the fire station at Patrington. A lady in the bus queue had been born in Somerset so she guided her till she had to get off at her stop. The lady behind said it was another 3 miles and they got off the bus together. Babs asked if she could be directed to the Parish Hall where she was due in an hour's time. Learning that she was the speaker for the W.I. Group Meeting, her new friend took her home, gave her the freedom of the bathroom, and presented her with a steaming cup of tea by the fire and a plate of scones—so delicious and so light that they melted in the mouth. Here is the recipe from a real Christian soul.

Mrs Blenkin, Patrington, E. Yorks

FRUIT SCONE

8 oz flour
2 medium-sized tablespoons
golden syrup
8 oz dried fruit (chopped
dates are good, but sultanas,
currants, peel etc. can be used)

1 heaped teaspoon
bicarbonate of soda
1 heaped teaspoon cream of
tartar

Melt syrup in about 1 teacup warm water. Allow to cool. Sieve flour with cream of tartar, add dried fruit. Mix to a soft dough with the syrup and water, adding the bicarbonate in the last of the liquid. Divide mixture into 2 greased sandwich tins. Bake till brown (about 10–15 minutes) at 425°F (Gas Mark 7). When cold, split and butter scone.

YOGHURT DROP SCONES

¼ *pint plain yoghurt*
1 *egg*

2 *level tablespoons plain flour,*
sifted with a pinch of salt
A little lard for frying

Beat the egg. Put the yoghurt into a bowl, add the egg and beat well. Add the sifted flour and salt, and fold into the mixture. Heat a little lard in a frying pan and when a haze rises from it, drop dessertspoons of the mixture into it. Cook until golden brown on underside, then, using a palette knife, turn to cook the other side in the same way. Drain on kitchen paper when cooked and keep hot, until all are cooked. Serve immediately with butter, jam or honey.

SCOTCH PANCAKES

3 *tablespoons plain flour*
1 *teaspoon cream of tartar*
½ *teaspoon bicarbonate of soda*

1 *egg*
1 *dessertspoon syrup*
A little milk

Sieve all dry ingredients then drop egg in centre and beat up. Then add syrup and beat up; if too thick, add a little milk. Cook on hot girdle.

Mrs Dunlop

DERBYSHIRE OATCAKE

½ *lb fine or medium oatmeal*
8 *oz plain flour*
Pinch of salt

1 *oz yeast*
1 *level teaspoon sugar*
½ *pint lukewarm water*

Sift together oatmeal and flour with salt. Cream yeast and sugar and add warm water. Stir into dry ingredients and leave in a warm place for 30 minutes. Heat griddle and grease lightly. Pour on a little batter and cook about 2 minutes. Turn and bake the other side. Serve hot with butter or dripping, or with crisp hot bacon.

NORFOLK GOLDEN RUSKS

8 *oz self-raising flour*
2 *oz fat – lard or margarine*
1 *egg*
1 *heaped teaspoon baking*
powder

Pinch salt – or more as
preferred
A little milk to mix, or milk
and water

Sift dry ingredients together. Rub in fat; mix to a soft dough – like a scone dough – with the beaten egg adding a little milk gradually as required. Roll out, cut into rounds about $\frac{3}{4}$ inch thick. Bake in a very hot oven, 475°F, (Gas Mark 9) about 8 minutes by which time they should be well-risen but *not* coloured.

At the turn of the century, no Norfolk tea-table was complete without a dish of crisp, golden rusks, thickly spread with fresh farmhouse butter.

SUFFOLK RUSKS

8 oz self-raising flour   **1 egg**
3 oz butter   **Milk or water to mix**

Rub the fat into the flour. Add the lightly-beaten egg, and work in enough milk or water to give a scone-like mixture. Roll out $\frac{3}{4}$ inch thick and cut into rounds. Bake at 450°F (Gas Mark 8) for 10 minutes. Split in half at once and put on baking sheets split side uppermost. Bake at 375°F (Gas Mark 5) until golden and crisp. These are delicious with cheese or with butter and jam.

26 *Large and Small Cakes*

He that will have cake out of the wheat must tarry the grinding.
William Shakespeare

Would'st thou both eat thy cake and have it ?
George Herbert

CHERRY CAKE

8 oz plain flour
1½ teaspoons baking powder
6 oz butter
6 oz castor sugar
Grated rind of 2 lemons
3 eggs
1 tablespoon milk
4 oz glacé cherries

Sift flour and baking powder. Cream butter and sugar until light and fluffy and work in the eggs one at a time, adding a little flour with each one. Add the lemon rind and fold in the flour and the baking powder, then the milk. Add the cherries which have been lightly coated with flour. Put into greased 7 inch cake tin and bake at 325°F (Gas Mark 3) for 1½ hours. Store in tin or freezer.

PARKIN

6 oz plain flour
1 level teaspoon salt
1 level teaspoon ground ginger
2 level teaspoons ground cinnamon
1 level teaspoon bicarbonate of soda
10 oz medium oatmeal
6 oz black treacle
5 oz butter
4 oz soft brown sugar
¼ pint milk
1 egg

Sift together flour, salt, spices and soda. Add oatmeal, and toss lightly to mix. Warm treacle, butter, sugar and milk until the butter has melted. Cool slightly, add egg and beat well. Pour into the centre of the dry ingredients and stir rapidly until smooth. Turn into a greased and lined 7 inch square tin. Bake at 350°F (Gas Mark 4) for 1 hour. Store in an airtight tin for 2 weeks before using.

APPLE GINGERBREAD

1 large cooking apple
6 whole cloves
1 dessertspoon sugar
3 tablespoons water
6 oz self-raising flour
2 teaspoons ground ginger
3 oz sugar
1 egg
4 oz black treacle
3 oz melted butter

Fudge icing:
1 oz butter
2 oz black treacle
2 oz icing sugar
Pinch of cinnamon

Peel, core and slice apple, and put into a saucepan with cloves, sugar and water. Cook until tender, remove cloves and mash apple with a fork. Leave to cool. Put flour and ginger into a bowl and stir in 3 oz sugar. Add the cooked apple, beaten egg, black treacle and butter and beat well together. Turn into 1½ lb greased loaf tin, and bake at 350°F (Gas Mark 4) for 40 minutes. Cool on a rack.

Make the icing by creaming together butter, treacle and sugar until light and fluffy. Add cinnamon and spread icing on the cake. Decorate with a scattering of chopped nuts or chopped crystallised ginger. Store in a tin, or wrapped in foil in the freezer.

SUGAR AND SPICE CAKE

4 oz butter
6 oz sugar
2 eggs
4 tablespoons hot water
10 oz plain flour
1 teaspoon bicarbonate of soda
8 oz raspberry jam, apricot jam or marmalade
1 teaspoon cinnamon
½ teaspoon mixed spice

Cream butter and sugar until light and fluffy. Add the eggs one at a time, then the water. Fold in sifted dry ingredients alternately with the jam or marmalade and beat thoroughly to blend the ingredients. Put into buttered 8 inch cake tin and bake at 325°F (Gas Mark 3) for 1 hour. Turn out and cool, and if liked, ice with a thin orange icing. Store in a tin or freezer.

MOIST CHOCOLATE CAKE

Cake:
8 oz butter
6 oz soft brown sugar
6 oz black treacle
4 eggs
6 oz self-raising flour
2 oz cocoa

For filling:
Fresh or butter cream,
flavoured as liked with orange
rind, peppermint or rum

For Icing:
Chocolate glacé icing, plain
or topped with slivers of
almonds or chopped walnuts

Cream together butter, sugar and treacle. Gradually beat in blended eggs adding tablespoon of sieved flour with last amount of egg. Sieve together flour and cocoa and fold into creamed mixture. Turn into two greased and bottom-lined 8–9 inch sponge sandwich tins; bake in moderate oven, 350°F (Gas Mark 4) for about 50 minutes. Turn out. When cold sandwich with fresh or butter cream and top with chocolate glacé icing.

EGGLESS CHOCOLATE CAKE

5 oz self-raising flour
1 tablespoon cocoa
1½ oz butter
2 oz sugar
1 tablespoon syrup or treacle

1 teaspoon cinnamon
½ teaspoon bicarbonate of soda
Sufficient milk or milk and
water to make moist
consistency

Cream sugar and butter. Add melted syrup. Stir cocoa, cinnamon, baking soda and pinch of salt into the flour, sift into other ingredients. Add milk until mixture is of moist consistency. Bake in greased tin in fairly hot oven, 375°F (Gas Mark 5). This makes a moist cake.

DUNDEE CAKE

8 oz butter
8 oz sugar
5 eggs
8 oz self-raising flour
½ teaspoon nutmeg

12 oz mixed currants and
sultanas
3 oz ground almonds
3 oz chopped glacé cherries
2 oz chopped candied peel
2 oz split blanched almonds

Cream butter and sugar and add eggs one at a time, each with a sprinkling of flour to avoid curdling. Beat well after each addition. Stir in most of the flour and lastly the fruit lightly coated with the rest of the flour. Turn into a 9 inch cake tin lined with greased paper, smooth the top and arrange almonds on surface. Bake at 325°F (Gas Mark 3) for 2–2½ hours.

MARMALADE CAKE

4 oz butter
4 oz sugar
2 eggs

2 rounded tablespoons
marmalade
8 oz self-raising flour
4 tablespoons milk

Cream butter and sugar and beat in eggs. Mix in marmalade, then add flour and enough milk to give a soft dropping consistency. Put in a greased 7 inch cake tin and bake at 350°F (Gas Mark 4) for 1 hour. For immediate use, this is good topped with whipped cream or orange butter icing, decorated with strips of candied peel.

SULTANA ORANGE CAKE

8 oz self-raising flour
Pinch of salt
4 oz margarine
4 oz castor sugar
2 large eggs

7 oz sultanas
Grated rind of 1 small orange
1 tablespoon strained orange
juice

Sift flour and salt. Cream margarine and sugar until light and fluffy, then add eggs one by one, beating well. Fold in half the flour, then the sultanas and grated rind. Fold in the rest of the flour, and add enough orange juice to give a stiff dropping consistency. Turn into a 6 inch cake tin lined with greased paper, and bake at 350°F (Gas Mark 4) for 1½–1¾ hours. It's good, too, if you substitute lemon juice and lemon rind.

CARAWAY SEED CAKE

6 oz butter
6 oz sugar
3 eggs

8 oz plain flour
¼ teaspoon baking powder
½ oz caraway seed

Cream butter and sugar until very soft, and gradually add beaten eggs. Gradually add flour and baking powder, and finally the caraway seeds. Turn into a greased 7 inch cake tin and bake at 350°F (Gas Mark 4) for 1¼–1½ hours.

DRIPPING CAKE

8 oz mixed dried fruit and
candied peel
3 oz clarified beef dripping
5 oz brown sugar
1½ gills water
8 oz wholemeal flour

1 teaspoon baking powder
Pinch of nutmeg
Pinch of cinnamon
Pinch of mixed spice
½ teaspoon bicarbonate of soda

Put fruit in a heavy pan with dripping, sugar and water, bring to the boil and simmer for 10 minutes. Leave to cool, then pour into the rest of the ingredients which have been sifted together. Blend well but do not beat. Put into a greased 6 inch cake tin and bake at 350°F (Gas Mark 4) for 1¼–1½ hours.

BOILED FRUIT CAKE

5 oz butter or margarine
6 tablespoons golden syrup
¼ pint milk
4 oz chopped dates
8 oz currants
4 oz sultanas
8 oz stoned raisins

4 oz chopped mixed peel
8 oz self-raising flour
1 teaspoon mixed spice
1 teaspoon nutmeg
Pinch of salt
2 eggs
½ teaspoon bicarbonate of soda

Put butter, syrup, milk and fruit into a saucepan and heat slowly until the fat has melted. Simmer gently for 5 minutes, stirring once or twice, then cool completely. Sieve together flour, spices and salt, make a well in the centre, add eggs, but do not stir.

Add soda to the fruit mixture and add to the dry ingredients, mixing thoroughly and beating well. Pour into a greased and lined 10 inch round tin and bake at 325°F (Gas Mark 3) for 1¾ hours. This is a moist, fruity cake which keeps well and is excellent for packed meals. It can be stored in a tin, or frozen when wrapped in foil or polythene.

CORONATION FRUIT CAKE
A moist cake that improves with keeping

8 oz plain flour
Pinch of salt
8 oz butter
6 oz sugar
1 lb currants
6 oz sultanas (or same
quantity of mixed fruit)
2–3 oz blanched chopped
almonds

2 teaspoons powdered
cinnamon
½ teaspoon each of powdered
cloves and nutmeg
½ teaspoon bicarbonate of soda
4 eggs
1 tablespoon black treacle

Sieve dry ingredients. Beat butter and sugar to a soft cream, add treacle, beat till well mixed. Add well-beaten eggs one at a time, beating each one well in. Fold in sieved flour mixture alternately with dried fruit and almonds. Put into a 7–8 inch tin well lined with greased paper. Make a hollow in the centre of cake to ensure a flat surface when cooked. Bake 3 hours, in a hot oven to start with, 375°F (Gas Mark 5) for 1 hour, then turn to 300°F (Gas Mark 2) for rest of time.

BROWN PLUM CAKE

10 oz butter
6 oz sugar
1 lb mixed cake fruit
Little candied peel
12 oz flour
Pinch of ginger

A little powdered spice, if
liked
2 eggs
½ teaspoon bicarbonate of soda
1 teacup milk

Cream fat and sugar, add fruit, peel, spice, flour then well-beaten eggs, and lastly milk with the soda dissolved in it. Bake in paper-lined tin for 3 hours in a slow oven, 300°F (Gas Mark 2).

VICARAGE CAKE

Melt 4 oz fat and put it to cool. When cool, mix the fat in 1 lb self-raising flour (brown is best) and add 6 oz sugar, 3 level teaspoons mixed spices and 4 oz fruit. Into a jug put 2 tablespoons treacle, ½ pint and 3 more tablespoons of milk. Stir to dissolve treacle. Make a hole in dry ingredients, put in the liquid and mix well. Bake in moderate oven 1¼ hours.

OLIVE'S CAKE

4 oz butter
4 oz sugar
2 oz golden syrup
2 eggs
8 oz flour
4–8 oz dried fruit (can be mixed)

2 oz dates
2 oz candied peel
1 dessertspoon marmalade
½ teacup milk
¼ teaspoon bicarbonate of soda

Cream fat, sugar, syrup. Beat eggs, add to creamed mixture alternately with flour. Add fruit and marmalade, lastly bicarbonate of soda dissolved in the milk. Line medium-sized tin with greased paper, put in mixture. Bake 1½–2 hours at 350°F (Gas Mark 4).

BROWN FRUIT CAKE

6 oz plain flour
1 tablespoon syrup
2 oz any fat
2 eggs
4 oz any dried fruit (dates and sultanas are excellent)

1 level teaspoon bicarbonate of soda
½ teaspoon nutmeg
½ teaspoon spice
2 tablespoons milk

Rub fat in flour, beat eggs well, add to mixture, put in treacle, fruit, spices, stir bicarbonate of soda in milk. add to mixture. Grease tin and flour it all over. Put in moderate oven 350°F (Gas Mark 4) for 1 hour. Turn out to cool on wire tray.

LIGHT FRUIT CAKE

4 oz butter
2 oz black treacle
2 oz soft brown sugar
3 eggs
6 oz plain flour
1 level teaspoon baking powder

1 level teaspoon mixed spice
Grated rind of ½ lemon
8 oz seedless raisins
2 oz glacé cherries, sliced
2 oz chopped mixed peel (or use 12 oz mixed dried fruit)
A few blanched almonds

Line 7 inch tin with greased paper. Cream the butter, treacle and sugar until fluffy. Add the eggs one at a time, beating well between each. Add the sifted dry ingredients alternately with the fruit, folding in lightly. Put into cake tin, and sprinkle nuts on top. Bake in a moderate oven, 350°F (Gas Mark 4) for about 1 hour. Allow to cool in the tin before removing.

RICH FRUIT CAKE

8 oz butter
6 oz soft brown sugar
1 teaspoon vanilla essence
1 teaspoon almond essence
Grated rind of 1 orange
4 tablespoons black treacle
4 eggs
10 oz plain flour

4 level teaspoons mixed spice
3 lb mixed fruit (raisins,
sultanas, dates, cherries,
candied peel, all well chopped)
¼ lb ground almonds
(optional)
4 tablespoons brandy, sherry
or orange juice

Grease and line cake tin, 9 inch across, with double thickness of grease-proof paper. Cream butter and sugar until light and fluffy; beat in essence and orange rind. Blend treacle with well beaten eggs and gradually beat into creamed mixture, adding 2 tablespoons sifted flour when half egg mixture is added. Lightly stir in sifted flour and spice. Add fruit and ground almonds and lastly liquid.

Turn into prepared cake tin. Bake in very slow oven, 300°F (Gas Mark 1) for about 4 hours, until a bright skewer comes out clean when inserted into middle of cake. Cook on cake rack, leaving on paper until ready to ice or to serve without frosting.

Double quantity is sufficient for tin 12 inch in diameter and takes 5½–6 hours in very slow oven, 275°F (Gas Mark ½).

Half above quantity is enough for 5 inch or 6 inch cake tin and takes about 2½ hours in slow oven, 325°F (Gas Mark 3).

Good for a wedding or Christmas.

TWO MINUTE CAKE

1 lb self-raising flour
8 oz sugar
Pinch of salt
1–1½ lb dried fruit

4 eggs
2 small cups milk
8 oz butter

Put all dry ingredients in a bowl and add eggs and milk. Melt the butter until quite runny and pour into the mixture. Beat well for 1 minute, and then pour into a greased lined tin. Bake 300°F (Gas Mark 2) for 3 hours. Add spice for extra flavour.

Mrs Cook, Church Allerton on Mendips, near Wedmore

BASIC RECIPE FRUIT CAKE

8 oz butter
About 4 oz sugar

About 4 oz golden syrup

Mix together sugar and butter and syrup. Add 1 or 2 eggs and milk, 12 oz self-raising flour, mixed fruit and almond essence. Cook 1¾ hours at about 300°F (Gas Mark 2).

DARK CAKE

1 lb mixed fruit
½ lb dark soft sugar

Enough warm tea to cover
Self-raising flour

Leave for a day to let fruit swell. Stir in as much self-raising flour as liquid will absorb. Well grease a bread tin and cook 1½–2 hours in very low oven (350°F, Gas Mark 4). Test with skewer.

GINGER STICKY-TOPPED CAKE

For topping:
2 oz butter
1 rounded tablespoon golden syrup
1 oz soft brown sugar
1½ oz flaked almonds
1½ oz glacé cherries, halves
1 oz sultanas

For sponge:
4 oz self-raising flour
1 level teaspoon baking powder
2 level teaspoons ground ginger
½ level teaspoon salt
4 oz castor sugar
2 eggs
4 oz butter

To make topping—Melt butter, syrup and brown sugar in a saucepan. Add almonds, glacé cherries and sultanas. Pour into the bottom of a greased 2 lb loaf tin.

To make sponge—Sift flour, baking powder, ginger and salt into a bowl. Add castor sugar, eggs and butter. Beat thoroughly for 2 minutes. Pour into the tin, carefully covering the topping. Place in a moderate oven, 350°F (Gas Mark 4) for 45–50 minutes, until firm to touch. Turn out and cool.

GINGERBREAD

4 oz plain flour
4 oz wholemeal flour
1 level teaspoon mixed spice
2 level teaspoons ground ginger
3 oz sultanas
4 oz margarine

1 gill milk
8 oz golden syrup
1 egg
1 level teaspoon bicarbonate of soda
1½ oz brown sugar

427

Sieve all dry ingredients (except soda) into a bowl. Add sugar and fruit, melt fat and syrup, warm milk and mix in soda; add the egg to dry ingredients, followed by fat and syrup; lastly add soda and milk. Pour mixture into greased tin (8 × 10 inches). Bake at 375°F (Gas Mark 5) for 45 minutes. The gingerbread will be 1 inch thick.

Mrs Joslin, Warwicks

DAMP GINGERBREAD

10 oz flour
6 oz butter
6 oz moist sugar
3 oz almonds
6 oz sultanas
1½ teaspoons ground ginger

1½ teaspoons cinnamon
¼ lb treacle
2 eggs
Warm milk
¾ teaspoon baking soda

Sieve the flour; clean sultanas; blanch and shred the almonds (blanch by steeping few minutes in cup of boiling water) and mix 1 teaspoon flour with the fruit. Cream the butter and sugar, add dry ingredients, treacle, beaten eggs and the baking soda mixed with a little milk. Add more milk if necessary to the whole. Turn into greased tin and bake at 325°F (Gas Mark 3) for 2 hours.

Mrs Biggar, Kirkcudbrightshire

BUTTER MILK CAKE

1 lb plain flour
½ level teaspoon mixed spice
½ level teaspoon ground ginger
½ lb butter
½ lb brown sugar
1 lb mixed fruit (raisins,

sultanas and currants)
½ pint buttermilk or sour milk
1 rounded tablespoon black treacle
1 rounded teaspoon bicarbonate of soda

Sieve flour and spices into a large mixing bowl. Rub in butter until mixture looks like breadcrumbs. Add sugar and prepared fruit and mix well. Heat buttermilk and add treacle and bicarbonate of soda. Stir until frothy. Add to the ingredients in the bowl and mix well together. Put into a greased and bottom-lined, round, 8 inch cake tin. Bake in a moderate oven, 350°F (Gas Mark 4), for 2¼–2½ hours, covering the cake with a piece of greaseproof paper after about 1 hour.

SUNDAY APRICOT CAKE

4 *eggs*
Butter
Castor sugar
Self-raising flour

Apricot icing:
5 *oz butter*
5 *oz icing sugar*
8 *oz can apricot halves*

Weigh the eggs and take their weight in butter, sugar and flour. Cream butter and sugar until light and fluffy. Work in eggs and flour, and pour into 2 8 inch sponge tins. Bake at 375°F (Gas Mark 5) for 25 minutes. Cool on a wire rack. To make the icing, cream the butter and sugar and gradually beat in a little juice from the can of apricots to make a really creamy icing. Spread half the icing on to one of the sponge layers. Cut the other layer in half and prop up on top of the filling with remaining cream. Fill the line between the halves with apricots and sprinkle top with castor sugar. This makes a delicious birthday cake.

Maisie Jones

HONEY CAKE

1 *lb thick honey*
6 *oz soft brown sugar*
4 *eggs*
1 *teaspoon powdered cinnamon*
¼ *teaspoon mixed spice*
12 *oz wholemeal flour*

1 *level teaspoon baking powder*
2 *oz sultanas*
2 *oz blanched chopped almonds*
2 *oz chopped peel*

Grease and line a 9 inch square cake tin with greased greaseproof paper. Melt honey and sugar over gentle heat in large saucepan. Remove from heat and cool slightly, then beat in eggs and spices and stir in the flour and baking powder until well blended. Stir in cleaned sultanas, chopped almonds and chopped peel.

Turn mixture into prepared tin and bake in hot oven, 400°F (Gas Mark 6) for about ¾ hour or until cooked through. Cool in tin, then turn out on wire rack and strip off paper. Store in an airtight tin and cut into squares to serve as required.

LUNCHEON CAKE

8 *oz self-raising flour*
¼ *level teaspoon salt*
4 *oz butter or margarine*
4 *oz soft brown sugar*
4 *oz sultanas*

2 *oz chopped peel*
Grated rind ½ lemon
1 *egg*
5 *tablespoons milk*

Sift flour and salt into bowl. Rub in fat lightly. Stir in sugar, the cleaned dry fruit, chopped peel and lemon rind. Beat egg with milk and stir into mixture. Put mixture into greased and floured medium size loaf tin. Bake in moderate oven, 375°F (Gas Mark 5), for $1\frac{1}{4}$–$1\frac{1}{2}$ hours, or until cooked through. Turn out and cool.

FUNERAL CAKE

8 oz soft brown sugar
8 oz butter
6 oz sultanas
6 oz currants
2 oz raisins
2 oz peel

2 oz ground almonds
3 eggs
12 oz self-raising flour
Nutmeg, lemon or mixed spice

Put sugar, butter and fruit into a saucepan with 1 tablespoon water and boil for 3 minutes. Cool and stir in ground almonds, eggs and flour, and selected flavourings. Put into 10 inch greased round tin and bake at 375°F (Gas Mark 5) for $1\frac{1}{2}$ hours, and then at 350°F (Gas Mark 4) for 30 minutes. Cool in tin before turning out. Mrs Davies says this is quick to make (for funerals) and rich and good for cutting. She also said it could be made weeks beforehand (presumably for Christmas and not for a funeral); the recipe came from her great-grandmother and has been in the family for generations. In Wales and bordering counties, dying is not 'kept to yourself'. Indeed everyone shares in it, and it's a drama above all else. 'We buried him decently with 'am and funeral cake', and of course *everyone* turns up, and a good time is had by all—well almost. Certainly in the case of a good old-aged person.

Doris Davies, Hay-on-Wye, Hereford

DUNDEE CAKE

8 oz plain flour
$\frac{1}{2}$ teaspoon baking powder
8 oz butter
8 oz sugar
3 oz sultanas
3 eggs

3 oz currants
3 oz raisins
1 oz candied peel
Grated rind and juice of 1 orange
3 oz almonds

Sift flour and baking powder. Cream butter and sugar. Add eggs, then flour, fruit, orange rind and juice. Put mixture in a greased paper-lined 8 inch tin. Blanch and slice almonds, and strew on top. Bake at 325°F (Gas Mark 3) for 2 hours.

Mrs Corrie, Burnside of Auchegool, Kirkcudbrightshire

TROUP CAKE

3 oz butter
1 tablespoon golden syrup
½ oz sugar

3 oz seedless raisins
6 oz plain chocolate
7 oz digestive biscuits

Melt the butter, syrup and sugar with raisins over a low heat. Melt the chocolate over hot water. Crush the biscuits with a rolling pin. Stir the crumbs into the butter mixture, together with a dessertspoon of the melted chocolate. Press the mixture into a shallow tin. Pour on the remaining chocolate. Leave to set and cut into small pieces.

MATTHEW'S CHOCOLATE CAKE

10 oz chocolate (plain)
6 oz butter
3 oz castor sugar

3 oz ground almonds
4 eggs
2 oz plain flour

Melt 6 oz chocolate over hot water. Cream the butter and sugar until light and fluffy and beat in the chocolate, ground almonds and egg yolks. Whip the egg whites stiffly. Fold in the flour and the egg whites, and pour into an 8 inch greased and floured tin. Bake at 350°F (Gas Mark 4) for 40 minutes. Cool on a wire rack and top with the remaining chocolate which has been melted over hot water.

CHOCOLATE TRUFFLE CAKE

4 oz margarine
1 tablespoon sugar
1 tablespoon syrup

2 tablespoons cocoa
8 oz sweet biscuit crumbs
2 oz plain chocolate

Cream the margarine and sugar. Add the syrup and cocoa and mix well. The biscuit crumbs should be very fine (they can be crushed with a rolling pin). Add gradually to the mixture and stir in well. Press down into a greased sandwich tin. Melt the chocolate over hot water and pour over the cake. Leave in a cool place for 5 hours to set. Cut in small pieces as it is rather rich.

FESTIVAL CAKE

1 lb mixed dried fruit
1 breakfastcup soft brown sugar
1 breakfastcup water
4 oz butter
1 teaspoon bicarbonate of soda

2 teacups self-raising flour
2 large eggs
2 oz nuts (almonds, walnuts)
12 glacé cherries
Squeeze of lemon
A drop of brandy also helps

Simmer together fruit, sugar, water, butter and soda for 5 minutes and leave to get cold. Add flour, beaten eggs, chopped nuts, cherries cut in half, and lemon juice with brandy. Mix well and pour into deep 7 inch tin greased and lined. Bake on middle shelf of oven set at 325°F (Gas Mark 3) for 2 hours. This recipe was given to Mrs Thompson by a very old lady who still makes it regularly. She *has* to, as her husband insists.

Helen Thompson, Newbury, Berks

VICTORIAN GINGER CAKE

8 oz butter	**8 oz crystallised ginger**
8 oz castor sugar	**Juice of 1 small lemon**
3 oz plain flour	**½ teaspoon bicarbonate of soda**
½ teaspoon salt	**1 dessertspoon boiling water**
4 large eggs	

Cream the butter and sugar until very light and fluffy. Sift flour and salt together and sprinkle a little on to the butter mixture. Add the eggs one at a time, adding a little flour at each addition. Cut the ginger into very small pieces and put into a bowl. Add the lemon juice, soda and water and stir well. Add to the cake mixture and stir until blended. Put into a greased and floured deep 7 inch cake tin. Bake at 325°F (Gas Mark 3) for 2 hours.

South Stoke Vicarage, Bath

VICTORIAN LUNCHEON CAKE

½ lb sifted self-raising flour	**3 tablespoons milk**
4 oz beef dripping	**1 rounded teaspoon baking**
4 oz soft brown (pieces) sugar	**powder**
1 egg	**8 oz currants**

Butter and flour the sides and base of a 6–6½ inch diameter, sliding-based cake tin. Cream the dripping thoroughly, add sugar, and cream down again. Sift flour and baking powder together. Add 2 tablespoons flour to dripping mixture, then the egg, and whip again. Continue adding flour gradually with single spoonsful of milk until both ingredients are absorbed. Turn into prepared tin. Flour currants and shake off surplus in a sieve. Turn on top of cake mixture and work in with a table fork, being careful not to let fork touch base. Thus fruit will not sink. Bake on middle shelf of oven, 325°F (Gas Mark 3) for 1 hour 10 minutes to 1 hour 15 minutes.

RAISIN PARKIN

12 oz medium oatmeal
6 oz plain flour
1 oz sugar
1 teaspoon ground ginger
¼ teaspoon salt

4 oz seedless raisins
⅛ pint milk
1 teaspoon bicarbonate of soda
1 lb black treacle
4 oz butter

Grease a meat tin (about 8 × 10 inches) and line the bottom with grease-proof paper. Put oatmeal, flour, sugar, ginger and salt into a bowl with the raisins and mix well together. Warm the milk to blood heat, and add soda. Melt together the treacle and butter. Add milk and treacle mixture to dry ingredients. Beat well and pour into prepared tin. Bake at 350°F (Gas Mark 4) for 45 minutes until firm to the touch. Cool a little and turn on to a cake rack. Keep in a tin for a few days before eating.

GINGER SPONGE WITH MARMALADE

4 oz butter
2 oz soft brown sugar
2 tablespoons warm golden syrup
2 eggs

4 oz self-raising flour
¼ teaspoon baking powder
½ teaspoon ground ginger
Marmalade

Cream butter, sugar and syrup and when light and fluffy, work in beaten eggs. Fold in flour sifted with baking powder and ginger. Put into two greased 7 inch tins. Bake at 400°F (Gas Mark 6) for 25 minutes. Turn out on a wire rack and cool. Sandwich together liberally with marmalade and sprinkle with icing sugar.

GILL'S SYRUP SPONGE CAKE

2 oz butter
2 oz sugar
4 tablespoons golden syrup

1 egg
2 tablespoons milk
4 oz self-raising flour

Melt together the butter, sugar and syrup. Beat together the egg and milk. Add egg mixture and flour alternately to the butter mixture. When well mixed, pour into greased 8 inch sponge tin. Bake at 350°F (Gas Mark 4) for 35 minutes. Cool on a wire rack. Do not split the cake, but top with a thin lemon water icing.

PHILLIDA'S BREAD PUDDING

8 slices bread (toast thickness)
½ pint milk
12 oz mixed dried fruit
2 oz mixed chopped candied peel
1 apple
3 tablespoons brown sugar
2 tablespoons marmalade
3 tablespoons self-raising flour
2 eggs
Squeeze of lemon juice
1 teaspoon ground cinnamon
4 oz butter

Soak the bread in the milk until it is really soft. Add dried fruit and peel, lemon juice, grated peeled apple, sugar, marmalade, flour, eggs and cinnamon. Beat very thoroughly together. Melt the butter and pour half into the mixture. Beat and put into a greased meat tin. Pour on remaining butter. Bake at 300°F (Gas Mark 2) for 1½ hours; then at 350°F (Gas Mark 4) for 30 minutes. Leave until cold, sprinkle with icing sugar, and cut in slices. It can also be eaten hot as a pudding with egg custard. A plate of this delicious 'rib-sticker' doesn't last long if it is left in the kitchen as a between-meals snack for hungry workers or sportsmen.

SEED SPONGE CAKE

3 teacups flour
2 teaspoons cream of tartar
4 oz butter
1½ cups sifted sugar
A few caraway seeds
2 eggs

Cream butter and sugar. Add flour, caraway seeds and eggs. Bake at 350°F (Gas Mark 4) for 1 hour.

Lewis' Mother's Cookbook, Mary Horrell, Exeter

ELLEN TREMLETT'S CHOCOLATE CAKE

4 oz chocolate
4 oz butter
4 oz castor sugar
4 oz flour
3 eggs
1 teaspoon baking powder

Grate the chocolate and let it get warm in the oven. Beat the butter to a cream with your hand. Add the flour, sugar and baking powder, then the chocolate. When it is cool, add the yolks of the eggs, and lastly the whites, which have been beaten to a stiff froth. Lightly bake for 1 or 1½ hours in a good oven.

Lewis' Mother's Cookbook, Mary Horrell, Exeter

POWDER CAKE

1 lb plain flour
2 heaped tablespoons baking powder

½ teaspoon salt
Milk to mix

Mix all together and mix to a fairly stiff dough. Roll out ½ inch thick and cut into rounds. Bake at 425°F (Gas Mark 7) for 20 minutes. Serve warm with butter and jam, or fry with bacon.

Mrs Biggar, Kirkcudbrightshire

CHERRY ALMOND CAKE

2 oz ground almonds
6 oz plain flour
6 oz butter
6 oz sugar

2 large eggs
¼ lb cherries
½ teaspoon baking powder
Almond essence

Wash cherries in very hot water, drain and cut into 3, dry in a little of the flour. Cream butter, sugar and eggs. Add ground almonds, flour and baking powder, and lastly cherries. Sprinkle top of cake with little fine sugar and blanched almonds. Cook at 275°F (Gas Mark 1) for 1½ hours. Cake should be pale golden colour, and stores well in freezer.

Pat Brown, Keynsham, Somerset

JOAN'S CAKE

12 oz self-raising flour
8 oz butter
8 oz granulated sugar
3 eggs
1 lb mixed fruit and few chopped cherries

1 oz ground almonds
Almond essence
1 heaped dessertspoon cornflour

Mix cornflour with a little milk and thicken by cooking with 1 breakfastcup water. Cool. Cream fat and sugar; add eggs, cornflour mixture and other ingredients. Bake about 1½ hours at 300°F (Gas Mark 2). Cool in tin, and store. Good to freeze.

Pat Brown, Keynsham, Somerset

SCRIPTURE CAKE

4½ cups 1 Kings IV 22v.
(Flour)
1½ cups Judges V 25v.
(Butter)
2 cups Jeremiah VI 20v.
(Sugar)
2 cups 1 Samuel XXV 18v.
(Raisins)
2 cups Nahum III 12v.
(Currants – figs to be correct)
1 cup Numbers XVII 8v.
(Almonds)

2 tablespoons 1 Samuel
XIV 25v. (Honey)
Season to taste 11 Chronicles
IX 9v. (Spice)
6 cups Jeremiah XVII 11v.
(6 eggs)
1 pinch of Leviticus II 13v.
(Salt)
1 cup Judges IV 19v. last
clause (Milk)
3 teaspoons Amos V 5v.
(Baking powder)

Follow Solomon's prescription for the making of a good boy, Proverbs
XXIII, 14v. (Beat it well.)

Mrs Harbord, Lincs

HONEY GINGERBREAD

4 cups plain flour
2 heaped teaspoons baking
powder
2 teaspoons ginger
½ cup each of sultanas and
halved cherries

A little chopped peel
4 oz butter
¾ cup honey
2 eggs
A little milk

Sieve the dry ingredients and add fruit; melt butter and honey in a pan,
add milk, and when cool add to the dry ingredients together with the
lightly beaten eggs. Mix, put in a prepared tin, and bake in a slow oven
for 1 hour.

CARAWAY ANGEL CAKE

5 oz plain flour
4 oz castor sugar
2 oz butter
1 gill milk
2 egg whites

1 teaspoon baking powder
2 oz mixed candied peel
1 large teaspoon caraway
seeds

Cream together the butter and sugar, add the milk gradually and when
smooth add the stiffly whisked egg whites. Sieve together the flour, baking

powder, and a pinch of salt. Very carefully fold into the egg fat mixture
with the peel and seeds. Put into a well greased 6 inch cake tin. Bake
$1\frac{1}{4}$ hours, 350°F (Gas Mark 4).

QUICK GINGER BREAD

4 oz self-raising flour   *3 oz lard*
$\frac{1}{4}$ *teaspoon salt*   *3 oz syrup*
1 level teaspoon ginger   *1 teaspoon warm milk*
2 oz brown sugar   *1 beaten egg*
1 oz oatmeal

Sieve the flour, salt and ginger into a bowl and add the brown sugar and
oatmeal. Place the lard and syrup into a saucepan. and melt. Add the milk.
Mix this mixture into the dry ingredients and add a beaten egg. Beat
thoroughly and pour the mixture into a 7 inch greased loaf tin. Bake for
$1-1\frac{1}{2}$ hours in an oven at 325°F (Gas Mark 3).

GLOUCESTER PLUM CAKE

4 oz butter or margarine   *Grated rind of $\frac{1}{2}$ lemon*
3 oz black treacle   *12 oz mixed dried fruit,*
2 oz sugar   *raisins, currants and*
3 eggs   *sultanas*
6 oz plain flour   *2 oz glacé cherries, halved*
1 level *teaspoon baking*   *2 oz chopped mixed peel*
powder   *2 oz chopped almonds*
1 level teaspoon mixed spice

Cream the butter, treacle and sugar till light. Add the eggs one at a time,
beating well between each. Add fruit and nuts alternately with the sifted
dry ingredients, folding in lightly. Put into a prepared 6 inch cake tin and
bake in a slow oven, 300°F (Gas Mark 2) for $2\frac{1}{2}$–3 hours. Allow to cool in
the tin before removing.

YORKSHIRE PARKIN

8 oz plain flour   *rolled oats*
$\frac{1}{2}$ *level teaspoon salt*   *8 oz black treacle*
1-2 level teaspoons ginger   *6 oz lard or cooking fat*
1 level teaspoon bicarbonate   *4 oz soft brown sugar*
of soda   *1 egg*
8 oz medium oatmeal or   *Approximately $\frac{1}{4}$ pint milk*

437

Sift together flour, salt, ginger and bicarbonate of soda. Stir in oatmeal or oats. Put treacle, lard and sugar into a pan and dissolve gently over a low heat. Make a well in the centre of the flour mixture, pour in melted ingredients then mix to a soft batter with the egg and milk, adding a little more milk if necessary. Stir briskly, without beating, to combine ingredients. Turn into a well-greased and lined 8 inch square tin, then bake in the centre of a moderate oven, 350°F (Gas Mark 4) for 20 minutes, then lower temperature to 325°F (Gas Mark 3) for 50–60 minutes. When cooked, the parkin should be an even brown and have shrunk away slightly from the sides of the tin. If possible keep in a tin for a week before serving.

APPLE GINGERBREAD WITH FUDGEY ICING

1 large cooking apple
3 oz sugar
4 oz black treacle
3 oz butter or margarine, melted

6 oz self-raising flour
2 level teaspoons ground ginger
6 whole cloves
1 egg, beaten

Peel, core and slice the apple and put in saucepan with the cloves, 1 dessertspoon sugar and very little water. Cook until tender, remove the cloves and mash well with a fork. Leave to cool.

Put the sieved dry ingredients into a bowl and add the cooled apple and beaten egg, treacle and melted fat and beat all well together. Turn into a $1\frac{1}{2}$ lb loaf tin and bake in a moderate oven, 350°F (Gas Mark 4) for 40 minutes.

Fudgey Icing:

Cream together 1 oz butter, 1 oz treacle and 2 oz icing sugar. Beat well until light and creamy. Add a little ground cinnamon to taste, if liked. Spread on the cake when it is cool and mark with a fork. Chopped nuts may be scattered over.

GINGER CAKE

6 oz self-raising flour
3 oz margarine
2 oz sugar
2 oz golden syrup
2 oz black treacle

1 egg
1 teaspoon ground ginger
$\frac{1}{2}$ teaspoon bicarbonate of soda
$\frac{1}{4}$ pint milk
Pinch of salt

Put fat and syrup and milk into a saucepan and melt. Add dry ingredients, then egg and lastly bicarbonate of soda dissolved in a drop of milk. Line a small meat tin and bake in a moderate oven. Test with skewer or knitting needle.

Self-raising flour was first used successfully in 1846, and was noted in *The Lancet* as an interesting invention. It was produced commercially in the 1880s, but does not seem to have come into general use until the 1920s. Curiously, it is still virtually unknown in many European countries, including France.

GRANDMA'S SUNDAY CAKE

2 eggs (beaten)
4 oz sugar
6 oz butter
10 oz self-raising flour

6 oz currants
2 oz mixed peel
A few cherries

Beat sugar and butter to a cream, add eggs. Stir in currants, peel, cherries, fold in flour. If not moist enough, add a little milk. This recipe has been used for years and is always a winner.

Mrs J. Keel, Chew Stoke, Somerset

FAMILY FRUIT CAKE

8 oz self-raising flour
¼ teaspoon salt
4 oz butter
4 oz soft brown sugar
4 oz sultanas and raisins

2 oz chopped peel
Grated rind of ½ lemon
1 egg
5 tablespoons milk

Sift flour and salt, then rub in butter until mixture looks like fine bread-crumbs. Stir in sugar, dried fruit, peel and grated rind, and mix lightly with egg and milk. Put into greased and lined 6 inch cake tin and bake at 350°F (Gas Mark 4) for 1½ hours. Cool on a wire rack. Do not cut for 24 hours.

CHOCOLATE SPONGE

4 oz margarine
5 oz castor sugar
2 eggs
1 tablespoon milk
4 oz self-raising flour
1 tablespoon cocoa

For the Filling:
6 oz icing sugar
1 oz cocoa
2 oz soft butter
2 dessertspoons hot water

Cream margarine and sugar and work in eggs and milk alternately with sifted cocoa and flour. Blend well and bake in greased 2 inch tin at 360°F (Gas Mark 4) for 30 minutes. Cool on rack and split in half. Cream together icing sugar, cocoa, butter and water until very soft and light and use to fill and top sponge. Mark with a fork and decorate with nuts or chocolate chips.

1898 BRISTOL CAKE

6 oz butter	**½ lb ground rice**
3 eggs	**2 teaspoons baking powder**
½ lb sugar	**1 lb fruit (less will do)**
½ pint milk	**¼ lb peel**
½ lb flour	

Beat butter to cream. Add sugar. Beat eggs separately and add milk, lastly flour and rice and fruit and beat for ¼ hour. Bake about 2 hours in a moderate oven.

Miss Jeffrey, Hambledon, Hants

YORKSHIRE SANDWICH

2 tablespoons ground rice	**2 eggs**
2 tablespoons flour	**A little milk**
1 tablespoon castor sugar	**1 teaspoon baking powder**
2 heaped tablespoons fats	

Cream fat and sugar. Beat in eggs, add dry ingredients and milk. Bake in moderate oven for 25 minutes.

CHOCOLATE FUDGE CAKE

4 oz margarine	**6 oz self-raising flour**
10 oz sugar	**2 oz cocoa**
2 eggs	**Vanilla**

Melt margarine in saucepan. Add sugar and beaten eggs. Add flour, cocoa etc. Pour into shallow *lined* tin and bake in moderate oven for 30–40 minutes. Really good—kids love it, but oven must *not* be too hot. Quick and easy.

GRANNY CROSSLAND'S COURTING CAKE

2 cups flour	**3 oz margarine or lard**
1 cup sugar	

Beat 1 egg well and put a tablespoon milk into it. Rub all ingredients into a paste and put on a bake sheet, spread well with jam. Bake in hot oven (not *too* hot). Cut into slices (fingers) in tin.

Made by Granny Crossland who lived till she was 94 (born 1848) at Newton-on-Trent and lived there all her life. She used to make this cake to take on holiday because the family, grandchildren and all, used to rent a house at Skegness or Cromer, taking from their farmhouse some of the food, but the rest was cooked for them by the seaside landlady. Farmer's wife and real martinet, Granny Crossland was still working, keeping her household in order, till she died. These recipes came from Granny Crossland's grand-daughter who lives at Crofthouse Farm, Beckingham, near Doncaster (on borders of Yorks and Lincs). Mrs Muriel Selby says she was newly married (1942) when she went to visit her grandmother for what proved to be the last time. The old lady kept saying that she was looking forward to visiting her to help her (Muriel) get her new house straight! But of course she never got there. However, Mrs Selby still makes these cakes to this day.

Mrs Selby, Doncaster

LINCOLNSHIRE CAKES

2 lb self-raising flour	**½ lb sultanas**
6 oz lard	**½ lb raisins**
6 oz margarine	**4 eggs**
1 oz sugar	**A little milk**
½ lb currants	

Rub in or cream. Cook in slow oven. Cut up into slices in tin.

Mrs Selby, Doncaster

GENOA CAKE

6 oz butter	**¼ lb currants**
6 oz sugar	**¼ lb sultanas**
8 oz self-raising flour	**¼ lb cherries**
3 eggs	

Cream butter and sugar together. Beat well for some time. Add eggs, flour, then fruit. Halve cherries and roll in some of the flour to prevent them sinking to bottom of cake.

Mrs Selby, Doncaster

QUICK ORANGE CAKE

4 oz melted butter
8 oz castor sugar
2 eggs
⅛ pint orange juice
8 oz plain flour
4 teaspoons baking powder

¼ teaspoon salt

Topping:
Rind of 2 oranges
3 tablespoons sugar

Add melted butter to sugar, then the beaten eggs and juice. Blend well, then add flour sifted with baking powder and salt, and beat well. Pour into 10-inch spring-form cake tin. Mix orange rind with sugar and sprinkle on top. Bake at 350°F (Gas Mark 4) for 75 minutes. Open sides of tin, leave cake to cool for a few minutes, then remove carefully to wire rack. If the quick topping is omitted, this can be iced, but the flavour is better with baked-on topping.

WALNUT MOCHA CAKE

4 oz butter
8 oz castor sugar
2 eggs
8 tablespoons milk
6 oz flour
2 teaspoons baking powder
Pinch of salt
2 teaspoons vanilla essence

4 oz walnuts

Icing:
2 oz butter
4 oz icing sugar
1 oz cocoa
Strong black coffee

Cream butter and sugar. Add beaten yolks of eggs and the milk. Sift flour with baking powder and salt and stir gradually into the egg mixture. Add vanilla essence and the walnuts lightly broken up and tossed in flour. Fold in stiffly-beaten egg whites, pour into greased rectangular pan and bake at 350°F (Gas Mark 4) for 40 minutes. Make the icing by creaming together butter, sugar and cocoa, softening the mixture with a little very strong coffee. Cover the cake and decorate with more walnuts if liked.

APPLE CAKE

4 oz margarine
4 oz sugar
2 eggs

5 oz self-raising flour
Enough cream or milk to
make a smooth mixture

This amount will fill 2 8 inch sandwich tins. Before baking, peel, core and slice enough apple to cover all over top of cakes, pressing slices in gently. Sprinkle a couple of tablespoons sugar and cinnamon (already mixed) over each cake. Bake at 400°F (Gas Mark 6) for about 30 minutes. This can be eaten warm as a sweet with cream or cold for tea.

Mrs Lye, Oxon

MARY'S CAKE

4 oz butter or margarine
4 oz castor sugar
2 eggs

Small amount vanilla essence
4 oz self-raising flour

Cream the fat and sugar, and beat in the eggs and essence. Fold in the flour. Use two sponge tins. Bake at 350°F (Gas Mark 4) for 25 minutes. This recipe came from the eleven-year-old deaf-and-dumb daughter of a farmer.

CHERRY AND ALMOND CAKE

6 oz self-raising flour
6 oz butter
6 oz castor sugar
4 oz ground almonds
8 oz glacé cherries

3 large eggs
Pinch of salt
Few drops vanilla essence
A little milk to mix

Cream butter and sugar. Then add all the dry ingredients, flour and ground almonds with the eggs. Then the cherries and sufficient milk to mix to a medium soft consistency. Cook in an 8 inch round tin slow oven, 325°F (Gas Mark 3) for 1½ hours. Allow the cake to cool in the tin 30 minutes before turning it out.
Note Rinse the cherries in warm water, cut in half and well dry; toss them in a little flour from the cake weight before using.

Miss Mabel Nokes, Priston Mill Farm, Bath

DATE CAKE

1 packet chopped dates
8 oz butter
3 eggs
4 oz sugar

8 oz flour
2 oz chopped walnuts
1 teaspoon bicarbonate of soda

Just cover the dates with *hot* water and the baking soda. Leave for an hour. Beat the sugar and butter, add the flour and beaten eggs, lastly the dates and walnuts. Bake in a shallow tin in a moderate oven, 350°F (Gas Mark 4) for 60 minutes.

Miss Mabel Nokes, Priston Mill Farm, Bath

ORANGE SPONGE

The weight of 2 eggs in flour, castor sugar, also butter. Cream the sugar and butter, add the flour. Then add 1 tablespoon warm water. Bake in 2 tins at 350°F (Gas Mark 4) for 30 minutes. Then, when cooling just pour over the juice of the orange leaving a little juice to flavour a butter icing.

Miss Mabel Nokes, Priston Mill Farm, Bath

FRUIT CAKE

4½ oz butter	*5 oz raisins*
4½ oz soft brown sugar	*7 oz currants*
1 oz peel	*3 oz cherries*
6 oz self-raising flour	*3 eggs*

Cream butter and sugar, add flour and beaten eggs, lastly the fruit. Bake at 325°F (Gas Mark 3) for 1½ hours.

Miss Mabel Nokes, Priston Mill Farm, Bath

ALMOND CAKE

3 oz self-raising flour	*4 oz butter*
4 oz castor sugar	*2 small eggs*
2 oz ground almonds	

Cream the butter and sugar. Then add the beaten eggs, also the flour and almonds. Bake in 6 inch tin for 60 minutes at 375°–400°F (Gas Mark 5–6).

Miss Mabel Nokes, Priston Mill Farm, Bath

CORNISH HEAVY CAKE

8 oz plain flour	*3 oz currants*
2 oz margarine	*¼ teaspoon salt*
2 oz lard	*Peel*
2 oz granulated sugar	*3 tablespoons water*

Sieve flour and salt well. Mix in fat roughly. Add sugar and fruit. Add water to make a fairly stiff dough. Knead out all cracks gently. Shape up and roll out to approximately ½ inch thick, keeping edges smooth. Criss-cross with knife over top. Bake at 375°F (Gas Mark 5) for 25–30 minutes.

CHOCOLATE CAKE

2 tablespoons butter   **1 cup sugar**

Cream together and add 1 beaten egg. Mix together 2 tablespoons cocoa, ½ cup boiling water and add to first mixture. Take ½ cup sour milk and mix in 1 teaspoon bicarbonate of soda. Add to above and fold in 1½ cups flour, ½ teaspoon lemon or vanilla. Bake for 45 minutes.

The icing: Cream 1 tablespoon butter, add 1 tablespoon warm milk, ½ teaspoon vanilla and icing sugar to desired thickness. Spread on top and sides and sprinkle on coconut.

This cake won first prize of £10 at the 1920 Cardiff Show.

Mary Giles, Marksbury, Somerset

VERY SPECIAL CHOCOLATE SPONGE CAKE

1 teacup sugar – castor, for preference
1 teacup self-raising flour

4 eggs
1 tablespoon drinking chocolate (added to the flour)

Whisk eggs to thick and creamy stage. Add sugar and beat again till thicker still. Then gently, with a fork, stir in the flour direct from the sieve. Have ready greased and floured, 2 8 inch tins and put the mixture evenly into them. Cook for 20 minutes in oven at 350°F (Gas Mark 4).

Icing:
½ lb butter

½ lb icing sugar
¼ lb drinking chocolate

Beat all together in bowl and spread on top and sides, making pattern with a fork.

This recipe came from the old cook of Lady Wills of Blagdon, Somerset, and was taught to Mrs Ball when she was a very young girl.

Mrs J. Ball, Compton Greenfield

KING EDWARD'S GINGERBREAD

½ lb brown sugar
½ lb butter
¾ lb treacle
12 oz flour
2 eggs

1 oz ground ginger
1 teaspoon lemon juice
Enough soda (bicarbonate) to cover a 6d.

Mix sugar and treacle and put in pan on fire to warm. Beat butter to cream. Beat eggs and add to butter and beat slowly. Add treacle mixture beating all the time. Fold in flour into which the ginger and bicarbonate of soda have been sifted. Bake in slow oven, approximately 325°F (Gas Mark 3) for 60 minutes. This was made at Sandringham for shooting parties given by Edward VII.

From the aunt of Mrs C. Dutnall, Cheam, Surrey
per Mrs A. Padgham, Minehead

KING EDWARD'S LUNCH CAKE

1½ *lb self-raising flour*	4 *eggs*
1 *lb granulated sugar*	1 *teacup milk*
½ *lb butter*	2 *teacups mixed fruit*

Cream butter and sugar. Add eggs with a little flour and beat. Fold in rest of flour and fruit. Bake in moderate oven, 350°F (Gas Mark 4) for 1½–2 hours.

A favourite at shooting picnic lunches at Sandringham.

From the aunt of Mrs C. Dutnall, Cheam, Surrey
per Mrs A. Padgham, Minehead

VICTORIA SANDWICH

2 *eggs*	4 *oz self-raising flour*
2 *oz margarine*	1 *teaspoon baking powder*
4 *oz sugar*	1 *tablespoon milk*

First prepare oven and tins. Remove browning sheet from oven (if one is used) and heat ready to 425°F (Gas Mark 7). Well grease 2 8 inch sandwich tins. Place margarine in oven to just melt, *do not let it boil*. Beat eggs and milk together, add sugar and beat well again (5 minutes with rotary whisk, less with electric beaters). Mix baking powder with flour; fold into mixture using a metal spoon; lastly stir in melted margarine. Now divide mixture into 2 tins and spread evenly. Place in oven one above the other and cook about 12 minutes. Take out upper tin and move under tin up for further 2 minutes.

FIVE GOLDEN RULES

1. Have tins and oven ready. Sponge must not be kept waiting.
2. Always fold in flour—do not beat—beating is already done.
3. *Melt* margarine and add last.
4. To test if sponge is cooked, press lightly with finger. If cooked, it will instantly rise.
5. When taken from oven sprinkle tops with castor sugar, leave 10 minutes before turning out. Spread with jam, sandwich together while still warm.

From Essex came this light-textured, conveniently-made sponge. Try using this recipe if you have had a patch of 'failed sponges' type cake-making—it's guaranteed to restore self-confidence and *the whole operation takes only* 30 *minutes flat*. It needs beating well.

WALNUT CREAM SANDWICH

2 eggs
Their weight in castor sugar,
butter and flour
Grated rind of ½ lemon
½ teaspoon baking powder

½ teaspoon lemon juice
2 tablespoons raspberry jam
2 tablespoons icing sugar
Few walnuts, shelled and
skinned

Put butter and sugar into a basin, well beat until it will drop off the spoon, and then add the beaten eggs and a little flour. Mix well, and then add the rest of the flour, the lemon rind and juice. Put in a tin lined with greased paper, and bake for 15 minutes. When cool spread jam on, ice top, and scatter walnuts over.

Mrs F. Webb, Loughton, Essex, 1911

OXFORD GINGER CAKE

4 oz butter
4 oz soft brown sugar
4 oz flour
4–6 oz black treacle

1 egg
1 teaspoon bicarbonate of soda
¼ teacup warm milk
Ginger to taste

Cream butter and sugar, add egg and treacle and mix well, add flour sifted with ginger. Dissolve bicarbonate of soda in warm milk and add last. Bake in slow oven, 325°F (Gas Mark 3) for 1½–2 hours.

I got this black, gooey ginger cake from Oxfordshire W.I. some years ago. It rises right up in the tin while cooking and then sinks in the middle—best looking in a round tin.

Mrs A. Padgham, Minehead, Somerset

DAMP GINGERBREAD

10 oz flour
6 oz butter
6 oz moist sugar
3 oz almonds
6 oz sultanas
1½ teaspoons ground ginger

1½ teaspoons cinnamon
¼ lb treacle
2 eggs
Warm milk
¾ teaspoon baking soda

Sieve the flour; clean sultanas; blanch and shred the almonds (blanch by steeping few minutes in cup of boiling water) and mix 1 teaspoon flour with the fruit. Cream the butter and sugar, add dry ingredients, treacle, beaten eggs and the baking soda mixed with a little milk. Add more milk if necessary to the whole. Turn into greased tin and bake 325°F (Gas Mark 3) for 2 hours.

Mrs Biggar, Kirkcudbrightshire

ICING FOR CAKES

1 heaped teaspoon of gelatine soaked in cold water, add ½ teaspoon of boiling water to dissolve it and make thick with ½ lb sifted sugar.

Lewis' Mother's Cookbook, Mary Horrell, Exeter

LEMON ICING FOR CAKES

Squeeze the juice of a lemon, mix with a tablespoon of water, and boil together. While boiling, pour over ½ lb icing sugar, stir until quite smooth. Spread the cakes while hot, and dry in a warm place.

Lewis' Mother's Cookbook, Mary Horrell, Exeter

CHOCOLATE ICING

1 oz grated chocolate　　　　　**½ gill water**
3 oz castor sugar

Put the ingredients into a saucepan and stir over the fire until it thickens. Pour over sandwiches and dry in a cool oven.

Lewis' Mother's Cookbook, Mary Horrell, Exeter

CHOCOLATE MACAROONS

4½ oz ground almonds　　　　**2½ oz melted plain chocolate**
7 oz castor sugar　　　　　　**Rice paper**
2 egg whites　　　　　　　　**Split blanched almonds**

Stir together almonds and sugar. Whip egg whites stiffly and fold into the dry mixture, together with the chocolate. Put in spoonsful on rice paper. Bake at 325°F (Gas Mark 3) for 30 minutes. Top with blanched almonds.

LEMON CHEESE NUGGETS

3 oz lemon cheese (curd)　　　**½ teaspoon baking powder**
8 oz flour　　　　　　　　　**2 oz butter**
2 oz castor sugar　　　　　　**1 egg**

Rub the butter into the flour, add the sugar, baking powder and lemon cheese, with one egg, mix into a stiff dough, place on greased tin in rough heaps. Bake in moderate oven 15 minutes.

Mrs Page 1899

GERTRUDE'S MACAROONS

4 oz ground almonds
8 oz castor sugar
2 teaspoons ground rice

2 large egg whites
Almond essence

Beat egg whites stiff, fold in other ingredients, put 1 teaspoon on rice paper and decorate with half almonds. Bake in cool oven, under 250°F (Gas Mark ½).

Pat Brown, Keynsham, Somerset

WELSH TEACAKES

½ lb self-raising flour
5 oz butter
1 egg
4 oz sugar
3 oz currants

2 oz sultanas
¼ teaspoon ginger
Little grated lemon peel
Milk to mix

Rub fat into flour, add sugar, fruit, peel and ginger, mix with beaten egg and a little milk to a stiff dough. Roll out ¼ inch thick, cut into rounds and bake on a bakestone, turning once. Sprinkle with sugar while still warm.

HOT APPLE MUFFINS

8 oz flour
1 teaspoon baking powder
3 oz lard

1 lb cooking apples
1 small egg
2 oz black treacle

Sift together flour and baking powder and rub in the lard. Peel, core and mince the apples. Beat the egg. Make a well in the flour and stir in the egg, minced apple and treacle. Work well together to a stiff, sticky dough. Add a little more milk if too dry, but on no account should it be too wet, as the apples moisten it in baking. Put on to a greased baking tray and bake in a moderate oven, 350°F (Gas Mark 4) for 30 minutes or till a light golden brown. While still hot cut in rounds and cool on a wire rack. Split open and butter, dusting with castor sugar before serving.

CRUSTY LEMON BUTTER BAKE

6 oz butter
6 oz castor sugar

6 oz self-raising flour
2 eggs

Topping:
Juice of 1 lemon
4 oz castor sugar
} *mix to a paste and stand aside*

Cut the butter into pieces stand in the warm until it begins to get soft. Add the sugar, also the beaten eggs, then stir in the flour. Turn into a shallow tin 10×7 inches (greased with butter) smooth the surface and bake at 350°F (Gas Mark 4) for 40 minutes. The surface should be soft, set and golden. Take the cake from the oven and while hot spread over the top the lemon juice and castor sugar. The juice of the lemon will sink and leave the top crispy when cold. (For myself I put 5 oz butter. Also after the cake is cooked. I just prick the top of the cake for the juice to go through.)

Miss Mabel Nokes, Priston Mill Farm, Bath

FOCHABERS GINGERBREAD

8 oz butter
4 oz sugar
8 oz black treacle
½ oz ground ginger
A little ground cloves
2 eggs
1 lb flour
4 oz currants

4 oz sultanas
1 teaspoon bicarbonate of soda
3 oz ground almonds
3 oz chopped candied peel
½ oz mixed spice
A little cinnamon
½ pint beer

Cream the butter with the sugar. Add the slightly warmed treacle, break in the eggs and beat the mixture well. Mix the flour with all the dry ingredients (except the soda). Dissolve the bicarbonate of soda in the beer and mix everything together thoroughly. Put into a large greased cake tin and bake in a slow oven for 2 hours.

GINGER CAKE

2 teacups flour
1 teacup golden syrup or treacle
2 oz margarine or cooking fat

2 teaspoons ground ginger
1 teaspoon bicarbonate of soda
½ teacup hot water
Pinch of salt

Mix together flour, ginger and bicarbonate of soda. Warm fat slightly and mix in treacle. Add hot water, mix in flour etc. quickly and bake in a moderate oven, 350°F (Gas Mark 4) for 1 hour. Fruit may be added if desired.

NUTTY GINGERBREAD

2 oz butter	*Pinch salt*
4 oz golden syrup	*Pinch bicarbonate of soda*
1 oz granulated sugar	*1 egg, beaten*
4 oz self-raising flour	*6 tablespoons milk*
½ level teaspoon ginger	*1½ oz walnuts, chopped*
½ level teaspoon mixed spice	

Heat butter, syrup and sugar gently until sugar dissolves. Sieve the dry ingredients together into a bowl. Add syrup. Add egg and milk and beat thoroughly. Stir in nuts. Divide mixture between 12 greased, deep patty tins. Bake in a moderate oven, 350°F (Gas Mark 4) for 25–30 minutes. Cool.

CONNIE COOPER'S CUMBRIAN CAKE

Line a Swiss roll tin with pastry.

Filling: Melt 1½ oz butter. Add 9 oz currants, 3 oz soft brown sugar, 1 teaspoon spice, ½ teaspoon cinnamon, ¼ teaspoon mace. Mix. Add filling and cover with pastry. Bake at 375°F (Gas Mark 5) for 45 minutes. Cut in squares.

BUNS FOR AFTERNOON TEA

½ lb flour	*1 oz sugar*
2 oz butter	*1 egg*
1 oz coconut	*A little milk*
½ teaspoon baking powder	

These are very easy to make, and very inexpensive. They are also highly appreciated. Rub the butter amongst the flour, then add the baking powder, sugar, and a pinch of salt, and mix well together. If preferred, currants or raisins may be added. Make into a paste with the egg, which has been beaten up, and a little milk. Knead slightly, and cut into small pieces. Form into buns, and place in a greased baking tin. Bake in a hot oven for 15 minutes. Wait till cool, then serve.

Miss Lily Jamison, Aberdeen, 1911

LEMON SPICE CAKES

4 oz plain flour
1 teaspoon baking powder
½ teaspoon ground cinnamon
¼ teaspoon ground nutmeg
4 oz quick cooking rolled oats
2 oz walnuts, finely chopped
6 oz butter
8 oz soft brown sugar
½ teaspoon vanilla essence
2 eggs

3 tablespoons milk
Finely grated rind of 1 lemon
2 tablespoons strained lemon
juice

Icing:
6 oz icing sugar
2 tablespoons lemon juice
Little milk

Sift flour, baking powder, cinnamon and nutmeg. Add rolled oats and chopped nuts. Cream butter with sugar until light. Beat in eggs with lemon juice and rind, a little at a time, mixing well after each addition. Fold in flour mixture with extra milk to make a soft consistency. Spoon into a greased and lined tin 10 × 14 inches and spread top smoothly. Bake at 350°F (Gas Mark 4) for 35 minutes.

Sift icing sugar, mix with lemon juice and little milk. Pour over top of warm cake and spread smoothly. Cut into squares when cold.

BANBURY PUFFS

8 oz flaky or rough puff pastry
2 oz butter or margarine
1 oz stale cake crumbs or
plain flour
1 egg yolk

2 level tablespoons black
treacle
4 oz currants, washed and
dried
1 oz mixed chopped peel
½ level teaspoon mixed spice

Melt butter in a pan then add cake crumbs or flour. Cook gently, stirring, for 3 minutes. Remove from heat and beat in egg yolk and treacle. Cool mixture then add remaining ingredients.

Roll out pastry thinly and cut into approximately 12 rounds with a 4 inch plain cutter. Divide filling mixture equally between rounds, moisten edges of pastry with water, then draw together so that filling is completely covered. Turn each over – with join underneath – on to a lightly floured board and press with a rolling pin into an oval. Transfer to baking trays, score tops into a diamond pattern (or make 3 diagonal slits in the top of each) then brush with lightly beaten egg white. Dust lightly with castor sugar, then leave in a cool place for 10 minutes. Bake just above centre of a hot oven, at 425°F (Gas Mark 7) for 15 to 20 minutes. Cool on a wire tray.

ALMOND APPLE-CAKES

For Apple Filling:
¾ *lb cooking apples*
½ *oz butter*
½ *oz soft brown sugar*
½ *level teaspoon ground cloves*

For Almond Sponge:
4 *oz self-raising flour*

½ *level teaspoon salt*
2 *oz ground almonds*
4 *oz butter*
4 *oz sugar*
2 *eggs, beaten*
About 2 teaspoons milk
12 *whole blanched almonds*
for decoration

To make apple filling: Peel, core and slice apples. Place in a large saucepan together with butter and sugar. Cook very gently until the apples are soft but not completely broken up. Stir in ground cloves and leave mixture to become quite cold.

To make almond sponge: Sift flour and salt together and add ground almonds. Cream butter and sugar until light and fluffy. Gradually add eggs, beating well between each addition. Add 1 tablespoon of the flour mixture with the last addition of egg. Gradually fold in rest of flour and almond mixture. Add enough milk to give dropping consistency. Spoon half the mixture into 12 2-inch paper cake cases.

Make a well in the centre of each and fill with 2 teaspoons of apple mixture. Cover very carefully with remaining sponge mixture and top each with a whole blanched almond. Bake in a moderate oven, 375°F (Gas Mark 5) for 25–30 minutes, until firm to the touch. Remove and cool.

NUTMEG HONEY CAKES

8 *oz plain flour*
½ *level teaspoon salt*
4 *level teaspoons baking powder*

1 *level teaspoon ground nutmeg*
4 *tablespoons clear honey, warmed*
1–2 *teaspoons milk*

Sift together flour, salt, baking powder and nutmeg. Rub in fat until mixture resembles fine breadcrumbs. Gradually add warmed honey, to form a stiff dough. Add extra milk if necessary. Knead lightly. Roll out to ¼ inch thickness and cut out rounds with a 2 inch plain cutter. Re-roll trimmings and cut out more rounds. Place on a greased baking sheet and bake in a hot oven, 425°F (Gas Mark 7) for 15–20 minutes. Remove and cool.

BURWASH DOUGHNUTS

2 oz lard	**1 egg**
1 oz sugar	**Milk**
8 oz self-raising flour	**Fat for frying**
½ teaspoon salt	**Castor sugar**

Rub the lard and sugar into the flour sieved with salt. Mix with the egg and enough milk to make a soft dough. Roll out ½ inch thick and cut into circles with a floured cutter. Cut out centres with a smaller cutter. Fry a few rings at a time in very hot fat, allowing 2 minutes on each side. Drain on absorbent kitchen paper, cool slightly and roll in castor sugar. Eat while very fresh. The small centres can also be fried and are delicious if cooled slightly, then iced with lemon or chocolate water icing.

CARAMEL CHOCOLATE SQUARES

4 oz butter	**1 cup flour**
2 oz sugar	

Cream butter and sugar and add flour, spread in a Swiss roll tin and bake until brown 400°–425°F (Gas Mark 6–7) for about 20 minutes.

Caramel:	**1 tablespoon syrup**
4 oz margarine	**½ tin or small tin condensed**
2 oz sugar	**milk**

Put all in a saucepan and bring to boil, boil for 5 minutes, spread over shortcake. Melt 4 oz chocolate spread over caramel. Cool and cut in squares.

Mrs D. Hurst, East Riding College of Agriculture

1903 ROCK CAKES

1 lb flour	**3 oz butter or lard**
6 oz sugar	**6 oz currants**
2 teaspoons baking powder	**1 egg**
Ginger	**A little milk**
Nutmeg	**Piece of candied peel**
Salt	

Bake in a rather hot oven for 15 minutes. 24 rock cakes.

Mrs Watson, Salisbury

CHOCOLATE CAKES

6 *tablespoons flour*   ¼ *lb margarine*
3 *tablespoons cocoa*   1 *egg*
4 *tablespoons sugar*   *Milk to mix*
1 *tablespoon baking powder*

Mix sugar, margarine and egg to cream, then add flour, cocoa, baking powder and a little milk. 12–15 little cakes.

Mrs Fordham, 1927

CHOCOLATE MERINGUES

2 *egg whites*   6 *oz castor sugar*
Pinch of salt   6 *oz plain chocolate or*
Pinch of cream of tartar   *chocolate chips*

Beat egg whites, salt, and cream of tartar until soft peaks form. Add sugar gradually, beating until peaks are stiff. Chop chocolate roughly, or use chocolate chips, and stir into the mixture. Cover baking sheets with plain paper and drop mixture on by rounded teaspoons. Bake at 300°F (Gas Mark 2) for 25 minutes, and cool slightly before removing from paper. Do not fill these meringues with cream. 12 meringues.

CHOCOLATE COOPER

4 *oz margarine or butter*   1½ *tablespoons golden syrup*
1 *dessertspoon white sugar*   2 *oz mixed dry fruit*
3 *dessertspoons drinking*   ½ *lb plain biscuits*
chocolate

Put all ingredients except biscuits into a small saucepan, heat ingredients until sugar and syrup have melted. Stir in crushed biscuits and put into a shallow baking tray. Melt 4 oz cooking chocolate and spread over.

Patricia Jones

CHINESE CHEWS

3 *oz flour*   4 *oz chopped walnuts*
3 *oz margarine or butter*   10 *oz chopped dates*
5 *oz sugar (brown if liked)* 2 *eggs*

Cream butter and sugar, and add flour. Add eggs, and fruit, cut fairly large. Spread in a small Swiss roll tin and bake at about 375°–400°F (Gas Mark 5–6) until firm and brown. Sprinkle with castor or icing sugar.

Leave in tin to cool and then cut into fingers before turning out on to a cooling tray. Recipe can be halved if necessary and then cooked in a square tin, sandwich-sized.

Margaret Jeffes

MELTING MOMENTS

5 oz self-raising flour　　　　**½ egg**
1½ oz margarine　　　　**½ teaspoon vanilla essence**
3 oz sugar

Beat margarine and sugar, add vanilla, egg and flour. Dip in rolled oats. Flatten top and cook in moderate oven for 15 minutes.

BERKSHIRE ALMOND SPOON-HANDLE CAKES

Rub 3 oz cooking fat (or mixture of fats) into 6 oz self-raising flour. Add 2 oz sugar (castor for preference). Mix 1 tablespoon water with ½–1 teaspoon almond essence and add to dry ingredients. Finish mixing by using fingertips, for kneading. Divide into pieces and roll into balls with hands. Make a circular dent with the handle of a wooden spoon and fill with honey or syrup (*very* little required).

Put mixture into well-greased fancy little tins or in paper baking cases. The latter keep cakes a better shape and look more festive. Bake 15–20 minutes in moderate oven, 375°F (Gas Mark 5). Do not make dent too deep with the spoon handle and take care not to overcook.

YORKSHIRE FAT RASCALS

1 lb flour (self-raising or plain　　**1 oz brown sugar**
with 1 heaped teaspoon baking　　**Pinch of salt**
powder)　　　　　　　　　　**4 oz currants**
8 oz butter or margarine　　　　**Little milk and water**

Mix flour with sugar and salt and rub in butter or margarine. Add currants and mix well to a soft dough with the milk and water. A fairly soft scone-type dough is required. Roll out dough to approximately ½ inch thickness. Cut into 2 inch rounds, dust with castor sugar, then bake for about 20 minutes in a hot oven.

SUSSEX FLEAD CAKES

1 lb flead (or fleck)　　　　　**Pinch of salt**
1½ lb flour　　　　　　　　　　**Cold water**

Remove all skin and signs of veins from the flead and cut into thin cubes. Sift flour and salt in a basin, add flead and mix to a stiff dough. Place on a floured board. Beat with the end of a rolling pin as hard and quickly as possible, turning over if necessary.

Leave 15 minutes, then repeat beating and rolling. Repeat above twice more—as for flaky pastry. Rest again for 15 minutes then roll out to 1 inch thickness, cut into rounds, bake in hot oven, 450°F (Gas Mark 8) for about 10 minutes.

These really do take quite a lot of energy, but if all goes well should be very light and fluffy. Best eaten warm, I think, with jam or sprinkled with salt according to taste.

My father loves these above everything—and, as a child I can remember buying them at a small baker's in Bexhill (the last place where they could be obtained). My own make were much appreciated by Canadian friends during the war.

Flead is the white fat from a pig—like a kind of flat sheet held together with a flat membrane, which needs pulling off. This 'flead' or 'fleck' is still obtainable from good butchers.

Mrs A. Padgham, Minehead, Somerset

ECCLES CAKES

6 oz flaky or rough puff pastry　　**¼ teaspoon allspice**
2 oz currants　　　　　　　　　　**A little grated nutmeg**
1 oz sugar　　　　　　　　　　　　**½ oz butter**
¾ oz peel

Slightly oil butter in saucepan, add currants, chopped peel, sugar, spice. Mix together, Roll out paste, cut into rounds, place in centre 2 teaspoons of mixture. Close up the rounds, flatten with rolling-pin, mark across top of each cake with knife. Brush over with white of egg, sprinkle on castor sugar. Bake in quick oven for 10–15 minutes, 450°F (Gas Mark 8).

SHREWSBURY CAKES

½ lb self-raising flour　　　　　**¼ teaspoon cinnamon**
4 oz butter　　　　　　　　　　　**Pinch of nutmeg**
4 oz sugar　　　　　　　　　　　**Pinch of salt**
½ egg or 1 yolk

457

Cream butter and sugar together until soft. Add egg and gradually the flour and cinnamon until stiff, smooth paste is formed. Roll out on floured board till about ¼ inch thick, cut into rounds 4–5 inches wide. Bake slowly 15–20 minutes on flat baking sheet, 300°F (Gas Mark 2).

27 Biscuits

Now stir the fire, and close the shutters fast,
Let fall the curtains, wheel the sofa round,
And, while the bubbling and loud-hissing urn
Throws up a steamy column, and the cups,
That cheer but not inebriate, wait on each,
So let us welcome peaceful evening in.

William Cowper

VANILLA BISCUITS

4 oz plain flour
4 oz flaked oats
4 oz margarine
3 oz granulated sugar
2 level teaspoons golden syrup

2 level teaspoons baking powder
2 small teaspoons bicarbonate of soda
½ teaspoon vanilla
2 teaspoons boiling water

Cream the margarine and sugar. Add all dry ingredients. Dissolve syrup in boiling water and add to mixture to make a firm consistency. (The cooler it gets, the firmer it sets.) Roll out to ⅛ inch thickness. Cut into shapes and bake in a moderate oven for about 15 minutes.

When cool, sandwich together with chocolate butter icing, made the following way: beat together 1 oz margarine or butter, 2 oz icing sugar, chocolate or cocoa to taste. A little milk or hot water facilitates the mixing and 'softens' the consistency.

Mrs Titley, Glos.

BOURBON TYPE BISCUITS

4 oz sugar	**Filling:**
4 oz butter	**1½ oz margarine**
6 oz plain flour	**2 oz castor sugar**
¼ oz baking powder	**1 teaspoon coffee essence**
2 oz coarse semolina	**1½ dessertspoons cocoa**
1 beaten egg	**Few drops vanilla essence**
1½ dessertspoons cocoa	

Sift together all dry ingredients *except cocoa*, stirring in lastly the semolina. Bind with sufficient of the egg to make a rolling-out consistency (i.e. dampish but not too wet). Roll out; fold and work in the cocoa powder. *This must not be added before.* Roll out again until ⅛ inch thick, then cut into fingers 3 × 1 inches, making 4 holes down each side of biscuits and then baking in hot oven, 450°F (Gas Mark 8) for 8 minutes. When cold, pair together with the filling.

To make filling: Warm butter, coffee (instant coffee with hot water will do) and sugar together until dissolved. Take off stove and beat well. Add cocoa and vanilla essence and beat well again. It is now ready, but if too stiff beat in a little milk or hot water.

A well-tried and proven recipe which has proved invaluable on a wet day for keeping the family quiet by letting them make these very more-ish biscuits.

POOR MAN'S PETIT FOURS

4 oz flour or semolina	**2 teaspoons almond essence**
2 oz plain flour	**About 4 tablespoons warm**
3 oz sugar	**water**
3 oz butter	

Rub fat into dry ingredients. Mix essence with half the water, mix to a pliable dough with that and with the rest of water. Roll out onto floured board to ¼ inch or even less thick, cut into shapes, fancy or plain. Decorate centres with nuts, cherries, or anything you wish, sprinkle with dragées and place on well-greased baking sheets. Bake about 20 minutes, 350°F (Gas Mark 4). This quantity makes 32 small rounds. Get off sheets fairly quickly as they may stick if left too long. Great variety can be made with any colour. A spot of melted chocolate makes a pretty finish, if a few are left unadorned for cooking and the chocolate added afterwards.

Ironically this recipe came, during wartime, from King's Road, Chelsea, and has proved a great standby when almonds are so expensive.

DATE FINGERS

3 oz castor sugar
4 oz rolled oats
8 oz plain flour

5 oz butter (melted)
6 oz chopped dates
⅛–¼ pint water

Put sugar, oats and flour in bowl. Add melted butter, mixing to a crumbly mixture. Put dates and water into a pan and cook for a few minutes until soft enough to spread. Put half the biscuit mixture into a Swiss roll tin, cover with date spread, and sprinkle remainder of mixture on top. Press down well. Bake in a moderate oven, 350°F (Gas Mark 4) for 55 minutes. Turn out and cut into 16 biscuits. Cool.

BROWNIES

2 oz lard
6 oz soft brown sugar
1 egg
2 oz melted unsweetened
chocolate

3 oz self-raising flour
¼ teaspoon salt
2 oz chopped hazelnuts or
walnuts
¼ teaspoon vanilla essence

Cream lard and sugar together. Add the egg and continue to beat. Mix in the melted chocolate and fold in the dry ingredients, vanilla and chopped nuts. Pour this mixture into a square baking tin and bake for 40–45 minutes at 350°F (Gas Mark 4). Cut into squares while still warm.

BRANDY SNAPS

2 oz butter
2 oz castor sugar
2 oz black treacle
1 teaspoon lemon juice

2 oz plain flour
1 level teaspoon ground
ginger

Melt butter, sugar, treacle and lemon juice together over gentle heat. Blend in sieved flour and ginger. Put teaspoons of mixture on well-greased baking trays, 5 inches apart. Bake 8–10 minutes in moderate oven, 350°F (Gas Mark 4) until rich brown and well spread. Remove from oven and leave to cool for moment until they are easily lifted. While still warm wrap each one around a wooden spoon handle, working quickly. Allow to become firm before lifting on to wire tray. Store in airtight tin.

CHOCOLATE MACAROONS

2 egg whites
4 oz ground almonds
4 oz castor sugar

3 tablespoons drinking chocolate
Blanched almonds
Rice paper

Whip the egg whites until the peaks are stiff, then fold in almonds, sugar and drinking chocolate. Spoon in small heaps on rice paper placed on baking trays, and put a blanched almond on each. Bake at 350°F (Gas Mark 4) for 20 minutes. If plain macaroons are preferred, mix them in the same way, using 2 egg whites, 6 oz ground almonds and 8 oz castor sugar.

CHOCOLATE CRISP BARS

2 oz self-raising flour
1 oz cornflakes
1 tablespoon cocoa

3 oz coconut
3 oz sugar
3 oz margarine

Grease 7 inch square tin with oil. Crush cornflakes into bowl. Add self-raising flour and cocoa then coconut and sugar. Mix *well*. Melt margarine and add to dry ingredients. Spread evenly in oven, 350°F (Gas Mark 4) for $\frac{1}{2}$ hour. Remove and cool. Cut into 18 bars. Very good for Sunday tea.

KRINKLES

4 oz plain flour
2 oz lard
2 oz sugar
1 level teaspoon baking powder
1 level teaspoon bicarbonate of soda

1 level teaspoon ginger and cinnamon
2 level tablespoons golden syrup (warmed)
Pinch of salt

Rub dry ingredients into flour, add warm syrup, mix well, roll into balls (walnut). Place well apart on baking tray and cook in top oven for approximately 7 minutes, then transfer to bottom oven.

DIGESTIVE BISCUITS

4 *oz porridge oats*	1 *oz sugar*
5 *oz self-raising flour*	1 *tablespoon syrup*
2 *oz lard*	*Pinch salt*
½ *teaspoon bicarbonate of soda*	

Mix together dry ingredients, melt lard, sugar, syrup, bicarbonate of soda in pan, add to dry ingredients. Roll out very thin, cut out and place on greased tray. Bake in moderate oven for 10 minutes till golden brown (transfer to bottom oven if needed).

HONEY WALNUT DROPS

6 *oz butter*	3½ *oz walnuts*
6 *oz castor sugar*	9 *oz plain flour*
1 *egg*	2 *level teaspoons baking*
10 *level tablespoons honey*	*powder*

Cream butter and sugar until light and fluffy, and add beaten egg, honey and chopped walnuts. Mix flour and baking powder and stir into creamed mixture. Drop small spoonfuls of mixture well apart on greased baking sheets, and bake at 350°F (Gas Mark 4) for 15 minutes. Lift off biscuits while hot, and cool on a wire rack.

HONEY DATE BARS

3 *oz butter*	1 *teaspoon baking powder*
6 *tablespoons honey*	½ *teaspoon salt*
3 *eggs*	6 *oz chopped dates*
6 *oz plain flour*	4 *oz chopped nuts*

Blend butter and honey until creamy. Beat eggs in one at a time. Sift in flour, baking powder and salt, and stir in dates and nuts. Spread on a greased rectangular baking sheet (9 × 12 inches) and bake at 350°F (Gas Mark 4) until golden brown, about 30 minutes. Cut into bars. These bars will keep well and are 'chewy' and moist – excellent for the lunch box.

DOROTHY'S FLAPJACKS

3 *oz fat (butter or margarine)*	*white)*
4 *oz sugar (mixed brown and*	5 *oz porridge oats*

Some golden syrup may be substituted for part of the sugar. Melt the fat and sugar together and work in the oats. Spread in a Swiss roll tin and bake at 350°F (Gas Mark 4) for 20 minutes. Cool in the tin and cut into squares. These are made in vast quantities for every money-raising event in a village in north-west Essex, and always add greatly to the profits.

GIANT CURRANT BISCUITS

4 oz self-raising flour	*Grated rind of 1 orange*
4 oz fine semolina	*4 oz currants*
4 oz butter	*2 eggs*
4 oz castor sugar	*1 tablespoon milk*

Sift flour and semolina together and work in butter until the mixture is like fine crumbs. Add sugar, orange rind and currants. Stir in beaten eggs and milk to make a stiff light dough. Turn on to a well-floured board and knead lightly. Roll out thinly and cut into large rounds with a biscuit cutter. Place on a greased baking sheet and bake at 375°F (Gas Mark 5) until crisp and golden, about 15 minutes.

CHOCOLATE OAT CRISPS

4 oz butter or margarine or	*1 level teaspoon baking*
white vegetable fat	*powder*
8 oz sugar	*½ teaspoon salt*
1 egg	*3 oz porridge oats*
2 oz plain chocolate	*1 teaspoon vanilla essence*
4 oz plain flour	*1 teaspoon almond essence*

Cream fat and sugar and add beaten egg. Melt chocolate and blend into mixture. Sift flour, baking powder and salt and stir into creamed mixture. Add oats and essences and mix thoroughly. Drop by teaspoons on buttered baking sheet. Flatten with a fork dipped in cold water. Bake at 350°F (Gas Mark 4) for 10 minutes.

OATMEAL NUT BISCUITS

6 oz butter	*4 oz plain flour*
6 oz brown sugar	*1 level teaspoon salt*
4 oz granulated sugar	*½ level teaspoon bicarbonate*
1 egg	*of soda*
4 tablespoons water	*9 oz porridge oats*
1 teaspoon vanilla essence	*4 oz walnut kernels*

Blend together butter, sugars, egg, water and vanilla until light and fluffy. Add flour sifted with salt and soda. Stir in oats and chopped walnuts.

Drop by teaspoons on greased baking sheets. Bake at 350°F (Gas Mark 4) for 15 minutes.

COFFEE CREAMS

8 oz butter	**Filling:**
4 oz castor sugar	**2 oz cocoa**
8 oz self-raising flour	**1 gill strong coffee**
2 oz cocoa	**2 oz butter**
	Sugar to taste

Cream butter and sugar and work in flour and cocoa to make a stiff mixture. With the hands, form balls the size of a walnut, put out on buttered tins and flatten with a fork dipped in water. Bake at 350°F (Gas Mark 4) for 12 minutes. Lift carefully on to rack and when cool, sandwich together with filling. Make this by cooking cocoa in coffee until the mixture is a thick cream. Beat in butter off the fire, add sugar to taste. Leave until cold before using.

SPICED COFFEE DROPS

8 oz butter	**1 level teaspoon bicarbonate**
1 lb brown sugar	**of soda**
2 eggs	**1 level teaspoon salt**
¼ pint cold strong coffee	**1 level teaspoon nutmeg**
1 lb plain flour	**1 level teaspoon cinnamon**
	1 level teaspoon ground cloves

Cream together butter and sugar, beat in eggs and coffee. Work in flour sifted with soda, salt and spices. Put in a cold place for 1 hour, then put in small spoonfuls on a greased baking sheet. Bake at 400°F (Gas Mark 6) for 10 minutes.

NORFOLK SHORTCAKES

8 oz plain flour	**1½ oz granulated sugar**
½ teaspoon baking powder	**1½ oz currants**
4 oz butter or lard	**½ teacup water**

Sieve the flour with the baking powder and rub in 2 oz of the fat. Divide the rest of the fat, also the currants and sugar, into 3 portions. Mix the flour etc. into a pliable paste with the cold water and roll it out into a long strip. Spread this with dabs of fat and sprinkle with sugar and currants. Fold into 3 layers, give the paste a half turn and repeat this process twice more. Roll out about $\frac{1}{4}$ inch thick, cut into rounds or squares and bake in a hot oven for 15 minutes at 400°F (Gas Mark 6) until golden brown. Dredge with castor sugar when cooked.

MRS BALDWIN'S BISCUITS

$\frac{1}{2}$ lb of flour, a teaspoon of baking powder, a teacup of cream and sugar sifted in to your taste made into a paste and rolled out very thin.

Mrs Garden, 1847

BUCKINGHAM BISCUITS

2 cups sugar
$\frac{1}{4}$ cup cocoa
$\frac{1}{4}$ cup milk
4 oz butter

$\frac{1}{2}$ cup peanut butter
2 teaspoons vanilla essence
3 cups porridge oats

Use a breakfast cup to measure the ingredients. Put sugar, cocoa, milk and butter into a saucepan and boil for 1 minute, stirring all the time. Add the peanut butter, essence and oats, and mix very well. Press into greased Swiss roll tin. Bake at 350°F (Gas Mark 4) for 25 minutes. Mark into squares and cut when cold.

Chris Sharples, Milk Officer

OLD SPICE BISCUITS

6 oz plain flour
$\frac{1}{2}$ level teaspoon bicarbonate of soda
$\frac{1}{2}$ level teaspoon ginger
1 level teaspoon mixed spice

1 level teaspoon cinnamon
3 oz butter, margarine or cooking fat
2 oz castor sugar
2 tablespoons black treacle

Sift together dry ingredients. Put fat, sugar and treacle into a pan and melt slowly over a low heat. Remove from heat, stir in sifted dry ingredients and work with finger tips till well blended. Roll mixture into small balls, transfer to greased baking trays—allowing plenty of room between each for spreading—then press flat with a knife or prongs of a fork. Bake in the centre of the oven, at 350°F (Gas Mark 4) for 10–15 minutes. Cool on a wire tray, then store in an airtight container.

SUGAR AND SPICE BISCUITS

10 oz plain flour
1 level teaspoon bicarbonate
of soda
1 level teaspoon salt
1½ level teaspoons cinnamon
½ level teaspoon nutmeg
6 oz butter or margarine

4 oz granulated sugar
6 oz brown sugar
2 eggs
4 tablespoons milk
9 oz porridge oats
4 oz chopped stoned raisins

Sift together flour, soda, salt, cinnamon and nutmeg. Add softened fat, sugars, eggs and milk. Mix until smooth, then stir in oats and raisins. Chill dough, then roll out on floured board ¼ inch thick. Cut in 3 inch rounds with a cutter. Put on greased baking sheets, sprinkle lightly with sugar, and bake at 375°F (Gas Mark 5) for 15 minutes. Remove from baking sheets immediately.

HUNTER NUTS

8 oz plain flour
1 level teaspoon ground ginger
3 oz butter

6 oz sugar
1 small egg
3 oz black treacle

Sift flour and ginger. Rub in butter. Stir in sugar and bind with beaten egg and treacle. Form into small balls about size of marble and place on greased baking sheet, an inch or 2 apart. Bake in slow oven, 325°F (Gas Mark 3) for 30 minutes.

GINGER NUTS

¾ lb self-raising flour
½ lb sugar
¼ lb butter
3 oz golden syrup

1 teaspoon bicarbonate of
soda
1 teaspoon ground ginger
1 egg

Melt butter and syrup to liquid in pan (do not boil). Add dry ingredients. Beat egg into mixture. Knead well and roll into balls the size of a walnut. Bake in a moderate oven. Leave plenty of room between each ball on the baking sheet.

Mrs Fred Harper, Holt Castle, Worcs.

GINGER SNAPS

1 lb plain flour
½ lb soft brown sugar
¼ teaspoon salt
1 level teaspoon bicarbonate
of soda

2 level teaspoons ground
ginger
3 oz lard
2 oz butter
8 oz golden syrup
1 egg

Mix all the dry ingredients. Warm the fats until they melt, then add syrup and beaten egg. Beat well into the dry ingredients, and form dough into a ball. Chill thoroughly, then roll out mixture thinly on a floured board. Cut into shapes and bake at 350°F (Gas Mark 4) for 10 minutes. Cool on a wire tray.

GINGER BISCUITS

10 oz plain flour
4 oz butter or margarine
4 oz sugar
1 tablespoon ground ginger

½ teaspoon bicarbonate of soda
3 tablespoons (6 oz) golden
syrup
Yolk of an egg

Beat butter and sugar to a cream, add other ingredients, mix to a dough, roll into small balls and bake in moderate oven about 20 minutes till wrinkled on top. Recipe about 100 years old and very good.

Miss Blackman, Stilton, Huntingdon

LINCOLN GINGER CRUST

Rub together ½ lb flour, 1¼ lb sugar, ¼ lb butter until it looks like breadcrumbs. Add 1 teaspoon ground ginger and 1 teaspoon baking powder. Beat 1 egg, add to mixture, working it with fingers, until sufficiently moist to spread (not runny). Grease flat dripping tin, put in mixture, making level about 1 inch thick. Bake in moderate oven, 375°F (Gas Mark 5) for ½ hour. When cooked cut into small squares. Do not take out of tin until cold.

CORNISH FAIRLINGS

4 oz flour
Pinch of salt
¼ teaspoon ground ginger
¼ teaspoon mixed spice
¼ teaspoon cinnamon

1½ teaspoons bicarbonate of
soda
2 oz butter
2 oz castor sugar
2½ level tablespoons syrup

Sift the flour, salt, ground ginger, cinnamon, spice and bicarbonate of soda into a basin. Rub the butter into the dry ingredients. Mix in the sugar. Melt the syrup and stir it into the mixture, to make a soft dough. Roll the mixture between the hands into balls about the size of marbles and place them on greased baking trays with a space between them to allow them to spread. Bake the fairlings at 350°F (Gas Mark 4) for 10 minutes. Take the tray out of the oven and hit it on a solid surface to make the fairlings crack and spread. Then put them back into the oven for another 5 minutes to finish baking.

CRUNCH BISCUITS

2 oz butter	*$\frac{1}{2}$ teacup flour*
1 teaspoon syrup	*$\frac{1}{2}$ teacup sugar*
1 teaspoon water	*$\frac{1}{2}$ teaspoon ginger*
1 teacup oats	*$\frac{1}{2}$ teaspoon bicarbonate of soda*

Melt butter, syrup and water and mix with dry ingredients. Bake about 20–25 minutes in moderate oven, 350°F (Gas Mark 4).

COCONUT CRISPS

4 oz butter	*$\frac{1}{2}$ teaspoon baking powder*
3 oz soft brown sugar	*$\frac{1}{2}$ teaspoon bicarbonate of soda*
4 oz granulated sugar	*$\frac{1}{2}$ teaspoon salt*
1 egg	*4 oz desiccated coconut*
1 teaspoon vanilla essence	*1 oz cornflakes*
5 oz plain flour	

Cream butter, add brown and granulated sugar, egg and vanilla essence and cream the mixture until light and fluffy. Sift together flour, baking powder, soda and salt and stir into the creamed mixture. Stir in coconut and cornflakes. Chill slightly, then shape into small balls, about $\frac{3}{4}$ inch diameter. Put about $2\frac{1}{2}$ inches apart on an ungreased baking sheet, and flatten with a damp fork. Bake at 350°F (Gas Mark 4) for 10 minutes. Cool slightly before removing from baking sheet. These are crisp and sweet biscuits, which store very well.

GOOD SHORTBREAD

1 lb plain flour	*8 oz butter*
8 oz ground rice	*8 oz soft margarine*
8 oz castor sugar	

Rub fats into mixed flour, ground rice and sugar. Roll $\frac{1}{4}$ inch thick, prick and put in refrigerator for 30 minutes. Bake at 350°F (Gas Mark 4) for nearly 30 minutes. It should be *pale* golden. Cool on trays. Good to store in freezer.

Pat Brown, Keynsham, Somerset

AYRSHIRE SHORTBREAD

4 oz plain flour	**½ beaten egg**
4 oz butter	**4 oz castor sugar**
4 oz rice flour	**2 tablespoons cream**

Sieve flour and rice flour and rub in butter, mix in sugar and bind to a stiff consistency with the egg and the cream. Roll out thinly, prick with a fork and cut into shapes. Bake in a steady oven for about 15 minutes until a pale brown colour.

Mrs Biggar, Kirkcudbrightshire

SHORTBREAD BISCUITS

1 lb plain flour	**Pinch salt**
10 oz butter	**2 egg yolks**
6 oz sugar	

Rub butter in, add sugar. Make well in centre and put in yolks. Knead. Roll to $\frac{1}{4}$ inch thickness. Bake 25 minutes at 350°F (Gas Mark 4).

Mrs Greenwood, Yorks

ALMOND SHORTBREAD

14 oz plain flour	**6 oz castor sugar**
2 oz ground rice	**2 oz chopped mixed peel**
2 oz blanched almonds	**10 oz butter**

Sift flour and ground rice onto a pastry board. Add chopped almond, sugar and peel and mix very well together. Have butter soft all the way through and put in the centre of flour mixture. Gradually knead the dry ingredients into it. Press mixture into two Swiss roll tins, prick all over, and mark into neat squares. Bake at 350°F (Gas Mark 4) for 1 hour.

GRASMERE SHORTBREAD

1 orange or tangerine	**8 oz plain flour**
10 oz sugar	**1 dessertspoon ground ginger**
4 oz butter	

470

On the day before making the shortbread, peel an orange or large tangerine. Remove white pith, and cut the peel into fine shreds. Make a syrup with 6 oz sugar and 4 tablespoons water, and in this boil the peel for 2 minutes. Leave the peel to stand in the syrup overnight. Rub the butter into the flour and work in the remaining sugar and the ginger. Add the peel drained of its syrup. Knead until all the ingredients are thoroughly blended. Pack the mixture into an ungreased baking tin to form a compact mass, and flatten evenly with the hands. Bake at 325°F (Gas Mark 3) for 25 minutes. Cut in small squares while still hot, but do not remove from the tin until cold.

OAT BISCUITS

4 oz self-raising flour	*2 oz lard*
4 oz porridge oats	*1 tablespoon golden syrup*
3 oz sugar	*1 teaspoon bicarbonate of soda*
2 oz butter	

Mix flour, oats and sugar together. Melt fats and syrup in saucepan and add bicarbonate of soda. Pour on to dry ingredients and form into small balls. Flatten these on a greased baking sheet with a fork. Bake at 375°F (Gas Mark 5) for 10 minutes. Leave in the tin until cold.

NORFOLK GINGERS

4 oz brown sugar	*1 small teaspoon bicarbonate*
4 oz margarine or butter	*of soda*
2 teaspoons ground ginger	*8 oz flour – plain is best*
½ teaspoon mixed spice	*About 2 tablespoons milk*
	1 egg

Sift flour, spices and sugar into a basin and rub in margarine or butter. Dissolve soda in warm milk. Add egg. Beat till blended. Stir into dry ingredients. Knead till smooth. Flour hands lightly. Roll equal-sized small portions of dough into balls. Place well apart on greased baking sheet. Press each ball lightly on top. Bake in a moderate oven, 350°F (Gas Mark 4) for about ½ hour. Leave on baking sheet until they cool, or they will break, then lift with a broad-bladed knife on to a wire tray.

NORFOLK GINGER DROPS

2 oz sugar
1 tablespoon golden syrup
1½ gills boiling water
1 egg
1¼ lb self-raising flour
1 tablespoon ground ginger

2 teaspoons ground
cinnamon
2 teaspoons mixed spice
2 tablespoons weak coffee
¼ teaspoon ground cloves
1 teaspoon ground mace
1 teaspoon bicarbonate of soda

Whisk egg and sugar in basin till fluffy. Dissolve syrup in boiling water. Add coffee. Stir in egg and sugar. Beat in carefully to all dry ingredients which have been previously sifted together. Have ready a greased baking sheet and drop mixture from a teaspoon on to it, keeping drops about 1½ inches apart. Bake for about ½ hour, 350°F (Gas Mark 4).

SUFFOLK OATEN WAFERS

6 oz plain flour or 6 oz
self-raising flour and take
only half the baking powder
1 teaspoon baking powder
½ oz sugar

½ teaspoon salt
1½ oz rolled oats (porridge
oats)
2 oz margarine
Enough milk to make dough

First mix dry ingredients, then rub in fat with finger tips. Mix to a firm dough with a little milk. Knead lightly on a lightly floured board. Roll out thinly. Cut into rounds. Bake on a greased baking sheet, a little apart, in a moderately hot oven at 425°F (Gas Mark 7) for about ¼ hour or till brown. Cool on a wire rack.

TOFFEE BARS

4 oz butter
3 oz brown sugar
1 egg yolk
2 oz plain flour
2 oz porridge oats

Topping:
3 oz plain chocolate
1 tablespoon butter
Walnuts

Beat together butter, sugar and egg yolk until smooth. Add flour and oats and stir well until smooth. Press mixture in a rectangular tin and bake at 375°F (Gas Mark 5) for 15 minutes. Cool slightly. Melt chocolate and butter over hot water, spread over warm biscuit mixture, and decorate with whole or chopped walnuts. Cut into bars while warm, but leave to cool completely in tin before removing.

GINGER BISCUITS

2 oz self-raising flour
1 oz fat
1 oz sugar

½ teaspoon ginger
½ teaspoon bicarbonate of soda
2 tablespoons melted syrup

Rub in and mix with melted syrup. Put in teaspoons on greased baking sheet and bake at 350°F (Gas Mark 4) for 15 minutes.

GINGERNUT MEN

6 oz plain flour
¼ level teaspoon salt
1 level tablespoon ground ginger
1 level teaspoon mixed spice

2 oz butter
4 oz demerara sugar
3–4 tablespoons syrup, warmed
Glacé cherries

Sift together flour, salt and spices. In a separate bowl cream butter and sugar. Mix in flour and enough syrup to form a stiff dough. Roll out to ½ inch thickness and cut out the men with a biscuit cutter. Place carefully on a greased baking sheet and bake in a moderate oven, 375°F (Gas Mark 5) for 15 minutes. Remove and allow to cool. Cut very small pieces of glacé cherry and use to represent buttons.

28 *Sweetmeats*

Sain Mihel byd bees, to be brent out of strife:
Saint John bid take honey, with favour of life.
For one sely cottage, set south good and warme:
Take body and goodes, and twise yerely a swarme.

Christmas take hede, if their hives be to light:
Take honey and water, together wel dight.
That mixed with strawes, in a dish in their hives:
They drowne not, they fight not, thou savest their lyves.

Thomas Tusser

PULLED TOFFEE

1½ *lb granulated sugar*   1 *teaspoon vanilla essence*
½ *gill vinegar*   1 *gill water*
½ *oz butter*

Pour the vinegar and water into a clean pan (not too small), add the sugar and boil for 15 minutes. Add the butter in little bits, and boil for another 15 minutes. Have ready a plate, greased with butter, turn out the toffee on it and sprinkle on the vanilla essence. Turn the edges inward (as if folding them) when cool enough to handle, smear the fingers with butter and hang the mixture over the hook. Pull the toffee lengthways, then hang it up again and again for 8 to 10 minutes until it is all white, or streaked with white. Then twist in sticks about ¾ inch thick and before it can set cut

474

into $\frac{1}{2}$ inch and 1 inch lengths with a pair of scissors. Place on greased paper to harden.

TREACLE TOFFEE

10 oz black treacle or golden syrup
$\frac{1}{4}$ lb brown sugar
$\frac{1}{2}$ oz butter
2 teaspoons vinegar

$\frac{1}{2}$ small teaspoon bicarbonate of soda
6 drops lemon essence or
1 teaspoon lemon juice

Mix treacle, butter, sugar and vinegar in a saucepan (a large one) and boil without stirring until a few drips will harden and snap if placed in a little cold water.

See that there are no lumps in the bicarbonate of soda when added—dry —to the mixture. Let all boil again for about 8 minutes, pour out on to a greased tin, sprinkle the essence of lemon or lemon juice over. When cool enough to handle, smear a scrap of butter on the hands and roll into small balls. Leave on the greased tin to harden.

YORKSHIRE BUTTER TOFFEE

1 lb demerara sugar
3 oz butter
1$\frac{1}{4}$ gills water

Lemon or vanilla essence
1 dessertspoon glucose

Dissolve sugar in water. Add glucose and $\frac{1}{3}$ butter and boil to 240°F. Add remainder of butter in thin flakes, one at a time, allowing butter to boil into the toffee quite undisturbed. Boil gently to 285°F. Remove pan to table and add chosen essence. Twist pan once or twice in rotary fashion to mingle the essence, but do not stir. Pour out on to oiled slab between bars, and when sufficiently set cut into 1 inch bars. Wrap in waxed paper and store in airtight tin when cold.

Mrs Bracewell, Northallerton, Yorks

RUSSIAN TOFFEE

1 lb castor sugar
$\frac{1}{2}$ gill cream or top of the milk
$\frac{3}{4}$ gill water
1 dessertspoon glucose

$\frac{1}{4}$ lb butter
$\frac{1}{4}$ lb honey
Lemon essence
Carmine

Dissolve sugar, cream and warm slowly. Add glucose, honey and a third of the butter and dissolve. Boil to 240°F stirring all the time. Add the

475

remainder of the butter, cutting it in thin slices so that it may boil quickly through the syrup and so no heat is lost. Add sufficient carmine to just tinge the toffee. Boil slowly and very carefully to 280°F. Add lemon essence to taste. Pour into greased tin or finish in bars. Russian toffee needs very careful cooking to avoid burning. Stir the toffee slowly and gently throughout the process.

Mrs Bracewell, Northallerton, Yorks

BONFIRE TOFFEE

1 *lb granulated sugar*
2 *oz butter*
1 *large tin condensed milk*

1 *tablespoon golden syrup*
1 *teaspoon lemon juice*

Put sugar, butter and syrup into a large heavy pan and stir over a low heat until they have melted together. Bring to the boil, add the milk and lemon juice and boil to 245°F (or until a little dropped in cold water forms a firm ball). Take the pan off the fire and leave to stand until the toffee stops bubbling, then pour into a well-greased tin. Mark into squares when nearly set, but leave until cold and hard before breaking up.

TREACLE TOFFEE

10 *oz sugar*
2 *tablespoons water*
2 *tablespoons black treacle*

2 *oz butter*
1 *dessertspoon vinegar*

Place all ingredients in saucepan. Boil steadily; about 12 minutes or until small amount dropped in cold water forms firm ball, 300°–310°F. Pour into shallow greased tin, about 8 × 8 inches. When beginning to set mark into squares with a knife which has been dipped in oil.

BUTTERSCOTCH (1)

1 *lb soft brown sugar*
2 *oz butter*
2 *tablespoons water*

3 *tablespoons treacle*
1 *teaspoon vinegar*

Put all in pan, boil till a little hardens at once in cold water. Pour in flat greased tin to set.

Mrs L. Booth, Weston-super-Mare

BUTTERSCOTCH (2)

1 *lb granulated sugar*
¼ *pint water*
¼ *level teaspoon cream of*

tartar
3 *oz butter*
½ *teaspoon vanilla essence*

Put sugar and water into a large pan, and heat until sugar dissolves. Add cream of tartar and boil to 240°F. (At this stage a little dropped from a teaspoon into cold water will form a hard ball.) Remove from heat, stir in vanilla essence. Pour into a buttered rectangular tin (11 × 7 × 1¼ inches) Cool slightly and mark into squares. When almost cold, turn butterscotch out, and break into pieces.

EXHIBITION TOFFEE

1 *lb granulated sugar*
8 *oz golden syrup*
1 *tablespoon water*

2 *tablespoons vinegar*
Flavouring

Put sugar, water, vinegar and syrup into a heavy pan, and stir occasionally until it boils, then boil gently without stirring 20 minutes. To ascertain if sufficiently boiled, drop a few drops into a large basin of cold water, and if in a few minutes you find it crisp, withdraw from fire and stir in flavouring to taste, then pour into a well-buttered tin, and before it is quite cold turn on to a cold dish and cut into pieces with a pair of scissors or knife.

Mrs Page, 1899

TOFFY

Take a lb of brown sugar, 3 oz butter, 1 teacup of water, 1 lemon. Boil the sugar, butter and water and half the rind of the lemon together. When sufficiently done (this you will know by dropping a little into cold water when it should be quite crisp) let it stand aside until the boiling has ceased, then stir in the juice of the lemon. Butter a dish and pour in the toffy. It should be a ¼ of an inch thick.

Lewis' Mother's Cookbook, Mary Horrell, Exeter

ALMOND BRITTLE

4 *oz sugar*
1 *teaspoon lemon juice*

2 *oz flaked almonds*

477

Dissolve sugar and lemon juice over a low heat until it is liquid. Boil until the liquid starts to colour. Add the almonds and mix thoroughly. Put into an oiled tin and press down with a cut lemon brushed with oil. Mark into squares at once. Break when cold.

EVERTON TOFFEE

Dissolve $\frac{1}{2}$ lb sugar, 4 tablespoons water and 1 tablespoon of syrup and 2 oz margarine in a pan, keep stirring. Add $\frac{1}{2}$ teaspoon cream of tartar and boil, don't stir. Add 2 oz margarine, slicing so that it will melt quickly. Lower the temperature and boil till light brown and just past hard ball stage. Pour into tin and set.

TREACLE TOFFEE

Place 3 oz sugar, 3 oz treacle, $\frac{1}{2}$ cupful water and 1 tablespoon vinegar in a pan. Heat until the sugar has dissolved. Boil for 2–3 minutes or until it is at the hard ball stage. Add 2 oz margarine, stirring so that it will melt quickly. Pour into a tin and set.

BUTTERSCOTCH

Put $\frac{1}{2}$ lb demerara sugar, 2 oz butter, 8 tablespoons water and 1 tablespoon vinegar in a pan. Heat until the sugar dissolves. Boil for 2–3 minutes, don't stir, until it is golden brown, quite thick and at the hard ball stage. Pour into tin and set.

SYRUP FUDGE

2 oz butter
4 tablespoons water
2 rounded tablespoons golden syrup

1 lb granulated sugar
8 level tablespoons ($\frac{1}{2}$ large can) sweetened condensed milk

Put all ingredients into a thick-based saucepan, and stir over gentle heat until sugar dissolves. Bring to boil, and boil gently for 10 minutes, without stirring. Remove from heat, and beat well until mixture begins to 'fudge'. Pour into a lightly buttered $7\frac{1}{2} \times 7\frac{1}{2} \times 1$ inch deep square tin. Leave until cold, then cut into squares.

CHOCOLATE FUDGE

Put 1 oz cocoa in a pan with $\frac{1}{4}$ pint milk and 1 oz margarine and $\frac{1}{2}$ lb sugar. Stir over a low heat until the sugar and the cocoa have melted, then simmer,

478

stirring frequently, till the mixture forms a soft ball when placed in cold water. Remove from heat. Add ½ teaspoon of vanilla essence and keep stirring until the mixture thickens. Pour into a tin and set.

W.I. FUDGE

1 lb sugar	**⅛ teaspoon cream of tartar**
½ pint milk	**2 oz butter**
1 oz cocoa	**½ teaspoon vanilla essence**

Dissolve the sugar in the milk over gentle heat. Add the cocoa and cream of tartar and boil until a little of the mixture forms a soft ball in cold water. Remove from heat and add butter and vanilla. Beat until creamy and smooth and pour into a greased tin. Cut into squares when cold. This recipe was demonstrated at a Women's Institute meeting many years ago, and has never been known to fail.

CHOCOLATE FUDGE

2 oz chocolate	**1 oz butter**
½ lb soft brown sugar	**½ lb icing sugar**
1 small tin condensed milk	

Melt chocolate over hot water, beat in butter, then stir in milk. Add soft brown sugar and stir in. Sieve icing sugar into mixture and knead it well until soft and creamy looking. Press into lightly buttered tray 6 × 4 inches. Leave to set and cut into 1 inch squares.

Mrs Bracewell, Northallerton, Yorks

SHERRY FUDGE

2 tablespoons seedless raisins	**4 tablespoons evaporated milk**
4 oz plain chocolate	**12 oz sieved icing sugar**
2 oz butter	**Sherry**

Soak the raisins in sherry overnight. Place chocolate and butter in a mixing basin over hot, not boiling water. Stir until melted and smooth. Remove from heat, stir in evaporated milk and drained soaked raisins. Gradually stir in sieved icing sugar until fudge is smooth and thick. Turn into a buttered and waxed paper lined tin. Leave to cool. When set, remove from tin, peel away paper and cut into squares.

MINISTRY CRUMB FUDGE

2 tablespoons syrup	Few drops vanilla,
2 oz margarine	peppermint or orange essence
2 oz sugar	6 oz dried crumbs
2 oz cocoa	

Heat the syrup, margarine, sugar and cocoa gently until all is melted. stir in the required flavouring and then the breadcrumbs (these are best lightly crisped in the oven). Mix thoroughly and turn into a well-greased 7 inch square tin. Spread evenly and mark lightly into fingers or squares. Leave for 24 hours and then use as a cake or sweet. The fudge improves with keeping for a day or two. This recipe comes from one of the many Ministry of Food leaflets issued during the 1939–45 War, and the few lean years afterwards. Many of them feature dried milk and dried egg, but some are still useful when budgets are low and ideas are needed.

GRANNY'S OLD-FASHIONED FUDGE

1 tablespoon golden syrup	4 oz chocolate chips
1 lb sugar	$\frac{1}{2}$ teaspoon vanilla essence
2 oz butter	1 teaspoon rum
$\frac{1}{4}$ pint milk	

Grease a heavy saucepan. Heat the sugar, milk and syrup, stirring gently until sugar has dissolved. Add chocolate and stir until melted and mixture is boiling. Cook to 238°F (or until mixture forms a soft ball when a little is dropped into cold water). Take off heat, add butter and cool without stirring. Add vanilla and rum and beat until fudge is thick and loses its shine. Put into a shallow buttered tin and cut into squares while warm.

FRUIT AND NUT FUDGE

$\frac{1}{2}$ pint fresh milk	2 oz raisins or sultanas,
2 lb granulated sugar	cleaned
$\frac{1}{4}$ lb butter	2 oz blanched or coarsely
$\frac{1}{2}$ teaspoon vanilla essence	chopped almonds

Soak sugar in the milk for 1 hour, then cook very slowly till sugar dissolves. Add the butter and when melted bring mixture to the boil. (Brush sides of pan with water to prevent graining from time to time.) Simmer steadily till a temperature of 238°F is reached, or till a little of the mixture forms a soft ball when dropped into cold water, (this can take up to 1 hour), stir frequently, especially when nearing 238°F to prevent burning. Remove from heat, cool slightly, then beat till fudge is thick and creamy. Add essence, fruit and nuts and pour quickly into a well greased shallow tin, smooth with a knife, mark into squares and cut when cool and set.

RUM RAISIN FUDGE

1 lb granulated sugar
2 oz butter
¼ pint evaporated milk

¼ pint water
1 teaspoon rum
4 oz seedless raisins

Put the sugar, butter, milk and water into a large saucepan. Heat gently till the sugar has dissolved and the fat has melted, then bring to the boil. Boil rapidly, stirring until a temperature of 240°F is reached (to the 'soft ball' stage). Remove from heat, add the rum and seedless raisins, beat well until the mixture becomes thick and creamy. As the sugar begins to grain, pour into a greased tin about 6 × 8 inches. When nearly set, mark into squares with a sharp knife.

SUGAR BALLS

4 oz plain chocolate
3 tablespoons single cream
16 sponge finger biscuits,

finely crushed
2 tablespoons sherry
2 oz castor sugar

Place chocolate in a basin over hot, not boiling, water. Stir until smooth. Remove from heat. Stir in cream and sugar. Add finely crushed sponge finger crumbs and sherry. Blend well. Leave mixture in a cool place overnight to stiffen. Roll heaped teaspoons of the mixture into balls; roll in castor sugar. Store in a screw-topped jar.

CHOCOLATE WALNUTS

Sandwich together 2 walnut halves with melted chocolate. When set, dip the whole walnuts into softened chocolate and place in sweet paper cases to set.

COFFEE WALNUT CREAMS

¼ lb icing sugar
1 level tablespoon double
dairy cream
1 teaspoon instant coffee

1 teaspoon lightly beaten egg
white
Walnuts

Work sugar, coffee and cream together to a smooth paste, adding egg white as required and more sugar if necessary. Beat until very stiff. Leave for an hour, then roll into small balls and flatten each on greaseproof paper to an oval with a quarter of shelled walnut.

481

CHOCOLATE TRUFFLES

8 oz plain chocolate
1 heaped tablespoon castor sugar

2 oz butter
2 tablespoons rum or cream
1 egg yolk

Melt the chocolate over hot water. Remove from heat and stir in sugar, butter, rum or cream and egg yolk. Beat until thick and cool. Shape into small balls and leave to dry. Roll in cocoa, chocolate vermicelli, hundreds-and-thousands or desiccated coconut.

NO-COOK FONDANTS

4 tablespoons evaporated milk
1 lb icing sugar

Flavouring and colouring

Put the milk into a bowl, sieve icing sugar and gradually work into the milk. Knead until smooth and shiny, and add flavouring and colouring to make a variety of sweets. To make *peppermint creams,* add a few drops of oil of peppermint, and a little green colouring if liked. For *orange creams* add orange-flower water and orange colouring. For *rose creams* add rose-water and cochineal. Oil of peppermint, orange-flower water and rose-water are all obtainable at any chemist. For *fruit rolls,* knead in 4 oz chopped mixed peel and 1 oz chopped glacé cherries with a little more icing sugar if necessary. Shape into 6 inch logs about 1 inch diameter and chill until firm before cutting each roll into 12 pieces. All the fondants may be shaped by this easy method, or else rolled out and cut with canapé cutters. Top of the sweets may be decorated with nuts, coloured balls, crystallised petals or angelica.

COCONUT KISSES

$\frac{1}{4}$ lb fondant
A few drops almond flavouring
$\frac{1}{4}$ lb desiccated coconut
A few drops green vegetable colouring

A few drops vanilla flavouring
A few drops raspberry flavouring
A few drops cochineal

Knead all but one tablespoon of the coconut into the fondant; divide the mixture into 3 parts. Into 1 work a few drops of vanilla; into the second a few drops of almond flavouring and green colouring; into the third a few drops raspberry flavouring and cochineal. Form each batch of mixture into small pointed rolls, using the remaining coconut to help press the soft mixture into shapes.

COCONUT ICE

2 lb lump sugar   **10 oz desiccated coconut**
½ pint water

Put sugar and water in a strong saucepan and stand over a gentle heat until the sugar is dissolved. Bring to the boil and continue boiling rapidly for 10 minutes, stirring all the time. Remove from the heat, stir in coconut and mix well. Pour half the mixture into an oiled rectangular tin (11 × 7 inches). Colour the remainder lightly with cochineal and press on top of the white ice. Mark into 12 bars when partly cool and finish cutting when cold. Wrap in Cellophane.

SPICED NUTS

Almonds and walnuts are good spiced. Mix in a bowl 2 oz castor sugar, 1 level tablespoon cinnamon, a good pinch each of nutmeg and powdered cloves. In another bowl, put a slightly beaten egg white, and dip the nuts in this, a few at a time, rubbing them in the fingers to coat them well with the egg white. Toss the nuts into the bowl of sugar and spice so they are covered completely; put on to buttered baking sheet and bake at 300°F (Gas Mark 2) for 30 minutes.

SUGARED NUTS

In a heavy shallow pan, boil together 8 oz sugar and 4 fluid oz water for 5 minutes. Add 8 oz blanched almonds, hazelnuts or walnuts and continue cooking gently, stirring well, until the liquid begins to look white and slightly sugared. Add 1 teaspoon vanilla essence and ½ teaspoon powdered cinnamon, and leave the pan on one side of the stove for 10 minutes. Put back on a very low heat and stir well until the sugar starts to melt. Pour on to a wire cake rack placed over waxed paper, and separate the nuts to allow them to cool and dry.

SALTED NUTS

Almonds, filberts and walnuts are very good toasted. Blanch and dry the nuts and sprinkle with olive oil. Brown on baking sheets at 400°F (Gas Mark 6) with an occasional stir, and while still hot, sprinkle with salt.

NUT BALLS

Mince finely, or chop in electric blender, 8 oz mixed nuts. Cream 5 oz butter and work in the nuts, 3 level tablespoons castor sugar, 4 oz plain flour and 1 teaspoon of vanilla essence. With the fingers roll the mixture into balls the size of marbles. Bake on lightly buttered tins at 375°F (Gas Mark 5) for 10 minutes, and roll while hot in powdered castor or icing sugar.

CANDY KISSES

6 oz granulated sugar
½ pint water
4 oz butter
4 oz finest semolina
2 oz ground almonds (or

fine cake or biscuit crumbs
or fine coconut)
½ teaspoon each of almond
and vanilla essence

Boil the sugar and water together till thick and syrupy but remove from heat before it changes colour. Melt the butter, stir in semolina and brown lightly; then add ground almonds and essences. Add this mixture to the syrup, stirring over low heat till thick and cook gently for 3 minutes. Leave to cool slightly, then divide into 4 portions and colour to taste with green, yellow and red colourings, but leaving one portion natural. Working fairly quickly so that the mixture keeps warm, form into assorted shapes. Roll some in coconut and decorate others with blanched almonds, walnut halves, hazelnuts, silver dragées and glacé cherries. Transfer to paper cases. Chopped cherries, dates and ginger can be added to the mixture for variety. This recipe is also delicious for stuffing dates and prunes.

CHOCOLATE BRITTLES

2 oz almonds
6 oz castor sugar

4 oz plain chocolate

The almonds need not be blanched. Dissolve 2 oz sugar over low heat until liquid. Add the almonds and boil together until light brown. Pour on to an oiled tin and leave until cold. Crush the mixture to a powder. Melt the chocolate over hot water. Remove from heat and mix with remaining sugar. Stir in the almond powder and form into small balls. Leave to harden and roll in a little cocoa or powdered drinking chocolate.

CRUNCHIE

4 oz syrup
4 oz sugar

1 oz baking powder

Boil sugar and syrup together till melted and thick. Take off gas, stir in baking powder. Pour out in greased tin.

484

29 *Jams, Jellies, Marmalades and Mincemeats*

Conserves of barberry, quinces, and such,
with sirops, that easeth the sickly so much.

Thomas Tusser

FOR EXTRA FLAVOUR IN JAMS

The flavour of plum jam, and, indeed, all jams made with stone fruits, is very greatly improved by the addition of a few bitter almonds. During the boiling process about $\frac{1}{2}$ a dozen almonds for every lb of fruit is enough, though more may be used if liked. The almonds need not be removed, but may be left in the jam and eaten with it. The addition of vanilla to stone fruit jam also improves its flavour, but vanilla essence will do instead.

APPLE MARMALADE

Cut as many pippins as you like into thin slices and put into a stone jar inside a pan of boiling water. Add an equal weight of loaf sugar, and

485

cinnamon to taste. Keep water boiling and shake jar frequently but do not stir. When smooth and clear, put into pots and tie down when cold. This is good to eat as an emergency pudding with cream.

Mrs Hill, 1864

APPLE AND BLACKBERRY JAM

2 lb blackberries	**½ pint water**
2 lb sour apples (windfalls of any variety)	**3 lb sugar**

Pick over and wash the berries, peel, core, and slice the apples. Put the fruit into a pan with the water and cook till tender. Add the sugar, stir until dissolved and bring to the boil. Boil until the jam sets when tested. Bottle and cover.

BLACKBERRY AND APPLE JAM

1½ lb blackberries	**¼-½ pint water**
1½ lb apples	**3 lb sugar**

Prepare fruit, simmer gently with water until soft. Add sugar, cook rapidly until setting point is reached. Pour into warm jars, cover with wax circle and cover.

BLACKBERRY AND APPLE JAM

This traditional country favourite is easily and quickly made, and is of course, very cheap. Peel and slice the required apples and boil in water, (allowing 1 gill for each lb of fruit) till they are pulped. Simmer the blackberries without water until soft and add to the apples. Weigh out 1 lb sugar for each lb fruit used, stir into the mixture till dissolved, then boil fast to setting point, testing after 20 minutes.

CAPE GOOSEBERRY JAM

Allow weight for weight of sugar and fruit; bruise ripest fruit in bottom of pan, boil without sugar for 15 minutes, add remainder of the fruit and sugar and boil for 1 hour.

CHERRY JAM

Cherry jam is a wonderful breakfast treat. To get a good colour and set, boil an equal weight of cherries and sugar for 5 minutes. Remove the fruit and cook the syrup for 12 minutes, add $\frac{1}{4}$ pint blackcurrant syrup. Add fruit and boil for 13 minutes before potting. The fruit is much better for being stoned first.

CHERRY MARMALADE

3 lb black cherries
$\frac{1}{2}$ pint raspberry juice

$\frac{1}{2}$ pint redcurrant juice
2 lb sugar

Put cherries, juices and sugar into a preserving pan, and simmer gently until sugar has dissolved. Cook gently, until a firm, clear jelly mingles with the cherries. Remove from heat and press cherries gently with the back of a spoon. Cool, and pot when cold.

DRIED APRICOT JAM

1 lb dried apricots
4 lb sugar
$3\frac{1}{2}$ pints boiling water

1 oz bitter almonds
Juice of 1 lemon

Quarter the apricots, pour the boiling water over, leaving them to soak for 24 hours. Then boil for 1 hour. Blanch the almonds and add, also sugar and the juice of lemon and boil again for $\frac{1}{2}$–$\frac{3}{4}$ hour.

DRIED APRICOT JAM

1 lb apricots (or any dried fruit)
5 breakfastcups boiling water

5 cups sugar
Juice of 2 lemons
Blanched almonds if required

Wash apricots thoroughly, cut in halves, pour the boiling water on, and let stand overnight. Boil next day until skins are tender, then add sugar and lemon juice and boil 20 minutes. A few blanched almonds added is an improvement.

FRESH APRICOT JAM

Cut fruit in halves and remove stones, put fruit aside for night adding some of the sugar to create a syrup (in total use 1 lb sugar to 1 lb fruit). Next day put on a gentle fire and boil for 1 hour; crack the stones and blanch kernels (in cupful boiling water) and add to jam to give extra flavour. Do not add any water, as it will be quite firm jam. A knob of butter improves all jams as it adds 'gloss' and prevents, to an extent, 'catching' the jam on bottom of pan.

FIG JAM

Cut the stalks off the figs and halve them. Put them into a large basin in layers, with a good sprinkling of sugar over each; let them remain for 12 hours. Next day put them in a preserving pan, boil for a short time, then add remainder of sugar and piece of lemon (or juice of 1 lemon). 12 oz sugar should be allowed for each 1 lb fruit. Boil all together until it jellies.

GOOSEBERRY JAM flavoured with ELDERFLOWER

Cut the gooseberries slightly, add $\frac{1}{4}$ cup of water. Boil for 15 minutes, add sugar, having allowed 1 lb 2 oz for every 1 lb fruit. Boil for $\frac{3}{4}$ hour. If the delicate flavour of elderflower is required, tie a bunch of flowers (one good sprigful) by the stem and suspend over side of the pan while fruit alone is boiling. Remove before the sugar is added.

GRAPE (ISABELLA) JAM

Using scissors to 'open' grapes, squeeze pulp out of skins, simmer pulp until tender, press through a colander, add skins, and then add $\frac{3}{4}$ lb sugar to every 1 lb of pulp and skins. Boil for about 1 hour.

GREEN GOOSEBERRY JAM

Wash, top and tail 6 lb gooseberries, and put in a pan with 2 pints water. Stew gently for about 20 minutes until soft and mushy. Add 8 lb warm sugar, dissolve slowly, and boil rapidly for 20 minutes. Skim and pour into warm dry jars.

GREEN TOMATO JAM

Take 8 lb green tomatoes and 6 lb sugar; tomatoes must be firm and sound with no sign of colour, cut into small pieces, mix sugar with a little water in saucepan, add fruit, boil as for ordinary jam; do not add any other ingredients whatever. This is a delicious jam. [Author's note: I can vouch for this—I had it as a child and have never forgotten it; how thankful I am that the recipe has, at last, come into my hands.]

LEMON AND APPLE MARMALADE

3 lemons	*3 lb cooking apples*
3 pints cold water	*4$\frac{3}{4}$ lb sugar*

Slice the lemons and soak in the water overnight. Cook until tender, then add the peeled and sliced apples. Continue cooking until the apples are tender but not broken. Stir in the sugar until dissolved, then boil rapidly to setting point. Cover when cold.

MARROW JAM

4 lb diced marrow	**1 pint apple juice (made from**
4 lb sugar	**windfalls, cores, skins and**
Ground ginger – if liked	**all, plus as little water as**
1 lb extra sugar	**possible)**

Overnight, in a big bowl, stand the diced marrow covered with 4 lb sugar. Next morning add 1 pint apple juice, and the 1 lb sugar. Boil until marrow is cooked and slightly transparent (about $\frac{1}{2}$ hour). Test for set in usual way, on a cold plate near window.

This recipe from Devon can be thoroughly recommended—it sets well, is of a very good flavour and above all in a wet season, is a wonderful way of using up a glut of marrows.

MARROW JAM

3 lb marrow	**Rind and juice of 2 lemons**
3 lb sugar	**2 oz root ginger**

Dice marrow flesh, cover with sugar, leave 24 hours. Bruise ginger, place in a muslin bag with the fruit and lemons. Cook slowly until sugar is dissolved, boil as before.

MIXED JAM FOR CHILDREN

Take equal quantities of gooseberries, red and black currants, cherries, raspberries and apples, pared, cored and cut up. Stew the cherries, then add the apples and finally the soft fruits. To every lb of fruit add $\frac{3}{4}$ lb sugar, weighing the fruit after it has been prepared for cooking. Boil altogether for 1 hour, allowing the apples and cherries about $\frac{1}{2}$ hour headstart. Pour into hot jars and cover when cold.

PEACH JAM

Peel and stone the peaches. To 6 lb fruit, add 1 quart (2 pints) water, and boil till very soft and tender (i.e. boil until nearly reduced to 6 lb again), add weight for weight of sugar, boil $1-1\frac{1}{2}$ hours.

PEAR AND GINGER JAM

4 *lb hard pears*   2 *oz preserved ginger*
3 *lb sugar*   2 *lemons*

Peel and core the pears and put into a bowl in layers with the sugar. Leave overnight, then put into preserving pan with chopped ginger, grated lemon rind and lemon juice. Heat gently until sugar has dissolved, then boil rapidly to setting point.

PEAR HARLEQUIN

3 *lb pears*   1 *orange*
1 *medium can pineapple* $\frac{1}{4}$ *pint bottle maraschino*
pieces   *cherries*
Sugar

Cut pears in $\frac{1}{2}$ inch cubes without peeling. Put into a bowl with pineapple, grated rind and juice of orange. Weigh the mixture and add 12 oz sugar to each lb. Cover and leave overnight. Put in preserving pan and cook gently (about 2 hours) until thick. Cut cherries in half and add with liquid from the bottle. Stir thoroughly and pour into jars. This is delicious with ice cream.

PINEAPPLE AND TOMATO JAM

4 *pineapples*   2 *lb tomatoes*

Grate or shred pineapples, skin tomatoes and cut them up fine; boil together for $\frac{1}{4}$ hour, then add cup for cup of sugar; boil $\frac{3}{4}$ hour or until it jellies, add juice of 3 lemons.

PLUM GUMBO

5 *lb plums*   3 *oranges*
2 *lb seedless raisins*   5 *lb sugar*

Cut plums into small pieces and put into preserving pan. Add chopped raisins and oranges cut in thin crosswise slices. Add warm sugar and bring to boiling point, then simmer until the consistency of marmalade. Cool slightly, stir well and fill jars.

PLUM RUM JAM

$3\frac{1}{2}$ *lb plums* $3\frac{1}{2}$ *lb sugar*
8 *tablespoons lemon juice*   4 *tablespoons dark rum*

Chop plums finely, and put into preserving pan with lemon juice and sugar. Bring to the boil and boil hard for 3 minutes, stirring constantly. Add rum and simmer for 5 minutes, stirring well. Pour into warm jars and seal.

RASPBERRY JAM

For jam with the whole-fruit flavour of raspberries, pick over 4 lb of the fruit and put into a pan which has been rubbed with butter. Warm an equal quantity of castor sugar, and when the berries start to bubble, beat in the sugar vigorously for 20 minutes, then put into jars; be careful to store this jam in a cool dark place.

RASPBERRY AND RED CURRANT JAM

Put 4 lb raspberries in a preserving pan with 1 pint of red currant juice, and bring slowly to boiling point. Simmer for 30 minutes and weigh the pulp. Add 12 oz of sugar for every 1 lb of pulp, boil, then continue simmering for 20 minutes, or until set.

RHUBARB AND BLACKBERRY JAM

4 lb blackberries   **$\frac{3}{4}$ pint water**
2 lb prepared rhubarb   **Sugar**

Use ripe blackberries for this, and simmer them in the water until tender, then put through a sieve. Cut rhubarb into 1 inch pieces, add to blackberry pulp, and simmer until tender. Measure and add 1 lb warm sugar to each 1 lb of pulp. Stir until dissolved and bring to boiling point. Boil for 10 minutes and test for setting. Pot and cover. This makes an inexpensive jam with a good blackberry flavour. It is very good used for tarts or jam slices with a meringue topping.

RHUBARB AND DATE JAM

To every pound of rhubarb add 1 lb sugar and if liked 2 oz dates. Cut the fruit in pieces about 1 in. in length, place in a basin, cover with sugar, allow to stand overnight. Next day put in preserving pan, add dates (if used) and green ginger (or ground ginger) to flavour, and boil till it thickens.

RHUBARB AND GINGER JAM

4 *lb rhubarb* *muslin bag*
2 *teaspoons ground ginger* 3 *lb sugar*
or 1 *oz bruised root ginger in* ½ *teaspoon citric acid*

Cut rhubarb into 1 inch lengths, and put into a bowl with sugar in layers. Leave overnight, then put into preserving pan. Add ginger and acid, bring to the boil, and boil rapidly until the jam jellies when tested (about 15 minutes). Remove bag of root ginger, pot and cover at once.

RHUBARB AND ORANGE PRESERVE

4 *lb rhubarb* 6 *oranges*
4 *lb sugar* ½ *teaspoon citric acid*
Grated rind and juice of

Cut up rhubarb into 1 inch pieces, grate rind from oranges, and squeeze out juice. Put into a bowl with sugar and leave for 12 hours. Put into preserving pan, add citric acid, bring to the boil and boil rapidly to setting point.

RHUBARB AND FIG JAM

2 *lb rhubarb* 3 *lb sugar*
½ *lb dried figs* *Juice of* 1 *lemon*

Cut rhubarb and fig finely, combine with sugar and lemon juice, and leave to stand for 24 hours. Bring to boil, and boil rapidly until a little sets when tested on a cool plate. Leave to stand for 30 minutes before filling jars.

RUDWAY RHUBARB JAM

Wipe the rhubarb and cut as for tarts. Then to every lb fruit add ¾ lb sugar and the peel of ½ lemon cut finely. Stand all together in a large pan all night to draw the juice, then place in preserving pan and cook fast for about an hour. Try it by putting some on a plate and if it is done, fill the pots whilst it is warm. Cover with paper soaked in brandy.

Lewis' Mother's Cookbook, Mary Horrell, Exeter

ROSE-HIP AND APPLE JAM

1 *pint rose-hips, really ripe* *until soft in* ¼ *pint water)*
2 *pints boiling water* 2 *lb sugar*
¾ *lb cooking apples (cooked*

Wash the rose-hips and put them into 2 pints boiling water. Simmer till soft. Mash with wooden spoon and strain through jelly bag, allowing it to drip overnight. Measure the juice and make it up to $1\frac{1}{2}$ pints with cold water. Cook the apples in water until they are reduced to a thick pulp. Mix juice and pulp and bring to boil. Stir in sugar and when dissolved, boil rapidly until the jam starts.

SWEET ORANGE JAM (1)

2 oranges   **10 lb sugar**
10 quarts water

Slice oranges very thinly, taking out the pips, cover with the water and leave overnight; boil down one-half (5 quarts) then add sugar, and boil till it will jelly.

SWEET ORANGE JAM (2)

Cut oranges in as thin slices as possible, picking out all the pips; put the cut-up oranges in a basin and add 1 pint water for each orange; put pips in another dish, cover with some of the water. Let these both stand all night, then strain the water off the pips and add it to the oranges, boil till skins are quite soft, let stand another night, then add weight for weight of sugar and boil briskly till it sets. To save mess, remember to *weigh pan* before the operation starts. It is then a simple matter to find weight of fruit before adding appropriate quantity of sugar.

THREE FRUIT JAM

Apples   **Sugar**
Pears   **Lemon rind**
Plums   **Root ginger**

Weigh out equal quantities of apples, pears and plums. Peel, core and slice apples and pears and stone plums and cook gently, allowing $\frac{1}{4}$ pint water to each lb of fruit until soft. Weigh the fruit and add warmed sugar in the proportion of 1 lb to 1 pint of fruit. Add the grated rind of a lemon to each lb of fruit, and suspend crushed root ginger in a muslin bag in the preserving pan. Dissolve sugar over a gentle heat, then bring to boiling point. Test for setting after 10 minutes' boiling, pot and cover. This makes an excellent tart filling, or a sauce for steamed pudding.

TOMATO AND LEMON MARMALADE

Allow 1 or more lemons and 1 lb sugar to each lb of tomatoes. Slice lemons very thinly, then take out pips and boil lemons in sufficient water to cover, until tender (test skins with matchstick). Put sugar into preserving pan with small quantity of water, as for toffee, and boil till it comes to crack degree, then add gradually the sliced tomatoes and lemons so as not to stop the boiling. Boil till it jellies.

TOMATO JAM (1)

Scald the tomatoes in order that they will peel easily; remove skins, weigh the fruit; put in the preserving pan with weight for weight of sugar; keep boiling steadily. When beginning to jelly add powdered orris root to taste; lemon peel or green ginger can be used as well, and pot it when it jellies well. Ground ginger may be used to replace green ginger—orris root, made from fragrant iris roots is now very rare.

TOMATO JAM (2)

12 lb ripe tomatoes   **Juice of 3 or 4 lemons**
16 lb sugar   **(according to size) or a little**
4 lb full-sized but quite   **citric acid and a few drops**
green tomatoes   **essence of lemon**
2 pints water

Boil altogether from $\frac{1}{2}$–$\frac{3}{4}$ hour briskly and it will jelly nicely. Small tomatoes are best for this.

TOMATO MARMALADE

To each 1 lb ripe tomatoes, peeled and sliced, add the juice of 1$\frac{1}{2}$ lemons and 1 lb sugar; boil for 1$\frac{1}{2}$ hours. This makes a most delicious preserve, not generally known.

APPLE CONSERVE

3 lb cooking apples   **1 lemon**
Sugar as required

Peel and core apples and cook very gently without water. Rub through a sieve when tender. Place in a saucepan with an equal weight of sugar and the strained juice and grated rind of 1 lemon. Stir over moderate heat till sugar has dissolved, then bring to simmering point. Simmer for 20 minutes to 1 hour, until the conserve sets when tested on a cold plate. Pot and seal.

APPLE GINGER

3 lb crisp eating apples
3 lb sugar

1¾ pints water
1½ oz essence of ginger

It is important to use pure essence of ginger for this, not a synthetic flavouring. This is for those who really love a strong ginger flavour. Peel and core the apples, and cut into neat pieces (as near to the shape of ginger in syrup as possible). Dissolve sugar in water, then bring to a slow rolling boil for 25 minutes. Raise heat and immerse apples, then simmer until fruit is just transparent and yellow but not broken. Remove from heat and stir in ginger essence. Lift apples carefully into jars (use preserving jars or screwtop honey jars), cover with syrup and screw down. Serve like ginger as a pudding, preferably with cream.

APPLE GINGER

4 lb apples
3 pts water

4 lb granulated sugar
2 oz ground ginger

Peel apples and cut in thin slices. Cook water and sugar together to a thick syrup. Add apples and boil until transparent. Stir in ginger, boil for 5 minutes and put into jars. Eat with toast, or use as a tart filling, or as a pudding with cream.

ORANGE CONSERVE

Cut some sweet oranges into 8, remove the centre pith; add a large cup of water to each orange, and let stand all night. Put the pith and seeds into a separate basin and cover with part of the water. In the morning, strain and add the liquid to the oranges. Boil till the skins are soft, about 2 hours, then add ½ lb sugar for each orange and boil for a further hour. Tie down in handsome glass jars or tumblers, especially if being used for Sale of Work or attractive personal present.

PLUM CONSERVE

3 lb stoned plums
3 lb sugar
6 oz stoned raisins

4 oz chopped blanched almonds

Put the plum stones into a muslin bag, and hang in cooking pan. Put plums, raisins, and a little water if necessary in pan, and simmer until soft. Add sugar, stir until dissolved, and boil rapidly to setting point. Stir in almonds. Pour into warm jars. This is good as a spread, makes a delicious tart filling, or with ice cream.

STRAWBERRY CONSERVE

Strawberries   **Sugar**

Weigh out equal quantities of strawberries and sugar and put in alternate layers in a bowl. Leave for 24 hours, then boil for 5 minutes. On the second day, boil for 5 minutes, and on the third day for 7 minutes. Put into warm jars and seal. The result is whole fruit suspended in thick syrup, delicious with puddings, or served on its own with thick cream.

SOMERSET CONSERVE

9 large hard pears   **1 cup water**
6 tart apples   **Preserving sugar**
1½ lemons   **2 oz stem ginger**

Peel, quarter and core pears. Peel and core apples and cut into slices ½ inch thick. Grate off rinds from lemons. Sprinkle over fruit. Sprinkle with ½ the lemon juice, add remainder of juice to the water. Weigh fruit mixture and for every lb weigh 1 lb sugar. Cut ginger into small pieces. Place sugar and water in a preserving pan. Stir over moderate heat till sugar has dissolved, then bring to boil. Boil steadily until of a syrupy consistency, then add the rest of the ingredients and boil until clear and thick for about 45 minutes. Pack into jars and cover.

WATER HALL QUINCE CONSERVE

2 lb quinces (weighed after   **2¾ pints water**
peeling)   **2¾ pints sugar**

Peel, core and cut quinces into small cubes. Put with 2 pints of the water into a pan and bring to the boil. Add the sugar, remove from heat and stir until the sugar has dissolved. Return to heat and boil gently until the fruit is soft but not broken. Meanwhile, boil the cores and peel of quinces in the rest of the water until all is soft and the liquid reduced to about half. Strain this into the quinces. Boil hard until the jam sets when tested. Cool a little, stir and pour into warm pots. The jam is like jelly with cubes of quince, and is a beautiful jewel-red colour.

Joan Smith

APPLE AND ELDERBERRY JELLY

3 lb cooking apples   **½ cinnamon stick**
2 quart elderberries   **2 pints water**
(weighed off stalks)   **Sugar**
Rind of 1 orange

Wash apples, cut into pieces and put into pan with elderberries. Add water, cover pan, and simmer to a pulp. Leave to drip through jelly bag. Measure juice and allow 1 lb sugar to 1 pint juice. Put into a pan, stir well and put in orange rind and cinnamon tied in muslin. Boil rapidly to setting point, remove orange peel and cinnamon, put into warm jars and cover. This jelly is nice if soft and not too firm, and is an excellent way of using elderberries.

APPLE JELLY

6 lb cooking apples
3 pints water

1 lb sugar to each pint of juice
Flavourings

Wash and cut up apples and simmer until soft in water. Put through a jelly bag, measure juice and add sugar. Stir over gentle heat until sugar has dissolved. Flavour with strips of lemon rind, boil rapidly to setting, pour into small jars and cover. Apple jelly is particularly delicious if a few rose geranium or lemon balm leaves are trailed in the liquid while cooking, but remove before potting. For herb jelly to serve with meat, use mint (for lamb) or sage (for pork) or bay (for ham). Hang a bunch of appropriate leaves in the jelly while cooking; remove them just before setting point is reached. For mint jelly, then add chopped mint; for sage or bay jelly, add a few whole leaves. Colour lightly with pure green colouring and pot in small jars.

APPLE MINT JELLY

2 lb tart green apples
1 quart cold water
Juice of 1 lemon
A bunch of fresh mint

Sugar as required
A little green vegetable colouring

Cut apples in slices, but do not core or peel. Place in a preserving pan with the water and lemon juice and several sprigs of mint. Bring quickly to boil. Cook to a soft pulp, mashing occasionally. Pour into a jelly bag and allow to drip overnight. Rinse pan and add juice with sugar, allowing $1\frac{1}{4}$ lb to each pint of juice. Wash a bunch of fresh mint thoroughly, bruise the leaves, then hold the bunch in the syrup for a few minutes while it is cooking. Add a little finely-chopped mint as well if you like. Continue boiling until jelly sets when tested, then stir in a drop or two of green colouring. Skim if necessary. Pot in small jars. Serve with lamb or mutton.

GOOSEBERRY AND ELDERFLOWER JELLY

Allow $\frac{3}{4}$ pint water to each lb of gooseberries. Simmer until berries are broken, then strain through jelly bag. Allow 1 lb sugar to each pint of juice. Allow warmed sugar to dissolve, then add 12 heads of elderflower tied in a muslin bag. Bring to boiling point, and boil for 15 minutes. Remove muslin bag, and pour jelly into small pots. This jelly has a muscat flavour.

GRAPE JELLY

Pick grapes off stems, put in a preserving pan, bruising some to make a liquid; boil for 15 minutes. Strain through a jelly bag, allow 1 lb sugar to 1 lb juice and boil quickly for 15 to 20 minutes. Jelly must not be made of fruit that is damp or picked during wet weather.

ORANGE AND APPLE JELLY

3 *large oranges*   **3** *large cooking apples*
4 *pints water*   **Sugar**

Peel oranges very thinly, and discard pith and seeds. Cut up the fruit. Boil peel, fruit and water for 1 hour, then strain liquid. Peel, core and cut up apples and weigh with the strained liquid. Put into a preserving pan, and allow 1 lb sugar to each lb fruit and liquid. Boil until apples are reduced to a pulp, and the mixture will set. Put into small jars and cover.

QUINCE JELLY

Cut up quinces with seeds and skin; cover with cold water and boil till soft, about 3 hours, add juice of 1 lemon. Strain, then add a cupful of sugar to cupful of juice, and boil till it thickens (hard boiling is necessary), about $\frac{1}{2}$ an hour. Skim well. Pour into hot jars and seal.

QUINCE JELLY

Take as many quinces as you like, don't peel or core them, but chop them roughly into a pan and just cover with water. Simmer steadily till very soft. Then hang up in a jelly bag and let drip until the juice is through. For each pint of juice add 1 lb granulated sugar, and boil steadily for about 45 minutes, removing the scum as it rises. When the jelly has jellied (pour a little on a plate to make sure), pour it into small pots. The residue left in the jelly bag makes a good jam for immediate use, if you boil it again with $\frac{1}{2}$ lb sugar to each lb of pulp.

If you have a japonica decorating a wall, use the fruit to make a jelly with an intriguing flavour. Follow the directions for quince jelly.

RASPBERRY AND APPLE JELLY

4 lb raspberries   **2 pints water**
2 lb cooking apples   **Sugar**

Cut up apples and put in pan with raspberries and water and cook until tender. Strain through jelly bag and add 1 lb warm brown sugar to each pint of juice. Bring to boiling point and boil for 10 minutes. Test for setting, pot and cover. Early windfalls can be used for this jelly.

RED CURRANT JELLY

Serve with mutton, ham, pork and game.

6 lb red currants will give a good quantity of juice if heated until tender, then strained and added to sugar, allowing $1\frac{1}{4}$ lb sugar to each pint of juice. The jelly will reach setting point quickly and should not be left long in the pan once it is removed from the stove.

RHUBARB JELLY

Stew some rhubarb in a jar in the oven until the juice runs freely from it. Strain the juice and to every pint add the thin yellow rind of a lemon and the juice of half a lemon and 1 lb preserving sugar. Boil till it jellies.

Lewis' Mother's Cookbook, Mary Horrell, Exeter

ROSE HIP JELLY FOR GAME

Provided birds do not get them, leave the hips to get fully rip and soft. Take off tops, cut them up and put in preserving pan with just enough water to cover. Bring to the boil, reduce heat and simmer to a pulp. Squeeze through a coarse jelly bag or cheese cloth then pass through an ordinary jelly bag. To the liquid obtained allow 1 lb of loaf sugar to every pint of juice. Put in preserving pan, stir till sugar is dissolved, then boil for 20 minutes or until a little will 'jell' when a teaspoon is dropped on a cold plate. This preserve is good with roast or jugged hare, also with turkey.

Queen Victoria always had a preserve made with wild rose hips at Balmoral to accompany game. Try the recipe mixing the dog rose hips with large hips of *Rosa Rugosa* from the garden.

ROWAN JELLY

Gather the berries on a fine day. Wash them in cold water, snip off stalks, put in preserving pan with water to barely cover, bring to simmering point and cook for 2 hours. Strain through a muslin bag, letting it drip until no more juice runs through. Measure juice and for every pint allow 3 large cooking apples. Cut up these without peeling or coring, put in preserving pan, cover barely with water, bring to simmering point and cook gently.

In Scotland, as well as 'Rodden Jelly' with game, the scarlet berries of wild barberries are used for jelly.

SUSSEX CONVENT CRAB APPLE JELLY

Cover Siberian (cherry-type) crab apples in water and cook in a casserole or jar in the oven until soft. Drain off juice and add 12 oz sugar to each pint of juice. Boil together to jelly.

If the fruit is left in the juice while it is being cooked to a jelly, it can be bottled separately and makes a lovely tart filling.

APPLE BUTTER

6 lb windfalls (any variety)   **1 teaspoon ground cloves**
2 pints water   **1 teaspoon ground cinnamon**
3 pints cider   **¾ lb sugar to each 1 lb pulp**

Wash the fruit, remove any damaged parts, and cut into pieces, simmer in water and cider until soft. Rub through a fine sieve. Weigh the pulp, return it to the pan, and simmer until thick. Add the spices and sugar, and boil, stirring frequently, until no surplus liquid remains. Pour into hot jars and seal. If poured into small, wide-mouthed jars, this preserve can be turned out as a stiff mould, and makes a good accompaniment to milk puddings.

APPLE CHEESE

1 lb pulped good white   **Juice and rind of 3 lemons**
`cooking apples   **4 well-beaten eggs**
1 lb white sugar   **4 oz butter**

Melt the butter in a pan. Add all other ingredients and cook for at least 30 minutes over slow heat. Makes about 3 lb but does not keep too long.

Pat Brown, Keynsham, Somerset

APPLE AND PLUM BUTTER

3 *lb apples*   **¾ *lb sugar to each pint of pulp***
1 *lb plums*

Peel and core apples and cut in slices, and cook in very little water until soft. Add stoned plums and cook until soft. Put through a sieve, measure and add sugar. Boil to setting point and put into warm jars. This may be used with bread and butter, of if put into straight-sided jars, it can be turned out, sliced and eaten with cream.

PLUM AND APPLE CHEESE

3 *lb apples*   ***Sugar***
1 *lb plums*

Cut up apples and plums without peeling or stoning. Add just enough water to prevent burning, and cook until tender, stirring often. Rub the fruit through a sieve and allow ¾ lb sugar to each pint of purée. Cook until mixture thickens and clears. Pour into pots. This may be used as a spread, or if put into jars without shoulders, it can be turned out and served in slices with cream.

APPLE AND PLUM CHEESE

Peel and core apples, and remove stones from plums, and weigh out an equal quantity. Put in thick pan and cook gently without water until soft. Add 1 lb sugar to each 1 lb of pulp, and boil slowly for an hour. Put into shallow baking tins or dishes. Dry out in a low oven temperature until the mixture is the consistency of soft leather. Cut in squares and store in tins with waxed paper between layers.

Miss Hill, 1864

BLACKBERRY AND APPLE CHEESE

This is a smooth version of jam, which can be cut with a knife, and is very useful for all sorts of pudding. Peel, core and quarter 2 lb cooking apples and cook in 1 gill water till tender. Add 2 lb blackberries and simmer till soft. Strain through a fine sieve, and measure the pulp. Add 1 lb sugar to each pint of juice, stir till dissolved, and boil the mixture until it sets when tested on a cold plate. It should be very firm. Put into warm pots and cover.

IVERSON CHERRY CHEESE

2 lb red eating cherries   **1 lb sugar**

Stone the cherries and chop the fruit finely. Crack a few stones and save the kernels. Put into a heavy pan with sugar and add just enough water to prevent burning. Simmer slowly, stirring all the time until a smooth mass of semi-solid consistency is formed. Add a few of the kernels. Pour into small jars and cover.

CRAB CHEESE

Siberian crabs make a pretty preserve. Fruit should not be peeled, but after it has been washed, dried, and stalks removed, is cooked whole in preserving pan with just enough water to prevent burning. When tender, press through sieve. Allow 1 lb sugar to same weight pulp. Boil up and then simmer for 45 minutes.

DAMSON CHEESE

Damsons   **Sugar**

Wash damsons, cover with water and simmer until soft. Put through a sieve and measure the pulp. Allow $\frac{3}{4}$ lb sugar to each pint of fruit pulp. Cook in a thick pan, stirring frequently, for 1 hour, until the pulp is thick enough to hold the impression of a spoon. Put into small straight-sided jars, and cover. When cold, this can be used as a spread, or turned out and cut into slices to serve with cream.

GOOSEBERRY CURD

This is similar to lemon curd, and should be put into small jars, being used within a few weeks. Prepare 3 lb green gooseberries and cook in $\frac{3}{4}$ pint water until tender. Put through a sieve, and then put into a double saucepan with $1\frac{1}{2}$ lb castor sugar, 7 lb butter and 4 beaten eggs. Cook gently, stirring until the mixture thickens.

BATH LEMON CURD

4 oz sugar   **1 egg or 2 egg yolks**
1 oz butter   **Rind and juice of 1 lemon**

Combine all ingredients in a double saucepan. Cook very gently until thick—the mixture must not be allowed to boil. Pour into warm jars and cover with wax circles. Put on covers when cold.

STANDARD LEMON CURD

6 oz butter
4 eggs (8 fluid oz when broken)

4 lemons (8 fluid oz juice)
1 lb sugar

Melt butter in a double saucepan, add lemon juice, sugar and thinly peeled lemon rind, and stir until sugar dissolves. Beat eggs lightly in a basin, cool the fat and sugar mixture slightly, and strain into the eggs, stirring all the time. Return mixture to double saucepan, and cook until it starts to thicken. Yield in saucepan: 2 lb 5 oz. Cool slightly before filling jars to top.

LEMON CURD

Beat up 9 oz butter, 2 lb sugar and the strained juice of 6 lemons. Heat gently till the sugar melts in a double saucepan. Stir 6 lightly beaten eggs into the butter mixture; heat, stirring all the time, till it is as thick as cream. Cook 2 more minutes and bottle in warm jars.

OXFORD MARMALADE

8 Seville oranges
Water

Sugar

Wipe fruit, put it into pan of cold water, boil gently until skins are soft and can be pierced with steel knitting needle. Drain, leave to cool, but retain water.

Divide into quarters, cut right through peel and pulp, shredding the orange coarsely into thick strips. Remove pips. Weigh fruit, and to each lb allow 1 lb sugar and $\frac{1}{2}$ pint of the water in which oranges were boiled. Should the water be objectionably bitter, it may be diluted slightly with fresh water. Let sugar dissolve in the water and boil all together steadily for about 35 minutes, or until marmalade sets when tested. Pour into jars, fasten down while hot.

MISS THOMPSON'S MARMALADE

1 lemon to every 6 oranges. Halve oranges, remove pips, squeeze juice in basin. Slice rind finely. Halve lemons. Squeeze juice into orange juice. Put rinds (not sliced) with orange rind. To every lb of sliced fruit add 3 pints water, soak all pips in $\frac{1}{2}$ pint of this water. Leave 12 hours, boil till tender, adding liquid from pips (after heating and straining it) and pips tied in muslin. Leave pulp 24 hours, remove lemon rinds.

To every lb of boiled pulp add 1¼ lb sugar (warmed in oven). Bring slowly to boil, boil till it jellies (about 50 minutes in all). Add orange and lemon juice, boil a minute or 2. Seal when cold.

MARMALADE

5 Seville oranges	*8 lb sugar*
2 lemons	*6 pints water*
1 large sweet orange	

Wash fruit and quarter. Extract pulp, put in a muslin bag, tie up. Cut peel very thinly and put into a bowl with bag of pulp and 6 pints water. Leave 24 hours. Place in preserving pan and boil gently 1 hour. Remove bag of pulp and strain off any liquid; add this and 8 lb sugar. Boil quickly 20 minutes and test for setting. Makes 12–13 lb.

Mrs Crimes, Anglesey

RUDWAY ORANGE MARMALADE

3 Seville oranges	*1 lemon*
1 sweet orange	

To every lb of fruit sliced, add 3 pints of cold water, and let it stand 24 hours, then let it boil until chips are tender. Stand another 24 hours, add 1½ lb of loaf sugar to every lb of fruit, as it is, then gently boil until the juice jellies.

Lewis' Mother's Cookbook, Mary Horrell, Exeter

GRAPEFRUIT MARMALADE

1 grapefruit	*1 orange*
1 lemon	

Cut all up finely, removing seeds. Pour over 4 pints of cold water and let it stand for 20 hours or more. Tie pips in a piece of muslin and put in with the fruit. Boil until it is tender, then add 4 lb sugar (remove seed bag first). Stir until dissolved then boil up again until it sets when tested. Makes 6 lb marmalade.

TRADITIONAL SEVILLE MARMALADE

2 lb Seville oranges	*4 pints water*
1 lemon	*4 lb sugar*

Wash and cut up oranges and lemon, putting the pips and pith in a muslin bag suspended from the pan. Cover with water and simmer until peel is

BILBERRY JELLY

Allow 3–4 pints of berries to get a pint of juice. Wash them, remove stalks, put in preserving pan or better still a large stone jar. Bruise them a little, then stand jar in a saucepan with water reaching midway up the jar. Bring to the boil and let them simmer till the juice runs out readily. Strain through a jelly bag, measure juice and allow $1\frac{1}{2}$ lb sugar to a pint. Put both in preserving pan, stir till sugar is dissolved, bring to the boil and boil rather fast for 10 minutes, or until a little will set when tested on a cold plate. This is very good with all kinds of game.

BRAMBLE JELLY

Wash 4 lb blackberries and put into a pan with $\frac{3}{4}$ pint water. Bring to the boil, and simmer very quickly until the juice has run out of the fruit. Strain and leave the juice to drip. Measure, and return to the pan with 1 lb sugar to each pint of juice. Heat gently till sugar dissolves, then bring to the boil and add juice of 1 lemon. Boil rapidly until setting point is reached, about 20 minutes. Put into warm pots and cover.

DAMSON JELLY

6 lb damsons   **1 lb sugar to each pint juice**
3 pints water

Simmer damsons in water until pulpy. Leave in a jelly bag overnight. For each pint of juice, allow 1 lb sugar, stir sugar until dissolved, then boil rapidly until the jelly sets when tested.

GREEN GOOSEBERRY JELLY

This jelly should be perfectly clear and bright. It can be used as a herb jelly if a few sprigs of herbs are plunged into boiling water, then added just before setting. Sage leaves, mint, rosemary and marjoram are particularly successful by this method.

To every lb of gooseberries, allow $\frac{3}{4}$ pint cold water. Prepare gooseberries and cook gently in water until the berries are broken. Strain through a jelly bag and measure the juice. Weigh out 1 lb sugar to each lb of juice. Boil juice for 15 minutes, then draw off heat and stir in sugar. Stir over gentle heat until dissolved, then boil for 20 minutes, until it jellies on the spoon. Remove scum from time to time. Pour into jars.

tender ($1\frac{1}{2}$–2 hours). Stir in sugar and warm gently until dissolved. Bring to the boil and boil rapidly to setting point. Cool for 15 minutes, stir and pour into warm jars.

DARK THICK MARMALADE

2 lb Seville oranges
1 lemon

4 pints water
4 lb sugar

Wash oranges and lemon and cut in halves. Squeeze out juice into a pan, remove pips and put in muslin bag, and cut peel and pulp in coarse shreds. Put peel, pulp, pips and water with juice, and simmer for 2 hours. Remove pips, add sugar, stir until dissolved and cook for about 1 hour until the colour has darkened slightly and the preserve sets firmly when tested. The addition of 1 oz black treacle will make the colour darker.

SWEET ORANGE AND LEMON MARMALADE

4 sweet oranges
5 lemons

5 pints water
4 lb sugar

Cut fruit into thin slices, removing pips and putting them into muslin bag. Put fruit, water and pips into pan and boil gently for $1\frac{1}{2}$ hours. Remove pips, add sugar and stir until dissolved. Boil for 10 minutes, or until setting point is reached.

LEMON MARMALADE

8 large lemons
8 pints cold water

Sugar

Peel lemons very thinly and cut peel into very fine shreds. Put pith and pips into muslin, and cut up the flesh of the lemons. Put fruit, peel and pips into a pan with water and boil until the contents of the pan are reduced by half. Remove pips. Weigh the contents of the pan and add an equal weight of sugar. Bring to the boil, boil for about 20 minutes until setting point is reached, and put into pots.

GRAPEFRUIT AND LEMON MARMALADE

2 large grapefruit
4 lemons

4 pints water
3 lb sugar

Peel the fruit and squeeze out the juice into preserving pan. Put lemon pips into a muslin bag but not the grapefruit pips, which will make the marmalade bitter. Cook the shredded peel in the water until the contents of the pan are reduced by half. Remove muslin bag, add sugar, and stir until dissolved. Boil rapidly for 20 minutes until setting point is reached.

TANGERINE PRESERVE

4 lb tangerines
3 lemons
1½ pints water
4 lb sugar

Slice tangerines and lemons thinly and simmer in water, with the pips in a muslin bag, until the peel is tender. Stir in sugar until dissolved, bring to boil, and boil hard to setting point. This is a delicious marmalade to remind us of that special Christmas scent of tangerines all through the year. It is particularly good with rolls or croissants for breakfast, or used as an ice-cream sauce.

PINEAPPLE MARMALADE

3 sweet oranges
1 lemon
1 large can pineapple chunks
4 lb sugar

Slice oranges and lemon, just cover with water and simmer until tender. Add the juice from the can of pineapple chunks and the finely cut fruit, and simmer until fruit is well blended. Add sugar, stir until dissolved and boil rapidly to setting point. This is a particular favourite with children who do not always care for the traditional marmalade, and is very good served with steamed puddings or with vanilla ice-cream.

CRANBERRY APPLE MARMALADE

1 large orange
½ pint water
1 lb cranberries
4 apples
1½ lb sugar

Slice the orange thinly and simmer in water until very tender. Put through the mincer with cranberries and peeled and cored apples, and return to the liquid with sugar. Cook over low heat until thick (about 25 minutes) stirring frequently. Put into hot jars and cover at once.

APRICOT MARMALADE

1 lb dried apricots
12 oz sugar
6 tablespoons lemon juice
1 tablespoon grated lemon rind
1 tablespoon grated orange rind

This is a thick preserve which is excellent for filling jam tarts or for spreading on slices of almond shortbread. Soak the apricots overnight in just enough cold water to cover them. Cook them in the water, then sieve both fruit and juice. Add sugar, lemon juice and grated rinds, and cook over a good heat for 15 minutes until thick. Put into hot jars.

TANGERINE MARMALADE

2½ lb tangerines
1 grapefruit
1 lemon

5 pints water
¼ oz tartaric acid
3 lb sugar

Peel the tangerines, shred the peel finely and put peel into a muslin bag. Peel the grapefruit and lemon, and put the peel through the mincer. Put into a saucepan with the chopped fruit pulp, the bag of tangerine peel, water and acid. Simmer gently for 2 hours, taking the tangerine peel out after 30 minutes. Wash this peel well, and drain. After 2 hours, strain the fruit pulp in a jelly bag. Put juice into a pan with sugar and heat gently until the sugar dissolves. Add the tangerine peel and boil rapidly to setting point. Skim, allow to cool slightly before potting.

APRICOT AND DATE MARMALADE

1 lb dried apricots
2 pints water
1½ lb dates

8 oz sugar
1 lemon
2 oz blanched almonds

This makes an excellent filling used between two layers of flaky pastry, baked in a hot oven and sprinkled with castor sugar. Soak the apricots overnight in 1 pint water. Add another pint of water, chopped dates, and sugar and the juice of a lemon. Cook slowly until the mixture is soft and thick, stir in chopped almonds and cook for 5 minutes.

MINCEMEAT

2½ lb suet
3½ lb soft brown sugar
3 lb currants
2¼ lb raisins
1½ lb peel
2 teaspoons salt
1 tablespoon mixed spice

2 teaspoons ground nutmeg
2 teaspoons ground cloves
4 lb apples (cooked day before)
½ pint sherry
4 lemons, rind and juice

Aunty Tommy's recipe, Gussage, Dorset

MINCEMEAT

Put into basin 1 scraped and sliced medium-sized carrot, $\frac{1}{2}$ lb peeled, cored and sliced apple, 8–12 oz mixed dried fruit (any kinds), 2 oz hazel or other nuts (optional), teaspoon mixed spice, pinch of salt and 4 oz suet or melted margarine.

Pass all through fine mincer twice. Return to basin and mix well with 3 tablespoons sugar, brown if possible, 1 tablespoon marmalade, 1 tablespoon treacle, 1 tablespoon spirit, sherry or vinegar, $\frac{1}{2}$ teaspoon lemon juice. Put into jars and cover like jam.

MINCEMEAT

$\frac{1}{2}$ lb each chopped raisins, sugar, sultanas, suet, apple (chopped), 2 oz candied peel or 1 tablespoon marmalade, 1 teaspoon lemon essence, pinch salt, 5 tablespoons ale or stout. Mix all dry ingredients, add liquids, mix well, put in jars, close down.

MINCEMEAT

$\frac{1}{2}$ lb butter
1 lb each currants, sultanas, raisins
4 oz peel
8 oz chopped, skinned almonds

$1\frac{1}{2}$ lb brown sugar
2 lb apples (weighed after peeling and coring)
At least 2 wineglasses rum or brandy

Put ingredients (except sugar and currants) through mixer. Mix well, stand overnight, remix and jar. Mrs Waggett says this recipe has been in her mother's family for several generations.

Mrs Waggett, Newcastle Emlyn

GREEN TOMATO MINCEMEAT

3 quarts chopped green tomatoes
1 quart chopped apples
8 oz shredded suet
$2\frac{1}{2}$ lb soft brown sugar
1 lb seedless raisins
$1\frac{3}{4}$ gills vinegar

$\frac{1}{2}$ lb chopped mixed candied peel
Salt to taste
$\frac{3}{4}$ tablespoon ground cinnamon
$\frac{3}{4}$ tablespoon ground cloves
1 small level tablespoon grated nutmeg

Chop tomatoes very finely; drain off liquid. Place in a preserving pan and add 4 quarts cold water; bring to boil and simmer for an hour. Cover and stand overnight. Next morning drain purée thoroughly; add apples, raisins, suet, vinegar, peel and salt to taste. Simmer for 2 hours. Add spice. Stir for a moment or two till thoroughly blended, then pot and seal. Store in a cool dry cupboard.

30 Pickles, Chutneys and Store Sauces

The squirrel gloats on his accomplished hoard,
The ants have brimmed their garners with ripe grain,
And honey bees have stored
The sweets of Summer in their luscious cells;
The swallows all have winged across the main.

Thomas Hood

INDIAN MIXED PICKLE

2 quarts green tomatoes
1 quart small onions
3 large cucumbers
1 firm medium cauliflower
½ medium head celery
2 large tablespoons salt
1 oz stick cinnamon
1 teaspoon allspice
½ teaspoon powdered ginger
20 cloves

½ teaspoon powdered mace
1 inch root ginger, cut up
finely
1 chilli pepper
1 dried red pepper
3 green peppers (optional)
1 quart vinegar
1½ lb sugar (use 1 lb if you do
not like a sweetish pickle)

Wash tomatoes, peel onions, cucumber. Remove seeds from cucumber, chop tomatoes, onions, cucumber, celery. Break cauliflower in neat pieces.

Put all in bowl, sprinkle with salt. Cover, stand overnight. Drain well next morning.

Tie spices in muslin bag, add to vinegar in which sugar has been dissolved, cook gently with vegetables in preserving pan 30 minutes. Remove bag, pour pickle into hot jars, cover, leave to mature at least a fortnight.

MILITARY PICKLE

1 *marrow*	7 *chillies*
1 *cauliflower*	1 *oz turmeric powder*
1 *lb beans*	1 *oz ground ginger*
1 *lb onions*	1 *breakfastcup flour*
1 *lb demerara sugar*	

Cut the vegetables up small and cover with salt. Leave to stand overnight, then drain. Put into saucepan, add 2 quarts of vinegar and boil 5 minutes. Mix to a smooth paste the dry ingredients and add while boiling. Boil for a good ½ hour. Stir well to save burning. Take up and bottle when cold.

SWEET MUSTARD PICKLE

1 *marrow, medium size*	½ *oz turmeric*
1 *cauliflower*	¼ *oz ground ginger*
1 *cucumber*	½ *oz ground nutmeg*
1 *lb onions*	10 *oz sugar*
1 *lb young French beans*	2 *oz flour*
2 *oz dry mustard*	2 *pints vinegar*

Chop vegetables into ½–1 inch chunks. Sprinkle with 1 oz salt, cover with water and soak overnight, then drain off water. Mix all dry ingredients with a little of the vinegar to make a smooth paste. Add remainder of the vinegar to the vegetables and simmer in a strong pan until barely tender, approximately 10 minutes. Add some boiling vinegar to the blended ingredients. Return to the pan and boil for 10 minutes stirring all the time and allow to thicken. Pot while hot. Yield: 9 lb.

PICCALILLI

5 *lb cauliflower*	1 *oz turmeric*
1 *lb onions*	1 *oz ground ginger*
Salt	8 *chillies*
3½ *oz mustard*	8 *cloves*
10 *oz lump sugar*	4 *pints vinegar*

Cut vegetables into small pieces and put in a pan. Sprinkle with salt and allow to stand overnight. Mix remaining ingredients. Put vegetables in stewpan, pour on the mixture, boil until tender. When cold it is ready for use. The 6 lb of vegetables can be varied. Marrow or green tomatoes instead of cauliflower.

Lewis' Mother's Cookbook, Mary Horrell, Exeter

CUMBERLAND BEAN PICKLE

6 lb runner beans
6 large onions
1 quart white vinegar
4 oz plain flour

2 oz dry mustard
1 lb sugar
1 teaspoon black pepper
1 teaspoon turmeric powder

Slice the beans and onions thinly and cook in a little water until tender. Drain thoroughly. Moisten the flour with a little vinegar, then mix together in a saucepan the vinegar, flour, mustard, sugar, pepper and turmeric. Bring to the boil and continue stirring all the time until the mixture is thick. Add beans and onions and continue stirring until the mixture boils again. Put into jars, and cover while hot.

PICKLED BEETROOT

8 medium size beetroot
¼ oz whole black pepper
1 horseradish (grated)

1 quart malt vinegar
¼ oz allspice
1 teaspoon salt

Bake beetroot in oven for $1\frac{1}{2}$–2 hours, when cool skin and slice; place in jars. Boil vinegar, horseradish, salt, pepper and spice together; when cool, pour over beetroot. Store in dry place.

PICKLED CABBAGE

Quarter a large firm red cabbage. Take out the stalk. Slice very thinly. Put on a large flat dish and sprinkle with plenty of salt. Leave overnight. In the morning turn all over to mix the salt. Drain. Fill clean bottles or jars. Sprinkle a quarter of a teaspoon of cayenne pepper on top of each jar. Cover cabbage with cold vinegar. Tie down securely and store. With this method the cabbage can be eaten at the end of 2 or 3 days. Some people make it with spiced vinegar, which is allowed to get cold before putting on the vegetable.

SWEET CUCUMBER PICKLE

3 lb cucumbers
1 dessertspoon powdered
alum
1 quart water

2 lb sugar
1 pint vinegar
2 tablespoons whole clove
2 inch stick of cinnamon

Make a syrup with the sugar, vinegar and spices tied in a muslin by boiling them together for 5 minutes. Meanwhile, peel the cucumbers thinly, cut into quarters lengthways and into 3 inch pieces. Cover with alum dissolved in water, and bring slowly to the boil, then drain and chill cucumber in ice water. When the syrup is ready add the drained cucumbers and simmer for 10 minutes. Leave till next day, then on 3 successive days drain off syrup, boil hard for 1 minute and then pour over cucumbers. On the last day, pack cucumber pieces into jars and fill up with boiling syrup. Cover when cold.

PICKLED EGGS

Add pickled eggs to your usual salad. Pickled eggs are popular down at the local. To make: just hard-boil eggs for 15 minutes, peel off shell, drop eggs in spiced vinegar and leave for 10 days.

PICKLED GHERKINS

Soak the gherkins in brine for 3 days, allowing ¼ lb salt to each quart of water. Then drain them. Place the gherkins in jars and pour boiling spiced vinegar over them, cover and leave 24 hours. Drain off the vinegar, boil it and pour over the gherkins as before. Repeat several times, until the gherkins are nicely green. Cork and store in a dark place.

NASTURTIUM SEEDS

These make very good mock capers. Gather the seeds on a dry day when quite young and soft. Wipe clean with a cloth. Put in a dry glass bottle. Cover with the following liquid: to 1 pint vinegar add 1 oz salt and 6 peppercorns. If you have not enough seeds ripe, you can add them from day to day till the bottle is filled. Seal well and resin the corks of the bottles. As they take from 10 to 12 months to get really pickled, they should be made 1 season for use the next.

PICKLED ONIONS

Small button onions
Vinegar to cover
To each quart of vinegar

allow 2 teaspoons of allspice
2 teaspoons peppercorns

Peel onions into clean dry jars, boil vinegar with spices, and when cold pour it over to fill jars completely; cover with parchment paper and store in dry place. Ready in 2 weeks. The pickles will be ready much earlier if the vinegar is used while hot.

IVERSON PICKLED GREEN TOMATOES

2½ lb green tomatoes
8 oz onions

8 oz sugar
1 pint white vinegar

Slice the tomatoes and onions. Sprinkle generously with salt. Leave for 24 hours and drain off salt liquid completely. Make a syrup with the sugar and vinegar and put in tomatoes and onions. Simmer until tender, pour into preserving jars and cover while hot.

VEGETABLE MARROW PICKLE

Prepare a large marrow as for cooking. Cut it in small square pieces, sprinkle with salt and let it remain overnight. Take 1 quart best vinegar, add to it a little pepper, and the marrow. Boil all together until the marrow becomes tender, then add 3 oz mustard mixed with a little cold vinegar and boil all together for 3 minutes.

Lewis' Mother's Cookbook, Mary Horrell, Exeter

MOCK OLIVES

These can be made from not-too-ripe plums. Pour over them a boiling brine made from 2 oz salt in ¾ pint vinegar. Let them stand 12 hours, drain off the brine, boil it up and pour over the drained plums. Bottle when quite cold.

APPLE CHUTNEY

6 lb cooking apples
2 lb onions
2 lb sugar
1 lb golden syrup
½ pint water

1½ oz ground ginger
½ oz ground cinnamon
¼ teaspoon Cayenne
1½ oz salt
1 quart vinegar

Peel and cut up the apples and onions, simmer in water for 20 minutes. Add the salt, spices and half the vinegar, and cook until softened. Add the sugar, syrup and the rest of the vinegar, and simmer until stiff. Pot and cover, using vinegar-proof discs underneath cellophane or screw tops.

MRS HAWKYARD'S APPLE CHUTNEY

5 *lb apples*
½-1 *pint vinegar*
1 *tablespoon salt*
8 *oz stoned dates*
8 *oz raisins or sultanas*

1 *small tablespoon ground ginger*
8 *oz onions*
1 *lb demerara sugar*
6 *chillies*

Peel and core the apples. Put the salt, ginger, chopped chillies and sugar into a pan with some of the vinegar. Add the apples and minced onions and bring to the boil. Add the chopped dates and whole raisins or sultanas and simmer until thick and brown, adding more vinegar as required (the apples make a lot of juice, and the chutney should not be runny). Put into warm jars, and cover well. The chillies make this a rather hot chutney, as Mrs Hawkyard's son liked very 'hot' spicy food. They can be omitted, but are really a good addition to what can often be a rather bland and boring type of chutney.

NORWICH APPLE CHUTNEY

2½ *lb apples, peeled and cored*
½ *lb onions, peeled*
½ *lb brown sugar*
¼ *lb sultanas*
½ *oz salt*
¾ *pint vinegar*

1 *tablespoon pickling spice*
½ *tablespoon dry mustard*
1 *teaspoon coriander seeds, optional*
2 *pieces root ginger*

Mince or chop finely onions and apples. Simmer with half the quantity of vinegar until tender. Add sugar, sultanas, salt, pickling spice, mustard, coriander seeds, ginger and remainder of vinegar. Simmer until thick, about 20 minutes. Remove ginger and turn into heated jars whilst hot and place on glass lids firmly. If ordinary jars are used, a cover should be used to stop the vinegar evaporating, i.e. good corks or a layer of thick waxed, vinegar-proof paper then a metal lid and clip, the clip being removed when the chutney is cold.

APRICOT CHUTNEY

1 *lb dried apricots*
1 *clove garlic*
3 *peppercorns*
4 *oz sultanas*

8 *oz sugar*
1 *orange*
½ *pint white vinegar*

Soak the apricots overnight, drain off the liquid and put the fruit into a heavy pan with chopped garlic clove, peppercorns, sultanas, sugar and the grated rind and juice of the orange. Bring to the boil, add vinegar, and simmer until the chutney is thick. Put into hot jars and seal at once.

BEETROOT CHUTNEY

2 *lb beetroot*
2 *medium-sized onions*
¼ *teaspoon ginger*
½ *lb sugar*

1 *lb apples*
½ *teaspoon salt*
1 *tablespoon lemon juice*
1 *pint vinegar*

Boil beetroot till tender and peel when cold. Cut into small cubes. Peel onions and apples and cut them up finely. Put them into a pan with sugar vinegar etc. and boil for ½ hour. Add the beetroot and simmer for a further 15 minutes. Bottle when cold.

BLACKBERRY CHUTNEY

Wash 6 lb blackberries and put in a pan with 2 lb peeled and chopped apples, 2 lb chopped onions, 1 oz salt, 2 oz mustard, 2 oz ground ginger, 2 teaspoons powdered mace, 1 teaspoon cayenne pepper, 2 pints vinegar, and cook gently for 1 hour. Put through a sieve to remove pips, add 2 lb brown sugar and cook till thick.

CHERRY RELISH

1½ *lb black eating cherries*
4 *oz raisins*
4 *tablespoons honey*

2 *teaspoons mixed spice*
¼ *pint white vinegar*
4 *tablespoons brown sugar*

Remove stones from cherries. Put all the ingredients into a heavy pan and simmer gently until the sugar has melted. Boil for 5 minutes, then simmer until thick, stirring all the time. Pour into small screw top jars and seal tightly. Very good with cold ham, chicken, turkey or duck.

ELDERBERRY CHUTNEY

1½ lb berries
1 onion
2 oz sugar (demerara is best)
½ pint vinegar
½ oz ground ginger
A few cloves

1 teaspoon salt
¼ teaspoon pepper
⅛ teaspoon mace
2 oz stoned raisins, if
obtainable

Pass berries through sieve, chop onion finely, and boil with other ingredients for 10–15 minutes. This makes up a small quantity.

GOOSEBERRY RELISH

Prepare 2 lb gooseberries, and add 12 oz seeded raisins, and 1 lb sliced onions. Put through a mincer and put into a pan with ½ lb brown sugar, 1 teaspoon dry mustard, 1 tablespoon ground ginger, 2 tablespoons salt, ¼ teaspoon cayenne pepper, 1 teaspoon turmeric and 1 pint vinegar. Bring slowly to the boil, then simmer for 45 minutes. Put through a coarse sieve, heat thoroughly, fill bottles and seal.

PEAR CHUTNEY

3½ lb pears
2 oranges
1 teaspoon powdered cloves
1 teaspoon powdered
cinnamon

1 teaspoon powdered allspice
1 lb seedless raisins
1½ lb sugar
½ pint vinegar

Peel, core and chop the pears. Grate the rind of the oranges and squeeze out the juice. Add rind, juice and pears to the spices, raisins, sugar and vinegar, and bring to the boil. Reduce heat and simmer for 2 hours. Pour into warm jars and cover tightly.

PEAR AND QUINCE CHUTNEY

4 lb cooking pears
2 lb quinces
2 lb onions
2 lb green tomatoes
1 lb stoned raisins
1 lb tender celery sticks
3 lb demerara sugar

½ teaspoon Cayenne pepper
½ oz salt
½ teaspoon ground ginger
10 black peppercorns
1 teaspoon grated
horseradish
4 pints vinegar

Peel, quarter and core the pears and quinces. Peel the onions. Put the tomatoes and raisins through a mincer into a deep saucepan. Cover, after stirring, and cook gently until tender, stirring frequently. Meanwhile, mince the celery and add the sugar, pepper, salt and ginger. When fruit is tender, stir in this mixture. Tie the peppercorns and horseradish in a small muslin bag and add to pan with the vinegar. Stir till boiling, then cook slowly, stirring frequently, until the mixture is thick, about 4 hours. Remove muslin bag. When contents are cooked, pot and cover.

PLUM CHUTNEY (1)

2 lb plums weighed after
stoning
1 lb carrots
1 pint vinegar
1 lb stoned raisins

1 lb soft brown sugar
1 oz chopped garlic
1 oz chillies
1 oz ground ginger
1½ oz salt

Stone plums and weigh out 2 lb. Mix with minced carrots and vinegar and simmer until soft. Add other ingredients, and simmer until the mixture is thick. Put into jars and cover tightly.

PLUM CHUTNEY (2)

2 lb any plums (or damsons
or pears)
¼ dried fruit (optional)
¼ lb onions
¾ lb sugar
½ pint malt vinegar

1 tablespoon salt
1 teaspoon pepper
1 dessertspoon mixed spice in
muslin bag (to be removed
after cooking)
1 teaspoon powdered ginger

Chop onions, stone and chop plums. Stew onions in half the vinegar until tender. Add all but sugar and vinegar. Add vinegar slowly, stirring, cook gently. Add sugar when mixture is soft. Boil steadily 10 minutes when chutney will be like thick jam. Pour into hot jars and seal.

PLUM CHUTNEY (3)

2 lb ripe plums
8 oz apples
8 oz brown sugar
1 lb raisins or sultanas

8 oz onions
½ oz chillies
1 pint best vinegar

Skin and stone the plums. Peel apples and onions and cut in pieces. Cook plums, apples and onions in half the vinegar until tender. Add remaining ingredients and vinegar and boil hard for 10 minutes until brown and thick.

LITTLE WYLLIE'S RHUBARB CHUTNEY

2 *lb rhubarb*
½ *lb onions*
1½ *lb brown sugar*
½ *lb sultanas*
½ *oz mustard seeds*
1 *teaspoon mixed spice*

1 *teaspoon pepper*
1 *teaspoon ground ginger*
1 *teaspoon salt*
¼ *teaspoon Cayenne pepper*
1 *pint vinegar*

Cut rhubarb into 1 inch lengths and chop onions finely. Put all ingredients into heavy pan and simmer gently, stirring frequently until mixture is of consistency of jam. Put into pots or preserving jars and cover tightly.

RUNNER BEAN CHUTNEY

2 *lb runner beans (after slicing)*
1½ *lb onions (after chopping)*
1 *heaped tablespoon cornflour*
1 *tablespoon turmeric*

1 *heaped tablespoon dry mustard*
1 *lb demerara sugar*
1 *lb soft brown sugar*
1½ *pints vinegar*

Prepare vegetables. Cook sliced beans in well-salted water until tender. Cook chopped onions in ½ pint vinegar. Mix dry ingredients to smooth paste with vinegar. Strain cooked beans, then add to rest of vinegar and cook for 10 minutes. Add sugar and rest of ingredients and boil for a further 15 minutes. Bottle and cover. Keeps well. Very good.

Mrs ap Gwynn, Welshpool

GREEN TOMATO CHUTNEY (1)

2 *lb green tomatoes*
2 *lb sharp apples*
1 *lb Barbados sugar*
¼ *lb shallots*
1 *oz garlic*

½ *oz salt*
¼ *oz red pepper*
½ *lb raisins*
Juice of 2 lemons
1 *pint vinegar*

Chop all the ingredients and mix in spices and flavourings. Add vinegar, and simmer gently for about 3 hours with the lid on until it is thick and pulpy. Put into jars.

GREEN TOMATO CHUTNEY (2)

2½ *lb green tomatoes*
8 oz brown sugar
2 teaspoons ground ginger
¾ *teaspoon Cayenne pepper*
6 nicely flavoured cooking

apples
2 medium-sized onions
A little salt
¾ *pint vinegar*

Slice the tomatoes, apples and onions and boil in vinegar for a little while. Strain, retaining the liquid. Chop the vegetables. Put them back in the saucepan with the vinegar and other ingredients and simmer for 4 or 5 hours. Pour into hot jars and tie down firmly.

Mrs Harding, Sixpenny Handley, Wilts

GREEN TOMATO CHUTNEY (3)

1½ *lb green tomatoes*
1 lb apples
¼ *lb sugar*
¾ *lb sultanas (or less)*
¼ *lb onions*

1 teaspoon salt
1 oz mixed spice
1 pint vinegar
Pinch of dry mustard

Chop these ingredients and cook all slowly together until the colour deepens. About 1½–2 hours. Use enamelled pan or casserole.

GREEN TOMATO SWEET PICKLE

2 lb chopped green tomatoes
¾ *lb peeled cored and sliced*
apples
¼ *lb chopped onions*
Saltspoon Cayenne pepper
¼ *pint vinegar*

4 oz sultanas or chopped
prunes
¾ *lb sugar*
1 small teaspoon ground
ginger

Boil all ingredients together till thick and stiff like jam. Pour into small pots. Seal and keep in cool, dry place.

RIPE TOMATO CHUTNEY

1 lb ripe tomatoes
8 oz onions
4 oz sour apples
1 lb stoned raisins
4 oz moist sugar

¼ *oz salt*
¼ *oz ground ginger*
Pinch of Cayenne pepper
½ *pint vinegar*

Skin the tomatoes and peel and core apples. Chop the tomatoes, onions, apples and raisins. Mix all ingredients and boil to a mash. This will take an hour or more. Put into small jars and close.

Mrs Harding, Sixpenny Handley, Wilts

SPICED TOMATO RELISH

1 *lb tomatoes*	*pepper*
1 *green pepper*	1 *level teaspoon Cayenne*
1 *lb onions*	*pepper*
1 *lb apples*	1 *level tablespoon mixed*
3 *cloves garlic*	*mustard*
¾ *lb white sugar*	½ *teaspoon mixed spice*
1 *level tablespoon salt*	½ *pint distilled vinegar*
1 *level tablespoon paprika*	6 *oz tin tomato purée*

Dip tomatoes in boiling water for 1 minute, remove skins and cut up. Remove pips from pepper and cut up with onions and apples. Chop garlic finely. Put in pan with vinegar and simmer until tender and thick, about 30 minutes. Add other ingredients, boil for 3 minutes. Pot while hot.

TOMATO CHUTNEY

2 *lb green tomatoes*	1 *tablespoon mustard*
1 *lb apples*	1 *teaspoon pepper*
½ *lb onions*	½ *oz salt*
½ *lb raisins*	1 *teaspoon ground cinnamon*
½ *lb demerara sugar*	*A little more than a pint of*
	vinegar

Chop up the apples and tomatoes or pass through a mincer and then boil all the ingredients together until it sets.

SWEETCORN RELISH

18 *ears corn*	1 *lb sugar*
1 *small cabbage*	4 *oz plain flour*
1 *head celery*	2 *oz salt*
4 *medium onions*	½ *teaspoon dry mustard*
2 *green peppers*	¼ *teaspoon Cayenne pepper*
4 *pints vinegar*	½ *teaspoon turmeric powder*

Cut corn from cob. Chop cabbage and celery, slice onions and chop peppers. Put into saucepan with half the vinegar. Mix remaining ingredients with the rest of the vinegar, combine mixtures, bring to boiling point and simmer for 40 minutes. Put into jars and cover at once.

VEGETABLE MARROW PRESERVE

Peel and take out the seeds, cut in slices $\frac{1}{4}$ inch thick, weigh the pulp, put equal quantities of sugar. If 8 lb, $\frac{1}{4}$ lb bruised ginger (put into a muslin bag), the juice of 4 lemons. If required hot, add $\frac{1}{2}$ teaspoon of cayenne pepper, boil 2 hours.

Lewis' Mother's Cookbook, Mary Horrell, Exeter

BATH CHUTNEY

2 lb apples or tomatoes	**$\frac{3}{4}$ pint vinegar**
$\frac{1}{2}$ lb onion	**2 pieces root ginger**
$\frac{1}{4}$ lb dates or dried fruit	**1 teaspoon coriander**
$\frac{1}{2}$ oz salt	**1 dessertspoon pickling spice**
$\frac{1}{2}$ lb brown sugar	

Prepare fruit and onions (weigh after preparation) mince or chop. Cook gently until soft adding a little vinegar if inclined to stick. Put spices in vinegar, infuse, strain. Add vinegar, salt and sugar to fruit. Cook until thick. Pour into hot jars and cover.

SOMERSET CHUTNEY

Peel 3 lb cooking apples and cut them up. Put them in a saucepan with 2 sliced onions, 1 lb brown sugar, $\frac{1}{2}$ lb seedless raisins or sultanas, $\frac{1}{4}$ lb currants, a dessertspoon ground ginger and 2 of mustard seed, $\frac{1}{2}$ pint vinegar and a tablespoon of salt. Stir all well together and bring to the boil. The mixture should boil gently for an hour or until the chutney is a nice brown colour.

Mrs Huxtable, Bath

CHUTNEY IN THE RAW

1 lb stoned dates	**Salt and pepper**
1 lb sultanas	**1 teaspoon curry powder**
1 lb apples	**1 lb brown sugar**
1 lb onions	**1 pint vinegar**

Mince the first 4 ingredients and stir in sugar and vinegar. Add 1 teaspoon salt, a sprinkling of pepper, curry and a small piece of root ginger in muslin. Stir mixture occasionally. Leave 24 hours. Remove ginger and bottle.

UNCOOKED CHUTNEY

1 lb sultanas or raisins or dates
1½ lb sugar
2 wineglasses of white wine vinegar

3 teaspoons mixed spice
1½ lb apples, peeled and cored
½ lb onions
3 oz salt

Mince the apples and onion and raisins or dates—the sultanas, if used, can be added whole. Add all other ingredients, mix well and pot. Keeps well and is best after several weeks.

SPICED APPLES (1)

2 lb apples
½ oz whole cloves
½ oz stick cinnamon
½ oz whole allspice

1 pint white vinegar
2 lb sugar
½ teaspoon salt

Put sugar, vinegar and salt into a saucepan, with the spices tied in a muslin bag. Bring to the boil and add the peeled, cored and sliced apples. Cook gently until the apples are tender, then take out the fruit, drain carefully and pack into warm jars. Boil the syrup until it thickens, take out the spice bag, pour over the apples and seal tightly.

SPICED APPLES (2)

2 lb small apples (firm)
2 lb sugar

1 pint spiced vinegar

Dissolve the sugar in the spiced vinegar. Prick the apples or cut in halves and simmer in the syrup until just tender, but do not let them break. Pack carefully into jars. Reduce the syrup by half, by gentle simmering, then pour it over the fruit while hot.

SPICED APRICOTS

1 lb dried apricots
½ oz whole cloves
½ inch cinnamon stick

½ oz whole allspice
1½ pints white vinegar
1¼ lb sugar

Soak the apricots in cold water overnight. Put the spices in a muslin bag and bring to the boil with the vinegar. Add the drained apricots and simmer for 5 minutes. Spoon the apricots into warm jars. Add the sugar to the vinegar, bring to the boil and continue boiling for 5 minutes until the mixture is syrupy. Remove the spice bag, pour the syrup over the fruit, and seal tightly. This is a good preserve to eat with ham or pork.

SPICED BLACKBERRIES (1)

This is an unusual use for blackberries, but extremely good with cold meats and poultry. Make some spiced vinegar by simmering gently together ½ pint cider or wine vinegar with ¼ oz each of allspice, coriander seed and cardamons, ½ stick cinnamon and 1 bay leaf. When the vinegar has reached boiling point, remove from heat, and leave to infuse for 2 or 3 hours. Remove the spices, and dissolve 1 lb sugar in vinegar. Add 2½ lb clean, ripe blackberries and 2 rose geranium leaves if possible. Simmer gently for 5 minutes till the fruit is tender. Lift out fruit, drain and put into warm jars. Boil the vinegar till syrupy, pour over the blackberries and seal firmly while hot.

SPICED BLACKBERRIES (2)

3 lb blackberries
1 lb sugar
½ pint vinegar

½ teaspoon each cinnamon
and ground cloves

Vinegar, sugar and spices are cooked together and the blackberries have cooked separately and are then added just before boiling point. Contents of pan are then allowed to simmer for 15 minutes. Bottle and seal down while very hot.

SPICED CRAB APPLES

4 lb crab apples (should be
uniform, ripe; avoid bruised
ones)
Whole cloves
¾ oz stick cinnamon

¼ oz ginger root
1 tablespoon allspice (whole)
½ pint best vinegar
¼ cup water
1½ lb sugar

Wash crab apples, leave stems on. Stick 2 or 3 cloves in each. Make syrup of vinegar, water, sugar, spices (tied in cheesecloth). Heat to boiling point, boil 5 minutes. Add fruit, cook gently until tender. Lift out whole, and seal down put carefully in jars. Boil syrup until thick, pour over. Seal.

SWEET SPICED DAMSONS

4 lb large damsons
1 pint vinegar

1½ lb sugar
1 oz mixed pickling spice

Prick damsons with a large needle. Put vinegar, sugar and spice in a pan and heat until the sugar has dissolved. Add the damsons, cook until soft but not broken, and then lift carefully into jars. Reduce the vinegar to a syrup by boiling, remove spices and pour over fruit. Cover tightly. Good with poultry or cold meat, particularly goose.

PICKLED DATES

Large dates
White vinegar
12 peppercorns

10 whole cloves
2 inch cinnamon stick
1 level teaspoon salt

Choose very succulent dates, and stone enough to fill the jars you want to use. Measure out enough white vinegar to cover them. For each pint use the quantity of spices indicated above. Put the spices in a muslin bag in a saucepan, add the vinegar and bring to the boil. Discard the spice bag and pour the hot vinegar over the dates in their jars. Leave to cool, cover tightly and leave for at least a month before using. Serve with all cold meats.

SPICED GOOSEBERRIES

Cook together 2 lb gooseberries with 8 oz brown sugar and 1 pint white wine vinegar. When the berries are tender, stir in 1 tablespoon dry mustard and 2 whole crushed garlic heads, 12 oz raisins and $\frac{1}{2}$ oz cayenne pepper. Add another pint of cold white wine vinegar, stir well and put into preserving jars, storing for at least 6 months before using.

PICKLED PLUMS

Sugar and vinegar are required. Place jars of plums in a moderate oven to heat through. Then cover the fruit with boiling syrup and seal at once. To make the syrup, dissolve sugar in spiced vinegar at the rate of 1 lb sugar to 1 pint vinegar. Boil 10 minutes. Keep the pickled plums 1 month before using.

PICKLED MELON

4 lb melon
2 oz salt
1 pint water
1 lb sugar

1 pint vinegar
8 cloves
1 inch cinnamon stick

Peel the melon and cut the flesh in $\frac{1}{2}$ inch cubes. Soak overnight in brine made from the salt and water. Drain and cover with fresh water. Bring to the boil, and simmer until tender and clear. Dissolve the sugar in vinegar with the spices and boil for 20 minutes until syrupy. Strain the syrup and bring it to the boil. Add the drained melon and boil for 10 minutes. Pour into preserving jars and seal at once. Excellent with ham or chicken.

SPICED ORANGE RINGS

6 firm oranges
$\frac{3}{4}$ pint vinegar
12 oz sugar

2 teaspoons cloves
3 inch cinnamon stick

Wipe the oranges and slice across in $\frac{1}{4}$ inch rounds. Put into a pan with water to cover and simmer for 45 minutes until fruit is tender. Put the vinegar, sugar and spices into the pan and bring to boil. Simmer and add rings a few at a time. Cook gently until the rind becomes clear and put fruit into hot preserving jars. Boil syrup until it starts to thicken and pour it over the fruit to cover completely. Add a few of the cloves and seal at once. Particularly good with ham and poultry.

PICKLED PEACHES

$3\frac{1}{2}$ lb peaches
$1\frac{3}{4}$ lb sugar
1 pint white malt vinegar

1 oz cloves
1 oz allspice
1 oz cinnamon

Wash the peaches. Dissolve the sugar in the vinegar, and add the spices tied in a muslin bag. Put in the fruit and simmer until tender but not soft. Drain fruit and pack into jars within one inch of the top. Boil the vinegar mixture until syrup, and pour on to the fruit, covering it completely. Seal at once. These are particularly delicious with cold ham and cold duck.

PICKLED PEARS

4 lb cooking pears
2 lb sugar
$\frac{3}{4}$ oz whole cloves
$\frac{3}{4}$ oz whole allspice

$\frac{3}{4}$ oz root ginger
$\frac{3}{4}$ oz stick cinnamon
1 pint vinegar
Rind $\frac{1}{2}$ lemon

Peel and core pears and cut into quarters. Dissolve sugar in vinegar. Crush spices and tie in a muslin bag and hang in the cooking pan. Simmer fruit in vinegar until tender. Drain off liquid and pack pears in preserving jars. Boil liquid gently until slightly thick, and fill each jar to cover fruit. Cover tightly, and keep for several months. These are very good with cold meat, poultry and ham.

SPICED PEARS

2 lb cooking pears
½ lb sugar
½ pint white vinegar
A piece of lemon rind

Small pieces root ginger and cinnamon stick
2 teaspoons whole allspice
Whole cloves

Peel and core pears and cut in half. Dissolve sugar in vinegar, and tie lemon rind and spices in a muslin bag. Stick a clove into each piece of pear, and then simmer pears in the syrup until they are tender and begin to look transparent. Pack them into clean hot jars, boil the syrup until it thickens slightly, and pour over pears. Seal tightly.

SPICED PLUMS

2½ lb firm plums
1 pint vinegar
1½ lb sugar
1 inch cinnamon stick

1 teaspoon cloves
Blade of mace
10 allspice berries

Prick the plums with a needle. Boil the vinegar, sugar and spices and pour over the plums. Leave overnight. Drain off the syrup and boil it for 10 minutes. Pour over the fruit again and leave for 12 hours. Bring to the boil with the plums. Remove the spices and put the plums into hot preserving jars. Boil up the syrup and pour over the plums, and screw on tops immediately. Delicious with all cold meat and poultry.

SPICED PICKLED PLUMS

1 pint white vinegar
1 oz cinnamon stick
¾ oz mixed pickling spice

¼ oz allspice berries
2 lb sugar
Victoria plums

Boil together vinegar, cinnamon stick, pickling spice, allspice, and sugar until the liquid is thick and syrupy. Wipe and halve plums, and remove stones. Prick well and put into jars. Pour over the cool syrup. Next day, strain off the syrup, reboil, cool and pour over fruit again. When cold, cover and store for at least 3 months before using. Good with poultry or cold meat.

SPICED PRUNES

1 lb large firm prunes	**1 inch cinnamon stick**
Cold tea	**1 teaspoon whole cloves**
1 pint vinegar	**10 allspice berries**
1 lb sugar	**Blade of mace**

Soak the prunes overnight in cold tea, and then simmer them in the tea until plump. Boil the vinegar and sugar with the spices. Add prunes and cooking liquid and cook for 5 minutes. Lift the prunes out with a slotted spoon, and pack them into preserving jars, or screwtop honey jars. Boil up the syrup, pour over the prunes, and seal at once. These are delicious with all kinds of cold meat, particularly pork.

TOMATO SAUCE (1)

4 lb ripe tomatoes	**2 oz peppercorns**
4 large onions	**½ oz cloves**
1 lb demerara sugar	**2 teaspoons Cayenne pepper**
1 oz salt	**1 pint vinegar**

Slice tomatoes and onions and mix with other ingredients. Simmer gently for 2 hours, stirring occasionally. Rub through a fine sieve, leaving nothing but spice, seeds and skin in strainer. Bring to the boil and boil for 5 minutes. Bottle when cold. This sauce will keep any length of time and improve by doing so.

Mrs Harding, Sixpenny Handley, Wilts

TOMATO SAUCE (2)

Put 4 lb ripe tomatoes in a pan with about ½ pint water. Boil until soft. Then rub through a sieve and put into a clean pan with a little cayenne, also 1 oz bruised ginger, 3 cloves, 1 teaspoon peppercorns and a blade of mace, all tied in a muslin bag. Boil all with the lid off till the sauce is thick as cream. When cold, bottle. Tie down securely.

TOMATAS KETCHUP

Have ripe Tomata. Bake, pour away the liquor that runs from them. to every pound put a pint of vinegar ½ oz Salt ½ oz White pepper ½ oz Shallot a teaspoonfull Cayenne. Boil it all together ½ an hour then press them thro a cullender when cold weigh it to every lb add the juice of 3 lemons, boil it up once cold bottle it.

Joseph Webb's book, 1823

PLUM SAUCE (1)

4 *lb plums or damsons*
½ *lb onions*
1 *pint vinegar*
1 *oz salt*

½ *oz each of ginger, allspice,*
nutmeg and mustard
8 *oz sugar*

Cut up plums and onions and cook with vinegar, salt and spices for 30 minutes. Sieve, stir in sugar and bring to the boil. Simmer for 1 hour, stirring occasionally, and bottle while still warm. This is a good way of using up windfalls, or a mixture of odd plums and damsons which are not good enough for table sauce.

PLUM SAUCE (2)

2 *lb cooking plums*
½ *lb sugar*
1 *pint vinegar*
1 *heaped teaspoon salt*

¼ *oz bruised ginger*
8 *cloves*
½ *teaspoon Cayenne pepper*

Boil for 30 minutes, sieve and bottle.

STORE SAUCE

For a cheap, tasty sauce, Hampshire housewives save spiced vinegar for the pickle jars. Onions, mixed pickles, gherkins, walnuts can all be turned to account. When a quart or thereabouts is available, chop up 1 onion, 3 apples, 3 tomatoes. Bring these ingredients to boil in the vinegar and simmer till contents of pan are a thin purée. Sieve and bottle.

THIN SAUCE

This goes well with grills and fish. To 1 pint vinegar allow 1 tablespoon sugar, ½ teaspoon treacle, 1 dessertspoon flour, 1 teaspoon each mustard and salt, 3 oz pickling spice. Bring vinegar and spices to boil. Mix remainder of ingredients to smooth paste with a little of the vinegar (cold) and then boil all ingredients for 20 minutes. Strain and bottle.

TARRAGON VINEGAR

Pick leaves as soon as the flower-buds appear on the plant, but before they begin to open. Pack a jar full of leaves and fill with white wine vinegar. Cover, and leave to infuse for at least 2 weeks. Strain, and pour into bottles. Put a branch of tarragon in each bottle. Basil, burnet, marjoram, mint and mixed herbs may be used.

GARLIC VINEGAR

Crush 8 cloves of garlic with salt. Bring 1 pint of vinegar to boiling point, and pour over. Put in jars, cool, cover, and strain after 2 or 3 weeks. Bottle.

SPICED VINEGAR

Crush or ground 1 oz each of mixed allspice, celery seed, mustard seed, cloves, black pepper and 1 oz of whole ginger, 2 or 3 dried chillies, 6 cloves of garlic. Sugar ($\frac{3}{4}$ lb) may be added for improvement though not essential. Heat all together to boiling point in 1 gallon of vinegar, and simmer for 10 minutes. After 3 or 4 weeks strain and bottle.

GOOSEBERRY VINEGAR

Having Bruised some ripe Goosebury add 3 Quarts of Water that has been Boild and coold to 1 Quart of Fruit and let it stand a day then strain it through a Flannel Bag. put 1 lb of Course Sugar to Gallon of Liquor. Stir it well together and let it stand for serverall months till it be fit for use it will Improve by Keeping and is good for Pickling.

Joseph Webb's book, 1823

RASPBERRY VINEGAR

To each lb of ripe fruit allow 1 pint of good vinegar. Pick over the raspberries, cover them with vinegar and allow to stand for 4 days. Strain through a nylon sieve, not pressing the fruit. To each pint of strained vinegar add 4–5 oz sugar. Simmer gently for 10 minutes and bottle.

JELLIED BEETROOT

Small boiled beetroot   **1 pint vinegar**
1 raspberry jelly

Boil the beetroot carefully to avoid 'bleeding'. When cool enough to handle, cut up and place in screwtop jars. Melt jelly in boiling vinegar and pour over the beetroot. Store in the dark, covering inside of screwtops with waxed paper, and making sure the beetroot is completely covered with vinegar and jelly.

31 Bottling and Preserving

> *What wondrous life is this I lead !*
> *Ripe apples drop about my head;*
> *The luscious clusters of the vine*
> *Upon my mouth do crush their wine;*
> *The nectarine and luscious peach*
> *Into my hands themselves do reach;*
> *Stumbling on melons, as I pass,*
> *Ensnared with flowers, I fall on grass.*
>
> *Andrew Marvell*

BOTTLING: GRANDMA'S WAY

Here are four methods of preserving fruit in ordinary jam jars.

1. Using pig's bladder drawn tightly over jars.
2. Melted mutton fat (this hardens like cement).
3. Layers of paper painted with flour paste.
4. Paper covers dipped in candle-wax melted down from ends.

Here is the old-fashioned way of sterilising the fruit:
Choose ripe, but firm fruit. Warm jars upside down in oven on newspaper.

Remove one at a time, fill with fruit, and replace in oven for about an hour, covering each jar with a patty-pan to prevent the top fruits getting scorched.

The fruit will shrink, so using one jar as a filler, shake fruit from this 1 into each of the others to bring level of fruit up to rim of jar. Now, 1 jar at a time, fill jars just to overflowing (stand on newspaper) with boiling syrup made from water and sugar—a quart of water to 8 oz sugar if you can spare it.

You can use just water, but you'll find that fruit bottled with even a slightly sweetened syrup takes far less sugar when needed for cooking.

Using one of the four methods above, cover the jars immediately. Tie bladder firmly down with string, or if you use melted mutton fat pour this on to the fruit and cover with greaseproof or brown paper.

If you use the flour and water paste method paint a circle of greaseproof with paste to lap over the jar rim to 1 inch below. Paint again with paste, then cover with a circle of newspaper. Finally, cover with a last circle of plain brown paper and tie down firmly with string.

Store your jars on open shelves in a cool, dry place, *and take great care not to tip them.*

PRESERVING: OVEN METHOD

1. Wash and drain the jars and lids.
2. Pack tightly with the prepared fruit to the top of the jar.
3. Place in a very slow oven on a piece of cardboard or several thicknesses of paper. The jars should be covered with the lids, to prevent the fruit from charring.
4. Leave in the oven about $\frac{3}{4}$ to 1 hour until the fruit appears cooked and has shrunk a little. Whole tomatoes take $1\frac{1}{2}$ hours. This method is not recommended for sliced tomatoes.
5. Remove the jars one at a time, place them on a mat or folded newspaper and cover the fruit with boiling water. Tomatoes require salted boiling water; use 1 teaspoon salt to 1 quart water and a little sugar, $\frac{1}{4}$ oz, may be added to the brine if desired.
6. Seal immediately with rubber ring, lid and clip or screw-band. As the jars cool, the screw-bands will need further tightening.
7. Test next day. Remove the screw-band or clip; if the seal is perfect it should be possible to lift the jar by the lid. If the lid comes off, the seal is imperfect and the fruit should be eaten within a few days or re-sterilised. Store in a cool, dark place. Remove screw-band or clip which may rust if left on the jar. Grease and store them for future use.

TOMATOES IN THEIR OWN JUICE

Follow oven method. Press the tomatoes, cut in halves, well down in the jar, sprinkling salt on each layer, 1 teaspoon of salt to 2 lb tomatoes, but add no liquid. A teaspoon of sugar to 2 lb tomatoes improves the flavour. Cover with lid and leave in the oven $1-1\frac{1}{2}$ hours until the juice in the jar simmers. Remove one at a time and seal immediately.

The Oven Method is not as satisfactory for Apples, Pears and Quinces, as Preserving in a Deep Pan.

PRESERVING IN A DEEP PAN

1. Wash and drain the jars and lids.
2. Pack the jars tightly with the prepared fruit. Apples and pears should be peeled with a stainless knife and put immediately into brine; use 1 teaspoon of salt to 1 pint of water and pack into the jars after rinsing.

   Shake soft, juicy fruits down; for hard fruits the handle of a wooden spoon is useful for arranging the fruit in layers and for packing tightly. Pack the fruit almost to the top of the jar.
3. Cover the fruit with cold water, filling the jars to overflowing. Add no water to tomatoes in own juice.
4. When the screw-band is used it should be given a half-turn back to allow for expansion.
5. Put some straw, newspaper, or cloth in the bottom of a deep pan or steriliser; place in the jars and completely cover with cold water. A large fish kettle, bucket or any container which is deep enough can be used. The jars should not touch each other or the sides of the container.
6. Bring the water slowly to simmering point. This should take $1\frac{1}{2}$ hours, then maintain at this temperature for 15 minutes. Pears and tomatoes require 30 minutes.
7. Remove the jars one at a time from the steriliser; place on a wooden table or board and tighten the screw-bands. As the jars cool, the screw-band will need further tightening.
8. Test the next day. Remove the screw-band; if the seal is perfect it should be possible to lift the jar by the lid. If the lid comes off, the seal is imperfect and the fruit should be eaten within a few days or re-sterilised. Store in a cool, dark place. Remove the screw-band which may rust if left on the jar. Grease and store them for future use.

PULPING

This is a simple way of bottling stewed fruit, whether soft or hard. Wind-fall apples or bruised plums can be bottled by this method if all the bruised parts are removed first. Apples and pears should be peeled with a stainless knife and put immediately into brine; use 1 teaspoon salt to 1 pint water.

1. Stew the fruit in a little water until thoroughly pulped, only enough water is needed to prevent the pan from burning. About 30 minutes' stewing is needed for soft fruit, longer for hard-textured fruit. Tomatoes should be stewed with seasoning; use $\frac{1}{2}$ teaspoon salt to 1 lb tomatoes, and about $\frac{1}{2}$ teaspoon of sugar.

2. Pour at once into hot, clean jars.

3. Seal immediately and when screw-band is used, give a half-turn back to allow for expansion.

4. Place the jars in a pan of hot water on a false bottom of straw, newspaper or cloth, bring to the boil and boil 5 minutes. Tomatoes should remain in the boiling water 15 minutes. The jars should be completely covered with water.

5. Remove, then tighten screw-band. As the jars cool, the screw-bands will need further tightening.

6. Test next day. Remove screw-band; if the seal is perfect it should be possible to lift the jar by the lid. If the lid comes off, the seal is imperfect, and the fruit should be eaten within a few days or re-sterilised. Store in a cool, dark place. Remove the screw-band which may rust if left on the jar. Grease and store them for future use.

USING CAMPDEN TABLETS

This method is suitable for most stone and soft fruits, provided the fruit is sound and not over-ripe.

Fruits not recommended to be preserved by this method are: Blackberries, cherries, pears, dessert apples, blackcurrants, gooseberries and tomatoes.

1. Dissolve the tablets in cold or tepid water, allowing 1 tablet to each $\frac{1}{2}$ pint water.

2. Pack the fruit in the jars, do not pack too tightly.

3. Pour in the solution until the fruit is entirely covered. At least $\frac{1}{2}$ pint of solution must be used for each lb of fruit and sometimes more is necessary.

4. Seal at once with screw-band. If metal covers are used, the metal must be protected by 2 or 3 layers of paper fitted into the lid or by smearing the inside of the lid with vaseline.

5. This method does not produce a vacuum, so it is not possible to test after sealing.

The fruit can be used for stewing, in puddings, pies, or for jam making. The fruit should be poured into an open pan and heated until there is no further smell of sulphur. If difficulty is experienced in getting rid of sulphur fumes in the case of plums, remove stones first. Do not throw away the liquid as this contains some of the fruit juices, sugar and protective substances.

N.B. Vegetables should not be bottled by any of these methods

PULPED TOMATOES

1 *lb tomatoes*   **1 *dessertspoon vinegar***
2 *teaspoons sugar*   **Dash of pepper**
1 *small teaspoon salt*

Melt in saucepan a small piece of cooking fat (not margarine). Skin tomatoes by immersing in boiling water; they then peel easily. Put in saucepan, cook until soft pulp; keep stirring, add sugar, salt, pepper and lastly vinegar. Bring to boil, boil 2 minutes. Place pulp in previously heated jars, fill right up to top and close down quickly with vacuum closures.

Now sterilise by placing jars in saucepan with newspaper in bottom of pan, just covering bottom to avoid a possible crack. Cover jars entirely with cold water and put lid on. Bring slowly to boil, then boil exactly 10 minutes.

PEASANTS' RUNNER BEANS

Fill a stone jar $\frac{4}{5}$ full with stringed beans. You may string and slice them if they are coarse or put in whole. Fill with brine made as follows: bring to boil a sufficient amount of water to cover beans. This will depend on size of jar. For every quart of water allow $6\frac{1}{2}$ oz of brick salt. As soon as it has come to boil, withdraw from heat, allow to cool, then pour over beans packed in jar. See that brine completely covers the beans. Cover well with several thicknesses of brown paper. Tie with string and keep in dark place. To cook beans, wash well in cold water and cook like fresh ones.

TO BOTTLE APPLES AND PEARS

Peel, core and slice the fruit. To prevent discoloration, put the peeled fruit into cold salted water (2 oz salt to 1 gallon), during preparation. Rinse quickly before packing into clean warm jars. Fill up with syrup (6 oz sugar to 1 pint water), fit rubber rings which you have previously soaked in cold water for 15 minutes. Fit screw bands, loosen by one *half turn*, then sterilise. To sterilise, put the bottles into a pan of cold water, bring slowly to simmering point and maintain at this 15–20 minutes. Take out and tighten screw band, test next day for seal.

Apple pulp may also be put into preserving jars, which are then put into a pan of cold water, brought slowly to simmering point maintained for 25 minutes. Apple slices may be preserved in the same way in a syrup of 6 oz sugar to 1 pint water. Pears are always better bottled in syrup, and the best varieties to bottle are good dessert pears which are fully ripe.

GINGER APPLES

Pare, quarter, core and cut enough apples into small squares to give 1 quart. Grate the rind from 1 lemon. Bring 2 cups water to boil. Add 2 cups brown sugar. Stir till sugar has dissolved, then add the juice of the lemon and bring again to boil. Boil until clear for about 5 minutes. Add the lemon rind, 6 pieces of ginger root and apple squares. Stir carefully till boiling, then boil for 2 hours, or longer, if necessary, until the mixture is thick and brown. Pour into sterilised jars and cover.

PRESERVED APPLES

Weigh equal quantities of good brown sugar and of apples. Peel, core and mince them small. Boil the sugar, allowing to every 3 lbs 1 pint of water. Skim it well and boil it pretty thick, then add the apples, the grated peel of 1 or 2 lemons or pieces of white ginger, boil till the apples fall and look clear and yellow.

Lewis' Mother's Cookbook, Mary Horrell, Exeter

BLACKBERRY AND APPLE PURÉE

Blackberries   **Sugar**
Apples

Wash blackberries and put over a low heat to extract juice. Strain the juice and measure liquid. Peel and core apples and cut into slices, and allow 4 lb apples to each pint of blackberry juice. Cook to a pulp, then add 12 oz sugar. Boil together, then put quickly into hot preserving jars and seal down. This purée is very useful for pies and puddings.

SPICED CRAB APPLES

4 lb sugar	**4 lb crab apples**
6 cups water	**¾ teaspoon whole cloves**
2 tablespoons lemon juice	**¾ stick cinnamon**

Place the sugar, water and lemon juice in a preserving pan. Stir over low heat till sugar has dissolved, then heat till boiling. Wash apples, cut into quarters, remove stems and cores. Add to syrup with spices tied in a small muslin bag. Stir occasionally till boiling, then stir till clear and tender. Remove spices, pour apples and syrup into clean hot jars and seal.

TO BOTTLE GOOSEBERRYS

To every Bottle of Goosberys put Six ounces of Loaf Sugar in powder. Tie a Bladder over the mouth of the Bottle and put them in cold water over the fire in the usual way till the Sugar is melted. Then take them out and put them they will not require a Cork.
Damsons done the same way are Beautifull

Joseph Webb's book, 1823

GINGER PEARS

8 lb pears
4 lb preserving sugar

4 oz stem ginger
4 medium-sized lemons

Pare, quarter and core pears and remove the stems. Cut quarters into small slices, add sugar, chopped ginger and the strained juice of the lemons. Cut lemon rind into long thin strips, add to fruit and mix. Cover and stand in a cool place overnight. Stir over moderate heat till sugar has dissolved, then bring quickly to boil. Cook very slowly for 3 hours till clear and thick. Pour into jars and cover.

BRANDIED PEARS

6 lb hard windfall pears
3 lemons
8 cloves

4½ lb granulated sugar
About 4 inch cinnamon stick
6 tablespoons brandy

Peel the pears, quarter them and take out the cores. Grate the rind off the lemons and squeeze out the juice. Layer the pears, sugar and lemon rind in a large bowl and sprinkle the lemon juice over the top. Cover the bowl and leave overnight.

Transfer the pears to a large casserole, covering them with the juice which has formed during the night. Add cinnamon and cloves. Cover with a lid and bake in a slow oven, 275°F (Gas Mark 1) for 6 hours until the pears are tender and are a golden amber colour.

Leave the casserole to cool, then stir in the brandy. Remove the cinnamon stick and cloves, and transfer the pears to jars, screwing them down for storing.

STEWED PEARS

Peel the pears and put them into cold water. To every lb of pears, add ½ lb of sugar, add cinnamon and cloves. To a dozen lb of pears add the rind of 3 lemons and sufficient water to keep them from burning. Stew them gently until quite soft. When done, add the juice of the lemons and 3 or 4 glasses of port wine. Tie them down tightly and they will keep for years.

Lewis' Mother's Cookbook, Mary Horrell, Exeter

SQUIFFY PRUNES

Cover the best prunes available with a port-type wine and seal down. After some weeks they are excellent. They make an ideal dessert after a good meal, if handed round in a dish with cocktail sticks to spear them. The liquid becomes really good and can be drunk as a dessert wine.

PRESERVED QUINCES

5 lb quinces   *3 lb sugar*
4 cups cold water

Peel, quarter and core quinces dropping each quarter into cold water to prevent discoloration. Cook the peelings and cores in boiling water to cover for 15 minutes, then strain off the liquid. Add quinces to liquid and cook slowly till tender. Remove quinces to a basin with a perforated spoon so that liquid can run back into pan. Add 3 lb sugar. Stir till dissolved, then bring quickly to boil. Add quince quarters, cook until clear, turn into heated jars and cover.

STEWED RASPBERRIES

Dreary, but if you want to bottle them for winter puddings, try mixing equal quantities of raspberries, currants and gooseberries in the jars— the flavour is excellent.

FRUIT MEDLEY

Use a few late strawberries or raspberries, 1 odd peach, a couple of Victoria plums. Keep in the refrigerator a preserving jar ⅔ full of cheap brandy. Add the fruit as you wish and use fruit and brandy together to enliven a fruit salad or pudding. It will keep for weeks.

EVERLASTING RUMPOT

1 bottle light or dark rum
Granulated sugar
Strawberries, cherries,

apricots, raspberries, plums,
redcurrants, peaches, grapes,
melon

The fruit should be sound, whole and ripe. The rumpot should not be overloaded with fruit and it is best to preserve a little at a time, using only the choicest fruits. Citrus fruits, apples, bananas and pears should not be used. Gently wipe the fruit, and do not peel or stone (except for melon which should be peeled, seeded and cut into large chunks). Put fruit into a large stone crock with its own weight of sugar, and cover with rum. Cover crock tightly with waxed paper and a lid and keep in a cool place. Continue adding fruit to the rumpot throughout the season. The fruit and syrup may be used in small quantities as required:

a) eat fruit as it is, or with cream or yoghurt;
b) add to fresh fruit salad with oranges, apples, nuts;
c) remove top of a melon, pierce flesh with a knitting needle, and fill 'case' with fruit and syrup. Serve chilled;
d) drain fruit, put into pastry case and top with whipped cream.

FRUIT SYRUPS

Make fruit syrups to use as a basis for winter fruit drinks, to serve as sauces for puddings, or to flavour mousses and ices. The usual problem is with sterilising and storage, since bottles tend to burst. The best ones to use are the lever-stoppered type with a china cap and rubber washer; second choice is the traditional sauce bottle with screw cap. Syrups should be stored in a cool dark place, or colours will fade, though a little vegetable colouring may be used for a more attractive appearance.

Latest answer to the storage problem is to use the freezer. Make the syrup in the usual way, cool, and pour into containers, leaving room for expansion, then freeze. Even better is to pour the syrup into ice-cube trays, freeze, then wrap each cube in foil, and put them together in labelled transparent bags. Each cube will be enough for 1 portion, to dilute with water.

Mixed fruit syrups

Syrups can be made from raspberries, strawberries, elderberries, blackberries, loganberries, and blackcurrants, or a mixture of fruit. Use clean ripe fruit, and avoid washing if possible. Add a little water to the fruit (about $\frac{1}{4}$ pint to 3 lb raspberries or strawberries, but $\frac{1}{2}$ pint to the same amount of blackcurrants). Cook gently for about an hour, crushing the fruit at intervals. Drain through a jellybag overnight, then measure and add $\frac{3}{4}$ lb sugar to each pint of juice. Stir until dissolved. Strain and pour into bottles, or into freezing containers. Make sure the bottles are securely topped and tied down.

Stand the bottles in a steriliser and fill with cold water to cover. Heat slowly so that the water reaches 175°F (simmering point) in an hour. Continue at this temperature for 30 minutes, remove bottles, cool, label and store.

Muscat Syrup

A delectable syrup, to make when gooseberries and elderflowers coincide, can be used for flavouring fruit cups with its scented muscat flavour. Use 3 lb gooseberries with 1 pint water cooked till soft, then add $2\frac{3}{4}$ lb sugar and bring to the boil. Infuse 8 elderflower heads for 10 minutes, strain through muslin, bottle and sterilise. The gooseberries can be used for a purée or fool.

RASPBERRY SYRUP FOR WINTER DRINKS

Squeeze fresh raspberries through double muslin, and add to every pint of juice a syrup made from 1 pint water and 1 lb sugar. Boil the mixture, then simmer for an hour, and when cold bottle and cork down, or put into preserving jars, and sterilise; this makes a delicious drink with water or soda water, or can be used to flavour winter puddings, or to use on sponge puddings.

FRUIT CORDIALS

These can be made from many fruits and form the basis of summer drinks or winter cures. The most suitable fruits are blackberries, blackcurrants, loganberries, raspberries and strawberries. This is the basic method. Put the fruit into a large earthenware basin and break it up with a wooden spoon, no water need be added, except to blackberries and blackcurrants. For these, add just enough water to start the flow of juice. Put the basin of fruit over a pan of hot water on the stove. Keep the water in the bottom pan on the boil, crush the fruit occasionally. When all the juice has been extracted put the fruit into a double muslin bag and leave to strain overnight.

Add $\frac{3}{4}$ lb sugar to each pint of juice and stir till thoroughly dissolved. Strain again into clean bottles, filling to within 1 inch of the top of the bottle. Cork securely, using new corks each year. Secure the corks with string, then sterilise. Put the bottles into a pan of cold water. The water must reach to within an inch of the top of the bottles. Bring the water to the boil and simmer for 20 minutes. Dip the corks in melted paraffin wax, and store the bottles in a cool dark place.

CHERRY BRANDY

Well worth the trouble and expense. To each lb of Morella cherries allow 4 oz sugar-candy, $\frac{1}{4}$ oz shredded bitter almonds and $\frac{1}{2}$ inch cinnamon stick. Prick the cherries all over and pack into jars with other ingredients. Fill the jars to the top with brandy. After 6 months, or better still a year, drain off liquid. Use cherries for puddings.

32 Storing and Drying

Season of mists and mellow fruitfulness,
Close bosom-friend of the maturing sun;
Conspiring with him how to load and bless
With fruit the vines that round the thatch-eaves run;
To bend with apples the moss'd cottage trees,
And fill all fruit with ripeness to the core;
To swell the gourd, and plump the hazel shells
With a sweet kernel.

John Keats

Let lay them dark as wind may come not near
And do fair straw upon them, crates them under
Or in heaps them save, a little space asonder,
And these heaps must ye now and now divide
Yet hath a third for them a fresh devise
Only their little feet to close in clay
And on a floor bestroon with chaff to lay
And others dip their little feet in pitch all warme
And so in order lay them on the table.

'Preserving Apples', Palladius

STORING VEGETABLES

Beetroot   Cover with straw, or put into a trench like potatoes, or into box covered with sand in a shed.

Carrots   Lift by mid-November and store in a cool shed in boxes raised above ground level.

Parsnips   Leave in ground, or store under a straw cover in a cool place.

Potatoes   Store in bags indoors. If you have a lot of potatoes, put them into a 3-foot wide trench, about 6 inches deep. Pile in the potatoes in a triangular heap about 3 feet high. Cover with straw and earth, leaving a little straw at the top so that moisture escapes.

Turnips   Put turnips into a trench like potatoes, or put into a big heap covered with straw or sand.

STORING FRUIT

Apples and Pears   As a general rule it is the apples which ripen latest which store best. An apple is ripe when it falls easily into the hand if lifted gently on its stalk. Do not put into store immediately after picking. Let the apples cool and sweat in an airy place before storing. The store should be dark, cool and very slightly moist.

Keep separate different varieties with varying keeping qualities. Store in trays in a frostproof shed, cellar or attic. Greengrocers' boxes, which can be stacked with space between, make useful trays. Special eating apples can be wrapped individually in sheets of newspaper and stored in boxes. Pears tend to ripen suddenly. Inspect fruit regularly and remove unsound fruit.

Marrows and Pumpkins   Store in a cool dry place away from frost.

Quinces   Store on shelves and trays like apples.

Another Way with Marrows. Vegetable marrows may be kept for months by cutting them when they are ripe, but not old, and leaving on plenty of stalk, and if the end of the stalk can be sealed with wax so much the better, though this is not absolutely necessary. Then tie a piece of tape, or something that will not cut the skin, round each end of the marrow, and loop the 2 together so that it can be hung up in a dry, cool place.

A STOCKINGFUL OF ONIONS

Leave outside to dry for a week or 2. Remove the tops and any loose skin and soil, pop them into an old nylon stocking and knot the top when it is full.

KEEPING GRAPES

Cut the bunches with a long stalk and a piece of stem, and stand them in tall jars in a cool larder with the grapes themselves supported if necessary. Put charcoal in the water and leave undisturbed. Keep for 6 weeks.

TO STORE FRESH LEMONS

Choose perfect fruit and pack it in layers in a wooden box with a lid. Separate lemons from each other and from the box by a good layer of silver sand. If the box is stored in a cool, dry place the lemons will keep for about 3 months.

STORING NUTS

Take off any outer husks—scrub walnuts and almonds—and leave to dry in a warm place. Chestnuts and walnuts can be packed in a crock with salt or dry sand between each layer. Small nuts can be packed in jars with a layer of cooking salt over the top and stored in a cool, dark place. Nuts to be used for cooking can be shelled, dried on a baking shelf in a cool oven, and packed into clean, glass jars.

FREEZING NUTS

Nuts kept in the freezer will be moist and fresh. They can be frozen whole, chopped, slivered or buttered and toasted, but they should not be salted. Small containers, foil or polythene bags can be used for packing, and nuts will keep for a year (4 months if buttered and toasted). To use, thaw at room temperature in wrappings for 3 hours.

DRYING FRUIT AND VEGETABLES

Drying is the oldest method of preservation. Suitable for drying are apples, dessert pears, grapes, sweet plums, peas, beans, onions, leeks and mushrooms. They can be dried in the oven, a warm cupboard or a rack over the stove, in a constant gentle heat with a current of air to carry away moisture (this is best obtained by leaving cupboard or oven door slightly open). Heat may be used after a baking session. Food should be spread on oven racks or wire cake trays spread with muslin, which should be scaled before use, or it may scorch during drying. The ideal heat for drying is between 120°F–150°F as the fruit or vegetables should be dried, not cooked or scorched.

APPLE RINGS AND PEARS

This is a useful way to keep apples if the freezer is full, or there is not the time or equipment for bottling. Pears can be dried, but the juicy varieties are rather difficult to handle.

Apples should be ripe but not over-ripe. Using a silver or stainless steel knife, peel and core the apples and cut into rings about ¼ inch thick. Put into a basin of salt water immediately (½ oz salt to 1 quart water) and leave for 10 minutes. The rings should be threaded on a stick which can rest on the runners of an oven, and the rings should not touch each other. Dry at 150°F, for some hours. Apples should be like dry chamois leather, moist and pliable. Cool in the air before packing tightly in paper bags, or in dry jars or tins. Store in a dry, dark place.

It is best to soak fruit for 24 hours before cooking, and to use the soaking water for cooking, flavoured with a little lemon or vanilla, a clove or a piece of ginger.

DRIED GRAPES

Use fresh, fully ripe fruit, to be dried whole. Spread out in a single layer, and test by squeezing. When they are dried, no moisture will appear; a lb of fresh fruit will give about 4 oz dried.

DRIED PLUMS

You can dry plums, too. They must be ripe. Halve and stone them. Stretch muslin on sticks to replace open shelves, and dry plums on these. Dry slowly, as for apples. Plums can also be dried whole.

DRIED BEANS

Leave haricot beans on the plants until dry and withered. Pull up plants and hang in an airy shed. Shell the peas and store as for seed. Young French and runner beans may be sliced, blanched for 5 minutes, drained, and dried in a thin layer.

DRIED MUSHROOMS

These dry very readily. Cut the stalks off short and peel. Lay them on the oven racks and when they are dried quite stiff, store them away. When preparing them for use soak them in water and simmer them in a little stock.

DRIED ONIONS AND LEEKS

These well repay drying, as so often they do not keep, so that when onions are showing signs of growing out or rotting, you know quite well it will not be long before they will all be gone. Peel them and take away any bad parts, and slice them on to muslin on oven racks. Leeks may be cut in strips lengthwise if preferred. Keep them moving about occasionally to help the drying, and when they are quite crisp take them out, and after a little while store them away.

DRIED PEAS

Leave marrowfat varieties on the plants until dry and withered. Pull up plants and hang in an airy shed. Shell the peas and store as for seed. For young, sugary peas, blanch them for 5 minutes, drain them and shake off excess moisture. Spread out in a thin layer and dry very carefully, without scorching.

33 *Candied Fruit and Crystallised Flowers*

Here you have that which in itself is good
Made better by the storing of it.

Fuller

CANDIED FRUIT

Try this with cherries, oranges, pears, pineapple and stone fruits. Canned fruits are very good, and easy to process.

Good quality fresh fruit should be gently cooked in water until just tender before processing. Canned fruit should be drained from its syrup. Fresh fruit should be processed with a syrup made from $\frac{1}{2}$ pint water and 6 oz sugar to each lb fruit. When using canned fruit, allow 1 lb fruit to $\frac{1}{2}$ pint liquid from the canning syrup and any necessary water.

Heat the syrup and use it to cover the fruit completely, keeping the fruit submerged with a saucer over the liquid if necessary. Leave to stand for 24 hours. Drain off the syrup, add 2 oz sugar and dissolve. Boil and pour over the fruit. Repeat this process twice more, adding 2 oz sugar each time. On the fifth day, add 3 oz sugar, and boil fruit for 4 minutes. Leave for 2 days. Repeat the process and leave the fruit to soak for 4 days. Drain off the syrup and put the fruit on a wire rack (such as a cake rack) to drain and finish off in a very cool oven or a warm airing cupboard for about 3 days. Store in boxes with waxed paper in a cool, dark dry place.

QUICK ORANGE PEEL

Peel of 3 oranges　　　　　*1 teaspoon water*
1 teacup loaf sugar　　　　*Granulated sugar*

Cut peel in sections, cover with water, boil until white pith can be scraped off with spoon. Make syrup of loaf sugar and water. Cook peel in this until transparent, when it will have absorbed nearly all the syrup. Lift with fork, roll in granulated sugar. Leave on wire tray until cool and dry. Store in airtight glass jar.

ORANGE POWDER

Remove as much pith from orange rind as you can, wash rind, dry slowly in cool oven. When quite crisp, break up in pieces and roll out until very fine. Put through a sieve. Store in tin in dry place. Delicious for cakes and puddings, and a little goes a long way. It does not lose its strength by keeping.

ORANGE PEEL SYRUP

Cut off as much pith as possible from orange peel. Put peel through a mincer or grate on grater. Place a layer of grated peel in a clean screw-top jar. Sprinkle a tablespoon of sugar on peel. Put in layers of peel and sugar till jar is filled. Screw down top tightly and leave for several weeks. Shake every few days. This will make a delicious syrup and flavouring for cakes, puddings and sauces. It sweetens as well as flavours.

ORANGE PEEL PRESERVE

The orange peel can be used to flavour cakes or puddings, but the longer it is kept the richer it becomes. One jar saved for a year matured a rich brown in colour and was as delicious as sweetmeat.

Wipe skins, chop finely or mince. Cover bottom of small jar with layer about $\frac{1}{2}$ inch thick, sprinkle with teaspoon sugar. Fill jar with layers. Fix top, shake well. During first week shake daily (this is important), and if jar is well sealed stand occasionally upside down, as top layers lose moisture. As the preserve sinks down, more peel and sugar can be added. If peel is very dry, add a little more sugar and a very small quantity of water. Use and replenish at any time.

KITTY FURZE'S WAY TO DRY ORANGE PEEL AND PRESERVE

Cut up peel and cover with cold water, 1 tablespoon salt. Soak overnight (or longer if you wish to collect over a day or 2). Drain, cover again with cold water, bring to boil for $\frac{1}{2}$ hour, cover with hot water, boil until tender ($\frac{3}{4}$ hour). Drain and measure and to each cup of peel add $\frac{3}{4}$ cup of sugar, return to saucepan with sugar and water and simmer until sugar is nearly gone. Store in jars covering with syrup.

Lewis' Mother's Cookbook, Mary Horrell, Exeter

CANDIED APRICOTS

4 lb just-ripe apricots   **1 pint water**
4 lb sugar

Cut the skin carefully at the top of each apricot and squeeze out the stones. Make a syrup with sugar and water and when it starts to thicken, add the apricots and bring to the boil. Remove from heat, then bring to the boil again. Do this 3 more times, then pour fruit and syrup into a bowl and leave overnight. On the next day heat the syrup and fruit and boil for 1 minute. Drain the fruit and put into a bowl. Boil the syrup and pour over the fruit. Leave overnight. Repeat this process twice more until the apricots are saturated and the syrup has been absorbed. Place apricots on a rack covered with paper and dry in the sun or in an open oven, turning the fruit occasionally. When dry, store in a tin or wooden box.

CANDIED CHERRIES

2 lb firm black cherries   **1 pint water**
2 lb sugar

The cherries should be weighed after stoning. Dissolve the sugar in the water over a low heat without boiling. When the syrup is clear, put in the cherries. Simmer very gently until the cherries are almost transparent. Drain the fruit and put on flat trays. Dry thoroughly in the sun or in a very cool oven with the door slightly open. Dust with icing sugar containing a pinch of bicarbonate of soda and store in a box with waxed paper layers.

SUGARED FRUITS

Use perfect fruits, ripe but not soft. Wash, cut each in half, stone. Prepare syrup by combining $\frac{1}{2}$ cup golden syrup, 2 cups sugar, 1 cup water. Bring to boil, stirring only until sugar is dissolved. Cook to 290°F or until syrup becomes brittle when dropped in cold water. Lower the prepared fruit pieces into syrup. Cook 5 minutes. Remove from heat, carefully skim out fruits, allowing to dry and cool on greaseproof paper.

CANDIED MARROW

2 lb ripe marrow flesh   **10 Cayenne pods**
2 lb sugar   **2 lemons**
1 oz root ginger

Cut the marrow into neat cubes. Cover with water and leave for 12 hours. Strain and mix with sugar and leave for 12 hours. Tie bruised root ginger, cayenne pods and the grated rind of the lemons into a muslin bag. Heat the marrow with the sugar and lemon juice until the sugar has dissolved. Put in the muslin bag, and simmer until the marrow is clear and the syrup is thick. Pour into a covered bowl and leave for 7 days. Strain off the syrup and put marrow on waxed paper on a wire rack in a warm place to dry. Roll cubes in castor sugar containing a pinch of bicarbonate of soda and cream of tartar.

CRYSTALLISED FLOWERS

Primroses, violets, polyanthus, roses, carnation petals, forget-me-nots, mimosa, cowslips, sweet peas, fruit blossoms are suitable for crystallising. Flowers which come from bulbs should not be eaten.
The flowers should be crystallised in a solution of gum Arabic crystals and rose or orange flower water. Allow 3 teaspoons crystals to 3 tablespoons rose water, and leave in a screwtop jar for 2 or 3 days, shaking sometimes, until the mixture is a sticky glue. A small soft paint brush is needed to paint the flowers. Large flowers should be taken apart and the petals reassembled when needed. The petals must be completely coated, or bare spots will shrivel and not keep. A little vegetable colouring may be added to the solution, but this must be very delicate to remain natural. When the flowers have been sugared, they should be dried for about 24 hours until crisp and dry. They are best stored in the dark.

CRYSTALLISED ANGELICA

Select young stems and stalks of angelica in April. Cut into 4 or 5 inch lengths and place in a glass or crockery vessel, pour over them a boiling solution of 1 pint water and $\frac{1}{4}$ lb salt. Cover and leave for 24 hours. Lift out, drain on a wire drainer, peel and wash in cold water.
Make a syrup of $1\frac{1}{2}$ lb sugar and $1\frac{1}{2}$ pints water and boil for 10 minutes.

Place the angelica in the boiling syrup for 20 minutes; lift out and drain for 4 days on a wire drainer.

Reboil again for 20 minutes in the same syrup. Allow to cool in the syrup, lift out and drain for 3 or 4 days.

Strew well with sugar and store in airtight jars.

CANDIED COWSLIPS

10 oz yellow cowslip 'pips'   *8 oz sugar*

This recipe was first used in 1700. The flowers should be gathered when the dew is off, and only the yellow blossoms should be used. Dissolve the sugar in as little hot water as possible which will absorb the sugar (about 4 fluid ozs). Bring to the boil and cook until the syrup starts to candy. Take off the heat and shake in the flowers gradually. Stir until the flowers become dry and sugary. Store in jars sealed with sticky tape.

CRYSTALLISED MINT LEAVES

Fresh mint leaves   *Granulated sugar*
Egg white

Use fresh green mint and well-shaped leaves. Beat egg white stiffly and coat both sides of the leaves. Coat with sugar and put on a wire rack covered with wax paper. Stand on the rack of a cooker until dry. Store in a tin between layers of waxed paper.

34 Food for Festivals

Turkeys, geese, game, poultry, brawn, great joints of meat, sucking pigs, long wreaths of sausages, mince pies, plum-puddings, barrels of oysters, red hot chestnuts, cherry-cheeked apples, juicy oranges, luscious pears, immense twelfth-cakes, and seething bowls of punch, that made the chamber dim with their delicious steam.

'A Christmas Carol' Charles Dickens

> *'Twas at the public feast and public day,*
> *Quite full, right dull, guests hot and dishes cold;*
> *Great plenty, much formality, small cheer,*
> *And everybody out of their own sphere.*

Byron

New Year in Wales

An old lady called Mrs Birkett told Maisie Jones how they had celebrated New Year's Day in Pembrokeshire. She was born in 1872, one of nine children, and her mother was a widow. They used to go to the houses and farms of any standing to collect a sort of bun, in pillow cases, one for each member of the poor family. This was called Pice Calennig and could only be collected between 6 a.m. and noon on New Year's Day. Most of the buns were pretty dry old stuff, but some kinder folk made better buns to give away. A rockbun perhaps, as Mrs Birkett said some of them you could throw against the wall and they wouldn't break, but perhaps this was just childish talk. You had to be up early, as all poor families were entitled to the New Year Buns.

When a baby was christened in the old days, rum butter was made to celebrate the christening, and a bowl of it was hidden, often on top of the grandfather clock. The young folk of the village used to come and hunt till they found it, then they ran back to the village pub, the good lady of the inn used to spread it on bread and butter and hand it around for all to share. When all the rum butter had been used up, the empty bowl was passed round for a collection then returned as a start in life for the baby. We were talking about this old custom the other day at our 'over-sixties gathering', one old lady said when her daughter was christened she got 18 shillings, quite a sum in those days. A friend tells me this custom still continues in a few villages on the fell sides.

Mrs M. Baxter, Carlisle

CUMBERLAND RUM BUTTER

4 oz butter
¼ teaspoon grated nutmeg

8 oz soft brown sugar
½ gill rum

Cream the butter and work in the nutmeg. Gradually work in the sugar, adding a few drops of rum at a time until it is finished. When the mixture is smooth and creamy, put into small pots and cover.

Cakes were very often made for religious festivals and many of our best-known recipes originated during Lent and the Easter festival. We all know Hot Cross Buns, but Sally Lunns were Good Friday buns too. Shrewsbury Cakes and Tansy Cakes, Johnny Cakes, Popovers, Pikelets and delicious mincemeat and pastry confections called variously Cumberland Cakes, Banbury Cakes, Eccles Cakes and Hawkshead Cakes. Doughnuts were a speciality of Shrove Tuesday, made with jam or fruit, plain or heavily spiced.

The Simnel cake, now associated with Easter, was presented on Mothering Sunday, to be eaten at Easter. The early Mothering Sunday cake was made with figs, the fruit representing 'fruitfulness in offspring' and Fig Cakes dedicated to Palm Sunday are still sometimes made.

EASTER CAKES

Rub 8 oz butter into 12 oz plain flour. Add 5 oz castor sugar, 3 oz currants, $\frac{1}{2}$ teaspoon cream of tartar, $\frac{1}{4}$ teaspoon bicarbonate of soda, and a pinch of salt. Mix well together, then beat in 1 egg and mix the dough with a knife. Form into a ball and roll out $\frac{1}{8}$ inch thick on a flowered board. Cut out with a fluted cutter, and put on a greased and floured baking sheet. Bake at 350°F (Gas Mark 4) for 15 minutes, put on a wire tray to cool and sprinkle with castor sugar. These cakes should be watched carefully as they should be only delicately brown.

SHREWSBURY CAKES

These are richer than the Easter Cakes and very good. Rose water gives a very delicate flavour and may be obtained from any chemist.

Rub together 8 oz plain flour, 8 oz castor sugar, 8 oz butter, $\frac{1}{4}$ oz caraway seeds and a pinch of nutmeg. Beat together 2 small eggs with 3 dessert-spoons sherry, 3 dessertspoons rose water, and mix with the flour a little at a time, blending carefully. Roll out thinly, cut into shapes and put on greased and floured baking sheets. Prick lightly with a fork and bake at 350°F (Gas Mark 4) for 15 minutes, without allowing them to colour.

SEDGEMOOR EASTER CAKE

Rub 4 oz butter into 8 oz plain flour. Add 4 oz castor sugar, 4 oz currants, $\frac{1}{2}$ teaspoon each of mixed spice and ground cinnamon. Beat an egg with 2 tablespoons brandy and mix with the dry ingredients. Roll out $\frac{1}{2}$ inch thick, cut in rounds and bake at 350°F (Gas Mark 4) for 20 minutes.

BANBURY CAKES

Roll out some puff pastry $\frac{1}{8}$ inch thick and cut in 6 inch rounds (use a small plate as a guide). Beat 2 oz sugar and 1 oz butter to a cream, then add 1 oz fine white breadcrumbs, 4 oz currants, 2 oz mixed peel, 1 oz biscuit crumbs (2 oz ground almonds may be used instead of the bread and biscuit crumbs), $\frac{1}{2}$ egg, and a pinch of allspice. Put a spoonful of the mixture on each round of pastry. Damp half-way round each circle and draw the edges up over the filling, putting the damp edge uppermost on the other edge. Press lightly together and form into an oval shape. Turn over, flatten slightly with the hand and reshape into an oval. Brush with milk and sprinkle thickly with castor sugar. Bake at 450°F (Gas Mark 8) for 25 minutes.

PALM SUNDAY FIG CAKE

Chop 6 oz dried figs roughly and stew in just enough water to cover until tender, then leave to cool. Mix together 6 oz plain flour, $\frac{1}{2}$ teaspoon baking powder, a pinch of salt and $2\frac{1}{2}$ oz castor sugar. Rub in $2\frac{1}{2}$ oz butter and mix to a batter with the cooled figs and water. Pour into greased and floured tin and bake at 375°F (Gas Mark 5) for 45 minutes. If liked, butter icing can be used to cover the top of this cake, but it is very good eaten plain.

SIMNEL CAKE (1)

This traditional cake has a layer of almond paste on top and in the centre, but is not iced. The cake may be decorated with eggs, chickens or flowers and a wide ribbon. Prepared almond paste is easily bought and very convenient to use for this recipe. Buy two $\frac{1}{2}$ lb packets and use one for the centre and one for the top. Before the cake is made, the almond paste should be rolled into two rounds the exact size of the cake tin.

Cream together 8 oz butter and 8 oz granulated sugar till light and fluffy. Sift together 12 oz plain flour with 1 teaspoon cinnamon, 2 teaspoons baking powder and a pinch of grated nutmeg. Slowly beat 4 eggs into the creamed mixture, blending in a little of the flour mixture at the same time. When thoroughly blended, add the rest of the flour together with $1\frac{1}{2}$ lb chopped dried fruit (currants, sultanas and raisins) and 4 oz chopped candied peel. The mixture should be stiff but may be softened a little with 2 tablespoons milk. Put half the mixture into an 8 inch tin which has been buttered and lined with buttered greaseproof paper. Cover with a round of almond paste and top with the rest of the cake mixture. Bake at 325°F (Gas Mark 3) for $2\frac{1}{2}$ hours. Cool in the tin. Remove from the tin and paint the top with 2 tablespoons thin jam. Put on the second round of almond paste. Brush the paste with egg-white, sprinkle with castor sugar and put under a hot grill for a few minutes to give a granulated crystalline surface. Decorate to taste.

SIMNEL CAKE (2)

Marzipan:
1 lb ground almonds
1 lb icing sugar
½ teaspoon almond essence
1 tablespoon lemon juice
4 egg yolks

Cake:
6 oz butter
6 oz demerara sugar

3 eggs
8 oz self-raising flour
1 level teaspoon nutmeg
1 level teaspoon cinnamon
1 level teaspoon mixed spice
Pinch of salt
1 lb currants
8 oz sultanas
4 oz mixed peel
Milk to mix

Mix the marzipan ingredients to a stiff paste and knead well; divide into 3 and roll out 2 of the pieces into circles 8 inch diameter. Put aside with remaining mazipan. To make the cake, cream butter and sugar together until light and fluffy, beat in the eggs one at a time. Sieve flour, spices and salt together and add to the mixture; finally add dried fruit. If the mixture is a little stiff, add enough milk to give a dropping consistency. Put half into a greased and lined 8 inch cake tin, then put in 1 circle of marzipan and cover with remaining cake mixture. Bake at 300°F (Gas Mark 2) for 3½ hours. Allow to cool. Brush top of cake with a little warm jam, and put on second circle of marzipan, pressing down well. Make 12 small balls from the remaining marzipan and arrange these around the edge. Brush lightly with a little egg and put the cake into a hot oven or under the grill for a few seconds to glaze lightly. Fill the centre with a little white glacé icing and decorate.

HOT CROSS BUNS

8 oz plain flour
Pinch of salt
¼ teaspoon mixed spice
¼ pint milk
½ oz yeast

2 oz butter
1½ oz castor sugar
1 egg
3 oz currants
½ oz finely chopped peel

Sieve the flour, salt and spice in a mixing bowl. Warm milk to blood heat. Add yeast and butter, stir until dissolved, mix in sugar and beaten egg. Pour on to the flour, and beat with hand until smooth. Turn on to a floured board, work in the currants and peel, and knead well. Put in a buttered bowl, sprinkle with flour, cover with a clean cloth, and put in a warm place to rise for 1½ hours or until mixture has doubled its bulk. Knock down with hand and leave to rise as before for 30 minutes. Knead the dough and shape into 8 rounds. Put on 2 greased baking sheets and on each bun put a paste cross made with flour and water dough. Prove in a warm place until nearly twice the size (about 15 minutes). Bake at 425°F (Gas Mark 7) for 15 minutes. While still hot, brush with a glaze made by boiling 1 tablespoon sugar in 1 tablespoon mik

EASTER BISCUITS

3 oz butter
3 oz castor sugar
1 egg yolk
Pinch of mixed spice
6 oz plain flour
2 oz currants

½ oz candied chopped peel
Milk to mix

Glaze:
1 egg white
Castor sugar

Cream butter and sugar until light and fluffy. Add egg yolk and work in spice and flour. Add fruit and peel and enough milk to give a stiff dough. Roll out thinly on a floured board and cut into shapes with cutter. Put on to greased baking sheets and bake in a fairly hot oven, 400°F (Gas Mark 6) for 15 minutes. After 10 minutes, brush with egg white and sprinkle with castor sugar.

GRANDMA BOY'S EASTER CAKES

1 lb flour
3 oz currants
3 egg yolks
Pinch of salt

6 oz butter or margarine (or half of each)
6 oz castor sugar
Vanilla or almond flavouring

Beat butter and sugar, and add egg yolks. Sieve flour and salt together and add to mixture. Lastly add the currants. Roll out and cut into rounds. Bake in moderate oven for 15 minutes.

Mary Giles

AUNT TOMMY'S EASTER CAKES

8 oz butter
1 lb plain flour
4 oz sugar
2 oz currants

3 egg yolks
1 egg white
5 drops lemon essence
1 tablespoon brandy

Rub butter into flour and work in sugar. Add all other ingredients and mix thoroughly to a firm dough. Roll out thinly and cut in large rounds (using the top of a tumbler). Bake at 350°F (Gas Mark 4) for 15 minutes. Cool on a wire tray and sprinkle with castor sugar.

EASTER CAKE

8 *large white egg whites*
1 *teaspoon cream of tartar*
10 *oz castor sugar*
4 *oz plain flour*
¼ *teaspoon salt*
½ *teaspoon almond essence*
1 *teaspoon vanilla essence*

Filling and Icing:
Apricot jam
2 *egg yolks*
2 *tablespoons butter*
1 *tablespoon grated orange peel*
1 *lb icing sugar*
3 *tablespoons orange juice*

Beat egg whites and salt until foamy, add cream of tartar and beat until stiff but still moist. Mix sugar and flour together lightly, and fold carefully into the beaten egg whites, 2 tablespoons at a time, with flavouring using a spatula and folding gently over and over until the mixture is even. Put into a 10 inch ungreased round tin and bake at 300°F (Gas Mark 2) for 1 hour. Invert the tin on a wire tray and leave the cake in the tin for about an hour until cold.

Leave until the next day, then split cake very carefully into layers, putting them together with apricot jam. To make the icing, combine softened butter, egg yolks, orange peel and orange juice, and gradually beat in the icing sugar, until the mixture is smooth and easy to spread. Spread thickly on top and sides of cake.

EASTER BUN RING

1 *lb strong flour*
1 *teaspoon salt*
3 *oz butter or margarine*
1 *oz fresh yeast*
8 *fluid oz tepid milk*
4 *oz castor sugar*
2 *oz walnuts (chopped)*

8 *oz stoned dates (chopped)*

Decoration:
4 *oz icing sugar (for glacé icing)*
Walnut halves
Glacé cherries

Cream yeast with the tepid milk. Sift flour and salt together. Rub in 2 oz of the butter. Melt the remaining 1 oz. Add sugar to flour. Beat egg, and add with the yeast liquid to flour. Knead well for 10 minutes. Cover and put to rise until doubled in size. Turn out risen dough on to floured board and 'knock back'. Roll out into a rectangle 18 × 18 inches. Brush with melted butter and sprinkle with nut and date mixture. Roll up tightly along long side. Form the roll into a circle on a baking sheet, seal the ends together well. With a sharp knife make 10 slashes halfway through dough at intervals all round. Leave to rise for ½ hour until well risen. Bake the bun ring for 25–30 minutes at 425°F (Gas Mark 7). Decorate with glacé icing, walnut and cherry halves.

CUMBERLAND EASTER CAKE

4 oz lard	½ teaspoon ginger
3 oz demerara sugar	7 oz self-raising flour
1 tablespoon golden syrup	Grated rind of 1 lemon
¼ teaspoon bicarbonate of soda	1 egg
1 dessertspoon milk	8 oz almond paste
¼ teaspoon cinnamon	Water icing

Melt the lard, sugar and syrup in a saucepan. Dissolve the bicarbonate of soda in milk and stir into the syrup mixture. Add the sifted dry ingredients, beat well, then stir in lemon rind and well-beaten egg. Bake in a greased and lined 7 inch cake tin at 325°F (Gas Mark 3) for 1 hour. Knead the almond paste until soft, then cover the top of the cake and the sides with a very thin layer. Mark the top and sides with a fork design, and ice a lattice pattern on top and sides with pale green water icing, using a large writing nozzle.

WILTSHIRE FIRMITY or FRUMENTY

1 pint prepared wheat	4 oz sugar (I use demerara)
1 quart milk	Grated nutmeg or cinnamon
1 oz flour	or flavouring to taste
A little cold milk	4 oz raisins
4 eggs (beaten)	4 oz currants

Cook the prepared wheat and milk in a double saucepan for 1 hour. Mix the flour with the cold milk and add—allow to boil for 5 minutes. Remove from heat and stir in the eggs well beaten with the sugar, return to heat and stir till thickness of custard. *Do not allow to boil.* Then add fruit which should have been previously cooked in a little water till tender. Usually served cold but very good hot on a winter morning.

To prepare wheat: put several handfuls into double saucepan; cover with plenty of water and cook gently until soft—then strain.

Used on Mothering Sunday. When we lived in Calne, we were able to take along a basin to Maslen's Café in Church Street on the Saturday before Mothering Sunday and get ready-prepared wheat. I think this custom must have been carried on for some long time—though I don't know if it is still.

Mrs Padgham, Minehead, Somerset

Note: Frumenty is common to many parts of Britain. In some areas it was a Christmas dish. A Firmity tea was served at the end of harvest in Suffolk.

HARVEST BREAD

Harvest bread is easy to make, and you do not have to be a splendid cook or a gifted artist to get effective results. The dough is a simple one, only proved once, and making the design is no more complicated than using plasticine.

Basic Dough:
3 *lb plain bread flour*
3 *level dessertspoons salt*
1 *oz fresh yeast (or ½ oz dried yeast)*

1½ *pints warm water*
A little beaten egg
A few drops gravy browning
Currants

Sift flour and salt. Mix warm water with yeast, pour into dry ingredients and work well together with the hands to make an elastic dough (if using dried yeast, leave it to stand in water for 15 minutes before adding to flour). Knead well until smooth, then prove the dough in a warm place until double in bulk, which will take about 1 to 1½ hours. The dough can then be formed into shape and baked immediately. It will lose its crisp outline if left to rise again.

For a large design, it is best to model the dough directly on to baking trays, upside down, so that the finished loaf will slide off easily. For a large piece of bread, model it on 2 baking sheets laid side by side, and placed on the oven rack on a table before beginning to form the shape.

Loaves and Fishes

Take half the dough, form into an oval shape, and roll about 1 inch thick, then place on baking sheet. Take half the remaining dough, form small flat fishes and tiny cottage loaves. Arrange on the base, and brush the whole design with beaten egg. Bake just above the centre of a hot oven, 425°F (Gas Mark 7) until it is set and golden brown (about 20 minutes) then lower the heat to 325°F (Gas Mark 3) for 20 minutes.

Wheatsheaf and Mouse

Take about 8 oz dough and form into a sausage shape about 12 inches long. Place on centre of baking trays and flatten the sausage slightly—this is the base on which the design will be modelled. Using 12 oz dough, form into a crescent shape and put it curving round the top of the stalk, flattening this shape too. Using about half the remainder of the dough, roll with the hands small sticks of dough a little thinner than a pencil and about 12 inches long, and lay each one along the basic stalk shape to cover it. Make a plait with 3 of these sticks. Cut a little v-shape out of the sides of the stalks, fairly high up, and bind the stalks with the plait, tucking the ends well under the sheaf.

Reserve about 2 oz dough for the mouse. With remaining dough, make small sausage shapes of dough, weighing about 1 oz each, and lay them round the top of the crescent, like the rays of the sun, and cover the crescent. Brush the whole sheaf with beaten egg. Clip each pair with a pair of scissors—these form the ears of corn.

Knead a little gravy browning into the dough for the mouse, and take off a tiny piece for the tail. Mould the dough into a pear-shape, then model the head and nose, and lift up small flaps for the ears. Make a thin tail and curl it round the mouse, and put in currant eyes. Bake as for loaves and fishes.

HARVEST BETSY CAKE

8 oz barley flour
8 oz plain flour
1½ teaspoons baking powder
½ teaspoon salt
4 oz butter

4 oz castor sugar
1 dessertspoon golden syrup
½ pint milk
8 oz sultanas

Sift the two kinds of flour together with baking powder and salt. Cream butter and sugar, and add syrup. Add the flour mixture and the milk alternately, then fold in the sultanas. Put into a buttered 7 inch cake tin, and bake at 350°F (Gas Mark 4) for 1½ hours.

SOMERSET HARVEST SUPPER (for 100 people)

PICKLED BEEF

40 lb brisket of beef (minus
high percentage of fat)
or a 30 lb silverside of beef
2 gallons water

2 lb salt
12 oz brown sugar
1½ oz saltpetre

Boil the brine ingredients for 10 minutes. Pour into earthenware crock and leave until cold. Remove bones from brisket if used. Place brisket or silverside in cold brine; leave in cold place for 10 days, turning every day. Wash meat well to remove excess salt. Place in pan of cold water; add 3 onions, 3 bayleaves, 6 cloves, 12 peppercorns. Bring to the boil and remove scum. Simmer—allow 20 minutes per lb. Leave in water until cold. Place on board or tin and press well. Some areas prefer to have beef or ham, in this case use half quantities of beef and serve a similar quantity of cooked ham.

APPLE FLAN

Pastry:
6 lb flour
1½ lb lard
1½ lb butter or margarine
1 lb castor sugar
½ pint (only) cold water

Filling:
12 lb cooking apples

2 lb sugar
2 pints cider
5 lb eating apples

Glaze:
2 lb apricot jam
2 pints cider
3 oz arrowroot

Rub fats into flour. Mix sugar with water. Add to form paste. Divide into 12 portions, and line 12 × 9 inch flan rings. Chill well. Peel and stew cooking apples in sugar and cider to form thick purée—cool. Pour into pastry cases. Peel and slice eating apples—toss in lemon juice. Arrange on top of purée. Sprinkle with sugar. Bake in moderate oven for 30–40 minutes. Boil cider and jam. Add blended arrowroot, cook until clear. Pour over fruit. Serve cold with whipped cream.

SOMERSET HARVEST CIDER CUP

3 gallons cider
3 pints sherry
3 pints port
½ bottle rum

½ bottle gin
7 bottles orange squash
7 bottles lemon squash
Ice cubes for hot day

Pour into large baby's bath or several plastic buckets. Add sliced red apple and sprigs of fresh mint. Stir and taste. Add sugar if necessary and taste again. Decant into large jugs each with apple and mint.

PUMPKIN PIE FOR HALLOWEEN

Short pastry
1 lb pumpkin flesh
6 oz brown sugar
¼ teaspoon powdered cloves
1¼ teaspoons powdered cinnamon

1¼ teaspoons powdered ginger
½ teaspoon salt
2 eggs
½ pint milk
1 tablespoon grated orange rind

Line a flan ring or pie plate with short pastry and bake at 400°F (Gas Mark 6) until just beginning to colour. Dice the pumpkin flesh, steam until soft and put through a sieve. Leave to cool, then stir in sugar, spices, salt, beaten eggs, milk and orange rind. Pour into flan case and bake at 400°F (Gas Mark 6) for 30 minutes.

PARKIN FOR GUY FAWKES

1 lb fine oatmeal
½ lb plain flour
¼ lb brown sugar
2 teaspoons ground ginger

1 teaspoon baking powder
2 lb black treacle
3 oz melted butter

This is a rich dark gingerbread which should be soft and sticky, and is very good eaten with a piece of cheese. Keep it for a week to mellow before eating, if possible in an old-fashioned bread crock. Mix all the dry ingredients together, make a well in the centre and pour in the treacle and melted butter. Beat thoroughly and bake in a buttered rectangular tin at 325°F (Gas Mark 3) for 1½ hours.

CHRISTMAS EVE WIGS

3 oz butter
8 oz self-raising flour
1 oz castor sugar
1 oz chopped mixed peel

2 teaspoons caraway seeds
1 egg
A little milk

Rub butter into flour, add sugar, peel and caraway seeds. Mix to a soft dough with egg and a little milk. Put into greased patty-pans and bake at 425°F (Gas Mark 7) for 20 minutes. Eat with mulled elderberry wine, or dip in ale.

BERKSHIRE ROAST SUCKLING PIG

These may be obtained nearly all the year round, but they should not be older than 4 weeks and they should be cooked immediately after they are killed. They make a very rich dish. Make at least 1½–2 lb good stuffing, stuff the pig and sew up the slit, using thin string or strong thread. It should be trussed in the same manner as a hare, with its forelegs skewered back to its hind legs, which have been brought forward. Brush all over with salad oil and if possible allow to stand in the oil for ½ hour or so, turning the pig round so that all parts have a chance to soak and soften a little. Put into a hot oven and baste continually until it is done. It will take about 2¾ hours to bake.

Remove it from the oven, dish onto a carving dish, pop a nice rosy apple into its mouth and pour over it some nice thick gravy. Make this with a little of the fat left in the roasting tin; sprinkle plain flour in to make a nice soft 'roux' with the fat, add a little lemon juice, some beef stock, cayenne pepper, nutmeg and extra water or vegetable water if necessary. Serve with apple sauce.

SUGAR AND SPICE BAKED HAM

1 gammon, 10–14 lb
8 oz moist brown sugar
1 tablespoon mixed spice ⎫
1 tablespoon ground ginger ⎬ mixed together
½ oz whole cloves ⎭

Well soak the gammon in cold water, drain and wipe dry. Rub the spice and ginger into the cut surface and into several incisions through the skin. Wrap in flour and water paste or aluminium foil and bake in oven for 20 minutes per lb, 350°F (Gas Mark 4). Remove from foil and strip off skin and rub over the hot fat with brown sugar and score with a knife into squares and insert cloves into each square. Return to oven 375°F (Gas Mark 5) for a further 30 minutes to glaze. Serve hot or cold.

BAKED HAM

1 ham (about 10 lb)   *½ lb dripping*
2 lb plain flour

Soak ham in cold water for about 24 hours. Make a paste with flour and water, roll out thin, then cover all over the ham, placing in a baking dish, put dripping over the paste. Bake in a moderate oven 4 hours, when it should be done. Take off paste, skin the ham, sprinkle with breadcrumbs and cayenne pepper, and ornament with cloves.

EASY CHRISTMAS PUDDING

8 oz self-raising flour
8 oz fresh white breadcrumbs
8 oz chopped beef suet
8 oz currants
12 oz sultanas
12 oz stoned raisins
8 oz brown sugar
6 eggs
Grated rind and juice of
1 orange
Grated rind and juice of
1 lemon

1 teaspoon salt
1 teaspoon mixed spice
½ pint old ale or 1 wineglass
brandy
4 oz chopped mixed candied
peel
4 oz chopped glacé cherries
1 small grated carrot
1 small grated apple
6 oz chopped blanched
almonds

Mix together flour, breadcrumbs, suet, dried fruit and sugar, then gradually work in all other ingredients. The mixture should be stiff but not dry, and a little milk may be added. The mixture makes 4 medium-sized puddings. Put into basins, leaving a 2 inch space above the surface of the puddings. Cover with greased paper and foil or pudding cloths, and tie tightly. Boil gently for 8 hours, adding boiling water to the saucepan from time to time. Cool completely and replace paper and cloth with clean ones for storage. Store in a cool dry place. Boil for 3 hours before serving.

SANDRINGHAM CHRISTMAS PUDDING

A receipt given to Hon. Albert Petre, a friend of the Royal Family.

1 *lb eggs*	1 *lb sultanas*
1 *lb plain flour*	1 *lb demerara sugar*
1 *lb white breadcrumbs*	$\frac{1}{4}$ *lb mixed peel*
1 *lb suet*	$\frac{1}{2}$ *oz salt*
1 *lb currants*	1 *dessertspoon mixed spice*
1 *lb raisins*	1 *wineglass brandy*

Beat eggs and mix all ingredients except brandy thoroughly *with hands* then stir in brandy. Cover with thick cloth and leave for 12 hours. Put into buttered basins, cover with 3 layers of greaseproof paper within bowls and completely cover with floured and buttered cloth. Boil 21 hours and a further 3 hours day of eating having, of course, removed damp cloth after first boiling, also top layer of paper and replaced with clean pudding cloth.

Mrs Padgham, Minehead, Somerset

CHRISTMAS PUDDING

$\frac{1}{2}$ *lb suet*	1 *tablespoon marmalade or*
$\frac{1}{2}$ *lb self-raising flour*	*grated orange peel*
$\frac{1}{2}$ *lb breadcrumbs*	1 *tablespoon black treacle or*
1 *lb mixed fruit (sultanas,*	*brown sugar*
chopped prunes, dates etc.)	4 *eggs*
1 *teaspoon mixed spice*	1 *pint brown ale or stout*
$\frac{1}{2}$ *teaspoon salt*	

Mix all dry ingredients thoroughly. Add treacle, egg and lastly ale or stout. Put into well-greased basins, cover with greased paper, steam for 5 hours. These were always served at an officers' convalescent hospital in the last war.

Miss Henry, Heathfield, Sussex

CHRISTMAS PUDDING WITHOUT SUET

This is dark and rich

4 oz each flour, breadcrumbs,
grated carrot, apple, sugar,
margarine
8 oz mixed fruit
½ teaspoon each ground ginger
cinnamon, grated nutmeg,
salt

1 tablespoon marmalade
2 dried eggs
1 teacup milk and ale mixed

Peel and grate apples and carrots, grate or cut up margarine, prepare dried fruits. Add all dry ingredients, let stand overnight. Next day stir well, add marmalade, blend with beaten eggs and milk mixture. Put into greased basins, tie down, steam 4 hours.

Mrs P. Macneill, Burwash

FESTIVE PLUM PUDDING

4 oz plain flour
1 level teaspoon each salt,
mixed spice, ground ginger
and ground cinnamon
½ level teaspoon grated nutmeg
4 oz fresh white breadcrumbs
8 oz shredded suet
4 oz soft brown sugar
4 oz each dried apricots,
prunes and dates
4 oz each currants and
sultanas

1 large banana, chopped
1 cooking apple, peeled, cored
and chopped
1 oz mixed peel
2 oz shredded almonds
Juice and grated rind of
1 lemon and 1 orange
½ teaspoon vanilla essence
4 oz black treacle
4 eggs

Sift flour, salt and spices, stir in breadcrumbs, suet and sugar. Chop apricots, prunes and dates and add to flour mixture, together with remaining fruit, peel and almonds and rind of lemon and orange. Beat lemon and orange juice, vanilla essence, treacle and eggs well together and add to other ingredients. Mix to moist consistency. Turn mixture into well-greased 2½–3 pint sized pudding basin, cover with greased greaseproof paper or aluminium foil and steam steadily for 5 hours. Steam further 2 hours before serving.

A RICH PUDDING

2 *lb each of currants, sultanas,*
raisins
2 *lb breadcrumbs*
2 *lb flour*
2 *lb demerara sugar*
¾ *lb mixed peel*
1 *lb minced apples*

2 *lb beef suet*
8 *eggs*
1 *tablespoon mixed spice*
1 *teaspoon nutmeg*
Salt
Brandy or milk

Prepare the fruit. Sieve the flour and spices into a bowl, add the bread-crumbs, the fruit, the minced apple and sugar. Add the suet and mix well with the beaten eggs and the brandy or milk. If you like a really dark pudding, dilute a spoonful of gravy browning with a little warm water and add this, stirring it well in. Mix the whole mixture very thoroughly and put into greased pudding basins, filling them ⅔ full. Cover each pudding with greaseproof paper and a floured cloth and steam for 6 hours.

If you have a slow combustion cooker you can put each pudding into a pan with enough water to come halfway up the side of the pudding, bring the water to the boil and cook on the hot plate for 1½ hours. Then transfer the pan to the simmering oven and leave it overnight.

1820 CHRISTMAS PUDDING

3 *lb raisins*
3 *lb currants*
¾ *lb orange and lemon peel*
¼ *lb citron*
1½ *lb suet*
1½ *lb flour*
¼ *lb almonds (grated)*
1 *teaspoon ginger*

1 *teaspoon salt*
6 *eggs*
2 *nutmegs (powdered)*
1 *breakfastcup sugar*
2 *lb breadcrumbs*
1 *wineglass brandy*
1 *quart old beer*

Mix all dry ingredients together. Add eggs (lightly beaten) and stout or old beer. Brandy last. Preferably, steam for 12 hours.

This recipe, which is the most delicious I have ever tasted, was given to me by the late Mrs May Dixon of Iron Acton, Glos., having been used by her great-grandmother. Mrs Dixon herself died in 1971 at the age of 87.

In 1820 it seems that sultanas were not available, and this was the only alteration I made to the original recipe. Instead of adding 3 lb currants, use half this quantity and introduce 1½ lb sultanas. The quart of 'Old Beer' may be difficult to get in some localities: I found that a glucose stout was a perfectly good substitute. Serve with Brandy Sauce.

Barbara G. Smith

LAST DAYS CHRISTMAS PUDDING

8 oz *sultanas*
8 oz *raisins*
4 oz *currants*
2 oz *chopped peel*
2 oz *grated raw carrot*
4 oz *plain flour*
1 teaspoon *mixed spice*
½ teaspoon *cinnamon*

4 oz *fine brown breadcrumbs*
4 oz *demerara sugar*
4 oz *softened butter*
2 oz *warm golden syrup*
Rind and juice of ½ lemon
2 *eggs*
4 tablespoons *brandy or milk*

Mix and steam for 4 hours; then for 1 hour on the day. This can be made at the last minute, or on the actual day.

CADOGAN PUDDING

This recipe for dark puddings was used throughout the war. Ingredients were varied according to the supply position, and the recipe is still useful. Alternative ingredients are given in order of preference.

½ lb *currants*
½ lb *sultanas*
½ lb *raisins*
4 oz *candied peel or dates or*
1¾ lb *total of available fruit*
½ lb *sugar*
4 oz *golden syrup warmed in*
drop of milk or honey or brown
sugar
½ lb *suet or cooking fat*
½ lb *breadcrumbs*

4 oz *ground almonds or other*
nuts or grated carrot
1 *lemon, rind and juice, or*
1 *orange or 2 teaspoons lemon*
essence
4 *beaten eggs*
1 *teaspoon each salt, nutmeg,*
mixed spice
4 oz *flour*
8 tablespoons *rum, whisky,*
stout or old beer

Clean and prepare dried fruit and chop peel. Grate suet, or if fat is used, rub into flour. Put all ingredients in large bowl. Mix thoroughly with well-beaten eggs and spirit or beer. Let each member of the family stir— this is 'for luck'. Well grease 2 fairly large or 3 smaller pudding basins. Fill with mixture. Steam or boil 8–10 hours, according to size. They should be steamed another 2–3 hours on Christmas Day.

BRANDY BUTTER

3 oz *butter*
3 oz *castor sugar*

3 tablespoons *brandy*

Cream butter, work in sugar and brandy. Pack into pots and store in a cool place, but not the refrigerator.

CHRISTMAS CAKE

8 oz butter
8 oz soft brown sugar
1 tablespoon black treacle
4 large eggs
4 tablespoons sherry, brandy
or cold tea
Grated rind of 1 lemon
½ teaspoon vanilla essence
4 oz self-raising flour
6 oz plain flour

1 teaspoon mixed spice
¼ teaspoon salt
Pinch of ground cinnamon
Pinch of grated nutmeg
12 oz currants
12 oz sultanas
8 oz stoned raisins
2 oz chopped peel
2 oz halved glacé cherries

Cream butter and sugar until light and fluffy, then beat together treacle, eggs, sherry or tea, lemon rind and vanilla essence, just enough to break up the eggs. Stir a little at a time into the creamed mixture, alternating with the flours sifted with salt and spices. Do not beat the mixture. Add the fruit and mix just enough to distribute evenly; the mixture should be just stiff enough to fall easily off the spoon. Turn into a 10 inch round tin lined with 2 thicknesses of greaseproof paper extending about 1 inch above the tin. Level off the mixture and leave to stand for an hour. Put into the bottom part of the oven set at 300°F (Gas Mark 1) and bake for 4-4½ hours, putting thick brown paper over the top about halfway through cooking if it is browning too quickly. The cake will be done when a depression no longer remains if the surface is pressed gently with a finger. Leave the cake in the tin until it is just warm, then cool on a wire rack. When cold, wrap in paper and store in a tin. The cake is moist, full of fruit and keeps almost indefinitely if not iced.

MRS GLEDHILL'S CHRISTMAS CAKE

This cake can be eaten nearly straight away, if necessary.

1 lb butter
1 lb soft brown sugar
1 lb flour, half self-raising,
half plain

8 or 9 eggs
¼ lb ground almonds
1½ lb dried fruit

As a rough guide cook for 6 hours at 250°F (Gas Mark ½) but most people know their ovens, some prefer to start a Christmas cake off at a higher temperature then turn the oven down. Mrs Gledhill says the secret of the moisture of this cake is to put a bowl of water in the oven.

RICH CHRISTMAS CAKE

1 lb 2 oz currants
8 oz sultanas
8 oz stoned raisins
6 oz glacé cherries, halved
4 oz peel
Grated rind of ½ lemon
10 oz plain flour
Pinch of salt

½ level teaspoon mixed spice
½ level teaspoon ground cinnamon
10 oz butter
10 oz soft brown sugar
6 eggs
3 tablespoons brandy

Grease and line a 9 inch cake tin. Chop the peel finely. Mix together currants, sultanas, raisins, peel and cherries. Sift the flour, salt and spices. Add lemon rind. Cream the butter and sugar until light and fluffy. Beat the eggs one at a time into the creamed mixture. Gradually fold in the flour and fruit alternately; towards the end add the brandy. Turn into the prepared tin, spread the mixture evenly, make a slight dip in the centre. Bake in the lower part of the oven at 300°F (Gas Mark 1–2) for 4½ hours approximately; to avoid over-browning of the top, cover with several thicknesses of greaseproof paper after 2½ hours. When cooked, carefully turn out of the tin and leave to cool on a wire rack. Prick the cake with a fine skewer and slowly pour 2–3 tablespoons of brandy over the cake before storing in tin.

LIGHT CHRISTMAS CAKE

6 oz glacé cherries
6 oz currants
6 oz sultanas
4 oz citron peel
4 oz glacé pineapple
8 oz butter
8 oz castor sugar

2 oz ground almonds
4 eggs
8 oz self-raising flour
Grated rind and juice of
1 lemon
3 tablespoons brandy

Grease and line a 9 inch tin with a double thickness of greaseproof paper. Wash glacé cherries to remove syrup. Slice peel thinly. Cut pineapple into small cubes. Cream the butter and sugar until light and fluffy. Stir in the ground almonds. Beat in the eggs one at a time. Add 3 tablespoons of the flour to the glacé cherries, currants, sultanas and peel, toss to coat. Fold these ingredients alternatively with the rest of the flour, grated rind and juice of the lemon into the creamed mixture. Lastly, stir in the brandy. Turn the mixture into the prepared tin. Bake in the centre of the oven or just below at 325°F (Gas Mark 3) for 2½ hours or till risen and just firm to the touch. Turn out and cool on a wire rack.

MATRON'S (ST THOMAS) CHRISTMAS CAKE (1941)

2 lb flour
½ lb sugar
2 lb raisins
A few chopped almonds
1 pint milk
2 teaspoons bicarbonate of soda

1 lb butter or lard
2 lb currants
1 lb peel
1 teaspoon cinnamon
4 eggs

Rub in fat. Mix with other ingredients. Bake 5–6 hours at 275°F (Gas Mark 1).

Lewis' Mother's Cookbook, Mary Horrell, Exeter

CHRISTMAS GINGERBREAD

1 lb plain flour
½ teaspoon salt
1½ teaspoons ground ginger
½ teaspoon bicarbonate of soda
6 oz butter
12 oz black treacle or golden syrup
8 oz soft brown sugar
1 egg
½ pint milk

2 oz citron peel
4 oz crystallised ginger
2 oz sliced almonds
Grated rind of ½ lemon
1 teaspoon coffee essence

Icing:
8 oz icing sugar
2 tablespoons lemon juice

Sift together flour, salt, ginger and bicarbonate of soda. Gently warm butter, treacle and sugar. Beat in egg and warm milk. Pour on to dry ingredients and mix well together. Add the peel and ginger chopped in small pieces, almonds, lemon rind and coffee essence. Mix thoroughly and pour into greased and lined meat tin. Bake at 325°F (Gas Mark 3) for 1½ hours. This cake keeps very well, and it can be iced before using with a mixture of sifted icing sugar and lemon juice.

Mrs Woolner

BILLY-THE-BUTCH'S WAY WITH THE CHRISTMAS TURKEY

To make your Christmas turkey remain in the memory of your guests for years to come, this method of improvement was given by that charming Welsh butcher, Billy-the-Butch of Haverfordwest, some years ago.

When your turkey is nicely cooked and golden brown on top but could do with about 15 minutes more, dish it onto the carving dish and quickly prick the skin all over with a fork. Pour over some green Chartreuse liqueur (or golden if liked) and replace in the oven for 15 minutes. Baste the 'juice' over the bird again just before taking to table, but don't waste any!

JANIE TWENTYMAN'S TIP FOR MINCEPIES-WITH-A-DIFFERENCE

When making your Christmas mincepies, pinch a little of your husband's whisky, enough to dip each top of your mincepies into, before covering up the mincemeat. Sprinkle the tops with a little sugar just before baking and the result is guaranteed to help the Christmas spirit considerably. If you are short of the hard stuff, mix it with a little milk—it is better than nothing, but not as good as 100% spirit.

JACK PAYNE'S WAY WITH FRESH SALMON

For a wedding or similar event. Some years ago, before he started catering for the passing motorist, Jack Payne took a course in cookery at his local Technical College at Bath. Here he learnt how to cook a large joint of beef to perfection, among many other things, and how to cook salmon fresh from the river without its being as dry as old cardboard—such as he had tasted in many a country inn. To this day he still cooks his salmon in this way to serve cold in the buffet section of The Red Lion at Beckington. Many of his regular customers are farmers, as this is bang in the middle of as rural an area as you will find, even in Somerset.

Have ready a fish 'kettle' or large saucepan with cold water, some clean rag, salt and oil. After cleaning your fish, or part of a fish, rub celery salt all over it. Then take your rags—pieces big enough to wrap the fish in, and soak them in oil, cooking oil or salad oil. Stuff one of the rags into the belly of the fish and wrap the other all round the outside of the fish and then place it in the cold water. See that the water entirely covers it. Add cooking salt and bayleaves to the water—12 for a whole fish. Now bring the fish gently to the boil and *no matter how large the piece is* cook it exactly for 10 minutes then take it off the heat. Leave the fish *untouched* in the water until the whole thing is nearly cold. Then it is ready. This method is suitable for using if catering for a wedding party or similar, as it may be done in advance if you have a suitably cold place to keep it in.

GRANNY HONEY'S TRERICE TREACLE TART

Granny Honey was driven out of County Cork as a young girl, with all the rest of her Protestant family, just before the turn of this century. Subsequently she became a lady's maid, but being fortunate in her employing 'family' she was taken into the schoolroom, along with the daughter-of-the-house and educated by the governess. She also learnt a great deal of first-class cooking at the hands of a German cook, who was a real battle-axe but knew her job. She was a wonderful mother-in-law and an exemplary housewife.

For 20 people

Have ready and 'rested' 3 lb pastry (see Mrs Hibberd's Easy Method). Line as many tins as you require having the pastry not too thick nor yet too thin, say $\frac{1}{8}$ inch thick. In a basin mix 8 oz breadcrumbs, juice of 1 lemon and a little desiccated coconut. Stir into this as much syrup as you will need for the total number of tarts, but do not worry if it is not enough at first sight. Share the mixture evenly between the lined but uncooked tins of pastry and tilt the tins to make the mixture spread around the whole surface. Have ready more syrup and fill up any deficiences as may be required. Make patterns with thin strips of pastry arranged on top of the tarts and bake in a fairly hot oven for 10 minutes and at a lower temperature until golden and set.

35 Herbs

Excellent herbs had our father of old,
Excellent herbs to ease their pain,
Alexanders and Marigold,
Eyebright, Orris and Elecampane.

Rudyard Kipling

What long hours
They gloat upon their steepling hollyhocks,
Bee's balsams, feathery southernwood, and stocks,
Fiery dragon's-mouths, great mallow leaves
For salves, and lemon-plants in bushy sheaves.

Edmund Blunden

GROWING HERBS

If we can't manage an elaborate Elizabethan herb garden, most of us can find a tiny patch of soil.

If it is possible to find a piece near the kitchen with small beds and plenty of paths, so much the better. Each herb needs to be near a path for easy cultivation and harvesting.

If you cannot use an isolated patch, try using herbs in flower borders. Angelica, tansy, lavender, sage, rosemary, hyssop and thyme are all decorative and useful.

Neat rows of herbs can be interspersed with vegetables and flowers for cutting to make a French-style housewife's garden, which is much more fun to work in and look at than serried ranks of Brussels sprouts.

A selection of herbs can be grown in windowboxes, tubs, the spokes of a cartwheel or in the pots on the windowsill. The plants do not need green fingers. They like clean, light, well-drained soil in sunny positions.

DRIED HERBS

The best time to gather herbs for drying is when the plant is just about to flower; the day should be dry and the sun should not have reached its zenith. Small leaved herbs, such as thyme and winter savory, can be loosely tied in small bundles in muslin, and hung near the kitchen fire to dry. Large leaved herbs, such as mint and sage, can be stripped from the stalks, any unsuitable leaves can be discarded and after dipping the leaves in boiling water for a minute, they can be dried in a slow oven for about an hour. Alternatively, after gathering, the herbs are washed and put on a wire rack to dry slowly in a warm room or the hot cupboard.

Parsley needs special treatment. It should be dipped in boiling water and immediately put in a hot oven, 400°F (Gas Mark 6), for *one minute* exactly. It is then finished off in a warm place. This method keeps both flavour and colour. The leaves of all herbs, when absolutely dry, are crushed and may be sieved. The finished product should be stored in airtight tins or dark glass jars with well-fitting screw top lids. Light spoils the flavour and colour of any dried herb.

National Federation of Women's Institutes

FREEZING HERBS

Mint, parsley and chives can be frozen, although their flavour will not be strong. They tend to wilt on thawing, so sprigs for garnishing should not be frozen. They should be chopped finely and packed into ice-cube trays, then frozen solid. Each cube can be wrapped in foil, and a number put into polythene bags for storage.

HERB VINEGARS AND JELLIES

Flavoured vinegars can be made which are delicious for mayonnaise and salad dressings but are expensive to buy. A half pint of herbs should be placed in a pint of wine vinegar for 4 days to infuse. Tarragon and fennel make good vinegars.

Most of us make mint jelly, but the same recipe can be used to produce jelly with thyme, sage, parsley and bay leaves. These are delicious with pork, ham and poultry.

HOW TO USE HERBS

Soups and Stews

Parsley, bay leaves, basil, carraway, celery seed, rosemary, lovage, chervil, thyme.

Sauces

Spearmint, parsley, mint, applemint, sage, lovage, fennel, chervil, dill.

Fish

Fennel, parsley, rosemary, marjoram, dill, thyme, basil.

Meat

Tuck sprigs of rosemary under skin of roast lamb and baste well—forget the mint! Knotted marjoram and winter or summer savory makes stews and ragouts succulent.

Stuffing

Thyme, rosemary, sage, alecost, lavender, lemon balm, savory.

Cakes

Carraway, tansy, aniseed, rose geranium (use a leaf in bottom of cake tin. Delicious with apple).

HERBS, SCENTED LEAVES AND FLOWERS AS FLAVOURINGS

Basil: Tomatoes, turtle soup.
Bay Leaf: Beef stews, spaghetti sauces, fish, milk puddings, custards.
Chives: Cream cheese, salads, stews.
Dill: Boiled beef, mutton, cucumber, old and new potatoes, salmon.
Elderflowers (muscat flavour): Gooseberries, custards.
Fennel: Mackerel, salmon.
Garlic: Salads, mutton stew, spinach, savoy cabbage.
Horseradish: Cream, apple sauce, beetroot sauce.
Lemon verbena: Apples.
Marjoram: Potato soup, pease pudding, lamb, pea soup, turnips, marrows, cod, hake, haddock.
Mint: Tomatoes, fresh fruit salad, lamb, peas, new potatoes, lemonade.
Parsley (more flavour in roots and stems than leaves): Sauces, soups, salads.
Rose Geranium: Apples, sponge cakes.
Rosemary: Mushrooms, spaghetti sauces, beef stews, chicken, duckling.

Sage: Duck, goose, pork, beef.
Tansy: Salads, veal.
Thyme: Chicken, turkey, lamb, spaghetti sauces.

HERB BUTTER

Put 1 teaspoon parsley, ½ teaspoon each of mint and chives, ¾ teaspoon tarragon, ¼ teaspoon marjoram, in as much lemon juice as the herbs will absorb. Allow 4 oz butter to soften in room temperature and cream it. Blend herbs with salted, creamed butter and set aside at room temperature for 1–2 hours so that the herbs can permeate the butter. Store in tightly covered jars in refrigerator. May be kept there until needed.

Use generously on bridge rolls, toast or sandwiches. Garnish hot steak, chops, escalopes, fish etc., with small rounds of really cold herb butter. Shape some herb butter into a roll, diameter approximately 1½ inches, pack into foil, twist both ends, place in refrigerator. Slices of this can be cut when needed.

HERB CHEESE

½ lb cheddar cheese (shredded)
1 dessertspoon each parsley,
chives, thyme, sage and

summer savory
2 tablespoons whipped cream
4 tablespoons sherry

Blend well cheese, herbs, cream and sherry. Allow to permeate. Can be used immediately or refrigerated for several days.

CHEESE OF THE SEVEN HERBS

This is an old Cumberland recipe and the name dates back at least 200 years. To 4 oz grated cheese, allow 2 tablespoons thick cream, 3 tablespoons sherry and 2 level tablespoons of the following herbs in mixture: finely chopped parsley, sage, thyme, tarragon, chives, chervil and winter savoury, also seasoning to taste. Put all the ingredients into a double saucepan and stir over very gentle heat till the mixture is creamy and pale green in colour. Whilst still warm, fill up small pots with the cheese and use when cold.

HERBY EGGS SERVED IN THE SHELL

Egg
Herbs
Butter
Saffron

Ginger
Sugar
Seasoning

Herbs used: Sage, mint, marjoram and other herbs as liked and chopped finely.

Take as many eggs as you wish to cook. Take off the end of egg shell and pour out the egg. Set aside the shells. Take the chopped herbs, fry them in butter, add the beaten eggs slightly seasoned with salt, and cook until set. Break up with fork or chop up on a board adding a little ground ginger and sugar. A pinch of saffron can be used to give a bright colour and failing this use a very little turmeric powder. Fill the shells with this stuffing and put them into the oven to heat through.

A nice way of serving is to cut thick slices of bread, cut out a circle from the centre and butter all over. The eggs can be put in these 'holes'. Place on a baking tin and warm in the oven while the pieces of bread crisp.

HERB LOAF

This is delicious for a winter party. Use second-day tin or sandwich loaf. Cut off crust; cut loaf in thick slices without quite severing at bottom. Spread each side with herb filling. Press loaf back into shape, wrap in foil, tie and bake in moderate oven, 375°F (Gas Mark 5), until slightly crisp on outside—about $\frac{1}{2}$ hour.

Filling

Chop finely such savoury herbs as parsley, chives, rosemary, thyme, mint, fennel, chervil, angelica. Mix well with butter. Fresh herbs are ideal for this loaf, but dried kinds may be used with discretion.

HERB SEASONING

To 2 parts of dried and pounded orange peel add 1 part each of dried thyme, marjoram and hyssop. This can be kept in a well-closed glass jar for months and gives the most wonderful flavour to stuffings and forcemeat; it will even cheer up the dullest rissoles.

CONCENTRATED MINT SAUCE

Pick enough mint leaves to fill a breakfast cup when well pressed down, and put $\frac{1}{2}$ pint of vinegar and 3 oz of sugar into a saucepan. Simmer for 2 or 3 minutes after the sugar is dissolved. Put the mint leaves into a colander, pour boiling water over them, and then dry them in a clean cloth; sprinkle them with 1 oz of sugar and chop up finely. Pack into small jars, adding enough vinegar to cover the leaves by $\frac{1}{2}$ inch, and tie them down. When using, dilute with a little more vinegar.

FRAGRANCE FOR LINEN

Fill small muslin bags with equal quantities of rosemary, thyme and bay leaves, rubbed small. Or try 2 parts each of powdered mint and rosemary to one part of thyme, tansy and powdered cloves.

SCENTED PILLOWS

Sleep sweetly on scented silk or satin pillows stuffed with pot pourri mixture. Try well-dried rose petals mixed with a teaspoon each of powdered dried mint and powdered cloves. Or try equal quantities of lavender, lemon verbena and rose scented geranium leaves, with a teaspoon each of powdered orris root and cinnamon.

LAVENDER STICKS

Lavender sticks were used to mark the dozens and half-dozens in our grandmother's trousseau chest, and they keep their fragrance for years. For each stick, take a small bunch of lavender and a length of narrow baby ribbon. Pick the lavender blooms on a fine day, and use them while the stems are still supple. Take an odd number of stems (13 gives a satisfactory 'stick') and tie them firmly together with one end of the ribbon immediately below the flower heads. Turn the bunch upside down and carefully bend the stalks out and down the heads from the point where the ribbon is tied so that the heads appear to be in a cage of stems. Space the stalks evenly, and then starting at the top where the stalks bend, weave the long end of the ribbon over and under the stalks so that the flower heads become completely enclosed in a kind of basketwork of ribbon and stalk. Make the weaving rather tight at the bottom and top of the heads and rather slacker in the centre to give a 'bottle appearance'. When the heads are completely covered, wind the ribbon firmly round the stalks for 1 to 2 inches, then tie in a bow. Leave about 3 inches of stalk below this bow, and trim neatly to an even length with sharp scissors.

POT POURRI

Pot pourri is a mixture of dried flowers, leaves and spices. The secret of success lies in the choice of scents, in correct drying methods, and in the use of the right container. Pot pourri can be used in small quantities to fill muslin bags or cushions, but it is more commonly kept in a jar. The jar needs a well-fitting lid and a stand, and special jars were once made for this purpose. Try a ginger jar, with a wooden lid and stand. The pot pourri should be kept in the shut jar all day, and in the evening should then be turned till pleasantly warm, moved to its stand and left to cool, when the scent will fill the room. When cool, the lid should be replaced till further use.

Roses are the traditional ingredients of pot pourri, but other flowers can be used to give colour and variety to the mixture. The flowers should be gathered freshly after the dew had dried, and the flowers should not be quite full out, as their scent is strongest then. The flowers must be dried, the scents fixed, and the blossoms blended with appropriate leaves, herbs and spices.

A box of fine sand is needed for drying the flowers. The petals should be placed on a layer of sand, then sprinkled with more sand, and so on in layers till the box is full, care being taken not to put too many petals into one box as they may mildew. The sand boxes should be kept in a warm dry place away from sunlight and draughts, and after a few days they will be crisp and retain their shape and colour. Different types of flowers and scented leaves should be kept in separate boxes. When they are ready for use, the sand can be sifted away. Flowers gathered at various times can be kept dried till the time comes to blend them.

If an extra fragrant mixture is required, the petals can be sealed, after drying, into jars with 2 tablespoons of kitchen salt. They should be left to stand for 3 weeks before mixing together. As a final fixative, powdered orris root is used. When the flowers, spices and fixatives have been mixed they should be sealed into jars or packets as required. The following are delightful mixtures:

Mixture 1

In a bowl, put alternate layers of rose petals, bay leaves and the powdered rind of two oranges, sprinkling each layer with a mixture of equal parts powdered cloves, allspice, cinnamon and mace. Finish with a layer of rose petals and a scattering of lavender flowers.

Mixture 2

Use alternate layers of lavender, lemon balm, thyme and mint, sprinkling each layer with a mixture of cloves and cinnamon. Leave for a few days before stirring and mixing together.

Mixture 3

Mix a quart of rose petals with a cup of marjoram, lemon, thyme, rosemary and lavender. Sprinkle with the powdered rind of an orange and a lemon, 6 broken bay leaves, 1 tablespoon cloves and 1 teaspoon allspice.

POT POURIE–GRANDMOTHER'S RECIPE

24 sweet smelling rose petals, 6 stems thyme, as many as possible of the following herbs: some rosemary, lavender, myrtle, balm, bay leaves,

mint, peel of lemon. Dry slowly in sun, rub to powder, put in wide necked attractive container. Add 2 oz each powdered cloves, musk, orris root, cinnamon. Stir well as pot pourie improves with an occasional stir.

Mrs M. E. Sanders, Lostwithiel, Cornwall

HERB OR CAPPALICK TOBACCO

2 oz of Coltsfoot
2 oz of Wood Bottoney
2 oz of Eye Bright
1 oz of Agrimoney

½ oz of Rosemary Flowers
½ oz of Lavender Flowers
2 oz of Lavender Cotton

Dry them in the Sun and rub them fine and mix them with 1 lb of the best Tobacco

Joseph Webb's book, 1823

36 Health and Beauty

Good Huswives provide, ere an' sickness do come,
of sundry good things, in her house to have some:
Good aqua composita, and vinegar tart,
rose-water, and treacle, to comfort the heart.
Cold herbs in her garden, for agues that burn,
that over strong heat, to good temper may turn,
White endive and succory, with spinage enough,
all such, will good pot herbs, should follow the plough.
Get waters of fumitory, liver to cool,
And others the like, or else go like a fool.

Thomas Tusser

CHILBLAIN MIXTURE

Mix 1 tablespoon of honey with equal quantity of glycerine, the white of an egg and enough flour to make a paste—a teaspoon of rosewater may be added. Wash the affected parts with warm water, dry and spread on paste. Cover with piece of linen or cotton material.

583

FOR CHAPPED HANDS

Every time after washing drop on them a little honey, and rub them together till the stickiness is entirely removed. The same may be applied to sore lips.

Grandma's Book, Mrs Margetts, Leics.

ESSENCE OF SOAP FOR SHAVING OR WASHING HANDS

Take 1½ lbs of fine white soap in thin slices, and add thereto 2 oz of salt of tartar; mix them well together, and put this mixture into 1 quart of spirits of wine, in a bottle which will hold double the quantity of the ingredients; tie a bladder over the mouth of the bottle, and prick a pin through the bladder; set it to digest in a gentle heat, and shake the contents from time to time taking care to take out the pin at such times to allow passage for the air from within; when soap is dissolved, filter the liquor through paper, to free it from impurities; then scent it with a little hergamot or essence of lemon. It will have the appearance of fine oil, and a small quantity will lather with water like soap, and is much superior in use for washing or shaving.

Grandma's Book, Mrs Margetts, Leics.

TO INCREASE THE GROWTH OF HAIR

Hartshorn beat small, and mixed with oil, being rubbed upon the head of persons who have lost their hair, will cause it to grow again as at first.

Grandma's Book, Mrs Margetts, Leics.

NEURITIS

Old remedy, recommended. 1 oz celery seed from chemist, 1 pint of water, boil to ½ pint. Strain, take 2 teaspoons twice daily, in a little water—for a fortnight.

I. Northey, Allet

CORNISH REMEDIES

Rope-yard worn around the legs and wrists for rheumatism and cramp. Hot roast onion in the ear for relief of earache.

New red flannel worn around throat to relieve sore and aching throat.

To cure corns apply fresh yeast on a cloth every morning.

Nettle rash is soothed by rubbing in parsley.

Mrs M. E. Sanders, Lostwithiel

HONEY FOR HANDS

Rub some honey on the sore parts and then cover with cotton gloves. For washing up, and for other wet jobs put rubber gloves over the cotton ones. Honey will soon heal the cracks and will soothe the soreness. Honey is also a marvellous face pack.

Another good thing for the hands is olive oil with just a sprinkle of sugar. If you use it regularly the sugar cleans the hands—and the olive oil makes them soft.

Mrs G. L. Morris, Ludlow

FOR CHAPPED AND ROUGH HANDS

Mix $\frac{1}{4}$ lb softened lard with 2 egg yolks and a tablespoon runny honey, a tablespoon ground almonds and a tablespoon rose water. Add a few drops of almond essence and work into a stiff paste. Keep in a pot by the washbasin. This paste is very healing and softening.

AT NIGHT

Olive oil and sugar to clean very sore, stained, ingrained hands. Cover with old tights or bags of rag.

TO REMOVE WARTS I

Rub the warts with the inside of broad-bean pods, after the beans have been taken out.

TO REMOVE WARTS II

Use juice of houseleeks to cure warts and corns. Apply the leaves to the excrescence.

SKIN TONIC

2 oz witch hazel
1 oz elder or orange flower water

1 oz rose water
Few drops tincture of benzoin

Apply with cotton wool every morning before make up.

Mrs Cox, Herts

SKIN BEAUTIFYING MASK

2½ tablespoons pure lemon *1 teaspoon ground camphor*
juice *Few drops glycerine*

Mix well. Cleanse skin and apply to face and neck. Leave on for an hour,
then wash off with warm water and a good soap. (Use upward movements
when washing *and* drying face.) Use once a week—twice, if skin is in poor
condition.

Mrs Cox, Herts

MOISTURISING LOTION

Elderflower water is a moisturiser, skin tonic and softener. Put 3 tablespoons dried or fresh elderflowers into ½ pint boiling water. Simmer a few
minutes. Cool and strain. Keeps for a week.

FOR A SPOTTY SKIN

Marigold flower water has healing and tonic properties. Make as for
elderflower water.

ROSEMARY TEA

Specially stimulating and good for digestion, rosemary tea makes a
delicious change. Use a teaspoon of dried rosemary to 1 cupful of boiling
water. Just stir and infuse in the usual way. This can also be used as an
astringent for the skin, leaving it feeling clean and refreshed, tingling with
new life.

LOSING YOUR LASHES?

For falling eyelashes blend together 3 teaspoons of castor oil and 1 teaspoon of rum. Coat the eyelashes with this using a soft, bristle brush and
taking care the mixture does not get in the eyes. Repeat every night for
as long as possible.

FOR TIRED EYES

Use cotton-wool pads wrung out in strong camomile tea or ordinary tea,
or cold milk. Place over closed eyes for 10 minutes.

FOR WRINKLED SKIN AROUND THE EYES

Finely grated raw potato packed between layers of gauze.

AMBRIDGE SOAP

My mother always made her own soap; not only was it cheaper than the recipes suggested, but it also found an excellent use for all the waste dripping and fat removed from the top of boiled meat.

The recipe was:

1 lb caustic soda
6 lb fat, clarified and free
from salt

Mix the soda in 3 pints of rain water and allow to get cool but not cold. Care should be taken not to get the soda on the hands as it boils when placed in water. Dissolve the fat and when lukewarm pour it into the soda water which should be the same temperature, stirring all the time with a wooden spoon until the mixture is of the consistency of honey. Pour into a box or tin lined with wet cloth as this prevents the soap sticking and makes it easier to lift out. Leave until next day, then cut in pieces and store.

Ammonia may be added if rain water is not obtainable, as this will soften the water and whiten clothes in washing.

Colouring and perfume can be added if desired to make a change from the hard, white soap which this recipe provides.

Godfrey Baseley, Ambridge

MISS ALICE ADDINELL'S HOUSEHOLD SOAP

3½ lb any fat   *2 oz borax*
9 pints water   *¾ lb caustic soda*
½ lb resin (powdered)

Boil together for 45 minutes and pour into moulds.

Lewis' Mother's Cookbook, Mary Horrell, Exeter

FOR NAUSEA

Mint tea made with fresh leaves is useful in allaying nausea. Put the leaves in boiling water, in a covered vessel. Let it stand near the fire for an hour.

Mrs Garden, 1847

RASPBERRY VINEGAR

A teaspoon of the above, in a tumbler of cold water, is a cooling beverage in case of thirst, cold or fever. To every pint of best vinegar put 3 pints of raspberries. Let them lie together for 2 or 3 days then mash them up and put them in a jelly bag to strain, but without using any pressure. To every pint when strained put a lb of powdered loaf sugar, boil it 20 minutes and skim it. Bottle it when cold.

Lewis' Mother's Cookbook, Mary Horrell, Exeter

EGG SHAMPOO

Whisk 4–6 yolks (according to thickness and length of hair). Use like an ordinary shampoo and rinse thoroughly. Use tepid water. Eau de Cologne in the rinsing water removes egg smell.

HAIR TONIC

A handful of stinging nettles or rosemary, or sage, boiled in a cup of cider vinegar and one of water. Cool, strain and bottle. Use daily on scalp with a piece of cotton wool.

TO EASE STIFFNESS

3 grapefruit	*2 oz Epsom salts*
2 oranges	*2 oz cream of tartar*
3 lemons	

Squeeze the juice from all the fruits and set aside. Put all the skins, pith and seeds through the mincer, and pour 2 pints of boiling water over it. Add the fruit juice and let it stand overnight. Squeeze through a fine sieve or cloth to extract as much juice as possible. Pour 1 pint boiling water over the Epsom salts and cream of tartar and stir thoroughly. The cream of tartar will not dissolve. Pour this into the juices, keeping it well stirred all the time. Bottle the mixture, stirring well all the time, and store in a cool place. Shake the bottle well before pouring out a dose, and take one wineglass before breakfast each day. Keep this up for a period of 27 weeks, by which time the system will have thrown off all stiffness of the joints. This recipe was given to an old lady in Sussex to give relief from arthritis and rheumatism; she thought it had originated in Canada.

A RECIPE FOR PRESERVING FRIENDS

Select those with round hearts. Don't bruise with unfeeling words. Add a heartful of the milk of human kindness and plenty of tact. Warm with sympathy. Don't overheat or it may ferment mischief. Knead with oil of unselfishness but beware of jars. Keep in a warm corner of the heart. Years will improve the flavour of this preserve.

Mrs Bracewell

MR KINGMAN'S SURE CURE FOR AGUE

2 ounces of Red Bark   *1 ounce of Salt of Wormwood*
1 ounce of Virgin Snakeroot

Put in treacle and take a large tablespoon when the Chills are coming on—
and if it does not abate, take again in 4 hours.

Joseph Webb's Book, 1823

ESTHER'S BEEF TEA

1 lb meat cut into dice, all fat taken off. ½ pint of water in a covered jar.
Let it simmer—no salt. It ought to look greasy. Leave it 12 hours. Give
teaspoon at a time if very ill. Put more water if for common tea.

Mrs Garden, 1847

TO EASE THE BROW

Pour ½ pint of boiling vinegar onto 1 bundle of chopped watercress.
Leave for 10 minutes, strain through muslin and keep, bottled, in a cool
place until needed. Sponge the watercress vinegar gently over the fore-
head and temples.

WATERCRESS TEA

Chop ½ bundle of well-washed watercress, put in a jug and pour over
½ pint of boiling water, leave to infuse for 4 to 5 minutes, strain and serve.
This can be drunk sweetened, neat, or with a slice of lemon in it.

COUGH MIXTURE

2 new-laid eggs   *1 oz salad oil*
3-4 lemons   *1 pint rum*
¼ lb brown sugar candy

Put eggs into a small basin and squeeze lemons on them. Let them remain
about 3 days, turning each day until the shells are dissolved. Beat well
together, add the candy, and when dissolved strain through a fine muslin.
Add rum and oil, put into a dry bottle and keep well corked. Shake well
before taking. Dose: ½ a wineglass night and morning.

ROYAL POSSET FOR A COLD

1 tablespoon groats   *½ pint sherry*
3 tablespoons cold water

Put the wine into a very clean saucepan, when hot pour in the groats mixed to a paste with the cold water. Stir and boil gently 6 minutes. flavour with a few cloves and sweeten with honey. Drink quite hot just before going to bed.

Mrs Page, 1899

ELDERBERRY CORDIAL

A grand stand-by against winter colds. Pick the fruit on a dry day. Stew fruit and stalks in water just to over them. Then strain through muslin, squeezing the bag to get all the juice. To each pint of juice add 1 lb sugar and 10 cloves. Boil for 10 minutes. When cold, pour into bottles and cork.

A MODERN MEAD

1 dessertspoon honey in tumbler boiling water. Stir well, sip very hot. The speedy effect on a tired heart is amazing. The ancient Britons drank mead—fermented honey and water. Recipe is for mead's unfermented counterpart. It helps sleep.

ELIZABETHAN or ELDERBERRY ROB

5 lb of ripe elderberries, simmered with 1 lb of sugar until it is the consistency of honey. Strain and bottle. 1 or 2 tablespoons to be taken at bedtime in very hot water. It is a mild aperient, will stop a cold, and bring on a sweat. It relieves all chest troubles. A tablespoon of whisky may be added if liked. A very old recipe, well tried.

VEGETABLES FOR BEAUTY

Every woman who owns a vegetable garden has a number of beauty secrets ready to hand. The most effective remedies for curing a bad complexion and for improving one's appearance can be obtained from vegetables.

Vegetables freshly cut are twice as valuable as vegetables which have been packed and stored before reaching your table.

The girl who wants a white skin should eat freely of carrots and parsnips. They have a whitening effect on the skin. Spinach and onions purify the blood. An old saying runs 'An onion a day keeps the doctor away'. Lettuce and watercress supply iron to the blood and give colour to the cheeks.

If you lose your beauty sleep—the stalk of the lettuce also has the added virtue of warding off insomnia. If you cannot sleep, you soon grow old and haggard looking. Eat a lettuce and a little thin brown bread and butter before retiring for the night and you will not lose your beauty sleep.

Eat the garnish—when a dish comes to table garnished with parsley, eat the parsley—don't regard it as an ornament. Parsley aids digestion, and you have never yet met a girl with a good, clear skin who suffers from indigestion. Also, if you have been eating onions, parsley will take any taint away from your breath.

Is your skin muddy?—tomatoes cleanse the liver, so the girl with the muddy complexion should count them her best friend. Eat them fresh with a little salt and pepper, but avoid vinegar as much as you can. Too much acid is bad for the complexion. The juice of the tomato is also valuable in removing stains on the hands caused by housework. The girl with a sun-scorched face or a florid complexion can obtain a wonderfully healing and bleaching skin food from cucumbers.

A cucumber wash—take 2 cucumbers, and cut them into small chunks without peeling them. Put into an earthenware basin, and pound to a pulp with a potato masher or other implement. Strain the pulp through a piece of coarse muslin, squeezing out as much juice as you can. Then into a clean enamelled saucepan put both juice and pulp, and simmer (do not boil) for 10 minutes. Strain again, and, when the liquid is cold, add one tablespoon of eau de Cologne to every pint of strained liquid. Pour this into a bottle, and sponge your face with the liquid 2 or 3 times a day.

Some hints from 1916

37 Around the House

Take weapon away of what force is a man?
Take huswife from husband and what is he then?
As lovers desireth together to dwell
So husbandry loveth good huswifery well.
Though husbandry seemeth to bring in the gains
Yet huswifery labours seeme equall in pains
Some respit to husbands the wether may send
But huswives affairs have never an end.

Thomas Tusser

Beechwood fires burn bright and clear,
Hornbeam blazes, too.
Keep the logs above a year,
And they'll be seasoned through.
Pine is good, and so is yew
For warmth through wintery days.
The poplar and the willow, too,
Take long to make a blaze.
Oaken logs will warm you well,
If they're bright and dry,
Larch will of the pinewood smell,
And the sparks will fly.

> *Birchen logs will burn so fast,*
> *Alder not at all.*
> *Chestnut logs full long will last,*
> *If cut and let to fall.*
> *Logs of pear and apple logs,*
> *Bring scent into the room.*
> *Cherry logs laid on the dogs,*
> *Smell like flowers in bloom.*
> *But ashen logs, so smooth and grey,*
> *You burn them green or old,*
> *Cut them, all you can each day,*
> *They're worth their weight in gold.*
>
> *Traditional Rhyme*

CHEESE TIP

It is always difficult knowing which is the best place for keeping the cheese fresh. The refrigerator makes it too dry and cold and the larder isn't cool enough, so why not try the Flower Pot Way ? All you need is a decent-sized clay flower pot which you then soak in cold water before popping the cheese, suitably wrapped, under the pot. In very hot weather, keep a moist cloth over the pot.

BAKING TINS

If possible wash all baking tins and patty tins while the oven is still warm —they can be dried most satisfactorily in the oven before all the heat goes.

FISHY SMELL

The smell and the taste of fish often remain on cooking utensils and cutlery. To cure this simply wash them in water to which a little vinegar has been added and the smell will disappear.

TONIC FOR INDOOR PLANTS

Don't throw away the tea with the tea-leaves; keep it. When it is cool, it makes a good fertiliser for indoor plants, but don't overdo it. Most plants prefer to be kept not too wet.

UNZIPPING THE UNZIPPABLE ZIP

It is so easy to get stuck in an outfit with an out-of-reach zip. To avoid being caught in this predicament, rub the troublesome zip with an ordinary wax candle or a 'soft' pencil—it is the graphite in the pencil which works the magic.

FIRST AID

Epsom Salts are an excellent thing to keep in the First Aid kit; many a farmer has taken the swelling out of a cow's injured foot by bathing it in a good strong mixture. Also this liquid is good for any swelling due to infection. But it is of the greatest help in helping to extract a splinter from a finger—simply soak the finger in a strong, warm solution of Epsom Salts for as long as possible and as often as need be; before long the splinter will easily be removed as the Salts 'lifts' it.

WAX STAINS

Remove as much of the dried wax as possible using a round-bladed knife. Place clean sheets of blotting paper on both sides of the blob of wax. Press with as hot an iron as the cloth, carpet or whatever will stand. The heat melts the wax which is then absorbed into the blotting paper. Any remaining stains may be treated with methylated spirits. If possible follow by washing, or, in the case of a carpet, shampooing.

INSTANT COFFEE STAINS ON CARPETS

The main object is to treat as soon as possible after the spilling. If a soda syphon is handy attack the coffee stain with this at once. Mop up lightly. Spray again and mop again. If this fails to work the coffee right out, of if the stain is of longer standing, use a mixture of alum and water to sponge the spot and dry out as well as possible. Often the vacuum cleaner will pick up the remaining moisture but newspaper placed over and under the spot, if this is possible, will absorb the rest.

MESSY MILKPANS

To make easier the task of cleaning an aluminium milk pan, transfer the milk, as soon as it reaches the required temperature, to another container. Wipe out the hot pan immediately with a soft dish cloth, then fill it with cold water—it will be no trouble to clean.

SAGGING CANE

To brace the sagging cane chair simply scrub it on the seat and under the seat, then dry, if possible, in the sun. It will now have a new lease of life.

SAGGING DRIVER ON LONG JOURNEY

Better by far than smoking (which tends in the end to make one sleepier because of the smoky atmosphere) is to have a supply of 2 kinds of boiled sweets made with glucose—bitter lemons and humbugs make a good contrast. The sugar quickly enters the bloodstream and gives one the necessary stimulus to carry on. However, the wise thing is still to pull into a lay by and have a short nap.

SCORCHING

A badly scorched garment or cloth can never be cured, but for milder damage try using a warm solution of borax and water—$\frac{1}{2}$ oz borax to $\frac{1}{2}$ pint water.

FURNITURE POLISH

Equal parts pure turpentine, vinegar and linseed oil.

Mrs F. Miller, Dorset

'Feed' oak on linseed oil and polish with plenty of grandma's recipe of grated beeswax and turpentine melted carefully over low flame.

Mrs N. E. Pow, Somerset

FLIES HATE BLUE

Are you troubled by swarms of flies ? Then did you know that flies hate blue ? Change your colour scheme to blue and you won't be bothered again. One farmer's wife tried this out and remarked that, though they had flies in every room in the house, she had no flies in the blue room. She told this to a friend of hers who said that this is fairly well recognised and in Holland many stables are painted blue inside to keep those pestering flies away from the horses. But no one has yet explained why blue is so effective.

CLEANING PEWTER (1900)

A thin paste of olive oil and powdered whitening rubbed on and left to dry, then polished.

FURNITURE POLISH FROM BEESWAX

3 oz beeswax
1 oz whitewax ($\frac{1}{2}$ a candle)
1 pint of white spirit
(turpentine substitute)

1 pint of hot water
1 tablespoon of washing-up liquid (more in hard water areas)

Using old saucepan or large tin stood in saucepan of boiling water, melt waxes. Remove from heat and gradually stir in the white spirit. Add washing-up liquid to hot water and then add to the waxes, stirring well. Stir occasionally until cold. Pour into suitable screw-top jars and label clearly.

TO PREVENT STEAMY WINDOWS IN KITCHEN

Soak a clean duster in a strong solution of detergent, allow to dry without rinsing. Use to clean windows; the film of detergent deposited will break down steam and leave windows clean for hours.

Mrs M. E. Sanders, Lostwithiel

IN THE GARDEN

St George's Day (23 April) is best day for picking *dandelions*—if the sun is shining.
Potatoes are traditionally planted on Good Friday—because the working man had this one day off as a holiday.
Runner beans should be planted on 1 May—May Day.
Apples should be picked by Marlborough Little Mop Fair Day (the Saturday before 11 October) and never later than Big Mop Fair Day (the following Saturday).
Blackberries must *never* be picked after 30 September, otherwise the Devil will have spat on them. (Irish and Cornish belief.)

TO TINT LACE

A few drops of coffee added to the rinsing water will give that creamy tint which is often spoken of as 'old'.

TO STIFFEN LACE

Never use starch for fine laces. A little borax dissolved in the rinsing water will give the desired stiffness. Or rice water is equally good for this purpose.

TO IRON LACE

Lay the lace on your blanket with the wrong side uppermost. Then with a cloth or a flannel placed directly over the lace it should be ironed. In thick lace, any raised flowers should be pulled into position with the tips of your fingers, taking great care not to tear the lace.

Miss L. A. Wheway, Hinckley, Leics.

TO WASH COLOURED EMBROIDERIES

Coloured embroideries, such as silk crewel work, should never be washed with soap, or the colour will come out. Have 2 basins of bran water. This is made by tying a lb of bran in a bag and putting in a saucepan of water. The bran may be used several times. Put the embroidered article in 1 of the basins and press it until the water is dirty. Then repeat the process in the other bowl of water. If the embroidery is very dirty, more than 2 bowls of water will be needed. Finally rinse the article in cold water, squeeze out as much water as possible, and hang it up. When it is nearly dry, iron it quickly on the wrong side with a hot iron.

Miss Mabel Nield

A GOOD WAY TO DRESS RICE

Soak the rice in cold water and salt for an hour; have ready a saucepan with boiling water, throw in the rice and let it boil briskly for 10 minutes, then drain it in a colander. Put it in the oven for a few minutes and then serve. The grains should be double the usual size and quite distinct from each other.

SCOURING POWDER

Shake up 1 lb whitening, 1 lb pumice powder and 1 lb soap powder. Store in clean, dry jars.

Mrs R. Evans, Merioneth

FOR PLANTS

Infusion of elder leaves poured over plants preserves them from caterpillars.

Mrs Garden, 1847

FOR CLEANING

For ormolu dip a soft brush in water, rub a little soap on it and brush the article for a minute or 2. Then work clean and rub dry near the fire. Finish with burnt bread nicely powdered. Mother of pearl should be washed in whiting and water—soap destroys its brilliancy. A solution of alum will clean ivory and bone.

Mrs Garden, 1847

HOMEMADE TRANSFER INK

3 *teaspoons castor sugar*
1 *teaspoon hot water*

1½ *teaspoons powdered laundry blue*

Mix in a cup and stand it in hot water to dissolve the sugar. For a dark material, use the same method, but substitute 3½ teaspoons powdered whitening for the blue.

Mrs Corrie, Burnside of Auchegool, Kirkcudbrightshire

MRS BOMPAS' WAY TO BOIL COCOA

A tea-cup full of nibs and a quart of water. Simmer them gently for 4 hours then pour off the liquid. Add to the same nibs a pint of water and simmer for 4 hours more. Put the 2 liquors together and warm it when required.

Mrs Garden, 1863

CAKE AND PASTRY MIX

3 *lb self-raising flour*
1½ *lb sugar*
1 *lb butter*
½ *lb lard*

Mix and store in plastic bag in refrigerator. I find the dewbin ideal.

For Pastry:
3 *lb self-raising flour*
1 *lb lard*
½ *lb butter*
Mix dry and store as for cake mix. Saves a lot of time.

Mrs Haynes, Isle of Man

REMEDY A FRUIT CAKE WITH A SUNK MIDDLE

by leaving it upside down on a wire tray in a warm room overnight.

Mrs Butcher, Cambs.

ALMONDS ON CAKES

Before putting the blanched almonds on the top of a Dundee cake, I dip them in milk. This keeps them tender and crisp and prevents them burning while the cake is baking.

Miss Christian Milne, Fraserburgh

BROWNING FOR SOUPS AND GRAVY

Take $\frac{1}{2}$ lb of coarse brown sugar, a tablespoon of salt, and nearly $\frac{1}{2}$ a pint of boiling water. Place the sugar and salt in a frying-pan with a very small lump of dripping, and stir well over a clear fire, till of a *dark brown*, then add the water; boil well, and when cold bottle for use.

Lewis' Mother's Cookbook, Mary Horrell, Exeter

GRASS AND MOSS STAINS

During the summer grass and moss stains are common, and as these are unsightly, especially on white garments, steps should be taken to remove them as soon as possible.

If the stains are on white material, damp the affected parts with cold water, then sprinkle with a mixture of equal parts of salt and tartaric acid. Allow the mixture to remain on the material until it is quite dry, then brush off lightly with a pad of soft cloth, or with a soft brush. Should any traces of the stains remain, repeat the process.

For coloured materials, rub the affected parts lightly with pure glycerine. Allow this to remain on the material for an hour or so, then wash the article or garment in the usual way. If the stains are old, it may be necessary to repeat the process 2 or 3 times.

ONION REMEDIES

The usefulness of the onion as a cooking agent is known to most house-keepers, but that it can be used for general household purposes is not so well known.

Rust stains on steel knives can be removed with the juice of a raw onion. Rub a slice over the affected parts, then polish in the usual way.

Try the juice of an onion for removing burnt foodstuff that clings to the sides of an aluminium saucepan. Rub well into the metal, then fill the pan with water and boil briskly for $\frac{1}{2}$ an hour. This will loosen the burnt food, leaving the inside of the pan quite clean.

Onion juice can be used for polishing tinware. Allow it to dry on the metal, then polish in the usual way.

Linen that has become slightly scorched through faulty pressing should be rubbed with slices of raw onion. Rub the juice well into the fabric, leave for a few minutes, then wash in a warm soapy lather and rinse in tepid water.

Index

Ham:
  and veal patties, 175–6
  cooking and preparation, 76–9
  curing, 272–4, 275
  freezing, 286
  sandwich, 244
  see also Bacon
Hampshire rabbit, 125
Hampshire six-cup pudding, 318
Hams, baked, 565
Hand-raised pork pies, 163–4
Hare:
  casserole, 109
  freezing, 286
  in beer, Cambridge, 110
  in wine, 110
  jugged, 111–12
  mock, 129
  pâté, 309–10
  pies, 171–2
  potted, 310
  pudding, 182
  roast, 109, 110, 112–13
  salmi, 104
  Somerset, with walnuts, 109–10
Haricot beans, 223
Harvest bread and cakes, 403–4, 561,
    562
Hearts, 64, 277
Herb(s), 575–82
  butter, 578
  cheeses, 300, 578
  loaf, 579
  tobacco, 582
  vinegars and jellies, 573
Herby eggs served in the shell, 578–9
Hereford orange and apple dumplings,
    343–4
Herrings:
  potted, 314
  soused, Welsh, 39
  stuffed, 44–5
  sweet-sharp soused, 39–40
  with mustard butter, 40–1
Hertfordshire:
  jugged hare, 111
  salmi of game, 104
High church pudding, 330
Hogs pudding, 14
Honey:
  and walnut sauce, 364
  and walnut scones, 413
  cake, 429

cheesecakes, 387–8
date bars, 463
for rough hands, 585
gingerbread, 436
glaze, 78
glazed chicken, 88–9
ice cream, 385
loaf, 407
nut and date puff, 353
nutmeg cakes, 453
pudding, 330
walnut drops, 463
Honeycomb mould, 381, 382
Horseradish:
  and beetroot salad, 231
  sauce, 235
Hot cross buns, 557–8
Hot pot:
  collar bacon, 84
  doctor's tripe, 71
  Lancashire, 59
  lamb and mushroom, 60
  lamb and potato, 59
  Welsh, 216–17
Hot sauce, 236
Hot tea punch, 266
Housewife's chicken, 95
Hunter nuts, 467
Hunter's beef, 54
Hunter's rabbit, 129

Iced plait, 402
Ices and ice creams, 383–5
Icing, 438, 445, 448
Indian mixed pickle, 511–12
Indoor plants, tonic for, 593
Instant breakfast rolls, 20
Instant pastry mix, 179
Invalid's fish pudding, 44
Irish griddle bread, 398
Irish roast rabbit, 128
Irishman's muffins, 413
Iverson:
  cherry cheese, 503
  grilled tripe, 71–2
  pickled green tomatoes, 515
Ivy cottage ice cream, 384

Jack Payne's salmon, 573
Jam:
  pancakes, 364
  sponge, 329
Jams and jellies, 485–508